A Corner
of the
Tapestry

A Corner
of the
Tapestry

A HISTORY OF THE
JEWISH EXPERIENCE
IN ARKANSAS
1820s–1990s

Carolyn Gray LeMaster

With a Foreword by Malcolm H. Stern

THE UNIVERSITY OF ARKANSAS PRESS 1994

98 97 96 95 94   5 4 3 2 1

Designed by Ellen Beeler

The paper used in this publication meets the minimum requirements of the
American National Standard for Permanence of Paper for Printed Library Materials
z39.48-1984. ♾

Cataloging-in-Publication Data

LeMaster, Carolyn Gray.
    A corner of the tapestry: a history of the Jewish experience in Arkansas,
  1820s–1990s / Carolyn Gray LeMaster: with a foreword by Malcolm H. Stern.
       p.   cm.
    Includes bibliographical references and index.
    ISBN 1-55728-304-4
     1. Jews—Arkansas—History. 2. Arkansas—Ethnic relations.
  I. Title.
F420.J5L46 1994
976.7'004924—dc20   93-48940
                                                        CIP

To Mother

Arkansas! We, thy loyal sons, salute thee!
Proud of the Wonder State we love—in which we live.
Proud of our heritage—we sons of manly men,
And of thy womanhood, to whom we love and homage give.
Thy beauteous lakes, thy rivers wide and deep;
Thy sun-crowned mountains, flower-strewn vales between,
Thy vine-clad hills, thy tow'ring oaks and pines,
Thy Glorious Land! No fairer one is seen.

Adolph Felsenthal, Camden, ca. 1930

ACKNOWLEDGMENTS

Without the inspiration that came from my dear mother, Erma C. Gray, this book would never have been written. I must first of all acknowledge my gratitude to her for not burdening her children with prejudice toward those of other races and creeds; she did this in a time when such prejudice was an almost all-pervasive heritage of children raised in the South. It was her love for the Bible and her shared faith with her children of God's promises to His Chosen People that first instilled in me an interest in biblical and post-biblical Jewish history. After studying both Jewish and Christian history and the historically deplorable treatment of Jews by Christians-so-called, I sought some way to offset the evil with good. The present work is a mitzvah—a good deed— that I offer as a Christian to the Jewish community in hopes that this effort will, in some minuscule way, help show true Christian love.

Although I began this work simply to record Jewish history in Arkansas, my admiration and respect for this group of people grew as I uncovered its history. The overwhelming majority of Jews added only good to our state. The inscription on the tombstone of Saul Salinger (1835–1883) in the Jewish section of Little Rock's Oaklawn cemetery says this succinctly: "His many virtues form the noble monument to his memory."

Special thanks must go to Rabbi Ira E. Sanders of Congregation B'nai Israel of Little Rock. He not only encouraged me in the work but was also a constant advisor to the project until his death in 1983. When I told him of my admiration for the deeds of Arkansas's Jewish settlers, he said they were but following the admonition given to them by the prophet Jeremiah: ". . . seek the peace of the city where I have caused you to be carried away and pray unto the Lord for it; for in the peace thereof you shall have peace."

Rabbi Sanders' introduction of me to Dr. Jacob R. Marcus (they were schoolmates at Hebrew Union College in earlier days), founder and director of the American Jewish Archives (AJA), was a blessing. Dr. Marcus became my friend and advisor and encouraged me when I almost gave up because of personal problems. He graciously read the manuscript as the sections were completed, and his corrections and suggestions have been invaluable. The staff of AJA, including Dr. Abe Peck and archivist Fannie Zelcer, were most helpful. I am grateful to Rabbi Malcolm H. Stern of Hebrew Union College–Jewish Institute of Religion, New York, for taking time from his busy schedule to write the foreword to the book. Rabbi Sanders also was helpful in soliciting needed financial support for the project's expenses. This was at first underwritten by grants from the Arkansas Endowment for the Humanities (AEH), and I appreciate the concern of its former directors, Dr. Andy Dube and Jane Browning, as well as the concern of other members of the AEH staff. After those grants were exhausted, Rabbi Sanders contacted Harry Solmson Jr. of Memphis, a former Arkansan whose family history was rooted in our state. "Harry B.," as he is affectionately called by his friends, undertook the solicitation for the project's support until its conclusion, and I am grateful for his tenacity in doing so.

Sincere appreciation is extended to others who contributed financially to the project's support: Alan J. Altheimer, I. N. Arnof, Mr. and Mrs. Isadore B. Baer, Zusman and Eda Bensky, Beth El Emeth (Camden) Perpetual Care Cemetery Fund (Edwin Horton, president, First National Bank of Camden, Fund administrator), Helen Berg, Berg Enterprises, Brunette Billstein, Noland Blass Jr., B'nai Sholem B'nai B'rith Lodge (Wynne), David and Cris Drexler, Bill Firestone, Mrs. George (Ella Tilles) Falk, Lois Ginsburg, Ellen Gray, Rosa Pfeifer Isacson, Robert Itzkowitz, the Jewish Federation of Little Rock, Sidney L. Kahn Jr., Kevin Kelly, Ira Lipman, Mr. and Mrs. Arnold Mayersohn, Edwin Mendel, Jane Mendel, Eugene Pfeifer III, Mr. and Mrs. Arthur Phillips, Harry and Adele Oppenheimer, Raida C. Pfeifer, Mr. and Mrs. David Reagler, Lena Rexinger, Louis Rhein, Louis Rosen, Mrs. Harry (Evelyn Levy) Rosenbaum, J. A. "Art" Sarason, Mr. and Mrs. Harold Sharpe, David and Miriam Solomon, Mr. and Mrs. Harold Steinberg, Mr. and Mrs. Morris Steinberg, Sam Strauss Sr., the Strauss-McCaskill Foundation, Mrs. B. J. Tanenbaum Sr., Mr. and Mrs. Joe Tenenbaum, the Tenenbaum Foundation, and the Zonta Club II of Dallas. Others contributed to the project through various organizations, such as the Arkansas Endowment for the Humanities and the Pulaski County Historical Society, and their concern and help are deeply appreciated.

Grateful thanks are extended to the contact persons in each of the Jewish communities in Arkansas who so graciously shared their local histories with me and answered unlimited questions. These included Charles

Elias, archivist, Temple B'nai Israel; Dr. Ray Biondo, and Joe and Evelyn Bernhard, Little Rock; George Heinneman, Joe Heinneman, and Lee Hummelstein, Jonesboro; George and Norma Fisher and Oscar Fendler, Blytheville; David and Miriam Solomon, Helena; Jerry Glatstein and Selma Golden, Pine Bluff; Ralph and Billie Brody, Texarkana; Mort Marks, Fort Smith; Jay and Faye Lewis, Fayetteville; Joe and Susi Rosenzweig, Hot Springs; Mr. and Mrs. Mannie Dreidel, McGehee; Elsie Phillips and Mr. and Mrs. Jerry Tanenbaum Jr., Dumas; Helen Berg, Camden; Harry Solmson Jr., Camden, Pine Bluff, and Little Rock; Louis and Gertrude Barg, Forrest City; and Joe and Janet Stuart, El Dorado. Special thanks go to the several rabbis besides Dr. Ira E. Sanders who helped on the project: Rabbis Seymour Weller, Gene Levy, Elijah E. Palnick, and Thomas J. Friedman. The hundreds of people who graciously gave oral interviews both in person and over the telephone and those who answered my many written requests for information are sincerely appreciated. Many contributed their family photos to the project as well. Ned Kirsh of New York, whom I have never met, was faithful over a ten-year period to send to me all the data on Arkansas Jewry he could find. The personnel at the various public libraries and archives have been most helpful, especially members of the reference departments at the Arkansas History Commission and the Central Arkansas Library. Hannah Sinauer, archival consultant, B'nai B'rith International, graciously answered many inquiries.

Several professors at the University of Arkansas at Little Rock (UALR) have offered valuable assistance on the project. Thanks go particularly to Dr. C. Fred Williams, who read over the manuscript, checking for corrections on Arkansas history in general. Dr. Dan Littlefield was the first to apprise me of the fact that no history of Arkansas Jewry had been written, which prompted my initial interest in writing such a book. Others who offered help or encouragement include Carl Moneyhon, Jim Parins, John F. Schell, and former UALR archivist Bobby Roberts.

Grateful thanks go to others who advised or gave encouragement to the work, including members of the Southern Jewish Historical Society as well as to Bernard Wax and Nathan Kaganoff of the American Jewish Historical Society and to Dr. Samuel Proctor. My sincere appreciation is given to Dr. Louis Schmier, who did the research in the R. G. Dun and Company Arkansas records at Baker Library, Harvard University Graduate School of Business Administration (research underwritten by an AEH grant) and to M. C. McCrory, who did research in the Sevier County, Arkansas, court record. Special appreciation is extended to Jeanie

Frauenthal, who meticulously edited the final manuscript (with its copious notes) before it was sent to the publisher. It has been my good fortune to work with the University of Arkansas press in the publication of this book. The staff of the press, headed by Miller Williams, is not only talented and professional, but congenial and personable as well. To University of Arkansas Press assistant production manager, Ellen Beeler, who did inspired work on the book's layout, and to press manuscript editor Conrad N. Sawyer, who meticulously edited the work and its copious notes, I offer my heartfelt thanks and appreciation.

Last but not least, I wish to thank my family for their long-suffering support while so much of my life was taken up with the research and writing of this manuscript. My husband, Robert, and children Rebecca and Glen helped gather material from all the Jewish cemeteries in Arkansas. Robert also helped in the prodigious task of condensing the mass of accumulated data into manageable form and helped program some of it into the database. Without my family's moral and financial support, I could not have continued through the dark days of personal and family tragedy (we lost my sister Jean and our beloved daughter Robin to cancer during this time, faced my own personal fight with cancer, and endured a number of other family crises).

CONTENTS

Section IV: Strengthening the Threads, 1930s–1950s
The Arkansas Jewish Assembly Years

Section V: The Warp and the Woof, 1940s–1990s
Merging of German and East European

FOREWORD

Major cities on the Atlantic seaboard have been home to most of America's Jews throughout our nation's history, so it is a surprise to many Jewish people to learn that for almost two hundred years Jews have been living in the heartlands of this vast country. In the colonial and federal period, individual Jews followed the rivers, chiefly the Ohio and the Mississippi and their branches, then set off along the better-traveled trails and roads to do what they knew best: carrying the merchandise of the populated areas to the more rural places and shipping back the products of the land. At first most of these travelers were English-speaking Jews, either native-born or from England, with a generous sprinkling of Dutch, but by the 1840s a growing majority of America's Jews were German immigrants. For them peddling merchandise supplied by an East Coast relative or *landsman* (person originating in the same European town as the peddler) became a way of life. As the peddler prospered, he would acquire a horse and wagon to carry more merchandise. Eventually he would open a store and become a significant contributor to the community.

The 1880s brought Yiddish-speaking Jews from the czarist empire. By World War I this immigrant population outnumbered the "established" Jews ten to one, overflowing the seaports and enlarging the inland towns. The lone Jewish migrant from the seaboard had to make religious compromises. His ancestral faith required many things of him that he could no longer fulfill: dietary laws that required meat slaughtered in a certain way, meat and dairy products not consumed at the same meal, the avoidance of pork; a cemetery plot that was separate for Jews; ten adult Jewish males over the age of thirteen needed in order to recite certain prayers, especially memorial prayers for deceased relatives. The impossibility of preserving these traditions made for the growth of the Reform movement in Judaism that had its widest development in America. Despite the difficulties, some tried to preserve their orthodoxy and eagerly welcomed the arrival of new Jews in their communities that made such observances possible.

The Arkansas story is, indeed, a paradigm of what happened in other

Jewishly less-populated states. Its teller is a lover of history who began delving into Arkansas Jewish history in college and who then decided that a written history is worth compiling. Starting with a paucity of hitherto published sources, Carolyn Gray LeMaster has labored over many years to ferret out every relevant item from court houses, cemeteries, synagogues, libraries, archives, and reminiscences of individuals to put together a masterly document, adding a "corner" to the colorful tapestry of American Jewish history. What is unusual in American Jewish historiography is that the author of *A Corner of the Tapestry: A History of the Jewish Experience in Arkansas, 1820s–1990s* is *not* Jewish. The end result is a valuable addition to the growing library of carefully researched, published communal and state histories of Jews in America. Everyone who cherishes that history is grateful to her for this labor of love.

Rabbi Malcolm H. Stern
Adjunct Professor of History
Hebrew Union College–Jewish Institute of Religion
New York, May 1992

PREFACE

Before the present study of Jewish history in Arkansas was undertaken, no comprehensive work on the subject had ever been done. There are several factors that can account for this oversight. One, southern Jewish history itself had been overlooked until 1976, when the American Jewish Historical Society encouraged the establishment of the Southern Jewish Historical Society (SJHS). The express purpose of the SJHS has been to encourage and engage in the collection, preservation, exhibition, publication, and popularization of materials relating to the history and life of Jews in the South and to promote research in and study of Jewish history and life in the region.

Besides the fact that Southern Jewish history as a whole has been overlooked, the reputation of the state of Arkansas historically has given no indication that its history and that of the Jew would have much in common. Arkansas was not important either culturally or commercially, and the Jewish immigrant as a rule settled in areas more civilized than Arkansas was reputed to be. Almost from the time Arkansas became a territory in 1819, it has been subjected to unfavorable publicity. By 1820 the editor of the *Arkansas Gazette* was complaining about prejudiced travelers who were spreading unfair accounts regarding the Territory. Such disparagement continued, and in 1834 one Arkansan noted that eastern newspaper editors evidently thought that Arkansas was "entirely out of the world"; one such editor described Little Rock as being "somewhere west of sunset." The state's reputation of being in a remote area where wild animals abounded was reinforced by various mid-century writers, and Arkansas later became known as "The Bear State."

The known history of Jews in Arkansas begins in 1823, but the history of the white man there precedes that date by some 282 years. During the years 1541–42 Hernando de Soto led a Spanish expedition that scouted Arkansas as part of an investigation of the southern part of America. After de Soto's visit, Arkansas did not see another white man until 1673, when a Catholic priest, Jacques Marquette, and a fur trader, Louis Joliet, explored the area for the French government. Nine years later, in 1682, the Frenchman La Salle claimed all the Mississippi Valley (including the area that became Arkansas) for France. He named it "Louisiana" in honor of King Louis XIV.

The first white settlement in Arkansas was a trading post established by Henri de Tonti, an Italian officer serving France, in June 1686 on a tract of land on the lower Arkansas River. The settlement was called Arkansas Post. In 1762 France ceded Louisiana Territory to Spain, in whose possession the area remained until a secret treaty returned it to France in 1800. France sold most of the territory between the Mississippi River and the Rockies to the United States in 1803, in what was called the Louisiana Purchase. From the time of that sale until 1819, Arkansas was part of Missouri Territory. In 1819 Missouri became a state, and Arkansas Territory was formed, which included what became the State of Arkansas (in 1836) and also part of what became Oklahoma. The population of Arkansas Territory in 1819 was approximately fourteen thousand.

Less than five years after Arkansas became a territory, the first known Jewish settler arrived. Although there was little Jewish involvement in Arkansas before statehood in 1836 or even up through the Civil War period, the efforts of the Jews that came at the close of the war and thereafter more than made up for any lack prior to that time.

This is a history of the Jewish experience in Arkansas from 1823 until the 1990s. It includes an account of not only the highly visible and successful Jews who settled in Arkansas, but also those who composed the more common warp and woof of society. Much of the data for this history are taken from the American Jewish Archives and other depositories, from more than two thousand articles and newspaper obituaries, some 450 oral history interviews, and hundreds of letters from present or former Arkansas Jewish citizens. Any errors that are included in the text are inadvertent and are sincerely regretted.

Because this is also a chronicle of Arkansas's general history as well, each section is fairly self-contained, and this on occasion causes a somewhat disjointed chronology of families and individuals. The material falls into five almost distinct sections: the history of the beginnings of Jewish involvement in the state, which includes the period from 1823 until the close of the Civil War; the congregational histories from 1865 to 1930, including those of the Reform (mostly from the Central European [German] Jewish migration) and Orthodox (mostly from the East European Jewish migration); the history and exploits of Jewish individuals and families who settled in Arkansas from 1865 until World War II and helped develop the state, including (1) the German-Jewish migration and (2) the East European migration; the history of the Arkansas Jewish Assembly, which sought from 1931 to 1951 to bring all the scattered Jews of the state together under one umbrella organization; and an examination of the changes in the Jewish communities of Arkansas from the close of World War II and the establishment of the State of Israel until the 1990s.

INTRODUCTION

J ewish history could well be viewed as a tapestry whose weaving began with the call of the patriarch Abraham around 2000 B.C.E. The weaving of Abraham's history and those of his descendants has included threads that are rich in color and inextricably intertwined, and this process has continued down through the centuries. Because of this intermingling of threads and colors, it is difficult to examine one section of the tapestry without at least a cursory explanation of how that particular segment fits into the overall work. Therefore, to have a proper appreciation of the history of the Jewish experience in Arkansas, some attention must be given to the matter of how this specific portion intertwines with Jewish history in general and American Jewish history in particular.

From post-biblical times to the present, wandering has been an integral part of the Jewish experience. Most often this has been brought about by persecution and expulsion, although at times it was self-imposed by those Jews who sought freedom of worship or greater educational and economic opportunities. The wanderings began with the dispersion of the Jews from their land (this land was at first called Canaan and was given to them by God, according to the biblical account in Genesis 13:14–17 and 17:8). The beginning of the dispersion actually began in biblical times when Israel, known as the Northern Kingdom, was taken captive by the Assyrians in 722 B.C.E. Then Judah, the Southern Kingdom, became a vassal state under the Babylonians in the years 605 to 604 B.C.E. and the majority of the population of Judah was subsequently deported to Babylon. After a seventy-year captivity, the Jews were allowed to return to their homeland. The general dispersion (called the Diaspora or Galut), however, is reckoned after the fall of Jerusalem in 70 C.E. For several centuries thereafter, their religious community was headed by a patriarch and centered in academies located in northern Galilee. It was here that the Jerusalem, or Palestinian, Talmud was compiled. The Talmud contains the Mishnah, a book of Halakhah (law) and Gemara (commentary on the Mishnah), and has been called the compendium of learning. The compilers of the Talmud were unaware that the Jews would be excluded from their homeland for centuries and that the Talmud would become the unifying factor in Jewish life down to the nineteenth century. The Talmud, together with the Torah, was to become a little sanctuary to the Jew wherever he went.

When Rome was divided in the fourth century and the Eastern, or Byzantine, half took control of Palestine, the Jewish homeland was slowly decimated by the oppressive practices of the rulers. Most of the Jewish community began to migrate across the Mediterranean and up through Europe. Those who settled from mid-Europe eastward became known as Ashkenasim (from the Hebrew word for Germany—*Ashkenaz*). As the Palestinian Jewish community dwindled, the religious mantle for the Jews shifted to Babylonia, where a large community of their coreligionists flourished. Academies were established there at Sura and Pumpedita, headed by religious leaders who were later called Geonim. Scholars at these academies compiled the Babylonian Talmud, which became generally preferred over the Palestinian Talmud.

After the rise of Islam in the seventh century and the rapid Muslim conquests through the Middle East and across the Mediterranean countries ending in Spain shortly after the beginning of the eighth century, the Jews began to leave Babylonia and migrate along the same routes as the Muslim conquerors. They flourished in Spain and produced writers, poets, physicians, religious leaders, and other professionals. Whereas their coreligionists had been expelled from Britain (in 1290), France (beginning in 1306), and various other localities, the Portuguese and Spanish Jews (called Sephardim, from the Hebrew word for Spain—*Sephard*) remained relatively secure until 1492, when they were expelled from Spain (and later, Portugal). Many of these exiles moved to the Ottoman Empire (which had conquered Byzantine Constantinople in 1453) and to South America.

The Jews who settled in this newly discovered hemisphere found a safe haven when the eastern tip of Brazil, including Pernambuco (Recife), was taken from Portugal by the Dutch in 1630. When the area was recaptured by the Portuguese in 1654, the Jews scattered again, some going back to Europe, some to Central America and the Caribbean Islands, and a few to North America. This latter group, consisting of twenty-three souls, landed at New Amsterdam (later, New York) in September 1654.

During the colonial period there were few Jewish settlers in North America, and those who did come settled mostly in the seaboard cities from Newport to Savannah. Many of these Jews were from Spain or

Portugal, but after 1720 Central European Jewish immigrants began to outnumber the Sephardim. In their religious practice in those early days, the Sephardic rite was adopted by all Jews in America. However, no ordained rabbi officiated here before 1840. These learned men considered the colonies as exile; lay leaders often conducted the services. There were some twenty-five hundred Jews in British North America by 1775, and six Jewish communities had been established with attendant synagogues, schools, and charity organizations.

After the Revolutionary War, the new freedoms won included the opportunity for Jewish involvement in American politics; Jews began entering state legislatures by the 1790s. By the 1840s there were still relatively few Jews in America; fewer than twenty thousand could be found among its settlers. However, because of political and economic unrest, Central Europeans had begun to emigrate to America in the late 1830s, and among these newcomers were an increasing number of Jewish immigrants. The few synagogues found in America at the time could not cope with the social and welfare needs of the Jewish newcomers, and Jewish agencies, such as the B'nai B'rith fraternal order, began to arise. Lodges sprang up and served as social centers, as the newcomers were for the most part not welcomed in Gentile circles.

During the Civil War, thousands of Jews served on both sides of the conflict. By war's end, approximately 150,000 Jews had made America their home. Most of these, of Central European extraction, had begun their business careers in the United States as peddlers and small store owners. They had come with little or no capital and slowly worked their way to success. By the turn of the century, they had made significant progress in various areas of commerce and manufacturing. Just as they were beginning to establish themselves in the American business and social worlds, they were faced with the challenge of helping their unfortunate kinsmen from East Europe. Between the 1880s and 1920s, some two million of these emigrés settled in America.

Before the arrival of the large number of East European Jews (who adhered mostly to Orthodox, or Traditional, Judaism), their brethren from Central Europe who had preceded them had developed a sort of symbiosis of Judaism and Americanism. What came to be known as Reform Judaism in America had begun as early as 1824 in Charleston, South Carolina. It had developed into an acculturated form of worship, which included organ music, choirs, Sunday schools, sermons in English, etc. When the East Europeans came, they insisted on keeping their traditional worship, their language (Yiddish), and their desire to remain in urban enclaves.

They appeared uncouth to the already settled and acculturated German Jews; the East Europeans deeply resented the patronizing attitude of their benefactors. The attitudes of the two groups toward each other and their concepts of worship eventually brought about three branches of Judaism in America—the Reform, the Orthodox, and the Conservative. The latter fell somewhat between the two former in belief. (Another branch of Judaism—Reconstructionism—developed after the 1920s.) During the time of the large influx of East European Jews, efforts were made by the Hebrew immigrant aid societies to send the newcomers away from the overcrowded seaboard cities into America's heartland and into the South.

The restrictive immigration laws of the 1920s initially helped to break down the wall of separation between German and East European Jews. With few immigrants to bolster the number of either group, they began to slowly accept each other and intermarry. But it was World War II, with the attendant trauma of the Holocaust and the establishment of the State of Israel that helped most to bond the two groups into one type of Jew— the American Jew.

Through the years, comparatively few Jews settled in the South, although there were some adventuresome souls who peddled throughout this part of the country. In the antebellum South, German Jews were found scattered throughout, and after the Civil War they settled in many of the smaller communities as well as in the larger towns and cities. Some established stores, brought in Jewish clerks, and a number of these in turn opened their own stores. The devastation in the South after the Civil War left a severe economic vacuum; the Jews who already lived there or who chose the region as their home helped in many and various ways to further the area's recovery. They not only entered into the business, civic, and educational life of their communities, but in many instances they brought with them their love for better things and provided opera houses or encouraged culture in other ways. After the Civil War, the German Jews who remained in the smaller towns often conducted furnishing (or outfitting) stores for the farmers of the areas. When the East European Jews began to arrive (from the 1880s to the 1920s), they stayed in the larger seaboard cities when possible, but some scattered throughout the states into the smaller towns and communities and opened small cash stores; these eventually superceded the large supply stores.

Whether German or East European, the Jews sought a better way of life for their children than they had themselves known. They worked hard to educate their children in the best schools possible. For the South, this eventually worked against a continued, vital Jewish presence, especially in the smaller towns. The well-educated children, along with their non-Jewish counterparts, sought better economic (and for the Jews, religious) opportunities elsewhere. Today, the Jewish population has almost disappeared from the rural South. But the history of their sojourn there remains a vital part of the American story.

SECTION I

Scattered Threads
1820s–1860s

A HISTORY

OF THE PIONEER

JEWISH SETTLERS

CHAPTER I

Abraham Comes to Arkansas, 1820s–1830s

Except for the general fanfare that greeted each boat that made its way up the Red River and stopped at Fulton, Arkansas, there was probably no special salute for Abraham Block when he first stepped foot on Arkansas soil in the early 1820s.[1] Yet his very coming had made the day special: what is known of Arkansas Jewish history began with his presence.

Abraham Block had been born in Bohemia on 30 January 1780,[2] and at age twelve had immigrated to America, settling in Richmond, Virginia.[3] As he grew up, he became established in the business community of that city, and on 2 October 1811 the thirty-one-year-old Abraham married fifteen-year-old Frances "Fanny" Isaacs.[4] The handsome, distinguished-looking Abraham had chosen a paragon as his wife. She was the daughter of the late Isaiah Isaacs, who had been a prosperous leader in the Jewish community and who was recognized as being the first known Jewish settler in Richmond.[5]

Isaiah Isaacs had been born in Germany in 1747 and had migrated to America by way of England, reaching Richmond by 1769. At the time he settled there, Richmond was a mere outpost with no synagogue. By diligence and hard work, Isaiah, a silversmith by trade, became a prominent and prosperous merchant and trader in land. Together with a partner, Jacob Cohen, he opened the first tavern in Richmond, called the "Bird in Hand." They also began to accumulate real-estate holdings, which included land in

Richmond as well as in the counties of Henrico, Powhatan, Albemarle, Norfolk, and Louisa.[6] They became interested in property in Kentucky and twice hired Daniel Boone to search out prime real estate there. (A letter from Isaacs and Cohen to Boone is still extant and contains a notation on the reverse side signed by Isaiah Isaacs: "Receipt of Colonel Boone for ten thousand acres land.")[7]

The land for the first Jewish burial ground in Richmond was donated by Isaacs, and he helped form Beth Shalome, the first congregation in that city. He had not only a love for Judaism but also an appreciation for secular education and was called a man of letters.[8] He contributed to a fund that established a college of arts and sciences in Virginia, with branches in Baltimore, Philadelphia, and New York. He was fiercely loyal to his new country and was one of the petitioners of a remonstrance from citizens of Henrico County, 11 June 1783, against those who took the part of Britain or who left the country during the hour of danger in the Revolutionary War.[9] In 1788, two years after Thomas Jefferson's bill for religious freedom was enacted as a Virginia statute, Isaacs was elected to Richmond's Common Hall, the forerunner of the city council, and served two terms. He also served on the grand jury.[10]

Isaiah Isaacs was a slaveholder, but this did not sit well with him. Both he and his younger brother David (who married a free mulatto woman, Nancy West) seemed to respect blacks with a regard unusual in that day. The older Isaacs made provisions for freeing his slaves, including instructions in his will for their emancipation at various dates.[11]

A look at Isaiah Isaacs' life and character gives some indication of the influence he would have on his family, friends, and community. No doubt his pioneering spirit was passed on to his children—at least to his oldest child, Fanny, who was born at Charlottesville, Virginia, on 27 February 1796.[12] Isaiah died at Charlottesville in April 1806, leaving Fanny and three younger children, all of whom were born to his second wife, Esther "Hetty" Hays. Hetty was the daughter of David Hays Jr. of Bedford, New York, who was a descendant of a distinguished Sephardic family.[13] In his will, Isaiah stipulated that, if he should die while his children were still young, none of his property of houses and lots were to be sold until the youngest child reached the age of twenty-one; then the property was to be divided among the four. He gave specific instructions regarding the children: they were to be educated to the full capacity of their talents and were to be placed with respectable Jewish families to ensure they would be brought up in the religion of their forefathers.[14] Of his four children, Fanny, David, Patsy, and Hays, only Fanny and Hays reached maturity.

Seven children were born to Abraham and Fanny Block during the time of their married years in Richmond. Abraham served in the War of 1812 and was referred to as "Captain" Block.[15] He also served in the Richmond Light Infantry Blues in 1813,[16] and by 1815 he was well ensconsed in the business community of Richmond. That year he and a number of other Jewish residents signed a petition to bring to the attention of the General Assembly the fact that the city's commercial progress was hampered because the navigation of the James River had not been improved.[17]

Although they were well settled into Richmond's commercial and religious life, the Blocks decided to pull up roots and move south and west. The couple might have decided to locate elsewhere because Fanny had reached her majority and received the inheritance of her father. Perhaps the pioneering spirit of Fanny's father, handed down to her through his tales of his life, also helped prompt the Blocks' plans toward a westward movement. When Captain Block heard from Eliezer Block, his cousin in St. Louis, regarding the booming trade with Mexico and of the potential trade on the Southwest Trail south from St. Louis, the decision evidently was confirmed.[18]

While Fanny was still expecting their seventh child, David (born 12 February 1823), Captain Block sailed on ahead to New Orleans. There he no doubt stayed with relatives, the Jonas family, and learned of the movement of white settlers, trappers, and traders up the Arkansas and Red rivers. When the Battle of New Orleans against the British had ended in 1815, this large push north had followed, especially when New Orleans merchants sought to dispose of goods left there after hostilities had ceased.[19] Captain Block was in Arkansas by 1823 and by 1825 had established a business in the village of Washington.[20] Hester, the Block's oldest daughter, who was born in Virginia in 1813, was residing in Arkansas with her father by 1825.[21]

Fanny and the other children followed Captain Block from Virginia by way of New Orleans, where Fanny evidently remained with relatives while her husband established himself in his Arkansas location. He visited his family on occasion, and a son, Virginius, was born to them in Opelousas, Louisiana, in 1828.[22] According to family tradition, Fanny had told her husband that she would not move to Arkansas until he had built a home for her. The Block's next child, a son, Eugene, was born in Arkansas in 1828, and the large two-story home that Captain Block built for the family was probably completed or nearly so by that time.[23] After Eugene was born, the Blocks had three more children born in Arkansas: Juliet, Ellen, and Laura.

The Blocks were not typical of the overwhelming majority of Jews who subsequently settled in the state. The Blocks were older, particularly Abraham, who was forty-three in 1823. They had a good-sized family, and they had already successfully established themselves elsewhere and came with means to set up a business. Most Jews who followed them came as energetic, single, and almost penniless young people who did not eschew starting out as peddlers, clerks, or farmers.

In retrospect, it may be wondered just why the Block family chose a remote location in which to settle that was so far removed from the hub of life, particularly Jewish life. And the remoteness of their location cannot be overemphasized. In Washington's early days, however, it held much promise. It was located advantageously on the Southwest Trail, which had been improved somewhat after the Louisiana Purchase in 1803 and was then called the Congress, or National, Road.[24] Later, President Andrew Jackson had the Trail widened to sixty-one feet, and it was used for the U.S. military and named the Military Road. The town of Washington has been called the "cradle of Arkansas history—all inclusive,"[25] and rightly so, for some of the state's most outstanding early settlers called it home. These visionaries included John English, the first judge to sit in the County Court; William Woodward, another judge; and early lawyers, such as Edward Cross, John R. Eakin, Augustus H. Garland, Albert Pike, Daniel Ringo, Daniel W. Jones, James K. Jones, Grandison D. Royston, B. B. Battle, and Charles Wheaton. Garland became governor of the state and attorney general of the United States; Daniel Jones also became Arkansas's attorney general and governor. Pike, Battle, and Eakin became members of the state Supreme Court, James Jones became U.S. senator, and Royston served as a representative in the state's first legislature and became president of the Constitutional Convention of 1874. Other notables included Joel Conway and C. E. Mitchell, circuit judges. Territorial politics was dominated by the men of Washington, which had become a town of lawyers.[26] The town also had an up-and-coming newspaper, *The Washington Telegraph*, which was the only paper in the state that did not suspend publication during the Civil War.

During the Block family's sojourn in Washington, they became acquainted with several luminaries of early Texas history, including Sam Houston, Davy Crockett, Jim Bowie, and Stephen Austin. Austin settled at Washington for a time, and the knife that Bowie made famous was forged by a neighbor of the Blocks—smithy James Black.[27]

At the particular time in the state's history when the Block family settled there, indications were that the area they chose could and would become one of the major locations in Arkansas and the Southwest. Many of the town's citizens prospered and built expensive homes, and their prosperity added to that of the Block family. Much of the tasteful and expensive goods with which the local citizens furnished their homes, their stylish clothes, their carriages, and at times even their slaves, were purchased from A. Block and his sons. (Although Fanny's father had seen slavery as evil, the Blocks kept a few family slaves and occasionally advertised the sale of slaves in the pages of a local newspaper.)[28] The goods listed in the Block advertisements in the *Washington Telegraph* give an indication of the diversity and amounts of merchandise the firm carried. The ads, noting that the goods came from New York and New Orleans, advertised "staple and fancy groceries, dry goods, hardware, cutlery, saddlery, clothing, hats, boots, shoes, crockery, glassware, iron, steel, nails, castings, tinware, carpenter's and blacksmith's tools, &c., &c., &c."[29]

Although far removed from his coreligionists, Abraham Block did not forsake his ties to Judaism. He made periodic trips to New Orleans, and when the first congregation, Shangarei Chesed ("Gates of Mercy"), formed in that city, Captain Block joined as a charter member.[30] He also kept up with the world of Judaism in America through the pages of a national Jewish periodical.[31] However, if the Blocks had made an attempt in their first years in Arkansas to keep the dietary laws, such efforts possibly were relaxed after a time. (According to excavations carried out by the Arkansas Archeological Survey and the Arkansas Archeological Society in the 1980s at the Block homesite in Washington, evidence showed that pork evidently was eaten on the premises by the 1840s.[32] Such food could have been eaten by servants, however, rather than by the Block household.)

It was in the 1830s and 1840s that the Block firm began to open branches in other towns and communities in southwest Arkansas. They prospered significantly, and credit for this success was attributable in part to the fact that efforts had been effective in clearing the Red River of the tangled mass of tree stumps, logs, and debris that blocked it for some 165 miles in northern Louisiana and southern Arkansas. Called the Great Raft, this almost impenetrable mass hampered river travel and made large areas of land unusable from trapped backwater. Before the Great Raft was cleared, the first steamboat to make the journey up the Red River from Natchitoches, Louisiana, to Fulton (just below Washington) did so in July 1831. The event was so unusual that it was greeted by men, women, and children with an elation that "bordered on intoxication."[33] The captain of the boat, Benjamin R. Milam of Long Prairie, Arkansas, had taken a circuitous route through the bayous and narrow cutoffs around the Great

Raft. It was a novel, daring undertaking, and no doubt those who greeted the boat, the *Enterprise,* included members of the Block family, for one of the steamboat's passengers was Abraham and Fanny's sixteen-year-old son, Simon.[34]

The clearing of the Great Raft, which was completed for the most part by the mid-1830s, was done by Capt. Henry N. Shreve, who served the U.S. government as superintendent for the improvement of the Missouri, Arkansas, and Red rivers. (Shreveport, Louisiana, was named in his honor.) Shreve reported to the War Department in 1839 that there were by then many flourishing cotton plantations on the part of the river where the raft had been located.[35] These new settlements came at an advantageous time for the Block firm, for they added prospective customers to the area. As his sons matured, Abraham first went into business with David, and later Virginius and Eugene joined the firm. The business branched out across the southwest corner of the state (and possibly into Louisiana) and Block concerns could be found at one time or another at Paraclifta (A. Block was the first merchant there),[36] Lafayette County,[37] Lanesport, Jackson Township, Centre Point, and the vicinity of Geneva.[38] The Block family could well have been the first chain-store operators in the state.

Abraham Block was devoted to his newly found home in Arkansas and encouraged others to settle in the area. For example, it was only after much persuasion on Block's part that Grandison D. Royston, noted above, decided to remain in Hempstead County.[39] Royston as well as his descendants proved to be outstanding assets to the state. Captain Block became firmly integrated into civic and social affairs as well as in the business life of the area. When Mount Horeb Masonic Lodge Number 4 was founded in 1839, Block joined as a charter member.[40] He also served as postmaster of Hempstead County.[41]

While the Block family members were busy establishing their enterprises in the southwest corner of Arkansas, the population within the territory was slowly growing. It had approximately 1,062 people in 1810, and this had increased to about 14,000 by 1819, at which time Missouri became a state and Arkansas became a territory. The pattern of settlement changed somewhat after 1821, when the administrative center and seat of justice was moved from Arkansas Post to Little Rock.[42] By 1830 the population of Arkansas stood at 30,388, more than double the number in 1820.[43]

When the territorial government first moved to Little Rock, there were only about a dozen houses at the new capitol. By 1830 the population of Little Rock was approximately 450. Washington Irving visited the town in 1832 and later described it as a flourishing village with three hotels and two rival newspapers.[44] It was here that sometime around 1830 the next Jewish settlers in Arkansas put down their roots. These were the Mitchell brothers, Jacob, Hyman, and Levi, who immigrated to America from Galicia.[45] The Mitchells settled in Little Rock at a time when other Europeans were coming, some in relatively large numbers. A group of 140 German immigrants from the Rhine River principalities came to Arkansas territory in 1833. With the population of Little Rock at about 550 at the time, these newcomers were welcomed as "respectable strangers."[46] The editor of the *Arkansas Gazette* described the new settlers as "intelligent and quite refined" and as being "full-handed," with some of them being wealthy; the editor expressed belief that anyone who was familiar with the German character would encourage such immigrants "by every means in their power."[47] Two Polish army officers had come with this latest influx, adding to the number of various countries represented in the territory.[48] Since almost all of the early Jewish settlers in Arkansas were from the German principalities, they found themselves welcomed by the populace in general and at home among the many others who spoke their native tongue.

The Mitchell brothers found acceptance, and their firm prospered. They had arrived in Arkansas just in time to see the state begin to blossom: seven new counties were being mapped out, the construction of a magnificent new state house was begun in Little Rock in 1833, and statehood was being earnestly discussed and would come about in 1836.[49] The Mitchells branched out and began doing business as far away as Fort Smith, located on the westernmost border of Arkansas.[50]

By 1836 there evidently were only a handful of German-Jewish settlers throughout the state. Besides the Block family members of southwest Arkansas and the Mitchells of the Central section, the others included Joseph Jacobs, Jeremiah Jacobs, and the sons of Abram Mordecai. Joseph Jacobs had the honor of having the temporary seat of justice of Monroe County located in his house in 1833. Both circuit and county courts were held there until the county seat was permanently established.[51] Jeremiah Jacobs fought in the Indian wars with the Alabama rangers and in 1836 moved west to settle in the little community of Mountain Pine, some twelve miles from Hot Springs.[52] That same year the half-breed sons of Abram Mordecai settled in Arkansas. Mordecai had been the first white settler in Montgomery, Alabama (which was first known as the old Indian town of Acochanta, "red earth"). He became a trader with the Indians and married a squaw. When the Indians were later assigned western lands for the Creek nation, Mordecai, then in his eighties, refused to follow his half-Indian sons to Arkansas.[53]

The adverse reputation that Arkansas had acquired, beginning almost from its first territorial days, may have discouraged prospective Jewish immigrants. The few who did come may have been enticed to the Mississippi Valley—and Arkansas—by the letters, books, and pamphlets that were circulated about the area at the time. The fertile, cheap land that was available, coupled with freedom of choice in government and religion, may have been the impetus that brought some, especially those faced by military service and political unrest in their native European localities. One German writer whose published descriptions of Arkansas may have repelled some and enticed others was Frederick Gerstaecker. This adventuresome foreigner traveled throughout the United States, then later wrote of his experiences. He visited Arkansas in 1838 and found its capitol city, Little Rock, to be a "vile, detestable place."[54] When he revisited the city again in early 1841, he noted that it had "increased and improved" since he was last there, but observed that he had never been pleased with the place.[55]

During Gerstaecker's 1838 visit to Arkansas, he traveled some ninety miles north of Little Rock and farmed for a period of time in the area around the softly rolling hills near Batesville. He then went to Cincinnati and wrote of his time in Arkansas, explaining why pioneers would brave the hardships of that state to settle there. Arkansas abounded in wet, swampy land, he said, but the dry areas yielded far greater returns than the European farmer could ever imagine. And because of such high yields, only small areas of land were needed for farming; the rest could be used to raise cattle, he noted.[56] Arkansas was, first and foremost, an agricultural state. Many of the Jews who would settle there became merchants, supplying needed goods to the state's farmers.

CHAPTER 2

The Search for a Safe Home, 1840s

Sometime in the 1840s, Jacob Mitchell of Little Rock bought a share in what later became Hot Springs National Park, located about fifty miles southwest of Little Rock. His title to the land was questioned, along with the title of others who held claim to the hot springs and their environs, and the claims were involved in litigation for many years. The matter was finally decided in favor of the United States government, which claimed title to the land and the springs.[1]

Jacob Mitchell, undaunted by setbacks, purchased a hotel in Hot Springs in 1846 and immediately began extensive improvements on it. He advertised that the hotel was open year round and would accommodate one hundred people. He also had bath houses in conjunction with the hotel that were advertised as being extended and improved.[2] His rates for room and board were listed as being twenty-five dollars per month, eight dollars per week, and a dollar and fifty cents per day. A customer's horse would be kept for twelve dollars per month, four dollars per week, or seventy-five cents per day. Jacob purchased a line of stage coaches that ran between Little Rock and "the Springs" twice weekly—on Monday and Friday mornings. One-way tickets were five dollars each.[3] Mitchell's rates remained the same through 1849.[4]

When Mitchell began prescribing herbs for use in connection with the baths, he acquired the sobriquet "doctor." He was described as being a "remarkably versatile" person, for he was not only a hotel owner and manager, a stage agent, and a livery stable owner but also a keeper of a barroom and billiard room and a justice of the peace.[5] "Dr." Mitchell also was manager of gala dances that included "sumptuous" meals and that drew rugged participants. At one of his balls, the resourceful Dr. Mitchell paid the fiddler five dollars for his night's work, but then proceeded to win ten dollars from him at poker. The musician had to play a second night to cover his debt.[6]

According to historian George Kohut, there were other Jews in Hot Springs at the same time as Jacob Mitchell, but almost all of these were visitors to the springs.[7] The U.S. Census of 1850 shows Jacob and his wife, Sarah, had moved to Van Buren, located on the Oklahoma border. No further mention of his brothers, Hyman and Levi, has been found in Arkansas after the 1840s; they evidently went elsewhere to seek their fortunes.

By 1840 the general population of Arkansas was 97,574,[8] with 5,350 living in Pulaski County.[9] At the time, only a handful of Jews were included in this number. Beginning with the 1840s, to study where the Jews settled in the state is to study the state's demographics in a microcosm. Although a few Jews scattered and lived almost to themselves, for the most part they located where they could set up their own businesses. A number came as peddlers who brought needed goods to isolated settlers. After scouting out a territory to find a suitable place—usually at some crossroads—they would then proceed to set up a permanent business. As did almost all the early pioneers, they generally followed the rivers, for these served as the routes of travel through the state's dense forests and swamps. Arkansas was blessed with several navigable rivers—the Ouachita, the Red, the White, the Black, the St. Francis, and the Arkansas, which cut entirely across the state's midsection. By 1836 steamboats were plying most of these rivers.

Some of the Jewish settlers of the 1840s included the families of Jonas and Isaac Levy, Abraham Kempner, Henry Jacobi, Edward Marcus, Henry Samuels, Edward Czarnikow, Nathan Levi, Edward Barinds, James and M. Benjamin, Adolph Radgesky, Solomon Franklin, Meyer Berg, Solomon Block, and a few others who were more remotely scattered. By examining the lives of some of these people, it can be determined where the Jews were settling in the state, what they were doing, and, at times, how they were perceived by others.

Jonas Levy had begun advertising fire and marine insurance in Little Rock by May 1841.[10] As an agent for the Protection Insurance Company of Hartford, Connecticut, he was the first to offer such coverage in the city. The fact that such protection was being offered just five years subsequent to statehood indicated that Little Rock, with a cosmopolitan population consisting of people from across the nation as well as several foreign countries, was beginning to grow up.[11] Jonas had come with two brothers and their mother from near Berlin. After they arrived in Little Rock, one of the brothers died; he was the first known Jewish person to be buried in Pulaski County. He was buried on a one-acre plot of ground that was donated by a philanthropist (from what data are extant, it would seem this individual was one of the Mitchell brothers) for a Hebrew burial ground. The exact location was lost during the Civil War. All that was remembered of it later was the fact that it was located a short distance from Little Rock on the road to Mount Ida toward Hot Springs.[12] (Some historians have incorrectly cited Jonas Levy as being mayor of Little Rock from 1860 to 1864; however, the city's records do not list Levy as ever having served as a Little Rock mayor.)[13]

Isaac, another Levy brother, who had been born in 1816, made his way to America as a young man by way of England. He stopped off in London in 1837 and witnessed the coronation of Victoria as queen of England before moving on to New Orleans and eventually settling at Little Rock.[14] A photograph of him taken after he moved to Arkansas captured the alert expression in his blue eyes, and his clean-shaven face revealed the determined way he held his mouth, giving some indication of the integrity that guided his life. When in 1850 he purchased the stock of the Little Rock firm of Elias and Company, he found that one of the dry goods boxes contained one thousand dollars in gold. He returned the money to the former owners of the business and refused to take any reward for doing so. The grateful beneficiaries of his honesty placed an ad in a local paper, apprising the general populace of Levy's "highly credible mark of honesty and integrity."[15]

Abraham Kempner, who had been born in Austria on 20 November 1817, came to Little Rock shortly after the Levys had arrived. Abraham had remained in Austria until he was past twenty, then visited England for three years before emigrating to Arkansas. He lived in Little Rock for two and a half years, then decided to make Hot Springs his home (he might have been influenced by Jacob Mitchell regarding this decision). He built up a prosperous mercantile business, and in 1854 he visited Europe, where he married Charlotte Reinsch. They returned together to Hot Springs and remained there until the Civil War, when they moved to Little Rock.[16] The Kempner family became an integral part of the Jewish communities of Little Rock and Hot Springs, and the family name was later numbered with the most prominent in the state.

Sometime in the 1840s, a Prussian Jew by the name of Henry Jacobi established a bookstore in Little Rock. The store was located at first on

Markham Street (where the Capitol Hotel now stands), but it was later moved to 116 Main Street.[17] A worker in leather goods, Jacobi established the only bookbindery in the city. Jacobi started out quite poor with a modest trade.[18] He gradually increased his stock and by 1859 offered light literature and books that were scientific, religious, historical, biographical, and educational. He also offered various bindings.[19] By that time, he had purchased not only his bookbinder, store fixtures, books, and stationery, but also 840 acres, four city lots, two horses, five cows, a wagon, a buggy, and plows. Part of the property he bought was forty acres in the area of Tenth and High streets, and here he had a park and grape orchard called Jacobi Grove. But times became hard for the Jacobi family on the brink of the Civil War, and Henry had to mortgage all his property in March 1860. To help out, his wife opened a millinery and fancy-goods store at 115 Main Street.[20] In 1845 Jacobi had married Sarah Jewel, a Protestant from Philadelphia, and their children were raised in her faith. During Jacobi's sojourn in Little Rock, he became good friends with a jeweler, Albert Cohen, and Henry named his seventh child Albert Cohen Jacobi. Another early pioneer settler of Little Rock was Hirsch Jacobi. According to family history, he may have been the cousin of Henry's who came over with him. Hirsch remained within the Jewish faith.[21]

Edward Marcus established a clothing store in Little Rock in the 1840s. When he realized he had a tendency to drink too much at times, he joined the Sons of Temperance. Such action was unpopular at the time, and it diminished his standing in the business community. He died a little over seven years later.[22] A contemporary of Marcus's named Henry Samuels was advertising a goodly number of articles for sale in his Little Rock store by September 1845; he died in 1849.[23] It is not known if these two men were also buried in the same place as the Levy brother.

Around 1842 Edward Czarnikow settled at Fort Smith, which bordered on Indian territory in the west, and built up a thriving trade with the Indians.[24] Arkansas had been home to the Osage and Quapaw Indians, and between 1803 and 1836 these were joined by the Cherokee and Choctaw Indians from Mississippi. The Osage were troubled by the migration of the Cherokees, and as the number of the latter increased, war broke out. In 1817 a new post was installed by Maj. Stephen H. Long on Arkansas's westernmost border to help establish order. It was named Fort Smith in honor of Gen. Thomas A. Smith. The number of Indians in the area swelled after 1830 with President Andrew Jackson's decrees to move the Indians east of the Mississippi River to reservations in the west. Between 1832 and 1839 thousands of Indians passed through Arkansas on their way west. This route was part of what was called the "trail of tears," so designated because of the Indians' suffering.

Edward Czarnikow had been born in Posen, Prussia, in April 1820 and came to America after stopping for a while in England.[25] Shortly after his arrival at Fort Smith, he was followed by his brother Louis and several other Jews, including Morris Price, Michael Charles, and Leopold Lowenthal.[26] Edward Czarnikow was popular with the Indians and became one of the most successful merchants who traded with them; some of them gave their children his name.[27] Edward sought out a Jewish bride and married Rose Happek, a member of the Moses Happek family of Little Rock.[28]

Nathan Levi, who had been born in Bavaria in 1826, came with his father to St. Louis in 1843.[29] By 1845 Nathan and a brother decided to strike out on their own and became competitors of the Block firm at Washington, Arkansas. After two years, the older brother left for California, and Nathan moved to a location in Sevier County about twenty-seven miles northwest of Washington. Henry Block, son of Captain Block of Washington, had previously owned a store in this location, but he moved to Fulton. Nathan opened his store there, and a post office was established in the building. The settlement had no name, and Nathan called it Centre Point (later, Center Point) since roads from several directions centered there.[30] Levi later sold his first store at Center Point and erected a second one, a large two-story building. The Masonic and Odd Fellows lodges of Center Point were organized on the second floor of his new building. Nathan served the town as both treasurer and marshal.[31] When the rigors of the Civil War forced him to close his mercantile business, he remained in the area and tried his hand at managing a cotton plantation, a livery stable, and a mail service.

Although Nathan Levi evidently became acquainted with the Block family of Washington and was the right marriageable age for some of the Block daughters, he married a non-Jew, Margaret E. Willis. It might have been that the prominent standing of the Blocks in the community intimidated Nathan. He had come as a poor foreigner at a time when the Blocks were well-settled, influential citizens. Levi and his wife had nine children, none of whom identified with Judaism.[32]

By 1846 Edward Barinds had been in business for many years at Arkadelphia, located on the Ouachita River in the southwest section of the state.[33] He was the first trader to open a business there, and he was considered an outstanding merchant who had the confidence of the entire community. He married Charlotte Levy of Little Rock in 1843. By 1851 his business, which consisted of groceries and dry goods, had grown quite large. He also became a land owner. But despite his excellent business and character reputation, he was still singled out because he was a Jew. The business report on him, which noted his excellent business practices and his high standing in the community, also noted that he was "absolutely fair, as Jews go." Barinds was one of a number of Jews who settled and prospered in Arkansas before the Civil War but who left around 1860.[34]

Barinds' success evidently attracted other Jews to Arkadelphia. It may have been that he hired some as clerks, which was a general practice among Jewish merchants (these young men often became prospects for any single girls in the family; the young clerks would learn the trade and then would branch out with their own businesses). At any rate, two Russian Jews, James and M. Benjamin, became merchants in Arkadelphia during Barinds' time there. The Benjamins prospered, and as James's business grew, he took in a partner named Sloane. Although, like Barinds, the business report on James was excellent ("honorable, tenacious and splendid character, not speculative, stands fair with people, punctual at home and abroad"), the report was qualified with a definite slur—"good character for a Russian Jew."[35]

Adolph Radgesky, who had the swarthy appearance so often associated with Jewish stereotypes, settled at Adam's Bluff in 1847 and went into business with his brother-in-law, Jacob Solomon. Adam's Bluff, in the eastern section of the state, was located advantageously on the White River, some forty-five miles almost due north of Arkansas Post. Radgesky and Solomon prospered in their business, which consisted of dry goods, groceries, and cotton. They also accumulated land. By September 1858 they had purchased thirty-four hundred acres, and it was noted that they "owned Adam's Bluff." And, similar to a handful of other southern Jewish settlers, especially those who were involved in the cotton business on a large scale, they owned slaves—two of them in 1858.[36] The devastation later brought on by the Civil War affected their business, and by the end of that conflict, they had moved to Memphis.[37]

Solomon Franklin was born in Posen, Prussia, in 1826 and came to America at age thirteen. He moved to the southeastern part of Arkansas in the early 1840s and tried his hand at a number of enterprises before eventually settling permanently near Pine Bluff. He initially began a career on the Arkansas River by building a little steamer, which he named Mary. He also ran a line of keel boats that took cotton and produce down the river to Napoleon, located at the mouth of the Arkansas River, where the shipment was transferred to Mississippi River steamers.[38] He also tried his hand as a merchant at Arkansas Post, but the business failed, and he sold out to Moses and David Blank, who were also Jewish merchants. Franklin then began trading about the area and eventually established another store at Richland in Jefferson County[39] (see section III, chapter 8).

Camden, Arkansas, located almost a hundred miles below Little Rock on the Ouachita River, had become one of the best business towns in south Arkansas by the late 1840s. It was here that the inhabitants of ten counties bought supplies and shipped their products on the boats which plied between there and New Orleans. As much as forty thousand bales of cotton were shipped yearly from Camden; in addition, wealthy planters and their families passed through semiannually on their way to New Orleans to purchase supplies for their plantations.[40] Meyer Berg moved to Camden from New Orleans in 1845 to open a mercantile business. His family was to become one of the outstanding Jewish families of that town, both in business and in Judaism[41] (see sections III, IV, and V).

A year after Meyer Berg settled at Camden, he was joined there by Solomon Block, a native of Bohemia. (There is no evidence that Solomon Block was related to Abraham Block of Washington, Arkansas.) Block's passage had been on the *Marie,* the same ship that brought Rabbi Isaac Mayer Wise to America. Rabbi Wise, who became a pioneer of Reform Judaism in America, was married to Solomon's first cousin, Theresa Bloch.[42] (Wise and Theresa had been married at Grafenried on 26 May 1844.)[43] As his business began to prosper, Block became a copartner with Edward Feibleman. The latter had already established a mercantile store at Lamartine, located some forty-five miles southwest of Camden. Block and Feibleman purchased a nineteen-hundred-acre sugar plantation on Bayou Teche in St. Mary's Parish, Louisiana, and Block managed this plantation while Feibleman managed their Camden firm.[44] In 1856 Block married Mary Levinson, daughter of Russian Jews Louis and Caroline Levinson of Washington, Arkansas. At the time of the wedding, Block was thirty and Mary was seventeen.[45] Block was a short, sturdy man, and his character was as firm as his build. He was intelligent, outspoken, solid, and aboveboard, and as the Jewish community grew in the Camden area, he led in their religious efforts.[46]

Other Jewish settlers in Arkansas of the 1840s included David Block (not to be confused with the David Block of Washington, Arkansas; no relationship has been discovered between them), who settled in Poinsett County in 1845. He had come with no means but his own determination. By hard work and diligence, he began investing in land and slaves and had accumulated goods worth ten to fifteen thousand dollars by 1860.[47] Henry Stegman settled in Lewisburg (later known as Morrilton) by the mid-1840s and developed a reputation for being honest and industrious.[48] C. Heinrich had settled at Batesville by 1848. He came almost penniless but established a grocery store that prospered. He became so esteemed that it was said that "only death could prevent him from fulfilling his word." Shortly after he took a partner in 1856, Heinrich died.[49] By early 1848 Mrs. C. Reinach, a widow, had her own small millinery shop in Pine Bluff. It was a typical business for women found in her circumstances. Her trade was described as being modest, amounting to about fifteen hundred dollars a year. Mrs. Reinach was considered a humble woman with small wants, and her trade was good.[50]

How the religious life of the early pioneer settlers fared can only be conjectured, for the most part. It is noted that Jonas Levy of Little Rock was acting as a minister of a "Jewish church" for "several years" prior to August 1843.[51] As such, he was allowed to marry those of the Jewish faith.[52] In his short history of early Arkansas Jewry, historian Alexander Kohut gives the terse statement that the Mitchells, Kempners, and Jonas Levy were followed to Little Rock by others and that a congregation formed about 1845.[53] This is substantiated by an article in the *Arkansas Gazette* in 1869 regarding religious edifices of Little Rock, which stated that:

The Jewish Synagogue, established here thirty years ago by the able and amiable Jonas Levy as its first Rabbi, is situated on Markham Street. It is a large hall very neatly furnished where large numbers of the most prosperous among our fellow citizens have been in the habit of congregating in the worship of God after the manner of the times of David and Solomon and the prophets. We are under the impression that they have no priest now.[54]

About the time Kohut mentions that a congregation formed in Little Rock, there was an attempt on the part of the Jews who had settled at Helena to at least keep the High Holy Days. Julius Freiberg, president of Bene Israel, the pioneer congregation of Cincinnati, authorized I. Ehrman of Helena on 13 September 1846 to borrow a Sefer Torah to be used in that city during the High Holy Day services that year.[55] If there were any other Jewish groups meeting in Arkansas during the 1840s, information on such has not been uncovered to date. From research into the religious condition of Jews who had settled elsewhere in America at the time, it is assumed that Arkansas Jewry, especially the many who were isolated from their coreligionists, followed the same general attitude. This attitude has been described succinctly by Dr. Jacob R. Marcus, who said that, although the early settlers "were devotees of traditional Judaism," they "nonetheless adapted their age-old faith to this westernmost Atlantic frontier by tacitly adopting a policy of salutary neglect."[56]

There were other Jewish individuals who also came to Arkansas in the 1840s whose stories are yet to be chronicled. The few described above give some insight into the events of those early days. What is missing from this history is their inner feelings toward being Jewish in a pioneer setting in which they were, for the most part, separated from all but perhaps one or two other Jewish individuals or families. No articles, letters, or diaries written by any of these early Arkansas Jewish settlers have been found, but based on the evidence at hand, it is certain that they entered the challenges of pioneer life with determination and zest.

As with the rest of the frontier lands of America in the 1830s and 1840s, there was a restlessness of movement, and this was reflected in Arkansas in the migration practices of the early Jewish settlers. In examining their business records, it is found that, after establishing themselves at a particular locality, they would then sell out and go to such places as New Orleans or Fort Smith or Memphis.[57] After the 1849 gold rush, there was a western movement from all parts of the country, like leaves blown by an autumn wind, and some of the Jewish settlers of Arkansas were caught up in that movement.[58]

CHAPTER 3

A Persistence Greater than Prejudice, 1850s

T he few who had braved the pioneer conditions in Arkansas prior to 1850 no doubt sent word to their friends and relatives in Europe about the possibilities of this sparsely settled state. The beauty of the Ozark Mountains in the northwestern part of Arkansas drew many of the earliest settlers, and the counties in that section led in white population by 1860. The greatest population growth was in the eastern and especially the southeastern parts of the state, however, where the rich, fertile bottom lands enticed farmers, and farms and plantations began to proliferate. This resulted in the need for more workers, which at that time meant an expanding slave population.

Settlers were also enticed to the bottom lands after 1849 because of the millions of acres made available by the Swamp Land Acts passed by Congress that year. The area involved in the Acts made up about a fourth of Arkansas's land. To increase the use of the land and draw settlers to it, the 1850 General Assembly of Arkansas set up a Board of Swamp Land Commissioners. The next decade saw much land reclaimed through the building of levees. Also during this decade, the Federal government gave away vast tracts of public land in Arkansas to former soldiers.[1] This did not affect many Jews (except perhaps Abraham Block of Washington, who had fought in the War of 1812), but it did bring in more settlers, and these were potential customers for the general merchandise stores that the Jews tended to establish.

The United States government helped in another way in the 1850s to spur migration into Arkansas. In that decade it began making land grants for the building of railroads, and the next few years saw some 2,600,000 acres, about one-twelfth of the state's land, come into the possession of three railroads: the Memphis and Little Rock, the Cairo and Fulton, and the Little Rock and Fort Smith. As it developed, another attraction that led to more migration into Arkansas came from the fact that the state took possession of a large amount of land after 1840 because some landowners failed to pay their taxes. The Donation Law of 1840 made it possible for settlers to obtain title to such land by simply paying the delinquent taxes. This possibility drew inquiries from distant states, and the supply could not keep up with the demand.[2]

Out of a general population of 209,897 in Arkansas in 1850,[3] Jewish residents constituted approximately four hundred of this number. This represented about a hundred families, since around two-thirds of the Arkansas Jewish settlers at this time were single men.[4] Although there was a good deal of movement on the part of immigrants to find a suitable place to locate, several of the Jews who came to Arkansas after 1850 put down deep roots, settled in, and became charter members of congregations that formed shortly after the end of the Civil War.

During the 1850 decade, Jewish businessmen were actively engaged in various enterprises in at least twenty-six counties in Arkansas. The fact that most of these were in the central, southern, and eastern sections of the state was an indication of the population pattern of Arkansas. More than 99 percent of these newcomers were from the German states, and their average age was around twenty-nine. About one-third of these were married, but at least three-fourths had other family members located somewhere in the state. About 44 percent of their businesses were in dry goods, 19 percent in grocery, and 18 percent in general stock. Only 5 percent were peddlers at the time, and 4 percent had confectionaries. These were followed in fewer numbers by those who were tailors, planters, livery owners, or owners of businesses that dealt in jewelry, furniture, riverboats, liquor, millinery, or books; one had a hotel.[5]

It is evident that, although the percentage of Arkansas citizens who were Jewish was quite small, almost 100 percent of them were establishing their own businesses, helping communities develop into towns by providing needed goods close at hand, creating jobs for others, and later helping to develop the state's natural resources. This is the pattern they would follow for the next hundred years.

These statistics become more meaningful when accompanied by some of the history of those whose lives were used to compile such data. Only a sample portion of what has been collected on the lives of Arkansas Jewry during the 1850s can be included here, but what is given is indicative of the industry and resiliency required of these early settlers.

David Block, who had settled in Poinsett County in the 1840s, moved to Cold Water Spring (present-day Coldwater), Cross County, which was situated advantageously at a crossroad near the St. Francis River on Crowley's Ridge.[6] (Crowley's Ridge, which is a formation of beautiful hill country about five miles wide, runs almost perpendicular to Arkansas's southern and northern borders, dividing its eastern delta farmland. Farming is done on both sides of the ridge.) The Block store prospered, and in 1851 David Block hired Maurice Block (the two were not related) as a clerk; after two years the men became partners. (Maurice Block had been born in Germany in 1819 and was educated there until age fifteen. When his father insisted he enter the bakery trade, which Maurice disliked, the young son left home and went to Paris, where he learned the trade of making fine ornamental brass clocks. At age twenty-one he married a Parisian, Bettie Bloom. In 1842 the couple emigrated to New Orleans, where Maurice began peddling. After bearing him two sons, Losso and Nathan, Bettie died of yellow fever. Maurice moved to Memphis with the boys and in 1849 married Anna Woubilman. They lived for a short while in St. Louis, where Losso died, then settled in eastern Arkansas.)[7]

David and Maurice were soon doing the largest crossroad trade on Crowley's Ridge. During 1858 they had a contract to furnish the city of Memphis with beef, and they shipped more than twenty-six hundred head that year. In 1859 their firm shipped seven hundred bales of cotton and more than ten thousand raccoon skins. After David Block retired in 1859, Maurice moved to Farm Hill, about forty miles north of Cold Water Spring (near present-day Harrisburg). He built up a large trade there and bought a farm.[8]

Another Jewish man who migrated into Arkansas in 1851 was Gabriel McCowan from Edinburgh. (The name was originally McCohn but became Anglicised to McCowan.) Gabriel, a congenial soul, was born 26 December 1813 at Edinburgh to Rabbi McCohn and his wife. The family was very poor, and Gabriel left his family as a young boy to make his own way. In his struggle to make a living, he traveled over most of Scotland and England. Although his education had been limited, he loved to read and became self-educated. He particularly loved the works of Shakespeare and of Sir Walter Scott and became proficient at reciting long passages from them. By the age of thirty he had come to America, and he opened mercantile stores at various times in both Mississippi and Louisiana. In 1849 he left with many others to seek gold in California. He built a store there, prospered, then lost all he had accumulated when the building burned. Undaunted, he headed back east and in 1850 chose Little Rock as his home. Here he established a dry goods store and later added a tannery. Alexander George, a German who had come with the 1833 migration to Arkansas, was McCowan's partner in the tannery business. McCowan married Elizabeth Mandel, a native of Hanover, at Port Gibson, Mississippi, and brought her back with him to Little Rock. They had five children. In 1859 the McCowan family lived briefly in New York, but as the North-South controversy heightened and it appeared that a confrontation was inevitable, the McCowans returned to Little Rock. Gabriel put down permanent roots this time and reestablished his dry goods store on Main Street.[9]

The growth of the Jewish community in Little Rock during the 1850s was indicative of the growth of the city as well. The names of some who helped build up the city in those early times have almost been lost to memory. Names such as Jacob Lehman, Simeon Joseph, F. A. Sarasin, tailor Louis Fisbell, and others whose last names only are known, such as Bloom or Simon or Cohn. But a few remained, and they as well as some of their descendants became the backbone of the Jewish community—and continue in that capacity to the present day. These included the Kempners and Levys, mentioned earlier, whose family members continued to migrate to Arkansas from Europe. They were joined by Morris and Abe Navra, Leo and Abe Pollock, Albert Cohen, Isaac Bott, and several others.[10]

Like all immigrants, the Jews had a number of obstacles to overcome when they settled in a new community. Not only did they need to learn the language, but they had to set up and establish their businesses and develop the confidence of their customers. Since Arkansas was an agricultural state from its earliest days, the merchants of the state were almost as much at the mercy of the harvests as were the farmers. It was not unusual for firms to go under after bad harvests, regroup, and then try again.[11]

An extra obstacle that Jewish merchants had to attempt to overcome was the prejudice so often leveled against them. For example, in 1853 Morris and Abe Navra had come from Vicksburg, Mississippi, to Little Rock, where Morris opened a small confectionary shop and Abe established a small tea and fruit shop. Although their shops were small, they paid their debts promptly and their reputation was said to be good, but the business report regarding A. Navra noted that he was "a Jew of Jewish proclivities decidedly" (whatever that meant), and that "as for confidences, he may betray as did Judas."[12] (Both men went on to establish reputable businesses, and their descendants are still active in the business and religious community of Little Rock.)

Shortly after Morris Navra moved to Little Rock, his son Jonas died, and Morris purchased a plot in Mount Holly Cemetery, which was located at the time at the edge of the city. A later account of this event stated that, at that time, there were not enough Jews in the area to form any social organization, which would have included a burial society and the purchase of a separate Jewish burial ground.[13]

Two brothers, Abe and Leo Pollock, came from Philadelphia to Little Rock on 31 March 1857 and soon, like the Navras, were the subjects of a prejudiced business report. The Pollock brothers had brought enough funds with them to set up their firms, and Leo established a furniture store while Abe opened a shoe firm. Both businesses quickly prospered, and they each gained a reputation as being temperate and "not a better . . . [merchant] . . . than you generally find."[14] Yet in a later business report, it was said of them that they belonged to a "class that could not be cheerfully recommended."[15]

Albert Cohen, born in Düsseldorf, 15 October 1834, came to America in 1856 and settled at Little Rock in 1857. He first worked in the jewelry establishment of D. C. Fulton and later established his own jewelry firm with a partner named De Episy (the latter moved to North Carolina a year later). Cohen continued the business, which consisted mostly of watchmaking. Although he was industrious and prudent, he struggled financially, mostly because there were a number of family members with him in Little Rock who were depending on him for support.[16]

Isaac Bott brought his family to Little Rock in 1858 from Fort Wayne, Indiana, where at least two of his children, Augusta and George, had been born.[17] Isaac opened the first bakery in Little Rock, and early photos of Main Street show his "I. Bott Bakery" sign at Second and Main. He acquired a considerable amount of property, part of which was later occupied by the Rock Island Railway Depot and its terminals.[18] Isaac also had another daughter (who later married Louis Volmer) and a son, Leo P., who was born at Little Rock in 1860.

There were other Jews in Little Rock in the 1850s as well. These included F. A. Sarasin and his partner, Frederick Kramer (who later became mayor of Little Rock). The men established a mercantile firm in 1857 and became known as good and reliable men. Members of the Bloom family came, two boys and their sister, and, with a partner, owned the small clothing store of Bloom and Fishell. D. B. Mendel was running a store for Gabriel McCowan in the early 1850s; Louis Fishell and L. Meyer and his brother-in-law Henry Hezekiah had tailor shops; Simeon Joseph was struggling with a small dry goods store, while S. H. Neiman was thriving in the same type of business; W. Levy and L. Ackerman both had small grocery stores; Samuel Alexander had a small confectionary—and had the misfortune of being burned out twice in one year; and L. Hynenar opened a little general firm and gave it the original name of "New Store."[19] While these and other Jews were moving into the area rather quickly, they were also moving out at about the same rate. Jacob Lehman was not atypical of the times. He had set up his store in Little Rock by 1853, prospered, then paid off his creditors and left for Colorado with plenty of cash in his pockets.[20]

Members of the Adler family came to Arkansas as early as the 1830s and continued to migrate into the state during the next four or five decades. They first settled in the eastern part of Arkansas, but some gradually moved farther west—to Fort Smith, Van Buren, and Fayetteville.[21] Toward mid-century, Samuel Adler settled first at Hot Springs, where he established a reputation as a man of good character,[22] then around 1855 he moved to Van Buren, across the Arkansas River from Fort Smith. Adler went East to New York or Philadelphia each year for the High Holy Days; on one such trip he met and subsequently married Sarah Sulzberger, daughter of a Philadelphia shochet (ritual slaughterer). Sarah's father, Leopold, gave Samuel Adler instructions on how to kill animals and fowl properly so that his daughter could keep a kosher home.[23]

After the wedding, Samuel Adler took his bride to Van Buren, where he continued his general store as well as a cotton plantation. Three children were born to the Adlers while they lived at Van Buren: two daughters in 1859 and 1861, and a son, Cyrus, who was born 13 September 1863. (Cyrus Adler became one of the most outstanding Jewish citizens born on American soil. He received a Ph.D. in 1887 from Johns Hopkins University, where he was an instructor in Semitic languages for several years. He was librarian of the Smithsonian Institution 1892–1905 and was honorary assistant curator of historic archaeology and custodian of historic religions at the United States National Museum, Washington, D.C., 1889–1908. He served as president of Dropsie College, 1909–40, and as president of the Jewish Theological Seminary of America in New York in 1924. He was an editor of The Jewish Encyclopedia and The American Jewish Yearbook and was a prolific writer.) In his later years, Cyrus Adler pondered the question why his father had settled in the "wildest part of this comparatively unsettled State of Arkansas."[24] He surmised that his paternal grandfather, who had served in Napoleon's army, was possessed of an adventuresome spirit that had been passed down to his sons, two of whom settled in Arkansas. Cyrus Adler also noted that his father might have been attracted to the idea of trading merchandise for furs with the Indians. Samuel Adler prospered to the point that he was soon able to purchase a plantation for ten thousand dollars and pay for it in gold. As the Civil War drew on, he invested in the Confederacy, and when he died, Confederate bonds and money worth eighty thousand dollars were found among his effects.[25]

Pine Bluff, located on the Arkansas River southeast of Little Rock, became home to more than a dozen Jewish families in the 1850s. Businesses with the names of Weil, Bloom, Blum, Lyons, Mandell, Reinach, Simon, Altschul, Aschaffenburg, Meyer, Meyers, Baker, Fies, Levi, and others began to take their places in the town. The earliest known Jewish settler there had been Jacob Wolf, who came in the 1840s but later moved to New Orleans.[26] In 1852 Max Weil, a native of Baden, Germany, opened a bakery in Pine Bluff. He was later joined in the enterprise by his brother, Charles.[27]

Isaac Altschul was an 1850s settler of Jefferson County; he opened a dry goods store in the area of Pine Bluff in 1852.[28] It is possible to catch a glimpse of what life was like for the early Jewish pioneers who lived in remote sections of Arkansas through an examination of the circumstances that surrounded the Altschul family. This glimpse comes from an autobiography written by Henry Morton Stanley, who became a noted journalist with a New York newspaper. As a young man, Stanley lived for a while with Isaac Altschul and clerked in his store. (Stanley was born in Wales and given the name John Rowland. His early life somewhat resembled that of Charles Dickens' Oliver Twist. He came to New Orleans in his youth and was adopted by a man named Henry Morton Stanley, who gave him a home and his name. As a journalist, the younger Stanley is best remembered for his locating the well-known missionary to Africa, David Livingstone.)[29] Stanley was nineteen when he was sent by his stepfather to learn the merchant trade at the Altschul store. At the time, Altschul had a store at Cyprus Bend, located in a rugged area on the Arkansas River several miles below Pine Bluff.

In his autobiography, Stanley described the Altschul store as being a one-storied building of solid logs, which had four compartments. Three of these contained general merchandise that gunners, grocers, drapers, and stationers were supposed to sell, and one of the rooms was used as an office by day and a bedroom at night for the clerks. The Altschul home was not far from the store, and the young physician of the neighborhood lived there with Isaac and his wife, Therese. The community around Cypress Bend consisted of log cabins and slave-worked plantations. These were all surrounded by huge pine forests and marshy wastelands—the breeding place of mosquitos. The climate was very unhealthy, and like almost everyone else in that area, Stanley contracted malaria. He had regular bouts with it two or three times a month, and his weight dropped to ninety-five pounds. Quinine was a staple part of the diet. Stanley noted that, in this unhealthy climate, tempers flared at the slightest provocation. At one point he marveled that "such a respectable man" as Altschul came to the point of feeling he had to defend his honor when he perceived he had been insulted by a casual remark from a "mean and ill-bred back-woodsman." All the men there carried guns, Stanley noted, and he described Altschul's attempt at learning to shoot a pistolette. After accidently killing an old sow that belonged to a nearby planter, Altschul gave up gun practice.

Although Stanley looked upon Altschul as a respectable man, he gives some indication of how others perceived Jewish merchants of the time. He said that it struck him as "being ridiculous for a servile German-Jewish peddler to fancy himself insulted" to the point of risking a duel that might lead to death or injury. Stanley noted that Altschul had already "trebly earned the ill-opinion of the planter community by being a trader, a foreigner, and a Jew." He observed that honor meant different things on the two sides of the Mississippi. On the east side, it meant probity in business, but on the west side it was signified "by popular esteem at the killing of a traducer, and . . . therefore, every peddler or clerk in Arkansas hastened to prove his mettle."

Stanley made note of the fact that Altschul, being an Israelite, kept his store open on Sunday for the benefit of the black people around. They flocked there, and Altschul himself took their orders since he exempted his clerks from Sunday duty. Stanley makes mention that Altschul had a slave, a "burly" man named Simon. Stanley hated the swamplands and decided that, in Arkansas, it would be much better to settle in a healthier location, such as Little Rock. He left Cyprus Bend in 1861 to join the Confederate army and did not return to Arkansas. (In 1895 Stanley marveled over the fact that the population of Arkansas had grown from 440,000 in 1861 to more than 1,250,000, and only about 10,000 of these were foreign born. He puzzled over the fact "that neither the dreadful ague, which exceeded the virulence of the African type; nor the Civil War," had been able to check the population growth.)

Another of the 1850s settlers in Pine Bluff was Gabriel Meyer, who settled there in 1856 as the result of fate in the form of Arkansas floodwaters. He had been born in Bavaria on 4 July 1834 to Hertz and Miriam (Came) Meyer and emigrated to America at age fifteen with his cousin Herman Meyer.[30] After a trip from Antwerp, Holland, to New Orleans that took seventy-eight days, young Gabriel began his career as a peddler in Louisiana. He applied himself to learning the language and customs, saving his money, and training himself for a mercantile career. From 1852 to 1856 he engaged in mercantile business at Marion, Louisiana, until he decided to visit his cousins who lived at Grand Lake, Arkansas. His trip on horseback was thwarted by the fact that the whole area through which he needed to travel was under water. He detoured by way of Napoleon, a small town located at the mouth of the Arkansas River, and then proceeded toward Pine Bluff. He intended to go on to Texas, he later said, but stayed at Pine Bluff, ordered a stock of goods from New York, and then opened the first store on Barraque Street. He may have been influenced to remain there by the friendship of the handful of Jews who had already settled in that location. Gabriel came to Pine Bluff just in time to see work begin on the Jefferson County courthouse, and his store joined about a half a dozen others that were already established in the town.[31]

In the early 1850s, Louis and Jacob Hanauer (also spelled Hanover) settled at Pocahontas, located in northeast Arkansas less than twenty miles below the Missouri border. They had come from Germany to America in the 1840s and to northern Arkansas by 1852. They worked as peddlers at first, offering hard-to-get merchandise from the East and abroad. They started from modest beginnings on Mill Creek and later moved into Pocahontas and opened a meatpacking house. They invested in local land and soon became known as "wealthy Jews."[32] Louis, the older brother, was credited with donating the site for the first Methodist church building in the town. Jacob and his wife, Mary, lost their little girl, Ellah Jane, in October 1855, and she was buried beside the Maria Stein Convent on Catholic Hill. About fourteen months later, Jacob was grief-stricken again when Mary also died. He placed her beside the grave of their little girl. The Hanauer brothers were active in the Masonic Lodge, and Louis served as past master in 1858, 1860, and 1861. As their work prospered, they invited their young nephew, Isaac Hirst, to join them at Pocahontas. (Isaac had been born in Greece of German parents, Jacob and Theresa Hanauer Hirst.)[33] Louis had at least one slave, Jim, who was known as a fine, trustworthy man who had been formerly owned by Benjamin Crowley, after whose family Crowley's Ridge was named.

(Evidently Jim remained with Louis even after the Civil War, for Jim was shot and killed by a lawless group of men in 1868 as he sat in Hanauer's cotton patch.)[34] Although Louis lived at Pocahontas less than twenty years, his memory was revered because of his many acts of charity.[35]

In 1853 J. and L. Beilenson joined I. Ehrman at Helena. The brothers rented a space on Ohio Street in the Zellner and Company Shoe Store and opened a small jewelry and watch-repairing business. After their careful and conscientious business practices became known, they were soon patronized by some of the best-known people in Helena. J. Beilenson remained in Helena to oversee the business, and L. Beilenson went back to Marion, Ohio, which was the family's original home.[36] Meyer Newman joined the other Jewish settlers of Helena in the latter half of the 1850s. He had been born at Hesse-Cassel, Germany, on 31 October 1837, was educated there, and came to America in 1856. He traveled over almost all of the United States, especially in the western and southern sections, and tried his hand at various businesses—mercantile, cigar, dairy, and saloon. In 1858 he visited Little Rock, then moved on to Helena, where he put down roots and married Bertha Platt. He opened a dairy and served as his own salesman. Many local people later recalled seeing Newman carry cans of milk around on his shoulders.[37]

Other river towns all over Arkansas saw Jewish-owned enterprises being established in the 1850s. At Batesville, on the White River, Aaron and Isaac Hirsch, natives of France, and Aaron's wife, Amelia (Blochman) Hirsch, a native of Heidelburg, settled in 1853 and opened a mercantile establishment there and at Jacksonport, some thirty miles southeast on the White River.[38] Also in 1853, Daniel Ottenheimer, a native of Germany, settled at Murfreesboro near the Missouri River. He was joined by his brother Phillip in 1855 (they went to Colorado and California around 1860 but later returned to make Arkansas their permanent home).[39] The year 1853 also saw the migration into Arkansas of David Felsenthal, who had been born in Bavaria on 8 January 1833. He first established a business at Woodlawn in the eastern section of the state but then moved on to Camden on the Ouachita River.[40] He was joined at Camden in 1854 by Henry W. Myar, who had been born in Germany in 1840 and emigrated to Arkansas with an older brother. Myar obtained land grants from the U.S. government and began his business career while a teenager, later becoming one of Camden's most successful and influential citizens (see section III).[41] Phillip Straus and M. H. Lippman were in Camden by 1854, John Lazarus and A. J. Sapp by 1855, and Jacob Jacobie by 1858.[42]

More than a dozen Jewish merchants were brave enough to open stores in the 1850s at Napoleon, located in Desha County at the junction of the Arkansas and Mississippi rivers. The town had the reputation of being the "wickedest place between New Orleans and Cincinnati."[43] Murder was a way of life in the town, and no one dared testify against the criminals. The danger of living there was overshadowed by the advantages brought about by the brisk business that came from traffic on the two rivers. Abraham Cohn and his partner, Mr. Sysicke, were in Napoleon by 1851. By 1853 they were joined by Wolf Cohn, Godfrey Tillman, partners Going and Cohn, Frederick Heinz, and Godfrey, Morris, and Henry Frank; by 1854 by David Thilman; in 1855 by Louis Volmer (who had been born at Rhinefalz, Bavaria, on 4 July 1841 and had settled at wild and wicked Napoleon at age fourteen);[44] and in 1859 by F. Solomon, E. Stern, Lewis Baer, S. Kalisha, and Mr. Radjesky.[45] By that same time Emanuel Burgauer had settled at Rockport in Hot Spring County.[46]

Chicot County, which was just south of Desha County and had the advantage of Mississippi River traffic, also drew a number of Jewish settlers in the 1850s. Almost all of them chose Grand Lake as the place to set up their businesses. This town was located on the Mississippi at the very southeast corner of Arkansas, where Arkansas touches Louisiana and Mississippi. A. Haas and a Mr. Cahn were there by 1850, and they were joined by Morris Frank by 1852 and J. Peak and Simon Weiss by 1856. Weiss's cousin, Emanuel Hoover, settled there that year as well, and he peddled over Chicot, Desha, and Drew counties. Abraham Cohn settled at Grand Lake in 1858, and I. Frank, Joseph and Rufus Steadman, F. and L. Baer, and H. M. Leftivich came in 1859.[47]

Fort Smith and Van Buren saw only a few more Jewish settlers in the 1850s, but these included Bernhard Baer, cousin of Samuel Adler (father of Cyrus Adler). Baer went to Van Buren in August 1857 at age nineteen and began his career as a clerk in his cousin's clothing store.[48] The 1850s also saw William Mayer and A. Cline settle at Fort Smith.[49] At that time the state's most populated areas were in the east and south, so most of the entrepreneurs either peddled in or set up their shops in these areas.

Some of the 1850s Jewish settlers chose farming communities away from the rivers as the sites for their enterprises. These included Herman Levy at Benton, A. Straus and a Mr. Cohn at Fountain Hill, I. C. Hirsh at Powhatan, Lewis Levinson at Spring Hill, Henry Kerchoff at Dover, Isaac and Julius Cohen at Berlin, and P. Cohen at Hamburg.[50]

Ferdinand Gates chose the little town of Hickory Plains for the general merchandise store he opened in 1855. He was born in Bavaria to

Henrietta and Mayer Gates. The elder Gates was a stock breeder and butcher, with extensive land holdings. Ferdinand was the first of the family to come to America. His brother Isaac came in 1856 and peddled throughout Prairie County until Ferdinand made him a partner in his store. According to a family history, the brothers may have stowed away in barrels in their effort to get to America.[51]

In 1859 Louis Salinger made his way to Brinkley in Monroe County, about thirty-three miles east of Hickory Plains. He and an older brother had first come to America in 1854 to seek their fortunes when Louis was just fourteen years old. They tried their hand at work in Indiana and Illinois for five years before coming to Arkansas, where they worked in both Woodruff and Monroe counties before Louis made Brinkley his home.[52]

Anias Ephraim Shoffner, born 18 April 1831 in North Carolina to German immigrants, came to Arkansas with his wife in 1858 and began farming on land about twelve miles south of Newport in Jackson County. He prospered and later opened a store and set up a cotton gin. He was particularly kind to black people and became known as the poor man's friend.[53]

Besides those mentioned above, there were other Jewish settlers sprinkled around the state, each one diligently seeking an opportune place to set up a business, put down roots, and enjoy, through diligence and hard work, the freedom that America allowed—freedom to be oneself, worship as one pleased, and put into practice without fear of reprisal the age-old religion taught them by their forebears.

While Arkansas in the 1850s saw a number of new Jewish faces among its citizens, it also lost its first permanent Jewish settler, Abraham Block of Washington. Captain Block died in New Orleans on 17 March 1857 during one of his regular visits there. He was seventy-seven years old. His obituary noted that he was almost universally known among the commercial community of New Orleans and the planters along the Red River and southern Arkansas and that he died without leaving a single enemy—as "guileless in his nature as a child."[54] The stores at Washington were closed for a week when Captain Block died; merchants there wanted to show their respect on the day of his burial but did not know the exact date.[55] Block's spotless character was left to his children as a goodly heritage. And they followed in his footsteps, becoming well known in their own right.

Considering the fact that during the 1850s decade so many Jewish newcomers had wandered into the state and either peddled goods or set up their shops (generally the first preceded the latter), it would seem that the fledgling congregation that prevailed in Little Rock in the 1840s would have flourished at this point. But many were birds of passage—drifting into the state and finding opportune locations, then moving elsewhere, looking for better health, education, and business opportunities. This followed the general pattern nationwide, particularly in the South. (For example, one of the numerous problems that plagued the early efforts to establish a congregation at St. Louis was the fact that so many of the potential members stayed in the city but a short time before moving on farther south or west.)[56]

The Occident, the only national Jewish periodical in America at the time, had two Arkansas subscribers in the 1850s.[57] In its December 1852 issue, the periodical mentioned that there were Jews in Arkansas. In the article, the question was posed, "What Can Be Done?" in relation to the state of Judaism in America. (This was the second such article dealing with the matter; the first one dealt with the "absolute necessity that existed in enabling piously disposed Israelites to come up to the requirements of Bible and tradition.")[58] The December article commented on the fact that the Jew, "the son of the weary foot," had penetrated the wildernesses of America ahead of other civilized people. In the eloquent writings common to the times, it noted that the Jew had been ". . . on the plains where the buffalo's hoof made the soil ring with his measured tread, before civilization had ventured to plant her standard by the banks of the silent Platte or the remote Arkansas."[59] (Evidently the writer could think of no place more remote for the Jew to settle in than Arkansas, which reflected a general attitude that changed little during the subsequent years.)

The December 1856 issue of *The Occident* listed the American cities that had Jewish congregations and noted that at the time there were about one hundred ten such localities. Around thirty of these were in eight southern states. It noted that there were "many of our people in Oregon and Washington Territories, as also many in Arkansas, Florida, New Mexico, and Kansas" that were not yet embodied in distinct communities.[60] The writer lamented that there was no cohesiveness in the congregations that had been listed. It was stated that

> our strength is frittered away by every community's acting independently of all others; since scarcely two congregations in any one city even, have a mutual good understanding between them.

The writer went on to chide his readers:

> Some may think that we are doing well enough in pursuing our present course, that we need no union, no schools, no literature, no educated preachers, no

religious guides, and no extensive charities. Men who have such a notion will be quite comfortable perhaps in having a synagogue, no matter how conducted, or, it may be, they will be equally satisfied in having not even this.[61]

It is not known if the few scattered Jews of Arkansas in the 1850s were at all satisfied with the fact that they did not have a synagogue, but it is known that the Jews of Pine Bluff began meeting by 1859. And the basic outward sign of the covenant between the Jew and his God, circumcision, was not neglected in the 1850s by southern Jewish citizens, including Arkansans. By 1859 an itinerant, horseback-riding mohel (ritual circumciser) was practicing his trade in several southern states, including Arkansas. That year an ad appeared in *The Occident Advertiser*, announcing that the Reverend L. B. Sternheimer of Columbus, Georgia, could "safely be recommended to our fellow Israelites" as a competent mohel. It noted that he had officiated in Memphis as well as in Georgia, Mississippi, and Arkansas, and that references by satisfied clients could be furnished on demand.[62]

The Jewish population of the United States was estimated in *The Occident* as being around 150,000 in 1859, with Arkansas being listed as one of the twenty-eight states which had Jews. All eleven of the states that would form the Confederacy are included in the 1859 statistics. Arkansas was grouped with Mississippi and Florida, and the total Jewish population of the three states was assumed to be around 1,200, compared with an estimated 18,000 for the remaining eight southern states.[63]

Abraham and Fanny (Isaacs) Block, first documented Jewish settlers in Arkansas (1820s).

"Col." Solomon and Goldina Franklin, early pioneer settlers to Arkansas, 1840s–1850s.

Isaac and Theresa Altschul,
1850s settlers in Arkansas,
near Pine Bluff. (Photos
courtesy of Irene Samuel)

*Samuel and Sophia Lyons,
antebellum settlers at Augusta
(later, Little Rock). (Photos
courtesy of Betty Wiener)*

Morris Navra, first president of Congregation B'nai Israel, Little Rock.

Congregation B'nai Israel's temple at Fifth and Broadway streets, Little Rock, was dedicated in May 1897 by Rabbi Isaac Mayer Wise, a founder of Reform Judaism in America.

Regina Kaplan served as administrator of Leo N. Levi Hospital, Hot Springs, from 1916 to 1951. (Photo courtesy of Betty Kaplan Uzick)

Party at the Progress Club, Fort Smith, 1920s; on floor, left to right: Dr. D. Goldstein, Dr. Marcus Sternberg, Zeke Levinson, Herbert Wolf, Marguerite Cohn, Gladys Ney, Dutch Rosenstiel, Alvin Tilles, Will Cohn, Avron Wein; second row: Mrs. L. Langfelder, Aggie Stern, Minnie Pohatski, Elizabeth Cohn, Florence Goldstein, Paul Isaacson, Rae Cohn, Mrs. Henry Kaufman, Tressie Phillips, Mae Pollock; standing: Henry Kaufman, Will Marks, Lester Ney, Mrs. Hazel Isaacson, Mrs. Will Marks, Nanette Wolf, Salene Marks, Katherine Krone, Bertha Sternberg, Harry Phillips, Cecil Hopp, L. Langfelder, Ernest Mendel, Elizabeth Stein, I. J. Friedman, Pauline Mendel. (Photo courtesy of Morton B. Marks Jr.)

The 1925 confirmation class of United Hebrew Congregation, Fort Smith; front step, Esther Sugarman; second step, left to right: Jeanette Sugarman, Henry Jaffe, Rachel Eisen; third step: Bill Gluckman, Ben Feenberg; top step: Louis Cohen, Rabbi William Stern, L. L. Langfelder. (Photo courtesy of Mrs. William [Rae] Stern)

Children of Congregation Agudath Achim in a Purim play in the early 1920s; front row, left to right: Elsie Scher, Ruth Schweig, Betty Goldberg, Max Itzkowitz, Leon Goldberg, Albert Snyderman, Selma Schweig, Abraham Schweig, Joe Bernhard; middle row: Buddy Schweig, Helen Schweig, Freda Glazer, Sam Kosten, Rosalie Schweig (queen), Harold Goldberg (king), Norman Siegel, Mary Unger, Ida Miller, Goldie Unger, Esther Riff (seated), the three girls with head garlands seated just in front of the middle row: Rebecca Riff, Mildred Schweig, Miriam Schweig; Back row: Sigma Weintraub, Rebecca Lulky, Abraham Riff, Ann Gilman, Charles Kluglose, David Riff, Julius Drayer, Hyman Ginsburg. (Photo courtesy of Joe Bernhard)

Jacob and Theresia Rexinger, shown here in 1918 with their daughter Lena and their son Isaac, were instrumental in the formation of a congregation, Bene Israel, at Eudora in 1911. Jacob served as its lay leader. (Photo courtesy of Lena Rexinger)

Moses and Henrietta Siesel (center) and their five daughters, left to right: Minnie (Mrs. James P. Franklin), Dolly (Mrs. Leopold Dreyfus), Ruby (Mrs. Leo P. Pfeifer), Weetie (Mrs. Louis Pfeifer), Brunette (Mrs. Jess B. Thalheimer). (Photo courtesy of George Franklin)

Mark M. Cohn, founder of the successful M. M. Cohn Department Store in Little Rock.

Joseph Pfeifer family; standing, left to right: Lucille Pfeifer, Dorothy Pfeifer, Eleanor Pfeifer, Lois Gottlieb, unknown, Albert Pfeifer, Harry Pfeifer, Leo Pfeifer, Albert Pfeifer Jr., unknown, Harry Isacson, Preston Pfeifer; seated at table: Bertha Lauman, unknown, Ruby Siesel Pfeifer, Heloise Pfeifer, Celia Gottlieb Pfeifer, Ruth Levy Pfeifer, Rosa Pfeifer, Mr. and Mrs. Joseph Pfeifer; bottom left: Evelyn Pfeifer, Nancy Pfeifer, Harry Pfeifer Jr. (Photo courtesy of Rosa Pfeifer Isacson)

Philip Pfeifer family of Little Rock; back row, left to right: Edith Pfeifer (Loeb), Bella Pfeifer (Cohen), Cecille Pfeifer (Landau); middle row: Arthur, parents Philip and Clara (Mandlebaum) Pfeifer, Louis; front row: James B., Eugene, Clarence. (Photo courtesy of Mrs. E. G. Levy)

Strauss family of Little Rock; standing, left to right: Frieda, unknown, Mose, Max, Alex, Alvin, Howard; seated: Ollie, Dora, Lisa, Sarita, Mae. (Photo courtesy of Dr. Alvin Strauss Jr.)

CHAPTER 4

Loyalty to a New Land, 1860–1865

At the beginning of the 1860s, Arkansas was making some advances in its move away from pioneer life. A feeling of relative progress and prosperity greeted the new decade, and except for the heightening controversy over slavery, the future looked bright.[1] The population of the state stood at 435,450,[2] and the large majority of workers, approximately 65,000, were found in the farming industry. This compared with carpenters, who numbered 1,613; merchants, 1,296; physicians, 1,222; blacksmiths, 1,094; and teachers, 933. A few people were engaged in other occupations.[3]

Despite the fact that urban growth in the state was thwarted by poor road conditions and many of its citizens worked on farms, by 1860 the population of Little Rock, the largest city in the state, had grown to 3,727. Camden, the next largest city, had a population of 2,219, and Fort Smith followed with 1,530. Although these figures seem relatively small now, at that time a settlement of more than 1,000 individuals was a rarity in the South. Van Buren, Fayetteville, Arkadelphia, Batesville, and Searcy had populations between 500 and 1,000. No other of the state's towns had a population of more than 500 hundred, and the combined total of the ten largest cities was about 13,000.[4]

Cotton farming took precedence over the farming of other crops, and Arkansas soon placed sixth in production among the cotton-growing states. Farmers depended almost entirely on river traffic for their goods, for the state faced monumental transportation problems overland.[5] As cotton production increased, the number of slaves in the state grew proportionately. There were only 1,617 slaves in Arkansas in 1820, but this number had grown to 111,115 by 1860. Most were located in the south and east on the flat cotton-growing delta lands. Slavery definitely was not a way of life for most Arkansans, however, as four-fifths of the families in the state owned no slaves.[6] The growth of slavery in Arkansas was a detriment to the state overall. Instead of investing in resource development, such as minerals, timber, and manufacturing, citizens with means bought land and slaves.

By 1860 there were only 518 factories in the state, with a total employment of fewer than nineteen hundred workers. Many of these factories, generally lumber mills, were located in the state's northwest corner, where water power sites were established.[7] No Jews have been found who were involved in the factories of the antebellum period; those who were in Arkansas during that time were generally in merchandising, cotton, or various other enterprises. The little resource development that had been done in Arkansas by 1860 was in the mining of whetstones in Garland County and the limited mining of iron, zinc, lead, manganese, and coal in the northern part of the state. The first geological survey of Arkansas was begun in 1857.[8]

The railroads had begun a slow, timid move into Arkansas, and by 1858 a thirty-eight-mile line had been run from Hopefield on the Mississippi to Madison on the St. Francis River. Another line was run between Little Rock and Des Arc a short while later. Telegraph service was available between St. Louis and Fayetteville, Van Buren, and Fort Smith by 1860 and between Little Rock and Memphis by 1861.[9]

Education had made little progress in Arkansas by 1860, although public schools had been encouraged by the Federal government since the 1820s. The population itself, for the most part, did little to encourage schools. Many farmers needed their offspring to work in the fields, thus education was not generally appreciated. The sale of public lands was to be the monetary resource for the support of public schools, but since land was inexpensive, the funds fell far short of the need. By 1860 there were a total of 727 public schools throughout the state, and most of these were supported by tuition or other private funds. According to the 1860 census, more than 23,000 white Arkansans past twenty years of age could not read or write. Private schools (called "academies") helped the matter somewhat, and a number of private colleges were opened. Some of the most important of the latter were supported by religious groups.[10]

Religion enjoyed a steady growth through Arkansas's early years, and by 1860 there were more than a thousand church buildings in the state. Half of these were Methodist, a fourth Baptist, and the others included Presbyterian, and Episcopalian, as well as other Protestant denominations. There were various branches within these groups, and there were Catholic churches.[11] No Jewish congregation had officially been recognized in the state at the time, although it was known that Jews had been meeting in Pine Bluff, Little Rock, and Helena.

The Jews of Little Rock in 1860 began to coalesce on a permanent basis, and some of them met on 14 October that year to form the Arkansas Jewish Burying Society. Their first burying ground consisted of several purchased lots in a section of the Mount Holly Cemetery. The first officers of the society were Morris Navra, president; Moses Happek, vice-president; Julius H. Levy, secretary; and A. Pollock, treasurer. Leo and A. Pollock and Isaac Bott made up the constitution and bylaws committee.[12] A social club, considered to be the first in Arkansas, was formed in 1864 among a number of Little Rock Jewish men. It was first known as the Little Rock Club and met in a building on the southeast corner of Markham and Commerce streets. The club, later known as the Concordia Association, rented quarters at several locations before constructing its own building.[13]

Arkansas, with its resources and its many needs, presented unlimited opportunities for growth, especially for entrepreneurs who had a compulsion to remain and help develop an area from its virgin state. Some Jewish entrepreneurs were no doubt drawn by the success exhibited by others, such as Abraham Block of Washington, who had succeeded in civic, social, and financial attainments and had set a fine example for others to emulate. It was said of his son David that he enjoyed a larger acquaintance in the county (Hempstead) than any man in it.[14] He was elected as county treasurer, serving from 1848 to 1854, and as a state representative for the years 1856–57.[15] He was entreated by many of his admirers to run for the state senate in 1862, but he modestly declined, saying that he had no aspirations for political office and did not trust his abilities to serve in the capacity of state senator.[16] (David's brother, Eugene, ran unsuccessfully as a state representative in 1858 on the Whig ticket.)[17] Some of the Blocks prospered on a grand scale, and David's stock was worth some one hundred thousand dollars by 1860.[18] Although the children of Abraham and Fanny Block did not find Jewish social and financial peers in their remote location with whom to wed, their prominent standing in the community assured excellent spouses (albeit Gentiles) for those who chose to marry. Hester, the oldest, married Dr. Benjamin P. Jett, a skilled surgeon who was well known professionally, socially, and politically throughout the state.[19] Rosina Block married Edwin Brittin of Washington, a grandson of two Revolutionary soldiers.[20] Juliet Pauline Block married Orville Jennings, who served as United States attorney for the Eastern District of Arkansas; and David married Amelia Trimble of Washington, the niece of Dr. Charles B. Mitchel, who was elected as a state senator in 1861 and again in 1863 as a member of the state's Confederate senate.[21]

The river towns in particular continued to draw Jewish settlers such as David Bluthenthal, who settled at Pine Bluff in 1860. He had been born in Germany in 1826 and had come to America in his youth, eventually finding his way into Arkansas. At Pine Bluff he set about opening the Bluthenthal Hotel, which particularly catered to a Jewish clientele. This no doubt attracted many of the peddlers and salesmen who were traveling about the state at the time.[22] Bluthenthal family members flocked to Arkansas, and some of them established a large mercantile business at Princeton, located in Dallas County less than forty miles southwest of Pine Bluff. David M. Bluthenthal, who had been born at Rheinfalz, Germany, to Henry and Amalie "Marmel" Rothschild Bluthenthal on 18 December 1842, came directly to Princeton to help his brother and cousins who had already settled there.[23] Youngsters from other families came as well. Sam F. Hilzheim, who was born in Mississippi in 1851, came to Pine Bluff when he was only nine years old.[24] Others who established businesses in Pine Bluff in 1860 included S. Mayer and A. Furst, C. Baker, and a Mr. Bloom, all of whom had begun as peddlers several years before.[25]

R. P. Cohen was born at Krotoschin, Germany, in 1829 and came to America with his parents as a young child. He eventually settled at Helena in 1860 and established a business.[26] He was followed shortly afterward by Henry Fink, who came to Helena and established a large, successful mercantile trade.[27]

By 1860 several Jewish merchants were advertising in the newspaper at Des Arc, located on the White River. These included F. Leptein, a jeweler; Leon Gans, Solomon J. Rosenberg, Samuel Lowenstein, H. P. Wolf, and Mr. Wilzinski, all merchants; and Isaac Gans, a carpenter and joiner.[28]

At this same time, several new Jewish stores were being opened at Camden. William Newman, with partners Fishell and Rich, rented a brick store for their enterprise in 1860.[29] That year, Sam Winter opened his little grocery business.[30] Samuel Stern joined the Meyer Berg company (established in the 1850s); Levi and D. Thal began their peddling ventures; and Joseph Hillman bought a lot for a store.[31] Twenty-year-old Henry Myar was dealing in land and cotton and had opened a mercantile business.[32]

Jews were locating in a number of Arkansas communities in the 1860s. In 1860 Isaac Cohen migrated from Texas and opened a small store in Berlin, a little community just north of the Louisiana border. About this same time, H. Hilbrom, who was described with a questionable compliment as being of "the tribe of Levi, but is rather popular," opened his general store at Rockport on the Ouachita River. Joseph Mayer also opened a small store in 1860 at Monticello after having peddled in the area for some time. The Kraft family settled at Jacksonport in 1860 and opened a store. And two Burgauer brothers, Moses and A., opened a new firm at Dover, located about halfway between Little Rock and Fort Smith. Moses was thirty and his brother twenty-five. They were single, industrious, and attentive, and they had what many of their other coreligionists lacked— enough capital (around five thousand dollars) to get their business off to a good start. In 1861 Sam Holheimer settled at Pocahontas and joined in the business community that included the Hanauer brothers and Isaac Hirst, while Phillip Ottenheimer tried his hand at business in the little community of Norristown (near present-day Russellville).[33]

Fort Smith, Hot Springs, and Little Rock saw few new Jewish faces during the early 1860s. S. Levy, who was described as one who might be "likely to have the tricky propensities of that ancient race," settled at Fort Smith in 1860.[34] He was followed by Jacob Reigler, who started with only a small amount of capital but developed an excellent reputation for his small store.[35] Hot Springs saw H. R. Auerbach's little store open in 1860. He developed a good reputation in his neighborhood and was considered honest, "as Jews generally are."[36] Those who settled in Little Rock during this period included Samuel and Augusta (Shiekowitz) Lasker and their three-year-old son Henry.[37] Pine Bluff had been Augusta's home. L. Meyer, a tailor, and his brother-in-law Henry Hezekiah opened a small store in 1860; I. M. Levy, a bookkeeper, opened a small business, but having no capital, he was forced to leave; L. Hynenar opened a cash store; in 1863 William Wolfe and family members opened a dry goods and grocery store and also invested in cotton crops; and in 1864 S. Ringelhaupt opened a small business in Little Rock.[38]

The Civil War Years

The presidential election of 1860 had given Arkansans little concern. Most were Democrats and their votes went to the southern candidate when the national party broke into northern and southern divisions. When Lincoln was elected (his name did not appear on the Arkansas ballot), Arkansas received delegates from South Carolina who urged it, as well as the other southern states, to secede. Since four-fifths of white Arkansans owned no slaves, the state hesitated to make such a commitment. Gov. Henry M. Rector called an election in January 1861 to let Arkansans vote on a convention to discuss secession. The vote passed, and the convention met at Little Rock on 4 March 1861. David Walker, who was against secession, was elected president. Although heated discussions arose on the matter, the opinion prevailed that secession would occur only if Federal troops made war on the Confederates. When the Confederates fired on Fort Sumter at Charleston, South Carolina, 12 April 1861, the Arkansas secession convention reconvened on May 6. This time it voted sixty-five to five in favor of seceding. The convention stayed in session long enough to prepare the state for war. Military boards were set up, officers were chosen, and a war loan was appropriated.[39]

Before the excitement of the Fort Sumter debacle, calmer thoughts had prevailed regarding the Union. For example, David Block of Washington, Arkansas, who was a true Southerner at heart, did not see secession as a solution to the North-South dichotomy. As early as July 1856, Block had pleaded in an article in a local newspaper:

> May these thirty-one states remain united as they are now, until time shall cease to be, and may the individual who shall first raise his voice for a dissolution of the Union, be the first to be transported from American soil.[40]

Block later acquiesced to the southern view, however, and his business acumen led to his appointment as general agent of the Produce Loan of the Confederate States for the State of Arkansas. And when the Hempstead County Confederate Association formed in 1863, Block was chosen president.[41]

Southern loyalty was evident in other Block family members. David's brother, Augustus, who had moved to New Orleans, showed his loyalty to the Confederacy by naming his son, born during the war, Robert E. Lee.[42] Devotion to the southern cause was passed on to the Block grandchildren as well. When a battalion of volunteers under the command of Lieutenant Colonel McNair marched into Washington, Arkansas, on its way north to assist Missouri, it was greeted by the ladies of Hempstead County and presented with a flag by Miss Emma Jett, daughter of Hester (Block) Jett and Dr. Jett. An article written at the time described the effect Miss Jett's "potent spell" had on the young volunteers. Their youthful eyes "gleamed with enthusiasm" as they sought expression to rise to the "very height of chivalry." Miss Jett waxed eloquent in her presentation to the

Confederate Guards. She reminded them that, while others might fight for pay or plunder, "the soldier of the South fights for chivalry," noting that the southern soldier doesn't bother to inquire as to the necessity of the conflict. In her stirring speech she said that "the haughty minions of a corrupt government" should be taught a lesson, and that "our sister state of Missouri . . . writhes beneath the insult of the heel of the oppressor and struggles for release." She closed with an ode to the southern flag.[43]

Aaron Hirsch of Batesville echoed David Block's prewar sentiments; at one point Hirsch said he would favor the "absolute abolishment of slavery with or without compensation from the United States Government" rather than see the destruction of the republic, which he asserted was the hope of mankind and of religious liberty. Although Hirsch commented later that he had been in danger of being mobbed for his outspoken views on the country's solidarity, he avowed that his love for the Union was so great that danger meant nothing to him. He described himself as being "full of life, full of business, and especially full of politics."[44] As did David Block, however, Aaron Hirsch also changed his viewpoint.

Hirsch had been in the state eight years when the war started and had been joined by a partner, Simon Adler. Their business prospered until they became the largest firm in northern Arkansas. In his memoirs, Hirsch said that it was the excitement at the beginning of the war that changed his views and had prompted every able-bodied man to volunteer for the Confederate cause. He and Adler raised a Confederate cavalry troop and supplied the horses and mules. Saddle blankets were made by cutting up a carpet that Hirsch had purchased for the Masonic Hall the year before. Medicine was hard to come by, and Hirsch told how he made the precarious 240-mile round trip to Memphis to bring back quinine and gold. Adler was elected quartermaster of the troop they had raised, but he became ill in Missouri and had to return home. He later took a good deal of the Adler-Hirsch merchandise to Texas until the war's end. Hirsch gave details of how a German cavalry troop galloped into Batesville and took particular vengeance on his store when it was found that the proprietors were Jewish. Hirsch appealed to Federal general Samuel R. Curtis for protection from the Germans, and Curtis graciously complied.

Hirsch's escapades in bringing medicine from Memphis for the Confederates caught up with him, and he was arrested on a visit to St. Louis. Because of favorable reports by Unionists, he was not put in prison, but he did have to make daily reports. Through the intercession of friends, he finally managed to join his family.[45]

The excitement mentioned by Hirsch and the enthusiasm generated by patriotic speeches like Emma Jett's, calling for young men to fight for the honor of the South, had the desired effect, and thousands of Arkansans joined other Southerners behind the Confederate banner. Among these volunteers were a number of Jewish Arkansans. Although they seem to have had no desire to fight for slavery, they did identify with "Southern honor," which to them meant the right for the South to make its own decisions. Many of these entered the war with the same zest that their northern coreligionists were exhibiting for the Federal cause. All across Arkansas, Jewish merchants left their stores to fight or help. If they were too old or were physically handicapped, other family members or their clerks left to join the battle.

When the war broke out, David Felsenthal of Camden closed up his business at Woodlawn, Ouachita County, and by doing so lost all of his property and accounts. He made this sacrifice in order to enlist, and he joined Capt. Marshall Purifoy's Company, which was part of the original Fifteenth Arkansas Regiment headed by Col. J. M. Gee. Felsenthal was captured at the fall of Fort Donaldson and was taken to Louisville, where he was kept under surveillance. He was then sent to prison at Springfield, but he was released on parole until exchanged.[46]

Louis Volmer of Napoleon enlisted at the outbreak of the conflict and served under Gen. Thomas J. Churchill throughout the war.[47]

Ferdinand, Isaac, and David Gates of Hickory Plains served in the Confederate army throughout the conflict. Isaac was quartermaster and commissary in Bragg's Division, and he was wounded both at Chattanooga and Murfreesboro (he suffered thereafter from paralysis and died in 1884). Gates served in Company A of Colonel Glenn's Regiment but later was moved to Woodruff's Battalion.[48]

Henry Myar of Camden served as a private in Company I of the eighteenth Arkansas Infantry Regiment.[49]

D. Aschaffenberg returned to Arkansas from Cincinnati, stayed at Napoleon until April 1862, then went to Pine Bluff, where he served as chief clerk for the quartermaster's department until after the close of the war.[50]

Isaac Hirst of Pocahontas joined the Confederate army and served in Missouri at Greenville; in Louisiana at Shreveport and Pleasant Hill; and in Arkansas at Prairie Grove, Jenkin's Ferry, and Helena. He participated in a number of skirmishes and was severely wounded in 1864 on the Saline River in Arkansas.[51]

A. K. Auerbach of Hot Springs joined the Confederate army at the outbreak of the war, as did Phillip Ottenheimer, who enlisted on 9 June

1861 at Van Buren. The latter served in Company H, Arkansas, General Churchill's Division. He was wounded at Wilson's Creek in August 1861 and transferred to Company C. He later joined Basham's company of the First Mounted Rifles and was captured in 1862. He was paroled at war's end from Company H, First Arkansas Mounted Rifles.[52]

Louis Salinger of Brinkley joined the Fifth Arkansas Infantry in 1861 and served under Generals Hardy, Johnston, and Beauregard. Just before the battle at Perryville, he was captured while on duty in Kentucky; he was released on bond shortly afterward and returned to his farming operations in Arkansas.[53]

Emanuel Hoover of Grand Lake joined the Confederate army at Napoleon in 1862, enlisting in West's Battery under Faries' Battalion, Polignas' Division. West's Battery never surrendered but disbanded after the war, and its men went to their respective homes.[54]

David M. Bluthenthal of Princeton, Dallas County, joined the Third Arkansas Infantry and served for one year. His brother Samuel enlisted in the Third Arkansas Cavalry and served throughout the war. He was twice taken prisoner and held in Federal camps.[55]

A. F. Dreyfus served as a member of Company A, Arkansas, eighteenth Regiment. He had enlisted at Pine Bluff in Captain Owen's Company. Dreyfus was wounded at the siege of Vicksburg.[56]

Some of those who served in the Civil War showed amazing courage and fortitude. Sam Winter of Camden received outstanding praise from Dr. Junius N. Bragg, a leader of the South Arkansas Confederacy. Speaking of Winter, Bragg said,

> Sam Winter was one of the bravest Confederate soldiers I ever knew. He would walk without hesitation to the mouth of a cannon if ordered to do so.[57]

Max Frauenthal of Germany, who lived in Mississippi before settling in Arkansas after the Civil War, was an unsung hero of that war. For those who knew him and served with him during the conflict, his name became synonymous with the word *bravery*. He had enlisted as a private in A. P. Hill's Corps, Mahone's Division, Harris's Brigade, serving first as a drummer before volunteering as an infantryman. He was known for his persistent attention to the wounded, and his comrades said he had no superior in bravery. He took part in a number of engagements with courage but distinguished himself particularly at the battle known as the "Bloody Acute Angle" at Spottsylvania Court House, Virginia, on 12 May 1864. At that battle, General Grant confronted General Lee and his army of 50,000 men with an army of about 130,000. During the heat of the battle, which has been described as the most "terrible and terrific musketry fire of the war," Max Frauenthal stood for several hours at the immediate point of contact. An observer said Frauenthal stood "amid the most terrific hail of lead and cooly and deliberately loaded and fired without cringing." The observer, Col. A. T. Watts (later of Dallas), said that

> After observing his [Max Frauenthal's] unflinching bravery and constancy, the thought occurred to the writer—I now understand how it was that a handful of Jews could drive before them the hundred kings; they were all Fronthalls [sic].[58]

Albert Cohen of Little Rock joined the Confederate cause and served as captain of the corps of mining engineers under Major Crump. Cohen, a jeweler, was familiar with minerals, and this proved to be of signal benefit to the southern cause. While his unit was in service at Magnet Cove, he processed sulfur, which was used to make powder for the Confederate army.[59] Another Little Rock jeweler, Michael Stifft, also helped in the rebels' war effort. He had seen military service previously while serving in the ordnance department in the Mexican-American War, during which he had been wounded in 1847 at Port Isabel. During the Civil War, he made swords for the Confederate soldiers.[60]

Although their part in the war effort might not have been quite as significant contributions to weaponry as Cohen's and Stifft's, Max and Charles Weil of Pine Bluff helped both the South and the North in another way. When Max had opened his little bakery shop in Pine Bluff in 1852, he could not have foreseen the need it would fulfill a decade later. Throughout the war, the Weil bakery supplied its goods to all the Confederate soldiers in that section of the state. And when Little Rock fell to Federal troops under General Steele, the Weils supplied baked goods to the Unionists until the war's end.[61]

Maurice Block, who had moved to Farm Hill in 1860, was compelled to close his store in August 1861. That fall the Confederate forces burned 139 bales of his cotton and a large amount still in seed (about 300 bales total) rather than let it fall into Federal hands. His ingenious wife and two black women saved two bales of cotton by disposing of the straw ticking in mattresses and refilling them with cotton. Less than six months later, Block sold the hidden treasure for $1.20 a pound at Island No. 37. He smuggled both cotton and cattle into Memphis during the war, and when he was able to get calico, coffee, and salt, he sold them, respectively, for a dollar a yard, a dollar a pound, and one hundred dollars a barrel.[62]

A Jewish Union soldier, August Bondi, whose unit saw a good bit of duty in Arkansas during the Civil War, left in his memoirs some details of life for a Jewish soldier during that period as well as some of his experiences with the Jewish community in Pine Bluff.[63] In 1861 Bondi joined the Fifth Kansas Cavalry, which included only two other Jewish soldiers. Neither of these two men, however, would profess to being Jewish. The religiously devout Bondi said he felt a deep sense of loss at being isolated from Judaism's influences during his years of military service. He noted that the only time his loyalties to Judaism were satisfied during that period was at Pine Bluff, Arkansas, where he had Rosh Hashonah dinner with Mr. Kahn. He later related that while he was at Pine Bluff he helped two Jews (whom he referred to as Jehudims [sic]) to recover their horses that had been taken by Company F soldiers. He noted that one of the two Jews was a Pine Bluff baker [which was evidently one of the Weil brothers].[64] Just as in the case of Max Frauenthal's kind deeds, the influence of Judaism's ethics in Bondi's life was shown on several occasions by his kindness to men, women, and helpless Confederates.[65]

Samuel Lyons, who served as an officer in the Confederate army, had settled with his family at Augusta, Arkansas, shortly before the Civil War began. It had taken the family several weeks of travel to make the journey from Louisville, Kentucky, to their new destination. After arriving, Samuel had engaged in the cotton and mercantile business. During the war the Lyons, like many others, found it necessary to bury their salt in order to keep it from the Federal troops. Sometime during the conflict, the family made a visit to Kentucky. On the return trip, their wagon was stopped by Federal soldiers near the Cache River. When the plucky Mrs. Lyons told the soldiers that she had nothing with her but a wagonload of children, the family was allowed to proceed. But sewn into numerous pockets and a vest worn by Mrs. Lyons was one thousand dollars in gold.[66]

Besides the three Gates brothers, noted above, two other Arkansas Jewish families had three brothers who served in the Civil War. These included the Gans brothers—Morris, Jacob, and Simon—and the Cohen brothers—Peter, Jack, and Pool.[67]

Bernhard Baer, a cousin of Samuel Adler (father of Cyrus Adler), joined the Confederate army in May 1861 as a private in the Third Arkansas Regiment. He was later promoted to the quartermaster's office and served there from July 1862 to May 1865. His regiment, under Generals McCulloch, Pike, and Cooper, served in Arkansas, Missouri, and Indian Territory and fought in the battles of Oak Hills on 10 August 1861, at Elk Horn Tavern, Pea Ridge, on 6 and 7 March 1862, and in several minor skirmishes. Defeat was not in Baer's vocabulary, and at the close of the war he went to Mexico, believing that it would not be safe to live in the United States under Federal control. After only three months at Monterrey, however, he was cured of his dislike for the United States and returned to make Fort Smith his permanent home.[68]

Samuel Adler of Van Buren faced financial and physical reverses when he became ill in 1863. His town was being continually defended and attacked as the Federal army sought to prevent any shipment of cotton down the Arkansas River. When the town fell to Union soldiers in 1864, it, as well as the Adler home, was sacked by Federals. Hoarded food, clothing, and furniture were hauled away by Union soldiers in a hearse, the only conveyance available. Although the Federals did not occupy the home because of Adler's illness, they did keep a mascot bear in his back yard. The fact that Adler was a Mason of high degree was a boon to him. When the Federal commander of Van Buren, also a Mason, realized the seriousness of Adler's illness, he arranged for a pass for the family through Federal lines to Philadelphia. (Samuel Adler later died, and the family did not return to Arkansas. They did continue to hold some ten thousand acres of land in the state until 1911.)[69]

A. E. Shoffner of near Batesville enlisted in Company I of Ganze's regiment in the spring of 1862 and served through the remainder of the war. His primary position was in the quartermaster's department, but he also took part in several battles.[70] Ed S. Stiewel, later of Little Rock, served in the Confederate army that went out of New Orleans.[71] Max Dampf, who was born in Hesse, Germany, in 1848, came to America in 1864 and joined the Union army. He was stationed in Little Rock until being mustered out, after which he made his home at Marshall.[72] Jacob B. Friedheim, the younger brother of Aaron, ran away as a boy and joined the Confederates in their last operations around Camden.[73]

In his book, *The Jew as Patriot, Soldier, and Citizen* (Philadelphia: The Levytype Company, 1895), Simon Wolf lists fifty-two Jewish Arkansans who fought in the Civil War.[74] Considering those mentioned above that Wolf overlooked, it would seem that well over seventy Jewish Arkansans fought on the Confederate side. Of the approximately two hundred Jewish merchants in the state in 1860, more than a third of them served the southern cause. Two Arkansas Jewish soldiers are known to have been killed—Isaac Burgauer, who died in 1863, and Julius Levy, who was killed at Shiloh.[75]

Several Jewish Civil War veterans, such as Max Frauenthal, noted above, made Arkansas their home after the war. He settled at Conway and established one of the largest stores in the northwest section of the state.

Jacob D. Goldman, who had clerked in a village store in Georgia, was stationed at Pensacola, Florida, where he met two enthusiastic Arkansans, Dick Davis and Jesse Gailor. After the war Goldman settled near his war buddies at Jacksonport (and later, Newport), where he became one of the state's leading businessmen and advocates.

Another veteran, Shields Daltroff of Memphis, served as a foreman in cannon molding and settled at Wittsburg (and later Wynne) after the war, becoming a well-known businessman and merchant. Frank Silverman settled at Pine Bluff, where he later served as sheriff and collector of Jefferson County. Louis Tilles served with the Federal troops and was stationed at Fort Smith. He liked the area and made his home there after the war. The Tilles family promoted the city's development in a number of ways.

These men, as well as other Jewish entrepreneurs, helped significantly in the state's recovery after the devastation of the War between the States (see section III).

The Threads Come Together

1860s–1930s

EARLY

CONGREGATIONAL

HISTORIES

.

CHAPTER 5

The German Migration, 1865–1930

From the 1820s (when the first known Jews settled in Arkansas) through the 1920s, there were two waves of Jewish immigrants to America. The first, which continued until the turn of the century, was a relatively small but steady flow from Central (the German states) and Western Europe. These came with a general migration of non-Jews from Europe who sought respite from economic and political unrest. The second wave, which began in the 1880s and continued until Congress enacted the immigration laws of the 1920s, were East Europeans. More than two million of the latter came, driven from their homelands by severe persecution. The outlook of the two groups were entirely disparate. The relatively well-educated German Jews had been exposed to some reforms in their religious thought and often considered themselves cultured and progressive. Although they were Orthodox in their beliefs when they came to America, they exhibited "a readiness, if not an eagerness, to adapt themselves to the life and culture" they found in their adopted land.[1] When a reform movement within Judaism arose in America, the German Jews, particularly in the South and West, eagerly joined it.[2] On the other hand, the more deprived Jews from East Europe, who had been forced to live in tightly knit groups in segregated areas for centuries, were more apt to cling to their religion and adhere to its rituals, regardless of how different they might seem to others. The study of how the threads from these two parts of the Jewish tapestry came together and formed congregations in Arkansas follows the history of the two migration periods.

In Arkansas, as elsewhere in the South and West, the Jews who came to America from the 1820s to the 1860s scattered, peddling goods, plying their trades, and opening small stores in isolated communities. Few areas during that period had large enough Jewish communities to form cohesive groups. The confusion and chaos of the Civil War wiped out many of the isolated stores, and after that conflict, some of the Jewish merchants of Arkansas, more than five dozen of whom returned as war veterans, moved to more populated areas that seemed promising. Between 1865 and 1900 the Jewish population of Arkansas rose from some fourteen hundred to around four thousand.[3]

After the devastation of the Civil War, the population of the South was decimated, and pamphlets and brochures were distributed in America and abroad to attract immigrants. Arkansas distributed such literature, printed in German and English, seeking to draw settlers. This effort met with only limited success,[4] but of those immigrants who did come to Arkansas during that period, most were from Central Europe.[5] The esteem German immigrants were afforded in Arkansas at the time is reflected by a Little Rock newspaper's statement in 1875 that ". . . no class of immigration [other than Germans] is more desirable."[6] Although there were not enough German immigrants to change the general pattern of Arkansas's population, the high esteem in which they were held carried over for the German-Jewish community as well.

The Jews of Arkansas began to merge into cohesive groups during the War between the States, one of the first being a social organization in Little Rock, known as the Little Rock Club. Formed in 1864, its membership consisted of "the elite of Jewish society." The club, which later changed its name to Concordia Association, was founded on the principal that "pleasure is a necessity for the progress of the human race."[7] The Little Rock (Concordia) Club was said to be the first social club to form in the city (and perhaps the state).[8] The facilities of the club, which met in several locations between its formation and the time it built its "magnificent" three-story building at Eighth and Scott streets in 1903,[9] were considered for many years as the most elegant in town and were used for the most prestigious occasions. When former president Ulysses S. Grant visited the city in 1880, the gala ball conducted in his honor was held at Concordia Hall.[10] That previous January, the Saltatorian Club, composed of some of Little Rock's non-Jewish elite, held its ball at Concordia Hall, where Saltatorian members went to "no little trouble to see that their

Jewish guests enjoyed themselves."[11] (About one-fourth of those attending were Jewish.) Other social groups often used Concordia facilities, thus strengthening a rapport between the Jewish community and non-Jewish groups, especially the German society. (There was a reciprocity between these groups. German Jews participated in non-Jewish German clubs, such as *Turn Verein*, a club that figured prominently in the city's postbellum social life.)[12]

As more Jews settled in Arkansas, they began concentrating on religious services, and between 1866 and 1930, as many as two dozen congregations formed throughout the state.[13] From nine to eleven congregations formed between 1866 and 1900, located at Pine Bluff, Little Rock, Helena, Camden, Hot Springs, Fort Smith, Texarkana, and Jonesboro.

Pine Bluff

The congregations at Pine Bluff, Little Rock, and Helena formed almost simultaneously in the years 1866–67. The Pine Bluff group, which chose the name Anshe Emeth (Men of Truth) purchased a lot at Third Avenue and Laural Street in Pine Bluff in May 1866 on which to build a house of worship. The gala occasion of its cornerstone laying in October that year was accompanied by a downtown parade and speeches by the town's mayor and Protestant ministers.[14] Anshe Emeth Congregation was the first Arkansas Jewish congregation to receive a charter from the state legislature. This occurred on 13 March 1867, five days before the Jewish congregation, B'nai Israel of Little Rock, received theirs.[15] The Civil War had hampered the official organization of Pine Bluff's congregation, although minyans had been held in the city on important holidays during the war's duration.[16] The early group met in homes, particularly that of Solomon Solmson on Pullen Street, and was led by Aaron Reinach and Max Weil.[17]

Just as the Jews of Pine Bluff were the first to officially form a congregation in Arkansas, they also were the first in the state to organize a lodge of the benevolent Jewish fraternity, B'nai B'rith (Sons of the Covenant). (The Independent Order of B'nai B'rith was organized in America in 1843 by German immigrants who sought safety and support through communal life. It met both spiritual and material needs, including life insurance for widows and children, and formed a meeting ground for diverse Jews in America. It grew rapidly, spreading worldwide. Serving the cause of Jewish philanthropy and charity, it also established the Anti-Defamation League to combat anti-Semitism and organized Hillel Foundations on university campuses to inspire Jewish students.)[18] Between 1866 and 1879, eight

B'nai B'rith lodges formed in Arkansas, three of which were located in Pine Bluff. The Levi Lodge of Pine Bluff was established in December 1866, more than four years before a lodge (Elias Navra Lodge) was established in Little Rock. Helena's Esther (later Aaron Meyers) Lodge was established in 1871. Both the Hot Springs Phoenix Lodge and the Camden Elah Lodge formed in 1877, and the Fort Smith Lodge (later Louis Cohen Lodge) formed in January 1879. The two other Pine Bluff lodges formed in April 1877 (the Phoenix, later Charles Weil, Lodge) and in January 1879 (the Pine Bluff Lodge Number 307).[19]

Considering Pine Bluff's relatively remote location, Anshe Emeth was fortunate in the quality of the rabbis who served it over the years. Those who served were well-educated leaders who sought to bring the Jewish community together, and most became well known for their work for the area's general good. Anshe Emeth's first two rabbis, Jacob Bloch (1867–71) and Moses Fluegel (1871–76), are examples of scholars who stood out in an area where higher formal education at the time was rare.[20] Rabbi Bloch taught in local public schools, and when the cornerstone was laid for a new city high school in 1870, he led the grand procession that included city officials and brass bands.[21] Rabbi Fluegel, a well-educated German immigrant with a heavy accent was described as having a "deficient delivery" although he was noted as being one of the "finest classical scholars in this country."[22] Non-Jews as well as Jews attended lectures and sermons given by the congregation's rabbis. Sermons at Anshe Emeth were conducted in German until 1874, indicative of the background of most of the Jews in Pine Bluff at the time.[23]

For the most part, the Jews of Pine Bluff enjoyed the freedom to practice their religion and observe Jewish holidays with open zest. Even the City Hall was used for their Purim balls.[24] If there was no public Jewish celebration of their holidays, that fact made the local news. For example, at one time when the congregation was without a rabbi, a local paper noted that, because of that fact, "none of the usual impressive public ceremonies" were carried out by the Jews.[25] At another time, a local paper described church life in Pine Bluff, noting that the "beautiful and stately temples" of the Protestants, Catholics, and Hebrews were open to all people, rich and poor alike, and referred to the houses of worship as "common meeting grounds."[26]

Although there was a general acceptance of the Jews in Pine Bluff, they did experience a shattering anti-Semitic incident in 1876. During the tenure of Rabbi Fluegel, who stressed sound religious training and a tolerant atmosphere, the Jewish cemetery of Pine Bluff was vandalized.

Stones and monuments were demolished, and a photo of the "inhuman and barbarous desecration" was sent to a national publication, *The American Israelite*. The journal's editors called on Jews nationwide to voice outrage against the "dastardly violators"; aid was encouraged to restore monuments and to plant flowers and "sweet shrubs, til the desert that has been made shall blossom as the rose."[27]

The congregation, which early joined the Reform movement, initially followed a more traditional worship. When a Jewish newcomer, L. Silverman, arrived in the city in 1873, members of his faith shunned him, although he bought and ran a local hotel and settled into the city's life. Their disdain stemmed from the fact that he was a Reform Jew.[28] Opinion changed over the next decade, however, as successive rabbis, trained in the Reform movement, led them into its tenets, which moved further and further from traditional Judaism. Rabbi Fluegel was followed by Rabbi Meyer Greenblatt (1876–85), an "enthusiastic elocutionist,"[29] who was quoted in a local paper as saying that the beliefs of the "old Orthodox Jews" had been "advanced and enlightened" and certain "peculiar rites" had been "very much modified."[30] Rabbi Greenblatt, a talented musician, strengthened Anshe Emeth's music program, consisting of Professor Eugene Ellinger, Pine Bluff's most accomplished musician at the time, organist and choir director Birdie Weiler, May Bluthenthal, and Mrs. Sam Franklin. Gentiles were later added to the choir.[31] (Rabbi Greenblatt was Anshe Emeth's only rabbi to die in office—of typhoid fever—and the only rabbi buried at Pine Bluff.)[32]

A Sabbath School was initiated at Anshe Emeth during the tenure of Rabbi Ferdinand Becker (1887–98).[33] Growing membership precipitated the need for larger facilities, and an impressive new temple was built at West Second and Poplar streets in 1902. Rabbi Joseph Kornfeld (1898–1904), who married a local belle, Josephine Bluthenthal, con-ducted the temple's dedication.[34] The congregation was generous with the use of its buildings over the years, allowing them to be used as classrooms for secular educators and by various churches on occasion. The First Christian Church was organized in the Jewish temple in June 1894. The local Musical Coterie used Anshe Emeth's piano and organ for instruc-tion, and Coterie programs were presented in the synagogue and temple.[35]

The Jews of Pine Bluff also were involved in cultural events in other ways. A Mendelssohn Club was formed in the city by the 1870s, and by 1876 there were thirty-three members. Composed of the "best talent in Pine Bluff," its members were "determined to persevere" until it was a credit and honor to the city. Members of the club included representatives of Jewish families such as Aschaffenberg, Hilzheim, Nathan, Leopold, and others. Jewish clubs also formed; the Bluff City Club (later known as the Harmony Club) became the "most prominent local Jewish organization" in the city by 1901. The Jewish women had a prominent social organization, the Entre Nous Eucre Club.[36]

One of Anshe Emeth's most noted spiritual leaders was Rabbi Ephraim Frisch (1904–12), who became an outspoken community leader. Frisch publicly opposed sectarian celebrations in the public domain, and in 1908 he publicly protested against the Christological expressions used by then interim Arkansas governor X. O. Pindall in his Thanksgiving Day proclamation.[37] Frisch was particularly interested in social justice and while at Pine Bluff became a longstanding friend of a young black educator, Isaac Fisher. The latter served as principal of Branch Normal College (later known as the University of Arkansas at Pine Bluff) from 1902 to 1911. Fisher sought to bring the black and white races together by quiet diplomacy and by stressing Negro self-improvement. When his position became unpopular, even among the blacks of the area, and prejudice against him mounted, he resigned his position in May 1911. Rabbi Frisch publicly defended Fisher, referring to his industry, integrity, and decorum.[38] Fisher left Pine Bluff in 1911 and Rabbi Frisch followed one year later, when he accepted a rabbinate in Far Rockaway, New York. Throughout his life, Rabbi Frisch (who died in 1957) continued to be active in social justice movements, and his scholarly activities included being yearbook editor of the Central Conference of American Rabbis as well as the author of several books.[39]

During Rabbi Frisch's tenure, the women of Anshe Emeth organized the Willing Workers, a Jewish charity with a charter membership of ninety-one. From the time of the congregation's formation, its distaff side had been as progressive as the men's. They had formed a Ladies' Benevolent Society in 1870, headed by Mrs. Sam Bluthenthal, with founding members Mesdames Jacob Bloom, John Bloom, Gabe Meyer, Aaron Reinach, Sol Rosenberg, and Charles Weil.[40] The organization was the forerunner of the congregation's Sisterhood.

Rabbi Joseph Jasin (1912–16), who succeeded Rabbi Frisch, helped found the Pine Bluff Associated Charities (which later became the Community Chest, then the United Way) and served for several years as its chairman. He also served as head of the City Beautiful Club, and his persistent efforts helped bring about the establishment of the city's public library.[41]

Anshe Emeth's congregation was split by dissention in 1921. Just four years earlier, it had been drawn closer together as a community during its fiftieth anniversary. The 1917 celebration was led by Rabbi Raphael Goldenstein (1916–19), who compiled the congregation's history and established a Sabbath School Library Association.[42] After Goldenstein left he was succeeded by Rabbi Leonard Rothstein, who soon nullified efforts of the former at solidifying the congregation. Before coming to Pine Bluff, Rabbi Rothstein had led for eleven years a congregation in Alexandria, Louisiana, where he had been aggressively active in civic work. Soon after joining Anshe Emeth, he made a number of radical changes in its constitution and its operating system. He abolished the old pew system, which entailed dues for specific seating, and opened membership to women, allowing them to serve on the board of trustees. Not one to mince words, at one time he denounced as "unwarranted and unjustified" the decision of Pine Bluff School Board members who voted to permit Dr. John H. Moore, a national lecturer for the Ku Klux Klan, to speak in the local high school auditorium. He called this action "a highhanded and flagrant abuse of authority" for using a public school for such a "lamentable, unbelievable and deplorable piece of business."[43]

Some members of the congregation viewed Rabbi Rothstein's courage of convictions as too extreme, and in the fall of 1921, fifty-eight members filed a petition to incorporate a new congregation, Temple Israel. Some of Anshe Emeth's most outstanding members joined the splinter group, including Simon Bloom, Henry Marx, Jake Stein, Henry Sonfield, E. B. Bloom, Mrs. Herbert Bluthenthal, Mrs. Ike Leitner, Harry Lewine, M. L. Reinberger, and Abe Soltz.[44] The membership lists of Anshe Emeth and Temple Israel at the time show that the congregation did not split evenly by families; family members were found in both congregations (e.g., Mrs. Gabe Meyer is listed as a member of Anshe Emeth, while her husband, Gabe, is found on the roll of Temple Israel).[45] Temple Israel continued to function until 1925. Rabbi Louis Brav, who served as its only leader, became well known in the community. The congregation held its services in the Shrine Temple and at the Harmony Club facilities. (The latter facilities also were used by the Young Men's Hebrew Association and the Temple Sisterhood.)[46]

Rabbi Rothstein continued his civic work in Pine Bluff for two more years after the congregation split, and his work at Anshe Emeth was described as "excellent." Like Rabbi Frisch before him, however, he became disillusioned with the citizenry of Pine Bluff and left there in 1923, citing the "narrowness and blindness of the community at large."[47]

When Rabbi Brav left, Temple Israel rejoined Anshe Emeth under the leadership of Rabbi Mayer Lippman.[48] After a short stay by the latter, he was followed by Rabbi Morris Clark, who was to serve the congregation for twenty-two years (1927–49)—longer than any other leader. Rabbi Clark's work with the Arkansas Jewish Assembly did inestimable good (see section IV).

From its inception, Anshe Emeth has been led by some of its outstanding lay members. Presidents who served the congregation through 1930 included David Aschaffenberg, John Bloom, Gabe Meyer, Joseph Altheimer, Solomon Miller, Charles Weil, E. B. Bloom, Ben Weil, Adolph Bluthenthal, Harry Rosenberg, Jay Levine, James Franklin, Henry Marx, Maurice Cohen, Charles Dante, W. S. Sherman, Morris Rosen, Leon D. Rutstein, Leonard L. Selig, Henry Levi, Robert N. Banks, Simon Joseph, David Bram, Dr. Sheldon Blau, Hubert Eisenkramer, and Sam Goldweber.[49]

Little Rock

Like their coreligionists in Pine Bluff, the Jews of Little Rock had met intermittently during the Civil War. A self-constituted committee collected three hundred dollars in the summer of 1865 and directed Scottish-born Gabriel McCowan to purchase a Sefer Torah (a scroll containing the five books of Moses) and a shofar (ram's horn) for the High Holy Day services that fall.[50] Morris Navra, who had settled in Little Rock in 1855, presided over the fall holidays of 1866 and was elected president of the new congregation. Originally, the group's name was "the Little Rock Congregation," but this was later changed to Congregation B'nai Israel (Sons, or Children, of Israel). Early officers and trustees included M. Caro, S. Erb, Louis Volmer, J. Bott, A. K. Auerbach, A. Kempner, M. Hilb, L. Lasker, Alex Meyer, N. J. Bunzel, and D. Rudolph. L. Landsberg and Jacob Menkus served as readers. Ninety charter members joined the new congregation, and 214 families and individuals were considered pioneer members.[51] Meetings were held in the Ditter Building and also in a frame building at Main and Water streets.[52] The first full time leader was the Reverend Samuel Peck (some early Reform spiritual leaders were known by the title *reverend*), who came in September 1867 and served as chazzan (professional cantor) and shochet (ritual slaughterer).

The economic struggle for livelihood after the Civil War apparently siphoned off a great deal of energy that otherwise would have gone toward congregational matters. Religious zeal waned quickly after the initial flurry of organization; few meetings were held and membership lagged even after monthly dues were greatly reduced. Enthusiasm revived when building plans were made, and a "dazzling" benefit ball was given to raise funds after a site was purchased at 304 Center Street in Little Rock. A local newspaper, commenting on the ball, said it was given to ensure that "the tribes of wandering foot and weary breast" would not be "shrineless." An observer of the festivities noted that "those feet were not in the least heavy with all their wandering" and it would be suspect that "there was any breast there that was weary."[53] The congregation's first temple was dedicated on 27 September 1872 by Rabbi Jacob Bloch, who had joined B'nai Israel a month earlier.[54] A Sabbath School, called Talmud Yelodim Institute (Institute for the Instruction of Children) opened that fall, led by overseers M.A. Cohn, M. Navra, and A. Simon Cohen. Within six months, sixty-nine children were enrolled. The first confirmation class, held in 1873, included Mollie Alexander, Anne Levy, Sarah Ehrenberg, Laura Wormser, Henrietta Lewis, Abe Weider, Simon Rudolph, Raphael Levy, and Moses Vogel.[55]

B'nai Israel established a Board of Relief in August 1873 that superceded the Society for the Visiting of the Sick and the Burial of the Dead, which had been formed in 1868 and had not functioned well. Five acres of land at Oakland Cemetery in East Little Rock were purchased from the city in 1875 for a burial ground. By that year, eighty-one children were enrolled in Sabbath School, and the choirs of B'nai Israel and Anshe Emeth of Pine Bluff began exchanging visits.[56]

Internal stress and storm plagued B'nai Israel during its first two decades as it sought to find its niche in American Jewish life. Some members insisted that all prayers be in Hebrew, but the majority were influenced by the free spirit of America that offered a new evaluation of Judaism. Slowly the leading changes in doctrine and liturgy were accepted, and the Minhag America (American Ritual prayer book) was adopted in 1872. Parts of the services that had been in German were changed, prayer was allowed in English, the women's gallery was abolished, family pews were established, worship was allowed with uncovered heads, and, finally, second-day holidays were dropped.[57] In May 1879 eight Christian men and women began serving as part of B'nai Israel's choir.[58] The latter seemed to be the last straw for those who adhered to more traditional inclinations, and that fall an Orthodox service was advertised in Little Rock for the first time. This well-attended service, held at Casino Hall, was conducted by S. Lasker, Lazarus Ehrenberg, and Isaac Adelman,[59] men who had been pillars in B'nai Israel. When Rabbi N. J. Benson, who followed Rabbi Bloch, was asked in 1883 to wear a robe and tallis (prayer shawl) at services and funerals, dissension grew until April 1884, when the congregation declared its pulpit vacant.[60]

When Reform Judaism in America, led by men such as Rabbis Isaac Mayer Wise and Max Lilienthal, held its first convention on 8 July 1873 in Cincinnati, Ohio, Temple B'nai Israel of Little Rock was one of thirty-two congregations that sent delegates. Although three B'nai Israel delegates were chosen to attend—Mathias A. Cohn, Abe Pollock, and Rabbi Bloch—only Bloch attended.[61] (It was later determined that Bloch failed to appear when a roll call of delegates was given on 9 July 1873, and B'nai Israel was therefore excluded from being considered one of the founding congregations of the Union of American Hebrew Congregations [UAHC]).[62] B'nai Israel officially joined UAHC on 7 September 1873 and became a faithful supporter of the new national organization and the rabbinical institute, Hebrew Union College (HUC), which UAHC established in 1875.[63]

Although controversy might surround some of the "progressive" changes in Judaism sought by adherents of the Reform movement, the basic ritual of the faith—circumcision—was never overlooked. The state was fortunate in having its own mohel (ritual circumciser) from 1880 to 1896. Jacob Menkus of Little Rock served in that capacity and during those years conducted the brith (or circumcision) of 246 babies statewide and two in Missouri. He carefully noted in his *Bereth Abraham* book the names of the children, their fathers, and the towns in which the Brith Milah (circumcision ceremony) took place.[64]

B'nai Israel's movement toward adhering strictly to Reform Judaism's rituals was brought about when Rabbi Joseph Stolz became leader of the congregation in 1884. A graduate of HUC, he was the congregation's first American-trained rabbi, and he was schooled in all the latest developments of Reform Judaism.[65] He completely reorganized the Sabbath School and opened the classrooms of the temple for public school night classes. He was a delegate to the UAHC convention in Pittsburgh in 1885, at which time Reform Judaism reached its apogee in liberalizing its doctrine. Rabbi Stolz immediately implemented what would be known as the "Pittsburgh Platform," on which Reform Judaism in America, including the Reform Judaism of B'nai Israel of Little Rock, rested for years to come.[66] The 1885 high water mark of Reform Judaism left a number of B'nai Israel members stranded, and the following year a schism split the congregation. The ones following traditional Judaism no doubt swelled the ranks of the Orthodox group that had been advertising since 1879.[67]

When Rabbi Stolz arrived in Little Rock in 1884, the city had a population of about 35,000. He later described the backwoodsy community that he found.[68] Only two or three streets were paved, and open bayous were still common. At the time he served B'nai Israel, he took note that the majority of the Jewish community were foreign born (German) and lacked higher education. Mathias A. Cohn and his son Morris M. and Jacob Erb were the only Jewish lawyers, a Dr. Deutsch was the only Jewish doctor, and Miss Hattie Cohn the only Jewish public schoolteacher. Simon Rudolph, a congregant, had sat under the teaching of Dr. Ludwig Philippson, and Mr. and Mrs. Mathias A. Cohn had lived previously in Cincinnati, where they had been taught by and were friends with Isaac Mayer Wise. (After leaving Little Rock, Rabbi Stolz also served as full-time leader to Arkansas congregations at Helena and Fort Smith.)

Rabbi E. Schreiber, a student of one of Reform Judaism's European founders, Abraham Geiger of Berlin, succeeded Rabbi Stolz as leader of B'nai Israel in 1889. Schreiber, who became noted for his "extraordinary scholarship, powerful eloquence, and irreproachable character," lectured at Christian churches, where his audiences included "highly cultivated . . . prominent lawyers, ministers, and doctors."[69] Under his leadership, B'nai Israel grew from 78 heads of families to 120, and the congregation was described as being "one of culture and refinement, holding liberal views."[70] Rabbi Schreiber served as a member of the Board of Visitors and Examiners for the Little Rock school system; other members included Mrs. Logan H. Roots, Mrs. Fay Hempstead, and Drs. M. B. Chapmon and J. H. Smith. Rabbi Schreiber also served as a professor of modern languages at Little Rock University, which was founded in 1882 by the Methodist Episcopal Church and located on Lincoln Avenue.[71] As did members of other congregations in Arkansas and the South, congregants were pleased when their spiritual leaders became well accepted and respected in the local communities.

During the tenure of Rabbi Charles Rubenstein (1891–97), B'nai Israel outgrew its facilities on Center Street and built a beautiful new edifice at Capitol and Broadway. The new temple was dedicated by none other than the venerable Rabbi Isaac Mayer Wise on 9 May 1897. Its spacious interior would accommodate about seven hundred people. A local paper covered the dedication at length; the edifice itself was described as "an architectural ornament . . . one of the most magnificent houses of worship in all the Southland." The building was of Romanesque design in cream-colored pressed brick, with terra cotta and limestone trimmings.[72]

Also during Rabbi Rubenstein's tenure, a Temple Aid Society, forerunner of the Temple Sisterhood, was formed on 6 October 1893. (A Ladies' Hebrew Benevolent Society had formed previously in 1867.)[73]

Like its sister congregation in Pine Bluff, B'nai Israel was fortunate in having well-educated spiritual leaders of high quality who served it through the years. Rabbi Harry H. Mayer (1897–99) later served Congregation B'nai Jehudah in Kansas City, where he confirmed and helped prepare for the rabbinate one Ira E. Sanders. Sanders would later become one of the most beloved and revered leaders of Little Rock's B'nai Israel congregation. Rabbi Louis Wolsey (1899–1907), who followed Rabbi Mayer, was named chaplain general of the Arkansas State Guard by Governor Jeff Davis in 1903; he served on the Little Rock Board of Education in 1906–07, and cofounded the Little Rock Public Library. His tenure at B'nai Israel was so successful that the temple had to be enlarged to accommodate increased membership.[74] (After Wolsey left Little Rock, he served the Euclid Avenue Temple in Cleveland for eighteen years, during which time the membership rose in that congregation from 180 to 1,225. He then served at Rodeph Shalom congregation in Philadelphia, known at the time to be one of the most powerful Jewish congregations in America. He also was active in the Central Conference of American Rabbis.)[75]

Judaism in Little Rock reached a new high during Rabbi Wolsey's period. When a survey was taken for religious preferences among the city's citizenry, "Jewish" was selected as ninth out of twenty-two groups that were specified.[76] Jews were generally well accepted in local organizations in the city as well. Of thirty-six Little Rock clubs and fraternities listed in 1900, twenty-five had Jewish members.[77]

A chapter of the Young Men's Hebrew Association (YMHA) was formed in Little Rock in 1902. Officers of the organization were Louis M. Samuel, Ralph Levy, William Levinson, and Gus Gans; directors were Charles Jacobson, Eugene Pfeifer, Herbert Wolf, and Cyril H. Friedham.[78] The organization, which was modeled after the Protestant Young Men's Christian Association, had been initiated in Baltimore in 1854. Its aims at first were social and recreational, but it later ventured into adult Jewish education.[79]

Rabbi Louis Witt (1907–19), who followed Rabbi Wolsey, was one of B'nai Israel's signal leaders. Shortly after he arrived in Little Rock, he organized the Arkansas Conference of Jewish Religious School Teachers.[80] Participants came from Little Rock, Camden, Pine Bluff, Fort Smith, Helena, and Hot Springs. The intensive studies helped strengthen

Judaism statewide, and through this organization, Witt became well known in Arkansas. Rabbi Witt and other Jewish individuals were active in the formation of an organized social agency in Little Rock. (This was a general trend, for Jews who settled in the state became active in charitable and social endeavors. For example, during the yellow fever scourge of 1879, several Jewish citizens—Dave Pollock, Gus Gans, Herman Kahn, and Professor Louis Cohen and his orchestra—helped raise needed funds.[81] And the Provident Relief Association, an early Little Rock charity organization, had Jewish officers and directors, including Gus Blass, Abe Ottenheimer, Rudolph Fink, E. Epstein, and M. J. Siesel.)[82] The United Charities Association was organized in December 1911, and its first state conference was held in Little Rock on 16 and 17 May 1912.[83] Rabbi Witt later served as president of the association.[84] (The organization was known variously as Arkansas Conference of Charities and Correction, Arkansas Conference of Social Work, and Arkansas Conference on Social Welfare.) Its first director was Murray A. Auerbach, a Jewish graduate of the New York School of Social Work, who been selected from about sixty applicants to head the organization. He later was recognized as the "father of professional social work in Arkansas."[85] Other Arkansas rabbis who served as president of the organization were Joseph Jasin of Pine Bluff, Charles Latz of Fort Smith, and Ira Sanders of Little Rock. Several other Jewish citizens were actively engaged in the formation of the work, such as Rabbi A. B. Rhine of Hot Springs (who served as an officer), J. F. Mayer, Mrs. Sol Schoenfeld, and State Senator Charles Jacobson.[86] Other Jews were also involved through the years.

In May 1916 Little Rock hosted the annual regional convention of B'nai B'rith. (The District Grand Lodge had met previously in the city in 1877 and in 1902.) About four hundred people attended the meeting, held at Concordia Hall. Keynote speaker to the forty-third annual convention, Dr. C. H. Brough, a Democratic nominee for governor of Arkansas, paid tribute to the civic and business achievements of the Jews of Arkansas. Convention delegates went to Hot Springs on 3 May to witness the dedication of the new Leo N. Levi Hospital, which had been established by B'nai B'rith (see below).[87]

During his tenure (1921–25) as B'nai Israel's rabbi, Emanuel J. Jack, a World War I veteran, served the Little Rock community as commander of Shoemaker Post No. 77 of the Veterans of Foreign Wars and as state chairman of the American Legion's Americanization Committee.[88]

Rabbi Ira E. Sanders, born at Rich Hill, Missouri, in 1894 and a graduate of Hebrew Union College in 1919, was called to B'nai Israel's pulpit in

1926. There he served the congregation as full-time leader for thirty-seven years and as rabbi emeritus for another twenty-two years. Serving first at Allentown, Pennsylvania, he then went to Temple Israel in New York as associate rabbi. The latter was a cosmopolitan congregation with a membership of fifteen hundred. On Decoration Day 1926, Rabbi Sanders happened to speak on the subject, "Why the North and the South Should Meet Together," noting that it was time that the wounds still being suffered in the North and the South from the Civil War should be healed. Unknown to him, a pulpit committee from Temple B'nai Israel of Little Rock was in the audience and was so moved by his lecture that its members determined he should come to Little Rock.[89] After accepting the pulpit at Little Rock and arriving by train on 1 September 1926, he said he was dismayed at what he found. The comparatively small city seemed like the hinterlands to him, and he was tempted to leave immediately. He found the city of Little Rock and the state of Arkansas to be semi-isolated sections of America where "newcomers from the North were looked upon as intruders in the highly homogeneous community and state."[90] Congregation officers who met him encouraged him to stay, and he decided to give it a try.

One of the first decisions Rabbi Sanders had to make after arriving in Little Rock was over the attitude of some of his congregants toward Palestine as a homeland for the Jewish people. He had been trained as a child to respect and love the Land of the Fathers, and when it was suggested that a separate congregation be established for those who opposed a Jewish state, Rabbi Sanders adamantly told those who proposed such an idea that it would be "over my dead body."[91]

But Rabbi Sanders saw Zionism as of minor importance to the needs he found in Little Rock at the time, one of the most pressing of which was in social-work education. He immediately began teaching an extension course in social work for the University of Arkansas. This developed into a School of Social Work, for which he served as dean from its inception in 1927 until lack of funds closed it during the Depression of the 1930s. When the school first opened, sixty-two students enrolled, two of whom were black women. At the close of the first session, several students informed Rabbi Sanders that in the South blacks and whites did not attend the same schools. Rabbi Sanders sternly rebuked them, but school policy was later enforced and only white students were allowed.[92] It could be viewed as providential that a school of social work was established at that time in the state's history. The greatest depression the state and nation had ever faced lay just ahead, and the social workers needed during that period were supplied by many graduates of the school founded by Rabbi Sanders. He also helped Rabbi A. B. Rhine of Hot Springs found the Arkansas Jewish Assembly and enthusiastically supported it (see section IV).

The majority of B'nai Israel's presidents were not only pillars of the Jewish community, but also were well known in the civic community as well. Those who served subsequent to first president, Morris Navra, through the 1930s were Philip Pfeifer, Abe Ottenheimer, Harry Ehrenberg Sr., Simon Cohn, Phillip Ottenheimer, Simon Gans, Louis Volmer, Mathias A. Cohn, Alexander Borg, Louis Blass, Mark M. Cohn, Max Heiman, Charles S. Stifft, Herman Kahn, Louis K. Mandlebaum, Arthur H. Pfeifer, Dan Daniels, Maurice J. Altheimer, Sidney Kahn Sr., Harry B. Solmson Sr., and Eugene M. Pfeifer Jr.[93]

Helena

No early records of Jewish congregational life in Helena are extant, but it is known that there were Jews in town by the 1840s. At the end of the Civil War, Jewish settlers included members of the Seelig, Meyer, Rosenthal, Trieber, and Wronke families.[94] These were joined by numbers of others, and by 1867 sixty-five Jews had formed a congregation.[95] There is some speculation that there might have been two groups originally, and these later coalesced. Indication of this comes from the earliest record— an inscribed yod (Torah pointer). Dated 14 November 1869, the group's original name is given as B'nai Jeshurun (a symbolic name for the Sons of Israel), with "United Hebrew Congregation" as part of the name. The yod was donated to the congregation by Maurice Meyer, an early leader in the Jewish community.[96]

Helena's Jewish congregation, later given the name Beth El (House of God), experienced a slump in interest shortly after it formed in 1867, just as B'nai Israel of Little Rock had. In 1873 a letter appeared in the national Jewish publication *American Israelite*, in which a Beth El member said that Judaism was "very much neglected" in Helena.[97] The congregation, composed of some twenty-five families and a number of young, single men, served in name only, the writer said. It had been meeting in a storeroom on Ohio Street, but interest was renewed after it purchased an abandoned Presbyterian church for a house of worship.[98] Churches had proliferated in Helena from the days of early pioneers who had founded the town around 1820. These settlers had established their religious life quickly and had passed down their spiritual devotion, helping to develop an "esprit de corps" later among the town's clergy.[99] For example, when the Jewish congregation needed the services of a spiritual leader (in cases of death, marriage, etc.) before a rabbi had been engaged, a local Methodist minister, the Reverend Dr. Garrison, officiated. The Jews considered him to be "high minded, with indefatigable energy."[100] Later Methodist and Episcopal congregations used the Jewish temple while their facilities were being built.[101] As the congregation progressed, it organized a Hebrew Benevolent Association, purchased burial grounds in November 1875, and held its first confirmation class about 1878.[102]

By 1880 the congregation was flourishing. At the wedding that year of Charles Meyers to Cecelia Weinlaub, a building project was initiated that culminated in the dedication in October 1880 of a new brick temple, located at Perry and Pecan streets. (Dedication invitations included the statement "Reform to the Limit!")[103] The congregation, although smaller and located in a more remote location than those of Pine Bluff and Little Rock, was fortunate in the spiritual leaders who served its members. The full-time rabbis who served from 1879 to 1930 were Abraham Meyers, L. Weiss, A. M. Bloch, A. Gerstman, Abraham Brill, Eli Mayer, Gerson B. Levi, Max Reichler, Joseph H. Stolz, Aaron L. Weinstein, Samuel Peiper, Peiser Jacobs, Jerome Mark, and Joseph Leiser. The men who served as Beth El's presidents were prominent business and civic leaders. Those who served from 1878 to 1932 were A. Meyers, H. Weinlaub, Henry Fink, Isadore Mundt, Isaac Frank, Meyer Newman, B. Selig, Isaac Ehrman, Mac Leiber, Eli Newman, L. Rothschild, Louis Solomon, Joseph L. Solomon, J. L. Altman, Mortimer B. Isaacs, and Sam Ciener Sr.[104]

Several organizations sprang up over the years among Helena's Jewish community, including a Hebrew Boys' Club, the Young Men's Hebrew Association (YMHA), the Excelsior Club, and the Helena Literary and Social Circle. In 1892 the latter group developed into a social organization, the Lotus Club, which purchased a residence on Ohio Street. A Temple Ladies' Aid Society was formed sometime after 1890.[105] Members of the various Jewish organizations were drawn from smaller towns of the area, including West Helena, Marianna, Marvell, Holly Grove, and Trenton.

In 1915 and 1916, during Rabbi Peiper's tenure and Joseph L. Solomon's presidency, the congregation built a new, impressive temple, sporting splendid Corinthian columns and Palladian windows. It cost less than $40,000.[106] The Jewish population of the area continued to grow, and by the 1920s between 100 and 125 Jewish families were listed in the Helena area.[107]

When the Helena Country Club was first formed in 1916, Jewish citizens of the area were invited to join. The club became "the center of social life" of Helena/West Helena.[108] The Jewish women of Helena were active in the community's civic and social affairs. A 1930s article noted twenty-nine Jewish women who were associated with Helena club events.[109] Although they were welcomed and were made a part of the local clubs, the Jews continued to maintain their own social club as well. In 1926 the Lotus Club moved to a "beautiful club house on the westerly outskirts of the city" between Helena and West Helena.[110]

Rabbi Carl Miller, who served Congregation Beth El in the 1930s, also helped establish the Arkansas Jewish Assembly (see section IV).

Camden

At least two dozen Jewish individuals and families had settled in Camden before the Civil War (see section I). Between 1865 and 1870, these were joined by others, including members of the families of Newhouse, Lazarus, Fisher, Rosenberg, Levy, Altschul, Felsenthal, Pollock, and Winter.[111] The early Jewish community in Camden was fortunate in having Aaron Freidheim join them; he could read services, deliver sermons, and teach Sabbath School. For such efforts, he was referred to as the "mainstay of the congregation."[112] The Jewish group remained rather loosely formed until 1869, when a synagogue was planned. They officially organized on 18 December 1869, naming their congregation Beth El Emeth (House of the God of Truth).[113] On Christmas Day a week later, officers and trustees were elected: Solomon Block, John Lazarus, Moses Winter, E. Feibleman, S. Levy, and David Felsenthal.[114]

By 1873 the synagogue was completed, and the Reverend M. Sukenheimer, hired as the first full-time rabbi, delivered the dedication address in October. To an audience of both Gentiles and Jews, the rabbi stressed the "perfect toleration of religious liberty in America," compared with the "intolerable persecution" the Jews had experienced and were experiencing in other parts of the world. The temple was debt-free by the time of the dedication, paid for by about fifteen congregation members.[115]

Rabbi Nachman I. Benson, who followed Reverend Sukenheimer as Beth El Emeth's spiritual leader, served only two years (1877–78). During his short tenure, the city's public schools could not be maintained, and Rabbi Benson taught the Jewish children, using the synagogue facilities. Thoroughly competent in both religious and secular studies, he left an indelible impression on the younger members of the temple. In later years those who were familiar with the congregation's full-time rabbis remembered him as its most outstanding leader.[116]

Beth El Emeth records between the years 1880 and the 1920s did not survive, and little is known of the congregation's history during that time. Toward the end of 1927, the congregation began contemplating the building of a new house of worship, and the old one was torn down in November of that year.[117] But, as fate would have it, a large new Jewish temple was not to be part of Camden's history. The congregation had begun to wane; children left home for higher education and did not return, and soon those who were left were caught in the throes of the Great Depression. It was not until the impetus brought about by the Arkansas Jewish Assembly that a small temple was built in Camden (see section IV).

Hot Springs

It is unfortunate for posterity that early records of the Hot Springs congregation were destroyed in three fires (1896, 1905, and 1913) and one flood (1924). What early record is available shows a very colorful beginning. In the fall of 1875, ten Jewish families organized a society to hold worship services during the High Holidays. Their plans almost went awry when two members of the newly formed group "revolted, in revolting language" and were expelled.[118] The details of the fiasco were reported in the national Jewish publication, *American Israelite*, whose editors commented that, if the offending parties had indeed used the terms reported, "they ought to be expelled from every decent community . . . [and] any Israelite using such words ought to be branded." Subsequent history of the congregation rests on the memory of older members who shared their reminiscences in the 1950s. (These included Dave Burgauer and the Mesdames Rena Welcher, Gertrude Newman, Mary Benedict, Mattie Bowman, and others).[119]

A group of Jewish settlers began meeting as early as 1872 in a small room in downtown Hot Springs, and High Holy Day services were held formally in 1875 in rented quarters. (The exact location is not known.) The name Beth Israel (House of Israel) was selected. Later, the second floor of a Central Avenue store was used. In 1876 the group purchased a burial ground, known as Jewish Rest Cemetery, in southwest Hot Springs. M. Hoffstadt, who died 7 September 1876 was the first person buried there.[120]

The B'nai B'rith lodge (Beth Israel Lodge), which formed in 1877, served as the center for Jewish life in Hot Springs for many years. The organization had rigid rules at the time and participation in its events was taken seriously; if an individual missed a meeting, funeral, or duty, the member was fined one dollar per miss. The first officers and trustees of the lodge, who were also pillars of the congregation, included Leo Mayer, M. Levy, B. Brown, Henry Fellheimer, Emanuel Burgauer, J. Karatofsky, Henry Cohen, H. Moscowitz, Jacob Kempner, and E. Lynes.[121]

Lay readers served the congregation in its early days; these included a Mr. Goodman and a Mr. Raphael. Some of the readers were itinerant teachers and some were passing peddlers.[122] In 1881 a house of worship was built at Central Avenue and Orange Street for a cost of $550. This was destroyed when a section of Hot Springs was devastated by fire in 1896. The facilities of the First Methodist Church were used until another temple was built. This too was destroyed by fire in 1913. Billy Gross (owner of Gross Mortuary in Hot Springs) dashed into the flaming building at that time and saved the Torah.[123]

The congregation's first full-time rabbi, Frank Louis Rosenthal (1894–1901), began advertising High Holy Day services after his arrival. During his tenure a Ladies' Aid Society formed (forerunner of the congregation's Sisterhood), headed by Mrs. Emanuel Burgauer. Rabbi Emanuel L. Schreiber, who had served Congregation B'nai Israel in Little Rock (1889–1891), also served at Hot Springs (1901–02).[124]

Rabbi Schreiber was followed in 1902 by Rabbi Abraham Benedict Rhine. The history of Congregation House of Israel as well as that of Hot Springs was intertwined with this spiritual leader for the next thirty-nine years (he served full time longer than any other rabbi in Arkansas). Born in Shavii, Lithuania, in 1876, Rabbi Rhine came straight from his graduation at Hebrew Union College to Hot Springs and assumed the rabbinate there for life. His first challenge was one presented by the fame of the local hot springs. With no restrictive immigration laws in place at the time, millions of foreigners were flooding to America. A certain number of these were afflicted with bone and joint disorders. As the fame of the healing thermal waters at various spas across America became known, many found their way to those at Hot Springs in hopes of miraculous cures. Along with others of all nationalities and creeds were indigent Jews. With no other means of help, they turned to the local rabbi for assistance. Rabbi Rhine, as had Rabbi Rosenthal before him, conceived of the idea of a charity hospital for these needy people.[125]

Rabbi Rhine, deeply touched by the thousands of indigents and frustrated at the limited resources and facilities that the relatively small Hot Springs Jewish community could provide, shared the tremendous need with the local B'nai B'rith lodge. They in turn appealed for help to the District Grand Lodge No. 7, of which they were a part. A petition was submitted at the 1902 annual convention, held that year at Little Rock, which stated that "this city [Hot Springs] is a veritable mecca for a large number of poor Jews who seek health," and that a hospital for them "is a crying necessity."[126] A committee was formed, headed by Charles S. Stifft of Little Rock, and in 1903 the first organized Jewish relief work was undertaken.[127]

The national B'nai B'rith organization set about a program of support for Hot Springs relief work in 1910, at which time an assessment tax of ten cents per member (later increased to twenty-five cents) was granted for the proposed hospital.[128] The Hot Springs lodge appropriated twenty-five hundred dollars to build and equip the hospital, which became the first national Jewish hospital in America for rheumatism and blood diseases. It was named in memory of Leo N. Levi, president of the International Order of B'nai B'rith (IOBB), who had become known worldwide as a champion of human rights and who had died in 1904.[129] The hospital's first patient, Morris Moscowitz, was accepted 1 November 1914. Although it was sponsored and funded by Jewish organizations and individuals, it opened as a nonsectarian facility, and the majority of patients through the years have been non-Jews.

In January 1916 twenty-eight-year-old Regina Kaplan of Denver, Colorado, became Levi Hospital's administrator; she remained in that position thirty-five years. Under Miss Kaplan's diligent direction, Levi Hospital grew from a twenty-five-bed ward with five "nurses—four of whom had less than a fifth grade education and who could scarcely read and write"—to a 125-bed, four-floor hospital. For years it operated an emergency room that served thousands of general cases, not including the tens of thousands who benefitted from arthritic research and aid. She persisted until a therapeutic pool, several clinics, and a nursing program (one of the first to accept male students) were installed or instituted. She also was instrumental in developing a National Arthritic Research Foundation.[130]

Rabbi Rhine met and married a local belle, Annette Wiener, and was actively involved in the educational system of Hot Springs, serving on its School Board for sixteen years. Without doubt, however, he became best-known for his founding of the Arkansas Jewish Assembly (see section IV).

Because the early records of Hot Springs' House of Israel were destroyed, a complete list of those who served as its presidents is not available. Some of those who served before World War II include Dave

Burgauer, Emanuel Burgauer, Leon Dinkelspiel, Henry Fellheimer, Leo Gartenberg, H. Goodman, Irving Greenberg, Billy Gross, Jack Grundfest, Harry Kupperman, Dave Laser, Phil Levy, David Lockwood, Leo Mayer, Albert Mendel, Ed N. Roth, Gus Strauss, Dr. Samuel D. Weil, and Samuel White.[131]

Texarkana

The city of Texarkana, located on the border between southwest Arkansas and northeast Texas, was formed when the St. Louis, Iron Mountain and Southern Railway Company built tracks in Arkansas to the Texas border. There it connected with the Texas and Pacific Railway Company in the years 1873–74.[132] The principal streets of the town were one hundred feet in width and joined at the border. During its early years of existence, Texarkana gained a reputation as being "wild and wooly."[133] Jews began settling in the town from its earliest days, including Bero Berlinger, a Jewish veteran of the Confederacy, who came in 1874. He encouraged the establishment of a Jewish "federation," and a Jewish cemetery was consecrated at that time by Berlinger, Marks Kosminsky, Joseph Deutschmann, Joseph Marx, and Sam Heilbron.[134] By 1876 enough Jews had settled in the area to celebrate the High Holy Days, and Mount Sinai Congregation was formed. That fall a local newspaper noted that the Jews of Texarkana had formed a synagogue for the first time.[135]

The initial religious leadership of Mount Sinai's congregation was unlike that of any other Jewish congregation in the state (or perhaps any other in the nation). What made it unique was the leadership of Rev. Charles Goldberg, pastor of the Cumberland Presbyterian Church of Texarkana. Goldberg, who had been trained as a rabbi in Germany, came to America in the 1840s. While peddling through Missouri, he became ill, and a Presbyterian family nursed him back to health. During his stay, the family shared their faith with him, and he subsequently converted to Christianity, becoming an ordained minister in 1847. He later served as a chaplain in the Confederate army and filled several pulpits before coming to Texarkana in 1874.[136]

When the Jews of Texarkana planned the High Holiday services in 1876, they had no spiritual leader to officiate, and they asked Reverend Goldberg to conduct the rituals. This he did, to the satisfaction of both Jews and non-Jews who attended, according to a local newspaper article; however, when the same notice appeared in *The American Israelite*, the editor noted that "There appears to be a mistake somewhere."[137] Although

Reverend Goldberg gained the respect and love of all segments of the Texarkana community, some Jewish visitors to the town were offended by his efforts for the Jews. When Charles Wessolowsky, a representative of a Jewish newspaper, visited Texarkana in 1879, he later wrote a scathing denunciation regarding Reverend Goldberg. Incensed that the Jews of Texarkana selected "an apostate Jew" as their leader, he said he hoped that "such hypocrites with their deceptive countenances . . ." would not be allowed in either church or synagogue.[138] Despite such criticism, Reverend Goldberg continued to gain respect by preparing some of the young Jewish boys for their bar mitzvahs. It was said that he never tried to convert the Jews to Christianity.[139]

By 1885 the Jews of Texarkana called on Camden's leader, Rabbi Friedman, to hold High Holiday services, and he was assisted by Marks Kosminsky. Services were held in English from the congregation's beginning. A Texarkana Hebrew Benevolent Association was meeting by 1885, with services held in Kosminsky Hall.[140] In 1890 the congregation purchased a vacant Episcopalian church at Eighth Street and State Line Avenue, located on the Arkansas side. A new constitution was adopted in 1893, with thirty members listed.[141] Less than two years later, their remodeled synagogue burned, and a new one was built and dedicated in 1894. Like other Jewish facilities statewide, this one was lent to other religious groups as needs arose.[142]

Mount Sinai's early leaders included Joseph Deutschmann, H. Brown, B. Fane, Sol Feinberg, Louis Josephs, Marks Kosminsky, Leo Krouse, Morris Sandberger, Ike Schwarz, and Max Wexler. Although the congregation was at intervals without a full-time rabbi, those who did serve were outstanding spiritual leaders who helped establish a rapport between the Orthodox and Reform Jews and also between the Jews and non-Jews. Those who served the congregation prior to 1930 were: A. Shriber (1890s), Joseph Bogen (1900–06), Israel L. Heinberg (1914–15), Rudolph Farber (1915–22), A. Rosenberg (1925–27), and Arthur S. Montaz (1928–29).[143]

The women of the congregation functioned under the title of Ladies' Aid Society and Ladies' Cemetery Society until 1923, when the Temple Sisterhood was organized.[144] A Zionist Association and Jewish War Relief organization were established by Texarkana's Jewish community in 1917. In 1919 more than eleven thousand dollars was collected from Bowie County, Texas, and Miller County, Arkansas, for the war relief fund. (Gentiles as well as Jews often contributed to these drives.)[145]

Fort Smith

Although Jewish pioneers were known to have lived in Fort Smith as far back as 1842, there is no record that any attempt at forming a congregation occurred before the 1870s. A Jewish cemetery became a necessity when Rosalie Tilles died in 1872, and a Cemetery Association was formed, officers of which were Bernhard Baer, Joseph Adler, and Edward Czarnikow.[146] This association may well have been the origin of a congregation. Simon Joel (who had settled in Charleston, Arkansas, in 1873) moved to Fort Smith in 1880 and founded a synagogue. It was known as Temple of Israel, and Joel served as its first president.[147] This synagogue was evidently one of two in Fort Smith that was formed, for in 1881, two Jewish factions in Fort Smith were noted, one of which was designated as "the reformers."[148] In April 1881 Rabbi N. I. Benson of Little Rock visited Fort Smith and lectured in both the Presbyterian Church and Odd Fellows' Hall. He established a "flourishing" Sabbath School for the children of sixteen Jewish families of the area.[149]

Jewish services were conducted in a store building on Garrison Avenue during the formative period, and the first confirmation service was held in the Christian Church of Fort Smith, located on the corner of Seventh and C streets. After an on-again, off-again start, the Jews of Fort Smith were assisted by Rabbi Messing of St. Louis in 1886 to formally establish United Hebrew Congregation (UHC). (Evidently the two early factions coalesced under the new name.) In 1892 UHC reorganized and that year built a lovely synagogue on the corner of Eleventh and E streets. The festive dedication ceremony was attended by local dignitaries, including Federal Judge Isaac Parker.[150] The second confirmation service was held in their new building that year.

Some of the congregation's early leaders and members were Ben Wolf, A. Fuller, Dave Tilles, George Tilles, Sam Tilles, M. Joel, S. Joel, Joe Pappenheimer, B. Baer, Herman Baer, S. Baer, Ben Wolf, M. Wolf, Isaac Kaufman, Mr. Stanuberg, L. Goldsmith, B. Schram, Gabriel Kaufman, J. Isaacson, Julius Jacobs, E. Phillips, P. Berman, Joseph Adler, Edward Czarnikow, Abraham Mayer, A. Silverberg, L. Samter, D. Schlessinger, Henry Wolf, M. S. Cohn, L. Pahotski, Herman Bejack, M. Kober, Isaac Cohn, Abe Meyer, M. Friedman, I. Isaacson, Rudolph Ney, Ike Apple, H. L. Cohen, L. Langfelder, Sol Cohn, and two women, Mesdames Nina Heyman and Winnie Silverberg.[151]

Dr. Abe Traugott was UHC's first full-time rabbi, serving from 1892 to

1896. Starting with forty-one members, the congregation doubled in size by 1909. Rabbi Edward S. Levy joined UHC as spiritual leader in 1907 and served in that capacity until his death in 1914.[152] He was succeeded by Rabbi Charles Latz, who became well known locally for his civic work. He was named president of a War Prison Council that was organized in December 1919, and he was actively involved in the city's public library. He served as a sort of circuit rabbi, organizing Sunday schools and holding services in small towns and communities in Arkansas and Oklahoma. He also prepared correspondence lessons.[153] Jewish families from various parts of eastern Oklahoma and the summer resorts and small towns in western Arkansas worshipped at UHC for the High Holidays.[154]

A charter for a B'nai B'rith lodge in Fort Smith was granted on 15 November 1878. The rules of the organization were adhered to religiously, and members were fined for not visiting the sick or for using strong language. After the turn of the century, the Lodge became particularly involved in helping the Galveston sufferers—Jewish immigrants who had fled to America from the persecution in Russia. Lodge members used a secret ritual until 1917, when it was abolished. Before that time, the password had been, "Guardian of Israel."[155]

Members of a Ladies' Hebrew Benevolent Society aided the poor and helped build the town's civic life. A Ladies' Auxiliary Society had formed by 1892, led that year by Mrs. Ben Wolf, Mrs. M. Sternberg, and Mrs. S. Joel.[156]

The year 1892 also saw the organization of the Progress Club in Fort Smith. Its purposes included the promotion of social activities, culture, good fellowship, and mental development of members. When George Tilles was elected president in 1910, he proposed the erection of a club building. Some nine thousand dollars was quickly raised, and a large three-story building, located on North Sixth Street, was completed by May 1912 at a total cost of forty-five thousand dollars.[157]

Rabbis who succeeded A. Traugott were Max Moses and Max C. Currick. When the congregation was without a rabbi in 1902, UHC president Abraham Mayer went to Hebrew Union College in Cincinnati and hired HUC graduate Emanuel Kahn, "one of the most promising young men in the country."[158] After Kahn, other rabbis who served UHC through the 1920s were M. Cahan, Charles Latz, Joseph H. Stolz, and William Stern.[159] Rabbi Samuel Teitelbaum, who joined UHC in the 1920s and served until the 1940s, also helped in establishing the Arkansas Jewish Assembly and was instrumental in its success.

Jonesboro

Two Jewish congregations were formed in Jonesboro in the 1890s, one Orthodox and one Reform. (For history of the Orthodox congregation, see next chapter.) About 1894 sixteen Jewish families organized a Reform congregation and began holding meetings irregularly in rented rooms.[160] From this early group, Temple Israel was organized in January 1896.[161] By 1897 the congregation had its own synagogue, which was dedicated on 2 January 1898. At the ceremony, Rosa Rosenfield (nee Schoenberger) presented the keys of the new temple to the president.[162] A local paper described the newly built synagogue as a "magnificent little temple of worship . . . [and] . . . in point of architecture no church in the city outclasses this one . . . the interior furnishings of the temple are the finest in the city."[163] Charter families of the congregation included those of officers Marcus Berger, Morris Berger Sr., R. H. Meyer, and Lewis Sachs, and members Emil Less, L. Sternheimer, Ben Schoenfield, Julius Weil, I. Goldstein, Gus Neustadter, Ferdinand Neustadter, Harry Miller, S. Levy, A. Arndt, and I. Jaffe. Single members included Alec Berger, Ben Berger, Joe M. Berger, Jacob Less, Mayer Schoenfield, Maurice Neustadter, Herbert Weil, Jake Schoenfield, Ralph Frapart, Ike Buttenstein, and Ralph Trepane.[164]

Religious school was started at Temple Israel immediately after it was organized, and the first confirmation was held in 1899, with Hannah Berger and Moses Sachs as confirmands. The first full-time rabbi of the congregation, Isaac Rubenstein (1897–99), encouraged the establishment of a Jewish cemetery in Jonesboro and, ironically, was the first person to be buried in it.[165] Other full time rabbis who served the congregation included M. S. Block (1899–03), Rabbi Michnick (1903), J. D. Braverman (1907–08), A. Sessler (1908–10), B. Schainberg (1911–12), (rabbi-layman) Saul Klarberg of Little Rock (1912–16), Louis Binstock (1917–18), and I. Farber (1920–22).[166] (Louis Binstock was not a rabbi when he filled Temple Israel's pulpit but had come to the city as an attorney and also taught at Arkansas State College at Jonesboro. He entered Hebrew Union College in 1918 and, after graduation, later became well known as an author and as a spiritual leader of Temple Sholom in Chicago.)[167] From 1922 until the 1930s, Hebrew Union College rabbinical students served on High Holy Days.[168]

Temple Israel was fortunate in having dedicated women in its ranks. When the congregation faced difficult times in the 1920s—a drop in membership, debts owed to the bank, repairs (including a new roof) needed on the temple, and little interest being shown by the male membership—the Ladies' Auxiliary pitched in, particularly Selma Smith and Marguerite Jacobs, and operated the temple. They made collections, conducted religious school, employed student rabbis, maintained the building, and took responsibility for the congregation's needs in general. A two-story house that had been built for the congregation's rabbis during the temple's thriving years was sold to retire the bank loan and make needed repairs to the temple.[169] General interest in the congregation was revived by the efforts of the Arkansas Jewish Assembly in the 1930s (see section IV).

CHAPTER 6

The East European Migration, 1880–1930

Because of the propensity of German Jews to adapt both their customs and their religion to American life, Orthodox (Traditional) Judaism was definitely on the wane in the United States by the 1880s. Events were occurring in Europe that decade, however, which would help stem that trend. In the early 1880s severe persecution broke out against the Jews of Russia. While their lot in East Europe and Russia had been both repressive and oppressive before the death of Alexander II of Russia in 1881, it became intolerable upon the succession of Alexander III that year. The enforced Jewish policy then became "one third convert [to the Russian Orthodox Christian Church], one third emigrate, one third starve."[1] With such options open to them, hundreds of thousands of Jews emigrated. America at that time had no immigration laws or quotas, and most of these East Europeans came to the United States. The Enlightenment that had prompted the Reform movement among the Central European Jews translated itself into the *Haskalah* ("intelligence," "understanding") movement among the Jews of Russia, but this teaching remained on more traditional lines religiously. As the East Europeans came to the United States, many bolstered the ranks of Orthodox Jewry, often establishing their own synagogues ("shuls") where none were available.[2]

Between 1881 and 1914, more than two million East European Jews flooded to American shores. (Those of other nationalities and creeds also came—more than twenty-two million migrating to the United States during the same period.) Immigration societies began to proliferate, including the Industrial Removal Office (IRO) and the Hebrew Immigrant Aid Society (HIAS).[3] The IRO, funded by the Baron de Hirsch fund, settled some 73,960 East European Jews in 1,731 American cities between 1901 and 1917. Of these immigrants, 261 were absorbed in seventeen Arkansas cities and towns.[4] Since many Jews coming out of East Europe adhered to strict Orthodoxy, those being considered for resettlement in areas sparsely populated by Jewish people, such as Arkansas, were screened as to whether they would work on Saturdays (the Jewish Sabbath) and would eat *trefa* (nonkosher foods).[5] Jewish congregations all over America were called upon to help absorb the overwhelming numbers. Local congregations in Arkansas—all but one of which were Reform at the time—followed suit, forming committees to help relocate the Russian Jews. Members of these committees generally came from the more affluent Jewish social and economic elite and often viewed the new immigrants, with their strange language (Yiddish) and lack of education, as "apparitions from the Middle Ages."[6] It is to the credit of the established German Jews that they raised funds to absorb their less fortunate kinsmen.

Congregation B'nai Israel of Little Rock's immigration committee was composed of some of the congregation's outstanding members, including Mark M. Cohn, Jacob Blass, M. Salinger, C. T. Abeles, C. S. Stifft, L. M. Levy, Max Heiman, Louis Volmer, and Arthur Pfeifer.[7] The committee of Pine Bluff's Anshe Emeth was composed of Charles Weil, Sidney Weil, Louis Roth, and Rabbi Ephraim Frisch. Rabbi Frisch was particularly sympathetic with the plight of the East Europeans. Having been brought to America by his devout Lithuanian family when he was eight years old, he had a deep respect for traditionalism. He said, that without the religious Jew especially, "any city would be palpably shorn of its virility . . . With him it is . . . more richly dowered with the resources that make for upward and outward growth."[8] He noted that the immigrants "became Americanized quickly" and rapidly learned the language.[9] The Orthodox Jews already residing in Pine Bluff were said to be especially friendly to the new arrivals.

Some of the earliest groups of East European Jews to come to America made a unique attempt at cohesiveness. Accustomed to the homogeneity of ghetto life, they sought to remain together after emigrating, and some attempted this through farming colonies in America. Between 1882 and 1900 numerous agricultural colonies were established in the United States, and one of these was in Arkansas.[10] Those who came to Arkansas were a segment of the *Haskalah* movement known as *Am Olam* ("Eternal

People"). This organization was composed of a small segment of intellectual, enlightened young people from Kiev, Odessa, and other Russian cities.[11] Coming to Arkansas by way of New York, their arrival was noted by *The Jacksonport* [Arkansas] *Herald* in February 1883.[12] The local announcement stated that "a group of Polish Jews" would locate near Newport in Independence County. About 150 people, families and single people, arrived. The saga of their short sojourn in Arkansas, here condensed, is one of the state's little-known tragedies.

The balmy spring weather and the virgin forest that awaited the former Russian ghetto dwellers near Newport, Arkansas, gave the newcomers a feel of what the Garden of Eden might have been like. They wrote back to Odessa of this paradise, and some thirty more immigrants left Russia to join them.[13] The second group bought a tract of thick forest near the first colony. But the ecstasy of both groups soon turned into a nightmare. For income, they contracted with a lumber company to sell staves at $20 per thousand. (The name of the lumber company is not known.) But it took two men two weeks at backbreaking labor to cut just $20 worth. They were paid $10 for cut staves, the other $10 to be paid on delivery. And delivery dates proved uncertain during that year's merciless prevailing floods. A hotter-than-usual summer (105 to 108 degrees in the shade) and humid conditions (weather that was totally unknown to the group, whose members were used to a more northerly climate) followed. Their living arrangements were quite primitive—two log shacks for the larger group and a ramshackle barn for the smaller one. The women and children slept in the crude buildings; the men slept on the ground. The men's bedfellows proved to be snakes and mosquitos; the frequent rains produced the latter in countless quantities. Malaria and yellow fever were their next unwanted guests, and by July 90 percent of the colonists were ill. Some eighteen to twenty of the group died, including the parents of three small children. Neighbors of the colonists helped, and a local physician cared for the sick while a local Jewish businessman helped bury the dead. (The names of the local men are not given in any report on the Newport Colony. The businessman may have been a member of the well-known Adler family of Newport.) With no livestock or fowl, starvation was a real threat to the group. The Arkansas colony was called by one historian "probably the most tragic of all the [Jewish farming] projects."[14] After a year of struggle, colony members received financial help that enabled them to pursue their dreams in other parts of America.

As large numbers of relatively uneducated East European Jews continued to come to America around the turn of the century, the American

German-Jewish elite began fearing a backlash of persecution from non-Jews. Too, they were ashamed of their poor relations, not wanting them in their well-established and well-accepted temples. The established German Jews therefore sought a way to absorb the East Europeans into American life without having to become the sponge themselves. Arkansas-born Cyrus Adler, an intellectual and semi-Orthodox Jew who became one of the giants in American Jewish history, conceived the idea of using Conservative Judaism as a means of Americanizing the Russian Jews.[15] Standing midway between Reform and Orthodoxy, and in theology and liturgy almost identical with Traditionalism, Conservative Judaism was more responsive to the needs of a consensus of its members.[16]

Since there were no Conservative congregations in Arkansas, the many East European Jews who came to the state increased the need for congregations with Traditional leanings. Between 1892 and the 1930s, fourteen new congregations sprang up, a half dozen of which were Orthodox "shuls." Although the others were established as Reform congregations, most of their adherents were from the Traditional East European background, and services often were more conservative in practice. These fourteen congregations were located at Jonesboro, Little Rock, Dermott (later at McGehee), Newport, Hot Springs, Pine Bluff, Eudora, Osceola (later at Blytheville), Fort Smith, Forrest City, Wynne, Marianna, and El Dorado (where two congregations were located).[17]

Jonesboro Shul

By the turn of the 1890 decade, East European Jews (mostly from Lithuania) had established a fair-sized settlement in Jonesboro. By 1892 an Orthodox congregation had formed, and a shul functioned there for a number of years. The group held its first High Holy Day services in the home of Morris and Rachel Schoenberger, and participants came from the nearby towns of Manila, Monette, and Trumann.[18] Others later came from Corning, Paragould, Newport, Wynne, Marked Tree, Lepanto, and Luxora.[19] Meetings were generally held at the Masonic Hall. As the Orthodox community grew, one of its members opened a kosher meat market.

An example of these early Jewish pioneers with traditional leanings was Lithuanian-born Nathan Blecker, who settled at Jonesboro around 1890 and established a dry goods business. He later opened branches at Lake City and Monette. After struggling for several years to remain Traditional in the remote location, Blecker, as well as others of the community, realized it would be easier for their families if they lived in a larger Orthodox community, such as those found in Memphis and St. Louis. Blecker moved his family to Memphis, while he remained in Arkansas to oversee his stores. He opened a store at Turrell, some twenty-five miles northwest of Memphis. Most weekends his family visited him there, where he became known familiarly as "Judge."[20]

After the Reform congregation, Temple Israel, formed in Jonesboro in 1896 and established its own cemetery, most of the Jews were buried there, whether from the Orthodox or Reform communities. One German-born member of the congregation, Lewis Sachs, was taken aback at the practice of the Reform in letting converts and non-Jewish spouses be buried in the Jewish cemetery. Sachs donated land contiguous to Temple Israel's cemetery for an Orthodox cemetery, Mount Zion. He was buried there at his death in 1938. Only eight others (all members of the Sachs family) are buried in the little Orthodox cemetery (which is one of only two such separate cemeteries in the state).[21] A garageman bought the land around the cemetery from Sachs and later surrounded the burial site with the chassis and parts of old automobiles.

Orthodox services were no longer held at Jonesboro after 1927; the few Traditional Jews who remained in the area merged with the Reform Temple Israel. The Jews of the area established a B'nai B'rith lodge, Zangwill Lodge No. 1063, in 1926. (Another B'nai B'rith lodge, Saul Bertig Lodge No. 1281, was established at Jonesboro in 1938.)[22]

Agudas Achim, Little Rock

The Orthodox community of Little Rock grew steadily as more East Europeans settled there, and in 1903 Traditional High Holy Day services were conducted by a Rabbi Wolfe at the Concordia Club.[23] By 1904 the group had selected a name, Agudas Achim ("Society of Brothers"; the spelling was later changed to Agudath Achim) and had acquired a full-time leader, Rabbi Samuel Katzenellenbogen.[24] Those said to be founders of the synagogue included David Scher, J. Harris Goldberg, and Barney Levin. Others known to be charter members were Morris Scher, Lippman Besser, Leopold Besser, Sam Bernhard, Max Itzkowitz, Nathan Harris, A. D. Kossover, Ike Tenenbaum, Sam Breier, Louis Siegel, and Dave Siegel.[25] Others considered pioneer members were William Back, Neuman Baum, Morris Green, N. Eisenberg, A. Sanders, Morris Kluglose, Sam Rosenbloom, Sol Ruff, Ike Meisner, Charles Alman, Joe Kosten, William Gilman, Max

Snyderman, Sam Schlesinger, Meyer Lulky, Frank Lulky, and Meyer Cohen.[26]

When Second Baptist Church of Little Rock moved in 1907 from its stone structure (built in 1886) at Eighth and Louisiana streets, Agudath Achim purchased the property and remodeled it as a synagogue.[27] Services were held at this site for the next seventy years. Some of the early meetings of the Congregation's Board might have amused an eavesdropper. For example, at a time when the Board discussed remodeling the synagogue and purchasing a new chandelier, board member J. Harris Goldberg objected, saying, "Even if we got one, no one would know how to play it."[28]

Rabbi Lazarus Lehrer became leader of Agudath Achim in 1913,[29] but Rabbi Katzenellenbogen rejoined the congregation after Lehrer left. Full-time leaders who served the congregation subsequent to Katzenellenbogen until 1930 included Rabbis Fenberg, Adelson, Aaron Colatz, Marks, Bunzell, and E. Z. Ekstein.[30] Each Orthodox leader also served as shochet (ritual slaughterer) and mohel (circumciser). From 1915 to the 1930s, the Orthodox conducted an active Talmud Torah (Hebrew school) for the congregation's children. It was held in the Young Men's Hebrew Association Hall, located in the one hundred block of East Seventh Street. Its Traditional religious training was "a world apart" from that of the Reform German-Jewish youth of Little Rock.[31] The Hebrew school was generally taught by students of the Medical School in Little Rock. Bertha Breier was one of the most active in seeing that the Hebrew school was continued.[32]

Rabbi Joseph Shapiro joined the congregation in 1930, remaining there seventeen years, longer than any other of the Little Rock shul's full-time leaders. He also worked with the Arkansas Jewish Asssembly.[33]

The Dermott Congregation

Eli Dante, a Russian immigrant who had come to America with several of his siblings, peddled goods in southern Arkansas and settled at Dermott, seventy-two miles south of Pine Bluff. There were a number of East European Jews in the Dermott area, and Dante, who had studied to be a rabbi in his native Russo-Poland, founded an Orthodox congregation at Dermott in 1905.[34] Services were held regularly for many years, drawing participants from McGehee, Arkansas City, Lake Village, Winchester, and other nearby communities. For the High Holy Days, as many as fifty to seventy-five people would attend. These included Abe Abroms, I. Pincus, Louis Zeno, Joe Weisman, Joseph Cohen, H. Greenberg, N. Joseph,

E. Schnelz, Nathan "Freedy" Friedman, Nathan Semack, Harry Roby, Ralph Raphael, Samuel Wolchansky, William Hamburger, Sam Nussbaum, the Shach family—Mike, Phillip, Irving—and the Dessent family—J. S., Morris, and Sam (who provided the Torah). The ladies, principally Mesdames Dante, Abroms, Pincus, and Cohen, prepared gefilte fish, roast goose, pastries, and other delicacies and also found overnight lodging for guests. When services outgrew the homes, they met above the town's movie theater. The services continued until the late 1920s, when adverse conditions prompted some of the families to move away.[35]

After a Reform congregation formed in the 1940s at McGehee, less than ten miles north of Dermott, those who wanted to maintain an Orthodox service would meet early and conduct their own, then join the Reform later for their services. There remained a close cooperation and congeniality between the Orthodox and Reform of the community, which often was unusual for the time. The Jews of southeast Arkansas established a B'nai B'rith lodge, Dave Meyer Lodge No. 1084, in 1927 at McGehee.[36] (For more information on the McGehee congregation, Meir Chaim, see section IV on the Arkansas Jewish Assembly.)

Newport, Beth El

The Jews who had been living in the Jacksonport-Newport area since prior to the Civil War were joined by others, and by 1873 seven Jewish families lived in Jacksonport. The pioneers had lived there for some fifteen years, and their "enterprising and industrious" hands had proved successful.[37] There was no synagogue, nor were any known meetings held, but the Jews of the town were avid readers of the national publication, *The American Israelite*, and they gloried "with delight in the progress of Judaism" which the magazine upheld. When an influx of East European Jews settled at Newport around the turn of the century, there were enough people to form a congregation, and Beth El (House of God) was established in September 1904. Rabbi Alfred Godshaw conducted services there for a short period.[38] Members of this group included S. Heinemann, H. Bernstein, Michael Jacobs, C. Meyer, S. Grossman, H. Salenfriend, Sam A. Goldberg, J. W. Shannon, and those known only by last names—Fels, Schneider, Waterman, and Wolf.[39] At the time the Beth El congregation formed, Newport was a thriving river town conducive to merchant activity. By the 1930s and 1940s, however, only a few Jewish families remained.[40]

Pine Bluff, B'nai Israel

By 1907 enough East European Jews had settled at Pine Bluff that a shul could be established. Known as B'nai Israel (Sons, or Children, of Israel), its services were held for many years in a room at 217 1/2 Main Street, next to Schlosberg's Tailoring Shop. Lay readers conducted services on Friday evenings, and a collection taken enabled the members to engage a rabbi or cantor each fall for the High Holy Day services, held in the Masonic Hall. These professional leaders came from St. Louis, Memphis, or Chicago. The fall services drew large crowds, as Jewish families from all over southeast Arkansas would attend.[41] Members of Pine Bluff's Orthodox community included the families of Barnett Bram (who served as shochet), Harris Bram, William Rosenzweig, Samuel Baim, Milford "Buddy" Sonnenschein, Max Schlosberg, Hyman Soltz, Samuel Soltz, Ben "Jake" Riesenberg, Abe Baer, Jake Rutstein, Henry Rutstein, Joe Webberman, Sam Levine, Morris Levine, Harold Davis, Jake Marcus, William Bilsky, and the families of Krumpner, Fink, Gurdin, Udes, and Cohen.[42]

As a youth in the 1920s, Burton Schlosberg, son of tailor Max Schlosberg, remembered his father sending him down Pine Bluff's Main Street to notify various Jewish businessmen that a minyan (a group of ten men) was needed for services or observances.[43] Rabbi S. Levine of Memphis conducted High Holy Day services for B'nai Israel in 1921, and the cousin of Louis Bram, Sol Sabludusky of Beaumont, Texas, conducted the services in 1922 and 1923. For almost ten years B'nai Israel was served by two or three full-time rabbis who taught Hebrew and the dietary laws to the young male members of the congregation. When the immigration laws of the 1920s closed the door to any further significant influx of East European Jews, the Orthodox community of Pine Bluff began to atrophy. Members of B'nai Israel began to die or move away; the latter was particularly true of the young people. The few who were left were slowly absorbed into the Reform Anshe Emeth Congregation, although they continued to observe yahrzeits (the anniversaries of the deaths of loved ones) for their members and also their own High Holy Day services. Even these rituals were merged with the Reform rituals around 1950.[44]

Hot Springs, Sheareth Israel

Enough East Europeans had settled in Hot Springs shortly after the turn of the century that an Orthodox congregation, Sheareth Israel (Remnant of Israel), was established with thirty members in 1907.[45] Its meeting place was at 224 Parker Avenue. Some of the members who helped form this group were P. Gartenberg, James Glass, I. Greenberg, L. Cohen, J. Karatofsky, C. Kerstein, Abe Krokow, H. Waldstein, P. Walkowitz, M. E. Weinberger, Pete and Clara Brockman, Aaron and Ethyl Kallsnick, and the families of Moscowitz, Zuckerman, and Wexler.[46] Several hotels opened in Hot Springs that catered to the Orthodox with kosher meals, and kosher meat markets opened as well. The congregation continued into the 1930s, and some of the hotels survived into the 1950s. But as other treatments besides the hot springs were found for bone and joint diseases, Hot Springs as a mecca subsided, and its Jewish population, particularly the Orthodox, dwindled as well. (There was a resurgence of Jewish population in Hot Springs after World War II, and enough Orthodox either lived there or visited Hot Springs that a small synagogue, Beth Jacob, was built in 1950.)[47]

Eudora, Bene Israel

Eudora, a delta town in Chicot County, located less than ten miles north of the Louisiana border, had seventeen Jewish families by 1911. These included twenty-five adults and numerous children. About half of these were German Jews who had migrated earlier from St. Louis, and the other half were East Europeans who had come after the turn of the century. German-born Jacob and Theresia (Strauss) Rexinger had moved to Eudora in 1904, and in 1911, when enough Jews had settled in the area, Theresia Rexinger encouraged the formation of a congregation. Her husband Jacob, well-trained in Jewish law, served as reader. The congregation was named Bene Israel (Sons, or Children, of Israel) and was properly organized: M. Cahn was elected president; M. Schwartz, vice-president; and Sol Meyer, secretary. Other charter members included the families of S. Marcus, M. Bluestein, H. Liebreich, S. Weis, A. Feibelman, M. Delugach, S. Delugach, Fritz Feibelman, H. Seelig, Abe Kahn, D. P. Stern, M. G. Stein, A. A. Fishel, and Miss Carrie Baer.[48] The Rexinger family was from a Reform congregation in Germany, and the Eudora group joined the Reform movement. Although the congregation did not become a member of the Union of American Hebrew Congregations, it did use the latter's literature.[49]

The Jews who lived in towns surrounding Eudora were invited to worship, and services were held in the Masonic Hall each Friday evening and on High Holy Days.[50] At times, the services were held at the Rexinger home. When the latter family rented a two-story brick hotel in Eudora's business district, which they named the Rex Hotel, services were held in it. In the 1920s Maurice Cohen, who had received "a marvelous Hebrew education" in his native Russia, moved to Eudora, where he helped with the services and taught a dozen children in the congregation's Sunday School.[51] The Eudora congregation continued to meet until the late 1930s.[52]

Osceola, B'rith Sholom

Osceola was the largest town in the northeast corner of the state after the turn of the century; by 1912 it had about twenty-five hundred residents. Eleven Jewish families had settled there at the time, and there were twenty Jewish children between the ages of five and seventeen. All of these families were from East European Orthodox backgrounds, but in 1912 they were visited by Rabbi M. Samfield, supervisor of the Reform-sponsored Synagog and School Extension for the area. He organized a congregation, B'rith Sholom (Covenant of Peace), with Isaac Miller as president and Harry Weinberg as superintendent of the newly organized Sabbath School.[53] It was expected that other Jews from the surrounding communities, particularly at Blytheville, less than twenty miles north, would join the group. This did not happen (the roads at the time were almost impassable), and the small congregation at Osceola was kept alive through the efforts of Annie Weinberg. Mother of thirteen children, only seven of whom lived to adulthood, Annie Weinberg was left a widow while in confinement with her last child, and she valiantly raised her children alone. Red-haired Annie owned a Torah, and she made sure there were the required ten men for a minyan to hold services in her home each Sabbath. She kept a kosher home until the flu epidemic of 1918, when several family members became ill and a diet change was suggested by the local doctor. She taught her children social graces and made them attend the Methodist Sunday School and church.[54]

Enough Jewish families had moved into the Blytheville area by 1918 that it was possible to establish a B'nai B'rith lodge, and the Menorah (S. S. Sternberg) Lodge No. 832 received its charter on 1 June that year.[55] In 1923 Annie Weinberg moved to Blytheville with her married daughter, Mrs. Walter (Lillian) Rosenthal, and Annie soon organized a Ladies' Aid Society in her home. She was joined by others: Mesdames Dave Dinkerspiel, H. Kleban, Ben H. Levy, P. H. Rosenthal, Ike Rosenthal, Harry Weisburd, S. J. Cohen, Max Meyers, Joe Isaacs, Sam Joseph, S. S. Sternberg, Joe Meyers, and C. E. Coulter, as well as Belle Meyers, Carrie Sternberg, and Addie Levy. From this beginning grew the congregation that became Temple Israel of Blytheville.[56] Although most of its members were East European and from Orthodox backgrounds, the temple joined the Reform movement. Because more traditional services that included prayer shawls and yarmulkes (skullcaps) had been held in the early days, many of the early members viewed the congregation as Conservative.[57] Lay readers for the meetings included Siegbert "Zeke" Jiedel of Blytheville and William Borowsky of Manila. This congregation was particularly nourished by the work of the Arkansas Jewish Assembly in the 1930s and 1940s.[58]

Fort Smith, B'nai Israel

As more and more East European Jews settled in Fort Smith after the first decade of the twentieth century, an Orthodox congregation, also named B'nai Israel, was organized in 1913.[59] It met on the second floor of a building on Garrison Avenue. Some of those who belonged were very devout in their worship; for example Ike Pahotski was remembered for taking off his shoes at the High Holy Day services.[60] Besides Pahotski, other members were the families of Louis and Sarah Kasten, David Sugarman, David Soifer, and Wolf J. Yaffe and his two sons. As many as thirty attended on High Holy Days, and the group had two Torah scrolls. As the members began to die and others moved away, the congregation atrophied by the 1930s, and a minyan could not be maintained. A member of the Reform United Hebrew Congregation recalled a time in the 1930s when several Orthodox men brought B'nai Israel's two scrolls to the temple. They formally donated the revered articles, joined their lot with the Reform, and became ardent supporters of the temple. One of the men, Louis Kasten, later served as a lay reader for the temple and, during World War II, assisted U.S. Army Chaplain Rabbi David Seligson with services at nearby Camp Chaffee.[61]

Forrest City, Tifereth Israel

A number of East European Jews settled in the east Arkansas town of Forrest City, located about forty-five miles west of Memphis. Most of these were Orthodox, and many belonged to the Traditional Baron Hirsch Synagogue in Memphis. Before 1940 the terrible road conditions in Arkansas made only limited travel to Memphis feasible, however, and local Jewish children often attended Christian churches. A concerned Methodist minister would alert the Jewish families when the Old

Testament was taught. One of the Jewish children, Jean Warshavsky, whose family had moved to Forrest City in 1906, attended Baptist meetings, but she wanted training in her own faith. She wrote to Rabbi Samuels in Memphis, telling him of the need for a Sunday School for the dozen Jewish children in Forrest City. In return he sent her literature, and her father gave her added instruction. She began teaching a Sunday School class for the local Jewish children. Rabbi Samuels also organized the Jewish men in Forrest City, and they hired a cantor for the High Holidays.[62] In 1914 a congregation, Tifereth Israel, was organized.[63] The congregation was soon neglected, and in 1920 Rabbi Jerome Mark of Helena, who was serving as deputy supervisor of the Reform Synagog and School Extension in Arkansas, reorganized the group and set up a Sunday School.[64] At that time, there were thirty-nine Jewish citizens with ten children living in Forrest City. Some of those who became members were Gus Levy, Harry Warshavsky, Max Yoffe, Isadore Yoffe, E. Snyder, Harry Dreyfus, and Frank Swartz. The Forrest City Jewish community was later joined by a number of other families, including those of Sol Cohn, Maurice Cohen, and Louis Barg.[65]

Although most of the East Europeans retained their memberships in Baron Hirsch Synagogue in Memphis, in Forrest City most lived the lives of Reform Jews. Their children grew up with Reform literature and, for the most part, remained in that branch of Judaism.[66] Samuel Sharpe, a Jewish tailor of Forrest City, had a black employee who helped teach English to Russian Jewish newcomers to the town, and one of the men taught the black man Hebrew. The latter became well versed in it, and when he later moved to Memphis, he would fill in for a minyan when needed.[67]

Wynne, Ahavah Achim

Wynne, Arkansas, which nestles next to Crowley's Ridge in east Arkansas and had been home to Jewish citizens from the time of its incorporation in 1888,[68] received a number of East European immigrants after the turn of the century. These included Mike Drexler, Hyman Steinberg, Herman Bornstein, Morris Reagler, Sol Meyer, Max Saripkin, and the families of Goldberg, Greenfield, and Speil. Russian-born Drexler migrated there in 1905, where he and his wife Dora raised eight children. Multi-lingual, speaking German, Russian, Hebrew, and Yiddish, Drexler was very religious and well taught in Jewish law. He became leader of the Jewish community, and in 1915 an Orthodox congregation, Ahavah Achim

(Brotherly Love),[69] was formed. It met on the second floor of Drexler's store, where a handmade ark housed its Torah. As many as thirty or more families from Wynne and nearby communities attended the services.[70]

In 1914 a B'nai B'rith lodge was established at Wynne, the Louis Barnett (B'nai Sholem) Lodge No. 754. It drew members from small towns in the area as well as from Forrest City. Picnics held by the lodge were well attended, and they were later remembered for providing fun, fellowship, and "scads of fried chicken, ice cold watermelon, and all such good things."[71]

The Wynne congregation continued until shortly before World War II. As road conditions were improved, travel to Memphis for worship became commonplace.[72]

Marianna and Clarkedale

During the same period that Rabbi Jerome Mark of Helena reestablished the congregation at Forrest City, he also visited the town of Marianna, some seventeen miles south. At the time there were forty-seven Jewish adults and their children living there. (The general population of Marianna was 5,074 in 1920).[73] Rabbi Mark organized both a congregation and a religious school.[74] Although almost all the Jews were from East European backgrounds, they joined the Reform congregation and religious school established by Rabbi Mark.

In 1920 Rabbi Mark also visited the town of Clarkedale, fifteen miles northwest of Memphis, where he organized a religious school. Max Friedman was named superintendent, and a number of women volunteered as teachers.[75]

The small congregations in east Arkansas near Memphis all came to an end as travel conditions improved and worshipers could attend services in Tennessee.

Texarkana

Among the East European Jews who settled in Texarkana was Zalmin (Salomon) Wexler, who came there via Galveston with his wife and family. Their presence in this Arkansas-Texas border town bolstered the number of Orthodox in that community, but there were never enough to make a minyan. There was a rapport here, however, between the Orthodox and Reform similar to that found at McGehee. Those who preferred a more traditional service met early at the Reform Temple, Mount Sinai, on

Saturday mornings and held services. Reform members of the Temple cooperated by filling in the needed number for a minyan. Some of the Orthodox, besides Wexler, included Victor and Ben Schiff, Sam Garber, Ben Friedman, Jack Scherer, W. M. Moss, and M. Silverman. By the 1940s the separate services were no longer held.[76]

El Dorado, Ohev Zedek and Reform Congregation

The oil boom that began near El Dorado, Arkansas, in the 1920s brought numerous seekers after wealth to that area. With the many others came Jewish businessmen. Their numbers swelled, and two congregations formed: a Reform congregation, and another, Ohev Zedek (Love of Justice), evidently Orthodox.[77] J. Ben Miller, an insurance agent who moved to El Dorado in 1925 and who was well-taught in Hebrew and Orthodox Judaism, led congregational life there (the two congregations merged). He also headed the active El Dorado B'nai B'rith Lodge No. 957, which had been established in 1922.[78] Members of the area's Jewish community included Sam Baum, B. H. Berk, Ike Goldstein, Morris Lewis, Morris Gurian, Irving Pesses, Morris Pesses, H. Packman, Dave Ostrich, E. D. Ritchie, Robert Rochmill, Harry Steinberg, Edward Rose, H. J. Warshavsky, Julien Weil, Stanley Weil, and the families of Mark, Baum, and Weiler.[79]

After the peak of the oil boom, El Dorado and its environs settled down and many of its newer citizens drifted away. The Jewish community also dwindled. A few stayed on, and at one time affiliated with the small group of Jewish citizens at nearby Camden. Encouraged by the Arkansas Jewish Assembly in the 1940s, another congregation, Reform Beth Israel, was organized in El Dorado.

The influence of Orthodox Jews on congregational life in many of the cities and towns of Arkansas proved to be inestimable. They helped swell the numbers in the various locations, making possible the building of temples, such as at McGehee and Blytheville, and a rejuvenation of Temple Israel at Jonesboro. Deep devotion to their religion prompted them to become stalwart members of the congregations they joined, whether Orthodox or Reform. And their presence in numerous Arkansas towns and communities made it possible for many citizens of the state to become acquainted with these people who followed the ethics and teachings of the patriarchs and prophets of the Bible.[80]

Adaptation of East European Jews

The adapting of the East European Jews to American life throughout the country was slower and more difficult than that of the German Jews before them. The former's language, customs, and determination to remain as Jewish as possible set them apart. This was particularly true in the small towns where there might be only two or three such families.

By the 1920s most Arkansas towns had at least one Jewish merchant. These Jews found a slow but steady acceptance from the local citizens as the latter discovered the Jews to be honest, hard working, charitable, civic minded, patriotic, and dependable. Most of the non-Jews were Christians, who viewed the Jews as authorities on the Bible. It was not unusual that a Jew be asked to teach the Old Testament for Christian Sunday School classes and for evening training services.[81] And Jewish children often accumulated perfect attendance records at the local Christian Sunday Schools. Such attendance was usually prompted by their parents, who wished for them some sort of spiritual training, and also by the youngsters' desires to be with their non-Jewish friends. They felt particularly welcomed in the Methodist churches.[82]

When East European Jews who settled in Arkansas were asked about any anti-Semitism they had experienced in the state, most could only mention a few "uneducated" remarks they or their children remembered from public school, such as being called "Jew-baby" and "kike."[83] In attempting to determine the amount or degree of anti-Semitism experienced by Jews in Arkansas, it became as difficult as describing "beauty," which has been said to be in the eye of the beholder. One man, for example, described an attempt to convert him to Christianity as the most despicable act of anti-Semitism he had experienced. Another, who had been awakened by a neighbor one morning at three during a rainstorm, was astonished to be told that his neighbor could not sleep. He felt compelled, he said, to wake up his Jewish friend to ask him to receive Jesus as his Saviour so he would not be "lost." Asked if that was not a very anti-Semitic thing for the neighbor to do, the Jewish man, a life-long bachelor, said no, that he was very moved " . . . to think that someone in the world cared enough to lose sleep over me!" Others were incensed over the well-worn "Jew him down" phrase, while others dismissed such talk as ignorant thinking, similar to the "as tight as a Scotsman" or "dumb Polack" phrases.[84]

The Jews who lived in small towns, who rubbed shoulders every day with the townspeople and whose lives could be well scrutinized, became somewhat of an enigma. Because almost 100 percent of the Jews were honorable, ethical, pleasant, and law-abiding citizens, they did not fit into the category of the stereotyped tricky Jew of jokes and prejudicial thinking. Because of this, they often were given the backhanded "compliment" that they were "not like the others." Knowing that the stereotypical Jew was the exception rather than the rule, the Jews very much resented this "compliment." One Jewish man, who had worked diligently to help build up one east Arkansas town, attended a dinner at which time he was given an award for his outstanding services to the community. While handing him the award, the master of ceremonies told him, as an aside, "You're not like the others." At that, the honoree walked out of the meeting and thereafter gave up his civic endeavors.[85]

While the East Europeans had expected some period of acculturation and prejudice in America and did not particularly look for succor from non-Jews, what came as their greatest surprise to many was the treatment they received from the well-established German Jews. The rapport found between the Orthodox and Reform, such as noted above in smaller towns, was totally lacking in cities with relatively larger Jewish communities, such as Little Rock, and Fort Smith. An almost unbreachable gulf developed between Orthodox and Reform. While the German Jews had been quick to form committees and help settle the East Europeans Jews, they found that the ever-increasing numbers of the latter who flooded to America made it "more and more irksome" to be identified as a Jew.[86]

But the East European Jewish adults did not dwell unduly on the discrimination emanating from the German Jews. Although they did not condone the superior attitude of the Germans, they were appreciative of the latter's efforts in helping them escape persecution.[87] Primarily, they were deeply grateful to be free, and their efforts were immediately turned toward making a living for their families.

Some of the children of the East Europeans, however, did not overlook such blatant discrimination. The little anti-Semitism the Jewish children found in Arkansas schools could not be compared to the class contempt shown them by German Jews. While the Germans viewed themselves as "progressive," they perceived the East Europeans as "uncouth, low-born, uneducated." Some of the children who grew up under this "powerful prejudice" retained a resentment for the "snooty, snotty" German Jews, who "looked down on us."[88] Although time diminished the sharp edge of resentment, years later some East European Jews still felt the hurt caused by the discrimination of fellow Jews during childhood.[89]

After the immigration laws were passed by Congress in the 1920s and the influx of East European Jews abated, Orthodox congregations became static. Events began to unfold that would eventually bring the various branches of Judaism to a mutual acceptance of one another. One of these involved the religious training of children. Such training for the offspring of Traditional Jews of Arkansas was rather spasmodic. The Agudath Achim Synagogue in Little Rock offered a Talmud Torah for its youth for several years, and the Orthodox shuls that sprang up across the state intermittently offered training to their children. In the 1930s the Orthodox began sending their children to the Reform congregations for a consistent instructional program. As the children grew up, many opted to join Reform Judaism. This became one of many bridges that brought the two groups together. Another bridge was the farsighted efforts of the Arkansas Jewish Assembly during the 1930s and 1940s, and an even stronger one was the creation of the State of Israel in 1948.

Colorful Threads
1860s–1940s

ECONOMIC AND

CIVIC PROGRESS

"May . . . the one who reads this first . . . speak often of our names so we are never forgotten in this world." [1]

INTRODUCTION

The history of the Jewish institutions in Arkansas, as recounted in section II, constitutes only a small portion of the story of their overall sojourn in the state. Because most of the Jews who came to Arkansas (and other parts of the South) were immigrants, they used both family and business to develop a social cohesion; the synagogue in the early days was almost ancillary to the importance of establishing economic progress.[2] And almost all Jewish men—immigrants and their offspring—were actively and deeply involved in fraternities, such as the Masons, Knights of Pythias, Odd Fellows, Elks, and Woodmen of the World, as well as social and charitable organizations. (The purview of this work does not include data on the extensive involvement of Arkansas Jews in the various fraternal organizations.) Between 1911 and 1930, when business clubs such as Kiwanis, Lions, Rotary, and Chambers of Commerce were established, almost all had Jewish promoters and charter members; many other Jewish businessmen who came later served as officers and active workers in the organizations.

There was an evident change in the business practice of the Jewish businessman in Arkansas after the Civil War. Before, it had been characterized by mobility (moving from one town or community to another in search of economic success) and frugality (expending resources on business efforts rather than on personal betterment). After the War, this practice changed to stability and expansion—the Jew had found a favorable home where he began putting down roots and investing in property.[3]

Not until the Great Depression of the 1930s was so large a section of the country so adversely affected as was the South after the devastation of the Civil War. The War had brought total destruction to the factorage system—dependent on the plantation, cotton, and slavery—and the tremendous vacuum it left crippled the agricultural economy of the South.[4] When the southern farmers—many of them war-wounded—returned home after the war, they were destitute, without equipment, capital, seed, and fertilizer. Those who were able to produce crops found that the most crucial necessity was missing: an organized market for their goods.

It was evident that what the South needed most at that crucial time was an ingenious and resourceful population to help rebuild the economy and to profitably exploit its natural resources. Knowing this, the southern states mounted mammoth campaigns between 1870 and 1900 to attract immigrants and Northerners. Results from such efforts were meager. Very few European immigrants came South, with the exception of a relatively good showing of Germans, and these included a fair number of Jews. The South, with its devastated economy and newly-freed slaves, had little attraction for newcomers. Jews fit nicely into this vacuum, however, for they generally were not competitive to either farmers or blacks. They seldom farmed or engaged in businesses that competed with blacks. (The Jews got on well with their black customers, treating them with respect and fairness.) Also, Jews were generally welcomed into areas like Arkansas that hoped to see commercial growth.[5]

While more than two hundred Jewish merchants had located in Arkansas by 1865, they were joined by at least four hundred others by the late 1870s.[6] The demographics of Arkansas Jewry in 1880 show that 95 percent of the Jewish immigrants to Arkansas between 1865 and 1880 were from Germany, and by 1878, half owned property. Most of these—some 63 percent—owned dry goods or general stores, 19 percent owned grocery stores, and 18 percent engaged in various other pursuits. A handful were professionals, but most of those engaged in other pursuits were planters, peddlers, bookbinders, jewelers, tailors, livery men, liquor store owners, furniture dealers, confectioners, and manufacturers.[7] Generally, their business evaluations were viewed positively by the credit agents of R. G. Dun and Company; some 72 percent received good or excellent ratings, 23 percent fair, and only 5 percent were noted as bad.[8] Almost 42 percent had partners, and these were generally Jewish.[9] The average age of the Jewish merchant at the time his business was assessed by an R. G. Dun agent was about thirty-two and a half. By 1878 Jewish merchants were found in about 100 towns or communities located in fifty-one Arkansas counties.

The Jewish settlers helped the economy after the Civil War not only in Arkansas's few urban areas, but also out in the countryside, where their help was more visible. A number of them became large furnishing (outfitting) merchants and cotton buyers. As such, they became agents of the highly speculative cotton trade, which enabled the staple crop system to function. Without such merchants, the farmer and cotton speculator could not have survived. It became the merchant's responsibility to keep account of crop conditions, growing seasons, reliability of the farmers, and the ability of his customers to purchase merchandise.

Although in afteryears the furnishing merchant came under much scrutiny and criticism, an examination of store records has shown that both the furnishing stores and the lien laws of the time had common failings.[10] The furnishing system was not originated by the merchant; rather, the needs of the times demanded such a supply source. Such merchants also helped to "channelize an enormous amount of extra-regional capital into the South."[11] The furnishing merchant has, in retrospect, been compared to robber barons, "avaricious rascals who . . . robbed investors and consumers . . ."[12] Although Jewish furnishing merchants of Arkansas usually were able to accumulate large amounts of land, foreclosures of the many farms were not caused by the merchant but rather by the fact that there were too many farms and a glutted crop market.[13] Almost without exception, the Jewish furnishing merchant of Arkansas was guided by a set of principles and ethics rooted firmly in Judaism and laws of the Tenach (Old Testament). In many instances, long after these men had passed away, their customers would continue to remind the merchants' descendants of their fathers' or other relatives' good deeds. Their help was noted to be particularly evident during hard times.[14]

Almost all the Jewish furnishing merchants in Arkansas before 1900 were from Central or Western Europe, but beginning in the 1890s, and particularly after the turn of the century, East European Jews began to migrate to the state. Their migration was caused by the severe persecution that arose in Russia in 1881, and between that year and 1924, more than 2.3 million flooded to America.[15] Although only a relative handful of East Europeans came to Arkansas (most preferred the large urban areas), they generally were sent to the state by the Jewish immigrant aid societies or were brought by relatives who had preceded them. Of those who came, a number settled in North Little Rock, a few in Little Rock and other urban areas, but most spread out across Arkansas—generally beginning as peddlers who eventually opened small specialty stores. They found a ready market throughout rural Arkansas, for by 1900 more than 90 percent of Arkansans lived on farms or in small towns.[16] The number of farms in the state grew from 39,044 in 1860 to 178,694 in 1900 and mushroomed to 232,604 by 1920.[17] Eventually, the small cash store, the type established by the East European immigrants, came to replace the large furnishing businesses.

The Jews who came to Arkansas were generally well accepted. The German Jews had migrated into the state along with other German settlers, and the common language and background helped their adjustment to their adopted home. They became well-respected members of the communities in which they settled, and this respect continued even after Germany fell into disfavor during World War I. The Jews were considered "progressive" and "dedicated to the common good."[18] Occasionally, an article would appear in a local paper extolling the Jews, such as one in the *Pine Bluff Graphic* in 1889 under the headline "The Jews, A Tribute to the Most Wonderful Race of People of the Green Globe."[19] Clifton R. Breckinridge, a former Arkansas congressman who served as U.S. Minister to Russia from 1894 to 1897, diligently attempted to help the persecuted Jews of that country during his tenure there probably because of his experience with Jews he had known in Arkansas. (Simon Bloom, mayor of Pine Bluff from 1913 to 1919, served as a secretary to Breckinridge; the latter served as a United States congressman from Arkansas in various years from 1883 to 1894.)[20] Jewish writer Harry Golden noted that Jews who settled in small southern towns were often viewed as special and called "our Jews" by the Gentile community.[21] This was true in many Arkansas towns.

Although the Jews were well accepted locally, their reputations did little to change the preconceived negative stereotype that most Americans held of Jews in general. Events that occurred in the twentieth century brought out a latent propensity toward anti-Semitism, which was seen in the explosive reaction in 1913 when Leo Frank, a northern Jew, was accused of killing young Mary Phagan in Atlanta, Georgia. Her murder precipitated the founding in 1915 of the Ku Klux Klan, an organization modeled on a secret society by that name established in the South after the Civil War.[22] During the height of the Klan in the 1920s, when Arkansas became one of the group's strongest bastions with some fifty thousand members, there was relatively little persecution against the state's Jewry.[23] It has been observed that large numbers of Southerners were not anti-Semitic for two reasons: they had such a deep-seated prejudice against blacks and Catholics that the Jews were generally overlooked, and Southerners tended to be schooled in the Old Testament, drawing their ethics from Judeo-Christian teachings.[24] The Jews as a whole were quiet, hardworking, helpful, and generous in their charity, and, for the most part, these qualities were taken into account by the communities in which they settled. Arkansas has had its share of anti-Semitism, however, and examples of where and what forms it took are interspersed in this text.

An examination of the close-knit structure of the Jewish families in Arkansas reveals that structure to be similar to a net spreading over the state. Just as a fishnet is simply a series of knots strung together, and if one knot is lifted the whole net moves; just so, in attempting to lift the history of a specific Jewish family in Arkansas, one often finds that it involves other Jewish families across the state, within whose families the first family had married. (This situation is not unusual among minority religious groups; for example, the same phenomenon would occur among a minority of Christians living in a Muslim country.) Relatively few intermarriages with non-Jews occurred between the 1860s and the late 1940s.

As the New South emerged, the immigrant Jewish newcomer grew up with it, and their histories became inseparably intertwined. The social and economic history of the South cannot be thoroughly considered without the inclusion of southern Jewish history.[25] Because the southern historian has neglected to include the Jewish entrepreneurs (except generally as a footnote) as a factor in the recovery of the South after the Civil War, their contributions have been difficult to measure. After a more thorough study, one can safely say that they played an important, crucial role in reestablishing commerce after that war.[26] This could well be said of Arkansas, where the contributions of the Jews have been superb, considering the fact that Jewish people have constituted such a small percentage of the state's population. What is striking is the weight of their contributions. Almost 95 percent owned their own businesses, were generating jobs, offering services, contributing to the economy, promoting culture and education, making use of natural resources, establishing banks and trust companies, and helping to keep revenues in the state.[27] And, as a people, they were unequaled in their contributions to charity and to the general good of the public. Active Jewish participants composed a comparatively fair share of almost every organization in the state that was seeking its development and betterment. David Y. Thomas, one of the first people to chronicle Arkansas history, wrote that Little Rock Jewish businessman Myron Lasker was a leader "among the Hebrews of the Southwest" and that "Little Rock and . . . the entire State of Arkansas owe much to [such types], the great progress made in recent times in so many directions [is] largely a result of their courage, faith, and vision."[28]

This section covers the period from the Civil War until the World War II era and gives an account of a cross section of the Jewish citizens and families that settled in Arkansas. For this study of economic and civic progress, the state has been divided into three geographical sections: Central Arkansas (Pulaski County), eastern Arkansas, and western Arkansas. Chapters seven through nine contain the history of the Central European Jewish settlers, who made up the greater number of the pioneers, and chapters ten through twelve give the history of the East European Jews, most of whom came after the turn of the century.

In order that the reader may gain better perspective on the various eras of people chronicled in this section, particularly the business and professional individuals, their life spans are given where known.

CHAPTER 7

German Migration in Central Arkansas

Pulaski County

Pulaski County was fortunate enough to survive the Civil War with few visible signs of physical ravages; both the Confederate and Union armies had occupied Little Rock and had actually helped in its expansion.[1] The population of Pulaski County grew from 11,699 in 1860 to 32,066 by 1870.[2] The citizens of Arkansas, along with the rest of the South, had hoped for a rapid and painless transition back into the Union, but those hopes faded in 1867 when the Reconstruction acts were passed by Congress. The state soon swarmed with Federal registrars, enfranchising some citizens while disenfranchising others. The result of this action was a new state constitution, which passed in March 1868. After narrowly passing, it made possible a six-year rule (1868–74) by the Republicans. A local newspaper called the new constitution "the sum of villainies."[3] The city of Little Rock was on the verge of financial ruin by the time the six years had passed under Republican control.[4] A local newspaper had noted that the ruling carpetbaggers were "parasites of fungus growth, the loathsome products of other soils . . . their only notoriety [was] their infamy."[5]

LITTLE ROCK

Although Little Rock was not plagued with race riots as were seen in Memphis and New Orleans during the Republican years, it had its own small civil war, known as the Brooks-Baxter War. In the governor's race of 1874, the liberal Joseph Brooks ran against Elisha Baxter. When the latter won the election, the results were contested by Brooks, who won a questionable court case in April 1874. A short period of conflict ensued, during which it is estimated that some two hundred people lost their lives, both to direct fire and to accidents.[6] Brooks marched his henchmen to the State House, where they ousted Baxter and barricaded the building.[7] For thirty-four days the usurper held the seat of government until President Ulysses S. Grant recognized Baxter as the winner and Brooks vacated the State Capitol.[8] During the conflict period, the Jewish-owned Concordia Club was used as a temporary hospital for the wounded, and several Jewish farmers—Jim Levy, William Levy, and L. Rosenberg—were wounded at New Gascony (a short distance from Little Rock).[9] Charles Pfeifer, brother of pioneer settlers Joseph and Philip, was so embarrassed by the political problems that he moved to Cincinnati.[10]

The mid-1870s brought other problems as well. Banks failed, and the value of money dropped so low on the exchange that saloon owners refused to accept it. Most immigrants gave the city and state "only a cursory glance."[11] At such a time as this, there were Jewish entrepreneurs who joined those already in Arkansas and who, in turn, distinguished themselves in signal ways in helping the area's recovery. One of the newcomers was Herman Kahn (1854–1929), who, it was said, came to Little Rock when Reconstruction was underway, and

> girded on the armor of industry, set his active brain to work, and with all the power of a vibrant nature helped to bring about a metamorphosis in commercial and industrial conditions. For this work he will never be forgotten. He left a name for civic accomplishment not exceeded in value by any of his compeers, a citizen of priceless value to the community.[12]

Kahn, who came to Little Rock in the early 1870s, began as a sales clerk, then opened a mercantile store with a meager stock of goods.[13] He prospered and by 1900 became president of the Bank of Commerce. In 1905 he formed the Hotel Marion Company, serving as its president. (The hotel was named for his wife, Marion [Cohn] Kahn.) The Arkansas State Senate praised those who established the hotel, saying they should be "entitled to lasting praise for having done so much to bring the state into the front rank of progress" with a facility "second to none."[14] The Marion Hotel became the state's focal point for political, civic, and social meetings for more than sixty years. (It was demolished on 17 February 1980, to make way for a new hotel, the Excelsior, and the State House Convention Center.) At the time the Marion was built, Little Rock was said to have been a "mealy, low-rise town on a slow river, and the hotel was the toniest, plushest place in it."[15]

Kahn became the single greatest builder in Little Rock up to that time, erecting at least six buildings in the city and being involved in the erection of several others.[16] Active in numerous civic organizations, he also served for eight years as a member of the Little Rock City Council and for six years on the committee that erected Little Rock's two bridges across the Arkansas River. When he died in 1929, it was noted that he had come to Arkansas as an immigrant youth from Germany and had built a fortune that "perhaps was not surpassed" by any other Little Rock man; he had based his career on his faith in the state and in Little Rock as a "safe and profitable place for investment." He was recognized for his "unusual gift for business affairs," for "ambition . . . vision . . . energy. His life showed what American opportunity means to one who has worth and merit, with devotion to constructive purpose." With all his success, however, it was said that his greatest satisfaction and reward came from his home and family.[17]

Herman and Marion "Mamie" Kahn passed on their love for Arkansas and their dedication to it to their two children, sons Sidney and Alfred. Sidney (1884–1972), a graduate of Harvard University, began his career as a banker in Little Rock, then went into real estate, where he became a leading figure in that field in Arkansas. He was an officer of the Little Rock Planning Commission for twenty years and president of the Little Rock Realty Association. He developed commercial property as well as subdivisions, including Prospect Terrace in Pulaski Heights.[18] Alfred Kahn (1886–1976) founded the Rose City Cotton Oil Company in 1914 and the Conway Cotton Oil Company. He served as president of Union Trust Company (later, Union National Bank) and was active in a number of other companies. Influential in Arkansas life, he was active in numerous movements to better Little Rock and the state. This included proposing a universal grading system on cottonseed and openly opposing gambling at Hot Springs.[19]

Industry and Natural Resources

Arkansas as a state was slow in developing its industry. It was distant from large cities, and railway charges were higher in the South. After 1884, when the state did not pay a considerable part of its debt, northern investors became wary of investing more.[20] The state's natural resources—timber, oil, and minerals such as coal, zinc, lead, and manganese—were exploited, but they were generally shipped out of state for processing and manufacturing, and the state thus lost considerable revenue. While most of the state's industry was owned by Northerners,[21] almost all Arkansas Jews owned their own businesses, and this helped keep revenues in the state. Several Jewish businessmen capitalized on the state's resources, such as lumber, ore, cotton, hides and furs.

Lumber

Arkansas had abundant forests, and by the turn of the century, three-fourths of the state was still covered in pine, hardwood, and cypress; as late as the early 1920s, some sixty percent of the state's wage earners worked for the lumber industry.[22] The most outstanding Jewish settler who capitalized on the state's lumber resources was Charles T. Abeles (1854–1933). Abeles came to Little Rock in 1874 and in 1880 opened the C. T. Abeles Company with partner A. B. Hendricks (whom he later bought out).[23] Within five years the Abeles Company had one of the most extensive trades in the state, and by 1887 it was competing with St. Louis manufacturers.[24] By 1908 Abeles had a three-story brick building at Third and Scott, employed 175 workers, and specialized in beautiful ornate staircases, cabinets, woodwork, and wood products.[25] Abeles became a foremost manufacturer in the Southwest, handling the largest stock of windows and plate glass in the area; he had two large woodworking plants, one of which covered fourteen acres. He furnished the sashes, doors and windows for the new state Capitol in Little Rock,[26] Camp Pike and Fort Logan H. Roots at North Little Rock, and Camp Eberts at Lonoke.[27] Abeles became prominent nationally in the lumber industry, capitalizing on the state's rich supply of high grade cypress, oak, and gum, which he sold locally, nationally, and overseas.[28] He was associated with several lumber firms, including Mechanics Lumber Company, as well as with regional and national lumber organizations. He gave liberally to civic causes statewide, and it was said that his "untiring efforts" to improve Arkansas and his "unimpeachable integrity . . . and sincere devotion to ideals" won him the affection of the state.[29] In 1911 Abeles built one of the city's first luxury apartment complexes, the Abeles Apartments, at 1403 Louisiana Street.[30]

Charles Abeles' brother, Sam, was a partner in the Abeles firm but later opened his own business.[31] (Sam Abeles' son, Julian, became a New York attorney who was involved in the music world, where he gained the trust of the National Association of Orchestra Directors and was given the title "Czar of Jazz." He had the responsibility of listening to each piece of music tried out by the big orchestras—such as those of Paul Whiteman,

Vincent Lopez, George Olsen, and Freddie Rich—and to reject any song whose lyrics were considered "vile, vicious, mean, low-down, or indecent," and such songs would not be played in the United States. The band leaders generally abided by his decisions.)[32]

Moses J. Ringelhaupt (1866–1918), a Little Rock native and brother-in-law of Charles Abeles, was associated with the Abeles Company and promoted the growth and expansion of the firm. He was president of Mechanics Lumber Company (an Abeles firm) and was associated with the Lasker-Morris Bank and Trust Company of Little Rock.[33] Theodore D. "Theo" Abeles, son of Charles and Delia (Ringelhaupt) Abeles, was associated with his father until the Abeles company was sold in 1926 to the Arkla Sash and Door Company. Theo then organized the Abeles Glass Company, which was the only dealer of flat glass in Arkansas at the time; he was also co-owner of the United Shoe Store.[34] The Abeles-Ringelhaupt family included members of other Little Rock Jewish families, such as Stifft, Jacobson, Blass, Simon, and Navra.

Morris Navra Ehrenberg (1890–1953) was also in the lumber business. He established the Union Lumber Company in Little Rock after World War I, but he lost it during the Great Depression and joined Mechanics Lumber Company.[35] Through marriage to Hortense Weil, Ehrenberg helped bring another industry to Arkansas. His father-in-law, Ben Weil, came to Little Rock in 1910 and opened a meat-packing plant. By 1913 it had become one of the most successful such firms ever launched in Arkansas. Weil built a large meat-packing plant on East Sixth Street, bought livestock statewide, and sent meats and hides to cities nationwide. Weil envisioned a plant in Little Rock that would be similar to the large stockyards in Kansas City but could not find adequate supplies of stock in Arkansas, so he later established several plants outside the state.[36]

The Franklin brothers, Siesel and John, were owners of Planters Lumber Company. Siesel (1897–1969), chairman of the company's board, served as president of both the local and the state lumbermen's associations. (Siesel was also an early Arkansas aviator. In the 1940s he operated a government-sponsored pilot training school at Ouachita Baptist College and at Henderson State Teacher's College. He was associated with Ellis Fagan Flying Service.)[37]

Other Jews who capitalized on Arkansas's timber products included Leo Pollock, Max Parker, Louis Leidinger, and Nathan Dreyfus. Pollock (1839–1906; see section I) came to Little Rock in the 1850s and, after serving in the Confederate army, became one of the city's first merchants when he opened a furniture store. (He also had an insurance business at

Marianna and at Forrest City.)[38] Parker (1836–1877) came to Little Rock in 1864 almost penniless. After saving frugally, he opened a wholesale and retail furniture store on East Markham, later adding a furniture factory and transfer company to his enterprise.[39] Leidinger also had a furniture store on East Markham that included a cabinet-making and upholstery department.[40] Dreyfus (1868–1946) came to Little Rock in 1888 and became involved in cabinet-making and upholstery, operating the Arkansas Upholstery and Cabinet Company for fifty-three years.[41] (His brother, Leopold Dreyfus, had a department store in Little Rock.)[42]

Holland-born Jacob Heiligers (1854–1900) found a way to capitalize on Arkansas's fruit trees; he established the Capitol City Cider Company in Little Rock in 1883 and manufactured "pure, sweet cider." He also made laundry bluing. Prior to his enterprise, only "foreign markets" supplied cider, and customers paid high prices for "an article that might be cider or might not."[43]

Mining

Coal was Arkansas's first-ranked mineral product from 1880 to 1920, when it was supplanted by oil, which was less expensive to mine and ship. Most of the state's coal came from a large coal reserve located in western Arkansas.[44] A Jewish entrepreneur who took advantage of Arkansas coal was Abe Stiewel (pronounced Steevel) (1840–1913). Stiewel came to Little Rock in 1872 with funds he had made from a moderately successful fruit business in New Orleans. He purchased a large number of shares in Arkansas coal mines and became owner of the Coal Hill, Eureka, Peacock, and Excelsior coal mines at the towns of Coal Hill and Spadra. They were operated by his brother, Edward S. Stiewel (1845–1909), who lived at Coal Hill for fifteen years before returning to Little Rock in 1899 as manager of Abe's holdings. Abe had also entered the brokerage and banking business. He bought both the Fones Building at Second and Main streets and the Park Theatre and held controlling interest in the Little Rock Trust Company and the Forest Park Amusement Company. (Abe was one of Little Rock's wealthiest citizens when he died in 1913.)[45]

Cotton

As an agricultural state, Arkansas's economy depended greatly upon cotton, and a number of Jews in the state dealt in cotton-growing, cotton-buying, and cotton-selling. In Little Rock Adolph Hamberg (1849–1936) became the most prominent Jew in that trade. Born in Holland, Hamberg opened a mercantile store in Little Rock in the 1880s and became a cotton and commission merchant in partnership with Max Mayer. As a cotton buyer, Hamberg paid merchants on the spot, helping to revolutionize the cotton trade. After the turn of the century, he, his son Harold, and nephew Walter Hamberg established the Ad Hamberg and Company Cotton Buyers. Ad Hamburg's ideas on handling cotton coincided with those of the Lesser-Goldman Company of St. Louis, and he became their state manager.[46]

Both Julius Lesser (1853–1908) and Jacob Goldman (1845–1922) had business careers in Arkansas shortly after the Civil War—Lesser at Forrest City and then at Marianna, and Goldman at Jacksonport. Both were highly successful in their respective towns. Lesser's mercantile firm handled sixty percent of the cotton grown in the area, and he was stockholder in several banks in Lee and Phillips Counties. He served as city treasurer and as an alderman in Marianna, and he owned several business blocks in the city.[47] He retained ownership of his holdings after he moved to St. Louis and founded the Lesser Cotton Company. It became one of the most successful cotton firms in the nation. Lesser bought several Arkansas compresses and built others.

After serving in the Confederate army, German-born Jacob D. Goldman settled at Jacksonport, having been invited there by two non-Jewish Arkansas soldiers who had befriended him during the war. He began his career in Arkansas as a clerk in the Simon Adler store. With a plan in mind to help Arkansas cotton growers, Goldman moved to St. Louis in 1875 and established the Adler-Goldman Commission Company. In 1892 he joined Lesser, and the Lesser-Goldman Cotton Company was established. The men sought to modernize the way cotton was handled, sending buyers out into the field to bid for cotton. Before this, the grower had to send his cotton to commission houses in New Orleans, Memphis, or St. Louis and take whatever they were offered, then wait weeks or months for payment. Small farmers had been selling to country merchants, who in turn sold to commissioners under less than desirable conditions. There were few banks and little money available locally, and messengers had to deliver the funds. Lesser-Goldman began using long distance phones, collaborating with banks so that cotton growers could be paid on the spot. Compresses were located for easy movement of cotton, and a system was established with the railway companies so that uniform freight rates were made possible. Their efforts revolutionized the cotton process, and over the years they helped wage battles in defense of producers and facilitated marketing to protect the growers from unnecessary hardships.[48]

The Lesser-Goldman Company became the largest domestic shippers of cotton in the nation. They specialized in Arkansas cotton, always believing it was the best in the world. Goldman loved Arkansas and always considered it his home; leaving it for St. Louis was "one of the hardest things" of his life.[49] He promoted migration to Arkansas, believing it had "a brighter future and present[ed] better opportunities" than any other state.[50] He had fliers printed and distributed nationwide that said "My Advice to Young Men, Based on 54 Years' Personal Experience, Is to Go to Arkansas!" In the flier, he enumerated sixteen good reasons he thought Arkansas was the best state in the Union in which to settle.[51]

Because of the importance of cotton to the area's economy, the Little Rock Cotton Exchange was organized in the early 1880s; the name was changed to the Little Rock Board of Trade in April 1886 to include other business and professional interests. In the Board's first annual report, Ad Hamberg, Joseph Wolf, and J. S. Pollock were listed as committee members, and of the eighty listed members of the organization, seventeen were Jewish.[52] Ad Hamberg later served as Board president (1902–03). Other Jewish businessmen were involved in the cotton trade. For instance, H. D. McCowan was associated with the Eagle Ginning and Cotton Company, which handled some four thousand to six thousand bales of cotton annually.[53] Jacob Jacobson, father of politician Charles Jacobson, was a Jewish settler of Perry County who later owned a farm in east Pulaski County. He and his son Adolph were cotton buyers, and Jacob became a respected cotton expert. He was involved in the state's purchase of the Cummins plantation southeast of Little Rock to be used as a penal farm.[54]

Hides and Furs

The abundant forests in Arkansas made it a haven for animals, and mink, otter, beaver, raccoon, deer, and bear were hunted for their hides.[55] Moses J. Siesel (1839–1906), who came to Little Rock in the mid-1870s, capitalized on Arkansas products of hides, wool, fur, and leather. He was known as one of the city's most reliable citizens, and his firm became one of the best-known in the Southwest.[56] (Siesel married Henrietta Oppenheimer, and their daughters married into the families of Pfeifer, Franklin, Dreyfus, and Thalheimer.)[57]

Manufacturing, Construction

The Ottenheimers and the Falks are prime examples of Jewish entrepreneurs who went into the manufacturing business. The Ottenheimer brothers—Daniel (1835–1916), Abraham (1838–1896), and Phillip (1839–1905)—had come to Arkansas before the Civil War (see section I), and they returned to Little Rock after serving in the Confederate army. In the 1860s they had a carpet and dry goods firm, but in 1886, Abraham "Abe" embarked on a wholesale and retail hat business with the Falk brothers, David (1857–1935) and Nathan (1866–1938). Known as the Falk-Ottenheimer Hat Company, it was the only establishment of its kind in the state in the 1880s and 1890s. By 1899 they employed twenty workers and were doing trade in several states.[58] David Falk served as a director of the Little Rock Board of Trade for a number of years; he was a charter member of the Travelers Protective Association and served as president of the Concordia Association. When he retired in 1928, the Falk-Ottenheimer Hat Company was dissolved. (Dave Falk married Abe Ottenheimer's daughter Jennie, and their son Randall played an important role in World War I and in the American Legion. Randall M. Falk [1895–1945] served as a captain in the U.S. Army in World War I; he later served as an executive of the War Manpower Commission and was the only Arkansan to attend the Paris caucus that created the American Legion. He served on several war boards in Little Rock during World War II.)[59]

Nathan Falk left the family hat business in 1897 and joined the Beal-Burrow Dry Goods Company as a stockholder and salesman. He traveled western Arkansas with a two-horse buggy; it required three or four months to cover his required territory (when he began using automobiles, he covered the same area in three weeks). He was known to be better acquainted with more small-town merchants in Arkansas than any other businessman at the time.[60]

The two sons of Dan Ottenheimer—Leonard (1892–1984) and Gus (1897–1985)—became well known for their efforts in manufacturing and in the development of Little Rock. Leonard worked in a dry goods company before founding Leonard J. Ottenheimer, Inc., a jobber of ladies' clothing. He was joined by his brother Gus in 1925, and the firm became Ottenheimer Bros. After the crash of 1929, the enterprise manufactured ladies' garments.[61] The Ottenheimer-Falk families were intermingled with a number of other Arkansas Jewish families, such as Cohn, Berger, Ottenger, Reutlinger, Storthz, DeFrance, and Berg. (For further data on Leonard and Gus Ottenheimer, see section V.)

Joseph Lyons (1862–1923), son of pioneer settlers Samuel and Sophia Lyons, became well known in Arkansas through his firm, the Joe Lyons Machinery Company. His business venture began in 1888, and in 1914 he began handling farm machinery. He was doing a million-dollar-a-year business by the end of 1918 and his firm was recognized as a leading jobbing house in the field in Little Rock.[62] He was joined by his sons, Maxwell (1896–1978) and Samuel (1898–), after World War I. (Maxwell Lyons served in the Marines in World War I, during which time he received the Silver Star with three additional stars and the Distinguished Service Cross as well as the Croix de Guerre and Fors a Guerre from France. He served as commandant of the Marine Corps League in Arkansas during World War II.)[63]

After Joseph Lyons died in 1923, the company left the farm equipment business and dealt solely in construction equipment for building roads and buildings. The state's roads were little more than dust or mud trails until the appearance of automobiles and, although a State Highway Commission was established in 1913, little was done to improve the roads until the 1920s.[64] The Lyons company was one of the first to carry heavy road equipment, and it provided vital equipment for road building in Arkansas for some sixty years. The Lyons family was active in civic and humanitarian organizations, and the firm's employees were encouraged to do the same. During World War II, the firm had a government contract to rebuild machine tools and equipment.[65] The Lyons family included members of other Arkansas Jewish families, such as Felsenthal, Cohn, Eichenbaum, Kronberg, Marks, Lasker, and Solmson.

In the late 1930s Edward D. Elias (1876–1958) and his family moved from Mississippi to Little Rock, where Mrs. Ed (Ruth Levin) Elias's family lived. Ed and his son Barney (and later, Ed's son Charles) established the Tri-State Construction Company; in the 1940s the company built the Governor's Mansion for the State of Arkansas. It also constructed commercial and industrial buildings, schools, housing developments, and communication facilities as well as public water and sewer facilities. The company continued until 1960.[66]

Department Stores

A number of Jewish businessmen, some of whom had been in business before and during the Civil War, helped Pulaski County's recovery after the war. Abraham Kempner, for example, came to Arkansas in the 1840s (see section I) and was later joined in business by his son Jacob as well as by Jacob's sons, Isaac "Ike," Abraham "Abe," David, and Melvin. By 1869 Jacob Kempner (whose wife Sophia was a sibling of the Blass brothers, Louis, Gus, and Jacob) had acquired a large amount of property statewide.[67] Both the Blass and Kempner names later became household words in the department store business in Arkansas and in the South. By the 1870s Kempner family members had established several Little Rock stores. The Ike Kempner and Brothers Shoe Store (later known as Kempner's) became known nationwide. When the store was destroyed by fire in 1916, the rebuilt edifice was described by a local paper as "the most beautiful store in America," and it noted that such an impressive structure was not expected to be found in Arkansas.[68] Ike Kempner was an indefatigable worker and became associated with as many as twenty-eight Arkansas firms at one time; these included realty firms, hotels, dairies, banking firms, utilities, cold storage companies, construction firms, transfer companies, and many others.[69]

The Blass family's sojourn in Arkansas was begun by Louis Blass (1844–1911), who migrated to Little Rock in 1867 and who was soon joined by his teenaged brother Gus (1849–1919). They started out at first with a box of goods on Main Street.[70] Another brother, Jacob Blass (1854–1922), joined them in 1869, opening his own store, which later drew a good trade among country folks. (His son Gilbert organized the Atlas Finance Company, and another son, Alvin, was owner of the City Hardware Company in North Little Rock).[71] Louis Blass brought his cousin, Pauline Heiman, from Germany as his bride. Known for his charity—he gave away thousands of dollars annually—Louis was said to have risked his own life to save others during a yellow fever epidemic while serving on the city's Board of Health and Humane Society and again when the Arkansas River flooded. When he died in 1911, his long obituary, which told of his unselfish deeds, began simply with the statement, "Louis Blass Is Dead."[72]

The name Gus Blass became synonymous with good citizenship as the man himself worked tirelessly for civic and social improvements in the city and state. As an ardent worker on the Board of Commerce (later, Chamber of Commerce), he drew a number of industries to Little Rock.[73] By the 1870s he had added a wholesale department to his retail store, and in 1913 he opened a new building at Fourth and Main streets, which was "resplendent with beautiful lights, sparkling with oriental splendor, and superb in its conception."[74] It was described as rivaling the shops of New York and Paris, and it offered the population in Little Rock and vicinity a taste of elegance not seen heretofore in Arkansas. Gus Blass believed that "nothing was too good for the city in which he lived."[75] His two sons, Julian G. (1876–1939) and Noland J. (1889–1979), followed in their father's footsteps. Julian became nationally known as a "sagacious" businessman as he led the Blass company; he was actively involved in a number of civic organizations, including the Little Rock Chamber of Commerce.[76] Noland also was civic minded and led the effort to establish the Pulaski Community Chest (later known as the United Way) and the University Hospital Blood Bank.[77]

Max Heiman (1853–1917), a cousin and partner of Gus Blass, was involved in a number of other businesses, including a shoe firm, a cold storage company, and a trust company. He sponsored the Arkansas Children's Home (later Arkansas Children's Hospital) and was the first president of the Little Rock Boys Club. He became known statewide for his financial, charitable, and social activities.[78] Gus Blass's daughter Essie married Joseph Berger (1874–1936) of Jonesboro (son of Marcus and Henrietta [Less] Berger), who founded the Norton-Berger Shoe Company. The company became one of the largest of its kind in Arkansas; its sales in 1920 exceeded $1 million.[79] Joe Berger also acquired the Pollack Company, which dealt in ready-to-wear clothes, that had ten branch stores in Arkansas, Louisiana, and Mississippi.[80] He was president of several other businesses, and he accumulated some fifty thousand acres of land in Arkansas.[81]

The Pfeifer name, which appeared on stores in Hot Springs and Pine Bluff as well as on the flagship store in Little Rock, became as well known in Arkansas's department store history as did that of Blass. Joseph Pfeifer (1835–1926) followed his brother Philip Pfeifer to Little Rock in 1864. Having come to America with only five dollars in his pocket, Joseph began his career in Little Rock in partnership with G. F. Miller; after one year, Joseph opened his own men's store, "Jos. Pfeifer."[82] By November 1874 Joseph was broke—as were many others who attempted to start businesses after the war—but he rallied again a year later and was on his way to success.[83] His sons Leo and Harry joined him in his clothing store, and in 1910 this was merged with a jewelry store headed by two others of his sons, Preston and Albert. Pfeifer's Department Store was born, and the enterprise grew until it became one of the most prestigious stores of its kind in the state.[84] Pfeifer family members were active in commercial and civic affairs, helping in innumerable ways the growth of the Little Rock area and the state.[85] When Preston Pfeifer donated to the Little Rock Kiwanis Club a large sum of money in memory of his father (who died in 1926) for an underprivileged boys' camp west of Little Rock, the camp was named the Joseph Pfeifer Kiwanis Camp.[86] The Pfeifer store became known for its charity and community service.[87] Both the Blass and the Pfeifer stores gave elaborate picnics for employees annually and chartered streetcars for the events.[88]

Leo Pfeifer (1871–1960) and his brother Harry (1873–1960) bought their dad's business interest at his retirement in 1909. Beginning in the business at age thirteen, Leo later became known as one of the state's fore-most retail merchandisers. He served on the boards of numerous organiza-tions and was an original member of the Donaghey Foundation.[89] He and his wife (Ruby Siesel) had one child, Eleanor, who married Sam Strauss. Harry Pfeifer began his career at age sixteen in his dad's store. He became interested in Little Rock's development as well and was in several real estate and business ventures that contributed to the growth of greater Little Rock.[90] His son Harry Pfeifer Jr. served as president of the M. M. Cohn Company (Harry Pfeifer Jr. had married the daughter of Albert Cohn). Leo's and Harry's brother Preston (1881–1961) served as president of Pfeifer Bros. from 1929 to 1934; he was succeeded by Sam Strauss.[91] Preston was active in the land purchase for what became War Memorial Park in Little Rock and served on other boards, such as those of the Pulaski County Flood Control and Navigation Association.[92]

In 1931 at the beginning of the Great Depression, the Pfeifer firm planned an ambitious expansion for what would have been an eight-story building at the southwest corner of Seventh and Main streets. It was hoped the effort would help the local economy, but the Depression cur-tailed the plans.[93] The Pfeifer family includes members of a number of Arkansas Jewish families, such as Levy, Dreyfus, Feinstein, Cohn, Strauss, Thalheimer, and Rudolph.

Joining the prestige of the Kempner, Blass, and Pfeifer names in depart-ment store history in Arkansas was that of Mark M. Cohn (1845–1923).[94] He came to Arkansas in 1872, first settling at Arkadelphia, some sixty-seven miles southwest of Little Rock. He, like so many other Jews, started on a very small scale, but by his "powerful will, strict integrity, unceasing energy, and indomitable perseverance" became successful.[95] After marrying Rachel Kempner, daughter of pioneer settler Abraham Kempner, he moved to Little Rock in 1880 and opened a clothing store. Just three years later it was described as being one of the most extensive and elegant of such stores in the city.[96] Mark Cohn's partner in Little Rock, Dutch-born Isaac Pareira (1840–1911), became a promoter of Little Rock real estate and helped develop the city.[97] (Pareira married Mildred Kempner, who was born at Hot Springs in 1855.)

Mark M. Cohn had two sons, Albert (1874–1926) and Victor (1878–1897). Victor, who was slated to succeed his father as head of the M. M. Cohn Company, died in 1897; so Albert, who was graduated as a civil engineer in 1894 and had worked on Arkansas's rivers with the U.S. government, gave up his engineering career to assume the family business when his father became ill. Although he was disappointed at leaving his chosen profession, he entered the company with zest and determination, and the store flourished under his management.[98] He became involved with civic affairs, serving as a director on a number of boards, including the Little Rock School Board. He gave generously to charity, often unbeknown to relatives or friends.[99]

As a graduate of Virginia Military Institute, Albert influenced decisions that greatly affected Pulaski County. One of his schoolmates at the Institute was Major (later Colonel) Kilbourne, who served as adjutant to General Wood when Wood was in charge of placing military camps during World War I. Kilbourne's high regard for Albert was an influential factor in the decision to locate the cantonment of Camp Pike in Pulaski County.[100]

Although it was through Albert Cohn's diligence and willingness to give up his own career that the M. M. Cohn Company survived and flourished, it extracted a terrible price from him later on. As he grew older and reflected on having lost the opportunity to practice his preferred profession of engineering, he became despondent and in July 1926 took his own life.[101]

Even though the economy was poor, there was a thirst for "quality and style" in the South in the years following the Civil War, and the Jewish-owned department stores, such as Kempner's, Pfeifer's, Blass's, and Cohn's, helped quench that need.[102] Albert Bloom also had a department store in Little Rock, although it did not reach the level of those listed above.[103]

Banking

Arkansas's dire financial straits after the Civil War were exacerbated by its lack of a viable banking system. The State Bank and the Real Estate Bank, both of which had been established by the General Assembly in 1836, had lasted little more than six years. The attempt at banking had been so disastrous (by 1843 the state was three million dollars in debt) that the General Assembly passed an amendment in 1844 forbidding any bank or banking institution to be established in Arkansas. Arkansas had no more banks until after the Civil War, and as late as 1882, only twenty-three banks could be found in the state.[104]

Between 1866 and the 1890s, some seven banks were established in Little Rock, and in five of these, Jews were either officers or board members.[105] The Merchants National Bank was established in Little Rock in 1866 as the first national bank in the city. (The name was later changed to First National Bank.) Col. Logan H. Roots served as its president, and

A. A. Mandlebaum, a Jewish merchant "well known . . . and far-famed for thorough-going and careful business qualities," served as assistant cashier. The German National Bank was established in 1873 with John G. Fletcher serving as president. Board members of the bank included Little Rock Jewish businessmen Isaac Wolf, M. Katzenstein, and Gus Blass; William Pollock served as teller. The Exchange National Bank was incorporated in 1882, with Jewish businessmen J. S. Pollock serving as cashier and J. W. Mandlebaum as assistant cashier and teller; bank directors included Philip Pfeifer and Isaac Wolf, and H. B. Pollock served as collector. J. S. Pollock later served as vice-president of the Exchange National Bank, A. A. Mandlebaum served as cashier, and Sol Gans served as a director.[106] When the Bank of Commerce was established, Abe Ottenheimer and Gus Gans served as two of its directors.[107] In 1898 the Bank of Commerce management changed, with Herman Kahn chosen as president and S. L. Kahn as vice-president; the firm grew from having assets of $165,000 to having assets of more than $3,000,000 by 1918.[108] The German National Bank, the American Bank, and the Merchants and Planters Bank merged in December 1911, with Jacob D. Goldman (of the Lesser-Goldman Cotton Company of St. Louis) named as president; five of the sixteen stockholders were Jewish.[109] The Lasker family of Little Rock, including Harry, Emmett, and Henry, established the Lasker-Morris Bank and Trust Company in 1915.[110] (The Lasker-Morris Bank changed its name to Commercial Trust Company in 1920, and this later merged with Worthen Bank.)[111] Aaron Frank, H. W. Pfeifer, Gus Gans, and A. R. Levy established the Southern Trust Company,[112] and Abe Stiewel established the Union Trust Company.[113] Other Jewish businessmen of Little Rock served in the banking industry over the years, especially on the various boards.

Education

Many Jews were active in the efforts to improve Arkansas's educational system, which was for many years almost an afterthought. Although the state's General Assembly of the years 1866–67 established a system of free public schools for white children and the Constitution of 1874 established free public schools, the state's citizenry did not promote or take advantage of what was offered.[114] One of the state's prominent citizens who worked to rectify this situation was Frederick Kramer (1829–1896), a pre–Civil War settler (see section I). A merchant by trade, his business took second place to his civic endeavors. He served as mayor of Little Rock during the

Reconstruction years 1873–75, was then succeeded by John G. Fletcher in 1875, but was reelected and served again from 1881 to 1887. Although his administration was considered one of the most important ones before 1920 and he was commended for his improvement of the city's streets, fire department, and sewage system, he was best remembered for his work in education. He served many years as a member and president of the Little Rock School Board. An elementary school at Seventh and Sherman streets was named in his honor. (Kramer, born in Halle, Prussia, came to America at age nineteen. He joined the U.S. Army and served in the Indian Territory from 1852 to 1857, after which he settled in Little Rock. Listed among the early Jewish merchants of the city and as a pioneer member of congregation B'nai Israel of Little Rock, he married Adaline Reichardt, a member of a German Christian family who had a plantation near the city. The family embraced the Christian faith. Kramer was a dedicated Mason and served many years as treasurer of the grand lodge of Arkansas.)[115]

Philip Pfeifer (1831–1897), brother of Joseph Pfeifer, also promoted education. German-born Philip had settled at Napoleon prior to the Civil War then joined the Confederate army and was wounded at the battle of Pea Ridge. In the 1860s he settled at Little Rock, where he established a wholesale grocery firm. His business was called a "boat store" because boat officers and crews congregated there and received their mail. It became a gathering place for local notables as well. An advocate of better schools, Pfeifer was elected to the Little Rock School Board. He donated land for a school for the east side of the city, and the Philip Pfeifer School was built on East Sixth Street.[116] Pfeifer, along with several other prominent citizens, served as a lay member of the State Medical Society. During the yellow fever panic of 1878, he provided food and supplies for passengers of a train stranded at a quarantine station east of Little Rock.[117] The Philip Pfeifer family later left the grocery business and bought the firm of Mechanics Lumber Company from Charles Abeles. By 1908 the firm was the largest lumber company in Pulaski County.[118] Arthur H. Pfeifer, one of Philip's sons, established a plumbing firm, later known as the Pfeifer Plumbing and Heating Company.[119] The Phil Pfeifer family married into the Arkansas Jewish families of Siesel, Katzenstein, Bott, and Levy.

Another signal promoter of education was Morris Levy (1852–1916), who settled in Little Rock in 1881, then moved to Argenta (North Little Rock) and purchased the Alexander Mercantile Company. He served on the Argenta school board for many years, including a number as its president. He was known for his generosity. When he kindly lent fifty dollars to "impoverished but ambitious produce peddler" Ernest Stanley, Stanley was so grateful that, when he established a small town outside North Little Rock, he named it "Levy" for his kind benefactor.[120] M. Levy's Dry Goods Company, engaged in dry goods, boots, shoes, and groceries, became the leading and "most representative" firm in Argenta [121] The Levy family included members of other Arkansas Jewish families, including Loebner, Vogel, Levy (not related), and Kahn.

Mathias Abraham Cohn (1824–1901; not related to Mark M. Cohn) was a promoter of higher education in Arkansas. He was elected as one of ten members of the first Board of Trustees of the University of Arkansas when it was established by the state legislature in 1871. He served as secretary of the Board as well as a member of the University of Arkansas Building and Grounds Committee. Cohn had first settled at Augusta, Woodruff County, where he was elected to several offices: state representative, county sheriff, and superintendent of the schools for the second circuit of Arkansas.[122] He was also editor of the *Augusta Sentinel*.[123] He moved to Little Rock in 1873, where he practiced law and where he sponsored a successful bill whereby rabbis could perform marriage services in Arkansas. Prior to that, only Christian ministers had had the privilege.[124] He and his wife, Theresa (Kobner) Cohn, had eight children, one of whom, daughter Marion, married Herman Kahn. A son, Morris M. Cohn, became a prominent Little Rock attorney. Morris also was interested in education, serving as a school director. He was city attorney and an organizer of the American Bar Association.[125] Morris, admitted to practice before the U.S. Supreme Court in 1883, wrote two law books published by Johns Hopkins University Press, and he wrote numerous articles for both law and Reform Judaism journals.[126] While serving as president of the Little Rock Board of Trade in the period 1897–99, he promoted the building of the Choctaw, Oklahoma and Gulf Railway (Rock Island) west of Little Rock.[127] His astuteness at law along with his courteous manner, strict integrity, oratorical abilities, and professional honor brought him recognition as "one of the leaders of the bar of the state."[128] He married Addie Ottenheimer, daughter of pioneer Jewish settler Abraham Ottenheimer.

Politics

Besides those already mentioned, a number of other Jewish businessmen were elected Little Rock aldermen, including Abe Ottenheimer, Daniel Ottenheimer, Albert Cohen, Ben Thalheimer, Frederick Kramer, Louis Volmer, Dan Daniels, and Max Hilb. (More information on these men is given elsewhere in this chapter.) Max Hilb (1828–1881), who settled in the city in 1864 and became known as a successful, charitable, "public-spirited" merchant, was elected several times as alderman and served as acting mayor during Kramer's administration. He was endorsed by a local newspaper for state representative on the Democratic ticket.[129] Dan Daniels (1848–1931) served as alderman for sixteen years, serving as acting mayor on occasion and later running for mayor.[130] Louis Volmer (1840–1914) served as a Little Rock alderman for eighteen years and as acting mayor under Mayor Warren E. Lenon (Lenon served from 1903 to 1908). Volmer had first migrated to Napoleon during the Civil War, then had served in the Confederate army. Coming to Little Rock after the war, he married Henrietta Bott, daughter of pioneer settler Isaac Bott. Louis became a partner with his brothers, Abe (1855–1918) and Simon (1855–1921). Their clothing firm had several failures during the tenuous postwar years, but they persevered and became successful, prominent men; a street in Little Rock was named in honor of Louis Volmer.[131] (One of Louis Volmer's sons, Leon, became a rabbi and served as superintendent of the Jewish Children's Home in New Orleans.)

Jacob Menkus (1840–1908) served as justice of the peace for twelve years. Judge Menkus, as he was known, had a successful mercantile store and was owner and proprietor of the Sprando Hotel, one of the first large hotels in Little Rock.[132] (Menkus also served as a mohel—ritual circumciser—throughout Arkansas and Missouri [see section II].)

New York native Jacob B. Erb, born in 1855, who received his law training in St. Louis, moved to Little Rock in the mid-1870s and established the law firm of Caruth and Erb. It became one of the leading such firms in the city.[133] Erb served as a Pulaski County judge before moving his law practice to Chicago.

Besides those hitherto mentioned, other Jews who served in public offices included J. S. Wolf, J. J. Strauss, Joseph Meyer, James Pollock, H. D. McCowan, Solomon Landsberg, Simon Ellenbogen, Joe Loeb, Rabbi Louis Wolsey, and Sam Storthz.[134]

One of the most outstanding men of Little Rock actively involved in politics was Charles Jacobson (1874–1957), who served as secretary to Governor Jeff Davis and later was elected state senator (1911–13). One of six children of Arkansas farmer Jacob Jacobson, Charles was the antithesis of the stormy demagogue Jeff Davis, yet for many years the two men worked together in seeming harmony.[135] During Davis's administration, Jacobson was named adjutant general of the state militia and, as such, brought the National Guard from an inefficient standing into an effective, disciplined organization.[136] A respected attorney, he wrote several books on both law and history. He was appointed U.S. commissioner at Little Rock in 1929 and served twelve years.[137]

(The two Arkansas Jews who reached the highest positions in the state's political and legal world were Judge Jacob Trieber [Federal judge, Eastern District of Arkansas] and Judge Sam Frauenthal [associate justice, Arkansas Supreme Court]. Trieber is discussed under Helena [eastern Arkansas] and Frauenthal under Conway [western Arkansas].)

Professional Organizations

Jews were consistently and actively involved in the business and professional organizations of both the city and the state. When the Little Rock Business Men's League was formed in January 1906 by twenty-seven businessmen, seven of these were Jewish; five of the organization's fifteen directors were Jewish, including the vice-president, Gus Blass.[138] Morris M. Cohn, Ad Hamberg, and Charles Stifft; all served as presidents of the Little Rock Board of Trade. And Jews helped promote the betterment of the city's utilities, streets, fire department, and other services. Mathias Cohn, his son Morris, and Meyer Pollock joined several other businessmen in promoting electric lights for the city.[139] Henry Levinson served as superintendent of public works in Little Rock from 1909 to 1914, during which time more than eight miles of city streets were paved, numerous sidewalks laid, and several buildings constructed, including the annex to the county courthouse (completed in 1914).[140]

Service Industry

Jewish businessmen also went about providing necessary services—such as insurance, laundry and cleaning, livery, lodging, and goods such as tobacco products, horses, mules, food, and real estate. Isaac Levy had been a pioneer in the insurance business in Little Rock (see section I), and Joe Altschul (1851–1917), son of Pine Bluff pioneer Jewish settler Isaac Altschul, became a well-known insurance agent in Little Rock.[141] The Ehrenberg name also became well known in the insurance business, beginning with Herman "Harry" Ehrenberg (1833–1912) in the 1890s; his son Mannie (1877–1965) later joined him.[142] Harry Ehrenberg had begun his career in Little Rock in 1868 with his brother Lazarus (1841–1921) in a tobacco and cigar manufacturing business; Harry had also sold "Pure lake ice."[143]

French-born Emil Levy (1847–1908) came to Arkansas in the 1860s and at first bought and sold hides at Batesville. He and his son E. G. Levy

(1875–1937) later established a wholesale cigar and tobacco firm at Little Rock.[144] Levy descendants married into a number of prominent Arkansas Jewish families, including Pfeifer, Kempner, Bloch, Tuchfeld, Baum, Marks, Johl, and Kaufman.

Henry Loeb (1872–1933) also was a cigar dealer in the city,[145] and two other cigar dealers, Joseph M. Frank (1846–1920) and Robert A. Furth, became better known for their philanthropy than for their businesses. Frank, who came from Cincinnati to Little Rock in 1870, became active in several business ventures besides tobacco, including real estate, a meat market, and a saloon. After succeeding at these ventures, Frank became active in charity work, and his donations of both finances and land helped make possible City Hospital in Little Rock; he also gave generously to the Benevolent and Protective Order of Elks No. 29 Elks Home at Fourth and Scott streets.[146] In 1880 he and Furth became partners in a cigar store, Joe's and Bob's Place. Furth also contributed generously to public causes and to the needy, so much so that he became well known in some of the larger cities nationwide.[147] (Furth's family included members of the Mandlebaum, Pfeifer, and Pollock families.) By 1888 Joseph Frank's brother, Lee Frank (1865–1908), had a butcher shop known as The Eclipse Meat Market at 203 West Fifth Street. Lee became one of the best known butchers in the city, and his improved refrigerating facilities brought trade with steamboats as well as with city customers.[148]

A number of Jews were involved with the laundry and cleaning business in Little Rock, and several of their enterprises grew to be the largest and most successful of their kind in Arkansas and the Southwest. The latter included Frank's Steam Laundry, Little Rock Laundry and Cleaners, Imperial Laundry and Cleaners, and Majestic Laundry and Cleaners. Aaron Frank (1864–1918) was the first Jew to enter the cleaning business in Little Rock, settling there in the 1880s and purchasing the only laundry in town (owned by Hogan and Ostrander). Aaron renamed it "Frank's Steam Laundry," and under his diligent care, it was highly successful.[149] As dedicated to civic work as he was to his laundry, Frank served on a number of the city's boards. In 1906 Nelson Frank (1873–1936) established his own cleaning and dyeing company and also established the Dixie Termite Destroyer Company.[150] (The Frank cleaning company was later purchased by Louis M. Samuel (1881–1933), a Little Rock native who had served as advertising manager for the *Arkansas Gazette* newspaper.)[151]

Little Rock Laundry and Cleaners was established by partners Harry Lasker (1865–1925) (a founder of the Lasker–Morris Bank in Little Rock in 1914) and Milton Loeb (1875–1957). They bought the Little Rock

Laundry at Third and Center streets and added a cleaning section; the business became highly successful.[152] (Harry's brother Henry, who owned a general merchandise company, developed the Lasker Addition in Little Rock.)[153] Myron B. Lasker (1875–1928) came to Little Rock in the 1890s and established the Imperial Laundry and Cleaners, which grew to be the largest and most successful business of its kind in the state. He built a 22,500 square foot building at Fifteenth and Main streets and had an employee force of 160 by 1930.[154] A founder of the Little Rock Towel and Supply Company, which flourished as well, Myron served on the boards of a number of business and civic organizations.[155] His son Myron Lasker Jr. (1910–1964), who later headed the Imperial company and established the Sno-White Diaper Service, also served on a number of business and civic boards.[156] L. Julian Alexander (who married Natalie Loeb, daughter of laundry and dry cleaning executive Milton Loeb) had Majestic Laundry and Cleaners, another highly successful firm; Alexander also was active in civic affairs.[157]

William B. Levinson (1878–1954) and Clarence P. Pfeifer (1888–1953) also were active in the laundry business in Little Rock.[158] Levinson had come in the 1880s with his parents, John D. (1836–1914) and Hannah Levinson, to Little Rock, where his father served as private secretary of the John Gould Fletcher estate.[159] Another of John's sons, Henry Levinson, was superintendent of public works of Little Rock (mentioned above). (The Levinson family included members of other Arkansas Jewish families, such as Silbernagel, Heller, McCowan, Cohen, Pollock, and Stiel.) Clarence Pfeifer, son of Phil Pfeifer, owned the Pfeifer Laundry and Cleaners, which had several outlets in the Little Rock area. He was active in civic affairs as well.[160]

In the days before the automobile, the livery business was a much required part of life, and Jewish merchants were found in this necessary trade. Ben S. Thalheimer (1850–1914) (mentioned above as a Little Rock alderman) came penniless to America at age seventeen in 1867. He first peddled in the Philadelphia area, then migrated to Arkansas in 1871. He settled at Fairmont, near Stuttgart, and dealt in horses, mules, hides, and furs. After buying a boat, he traded and hauled freight on the Arkansas River, then went into the grocery and mercantile business. In 1884 he moved to Little Rock and established a horse and mule firm. His reputation as an honorable and honest man became known throughout the state, and he built up a considerable trade. He also bought farm land close to Little Rock, sectioned it, and sold it on reasonable terms to settlers.[161] He handled elegant carriages, buggies, livery fixtures, feed, and livestock.[162]

He and his wife, Fannie (Mayer) Thalheimer, had five children: Sidney, Sol, Jesse, Abe, and Pearl. Sidney, who later joined his father in business, was selling automobiles by 1921. Abe Thalheimer opened three tobacco stores in Little Rock and also dealt in real estate.[163] Some of Arkansas's other Jewish families that became intertwined with the Thalheimers were the Heiman, Oppenheimer, Felsenthal, and Dreyfus families.

Louis Reinman (1861–1951), who came from Germany to Little Rock at age fourteen in 1875, began dealing in mules, and by 1888 the company he established merged with the Davis and Son Company to form the Davis-Reinman Company. Other partners included William Davis, Charles Sommers, and Gus Straus (formerly of Lonoke). Reinman became an admired sight in Little Rock when he would display his expert riding ability on his "splendid" horses on Markham Street.[164] After Louis W. Wolfort (1868–1938) came to Little Rock in 1898, he became a partner of Louis Reinman, and the firm, Reinman and Wolfort, became one of the best-known stock businesses in Arkansas. In 1914 the firm received a contract with British buyers to ship Arkansas mules to England to be used in World War I. They shipped thousands, sending 120 a week to a stockade in North Little Rock, where British buyers inspected them and sent them overseas. In 1918 Reinman and Wolfort started selling autos and were soon doing the largest volume of truck and car business in the state. Louis Reinman was known as a leader in helping to advance community efforts.[165] Louis's father, Lipman Reinman, and his uncle, Joseph Reinman, also were well-known Little Rock stockmen. Julia Reinman, Louis's sister, married Charles M. Simon, who came to Little Rock in the 1880s and founded the Arkansas Transfer Company.[166] The family married into other Arkansas Jewish families, such as McCowan, Selz, Phillips, and Weisman.

Some of the other Jewish citizens who were involved in the livery business in Little Rock were Samuel R. Cohn (1866–1925) (a number of Cohn families settled in Arkansas, many of whom were not related) who came to Little Rock in the 1890s and established the Southern Livery Stables, and Sam J. Meyer (1885–1960) who came to Little Rock before the turn of the century and established a livery stable and a horse and mule trading business that continued until the late 1920s.[167]

Some of the leading hardware stores in Little Rock have been Jewish owned. One of the earliest such stores was owned by the Mandlebaum brothers, Louis K. and John W. They were sons of Samuel E. Mandlebaum, who settled in Little Rock in 1871 with his family. James Mandlebaum (1847–1929), another of Samuel's sons, was president and treasurer of the well-known Fones Brothers Hardware Company.[168]

Beverage, Food, Lodging

Several of Little Rock's early Jewish pioneers went into various kinds of beverage and food businesses, from saloons to coffee companies. In the 1870s and 1880s there were several Jewish-owned saloons in Little Rock. One of these was run by Max Elkan, proprietor of the Board of Trade Restaurant and Saloon, which was furnished in "handsome style."[169] Elkan was joined by a partner, Simon Ellenbogen (1847–1931), who came to Little Rock in 1872, and they soon established an "elegantly appointed" billiard parlor and restaurant. By 1888 it was called the Grand Opera House Saloon, having been remodeled with embossed glass swinging doors; the colorful glass and design were new for the times.[170] Ellenbogen, who served as a Little Rock justice of the peace for twenty years, was the son of Elias Ellenbogen (1813–1898) and the brother of Emanuel Ellenbogen (1856–1949).[171] Their family included members of other Arkansas Jewish families, such as Pollock, Gans, Cooper, Ottenheimer, Wormser, Berger, and Stern.

Nathan Ackerman (1846–1895) had a saloon at Fifth and Center streets,[172] and Louis Katzenberg (1851–1922), who settled in Little Rock in the early 1870s, opened a restaurant and saloon at Fifth and Main streets. The establishment opened with a big "blow-out," which included oysters and wine for all who attended.[173] Katzenberg married Jennie Mandlebaum, whose sisters married into the prominent Little Rock Jewish families of Pollock, Furth, and Pfeifer.

Isaac Bott, one of the city's first Jewish settlers (see section I) had opened Little Rock's first bakery.[174] Simon Samuels (1828–1904) and his son Joe Samuels (1857–1914) also had a bakery as well as a general store in Little Rock.[175]

By 1875 Daniel Hochbaum (1845–1914) had opened a confectionery store at Eighth and Main streets; his son Jake (1881–1919) later joined him in business.[176]

By 1885 Louis L. Mivelaz (1872–1918) was managing the Capitol Hotel Restaurant, where, under his leadership, it became one of the city's leading eateries; he was known to hire only the best cooks, and his cuisine was known for its high standards.[177] A relative, P. L. Mivelaz, operated the Mivelaz Merchants Hotel for a number of years.[178]

One of the best remembered Jewish-owned eateries in the Little Rock area was Summerfield's Ice Cream Parlor. It began when Will Terry, a local dairyman with one wagon, wanted to branch out. Jewish businessmen Harry Lasker and Seymour Summerfield (1883–1938) joined Terry as partners, and Terry Dairy grew until it was the largest such facility in the state. (The dairy was later sold to Borden's Dairy.) When Summerfield lost his interest in the company after the stock market crash of 1929, he opened the Summerfield Dairy and Ice Cream Parlor in Little Rock. After Seymour died in 1938, his wife, Nona (Pollock) Summerfield (1894–1948), continued the business, then later sold it to Swift, Incorporated.[179]

Sol H. Johl came to Little Rock from Germany in the 1870s and opened a saloon at Third and Main streets; he later founded the Sol Johl Coffee Company.[180] Lester S. Marks (1892–1983) established the Marks Consumer Coffee Company in Little Rock sometime after World War I.[181]

Besides Herman Kahn, the best-known Jewish hotel owner in Arkansas was Samuel J. Peck (1904–1967). His father, German-born Isaac Peck, settled at Magazine, Logan County, where he was a merchant and a banker. After college, Sam helped manage the Goldman Hotel of Fort Smith. He later bought hotels at Tonkawa, Oklahoma, and at Fayetteville. In 1938 he bought the Frederica Hotel at Little Rock and renamed it the Sam Peck. He remodeled it through the years until it became one of the finer hotels of the city.[182]

Real Estate

Most of the Arkansas Jewish settlers became land and property owners, some helping to develop areas of their respective cities and towns, and several becoming full-time real estate brokers. The best-known Jewish name in this field was that of Block. Joseph F. Block (1860–1953), born in Camden, Arkansas, to early Jewish pioneer Solomon Block (see section I), came to Little Rock around 1905 and handled cigars and insurance and later went into real estate. He and his sons, Sam (1893–1981) and Lewis (1898–1983), established Block Realty Company in Little Rock in the early 1920s. They were cited as having started the idea of yard signs, newspaper advertisements, and the "open house" selling technique in the Little Rock realty market.[183] The company grew to become one of the largest in its field in the metropolitan area. The Block family married into several of the local Jewish families, including those of Wolfe, Loeb, Meyer, Cohn, Tuchfeld, Levy, Baum, Bloom, Scharff, Eisenkramer, Weinstein, and Bloch. (Abraham Bloch [1810–1892] had migrated to Little Rock in 1862 and opened a mercantile store).[184] Sam Blum (1857–1940) was also a Little Rock real estate broker. He came to the city in 1880 and was in the real estate business for sixty years—until his death in 1940.[185]

Culture and Entertainment

Known for their sense of refinement, Jewish citizens of Little Rock helped supply both entertainment and culture to the community through the years. Professor Louis Cohen (1834–1924) came to Little Rock from Germany via St. Louis in 1863 and taught music and language in Little Rock schools for a number of years (he had mastered nine languages). He was an organizer and first president of the Arkansas Music Teachers Association, founded in 1889, served as a member of the Little Rock School Board from 1893 to 1900, and was active in several civic organizations, presenting music programs throughout the city. He was active in the Masons and the Odd Fellows, serving as grand master of the Arkansas Independent Order of Odd Fellows. He served as chaplain to the group and received an honor medal in 1915; only 717 of the 2,000,000 membership worldwide had ever received such an honor up to that time. He also owned the Musical Instruments Store on Main Street.[186]

Cleve Moses (1880–1949) established the Moses Melody Shop in Little Rock shortly after World War I. It was one of the most popular stores of its kind for more than sixty years and was continued by Cleve's sons, Cleve Moses Jr. and James. (Cleve Moses Jr. moved to Houston after World War II and established a music store there.)[187]

Ike Kempner, one of Little Rock's most industrious business and real estate developers, promoted entertainment in the city. He built the Gem and Royal theaters, and with his brother Dave built the magnificent Kempner Theater on Louisiana Street in 1910. The latter was three stories high, with elegant suites on the upper floors. At its dedication, then Governor George W. Donaghey, Little Rock Board of Trade president H. L. Remmel, and Attorney General of Arkansas Hal L. Norwood gave the opening comments. The first play presented in the theater was "Billy," a Lee and Sam Shubert production. The Theater scheduled as many road shows as possible. It also scheduled lecturers such as William Jennings Bryan, who spoke there in 1915. After the 1920–21 season, the Kempner was used primarily as a movie theater. It was later known as the Arkansas Theater.[188]

When Joseph Kuttner (1835–1894) and his wife Othelia came to Arkansas in 1877, they brought with them their seven-year-old son, Edward (1870–1922). In time, the young Kuttner excelled in music, hired musicians, and established Kuttner's Orchestra. He was quite popular at the time and furnished music for numerous events statewide. He also served as manager of two local theaters, the Kempner and the Gem. He was killed in an accident while on a fishing trip near Little Rock, and a band composed of members of the American Federation of Musicians played at his funeral.[189]

Saul S. Harris (1880–1943) came to Little Rock in 1906 and served as manager of the Majestic Vaudeville Theater; he later became partner and manager of the Gem Theater. He served as publicity manager for the War Camp Activities Committee at Camp Pike during World War I.[190] Phillip Epstein (1868–1924) came to Little Rock in 1916 and served as director of music at the Majestic Theatre and the Capitol Theatre. His talents led him to New York, where he was rated as one of the greatest arrangers in musical circles in America at the time. He was associated with Victor Herbert and the Schubert circuit in supervising musical numbers.[191] Jack A. Rosenthal (1907–1960) of North Little Rock began his music training at age two. He and his brother Leroy organized their own dance band in high school and later recorded their own compositions, which were broadcast nationally on radio and television. Rosenthal wrote a music column for a local newspaper, entitled "Music Box Review."[192]

Little Rock native Max Aronson (1881–1971; better known as Gilbert M. Anderson—"Bronco Billy") was one of the most popular entertainers in America. He took the name of Anderson when he entered vaudeville, and by 1903 he had become involved in movies, working for director Edwin S. Porter. Films were fragmentary at the time, and Anderson conceived of making a long picture—of one thousand feet of film. Deciding it should be something exciting, he called it The Great Train Robbery. He subsequently made more than seven hundred one-reel films. By 1917 he had made 385 Bronco Billy films, starring himself. He innovated the "stand-in" or "double," because he had no experience with guns or horses. He teamed with George K. Spoor and made films with Charlie Chaplin, Gloria Swanson, and Wallace Beery. By the 1920s William S. Hart had captured the western-film market, and Anderson drifted into oblivion. But his fame again came to light in 1958, when he received an Oscar for his early achievements in the film industry.[193]

Professional baseball in Little Rock benefitted from the interest and efforts of several of the city's Jews. Aaron Frank (previously noted for his steam laundry) helped in efforts that gained the admission of the city's baseball team to the Southern Baseball League. He was also a charter member of the Arkansas Travelers baseball club, along with Jacob B. Hirsch (1861–1939, son of early pioneer Aaron Hirsch of Batesville and Newport) and Ike L. Weil (1863–1915).[194] Frank served as the club's president, Hirsch as treasurer, and Weil as sergeant-at-arms.

The Professions

Although it was the subsequent generations of the pioneer Jewish families that began going into the professions, a few professionals, such as Professor Louis Cohen (noted above) and Dr. J. J. Auerbach, were found early on. The latter had served as a post surgeon at Houston during the Civil War and at the United States Hospital at New Orleans during the 1867 yellow fever epidemic and came to Little Rock to practice in 1869.[195] Theodore R. Fox (1857–1944), a certified public accountant who married Flora Oppenheimer of Paris, Arkansas, opened a store at Dardanelle. The business failed during the depressed economy of the early 1890s, and they moved to Little Rock, where Fox was associated with the Gans store.[196] The Fox-Oppenheimer family included members of prominent Arkansas Jewish families, such as Siesel, Franklin, Pfeifer, Dreyfus, Thalheimer, Wolf, Pollock, Sternberg, and Mendel.

Several Jewish doctors became prominent in Little Rock after the turn of the century. These included Dr. Roscoe C. Kory (1885–1951), an ear, nose, and throat specialist who came to Arkansas in 1920.[197] Dr. Alexander H. Cohen (1883–1923), a dentist, practiced in Hot Springs, eastern Arkansas, and at Little Rock.[198] Hyman Rosenblum (1892–1969) came to Little Rock in 1921 as a graduate from the podiatry college in Chicago. At the time he came, there was no state law governing his profession. He wrote a law for the state examining board, which was enacted; other states copied it in whole or in part.[199]

Although most of the early pioneer Jews were found in mercantile and dry goods stores, they generally sent their children to the best schools they could afford, and their offspring often went into the professions. Examples of these include the families of Pollock, Strauss, Loeb, Rose, Ehrman, and Berger. Second generation offspring who became doctors included Manuel D. Pollock (1877–1953), son of early pioneer Abraham Pollock, and Manuel's son, Alan E. Pollock (1907–1986). Both were chiropodists.[200] Dr. Alvin Weil Strauss Sr., son of Pine Bluff settlers Alexander and Mae (Weil) Strauss, became a prominent Little Rock physician after beginning his practice there in 1919. He was the first chairman of the board of McRae Sanatorium for Negroes at Alexander, Arkansas. He was considered one of Little Rock's "beloved doctors," providing medicine for his needy patients and showing compassion to people of all races and creeds.[201] (Dr. Strauss's son, Alvin W. Strauss Jr. and his grandson, Mark Strauss [son of Alvin Strauss Jr.], both became Little Rock physicians.)

Joseph Loeb (1896–1931) was one of many second generation Jews who went into the law profession. His father was Lehman Loeb (1838–1916), who came from Hesse, Germany, to Little Rock in 1870 and established a grocery and wholesale clothing business.[202] Joseph became a Little Rock attorney and was associated with the First Division Circuit Court for more than twenty years.[203]

In the 1870s Daniel F. Rose (1850–1914), born in Alsace-Lorraine, came to Little Rock, where he established the Rose Real Estate Company and the Chemical Floor and Tile Company. He married local belle Augusta Bott, and one of their three sons, Milton B. Rose, an 1899 law graduate of the University of Arkansas, taught Latin and Roman history at Little Rock University and became known as a "scholar of broad attainments." He was admitted to practice before the U.S. Supreme court in 1903. He became a land title expert on titles of zinc and lead acreage in North Arkansas and also specialized in commercial law in Little Rock; he and his father became two of the city's largest land owners. Both were civic minded, helping to build up the city and the state.[204]

Albert A. Ehrman (1859–1917), a native of Hillsboro, Mississippi, came to Little Rock in 1899 and engaged in the livery business and, later, a meat market. He married Esther Lasker. Their son, S. Lasker Ehrman (1894–1946), was a graduate of Arkansas Law School and Columbia Law School. After serving in World War I, Lasker Ehrman formed a law partnership in Little Rock with Grover T. Owens. Ehrman was active in various civic organizations and served a number of years as chairman of the examining board of the U.S. District Court.[205]

Lawrence J. Berger (1891–1963), son of early Malvern, Arkansas, pioneers Henry and Carrie (Ottenheimer) Berger, practiced law at Malvern and, after 1920, in the Greater Little Rock area. He was the first director of the North Little Rock Housing Authority and served as its director and legal advisor for many years. He was city attorney of North Little Rock under mayors U. E. Moore and Ross Lawhon. He also served as secretary to Governor Harvey Parnell in the late 1920s. He was president of the North Little Rock Boys' Club and a member of that board for thirty-one years.[206]

The Eichenbaum brothers, E. Charles and Howard S., sons of Ephraim and Sadie (Cohn) Eichenbaum, became prominently known in the fields of law and architecture. Charles (1907–1993) established a law firm in Little Rock in 1928 after graduating from Washington University in St. Louis. Although he began his career as a defense counsel for casualty insurance clients, he moved into the area of bankruptcy and tax law as the Depression brought about such a need. The firm began practicing in the area of real estate expansion and shopping centers in the late 1930s.[207] Howard Eichenbaum (1904–1973) also was a graduate of Washington University in 1924 and began an architectural career in the firm of Mann and Stern. Together with Frank Erhart, he founded the Erhart and Eichenbaum firm in 1929. As a young architect, Howard designed three- to five-room houses for the Dyess Colony in Greene County, Arkansas, in 1934. His firm also designed some nine hundred houses built in the Bauxite area of Saline County in the 1940s.[208] (See section V for more data on the Eichenbaums.)

Some other Jews of Arkansas distinguished themselves in the field of architecture, including Theodore M. Sanders (1879–1947) and Morris B. Sanders Jr. (1904–1948). They were members of a Little Rock family with quite humble beginnings. German-born Fred and Fannie Sanders settled at Mountain Home in 1871 and attempted to farm for a living. They lived forty miles from a railroad on poor, rocky soil. Fred built a small log house and struggled to make the ground produce, but his health failed. The starving family was rescued by a kind relative who traveled from Mississippi by boat, train, and horseback and helped resettle the family at Little Rock. There Fred opened a photography business and, being fluent in four languages, served as a court interpreter for foreign cases. He took an active interest in the city and its development.[209] Sanders had nine children, four daughters and five sons. Two sons, Louis A. and F. W., became well-known for their chinaware business in Little Rock,[210] and Morris B. Sanders Sr., who married Mark M. Cohn's daughter Mabel, owned the M. B. Sanders Plumbing Company and was a director of the American Exchange Trust Company.[211]

Fred Sanders' son, Theodore M., was a graduate of the University of Illinois School of Architecture and studied at the Beaux Arts Institute of Design in Paris. After graduation, he practiced at Little Rock, where he was associated with Frank Gibbs. After Gibbs' death, Frank Ginocchio joined the firm, and in 1927 Charles Thompson became a member.[212] The firm and its members became prominent statewide. Sanders designed such buildings as the Arkansas-Louisiana Gas Company, the Hall Building, the Women's City Club Building, the Union National Bank (at Fourth and Louisiana streets), the M. M. Cohn Building, the Stifft Jewelry Building, and numerous other buildings statewide, including county court houses and private residences. He served as an officer in several architectural organizations, and in 1946 he founded the Theodore M. Sanders Art Exhibit, which sought to inspire juvenile art activities. He promoted the public library, and he taught descriptive geometry at Little Rock Junior

College.[213] He married local belle Irene Pareira, daughter of Isaac Pareira, and they had two children, Arthur and Miriam.

Morris B. Sanders Jr., grandson of Fred Sanders, was graduated from Yale University in 1925 and from the Yale College of Fine Arts in 1927. In 1935 he established an industrial design firm in New York and designed a variety of industrial products, including Module furniture for the Mengel Company, Fluoro-color for Franklin Lamp and Shade Company, and VariVase for the Johnson Ceramic Company. He also designed his own home on Forty-ninth Street in New York, which was a four-story modernistic building of glass and glazed royal blue brick. Before his untimely death at age forty-four in 1948, it was hoped that he would achieve the reputation of a Frank Lloyd Wright.[214] From its humble beginnings, the Sanders family became one of the Little Rock's most prominent, and members married into such noted local Jewish families as those of Pfeifer, Cohn, Levinson, and Phillips.

Eugene John Stern (1884–1961) was another Arkansas Jewish architect who became prominent in that field. He was born in Austria to Jacob and Helena (Roth) Stern and received his training in New York. He came to Little Rock in 1913 and formed an architectural firm with George Mann. The firm designed the Albert Pike Consistory at Little Rock, the Arlington Hotel, at Hot Springs, and numerous other buildings throughout the state. Stern bought out Mann in 1925. He was active in civic groups and organizations and served as first president of the Arkansas chapter of the American Institute of Architects. He was considered an outstanding citizen and one of the leading architects in Arkansas and in the Southwest.[215]

Advertising

Jews were pioneers of the advertising industry in Arkansas. Sidney M. Brooks (1886–1985), a Memphis native and a Harvard graduate, stopped in Little Rock in 1910 during a train trip from Chicago to Texarkana to visit a friend, Little Rock newspaper executive Fred Allsopp. The latter suggested that Brooks open an advertising agency. Back in Chicago, Brooks resigned his position after telling his superior of his plans. The man advised him that he would "starve to death in Arkansas . . . Of all the God-forsaken places in the world, what would you want to go to Little Rock for?"[216] Undaunted, in July 1911 Brooks founded the S. M. Brooks Advertising Agency in Little Rock, the first such company in Arkansas. Under his able guidance, the agency achieved local and national prominence. Brooks was a charter member and a director of the Little Rock Chamber of Commerce and served on numerous other civic boards. He served in the Army Intelligence Service during World War I, and he was appointed by President Herbert Hoover as state chairman of the Citizens Reorganization Committee for Arkansas for the years 1931–32.[217]

A second Jewish pioneer in the advertising field was Leo P. Bott Jr. (1897–1987), grandson of pioneer Little Rock settler Isaac Bott. Leo founded the Bott Advertising agency in 1917 and began promoting Arkansas and its products and services, such as Niloak Pottery, Hot Springs bath houses, Mountain Valley Water, as well as Arkansas dentistry and Arkansas professional baseball. Leo Bott was said to have originated the "smiling face" advertising idea and had a typewriter made with the symbol on one of the keys. After visiting Alaska in the 1920s, his ad agency prepared some of the earliest promotional literature for that territory. He was an early promoter of direct-mail advertising and wrote articles on the subject. He also wrote articles and short stories that appeared in a number of national magazines. In the 1930s Bott moved his ad agency to Chicago, where he became well known.[218] (Bott retired to Little Rock in 1986 and died a year later.)

Jewelry

Several Jewish-owned jewelry stores became well known in Little Rock. Albert Cohen (1834–1892) established one of the first such stores in the city when he came in 1858 (see section I). After serving in the Confederate army, he resumed his jewelry business. He was interested in scientific and literary pursuits and was an accomplished linguist, serving as an interpreter and translator. As did many other Jews from Germany, Cohen proudly joined in the German organizations in the city.[219] He served on the City Council and on the Little Rock School Board and was remembered for his generosity and public spirit—and also for the green spectacles sign that fronted his store.[220]

No name in jewelry became better known or respected in Arkansas than that of Stifft Jewelers. The Stifft family had its beginnings in Little Rock in 1878 when Michael Stifft (1822–1905) left New Orleans for greener pastures in Chicago. A bad cold on the train ride north prompted him to get off in Little Rock to recuperate. Mrs. Herman (Rosa) Summerfield (1848–1915) took him into her home until he was well. He liked the city so much that he opened a jewelry store and later sent for his son Charles in Chicago to join him.[221] Michael Stifft, who subsequently established the first engraving plant in Arkansas, became a familiar sight in Little Rock by the 1890s. Known as a "lovable old gentleman" and affectionately called "Grandpa Stifft," he would recount bygone days of Little Rock to anyone who would listen.[222] He died in 1905 leaving six children, including sons Charles and Nathan. Both men were associated with the Stifft firm, although Charles (1856–1926) became the better known. He became a leader in Little Rock's development, serving in building and loan associations, in trust companies, and in land development (one section became known as Stifft addition in Pulaski Heights).[223] He served four years as president of the Little Rock Board of Trade. A self-taught man, he collected a large private library. By 1912 his company was doing a larger volume of business in Little Rock than all his competitors combined.[224] Charles and his wife Rebecca (Mailhouse) Stifft had five daughters and one son. The parents provided a delightful childhood for their youngsters, all of whom remained in Little Rock and continued to help in its development and growth; many of the grandchildren also did the same.[225] The family married into other Arkansas Jewish families, including those of Frank, Pfeifer, Cohn, Abeles, Phillips, Haas, Cohen, and Storthz.

Other Jewish-owned jewelry stores in Little Rock included those of Jacob Ben Mayer Jr. (1898–1958) and Stanley Lasker Alexander (1896–1958).

Grocery, Mercantile, and Dry Goods

Several Jewish businessmen were found in the grocery business in Little Rock's early history. These included Sam Lyons (1824–1897), who had come to Arkansas in the late 1850s (see section I; his son founded the Lyons Machinery Company discussed above). After first settling in Augusta, the family moved to Little Rock in 1874, where they opened a grocery store that specialized in poultry. Lyons had been wounded in the Civil War and walked with a cane. After his beloved wife Sophia (Kahn) Lyons died in 1877, Sam grieved for twenty years and finally went to her grave site and there took his own life.[226] Several of their seven children remained in Arkansas and became involved in its growth. Descendants included the families of Levinger, Badt, and Eichenbaum (noted above).

Max Mayer (1856–1932), born and raised in Indiana by Bavarian-born parents, Jacob and Barbara Mayer, heard of the advantages offered in Arkansas for those with initiative and vision. He moved to Des Arc in 1877 and worked for Frolich Mercantile Company for thirteen years.

Moving to Little Rock in 1890, he entered the cotton business, and in 1895 he and S. P. Scott established a produce business, the Scott-Mayer Commission Company. It became one of the most successful firms of its kind and remained so for many years. The company erected a three-story building at 806–820 East Markham in 1905. Mayer was active in a building and loan association and in the Little Rock and U.S. Chambers of Commerce. Two of Mayer's three sons, Jacob and Nicholas, were active in the Scott-Mayer firm; a younger son, Theodore, owned the Black and White Food Stores.[227] August S. Vogel (1889–1945), son of early Little Rock pioneer George S. Vogel (1832–1877), became associated with the Scott-Mayer Commission Company around 1917, and his sons, Sam and George, also became involved with the company. Sam later established Vogel Enterprises (see section V).

Henry Silbernagel (1858–1942) came to Little Rock in 1877 and opened a grocery and feed store that was well known in the city for more than forty years. He sold the company in 1917, and he and his wife then lived at De Witt with their daughter, Mrs. Theodore Loeb, and her family.[228]

The majority of Jewish-owned businesses were either mercantile or dry goods stores. One of the earliest mercantile enterprises was established by Gabriel McCowan (1813–1870), who had come to Arkansas in the 1850s (see section I). He became known for his long, flowing beard, which reached to his waist, and for his generosity to the many children who came into his store, to whom he gave trinkets. He was one of the first four men in Arkansas to receive the thirty-third degree of the Scottish Rite. He was a trustee of St. John's College, which had been established in 1859 as a military school by the Masonic order, and a street near the college (located in East Little Rock) was named McCowan in his honor. (At McCowan's funeral in 1870, it was noted by Elbert N. English, a former chief justice of the Arkansas Supreme Court, that the street named for McCowan would be an enduring monument to him—that "only an earthquake or thunder of the last day would jar down the ground on which the college stood." The college later burned, and in the 1970s the Interstate 30 Freeway became the "earthquake" that removed most of the street. No marker is found on the remaining short span of street, and if there were, the name would be misspelled. Evidently, an accidental distortion changed the spelling to *McGowan* on city maps).[229] McCowan helped organize one of Little Rock's fire departments and served as a foreman and chief engineer; he was chief of the Pulaski County Fire Company when he died. At his death, his funeral was one of the largest held in Little Rock up to that time. McCowan developed a medicine called "McCowan's Eye

Water" that became rather successful when it was promoted after his death by a brother-in-law, D. B. Mandel.[230]

David Rudolph (1817–1909) came to Little Rock in 1865 and opened a mercantile store.[231] His sons Charles (1855–1937) and Sam (1859–1939) operated a men's clothing store from 1891 to 1910, then went into the real estate business under the name of Sam Rudolph and Co. Another son, Joseph Rudolph (1861–1938), had his own dry goods store in Little Rock until 1908, when he moved to Akron, Ohio, and opened a chain of men's clothing stores.[232] David Rudolph's daughter married Joseph Pfeifer, the department store owner.

Other Jewish mercantile owners included Charles S. Shiekowitz (1823–1909), who came to Pulaski County in 1869 and established a store in North Little Rock (known as Argenta at the time).[233] Members of the Elias family—Raphael, Aaron, and Henry—were merchants at 18 Main Street in Little Rock in 1871.[234] Jonas H. Epstein (1829–1909), opened a mercantile store in Little Rock in 1875. His son Ephraim (1851–1935) later had stores at Atkins, Ozark, and Little Rock; Ephraim married Sally Lasker.[235] Sally Epstein's brother-in-law, Louis Julius Alexander (1866–1904), who had married her sister Bettie, opened a general merchandise store in Little Rock in 1887 and moved it to North Little Rock in 1898. He became successful in that city and was running for the position of alderman when he was struck by lightning and killed in 1904 while on a fishing trip near North Little Rock.[236]

Joseph Scholem (1858–1931) came to Little Rock in the late 1880s and opened a general store. He married Ray S. Parker, and their family became intermingled with the Arkansas Jewish families of Altschul and Abowitz.[237] Well-educated Adolph Schwartzbart (1852–1907), a university graduate in Austria, came to Little Rock in 1888 and opened a mercantile store, which continued until his death in 1907.[238] Charles Lowenfield (1850–1894), also of Austria, settled first in Fort Smith, then came to Little Rock in the 1880s, where he was in the mercantile business. He married Esther Epstein, daughter of Jonas Epstein, and their four sons, Julius, Ike, Joe, and Sidney, were active in the business life of Little Rock.[239] Their daughter married Harry Hanf of Pine Bluff.

Charles W. Kaiser (1852–1926) came from Obernich, Germany, in 1894 and established a mercantile store in Little Rock. He became affectionally known as "Uncle Charlie" and his wife as "Aunt Fannie."[240] Joel Tuchfeld (1868–1909) came from Galicia, Austria, to America in 1888 and settled in Little Rock in 1897, where he opened a mercantile store. He married Grace Levy, daughter of Emil Levy of Batesville and Little

Rock. Tuchfeld died at age forty-one of typhoid fever.[241] Solomon Reutlinger (1845–1891) came to Arkansas in the 1880s and was in the mercantile business. The Reutlinger family included members of the Ottenheimer, Cohn, Storthz, Salinger, and Falk families. Solomon's sons, Ralph and Sigmund "Sig," lived at England, Arkansas, and Perryville, Arkansas.[242]

By 1880 Jewish merchants were dominating both clothing and cigar and tobacco firms in Little Rock. Of the advertised clothing concerns of the time, all but one were Jewish owned, and of the sixteen advertised cigar and tobacco stores, ten were Jewish owned.[243] Some of the early dry goods merchants included Simon Gans (1840–1903), who came to Little Rock in 1860 (see section I). In 1864 he returned to Little Rock as a Confederate veteran and opened a clothing store that expanded to three stores by 1891.[244] He married Mary Ellenbogen of Philadelphia. The business was continued in Little Rock until the 1930s by their son Felix (1872–1924) and their grandson Leon (1905–1966).[245] Emanuel Gans (1874–1937), another of Simon Gans' sons, operated a wallpaper store on Main Street.[246] Jacob Gans (1825–1900), a relative of Simon, came to Little Rock in 1872 and established Gans and Son clothing store, located from 1892 to 1908 on the first floor of the Masonic Temple at Fifth and Main streets.[247] Jacob had married Bluma DeYoung of Philadelphia (see below), and when they celebrated their silver wedding anniversary at Concordia Hall in 1880, a local paper said that "all feasts heretofore given in Little Rock failed in comparison to the *soiree*."[248] Among the 350 guests who attended were mayors, judges, and other members of Little Rock's elite—both Jews and gentiles. Their sons, Solomon (1859–1926) and Gus M. (1866–1919), became successful, well-known businessmen as well. Sol Gans built an impressive home on West Third Street in Little Rock and also the Gans Building at 217 West Second Street.[249] The Gans family included other Arkansas Jewish families, such as Back, Altman, Frank, Solomon, Becker, and Blass.

Several pre–Civil War settlers continued their dry goods businesses after the war, including Moses Katzenstein (1837–1895), Isaac Levy (1817–1907), and Abraham Pollock (1834–1899; see also section I). Katzenstein was a partner with Simon Gans in the Gans and Katzenstein firm. He was joined by Aaron Katzenstein (1832–1891) in Little Rock in 1878, and they became successful merchants. Four of their daughters married some of Arkansas's leading Jewish men—Gus Blass, Max Heiman, L. E. Goldsmith (of Pine Bluff), and Arthur Pfeifer.[250]

Isaac Levy continued his dry goods business after the war. His son, Louis M. Levy, did not succeed in the several business ventures he tried, and in a fit of despondency took his own life in 1907, two months after his father had died. One of his daughters married Preston Pfeifer and another married Victor Gates of De Valls Bluff.[251]

Abe Pollock changed from dry goods to shoe sales after the Civil War, and he built up one of the largest trades of its kind in the state.[252] He married Pauline Ellenbogan of Philadelphia. Other Pollocks settled in Little Rock as well. William Pollock (1857–1909) was associated with the German National Bank, and Meyer Pollock (1844–1925) was a clothing merchant and also president of the Little Rock Incandescent Electric Light Company.[253] The Pollock family included members of the Hirsch, Gans, Cohen, Turner, Boone, and Summerfield families.

Another dry goods merchant, William Wolf (1834–1889), came to Arkansas in the 1860s with his brothers Henry (1839–1890) and Joseph (1844–1914), and they established the Wolf and Bros. Wholesale Dry Goods Firm. It was said to be the leading business of its kind in Arkansas by 1889.[254] Another brother, Isaac Wolf, joined them in Little Rock. Herbert Wolf (1882–1943), one of Isaac's sons, operated the Wolf company until 1912, when he joined the M. M. Cohn Company. He was later named president of the latter company and also served as chairman of its board. He was active in a number of civic organizations and served as chairman of the Retail Merchants Division of the Little Rock Chamber of Commerce.[255] The Wolf family included members of the Ottenheimer, Louchheim, Pollock, and Lasker families.

Another familiar name among Little Rock Jewish clothiers was that of Bauman. Simon E. Bauman (1884–1957) came to Little Rock in 1909, and after working as a salesman ten years, founded the Bauman's Men's Shop. It became a popular store on Main Street.[256] Simon's cousin, Stanley M. Bauman (1892–1955), was involved in the mercantile business in Arkansas and served as secretary-treasurer of the Busy Department Stores.[257] His wife, Sadee Alexander, was the daughter of L. Julian and Bettie (Lasker) Alexander.

Several others who were active in the dry goods business in Little Rock included Louis C. Bernays, who was well known by 1871.[258] Phillip H. Bernays owned a men's clothing store with a partner, John E. Maxwell, and their excellent ads appeared in local papers in the 1880s.[259] Although it was unusual for the time, the family intermarried and left Judaism.[260] John Samuels (1832–1882) and Louis A. Samuels (1864–1922) had a clothing store on Main Street for a number of years, from the mid-1860s until after the turn of the century.[261]

Walter A. Marx (1883–1921) worked with a department store in Little Rock before purchasing the Miller Ready-To-Wear shop in 1922; he became recognized as one of the most progressive garment men in the South.[262] Solomon Landsberg was listed as a dry goods merchant ·on Commerce Street in 1871. During the period 1883–87 he served as a justice of the peace.[263]

Several Jewish tailors also had dry goods stores. Merchant-tailor Adolph Kasselberg (1847–1922) came to Little Rock in 1887 and conducted his own business at 108 Louisiana Street for a number of years.[264] Al Cohn (1867–1925), who married Bertha Kronberg, was manager of the Knickerbocker Tailoring Company.[265] Max Salinger (1853–1915) came to Little Rock in 1900 and founded the Hub Clothing Company; he sold this and opened a tailoring shop on Main Street that continued until his death.[266]

Several Jews were in the crockery business, which provided much needed cookware, dishes, and other kitchen items. The most well known Jewish men in this type of enterprise were the Navra brothers, Prussian-born Morris (1823–1883) and Sam (1832–1892). They were pioneer settlers of the 1850s (see section I), and their queensware, crockery, and dry goods business was quite successful.[267] It became a jobbing firm, and the reputable, quality goods it carried helped it become one of the largest china "emporiums" in the city.[268] Morris Navra was an organizer and first president of Congregation B'nai Israel in Little Rock (see section II). His son Elias (1850–1937), who married Emma Cohen, daughter of jeweler Albert Cohen, continued the family business. Elias was known for his civic and congregational leadership, and the Little Rock B'nai B'rith Lodge was named the Elias Navra Lodge in his honor.[269] The Navra family included members of other Arkansas Jewish families, such as Ehrenberg, Jacobson, and Slager. A. K. Auerbach (1835–1870) was a partner in the Navra queensware and crockery firm for several years.[270]

Bernard Cohen (1833–1904), a brother of music professor Louis Cohen, came to Little Rock in the 1860s and opened a general merchandise store on Main Street between Markham and Second streets. He married Rebecca Navra and was in partnership with his brother-in-law, S. Navra, in the crockery business. He was cited as a founder of one of the first pottery businesses in Arkansas at Benton. He operated a steamboat business from 1875 to 1886, with boats running from Pine Bluff to New Orleans. His steamboats included the *Katie Kountz*, *Big Rock*, and *J. A. Van Etten*. From 1886 until his death in 1904, he remained in the crockery business. Both he and his sons were active in the business and civic life of the city, and a daughter, Flora, became prominent in its educational circles (see below).[271]

Frederick W. Sanders (1872–1954), son of Fred Sanders of Mountain Home and Little Rock, owned and operated a glassware store in Little Rock for a number of years after the turn of the century, then opened Sanders Variety Store in the Hillcrest area of Little Rock.[272]

Philip Charles Prousnitzer Jr. (1915–1983) established the P. C. Hardware and Machine Company, which became one of Little Rock's well-known hardware stores. P. C. Prousnitzer Jr., who served in the military in World War II, was the son of P. C. Prousnitzer Sr. (1877–1952) and Hatty (Franklin) Prousnitzer (1881–1936). Hatty was a member of the prominent pioneer Jewish Franklin family of Pine Bluff.[273]

When a tornado hit the downtown section of Little Rock (which centered around Markham and Main at the time) in October 1894, the material damage sustained by Jews showed the concentration of Jewish businessmen in that area. Firms that suffered from the estimated $1 million in damage to buildings and goods included Pollock and Sons' shoe store, A. Storthz's pawn store, E. Ellenbogen's eatery, Falk-Ottenheimer and Company's hatters and milliners, Wolf and Bro.'s dry goods, Volmer's dry goods company, C. T. Abeles' sash and door factory, Adelman's store, S. Rudolph's store, Adolph Kahn's, Harris's jewelry store, Siesel Building, Epstein and Alexander's dry goods store, Levy's dry goods store, Mrs. Erber's store, Gans Building, and Louis Reinman's livery stable.[274] Four (non-Jewish) people were killed and thirty-four injured, including Mrs. Louis Volmer. Of the twenty-six residences that were damaged, six were Jewish owned.[275]

In all the countries where the Jews had been scattered since the beginning of the Diaspora, they had seldom found justice in the various secular courts. They had, therefore, established their own courts (called Bet Din—court of law) within their individual communities. In America, they found not only religious and secular freedom, but they also found justice in the country's judicial system. Because of this, on occasion, Jewish merchants could be found taking each other to court.[276] Also, on extremely rare occasions, they could be found in trouble with the law as well; one case in 1884 involved Mollie Cohn's house of ill repute on lower Markham Street. One of her customers was arrested for giving a girl named Lizzie a black eye.[277]

During the Depression years of the 1930s, there were a number of suicides in Little Rock, and several of these were Jewish businessmen. The latter included M. H. Benson (1872–1931), James J. Pfeifer (1886–1931), whose suicide was attributed to ill health, and Nathan Adler (1882–1932). Adler's death was especially poignant, in that he took his own life seeking to insure his family's financial well-being. Son of Simon Adler of Batesville, he had headed his father's bank in that city before moving to Little Rock, where he became president of the White Diamond Fertilizer Company. Nathan Adler had married Helen Albright, an Episcopalian; they had two daughters and a son, Nathan Adler Jr. One of the daughters, Ray (Mrs. Foster Cochran), followed her mother's faith, and their other daughter, Marie (Mrs. Lawrence Kessel), followed her father's.[278]

NORTH LITTLE ROCK

When the railroad was first brought to central Arkansas from Memphis, it terminated at North Little Rock (Argenta) for some time. Passengers were then ferried across the Arkansas River to Little Rock. As a termination point, Argenta began to grow, and Main Street and East Washington Avenue saw the establishment of a number of Jewish-owned stores. Argenta served as a gateway to the delta farming country to the south and east, and furnishing merchants sprang up as well. Among these was Morris Levy's son, Roy (1884–1951), who established a furnishing store on Washington Avenue with business partner Joe Loebner (1892–1972). Because of the large volume of business the Levy-Loebner store did with both farmers and employees of the nearby Missouri Pacific Railway Shops, the company prospered.[279]

Nathan Gershner (1874–1950), who came to Little Rock with his Austrian-born parents in 1880, established a large furnishing store in North Little Rock that continued until 1930.[280] Nathan's brother, Morris Gershner (1873–1941), was in the furniture business but joined the North Little Rock Police Department and was desk sergeant and a detective from 1927 to 1941.[281] Morris's son, Leon Gershner (1906–1977), served with the Arkansas State Police for twenty-five years and retired as a captain.[282]

There were several Jewish-owned saloons in North Little Rock before the Prohibition era. R. Gershner and Adolph Kahn had saloons on Washington Avenue, and M. Gershner had one on Main Street.[283]

Austrian-born James B. Gross (1881–1940) conducted a plantation supply business in Little Rock. He moved his store to North Little Rock in 1923, buying out the Topf and Wright firm. He was active in civic organizations and was a stockholder and director of several banks.[284] He married Hazel Blass.

David Jesse Michael (1857–1930) came to Little Rock in 1880 as a traveling salesman and married Charlotte Reinman, sister of livery-owner Louis Reinman. David and his son Louis Michael (1888–1941) later became partners in the Michael and Reinman firm of North Little Rock. They also established the Michael Fish and Commission House on East Washington in North Little Rock.[285]

The Distaff Side

As did their male counterparts, a number of Jewish women distinguished themselves in various ways in the betterment of Arkansas. Some of these women had left home and family in Europe and had been brought to America by their enthusiastic husbands. Others were daughters, sisters, aunts, cousins, or other relatives of those who had settled in this new world. On occasion, they could be found as spinsters, although there was usually a shortage of potential wives available. Listed below are a few of those women in Pulaski County who should be remembered. (Others are listed with the East European migration, and also in other sections of this book.)

Cecelia Schwartz (1847–1929) was born in Austria but was brought to New York by her parents when she was two years old. She was educated there and was graduated as a teacher in 1864. That same year she came to Little Rock and married merchant John M. Samuel. They had five children before John died in 1882. Cecelia then married widower Max Parker, a Little Rock furniture store owner and furniture manufacturer. He had had four children by his first wife, Carrie Davidson of Washington, Arkansas. Cecelia and Max had one son of their own before Max died in 1887. Left with ten children to raise, Cecelia did so with zeal and love. Multilingual, she also found time to teach a free night school at the Temple for foreigners who settled in the area. She helped in the organization of Temple B'nai Israel, the Temple Ladies' Aid Society, and the local chapter of the Council of Jewish Women.[286]

There were a number of other Jewish women who were vitally interested in education and who taught in the Little Rock schools. Some of these included Flora L. Cohen, Brunette Fox, Sarah Ehrenberg, Harriet Cohn, Hattie Bloom, Nathalia Kauffman, Vera Levy, and Gladys Ottenheimer.

Flora L. Cohen (1875–1938), daughter of Bernard and Rebecca (Navra) Cohen, became prominently known in the educational circles of Little Rock. She taught in nine local public schools during a forty-five-year span. She was appointed principal of Pulaski Heights Grammar

School when it was established in 1923 and continued in that position until her death. She was a founder of the Woman Teachers' Association and served as president of the Principal's Roundtable. She became known for her happy disposition and her "loyal, faithful, untiring" efforts in the field of education.[287] (A sister, Mabel Cohen [1884–1962], was a businesswoman and was active in civic affairs.)[288]

Brunette Fox (1895–1988), daughter of Theodore R. and Flora (Oppenheimer) Fox, was a Little Rock schoolteacher who began practicing social work before it had a name. She checked on absentees, going to their homes if they had no telephones, and provided clothes for those who missed school because of a lack of them. When Rabbi Ira Sanders began a School of Social Work in Little Rock in the late 1920s, Brunette was a student. During World War II she helped at Camp Robinson, where she befriended a young soldier with pneumonia and called his widowed father, Alfred Billstein, in Toledo to report the serious illness. Alfred came to Little Rock to see his son, and he and Brunette later married.[289]

Mrs. Milton (Sarah Ehrenberg) Loeb (1881–1927) was a Little Rock schoolteacher,[290] as was Harriett Cohn (1850–1928), daughter of Mathias and Theresa (Kobner) Cohn. Harriett taught in the city's schools for thirty years.[291]

Hattie Bloom (1874–1919) taught in the Little Rock public schools for some twenty-five years and was principal of Rodney H. Parham School.[292] Mrs. Samuel (Nathalia Kauffman) Etheridge (1889–1977), daughter of Charles and Ernestine Kauffman, was supervisor of public education and a Little Rock school teacher from 1915 to 1955 and taught confirmation classes at Temple B'nai Israel for some fifty years.[293] Nathalia's sister, Mrs. Henry (Fannie Kauffman) Cline, also taught in the city's public schools from 1915 to 1951. A member of several social and literary clubs, she was a longtime principal of Temple B'nai Israel's Sunday School.[294] Mrs. Irvin (Vera Brewer) Levy (1905–1980), a North Little Rock public school teacher, was also active in the Parent-Teacher Association, serving as president of the PTA Council. She was a leader in a number of civic affairs, such as March of Dimes, Committee on Women's Public Affairs of Arkansas, Governor's Commission on Status of Women, and many educational organizations.[295]

Gladys Ottenheimer (1895–1983), daughter of pioneer settler Daniel Ottenheimer and sister of Leonard and Gus, taught at the old Peabody School on West Capitol Avenue from 1913 to 1928. She was principle of Temple B'nai Israel's Sunday School for twenty years and taught there for forty years. She married Joe B. Hirsch, and they were associated with the

Ottenheimer Brothers Manufacturing Company. She served as secretary of the company until 1954 and was a director and vice-president of the Ottenheimer Brothers Foundation.[296]

Other Jewish women were active in the support of education in Little Rock. Mrs. Philip (Clara Mandlebaum) Pfeifer (1849–1920) was active in the Philip Pfeifer School and served as president of its School Improvement Association.[297] Mrs. Joe (Ray Ullman) Navra (1885–1923) was well known for her active work in public school activities, which included being an officer of the Parham School Improvement Association.[298] Irene (Pareira) Sanders (1885–1916), wife of architect Theodore M. Sanders, was prominently known for her civic work, particularly in educational circles. She was president of the U. M. Rose School Improvement Association and was active in the Girls' Industrial School Association.[299] Mrs. Stanley (Sadee Alexander) Bauman Sr. (1899–1974) served as president of the Little Rock PTA Association; she was also active in the Goodwill Industries and was made a lifetime member of its board.[300]

Many Jewish women of the greater Little Rock area were active in its civic affairs, and it is not possible to cite them all for their efforts. A few are given here as examples of the magnanimous and civic-minded spirit found among them. The women of the Blass family of Little Rock set a precedent early on in giving of themselves for others. Mrs. Louis (Pauline Heiman) Blass (1847–1915) and her husband had no children of their own, but they helped raise a number of orphans. Pauline served on the board of the Ada Thompson Memorial Home (for elderly women), and her charity work was "unlimited."[301] She and her husband had a love for animals as well and worked with the Little Rock Humane Society.[302] Mrs. Gus (Bertha Katzenstein) Blass (1856–1945) was a philanthropist and civic leader who served on a number of civic boards. She was a founder and a continuous officer of the Provident Relief Society and its successor, the Welfare Bureau. She was also a member of the Daughters of the American Revolution. It was said that she gave to every civic cause or project, local or national, that was recommended to her.[303] Mrs. Noland (Isabel Ringelhaupt) Blass Sr. (1897–1979) shared her husband's interest in social welfare. She was a founder of the Pulaski County Family Service Agency and served on a number of boards, such as the Pulaski County Welfare Board (more than twenty years), the Ada Thompson Home, the Senior Citizens Activities Today (SCAT), the Grey Ladies of the American Red Cross, and the YWCA. She was an honor graduate of the National Cathedral School at Washington, D.C.[304] Mrs. Julian (Lea Gans)

Blass (1890–1936) was a leader in civic, club, and musical affairs, and was particularly active in the Little Rock Orphan's Home.[305]

Several Jewish women were involved with the organization of the State Federation of Women's Clubs, including Mrs. J. B. Hirsch, Mrs. Herman Kahn, and Mrs. Morris M. Cohn. Mrs. Jo (Ida) Frauenthal of Conway served as president of the organization from 1912 to 1914.[306]

Other Jewish women involved in civic affairs included Mrs. Henry (Minnie Ehrenberg) Lasker (1876–1939), daughter of Lazarus Ehrenberg. She was a board member of the Pulaski County Tuberculosis Association, the Women's City Club, and the Blind Women's Home, as well as the Little Rock Chapter of the Council of Jewish Women.[307]

Mrs. Herbert H. (June Maas) Wolf (1895–1978) was active in youth work, serving as a member of the Girl Scout Council. In 1938 she was instrumental in obtaining cabins for the Girl Scout Camp at Lake Sylvia, and she was noted as being the first Cub Scout den mother in Little Rock. She was named by Governor Carl Bailey as the state representative at the White House Conference on Physical and Mental Health in 1930. During World War II, she was actively involved in the United Service Organizations (USO) Council.[308]

Mrs. Harry W. (Helois Kaufman) Pfeifer Sr. (1875–1956) served on the boards of the Arkansas Children's Hospital, the Working Woman's Home, and as president of the Women's City Club.[309]

Mrs. Sidney H. (Bertie Stifft) Florsheim (1878–1951), daughter of Charles and Rebecca Stifft, founded the Women's Auxiliary of the Little Rock Boys' Club in 1923 and served as its president for many years. She was a board member of the Lady Guardians of the Ada Thompson Home.[310] Another Stifft daughter, Mrs. Albert D. (Marcuse Stifft) Cohn (1885–1946), became a "leading spirit" in the city's educational, civic, and cultural efforts.[311]

Mrs. Morris B. (Mabel Cohn) Sanders (1881–1932), daughter of Mark M. Cohn, was a board member of the Ada Thompson home and was active in a number of civic and social affairs.[312]

Mrs. Harry B. (Gertrude Myar) Solmson Sr. (1880–1974), daughter of Camden pioneer Henry Myar, was a Grey Lady in both World Wars and was a board member of the Trebing Memorial Home for Blind Women, Working Women's Home and Day Nursery, Little Rock Women's Club, and other civic organizations.[313]

Mrs. Alvin W. (Tracye Altschul) Strauss Sr. (1893–1961), wife of a prominent Little Rock physician, was active in the Pulaski County Medical

Society Auxiliary, St. Vincent's Infirmary Auxiliary, the YWCA, and the Boys' Club Auxiliary.[314]

Mrs. Roscoe C. (Rose Bernwald) Kory (1895–1982), the wife of a Little Rock physician, was a board member of the Women's City Club and Federation of Women's Clubs, Pulaski County Medical Society Auxiliary, Easter Seals, Arkansas Jewish Assembly, and served as a PTA president.[315]

Mrs. Ephraim H. (Sadie Cohn) Eichenbaum (1880–1951) was active in Jewish and non-Jewish circles. In 1926 she was elected president of the Council of Jewish Women that covered an eight-state area. She helped in the teaching and placement of immigrants from Ellis Island, where she was greeted by President Calvin Coolidge when she visited. She was dedicated to the underprivileged, and she took her daughter Betty with her, beginning at an early age, to visit people at the School for the Deaf, in the state prison, and in old folks' homes.[316]

Mrs. David W. (Esther Loveman) Kempner (1891–1959) was an organizer and the first president of the Little Rock Drama League and also served as president of the Little Rock Council of Jewish Women. She was a founder and board member of the Memphis (Tennessee) Orchestral Society. She was the first woman appointed to the Arkansas Penal Board.[317]

A few Jewish women excelled in the business world, long before such involvement (or success) was generally pursued. One of the most successful such women before the turn of the century was Mrs. Jacob (Bluma DeYoung) Gans (1835–1915). Mrs. Gans was born in Philadelphia and came to Little Rock in 1875. She was possibly the first woman in Arkansas to have her own factory. By the early 1880s she had established a millinery, fancy dry goods, and dressmaking business at 108 Main Street. She had eighty-six employees, who worked in dressmaking, millinery, and as salesclerks. Her establishment, the Mrs. B. Gans company, considered one of the most extensive of its kind south of St. Louis, was expanded in 1884. The store was considered a "delightful" place to visit; even the little girls who accompanied their mothers were overwhelmed by the beauty of all that was offered.[318] Her store was a beehive of activity and crowded with customers. Mrs. Gans personally selected her stock from Eastern markets; she bought materials in Paris and from there brought back seamstresses who would "do justice" to the lovely fabrics.[319] When her husband, Jacob, died in 1900, Mrs. Gans eventually moved to New York to be near their daughter, Mrs. William Katzenberger. The Mrs. B. Gans company was continued in Little Rock by Gans family members. In 1912 the Little Rock Board of Trade reported that no dry goods or millinery house in Little Rock could surpass the "well stocked and enterprising establishment of Mrs. B. Gans"; the company's slogan was "Outfitters for All Womankind."[320] At that time the firm had thirty-three assistants and was one of the leading houses in the city for revenue. When she died in 1915, Mrs. Gan's body was returned to Little Rock and buried beside her beloved husband.

Mrs. Hirsch (Amalia Kahn) Jacobi (1834–1926) conducted a millinery shop in Little Rock for a number of years, and Hattie M. Cohn (?–1931), daughter of Simon Cohn, operated a millinery store in Little Rock for a quarter of a century.[321] Mrs. Nelson (Eugenie Stifft) Frank (1883–1963), daughter of Mr. and Mrs. Charles Stifft, began selling corsets from door to door in the 1920s, then opened her own small shop in 1928. Increasing her stock to include fine lines of hats and dresses, she established the Eugenie Frank Shop, which became an exclusive women's fashion store that was considered haute couture.[322]

Etta Marian Simon, daughter of Felix and Minna Simon, was a journalist and served as society editor for the *Arkansas Democrat* during the second decade of the twentieth century.[323]

CHAPTER 8

German Migration in Eastern Arkansas

T he story of rural and small-town Arkansas from the time of the Civil War until World War II centers generally around cotton growers and buyers, timber industry workers, and the local merchants who supplied each community's needs. Life was often harsh and crude for rural Arkansans during that period, travel was difficult, and each little community was, for the most part, autonomous. Farmers and timber workers were often hard pressed for supplies for their generally large families. The farmers also had farming needs, and with only one pay period annually at harvest time, credit was an essential necessity of life. With no State Banking Department in Arkansas until 1913, and with only thirty-nine banks reported in Arkansas by 1900,[1] the outfitting (or furnishing) store was developed to meet this crucial need. This section chronicles some of the Jewish merchants who settled in Arkansas, what they did, and how they were perceived by their fellow citizens. The history begins at Batesville and moves somewhat clockwise around the state. (The Western portion is included in chapter 9.)

Northeast Arkansas

Simon Adler (1832–1904), who had settled at Batesville in the 1850s (see section I), had left the Confederate military because of ill health and had gone to Mexico until after the war. He was against slavery, yet did not want to fight against the South.[2] He returned to Batesville in 1866 and resumed his popular mercantile business. To meet local needs, he initially made private loans, then opened the People Savings Bank.[3] Adler brought relatives into his business with him as well as other bright young Jewish workers, some of whom Adler helped to open their own stores. Those who came to Batesville included Louis and Abraham Baum, Samuel and Max Siesel, Robert Schwarzkopf, B. Loebner, James Loewen, Max Blumenthal, Herman Schott, Sigmund Bacharach, Abe Volmer, Michael Jacobs, Joshua Rich, and Charles Meyer. At Jacksonport, less than twenty-five miles east of Batesville, Simon Adler was joined in a business firm by Adler family members Sol, Benjamin, and Nathan, as well as by his pre–Civil War partner, Aaron Hirsch. They later opened branches at Clarendon, Evening Shade, and Newport; they also invested heavily in other small mercantile stores in north Arkansas and as far away as Hermanville, Mississippi.[4]

As was often the case with other Jewish merchants in Arkansas, Simon Adler helped his community culturally as well as economically, civically, and through charity. On the second floor of his two-story brick building at Batesville, Adler constructed an opera hall, which was referred to as the "Daisy of the Town." Included in the events at Adler Hall were the grand Christmas dress balls of the Knights of Pythias, dramatic productions, and concerts that benefitted the Methodist Church.[5] Simon Adler became known for his integrity, generosity, and charm, and a local newspaper referred to him as "our good friend"; at least seven local residents named their sons for him.[6] When Adler died in 1904, a local newspaper extolled him as an outstanding businessman; it was noted that no one in that section of the state "ever held the confidence of the people in a greater degree."[7]

NEWPORT

What was said of Simon Adler became the norm in almost every place in which Jews settled, for they entered community life and helped build up each area. They helped develop the town of Newport, located about five miles south of Jacksonport. With the coming of the railroad to the town and the lessening of river traffic, Newport's importance later superceded that of Jacksonport. In the 1870s Lazar Hirsch, son of early pioneer Aaron Hirsch, settled at Newport, where he established a mercantile company and helped found the White River Telephone Company, White River Ice Manufacturing Company, and the Newport Compress and Storage

Company. He served as city treasurer, recorder, deputy sheriff, and deputy clerk. He was said to be one of the "ablest" young men in the county and was interested in all that affected it. "Intelligent, enterprising" J. B. Hirsch, another son of Aaron Hirsch, worked in his father's furnishing store, then opened his own such store in Newport.[8]

In 1880 Sigmund Wolff and Isaac Goldman, who had come to Newport as clerks in the Adler store, bought the general mercantile store established by Lazar Hirsch in 1874. Renamed the Wolff-Goldman Mercantile Company, it grew to become the largest store of its kind in the area.[9] A large new store was constructed in 1909, designed by noted architect Charles L. Thompson of Little Rock. Wolff and Goldman became enthusiastic promoters of the town and their investments in Jackson County were substantial. Their enterprise grew to include furniture and a farm supply business. Wolff became president of both the Jackson County Bank and the First National Bank of Newport. After Sigmund Wolff (1856–1909) and Goldman moved to St. Louis (where they established the Marquette Cloak and Suit Company), Wolff's son, Norman C. Wolff (1886–1952), stayed in Newport as head of the enterprise there. He became an official in the Wolff-Goldman Realty Company and the First National Bank.[10] When farmers came to town to buy supplies from the Wolff store, on occasion they also ordered suits for themselves and dresses for their wives. After giving the approximate size and weight of the latter, the farmers let the merchants select the proper fit.[11] The Wolff-Goldman Company was sold to P. K. Holmes of Newport in 1927.

Charles Meyer (1859–1926), who also started his career at Newport as a clerk in the Adler store, and his wife Jeanette (Heiligers) Meyer owned a dry goods store at Newport for twenty years before moving it to Jonesboro.[12]

Anias Ephraim Shoffner (1831–1903) had settled near Batesville in 1858 and, after serving in the Confederate army, developed a farming enterprise of some two thousand acres about twenty miles south of Newport. The town of Shoffner grew up around his furnishing store. His son, Mann Shoffner, dealt in mules and became one of the largest mule dealers in the South. A. E. Shoffner was civic minded, serving as a justice of the peace, town constable, and school director of his township.[13] A. E. was kind to the thirty or more black families that lived in the area, and some members of those families served as pallbearers at his funeral in 1903. When President McKinley died in 1901, blacks at Shoffner said they were glad it was not Mr. Shoffner, who was so kind to them. A. E. Shoffner intermarried, and his family followed the Christian faith.[14]

Leopold Thalheim had a general store at Newport by 1887, and he and

Levi Hecht of Pocahontas were on the board of the Reyno, St. Louis and Iron Mountain Railway. Jacob Heiligers, who had established a cider company in Little Rock in the 1880s, later moved to Newport, where he opened a general store and became well known for his commercial interests.[15]

By 1900 German-born Sol Heinemann had opened a mercantile store at Newport and had begun buying cotton. He had tugboats on the White River that hauled sand and gravel, and he also harvested mussels from the river for making pearl buttons.[16] Other Jewish merchants who located at Newport around the turn of the century included M. Bach (grocery), H. Bernstein (hotel), and B. Cohn and C. Cohn dry goods stores.[17]

WALNUT RIDGE

Many of the Jews who settled in the rural areas of Arkansas began their careers as peddlers, or foot merchants. Jewish peddlers were unsung heroes, which has seldom been noticed by historians, as they brought goods and news to isolated families and country communities.[18] One of these foot merchants who came to Arkansas in the early 1870s was Isaac Less (1849–?). He peddled his goods in northeast Arkansas and by 1875 had established a general store at Walnut Ridge, a town that was established less than forty miles north of Newport when the Iron Mountain Railroad came through that section of the state in 1873. (By 1919 it was the leading town in Lawrence County.)[19] Isaac's fair dealing and hard work became well known, and he became one of the largest landholders in Lawrence County, accumulating more than nine thousand acres by 1890.[20]

The Bloom family—David, Dolph, and Charles—established a store at Walnut Ridge that grew to be one of the largest department stores in that section of the state by 1919. At the turn of the century, Jacob L. Reinach (1863–1908), whose family had originally settled at Pine Bluff, served as superintendent of the Hoxie, Pocahontas and Northern Railway at Walnut Ridge.[21]

JONESBORO

Jonesboro, county seat of Craighead County in northeast Arkansas, was incorporated as a town in 1883. It grew from a wilderness "inhabited by hoot owls" to a thriving first class city by 1930. In 1910 it had a population of more than seven thousand and a population of more than ten thousand in 1930.[22] In 1881, before the town was incorporated, Rudolph H. Meyer (1859–1945) peddled in the area, then opened a store, The Grand Leader.

(Before moving to Jonesboro, German-born Rudolph had first joined his brother, Adolph Meyer, in 1874 at Grand Lake in the southeast corner of the state and had been a landing keeper on the Mississippi River in the days of steamboats.) Rudolph's department store in Jonesboro grew to be the largest in the town; by 1903 it covered a half acre of floor space and had ten departments. It had steam heat and electric fans and was described as "one like those found in cities ten times larger."[23] Rudolph also helped found a bank in Jonesboro.[24] Rudolph's younger brother, Maximillian "Max" Meyer (1861–1946), at age fourteen had also begun his career with his brother Adolph at Grand Lake. Max completed his education at nearby Eudora, then moved to Jonesboro, where he established a grocery business that also dealt in furs, hides, cotton, and buggies. He built a large warehouse, and his was the first business in the city to have an elevator. He also had a large rice farm near Newport. Max married Camille Neustadter, sister of Gus Neustadter (see below), and they had four children.

Joseph Heinemann (1876–1931), who had come from Germany at age seventeen and had worked as a foot peddler in Louisiana and Mississippi, joined Rudolph Meyer's Grand Leader company around 1910. In 1914 he established Heinemann's Department Store, which became one of the largest stores in Northeast Arkansas; it had the largest display windows of any enterprise in Jonesboro. In 1937 it was the city's largest store, employing forty-five workers.[25] It was said that the store was responsible in a great measure for keeping Jonesboro trade "at home where it belongs."[26] The firm continued in the Heinemann family until 1944.[27]

The Jews who settled in the Jonesboro area helped develop the town and were said to have done it "untold good."[28] Lewis Sachs (1850–1938) was one of these. Coming to the area in 1888, he envisioned its future at a time when there were only a few wooden shanties in the town. He accumulated vast land holdings and became a real estate broker, handling only his own property; he also had a brick factory. He became known as a "very generous, public-minded man," and men of his foresight were said to be welcomed in the area.

Marcus Berger (1844–1906) became a partner of Isaac Less at Walnut Ridge in the 1880s, but in the early 1890s he moved to Jonesboro, some twenty miles southeast, and opened the first wholesale supply house there. Selling merchandise at prices as low as those in St. Louis, Berger drew customers from a seventy-five mile radius. A relative, Morris Berger Jr. (1865–1932), also settled in Jonesboro in the 1880s and, with John M. Johnson, established a furniture business—Johnson, Berger and Company—

which did business all over northeast Arkansas. According to a local newspaper, Jonesboro owed its progress to such men.[29] The Johnson-Berger firm, cited as the oldest and largest furniture company in Eastern Arkansas, remained as such until the Depression and the death of Morris Berger in 1932; that year his son Jake opened the Berger Furniture Company.[30] Morris Berger's daughter Sadie married Ashley Sales (son of Rabbi Samuel Sales of Emanuel Temple in St. Louis), who was proprietor of a grocery store in Jonesboro.[31] In 1932, when Jonesboro was without a bank because of the Great Depression, the Berger brothers, Ben and Alec, were leaders in the establishment of the Mercantile Bank in Jonesboro. Ben H. Berger (1880–1943) served as president of the bank for many years, and Alec Berger served as chairman of the board.[32]

Ben Schoenfield (1864–1940) opened what became a successful mercantile store in Jonesboro in 1892 and helped organize a Jewish congregation (see section II). He married Clara Weiss, and they had four children. Their son Morris, who married Sadie Euster of Middleboro, Kentucky, continued the family business. (Four Euster girls married Jonesboro men; besides Sadie, Pearl Euster married Sam Hummelstein, Florence married Maurice Rubenstein, and Evelyn married George Heinemann.)[33]

Members of the Less family, Emil and Jake, had a clothing store at Jonesboro. Emil opened the Star Clothing House in 1888 and Jake (1868–1941) later joined him. They had a branch at Newport as well. Emil made semiannual trips to New York, and their store was the first in Jonesboro to offer such "high class" custom-made clothing as Manhattan shirts.[34]

Abe Hummelstein came to Jonesboro in 1907 because Arkansas was a fur-producing state. He established the Jonesboro Hide and Fur Company and was joined by his brother Sam. Abe married Oneida Neustadter, whose father Gus Neustadter (1870–1931) had a grocery store in Jonesboro with a partner, L. H. Sternheimer. (Gus also had a store at Walnut Ridge.) Sternheimer and Neustadter grew to become one of the largest and most successful stores in Jonesboro. The two civic-minded men were said to have done all within their power to improve conditions in the Jonesboro area.[35] Ferdinand "Ferd" Neustadter (1865–1926), Gus's brother, established a dry goods and clothing store, The Famous, in Jonesboro in 1902 with a partner, H. D. Miller. Miller had founded The Bell clothing store in Jonesboro in the 1890s.

Moses Stonefield (1853–1922) established a grocery store that carried a good grade of merchandise. Ben Stonefield (1890–1955), Moses' son, succeeded his father in the store. During the Great Depression he was known to carry past-due bills so that his customers would not go hungry. J. Cohen and J. Steinfield bought the Rosenfield Department Store and renamed it the C and S Department Store. They carried a large stock of clothing and general merchandise; their customers thought so much of them that some named their children after them.[36]

Jews who grew up at Jonesboro noted that they found little or no anti-Semitism; rather, they socialized generally with all religious groups. Even in the days of the Klan, it was known that a Jewish dry goods merchant was aware of the fact that he was selling sheets to be used by the Klan. Jewish businessmen were welcomed as members of the local country club.[37] A federated club, "Sixteen Jolly Girls," which was founded in Jonesboro by a Methodist, Mrs. C. M. Ludlow, gave performances locally. Girls of various religious backgrounds were allowed to join, and Jewish members included Doris Goldstein, Oneida Neustadter, and Thelma Meyer.[38]

MONETTE

At Monette, some twenty miles east of Jonesboro, D. Gottfried and his partner, Mendelson, peddled in the area in the 1890s then opened the New York Store in the small town. By 1903 their business was called a "splendid" enterprise. In a backhanded compliment to the town, a local writer said that "A Jew never locates in a dead town; they have too much business sense."[39] H. Simon also peddled in the Monette area and established a general mercantile store there. It was said that the Jews helped both to promote and to improve the town.

PARAGOULD

A. D. Bertig (1853–1926), a native Austrian, came to Arkansas as a pack peddler in the 1870s and was later joined by his brother, Saul (1863–1945). Together they would make a circle on their travels, beginning at Little Rock and going west to Ozark, then northeast to Walnut Ridge, then to Paragould. At the latter town, located in Greene County on the eastern slope of Crowley's Ridge (a ridge of high ground that runs perpendicular through Arkansas's flat delta land), they spent their nights at the home of Raymond Frey. In 1884 they opened one of the first businesses at Paragould, and in the early 1890s they, with W. C. Hasty, purchased a tramway that went east from Paragould. They extended it across the St. Francis River, and, assisted by the Cotton Belt Line, their railroad became known as the Paragould Southeastern Railway. They established the town of Bertig at the end of the line, and three lumber companies located there, shipping millions of feet of lumber yearly. A post office was established in June 1894 and continued until 1914. By 1926 the town had dwindled to one grocery store and four houses.[40] The Bertigs established branch stores at Marmaduke, Piggott, and Blytheville in Arkansas and at Cardwell, Missouri. They eventually had thirteen cotton gins and accumulated some seven thousand acres of land. A. D. was president of the First National Bank of Paragould and president of the Board of Trade. He promoted an electric street car between Hoxie and Walnut Ridge and built the "most complete ice plant in the southwest" (which housed a new electric light plant) and a bottling works. The Bertig brothers were said to be interested in almost every enterprise in Northeast Arkansas. Their large general mercantile stores furnished farmers across an extensive area of the state.[41]

Simon L. Joseph (1854–1909) came to Arkansas in 1878. At first in partnership with Isaac Less at Walnut Ridge, he then opened a business in Paragould in 1885 with a partner, Mr. Harris, whom he later bought out. Joseph was joined in his firm by his brother-in-law, Joseph Wolf. (Both men had married sisters of J. D. Goldman—a founder and partner of the Lesser-Goldman Cotton Company. Simon Joseph wed Setta, and Joseph Wolf [1856–1932] wed Ida.) They also had farms and a cotton gin. Their large firm, located across the street from the Bertig company, continued into the 1930s. Around 1900, Alvin Samuel, a nephew of the family, settled at Paragould, where he farmed and had a cotton gin.[42]

Other German Jews who settled at Paragould included Dave Loeb (1859–1939), and Block family members, J. D. and M. F. "Dave" Loeb came from Germany to Paragould in the late 1880s and had a mercantile store there from 1890 until his retirement in 1939.[43] Sons of Maurice Block of Wittsburg, J. D. and M. F., had businesses at Paragould. J. D., an attorney, maintained a law office there, and M. F. and his son William had an insurance firm at Paragould and Jonesboro.[44]

RECTOR

Austrian-born Sigmund Unterberger settled at Rector, about twenty miles northeast of Paragould, in 1895 and established a mercantile store with branches in two nearby towns. He had two cotton gins as well. Sigmund married Gertrude Meyer (whose parents had come from England), and they had four girls, Adele, Phyllis, Rosalind, and Jane. Gertrude belonged to the Methodist church choir that presented dramatic productions for local schools. The Unterberger's children went to the Methodist church as well. (When daughter Rosalind was visiting the Methodist church at age nine, she was told that she would burn in hell because she hadn't been baptized a Christian; she never went back.)[45] Sigmund brought his two sisters from Europe, and the younger one, Minnie, married Gertrude's brother, Louis Meyer. Louis (called "Uncle Louie" by family and friends) became well known and loved in Rector. A talented singer and musician, he was considered the "Al Jolson type" and provided local entertainment, with Gertrude accompanying him on the harpsichord. There was an aura about the Unterberger family that made some of the local people view them as "aristocrats."[46] They helped promote utilities in the town, and theirs was the first home to have indoor plumbing. Visiting farm friends would come by on Saturdays and ask to see the bathroom fixtures. When the Unterberger daughters became old enough to date, Sigmund moved the family to St. Louis and commuted back to his stores in Arkansas. He lost his Arkansas holdings during the Depression.[47]

POCAHONTAS

At Pocahontas, a lumber town and the county seat of Randolph County in Northeast Arkansas, the Hanauer brothers, Jacob and Louis, had settled before the Civil War (see section I). Their nephew, Isaac Hirst (1842–1917), who had come to live with them and who was wounded in his service in the Confederate army, returned to Pocahontas after the war. (The Hanauers had moved away—Jacob to Cincinnati and Louis to Memphis.) Hirst married a local Gentile, Nora Hubble, opened his own store, and accumulated both town and rural property.[48]

Austrian-born A. Z. Schnabaum (1865–1923), who began peddling as a young boy in northern Arkansas, settled at Pocahontas in the early 1880s. He established a general store and cotton gin and "amassed a great fortune" in merchandising, cotton, and land.[49] He was lauded for his high ideals, lack of deceit, and generosity. His children intermarried and his descendants were scattered across Arkansas.[50]

Levi Hecht was one of the first merchants of Pocahontas; he established what became a prosperous mercantile store.[51]

BLYTHEVILLE

Although most of the Jews who settled in the Blytheville area were from East Europe (see chapter 11), several German-Jewish families made it their home. These included the Sternbergs, Josephs, Jiedels, Rosenthals, and Rosenbergs. Silvey Sternberg (1877–1928), son of Mark and Sarah (Oppenheimer) Sternberg of Ozark (Arkansas) and Fort Smith, became a traveling shoe salesman around the turn of the century. One of his customers was the Bertig store at Blytheville. After being offered a better job with the Bertig enterprise, he worked there several years, then opened a cotton brokerage business. It became one of the largest cotton-ginning companies in the area. He also had large land holdings. When he became bedfast with stomach cancer in the mid-1920s, it was said that he bought and sold more cotton, even in bed, than any other man in the state. He married Mollie Weinberger, and they had two children, Harold (1910–1992), who worked with the family business until it was sold in the mid-1930s, and a daughter, Helen. The Sternberg family was quite civic minded. They provided free milk to the town's school children, and Mollie helped organize the Blytheville Women's Club. (The Sternberg family was related to a number of Arkansas Jewish families, including those of Fox, Siesel, Krone, Wolf, and Lewis.)[52]

Sam Joseph (1867–1960) and his wife Olga Sternberg (a cousin of Silvey Sternberg) moved to Blytheville around 1913 and opened a hardware and paint store and a sheet metal shop, which continued for some forty years. They had two sons, Charles and Simon (see section V).[53] The Jiedel brothers, Siegbert and Richard, moved to Blytheville in the 1920s. Siegbert "Zeke" (1902–1955) had the Jiedel Cotton Company, a cotton brokerage business, and Richard owned a dry goods store. The brothers were active in the religious and civic affairs of the city.[54] Walter Rosenthal, who owned a ladies' dress shop at Blytheville, married Lillian Weinberg of Osceola (see chapter 11).

MANILA

Leopold "Lee" Rosenberg (1881–1960), a native of Meisenheim am Glan, Germany, came to America at age thirteen and joined his uncles Joseph "Joe," Gus, and George Rosenberg, who were merchants and land and cotton dealers in the Hope-Fulton-Texarkana area of southwest Arkansas (see chapter 9). After a ruined cotton crop in 1911, Lee and Joe established a dry goods store at Kennett, Missouri, then relocated the store to Manila, Arkansas, in the 1920s. Lee bought a cotton gin which he continued until the mid-1940s, when he and his family (wife Florence [Quertermous] and daughters Jo Ann and Frieda) moved to Memphis. (Joe Rosenberg had joined his family earlier in St. Louis).[55]

WITTSBURG, WYNNE

At Wittsburg, located at the head of navigation on the St. Francis River in Cross County, a thriving community was established.[56] Block family members, who had migrated from Alsace, first settled at Wittsburg in the 1850s (see section I). After the war, Maurice Block, David Block, J. J. Hamilton, and A. A. Lucky established a large store known as D. Block and Company. It became the largest commercial business in that section of the state. When the railroad later bypassed Wittsburg, the town moved to nearby Wynne Station. There, Maurice's son, Isaac Block, built a sawmill and cotton gin. He bought more than seven hundred acres of land, building neat tenant houses on each forty acres.[57] Isaac and several men, including W. M. Kennedy, J. R. Kennedy, and J. E. Badinelli, formed the Cross County Bank in 1891; Isaac served as president.[58] Two of Maurice Block's sons (Maurice and his wife, Anna Woubilman, had ten children; one died in infancy) were in politics in the town. William served as deputy county clerk, deputy collector of taxes, and as a justice of the peace. J. D. was elected prosecuting attorney of the second circuit (which included seven counties in 1888) and was elected a state representative in 1886.[59] His son, Maurice F. (1892–1965), a graduate of Washington University Law School at St. Louis, practiced law with his father, and, after serving in World War I, founded the M. F. Block Insurance Company at Jonesboro and Paragould.[60] Solomon Meyer, who worked in the Block furnishing store, married Maurice's daughter Julia. Meyer later opened his own dry goods firm at Wynne.[61]

Shields Daltroff was a clerk in the Block store at Wittsburg in 1875. He later bought out the firm, renaming it Daltroff, Sparks and Oliver. It was moved to Wynne in 1888, where a large brick building had been constructed for it. (Isaac Block and Daltroff had their houses dismantled at Wittsburg and moved to Wynne.)[62] Daltroff served as a justice of the peace at Wynne. He married Gentile Willie Malone, daughter of the Reverend W. C. Malone; when Willie died, he married Rosa Ackerman of Pennsylvania in 1887.[63]

German-born Louis Friedberg (1874–1945) and his family—wife Paula and daughters Esther and Leona—settled at Turrell in Crittenden County around the time of World War I and conducted a mercantile store. Paula (1879–1945), affable and civic minded, joined in war efforts and in club activities of the town, which had a population of about two hundred. The family was well accepted, and the daughters intermarried.[64]

East-Central Arkansas

St. Francis County in eastern Arkansas was one of the state's early counties and named for the St. Francis River that drained it. Forrest City, some fifty miles west of Memphis, became the county seat in 1874; at that time the county had a population of some 7,000; by 1880 Forrest City had a population of 903.[65] In 1875 the Beckers and Lewises arrived at Forrest City. The family consisted of Benjamin and Sarah (Becker) Lewis, and sons Sol and Charles, and Sarah's twenty-six-year-old brother, Alexander Becker, and his wife, Fannie Lewis. Becker and Lewis became partners in establishing what became a large dry goods and general store as well as an opera house located on the second floor of their building. They helped establish the Bank of Eastern Arkansas and became involved in farming and real estate.[66] Charles became involved in the family enterprises as he grew up and became a "very valuable citizen" of Forrest City. Alexander Becker and Charles Lewis served as directors of the Forrest City Ice and Power Company and Forrest City Gin Company, both of which they helped establish. They were directors of several trust companies located in Little Rock and Helena and in three other states.[67]

Other Jews were drawn to Forrest City, including A. Jastrawer, who came there from Prussia in the 1870s and opened a shoemaking firm. He later moved to White Hall in Lee county and opened a successful mercantile store. He helped develop that area, accumulating some one thousand acres of land.[68] Max Yoffe, born in Amsterdam in 1872, settled in Forrest City in the 1890s and opened a mercantile store. (Yoffe's parents, Nathan and Rebecca [Burrik] Yoffe, were said to have moved to Russia when Max was a boy. Nathan worked in the large timber holdings of Baron Rothschild. The Baron closed his works in Russia in 1889 and paid the expenses for some two thousand of his workers to travel to New York.)[69] Max Yoffe prospered and became a well-respected citizen of Forrest City, serving on its city council. Isadore Yoffe, a relative, took over the store in 1914.[70]

BRINKLEY

At Brinkley, twenty-five miles west of Forrest City, members of the Prussian-born Salinger family settled in the early 1870s. There they became involved with the business life of the town for the next 120 years. Louis Salinger lived for a short while in Augusta in the 1860s, then settled at Brinkley in 1872.[71] He was joined by other family members, including brothers Selig and Sol, and a sister, Bertha (Mrs. Harry Goldberg). Their firms prospered and they engaged in land development. The Goldberg store was located at nearby Goodwin. Sol Salinger and Harry Goldberg were killed in a train wreck near Forrest City in 1883.[72] Joseph Sholem, who first settled at Fort Smith after the Civil War, moved to Brinkley, where he and his brother, I. Sholem, conducted a prosperous general mercantile store.[73]

DES ARC

The town of Des Arc, county seat of Prairie County and located on the White River in the east-central section of the state, saw a number of Jewish merchants in its early days. Drawn there by the timbered and fertile region, those who settled there between 1860 and 1880 included F. Leptein, Isaac Gans, Leon Gans, S. Rosenberg, Samuel Lowenstein, H. P. Wolf, Ferdinand Gates, Alex Dreyfus, L. Freidenberger, Adolph Goodman, and Simon Blum.[74] Most of these men later relocated to other cities and towns in Arkansas.

LONOKE

Lonoke, county seat of Lonoke County, was incorporated as a town in 1872. Located on flat prairie land about twenty-five miles east of Little Rock, it was an ideal agricultural site. In 1856, long before the town was incorporated, German-born Isaac Gates settled there (see section I). He began as a peddler, then opened stores at Lonoke, De Valls Bluff, and Des Arc. His brothers, Ferdinand and David, joined him as partners, and their firms became thriving furnishing stores.[75] Ferdinand married Sally Mayer, sister of Max Mayer of Little Rock, and three of their sons, Elias, Jacob, and Victor, later formed the Gates Mercantile Company, which had a two-story building at Lonoke. The brothers acquired considerable land holdings in the area.[76] Jacob "Jake" Gates (1878–1930) was a Harvard graduate who became a leader in political circles of Lonoke County. He was chairman of the Democratic Central Committee, was named county judge after the death of Judge E. C. Holt in 1918, and served as a state representative in the 1920s.[77] Jake Gates was an organizer of the Lonoke Chamber of Commerce in 1917 and helped in its efforts to promote a diversified farming program.[78] During World War I an aviation training field, Eberts Camp, was initiated at Lonoke, and Gates Mercantile stockpiled large amounts of military supplies. The camp was still under construction when the war ended,[79] and the Gates' family, caught with the then unneeded merchandise and, refusing to accept bankruptcy, lost much of their accumulated property and wealth. Victor (1879–1937) continued to oversee the family's farming interests until he was murdered by a hitchhiker in 1937.[80]

During the 1870s other Jewish firms were opened at Lonoke. One of these, Daniels and Straus, included the partners Dan Daniels and Gustav C. Straus (both of whom later moved to Little Rock). The firm, which handled a "vigorous" trade in stock, lumber, and machinery, prospered, drawing customers from Memphis to Texas.[81] Daniels had first peddled in the Lonoke area before opening a store. He later served both as mayor of the town and as a school board member and was a builder of the Lonoke County courthouse.[82] When the circus came to Lonoke in the 1880s, the company's horses were boarded in the Straus stables.[83] After Straus moved to Little Rock in 1887, he became a partner in the Davis-Reinman Company, which had the same line of business as his Lonoke firm.

As did almost all the other Jewish stores that flourished in Arkansas, the Daniels and Straus firm of Lonoke hired bright young Jewish men as clerks. One of these, Dutch-born Alphonse Hamberg, frugally saved his money and later opened what became a successful dry goods firm at Lonoke. Having served in the Dutch Border Guard during the Franco-German war in 1871, Hamberg was interested in the military. He organized a company of the Arkansas National Guard at Lonoke and served as its captain.[84] In the 1890s Ike May (1859–1938) settled at Lonoke, where he established a hardware store.[85]

David Gates (1845–?), brother of Ferdinand, came to America in 1857 and helped in his brother's Lonoke enterprises, especially in helping raise pure-bred Hereford and short-horned cattle and in farming. Several years after the Civil War, he opened his own store at De Valls Bluff, about twenty-five miles east of Lonoke. He bought some twelve hundred acres of land and raised horses.[86] Jacob Frolich (1863–1932), a nephew of Ferdinand Gates, also worked in the Gates' Lonoke store. After the turn of the century, he and partner R. H. Sanders established a firm at De Valls Bluff, and by 1922 it was the largest general store in town.[87] Frolich also owned the De Valls Bluff Gin and Milling Company. Frolich was a member of the De Valls Bluff School Board and was appointed by Governor Charles H. Brough as a state representative from Prairie County in 1917 to fill the unexpired term of W. H. Bland when the latter died. Frolich was chairman of Liberty bond sales as well as the Jewish War Relief during World War I.[88] Max Frolich, Jacob's brother, had a livery business at Lonoke in the early part of the twentieth century.[89]

DE WITT, STUTTGART

Arkansas County was one of five counties formed when Arkansas became a Territory in 1819. Arkansas Post, around which the early history of the state centered, was located there. The town of De Witt, situated amid fertile fields and timbered lands, was selected as the county seat.[90] It was here that the German-born Loeb brothers, Gus and T. M., established a dry goods store around 1900 and, later, a rice mill. T. M. married Jeannette Silbernagel of Little Rock. After the rise of Hitler in the 1930s, they brought over other members of their family to Arkansas, including the Frenkels—Edmund, Elma (Loeb), and their son Herbert—who settled at Conway.[91] Other German-Jewish merchants settled at Stuttgart, located in Arkansas County in the geographical center of the Grand Prairie region of eastern Arkansas. These merchants included Alvin May and the Oberdorfer brothers, Sam (1886–1948) and Hugo (1893–1973). The Oberdorfers had general mercantile stores at both Stuttgart and North Little Rock.[92] (The Oberdorfer sisters, Misses Olga and Frieda, also settled at Stuttgart. All of Sam Oberdorfer's siblings died at Stuttgart in the 1970s.)

Southeast Arkansas

Lee County, which is bordered by the Mississippi River to the East, was formed in 1873 and was named for Gen. Robert E. Lee. Centrally located Marianna was named as county seat, but it was little more than an "insignificant hamlet" until the 1870s, when the town was incorporated.[93] Jacob Shaul (1849–1925) peddled in the area of Marianna shortly after the Civil War, then opened a store in the little town and began handling cotton. His son Lee (1880–1948) also went into the cotton business and later opened a department store in Marianna.[94] Jacob Shaul's daughter married a Mr. Katzenstein, who opened a department store in Marianna.[95] Julius Lesser had established a business in Marianna in the 1870s and later opened the Lee County Bank. He was vitally interested in the cotton industry in Arkansas and went to St. Louis, where he established the Lesser Cotton Company (later, the Lesser-Goldman Cotton Company). Lesser continued his interests in Marianna—the bank and a mercantile company—for many years.[96] (See chapter 7 for more data on the Lesser-Goldman Cotton Company.) Harry Yoffe had a dry goods store at Marianna around the turn of the century.[97]

HELENA

The town of Helena, located on the Mississippi River about seventy-five miles below Memphis, Tennessee, sits advantageously on the lower end of Crowley's Ridge, making it an ideal location for development. The county seat of Phillips County, Helena was incorporated in 1833.[98] Farming was the all-important occupation of the county, and almost everyone was or became involved with it. Professionals and businessmen generally became farmers as well.[99] Use of the land for farming was enhanced when the construction of levees began after 1851.[100] The town was taken by Federal troops early in the Civil War and suffered little damage.[101] The town thrived, shipping cotton from its rich farming lands and timber from nearby forests; steamboats plying the Mississippi between Memphis and New Orleans stopped often.[102]

Although only a few Jewish pioneers settled in Helena before the Civil War, a number came during and shortly after the conflict and began opening stores and businesses (see sections I and II). These included Aaron Meyers, Moses Solomon, Selig Goldsmith, Henry Fink, and the Trieber family. In the 1860s Aaron Meyers (1841–1914) and his wife, Johanna (Potsdamer), established a successful wholesale and retail grocery firm. Aaron became active in civic affairs and was elected city marshal, city tax collector, mayor, and city treasurer. He also served as secretary of the Helena School Board and was treasurer and a stockholder in the Helena Grand Opera House.[103] Meyers' brother-in-law, Moses Levi Solomon (1835–1895), and his wife, Pauline (Potsdamer) Solomon, also settled in Helena in the 1860s. The Solomons were generous to the needy of all races, and when Pauline Solomon died in 1903, the family established in her memory a playground located on Market Street. The family later donated a plot in north Helena for a black playground.[104]

Moses and Pauline Solomon had eight children, all but one of whom were self-taught with minimal formal education. Henry R. Solomon (1883–1947), Moses Solomon's youngest son and the only one to attend college, settled at Memphis, where he was in the shoe business.[105] The other Solomon sons were Joseph, Phillip, Louis, David, and Lafe, and these men played important roles in the history of Phillips County. Joseph (1869–1927) began clerking at age nine to help support the family, and in 1895 he, his brother Lafe (1879–1949), and a partner formed the Solomon-Johnson Grocery Company. Joseph acquired interest in the Lesser-Goldman Cotton Company in 1902, and thereafter became the kingpin of the cotton trade in the Helena area. He bought a number of farms, and he and the local Straub family built the first concrete highway from Helena to the Mississippi River crossing; it was known as the Solomon-Straub Pike. He built a five-story "skyscraper" office building, the "finest in the state outside of Little Rock."[106] It was said that Joseph Solomon contributed more toward the commercial prosperity of Helena than any other one man.[107] The Solomon-Johnson Grocery Company was succeeded by the Solomon and Altman Dry Goods firm. Phillip Solomon (1871–1930), with partner John Ware, established a department store that became the largest in Helena; Phillip also owned a shoe store.[108] Louis Solomon (1873–1926) was a member of the Security Bank and Trust Company and served in the Helena Light Guards.[109] David Solomon Sr. (1875–1952) was associated with the Ware and Solomon department store and was also a successful farmer known as one of the county's largest shippers of spinach. Civic-minded, as were his brothers, David served on the Helena School Board for many years. (During the days of the KKK, a Klan-backed candidate ran against David unsuccessfully.)[110] Brothers Lafe and David, together with Sam Ciener, founded the Helena Dry Goods Company, which supplied merchants from as far as three hundred miles away.[111] Lafe was elected a director of the Helena Improvement District, an organization for building and maintaining levees. The Moses Solomon daughters were Mrs. Meyer (Ella) Cook (1868–1922), who was active on the Helena Hospital Board, and Mrs. Louis (Sarah) Shapira (1877–1947), whose husband was a partner with David Solomon Sr. in the clothing store, The Leader.[112] Joseph Solomon's daughter Myrtle married Irving A. Metz, who had first settled at Wynne. Irving worked with the Solomon enterprises in Helena until the 1930s, when he and his family moved to Memphis.[113]

Selig Goldsmith (1843–1916) settled in the Helena area in the 1860s and established a general mercantile store. The family entered the cotton trade, and Selig's son Milton W. "Pete" (1899–1949), who owned and operated extensive farming interests, became one of the best-known cotton factors in the mid-South and a leading cotton factor in Arkansas. He was a director of the Helena Terminal and Warehouse Company, the Helena Cotton Oil Mill, and the Helena National Bank.[114] Abe Goldsmith, who owned a general merchandise store, also was involved in the cotton trade.[115]

The Grauman's were cotton men as well. Harry Grauman (1867–1948) first had a store at Marvell (about fifteen miles west of Helena) then opened a cotton business in Helena in 1909. Edward Grauman (1896–1948) became a senior member of the Grauman Cotton Company, which owned and operated extensive farm lands. Edward became known as one of the "best authorities on cotton in Eastern Arkansas."[116] Dave Grauman (1871–1963) became a well-known Helena pharmacist.

Henry Fink (1833–1896) settled in Helena in 1862 and developed a large, successful mercantile business. His two older sons, Morris and Isidor (1860–1923), later joined the Fink enterprise, and part of its proceeds were used to educate the two younger brothers, Jacob and Montague. Jacob (1862–1923), a graduate of the University of Virginia Law School, became a Helena attorney, serving as police judge, mayor, and school board member. He was especially cited for his faithfulness on the school board; it was during his association with it that the schools saw tremendous growth.[117] Montague Fink (1866–1957), a graduate of the University of Virginia Medical School, was a general practitioner in Helena and became an authority on the treatment of tuberculosis. He served as president of the Phillips County Medical Society and was one of five men in 1903 to sponsor a successful bill requiring state licenses rather than county licenses for physicians. He served as the first health officer of Phillips County. As president of the city's Board of Health in the year 1905–06, he helped persuade Helena to replace its system of dumping sewage in the Mississippi River.[118]

Jacob Trieber (1853–1927), an 1860s settler in Helena, became one of the most noted men of Arkansas, Jewish or non-Jewish, in the judicial field. In 1900 he was appointed by President William McKinley as a federal judge and thus became the first Jewish person in America to hold such a position. He became known nationwide for his judicial abilities and astuteness at law. Born at Raschkow, near Breslau, Germany, and educated in the gymnasium there until the age of thirteen, he emigrated with his parents, Morris (1814–1898) and Blume (1812–1885, daughter of Rabbi David Brodeck) Trieber, to St. Louis. The Triebers settled at Helena in 1868, where Jacob began his career as a bookkeeper in a mercantile house. He studied law under Judge M. L. Stephenson of Helena, a former justice of the Arkansas Supreme Court. Trieber helped organize the First National Bank of Helena in 1887, serving as its president from 1893 to 1897. (He became proficient in banking law and in 1913 was a moving force in the establishment of a state banking law.)[119] He was elected to Helena's city council in 1882, was named superintendent of the state census in 1890, elected treasurer of Phillips County in 1892, and was appointed as U.S. district attorney for the Eastern District of Arkansas in 1897.

Trieber's appointment in 1900 to a federal judgeship was "a miracle of no small proportions," considering he was an immigrant with a heavy

German accent, of modest means, with no formal college or law school training, and from a small town in rural Arkansas.[120] This rather short man (five feet four inches), a staunch Republican, proved his worth. Many of the cases that he presided over as a federal judge stemmed from problems with the railroads, racial prejudice, and bootlegging. Having come from a childhood in which he saw firsthand the results of racism and intolerance, he had compassion for peoples of all races and creeds. He was touched by the tragic lynching of blacks in Arkansas and the rest of the South, and he disapproved of the job discrimination posed against black people by Caucasians. Trieber's several innovative interpretations of the law regarding civil rights included the first decision holding that blacks were entitled to equal employment opportunities. His noted opinion in *United States v. Morris* stated that he believed Congress had the power to protect citizens' rights "to lease lands and to accept employment for hire . . ." regardless of race or color; he saw it as "indisputable" that such protection was a fundamental, inherent right for all free citizens.[121] His ruling in *United States v. Hodges* against job discrimination was overturned by the United States Supreme Court in 1906.[122] For sixty-two years after Judge Trieber's ruling was overturned, prejudice was condoned, which allowed for the rise of the Ku Klux Klan and years of hardship and suppression for blacks. It was not until 1968 that Judge Trieber's rulings were vindicated and his reasoning in *United States v. Morris* upheld.[123] Other rulings of Trieber with latter-day results were those regarding the regulatory rights of Congress that helped establish present-day migratory bird laws.[124]

Judge Trieber served as Masonic Grand Master of Arkansas and as president of the Arkansas Bar Association. He married Ida Schradski, and they had two children. Known for his lucid, concise opinions and the ability to clear dockets quickly, he was invited to New York in 1927 at the suggestion of Chief Justice William Howard Taft to help ease the congested docket of the federal courts there. He died while in New York. Judge Trieber, a devout follower of the ethics found in Judaism, was noted to have said that he would give stiffer fines or sentences to any Jew convicted in his court because they knew, or should know, he said, right living as found in their religion.[125]

A number of the early Jewish settlers became involved in Helena's political life. Besides those noted above, others included Isaac Ehrman, Leo J. Mundt, and Eli Newman. Ehrman (1836–1917) settled at Helena in the early 1870s and established a wholesale and retail liquor firm. Civicminded, he served as a city alderman and was a stockholder in the People's Savings Bank and the city's Grand Opera House and Fair Association.[126]

Leo Mundt, a lawyer, served as a municipal judge in Helena. His father, Isadore Mundt (1838–1918), had come to Helena in the 1860s and established a wholesale dry goods business. Isadore's other sons, Seelig (1876–1939) and Hugo (1878–1934), established one of Helena's largest general stores.[127] Seelig served as secretary of the Helena Retail Merchants Association and helped the organization in staging some of the largest trade events ever held in the city.[128] He held several other prominent positions. The Mundts married into the Seelig family of Helena. Simon Seelig had begun as a struggling Helena merchant in 1865 but built up a "great reputation" and business in a few years.[129] He was joined by family members Edward Seelig (1845–1881) and Baruch Seelig (1856–1928). Simon accumulated large land holdings, and a community known as Seelig sprang up near Helena. (Simon Seelig and his wife had no children, and they adopted Major Mundt, giving the child the Seelig name. Major Seelig was a graduate of Harvard Medical School and was affiliated with the Washington University School of Medicine in St. Louis.)[130]

Eli Newman (1868–1922), son of Helena's 1862 pioneer Meyer Newman (1838–1899), served as a member of the city council. Known throughout Eastern Arkansas as one of the "most popular" of Helena's sons, he was manager of the Rex Theater and the Grand Opera House.[131] The Newmans headed the Newman Coal Company, Helena Bill Posting Company, and Newman Steam Bottling Works.

Some of Helena's Jewish businessmen who began as peddlers in the area included Edward Sonfield (1854–1927), who first came to Phillips County in 1870, then later established successful general stores at Trenton, Marvell, Holly Grove, and Poplar Grove, as well as at Helena.[132] After beginning as a foot merchant, Albert Ball (1852–1928) established his own business and became "prominent in all circles" of Helen's civic and business life.[133] Samuel Bender (1840–1892) saved his earnings and opened a store in Helena in the mid-1860s. One of his clerks was Mace Lieber, who, with his brothers, Isadore (1850–1909), Eli, and Nathan, established Lieber Brothers dry goods firm. Eli and Nathan moved to Knoxville, and Mace and Isadore built up what was called "Helena's most progressive dry goods establishment" by the turn of the century.[134] Ike Mannheimer (1856–1930) and Louis Kahn (1862–1926) came to Helena in the early 1880s, built up a trade, and became partners in the Garner Stave Company out of Marvell.[135] Mosler Kahn (1891–1956), son of Louis and Nellie (Grauman) Kahn, had a clothing business in Helena and accumulated large real estate holdings countywide.[136] B. M. Isaacs (1858–1921) came to Helena in the 1880s, established a business, and became a prominent merchant. He was joined later by his son, Mortimer (1886–1949).[137]

Not all peddlers succeeded, and some, such as Solomon Silverstein and Louis Weinlaub, met tragic fates. Silverstein was "brutally murdered" as he peddled near Poplar Grove in June 1881.[138] Silverstein left a wife and eight children, who were cared for by the Jewish fraternal organization, B'nai B'rith. Louis Weinlaub (1859–1895) drowned when he sank in the Mississippi River in 1895 with his pack on his back.[139] His brother, Herman Weinlaub (1827–1896), who had settled in Helena in the early 1870s, established a successful business there.[140]

By 1880 the business life of Helena was flourishing, and it was said to be conducted "principally by the Israelites."[141] Some of the other Jewish businessmen of the town included Isadore Rothschild (1874–1949) and his partner Jacob Jiedel, co-owners of the Jiedel and Rothschild dry goods firm. The firm continued until 1937. (Jiedel had come from Germany with his sister Eva and brothers Raphael, Siegbert, and Richard; the latter two settled at Blytheville.)[142] Harry Barnett (1876–1948) established Barnett's Ready-to-Wear, and David A. Halpern (1865–1931) joined Isidor Fink in the Fink and Halpern dry goods company. Halpern bought out Fink in 1914 and ran the firm under the name "D. A. Halpern" until the business closed in 1930.[143] The Levy brothers, Emanuel (1859–1939), David (1860–1946), and Silas (1860–1942), had grocery and liquor stores. Zollie Brush (1869–1957), who was brought to Helena as a child by his parents, later opened a livery stable and became known as the "best mule dealer in Phillips County."[144]

By 1909 there were at least twenty-two Jewish businesses in Helena, most of which had one or more partners in the firms. Several Jews were involved in Helena banks by 1914, including Aaron Meyers, B. Seelig, J. L. Solomon, and Louis Solomon. Edgar Bacharach and Leonard Kern established a clothing store in Helena in 1919, and Raphael Jiedel was manager of Helena's Grand Opera House in the 1920s.[145]

The Jews of Helena found it to be a safe, comfortable home. They were, for the most part, well accepted and became prominent in almost every walk of life. Their efforts did not go unappreciated. For example, when Edward D. Weil (1866–1934) came to Helena, he was associated with the successful Seelig Dry Goods Company and married Vera Mundt, twin sister of Judge Leo Mundt. When Weil died in 1934, it was said of him that he had "no superior in energy and ability in the mercantile business . . . [he] had no enemies, but had friends from all classes—white, colored, rich, and poor. He did not seek the limelight, but where true value is valued, his name will be long remembered."[146] Alvin Solomon, whose father, Sam Solomon (1865–1912), came to Helena as a tailor around 1900, viewed the Helena community as an "outstanding example of good relationships among the various religions."[147] Jews were accepted as members of the local country club when it was established in 1916, and some served as its president at various times. Solomon noted that there was a certain amount of prejudice in every community (for example, in Helena, Jews were not allowed in the city's high school fraternities or sororities) but felt that Helena was "one of the bright spots" in having so little prejudice.[148]

Growing up as Jewish in Helena was viewed as a pleasant experience according to Leslie Mundt, who became a prominent New Orleans dermatologist. He remembered his life in Helena as a happy time. The family prospered until it could afford three or four servants, an automobile (with a private gas tank in the back yard), and a chauffeur. He remembered no anti-Jewish prejudice except the hurt of not being allowed into high school fraternities.[149] The Jewish youth of Helena enjoyed barge parties on the Mississippi River. On one such event, during which the group went as far as the mouth of the St. Francis River on the steamer *Grace Velie*, they were chaperoned by the Sam Solomons, Eli Newmans, and Albert Newmans. Parties were also given at the Jewish-owned Lotus Club.[150]

MARVELL

About fifteen miles west of Helena, German-born Adolph Hirsch established a store in the community of Marvell, which had begun as a small village shortly after the Civil War. He established an immediate rapport with the local community when, after building his store, he hosted a dance before putting in fixtures or merchandise.[151] Adolph, said to be a "born merchant" of boundless energy who had "fine business acumen," often allowed his clerks to become business partners, and his firm became the parent company of several others that sprang up in the area.[152] The Hirsch firm grew until it was doing an "immense" business and began buying up valuable land.[153] Adolph brought from Germany family members, including his brothers Max and Morris (both of whom died in their twenties) and relatives Edmund Hirsch (1903–1974) and Ludwig Hirsch (1879–1951). (Adolph Hirsch's immediate family did not want to leave Germany, and he eventually returned to be with them; he then came to Arkansas once a year to check on his holdings.) Ludwig came in 1897 and became a member of the Hirsch firm. He bought and operated extensive farm interests in the Marvell area, which was continued by his son Max Hirsch (1915–1979).[154] Edmund Hirsch became a cotton merchant and was a charter member and president of the Marvell Rotary Club.[155] A. Hirsch and Company was cited as being instrumental in extensive land development and real estate improvement in the Marvell area.[156]

TRENTON

Simon Krow (1837–1901) began peddling in the Helena-Marvell area in the 1860s and established a successful mercantile and furnishing store at the little town of Trenton, about five miles from Marvell. He became one of the most prosperous and influential citizens of the Trenton area.[157] In 1869 Simon and a partner, Mr. Neumann, opened a branch store at Marvell, where the men became leaders in the Marvell area.[158] The small community grew to become a banking town, lumber center, and shipping and trading point for the surrounding rich agricultural area.[159] By the 1890s the town had several Jewish-owned stores—those of Hirsch, Krow and Neumann, and S. Goldsmith (1843–1916). It also had a cotton gin, a school, a church, and a doctor. The nearest phone was at Helena, some twenty miles away, and the local population from miles around gathered at the stores to hear the news, such as the beginning and the end of the Spanish-American War. So busy were the stores that a one-dollar fine was imposed for illegally using the hitching posts in front of them.[160] Simon Krow provided a "bachelors' house" for his clerks, and some of these eligible young men married his daughters.[161] Simon's son, Ira (1876–1951), joined his father in the Marvell store and bought farmlands in the Marvell-Trenton area. He and German-born Victor F. Neumann (1868–1941), who became a partner in the firm, moved to Helena in 1922 and ran the Krow and Neumann mercantile firm established there.[162]

Ike Mannheimer (1856–1930), who was associated with the Hirsch firm, was another Jewish businessman who helped build up the Marvell area. He and Frank R. Garner established the Garner Stave Company, which was doing a hundred-thousand-dollar business annually by 1904. Mannheimer, who had business connections in Helena as well, was considered an "outstanding citizen" of Marvell and was said to be a "great factor in the civic organization" of the town. Other Jewish men in the Marvell area included Harry Grauman (1867–1948), who had a furnishing store; I. Maas, who served as postmaster around the turn of the century; and Abraham Hanft (1852–1909) and Morris Hanft (1873–1919), who were associated with the Hirsch firm.[163]

HOLLY GROVE

Monroe County, which lies just west of Phillips County in Eastern Arkansas, was formed in 1829. Named for James Monroe, America's fifth president, the business of the county was first conducted at Lawrenceville.[164] Prussian-born Rudolph Abramson settled in this little town in the 1860s but moved to nearby Holly Grove when that town was incorporated in 1876. He established what became a prosperous furnishing store, and in the 1890s opened a branch store at Maddox Bay.[165] His son Rudolph "Rue" Abramson (1880–1940) continued the family business and became prominent in the area. He was president of the Bank of Holly Grove when it closed in 1932, after which he spent most of his life savings paying off depositors. Cited as "an inobtrusive philanthropist," he became one of the most "highly respected and best loved" citizens of the county.[166]

CLARENDON

In 1856 the county seat of Monroe County had been moved to Clarendon, located on the White River, and the importance of the town as a lumber shipping point grew when the railroads came through, especially when a branch track was laid to Helena and the Mississippi River.[167] It was here in the 1860s that Sol Bondi established a store that grew and flourished, and the Bondi family played "quite an important part in the history and development" of the area.[168] Sol was later joined in the firm by his four sons, Edward, Sam, Ike, and Isadore. Around the turn of the century, two of the sons opened stores in Yell County—Sam at Danville and Isadore "Issie" at Dardanelle. Edward and Ike remained in charge of the Clarendon store until their deaths in the 1940s.[169]

Isaac Halpern (1827–1898) was another pioneer settler in Clarendon; he established what became a successful mercantile business and later branched out into other business interests across eastern Arkansas.[170] A branch of the Bacharach and Kern clothing store of Helena was opened in Clarendon in 1935. The partnership dissolved, and Bacharach retained the Helena store, and Leonard Kern (1895–1976), who married Theresa Jacobs of Batesville, kept the one at Clarendon. Kern's son Leonard Jr. (1925–) continued the family business.[171] Jewish businessmen who had stores at Clarendon after the turn of the century included A. Blacker, J. G. Mayer, Leon Katz, and L. Bernstein; the highly successful Goldman and Company also was located there.[172]

WINCHESTER

The Bavarian-Jewish family of Zeno settled in the eastern Arkansas town of Winchester in Drew County. They came around the turn of the century and were involved in the mercantile business as well as in farming and cattle. Abraham Zeno (1871–1963) was a livestock dealer, and three of his four sons settled in Arkansas—Arnold and Max at McGehee and Norbert at Little Rock.[173]

STAR CITY

Louis Silberstein (1863–1904) migrated from Germany to Fort Smith, where a Baptist minister, Reverend Ross, took him under his wing and cared for him. Louis later converted to Christianity and became a traveling evangelist in his horse and buggy. He founded a church at Dumas and was preaching at Star City (Lincoln County in eastern Arkansas) when he met a local belle, Charley Lyman. They married in July 1903, and two months after their son, Ross, was born in September 1904, Louis died of pneumonia. Silberstein's widow never remarried; she and her son, and later, his family remained in Star City.[174]

ARKANSAS CITY

Desha County, just south of Phillips County, is bordered on the east by the Mississippi River. The county was important in the state's early history because of the prolific river travel. The wild, thriving little town of Napoleon was located here, but it later washed away when the river changed course. The county seat was moved to Arkansas City in 1879, and a number of Jewish stores sprang up there. Most of these early pioneers began as peddlers, and only a few had time to establish businesses before the Civil War began. Some Jews served in the Confederate army, then returned to southeast Arkansas, where both farming and river trade made it an ideal location for business prospects.

One such man, Emanuel Hoover, peddled in southeast Arkansas, beginning in 1856. After serving in the Confederate army, he opened stores in several locations in that section of the state before settling at Arkansas City in Desha County.[175] He married Pauline Cahn, and they had two children, Samuel and Lillie. The latter married Abraham Dreidel, who had clerked in the store of Samuel Marks in Arkansas City. Dreidel joined Samuel Hoover in the Hoover confectionary firm, together with

Henry Townsend (who served as Desha County judge and sheriff). Their firm was highly successful, and they opened branches in Dermott and Warren. They also branched out into real estate.[176] Dreidel served as mayor of Arkansas City in the years 1901–05 and later in the years 1910–11; he also served as city marshal. He was the first Jew to serve as a state senator, being appointed by Governor Jeff Davis in 1907 to fill the unexpired term of Senator Howard Robb of the Seventeenth Senatorial District.[177]

MCGEHEE

As river traffic lessened and the railroads proliferated, the nearby railroad town of McGehee began to grow after the turn of the century.[178] After the devastating flood of 1927, much of the business life of Arkansas City moved to McGehee. Samuel Friedman (1848–1916) was one of the early McGehee settlers; he conducted a mercantile store there and was later joined in it by his son Isadore.[179] Bavarian native William "Bill" Hamburger (1889–1984) came to America as a youth and began peddling in Oklahoma. He went into horse-trading as well, and after making a business trip to McGehee, he liked it so well that he returned to stay. He sold cattle and horses, began buying land, and dealt in cotton and built a gin.[180] Bill Hamburger was joined in McGehee by his brother Adolph (1887–1964). Their brother Henry (1892–1966) and his family were brought from Germany during the 1930s after the rise of Adolph Hitler.[181]

Leopold Pfeifer Dreyfus (1866–1942), who came from Germany to Arkansas at age fifteen, was a Little Rock merchant. In 1927 he went to McGehee and established the Dreyfus Company that dealt in hides, furs, pecans, and junk. Leopold's son Martin (1908–1975) continued the firm and built it into a large grain company. Martin was a charter member of the McGehee Lions Club and served as its president; he was also a member of the Arkansas Seed Dealers Association. He married Rosa Belle Yout of Little Rock, and their son Lewis continued the Dreyfus firm. Both Martin and Lewis served in the military.[182]

GRAND LAKE, EUDORA

Chicot County, located in the southeasternmost corner of the state and bordering on the Mississippi River, is one of the state's most fertile sections. Drawn by the natural business advantages of the area, Jewish pioneers began trading there by the late 1840s, and at least twenty were doing business in the county by 1860. (see section I) Most came as peddlers, as did Adolph Meyer (1845–1928), who came virtually penniless as a lad to America and began selling wares all over the delta area of Louisiana, Mississippi, Tennessee, and Arkansas. He bought and sold junk up and down the Mississippi River and saved enough to open a mercantile store at Grand Lake, Arkansas, with his nephew, Isaac Dreyfus.[183] At Grand Lake, Adolph established Cariolla Landing, which became one of the largest shipping points south of Helena on the Mississippi River. (Adolph named the Cariolla Landing after his wife, Carrie, and the wife [Ola] of his partner, Peter H. Ford.)[184]

As river traffic lessened, however, and rail lines were laid in the 1890s, the nearby railroad town of Eudora began to thrive, and Adolph Meyer moved his store there after 1900. (In 1911 the state legislature made one large drainage district of Chicot County, thereby laying the foundation for making about a hundred thousand acres available for agriculture.)[185] Adolph's customers were drawn from a wide area; for many years the roads were so bad that he provided a camp house where the travelers and their wagons could spend the night.[186] Adolph began buying property and at one time owned thirty thousand acres of farm land, plus town property and holdings in Missouri.[187] Adolph and his wife and younger children moved to St. Louis in 1905, leaving the older sons in Eudora to care for the family business—Meyer, Son and Company Merchants and Planters. Adolph's son Reynold H. Meyer (1884–?) built a home at nearby Readland and served as mayor and postmaster. He later served thirty years on the Eudora School Board. For more than half a century, R. H. Meyer was part of "every worthwhile movement" of the area.[188] He served for twelve years as president of the First National Bank of Lake Village, which he helped to organize, and as vice-president of the First National Bank of Eudora.

Alvin Meyer Sr. (1908–1988), son of Reynold Meyer, was civic minded like his father and grandfather, serving as president of the Eudora School Board for a number of years and as president of the Eudora bank. Alvin said that he experienced some anti-Semitism, having heard people say "That damn Jew," but he tossed it aside as ignorance.[189] Carroll Meyer (1897–1988), Adolph's youngest son, worked for Burdolph Meyer at Sikeston, Missouri, and returned to Eudora in 1928, opening the M and W store with partner Ewell Weinberg of Osceola. Carroll, who also farmed, served on the Eudora City Council for eighteen years. (Carroll later shortened the spelling of his first name to Carrol.) Adolph Meyer's sister Lena married Ben Sandstein, and they had a store at Gould in Lincoln County, where they raised their two sons.[190]

The Weiss brothers, Herman and Ferdinand, and their brother-in-law, Abe Kahn, were three of the first mercantile merchants at Grand Lake (they later moved their store, H. Weiss and Co., to nearby Eudora). Kahn (who came to be known locally as "Uncle Abe") was Eudora's first elected recorder. Other early Jewish settlers of the Eudora area included Mrs. Ernestine Friedlander, who served as postmaster of the town in the 1890s. Another Friedlander, who owned a store south of Eudora, was killed when a tornado hit the area in 1892. M. B. Block and M. Schwartz had stores at Eudora after the turn of the century. Block was the first to erect a store building on Eudora's Main Street. His sister, Lizzie Block, was the first teacher in Eudora's first school. Schwartz served as city recorder and was commissioner of the district when water and sewerage systems were initially implemented in Eudora; he also served as president of the First National Bank of Eudora. Schwartz's brother-in-law, B. Abrams, erected Eudora's third brick building. A. Feibelman served as vice-president of both the First National Bank of Eudora and the Merchants and Planters Bank, and A. A. Fischel served as secretary of the latter. Sol Levy also had a dry goods business at Eudora and erected a new brick building for his store in 1916.[191]

Jacob Rexinger (1866–1948) came from Germany to Eudora in 1904 to work for A. Feibelman. He married Theresia Strauss of Tupelo, Mississippi, and they became involved in the religious and civic life of Eudora. He was lay leader of a congregation he helped organize (see section II) and served on the city council, school board, and other civic organizations. Theresia helped organize a School Improvement Association. Jacob later ran the Rex Hotel at Eudora, then opened a furniture store. During the 1930s, the Rexingers helped bring from Germany members of Jacob's family, Louis and Edwin Rhein, and their sister and her family, the Edward Strausses. The Rhein and Strauss families later settled at Little Rock.[192]

DERMOTT

Dermott, located in northern Chicot County and situated in a higher, timbered area, became the metropolis of the county when two lines of the Missouri-Pacific System formed a junction there.[193] The Iron Mountain Railway came through the area in the 1880s, and the town of Dermott was incorporated in July 1890.[194] Ben Kimpel, who had begun as a peddler there in the 1870s, established one of the town's first general mercantile stores.[195] Ben's brother, Dave Kimpel (1856–1929), came to Arkansas from Germany in 1878 with no material goods and began his career as a peddler. He became "outstanding" in the community, having used his "industriousness, initiative, persistence, and good business acumen" to gradually accumulate extensive farming and mercantile interests.[196] His business interests included being a senior partner of Kimpel and Bynum, general merchants, and Kimpel and Lephiew, ginners and cotton buyers. In the 1890s he served as the second mayor of the town; he also served as an officer in the Bank of Dermott and as a director of the Dermott Grocery and Commission Company. Kimpel held a special regard and respect for the blacks of the Dermott area, and they considered him their friend and benefactor.[197] Dave married Beulah Godwin, a Methodist, and they had four children. Daughter Bertha married Bert Shafsky, who managed Dave's Dermott drug store. The three other children, Ben, Lenora, and Ernest, married non-Jews.[198]

DUMAS

The town of Dumas, located in the northeast corner of Desha County, was not established until the 1880s. Before that time the area flooded each year and settlement was not practical. Gustave "Gus" Waterman (1848–1918) migrated from Germany to the area in the late 1870s and became one of its first settlers. He established a mercantile store and started clearing swampland and building levees. He served as postmaster of the community from 1882 to 1887. He was called the "Father of Dumas" and served as the town's first mayor when it was incorporated in 1904.[199] He also served as chairman of the Linwood and Auburn Levee Board and as a member of the Southeast Arkansas Levee District. He became one of the most prominent businessmen and planters in southeast Arkansas. Gus married Rachel Ulman of Memphis, and they had three sons and three daughters. Three of their children died young; a daughter, Jessie, married Morris Herrman of Memphis. Their son Lawrence (1889–1948) was a lifelong Dumas citizen and businessman, and another son, Julian (1891–1943), became the first dean of the University of Arkansas Law School at Fayetteville in 1924. (see chapter 9.)[200]

PINE BLUFF

Pine Bluff, Jefferson County, was incorporated as a town in 1846, and by 1860 the population had reached 1,396. Although no fierce fighting took place in Pine Bluff during the Civil War, the conflict badly hurt the town. It rebounded quickly, however, and improved means of transportation to the fertile agriculture and timbered area during the 1870s to 1890s brought about a remarkable increase in population, which stood at 11,496 by 1900.[201] Immediately after the Civil War, it took farsighted men to envision what Pine Bluff could become, considering its depressed economy, rutted dirt streets, frame buildings, and low-lying lands that tended to flood in the spring. Among those visionaries who helped develop the town were a number of Jewish merchants who had settled there prior to the early 1860s. These included, among others, Isaac Altschul, Max and Charles Weil, Sol and Sam Franklin, several members of the Bluthenthal family, Gabe Meyer, David Aschaffenberg, and John Bloom.

Bavarian–born Isaac Altschul (1825–1898), who had conducted a store on the Arkansas River in Jefferson County during the 1850s and 1860s (see section I), moved his business to Pine Bluff after the war, where he became a successful merchant.[202] He brought several other members of the Altschul family to the area, including Samuel (1816–1878), Solomon (1824–1910), and Adolph (1841–1901). Samuel and his son F. Morris (1851–1933) established what became a large retail and wholesale tobacco and candy business.[203] Solomon opened a store at Hampton in Calhoun County and remained there. His son Joseph (1845–1923) opened the first confectionary store in Pine Bluff in 1868 and handled fancy groceries, tobacco, toys, and sporting goods. Joseph was succeeded in the business by his son Bertrand (1877–1917) and his son-in-law, C. A. Parker (1881–1939).[204] Adolph Altschul was a Pine Bluff merchant, who, to the family's consternation, married a light-skinned mulatto, by whom he had five children.[205] A number of the Altschul family settled in Pine Bluff and became a vital part of the business and civic community. Charles Altschul (1859–1922) served as vice-president of the Citizens Mortgage and Security Company.[206]

After the Civil War, Max Weil (1829–1908) continued the bakery he had established in the 1850s (see section I). It had been the first shop of its kind in Jefferson County before the war, and as late as 1896 it was said that Weil's bakery goods were the finest in the city.[207] Max's brother Charles (1840–1914), who had joined him in the bakery business prior to 1865, opened a furnishing store after the war. His "honest dealings" enabled him to build up an extensive trade with farmers.[208] Charles was elected to the Pine Bluff City Council, serving for twenty years and, on occasion, serving as acting mayor. Becoming affectionately known as "Uncle Charlie," he was cited for his charity and for his efforts in building up the city. He was vice-president of the Cotton Belt Savings Bank and Trust Company and a director of the Merchants and Planters Bank. It was said that his name was synonymous with "uprightness, kindness, devotion to duty and to the principles of right."[209] Charles had nine children, five of whom were sons, and four—Sidney (1874–1943), Ben (1883–1927), Dave

(1889–1965), and Henry—joined him in his firm. (Charles Weil's first wife, Sarah Hart [1852–1871], died after giving birth to their first child, daughter May [1870–1953]. At the time, when a wife died, the widower often married the late wife's sister. Charles married Sarah's sister Amelia, and they had eight children.) Charles's son Ben also served on the city council, and Charles's daughter, May, married Alexander "Alex" Strauss (1862–1932), who founded a cotton company in Pine Bluff and was active in it for fifty years. Alex Strauss served as president of the Pine Bluff Cotton Exchange. (Strauss was killed in a fire that destroyed his home in 1932.[210] His descendants became prominent Little Rock physicians.)

Solomon "Col. Sol" Franklin (1827–1895), who had settled at Arkansas Post in 1842 and worked as a blacksmith, relocated to Noble Lake below Pine Bluff after the Civil War. He bought two steamers, the *Juliet* (renaming it *Goldina*, after his wife) and, later the *Miami*. Both steamers sank, the latter from a boiler explosion that killed sixty people and almost took Sol's life as well.[211] Leaving the steamer business, he established a plantation at Noble Lake and built a cotton gin, to which he attached the whistle of the steamer *Rosa Miller*. (A local paper noted that, if he couldn't run a whole steamboat, "he must have part of one.")[212] Sol became one of the largest cotton planters in the state, having as much as twenty-four hundred acres under cultivation. He was interested in politics and was a delegate to the Second Democratic Congressional Convention in 1872.[213]

In 1872 Sol Franklin offered to help settle two hundred of his "unfortunate brethren" of Rumania on his then fifteen-hundred-acre farm. He offered to provide all necessary accoutrements—cleared land, houses, etc.—free of charge, and he would let them work on half shares of any produce, or they could work for regular wages of fifty dollars a month for three years. The editors of *The Jewish Times*, in which Sol Franklin's letter was published, had misgivings about his offer. Not knowing the latter's magnanimous character—that he would not take advantage of any man—they perceived that he only wanted the emigrés for his personal service. His proposal was given serious attention at first by the noted French-Jewish statesman, Adolphe Cremieux, who promoted the welfare of Jews worldwide.[214] Sol Franklin was known for his lavish generosity to friends and the needy. When the prosperous tide of business took a downturn in the 1890s, businessmen in the Pine Bluff area were sorely affected, including Isaac Altschul, Joseph Altheimer, and the Franklins, Sol and Sam.[215] Sol died of heart failure the day his beloved plantation was sold to satisfy a fifty-six-thousand-dollar debt. Described as a "soul of honor," he left behind "an untarnished name."[216]

Sol and Goldina (Hilzheim) Franklin had ten children. Some of their offspring remained in the Pine Bluff–Little Rock area and became well known. David L. Franklin (1863–1919), who married Charles Weil's daughter Sarah, became a leading figure in the commercial life of Pine Bluff, heading the Gould-Galbraith Supply Company of the city. David's son James Gould Franklin (1906–1946) was a graduate of the Washington University School of Architecture in St. Louis and became a well-known Pine Bluff architect. He worked with the Pine Bluff Arsenal's drafting department of engineering services during World War II.[217] Another of Sol's sons, Benjamin (1875–1937), had a steam laundry in Pine Bluff, and later, one at Little Rock. After moving to Little Rock, he served as a deputy sheriff and was a dedicated supporter of the Little Rock Travelers baseball club.[218] Sol's son James (1868–1921) married Minnie Siesel of Little Rock and became owner of the M. J. Siesel Company (see chapter 7). Sol's daughters married into the Prousnitzer, Cook, Eisenman, and Weiler families.

Sol Franklin's brother, Samuel (called variously "Colonel" Sam or "Captain" Sam) (1836–1893), who had followed Sol to America in 1852, served in the Confederate army and then settled at Pine Bluff. He returned penniless as a veteran, but with an "iron will to succeed," he soon prospered.[219] He bought and sold the well-known Spadra coal of Johnson County and established a sawmill just east of Pine Bluff. He, together with W. B. Ragland and M. L. Bell, established the Pine Bluff Gas Works and laid gas pipes up Barraque Street. (Coal was used to make the gas used in homes, businesses, and street lamps.)[220] Sam Franklin erected one of the first cotton oil mills in the South and became known as a leading financier of the area.[221] He was known as a gifted writer and orator; in 1880 he served as president of the Hancock and English Club of Pine Bluff, an organization that encouraged harmony between the races and included black members.[222] As was his brother Sol, Sam was interested in politics and ran (unsuccessfully) as a state representative in 1876.[223] He too suffered severe financial losses in the 1890s, but it was said that even during this hardship, he continued to help others.[224] Sam and his wife, Rebecca, were childless.

Members of Goldina (Hilzheim) Franklin's family settled at Noble Lake for a time. These included her parents, Samuel Hilzeim and his wife, Henrietta, and Goldina's eight siblings, which included only one brother. Her sisters married into local Pine Bluff families—Altschul, Weiler, Cook, Nathan, Jacobson, and Walloch—and her brother, Sam F. (1851–1926), had a varied career. After being educated at Georgetown University, he returned to the state during the Brooks-Baxter War. He joined Gen. King White's "rough riders" and was promoted to captain. He then joined the Garland Greys, a crack military outfit, where he rose to the rank of major (although he preferred being called "captain.")[225] He was described as a handsome, dashing fellow in his uniform, and he became known for his "irreproachable" character.[226] After serving in the military, he was manager of the Pine Bluff Opera House and the Arkansas River Packet Company. In the 1890s he served in the state legislature, where he was placed on the committee on railroads, cities, and towns. He sponsored several successful bills, one of which added Thanksgiving, New Year's Day, and Washington's Birthday to the list of legal holidays in the state. (He was known for his humor as well: he introduced a bill against wearing high hats in theaters.) At one time, when a House member made a derisive remark about Jews, Sam gave a "stinging and eloquent rebuke."[227]

Members of the Bluthenthal family also were in the Pine Bluff area in the 1850s. Samuel Bluthenthal (1833–1917), born in Munchweiler an der Alsenz which is now in Rheinland-Pfalz but was then in Bavaria, to Henry and Marmel "Amalie" (Rothschild) Bluthenthal, came to Arkansas and began as a foot merchant in the Princeton and Lanark areas southwest of Pine Bluff. He accumulated two horses and a wagon and became known as a "wandering Jew peddler," going from house to house. He established a store at Princeton in Dallas County and began inviting relatives to join him. His brother David M. (1842–1915) came penniless at age thirteen to join him. Both Samuel and David M. served in the Civil War; the former was both captured and wounded. The war ruined their business, and after the conflict, the family settled at Pine Bluff, where Samuel opened the S. Bluthenthal and Company mercantile store. It was rated as a "very respectable" firm by 1878.[228] As the firm grew to be a large enterprise, it included the business of cotton factorage.

David M. Bluthenthal was one of five men who founded the Citizens' Bank of Pine Bluff. He was a "genial, jovial man of strict integrity," and it was said that few men were more prominently connected with Pine Bluff's early life than he was.[229] Other family members joined them, including David S. Bluthenthal (1836–1908) and his nephew Adolph (1865–1927). The latter, with partner Leo Kastor, in 1892 established what became a prosperous men's clothing store. Another David Bluthenthal (1827–1902) settled in Pine Bluff around 1860 and established the Bluthenthal Hotel, which was said to be "one of the best known hotels for Jewish people in Arkansas." (The three David Bluthenthals were first cousins and were known as "Little Dave," "Long Dave," and "Dicka [Large] Dave.")[230]

Several of the Bluthenthals became some of the city's wealthiest and "most influential" citizens.[231] (Samuel Bluthenthal's daughter Josephine married Rabbi Joseph Kornfeld, who served Pine Bluff's Anshe Emeth Congregation from 1898 to 1904.) Harold E. Bluthenthal (1884–?), son of David M. and Sophie (Simons), was associated with his father's firm and became a community leader. He was also credited with rescuing approximately fifty people marooned on the free bridge at Pine Bluff during the disastrous 1927 flood.[232]

Gabriel "Gabe" Meyer (1834–1917), a pre–Civil War settler at Pine Bluff (see section I), was the first to establish a store on Barraque Street, which became a main business thoroughfare of the city. His mercantile store flourished, and he branched out into land ownership and planting. At one time it was said that he paid more taxes than anyone else in Jefferson County; he owned twenty-one plantations, several of which were among the largest in the state.[233] The epitome of civic mindedness, Gabe became involved in any movement that advanced the growth or development of the community. He served both on the city council and on the school board for some twenty-five years. In the 1860s, during a time when the city lacked funds to pay its teachers, he advanced eight thousand dollars to pay them, then went East to negotiate for the needed total of ten thousand dollars. He was thought of as the father of the Pine Bluff school system, and until 1917 he handled all the land deals for the school system.[234] An elementary school was named for him, and for years after his death, family heirs donated medals of honor to students who excelled at the school. Gabe Meyer also served as a justice of the peace for six years.[235]

Gabe Meyer's daughter Florence married Leo Kastor, who, with partner Adolph Bluthenthal, had established the successful Kastor and Bluthenthal men's clothing store. Leo Kastor (1862–1915) had come from Germany to join his brother Isador at Evanston, Wyoming, in the 1880s, then had gone to Pine Bluff. Isador had first settled at Pocahontas, before moving to Wyoming.[236] Leo became known as one of Pine Bluff's most dependable citizens, seeking to help its growth and development.[237] Dolph "Dolf" Kastor (1893–1988), son of Leo and Florence, was a talented vocalist who studied voice in New York. He became a featured soloist with the Al G. Field Minstrels for twelve years, beginning around 1915. At the performance of the group at the Saenger Theater in Pine Bluff in November 1924, a local newspaper headlined the show's review with, "Dolf Kastor came home yesterday, and brought the Al G. Field Minstrels with him."[238] The rise of the motion picture industry, followed by the Great Depression, spelled doom to such shows, and Dolf returned to Pine Bluff. There he served as floor manager of the Saenger Theater and performed at special functions.

David Aschaffenberg (1831–1890) was another 1850 emigré who came from Germany to Arkansas (see section I). He served in the Confederate army, then settled at Pine Bluff, where he became a successful business-man. He was also civic minded and served as a justice of the peace, on the city council, and as city clerk and recorder. He was frequently visited by his brother Leopold, who had settled in Louisiana and later became one of the largest cotton planters in that state. (Leopold helped pioneer the con-struction of a chain of levees in Louisiana along the Mississippi River.)[239]

Pine Bluff had two Jewish mayors, L. E. Goldsmith and Simon Bloom. Goldsmith (1852–1910) served one term as mayor in the 1890s and declined a second term because of ill health. His term in office was said to have been one of the best recorded, and he was numbered with the city's most constructive mayors. He revolutionized the financial department, which "raised the value of scrip from fifty or sixty to almost par. . . ."[240]

Simon Bloom (1861–?) served as Pine Bluff's mayor from 1913 to 1919. His father, John Bloom (1832–1883), and his Uncle David (1824–1889) had come to the Pine Bluff area in the 1850s as peddler-merchants.[241] Simon began his career as secretary to Congressman Clifton Breckinridge; he later was a commercial agent for the Iron Mountain Railway at Pine Bluff. From 1904 to 1912 Bloom and W. R. Kirby had a business at Varner in Lincoln County, then Simon returned to Pine Bluff, where he was elected mayor and served six years. (When he ran for mayor in 1913, he was opposed by W. D. Boies, who used anti-Semitic tactics in his cam-paign, but Bloom won the race.)[242] After serving just two years as mayor, it was said that Simon Bloom had "accomplished more good with a depleted treasury than any of his predecessors who had money at their com-mand."[243] He added better streets and more improvements than had been known in the city's history prior to that time. He became well known and respected statewide as he worked for an amendment that would give first- and second-class cities and towns in Arkansas the right to issue public improvement bonds.[244] He was considered as a candidate for governor in 1915. When Pine Bluff voted "wet" on alcoholic beverages, Bloom invited Carrie Nation to speak in the city, but local saloon keepers and some busi-nessmen opposed her visit.[245] During World War I Bloom served as a sec-ond lieutenant. He was also a well-known cotton grower, owning some thirty-two hundred acres of cotton land at one time, and he actively pur-sued a cotton-spinning plant for Pine Bluff. He was cited as contributing substantially to the upbuilding and advancing of the city. Simon and his wife, Sophia (Rhine) Bloom, had one son, Sol N., who retained the business at Varner.[246]

E. B. "Buck" Bloom (1865–1938), another of John and Fannie Bloom's sons, was also active in the political life of Pine Bluff. He was elected as city clerk, city treasurer, and county clerk; he also served as secretary of the Pine Bluff Chamber of Commerce. Buck helped in other ways: he promoted a free bridge across the Arkansas River at Pine Bluff, made strong pleas for better city streets and roads, and lobbied the state legislature for the Pine Bluff business community.[247] In 1908 he, with his son Frank R. Bloom, established what became one of the largest independent general insurance agencies in the Southwest. He became known for his lavish generosity and was cited as being one of the most charitable men who ever lived in Pine Bluff: "A barefoot child on a cold day never remained barefoot for long after 'Buck' Bloom saw him . . . and [from him] the hungry received food and medicine . . . "[248]

Other members of the Bloom family settled at Pine Bluff, and these included several Jacob Blooms. Jacob Bloom Sr. (1824–1889) exemplified the perseverence needed to establish a business in the perilous times after the Civil War. He began with a small business in 1866 and subsequently went bankrupt three times before becoming well established.[249] By the time he died (of blood poisoning), he had become an "old and respected" Pine Bluff citizen. Another Jacob Bloom (1833–1900) (who also died of blood poisoning), became one of the city's largest merchants and one of its "most progressive citizens." Jacob Bloom Jr. (1846–1892) operated a meat market and became well known as a "respectable and industrious" citizen.[250]

Aaron Reinach (1822–1895), another Pine Bluff butcher and meat market operator, came to the city before the Civil War. A number of the Reinach family members also settled in Pine Bluff and were involved in various enterprises.[251]

Isaac Dreyfus (1850–1934), who had worked as a youth with his uncle, Adolph Meyer, at Grand Lake, prospered there and opened a store with a partner, C. Baer; they also cleared land worth five thousand dollars.[252] Dreyfus sold out to Baer and moved to Pine Bluff, where he became a "beloved" citizen.[253] The small store he opened at Pine Bluff grew to become a large department store, and by the 1920s he was said to be one of the oldest merchants in continuous service in the area; his slogan was "Your Grandparents Traded Here."[254] Isaac Dreyfus and Charles Weil were two of seven men who formed and became directors of the Merchants and Planters Bank of Pine Bluff.[255] Dreyfus's sons, H. (1885–1930) and David

(1890–1951), continued their father's business. James M. Dreyfus (1838–1905) established a furniture and hide business in Pine Bluff, where he became an influential and respected businessman of the city.[256]

Members of the Rosenberg family settled in Pine Bluff by December 1865. Sol, Simon, Abe (1826–1914), and Felix (1853–1920) had contacts in Philadelphia and New York who helped them get established.[257] Charles Miller and Isaac Wise Miller became partners in the firm, which became Rosenberg, Miller, and Company.[258] It grew to become a furnishing store. Their business fluctuated with the times, and their credit reports stated [seemingly pejoratively] that they dealt mainly with "niggers and transient persons"; they were bankrupt in 1874 but rebounded by 1877.[259] In 1874 Sol Rosenberg lamented in a letter that he had experienced a "good many ups and downs" in his life because he had placed "too much confidence in strangers—particularly commission merchants."[260] Sol said he was, by 1874, a man "broken financially and in spirit." Although he had been thrifty and had made money, he could not hold on to it, he said, but he had learned to associate with men of "honest and sterling" qualities, such as the Altheimer brothers, Louis and Joseph. He made a poignant request, asking that the "one who reads this [letter] first . . . speak often of our names so we are never forgotten in this world . . . " Although Sol and Simon later moved from the Pine Bluff area, Abe and Felix remained. Harry Rosenberg (1882–1936) owned and operated the Pine Bluff Produce and Provision Company, and other Rosenberg family members continued to live in the area.[261]

Morris Hanf (1848–1911) came to Pine Bluff in the late 1860s and opened a fur business; he later added furniture to his stock, and by 1883 the business was noted to be the oldest such store in Pine Bluff.[262] Morris was joined by family members Edward (1844–1900), Isaac (1855–1878), and Dina (1856–1913). They also brought their mother, Eliza (1818–1898), to Pine Bluff. Moses Bernath (1826–1902) and Joseph Bernath (1855–1910) were early settlers of Pine Bluff. Moses' son Henry (1866–1948) was a member of the Southern Ice Company for fifty years.[263] The Hanf and Bernath families were followed by the Silverman family, which came to Pine Bluff in the early 1870s. Frank Silverman (1843–?) was born in Wooster, Ohio, son of Lyon and Mary (Troutman) Silverman. He was well educated and, after serving in the Civil War, migrated to Pine Bluff, where he became editor and owner of the *Jefferson Republican*. He was elected to several offices: county and probate judge in 1876, land commissioner of the Little Rock–Texas road, deputy sheriff, and sheriff and collector of Jefferson County.[264] He married Lizzie Swords and slowly drifted from Judaism. One of his sisters married E. Joseph and another married Leo Pollock of Little Rock.[265] Other Jews who served as elected officials of Pine Bluff included Harry Hanf, Sol Miller, and Henry Nathan, aldermen; Ed Levy, police judge; and Nathan Cook, an undertaker who served four terms as Jefferson County coroner and two terms on the city council.[266]

A number of Jewish-owned businesses sprang up from the 1870s to mid-1880s. Most of these were mercantile stores, and their fortunes fluctuated with the local agricultural economy. The owners persevered and for the most part succeeded. They became respected and influential citizens. These German-born men included the Thalheimer brothers, Sol (1855–1916) and Ben (see chapter 7). They first settled at Fairmont in Prairie County, then came to Pine Bluff in the mid-1880s. At first in the grocery business, they later went into livestock and opened a meat market. Ben moved to Little Rock, but Sol remained in Pine Bluff, where he became one of its "beloved and popular" citizens. Ben's son, Abraham "Abe" (1884–1973), also remained at Pine Bluff, where he dealt in horses and mules.[267]

Other settlers included Jacob Wertheimer (1827–1902), a "highly respected . . . influential" businessman;[268] Gerson May (1831–1894), who came "as a stranger . . . gained the friendship of the community" and died "universally respected";[269] Samuel Friedman (1848–1916), a mercantile owner;[270] Leopold Rosenbaum (1852–1894), who became one of the city's "prominent merchants";[271] Leon Eilbott (1857–1910), a successful merchant at Pine Bluff and Altheimer;[272] Jacob Reinhardt (1852–1902), a sawmill owner and well-known lumberman;[273] Joe K. Krumpner (1859–1912), a well-known junk dealer and grocery store owner; Charles Levi (1881–1918), owner of a men's shoe store; and Meyer Weiler (1846–1910).[274]

August Blum (1846–1900), who had begun his career at Pine Bluff in 1870, almost penniless and with no backing, relied on his "large energy," to succeed. He married Amalia Altheimer, sister of Joseph and Louis, and established the Blum Dry Goods Emporium, which became one of the largest stores of its type in the state. (Blum designed unique displays for his store windows. For example, for an Easter 1890 display, he used a large white cross surrounded by a wreath of flowers; at its base he placed moss, sod, and an artificial hen and chicks. He also had two live white pigeons to perch on the cross "for added attractiveness.")[275] Several early pioneers of Pine Bluff, such as Sam Fies (1841–1919), Henry Fies (1855–1873), and Mose Brown (1846–1916), migrated from Alsace-Lorraine and became prominent businessmen in the city.[276]

Other 1870s–1880s settlers included members of the Silbernagel, Gottlieb, and Oppenheimer families. Sam Silbernagel (1844–1908) migrated to Jefferson County, settled briefly at Dermott, then returned to Pine Bluff. His general mercantile store prospered, and he married Hannah Kimpel of Dermott. Sam became a prominent merchant and was joined in the city by a number of other family members. Morris Silbernagel (1861–1922) opened a general mercantile store in Pine Bluff in 1892 that grew to become the largest of its kind in that section of the state by 1920. He served as founder and president of the Silbernagel Company, Inc., a wholesale grocery firm, and became one of the leading merchants in Southeast Arkansas.[277] Morris's son Dan (1888–1946) served as president of the family business, which had branch offices at Little Rock and Dermott, and its trade area included Central and South Arkansas and Northern Louisiana.[278] Bernard "Ben" Silbernagel (1863–1909) also was a Pine Bluff merchant.

Max Gottlieb (1857–1923), who came from Germany to Pine Bluff in 1883, established a jewelry store that became one of the largest and most attractive mercantile houses in the city. His son Joe (1887–1950) continued the business and became prominent in business circles.[279] J. Oppenheimer was a junk dealer in Pine Bluff in the 1880s.[280]

In 1881 more than thirty Jewish firms were listed in the Pine Bluff city directory.[281] By 1885 the Pine Bluff telephone directory was listing 102 customers, and one-fifth of these were Jewish.[282] Other Jews were drawn to Pine Bluff and opened businesses. These included Solomon "Sol" Solmson; Henry Marx; Ferdinand Baer; the Eisenkramer brothers, Max, William, and Gus; J.B. Simon; Simon Strauss; Samuel Katzenstein; and Jay Levine.

Sol Solmson (1838–1892), whose German-born family had settled at Dyersburg, Tennessee, after the Civil War moved to Pine Bluff during a yellow fever epidemic in the 1880s. Sol became a respected businessman and civic leader, serving as a justice of the peace.[283] He married Henrietta Berlin, and their children became prominent in the Pine Bluff community. Their daughters married into the families of E. B. Bloom, J. C. Schloss, Adolph Bluthenthal, and Henry Fibus. The Solmsons had four sons, Mose Solmson (who moved to St. Louis); Sam Solmson (1873–1962), a Pine Bluff businessman; Harry Solmson (1875–1939), an insurance man of Pine Bluff and Little Rock; and Meyer "Boy" Solmson (1880–1938). Meyer became a reporter for the *Pine Bluff Daily Graphic* at age seventeen and became managing editor of the newspaper at age twenty-one. (In 1901, when Meyer wrote an article about a local citizen, J. E. Simmons, who had left the city owing a number of debts, Simmons sought out Meyer and threatened him. Solmson shot and killed Simmons in self defense.)[284] Meyer built an excellent reputation in journalism in Pine Bluff, and from there he worked with a St. Louis newspaper. He then became managing editor of the *New York Morning Telegraph* and was editor of the theatrical publication, *Variety*. He was a district Tammany leader and became acquainted with noted political leaders of the time; he also was a publicity agent for William Jennings Bryan's presidential campaign. He was later appointed assistant finance officer for the Resettlement Administration for four western states, with headquarters at Berkeley, California.[285]

Henry Marx (1873–1950) came to Pine Bluff as a lad of sixteen, worked for a relative, then opened a men's and boy's clothing store. He also accumulated some twelve hundred acres of cotton land. He served as a director of the Cotton Belt Trust Company and was active in the civic life of the city.[286] Sam Levi (1887–1951) worked with Henry Marx in a clothing store at Texarkana; Levi later worked with the Pine Bluff store.[287]

Ferdinand Baer (1866–1832) was educated in Germany and came to Pine Bluff in 1896, where he engaged in the feed business. He became one of Pine Bluff's most respected citizens.[288]

Max Eisenkramer (1872–1941) migrated from Germany to Pine Bluff at age sixteen. He studied to become a certified public accountant and conducted business in Pine Bluff until he retired in 1933.[289] Max's brothers William (1874–1945) and Gus (1875–1919) also had businesses in Pine Bluff. William had a tailoring shop and clothing store that was continued by his sons Hubert (1912–1973) and Jack.[290]

J. B. Simon (1865–1953) became a prominent member of the Pine Bluff business community, becoming familiarly known as "Uncle Jake." He had a clothing store, which he later sold, and opened a movie theater called the Best Theater.[291] Simon married Carrie Katzenstein, three of whose sisters married prominent Arkansas businessmen: L. E. Goldsmith of Pine Bluff and Gus Blass and Max Heiman of Little Rock.

Simon Strauss (1866–1901), a Pine Bluff native who began his career at age eighteen as a clerk for L. E. Goldsmith, later joined I. W. Miller in the Strauss and Miller store. He then bought the Goldsmith firm.[292]

Samuel Katzenstein (1869–1954) settled in Pine Bluff in the 1880s, worked for the branch of the Gus Blass Company there, then established the Katzenstein Shoe Company, which continued until 1950.[293]

Jay Levine, son of Max Levine, a prominent cotton factor in Louisiana and Texas, joined his father in the cotton business, and on a buying trip to Arkansas, became impressed with the Pine Bluff area. He settled there in

1913 and established a cotton brokerage firm and a trucking company.[294] His brother Sam, an attorney, liked small town life, saw Pine Bluff's potential, and also settled there. (For more data on Sam Levine, see section V.)

Irving Reinberger (1860–1925), son of John Reinberger of Little Rock, was an outstanding attorney in Pine Bluff and El Dorado. In 1892 he moved to Pine Bluff, where he served as deputy prosecuting attorney and then as city attorney. His sons, Maurice (1887–1960) and Charles, became attorneys and joined their father in the firm Reinberger and Reinberger. Maurice began his practice in 1908 after graduating from the University of Arkansas and the Cumberland University School of Law. After serving in the U.S. Army in World War I (he entered as a private and was mustered out as a second lieutenant), he became widely known as a criminal lawyer. Although he believed in capital punishment, he represented more than one hundred alleged criminals who faced the death penalty, and he had only one such conviction. He defended clients in almost all the state's courtrooms, and he drew crowds of spectators wherever he went. One of his most famous cases involved getting light sentences for a group of Chicago hoodlums that had robbed the old People's Bank of Pine Bluff in the "roaring twenties." He served on the State Selective Service Appeal during World War II and as commander of the Hearin-Connelly American Legion Post of Pine Bluff.[295] Irving Reinberger's sons were all professionals: two were certified public accountants— Mannie J. (1902–1984) and Edgar S. (1889–1940), both of whom served terms as president of the Arkansas State Board of Accountancy—and another son was Dr. James Reinberger of Memphis.[296]

ALTHEIMER

Two towns in Southeast Arkansas, Altheimer and Goldman, were named for Jewish settlers, as were the two sawmill towns of Waldstein and Abeles. The town of Altheimer, located ten miles east of Pine Bluff, was created by the efforts of the Altheimer brothers, Joseph (1842–1912) and "Colonel" Louis (1849–1922).[297] A forebear of the Altheimer family had been Don Jose Alvers, who had fled from Spain in the great expulsion under Ferdinand and Isabella in 1492. The family migrated to Altheim, Germany; later, when forced to take a German surname, they chose Altheimer.[298]

Louis Altheimer formed his first impressions of Arkansas in his early youth after reading the travel memoirs of Germany's Frederick Gerstaecker, an early visitor to the state. Coming almost penniless as a boy of fourteen, Louis emigrated to America with his two cousins, Simon (age 15) and

Jake (age 13) Bamberger. (Simon Bamberger eventually settled in Utah and later became governor of the state.)[299] After brief careers in several places—Indiana, Mississippi, and Wyoming—Louis returned to Germany, married Julia Sussholz, and brought her to Arkansas in 1868, accompanied by his brother, Joseph. Confident in the area's future, they opened a mercantile house in Pine Bluff and began buying and developing surrounding land. They cut forests, dug drainage ditches, converted swamps, and developed farmland. In 1886 Louis prevailed upon R. C. Kerens of St. Louis to build a section of the St. Louis, Arkansas and Texas Railroad (Cotton Belt Railroad) to the area where the town of Altheimer was built.[300] Although Arkansas had but one short railroad in the state when the Altheimer brothers came, they lived to see it, as well as Jefferson County, gridded with railroads.

By 1904 the Altheimers had directly or indirectly cleared some twelve thousand acres of land.[301] It was said of Louis in 1904 that he had "cleared more land for agricultural purposes than any man in Arkansas" and had brought hundreds of workers from other states to work his plantations.[302]

Louis Altheimer died in 1922, but one of his sons, Maurice (1872–1937), a graduate of the Washington University School of Law at St. Louis, continued the family enterprises, which, by that time, included a thriving department store in Little Rock, Altheimer Supply Company at Altheimer, a store at Humphrey, and plantations at Altheimer and Pine Bluff.[303] Maurice also served as president of the Twin City Bank of North Little Rock for twenty years. He was known as an advocate and promoter of Arkansas as a place in which to settle.[304] Louis and Joseph brought over a number of relatives from Germany, and, at one time, some sixty members of the Altheimer family lived in the Pine Bluff area.[305] Brothers Gus, Sol, and Leopold "Lee" had joined Louis and Joseph in their early years in Pine Bluff, but they later established a wholesale trade in St. Louis.[306]

Ben J. Altheimer (1878–1946), son of Joseph and Matilda (Josaphat), grew up at Pine Bluff, where he attended the Jordan Academy and then studied law under F. G. Bridges and Judge W. T. Wooldridge. He established the law firm of White and Altheimer, which continued until the Joseph Altheimer family moved to Chicago in 1909. (Joseph made this move after several Arkansas banks failed during the crisis year of 1893 and he lost his holdings over that decade.) Although Ben J. practiced law in Chicago for twenty years, he never forgot his Arkansas roots. After retiring in 1939, he returned to Arkansas and began buying up the land his father had lost so many years before. He accumulated some twenty-five thousand acres of timberland in Louisiana and more than fifteen thousand

acres in Jefferson County.[307] He also remodeled "The Elms," a local plantation home near Altheimer.[308] Ben J., who was said to have resembled
Douglas Fairbanks in appearance, was interested in the hundreds of share-
cropper families that lived on the land he purchased, and he was known to
treat them in a just and considerate way.[309] Prior to his death in 1946, he
established the Ben J. Altheimer Foundation, which continued to benefit
various aspects of Arkansas life, particularly the town of Altheimer as well
as education in Arkansas. He has been remembered as a "real trailblazer" in
agricultural research and development in Arkansas (see section V).[310]

The town of Altheimer itself grew slowly; by 1930 it had a population
of only 475.[311] Around the turn of the century, German-born Jacob Cohn
(1879–1971) had settled at Altheimer and had opened a general store.
Since the town had no utilities until the 1920s, Jacob improvised with a
deep well, a one cylinder gas pump, and a large water tank. With this, he
had running water and flush toilets, much to the curiosity of the local
farmers.[312] After the devastating flood of 1927, bad cotton crops, and the
market crash of 1929, the Cohn family, like many other individual Jewish
store owners in rural Arkansas, were forced to seek livelihoods elsewhere.
(For more information on the town of Altheimer, see section V.)

GOLDMAN

The town of Goldman in Arkansas County was named for Jacob D.
Goldman of St. Louis. Locals called him the "wealthy Jewish railroad man
from St. Louis."[313] He was one of the original directors of the St. Louis
Southwestern Railway Company that went through the town. Over the
years, the origin of the town's name became lost to some of the local
people. A writer for a newspaper in the nearby town of Stuttgart said in
1939 that "We don't know where Goldman got its name . . . Sounds kinda
yiddish, but anyway, it isn't Irish."[314]

WALDSTEIN

When the railroads began to cut through the state's grand virgin forests,
lumber companies established sawmill towns. One of these, Waldstein,
was named for the developer of the area, Jewish settler Joseph Waldstein.[315]
Joseph and his brother had a large sawmill on a spur of the Cotton Belt
Railway. Old-timers of the Waldstein area remembered that a fair-sized
town was established there, with a commissary run by Asa Seymour.[316]
Joseph's sons Victor and Henry operated the family's extensive plantation
property, located in the Linwood section of Jefferson County, and the

Waldstein family was prominent in the business and social life of Southeast Arkansas for a number of years.[317] In nearby Pine Bluff, Joseph's daughter Amanda became one of the "best known women of the community."[318]

ABELES

The small lumber village of Abeles, named for Charles Abeles of Little Rock, was located a few miles southeast of Stuttgart in Arkansas County. Charles owned timberland in the area and established one of his sawmills there. The village of Abeles appeared on state maps in the late nineteenth and early twentieth centuries.[319]

The Distaff Side

For almost every successful Jewish businessman in Arkansas, there was a supportive, devoted wife. Many of these women were active in the local community, especially in the area of religion. Most supported the local schools and charities. Three women of eastern Arkansas are cited here for who they were and what they accomplished: Mrs. Seelig L. (Josephine "Josie" Krow) Mundt of Trenton and Helena, Mrs. Max (Irene Straus) Eisenkramer of Pine Bluff, and Mrs. Joseph (Matilda Josaphat) Altheimer of Pine Bluff.

Josie (Krow) Mundt (1886–1943) was born and raised in the small town of Trenton in Phillips County. Her father, Simon (noted above), had peddled in the area around Helena in the 1860s and had opened what became a prosperous furnishing store at Trenton, a small village about twelve miles west of Helena. Simon married Rose (Ricka Seelig [1843–1910]) and they had four children, Sallie, Ira, Bertha, and Josephine "Josie." The parents were not content just to make a living for their family; they wanted them to have culture as well. They brought teachers to Trenton who taught piano, violin, and elocution to the children. Simon and Rose housed the teachers and allowed other local citizens to use their services as well.[320] The Krows entertained royally in their remote location, bringing visitors from as far away as Pine Bluff and Helena, Arkansas, Nashville and Memphis, Tennessee, and Cincinnati, Ohio. During such times, the evenings would begin with piano and violin solos and recitations of "sweet" pieces; at eleven o'clock, frozen "dainties" were served, and all of this was followed by dancing until the early morning hours.[321] The Krow's commodious nine-room frame house had a porch across the front and side, and large magnolia trees grew in the yard.[322]

When Josie married Seelig Mundt of Helena, she became the driving force that brought about the Helena Civic Music Association. It was through her efforts that the organization was maintained, and she worked tirelessly to sell tickets and to raise needed funds.[323] After Josie Mundt died in 1943, the Association "limped along," then folded after the Warfield Concerts were established. (Samuel Drake Warfield was a lifelong resident of Helena. When he died at age sixty-six in 1967, he left his estate to fund free concerts at Helena. These have included outstanding national and international musicians and vocalists. Since 1972 these have been held in the Lily Peter Auditorium at Phillips County Community College, Helena.)[324] Josie Mundt and her husband had four children, Rosalind, twins Vera and Leslie, and Ira. Josie passed on to her children her love for music and culture, and the Krow family legacy for the fine things of life continued on through its descendants (see section V).

Irene (Straus) Eisenkramer (1875–1939), born in Pine Bluff to Abraham (1834–1894) and Hannah (Levy) Straus (1849–1905), became a noted leader in civic and club work in her native city. She taught civics and American citizenship in the Pine Bluff high school and served on the executive committees of the Pine Bluff Musical Coterie, the city's Federation of Women's Clubs, and the City Beautiful organization. She was chairman of the Coterie Chorus in 1924. A writer and poet, she had works published in local newspapers and educational publications. She also composed a number of songs, one of which appeared in military publications during World War I. Irene Eisenkramer continued her civic work until her death.[325]

Matilda (Josaphat) Altheimer (1844–1935) was born in Stendal, Altmaer, Germany, to Sigmund and Fredricka (Meyer) Josaphat. Although her father trained for the rabbinate, he became a university professor instead. Matilda received an excellent education and was multilingual, speaking German, French, Spanish, and English. She and her sister Emma were aided financially in their education by their uncle, Israel Beer Josaphat, who was one of many European Jews who left their own Jewish communities and joined the outside world. He was baptised a Christian in 1844 and assumed the name Paul Julius Reuter; he later founded the British news agency Reuters.[326]

Matilda married Joseph Altheimer in Germany amid the cultured surroundings of her family life. She came with him directly to Pine Bluff as a young lady in her early twenties. Pine Bluff, at the time of her arrival, was described as:

a city of rutted streets and few pavements, many frame business structures and a few brick blocks, a few artificial gas lights, a dilapidated horse-car line and only the beginning of decent roads to the surrounding fertile country . . . a none too attractive place, lacking the commonplace conveniences of living.[327]

What she thought of her new surroundings is not known. But it was noted that she lived "many happy years" in Pine Bluff.[328] A talented and prolific writer, she wrote numerous poems and more than sixty plays and scenarios, several of which she translated into German and French. She also raised her children, Ben J. (noted above) and Henrietta (1880–1930), to appreciate culture and education. They were both well educated for the day (Henrietta attended an academy in Pine Bluff; she later married I. B. Jacobs around 1900). Although the family lost their holdings in Arkansas (and Joseph died shortly after leaving the state), they continued their interest in Arkansas, and some of Matilda's poems appeared in Pine Bluff newspapers. At the age of eighty-eight, she published a small book of poems entitled *Pastime Poems*. She died in Chicago at age ninety-two, but the legacy she left through her children, especially her son, Ben J., through his foundation, continued to benefit and advance the state of Arkansas into the 1990s (see section V).[329]

CHAPTER 9

German Migration in Western Arkansas

Southwest Arkansas

Because the business opportunities were greater in the central and eastern sections of Arkansas, more Jews located there than in the western portion. Continuing clockwise around the state, in its southwest and western sections, Camden, Texarkana, Hot Springs, and Fort Smith drew fair-sized Jewish communities, where congregations were established. A few Jews also could be found in some small towns, such as Fulton, Malvern, Prescott, and Ashdown. In the 1920s when the oil boom hit El Dorado, thirty-two miles below Camden, the resultant influx of people brought about a need for more stores, and Jews were found among these merchants as well.

CAMDEN

The pioneer Jewish settlers of Camden were some of the leaders in that town's development. Located in Ouachita County (named for the Ouachita River that drains it) in the south central portion of the state, Camden was incorporated in 1844, and by 1860 it had a population of more than two thousand, making it the state's second largest city. (Little Rock had a population of 3,727 at the time.)[1]

Henry Myar (1840–1912), who could be designated the quintessential Jewish settler, settled in Camden in the 1850s (see section I). Coming as a poor, untrained boy, it was said his hard work and diligence were rewarded; he became one of the wealthiest men in Arkansas and one of Camden's most important citizens.[2] He invested heavily in land development, accumulating some twenty thousand acres, most of which were in cotton and timber. He served as president of the Camden National Bank, which he helped establish, and was a stockholder in several other banks. Called "Colonel" Myar and referred to as "the merchant prince," he was an investor in the railway from Little Rock to Linwood, south of Pine Bluff.[3] He had deep cultural interests as well. In 1886 he bought property in El Paso, Texas (where his sister and brother-in-law, Mr. and Mrs. Herman Kayser, lived), on which he had the Myar Opera House erected. It was considered the pride of theater goers in El Paso for almost two decades. (Myar lived in Camden until he died in 1912; he attended the Myar Opera House only once—at its opening performance.)[4] Myar, who was remembered for his "intelligent fidelity" to his word, married Lena Davis of New Orleans. She shared his intense interest in Arkansas's development and its citizens, as did their descendants.[5] Their sons, John (1842–1884) and Sam, continued the "Colonel's" work in Camden. Claudia, one of their three daughters, married Dr. Samuel H. Goldenson, rabbi of a leading Reform congregation, Temple Emanuel of New York; daughter Hannah married Joe Franklin, son of Sol Franklin of Pine Bluff; and daughter Gertrude married Harry B. Solmson, also of Pine Bluff. (For more data on the Solmson family, see sections IV and V.)

The Jews were well accepted in Camden and experienced little prejudice. Even during the Klan days after World War I and into the 1920s, the Protestants of Camden devised a double primary during elections in order to defeat Klan candidates.[6] As at Little Rock, Helena, Pine Bluff, and other cities and towns noted above, Jews were well represented in Camden's elected offices. Some of those who served in public office there included Adolph Felsenthal, Abe Lazarus, Leo Berg, Jacob Friedheim, Mose Stern, Leonard Stern Sr., and Joseph Levy.

Adolph Felsenthal (1863–1942), one of nine children of pioneer Arkansas settler David Felsenthal (see section I.),[7] served as Ouachita County assessor and as state president of the Arkansas Assessors Association. Adolph was interested in politics and promoted a number of voting laws, including the absentee ballot law. He began pursuing and promoting a quorum court system as early as 1911. He worked diligently to help effect needed changes for a more equitable and lower taxation basis.[8] Adolph began his career in Camden as manager of the large Bry and Brothers mercantile firm (see below); in 1908 he, with Dr. E. H. Carson, Louis

Bauerlein, and others, established the Carson Dry Goods Company, located at Camden and El Dorado, which became one of the largest enterprises in south Arkansas.[9] Adolph was best known as an outstanding developer of that section of the state. He conceived of, promoted, and expended tremendous effort and funds toward the development of navigation on the Ouachita River.[10] He was one of the promoters of a power plant, dam, and reservoir on the Ouachita River near Hot Springs; such effort culminated in the Remmel and Carpenter Dams, constructed by Harvey Couch, and in the Blakely Dam.[11] He was called the "father" of river navigation on the Ouachita River and cited as being largely responsible for its locks and dams. He almost "lone-handedly" promoted the Federal government into such construction, and his contribution to Camden was compared to the work of those who created the port at Houston, Texas: Adolph Felsenthal "did for Camden all that better-known men ever did for Houston."[12]

Abe Lazarus (1863–1930), son of pioneer Camden settler John Lazarus (1834–1904), served as president of the Camden School Board for more than a dozen years. One of the clerks in John Lazarus's mercantile store was John C. Ritchie, who became friends with Abe, and the two young men became partners in the Ritchie Wholesale Grocery Company. The business prospered and expanded into multiple branch houses in Arkansas and Louisiana. By the mid-1930s the company was doing an annual trade of ten million dollars.[13] Known for his liberality and charity, Abe Lazarus, who looked and dressed like Abraham Lincoln, was lauded for his civic work. A tribute to him at his death noted that "Some men remember themselves into oblivion, Abe Lazarus forgot himself into immortality."[14] (John Lazarus's daughter, Laura, married Rabbi N. J. Benson, who served both at Camden and later [1881–84], at Little Rock. The Benson's son, Ralph, served as president of Ritchie Wholesale Grocery Company at El Dorado, where he was elected county and probate clerk.)[15]

Leo Berg (1868–1931) served as Camden's mayor in the 1920s; he was the son of Meyer Berg (1829–1881), a pre–Civil War settler in Camden. Meyer Berg was a hard worker, and he became a highly regarded businessman.[16] When he died of pneumonia in 1881, he left five children, all of whom became successful. Two of his sons, Henry (1866–1950) and Leo, began their business careers as young teenagers in the Henry Myar store, where they learned sound business practices.[17] They invested heavily in land and property and were in banking. Both served as bank presidents—Leo at Merchants and Planters Bank in Camden and Smackover and Henry at the First National Bank of Camden.[18] Leo became well known in southwest Arkansas as owner of the largest jewelry store in that section. At the height of the Klan days in the 1920s, Leo served as Camden's mayor for six years. During his tenure he led in the advancement of the town, and it was raised to first class city status in 1925; by 1930 Camden's population was 7,269.[19] Leo helped a number of young men establish their own businesses, and the blacks who worked for him held him in high esteem.[20] The Camden Chamber of Commerce cited him as a man of unblemished character and one of its "most useful and valuable members."[21]

Jacob B. Friedheim (1848–1899), who served as a Camden school board official, settled in the town in 1866 and became one of its well-known developers. He was one of the first to direct northern capital to the town after the Civil War and was an initial promoter of the undeveloped lignite coal deposits of the Ouachita Valley area.[22] A practicing attorney, he was active in Republican politics and lost in a race for Congress against Thomas C. McRae. He served as commissary general of the State Militia, as register of the U.S. Land Office, and as chief clerk to the U.S. Marshal. He served on the board of the city's utility companies and promoted them and was general manager of the Camden, Louisiana and Saline Passenger Railway Company.[23]

Moses "Mose" Stern (1852–1925), who served as a member of the city council, was brought to Camden by his brother Samuel (1847–1891) in 1874. Samuel had come there as a thirteen-year-old in 1860, had clerked, had opened his own meat market, and had become one of the town's developers.[24] Mose initially joined in his brother's meat market, which was continually modernized, then established a fur business. He became a prominent civic leader, serving as president of the Board of Trade. He helped found the Ouachita Valley Bank and served as one of its directors. He was known for his kindness and for his "generous impulses."[25]

Leonard M. Stern (1885–1951), son of Samuel Stern, served a number of times as Camden police judge and as an alderman and was elected municipal judge in 1945. After graduating from Cumberland University Law School in 1907, the young Stern bicycled through Europe, then served in the Department of Justice in Cincinnati for two years. When he returned to Camden, he became politically prominent and accumulated an "enviable record" as a judge. He also was a sports enthusiast and personally funded a semi-pro team for the city, which became one of the best in the south Arkansas League.[26]

Joseph Levy (1839–1903), another pioneer merchant of Camden, served on the city council. Two of his sons became prominent druggists,

Arthur (1874–1934) at Camden and Isadore "Peeny" (1871–1926) at Hot Springs.[27]

After the Civil War, the Bry brothers, Nathan and Louis, came to Camden with honesty and industriousness as their only assets, but they soon established what became a "colossal" metropolitan type of mercantile store in that area of the state. They drew customers from as far away as northern Louisiana and the Indian Territory, even in that ox-wagon period. The Bry brothers had a number of "firsts" for south Arkansas: the first modern department store, the first strictly cash store, the first store with plainly marked prices, the first store to use women as clerks, the first store to use cents in price making, and the first store with "money back" guarantees. When they had expanded as much as they could in Camden, they hired managers for the store and moved to St. Louis. There, in 1893, they began manufacturing ladies' garments. In Memphis they established "Bry's," a popular retail store.[28]

Other Camden pioneer Jewish merchants included Solomon Levy (1829–1881), auctioneering; Levi Thal and D. Thal, produce business; Samuel Winter (1838–1898), grocery; Henry Heller, dry goods; A. Lowenstein, ladies' ready-to-wear; Simon Weil (1833–1894), merchant; and Adolf Feibelman (1869–1953), cotton buying. Louis Wagner (1834–1908), a pioneer Camden merchant, had two of his sons open stores in Arkansas towns—Eli at Marianna and Joe at Nashville.[29]

A later arrival on the Camden scene was Adolph "Kid" Newman (1869–1940), who traveled over the state as a salesman for the Watson and American Ice Cream Company of Little Rock. Around 1920 he settled at Camden, where he opened an ice-cream factory and a kiddie park. A friendly, cheery person, he performed in minstrel shows and other productions. He also owned a cafe, which became one of Camden's popular places. He married Bella Woolf (sister of Mrs. Henry Berg), who became known as a "beloved woman" of Camden.[30]

Al Rose was a writer and editor for the *Camden News*, and for years wrote a column, "Al's Alfalfa," which included homey topics and poems. He married a non-Jew and converted to the Methodist faith.[31]

FELSENTHAL

The Felsenthal Land and Timber Company in south Union County was established by the Felsenthal brothers, Adolph, Isaac (1870–1939), Sidney (1882–1971), and Lee (1884–1964), around the turn of the century, and in 1904 they established the town of Felsenthal in the county's southeast section. In 1905 two excursion trains from Little Rock were used to bring prospective buyers to the town; Governor Jeff Davis was one of the visitors.[32] The town grew to a population of twelve hundred, and it boasted public schools, a bank, an opera house, a post office, three hotels, a brick company, and two newspapers. Although prospects were bright for the new town and a judicial seat was established there for the eastern district of Union County, flood waters of 1906 prohibited the court from ever meeting. The frequent floods and the rise of the nearby sawmill town of Huttig doomed the town from becoming the metropolis the Felsenthal brothers had envisioned.[33] By 1911 the town became unincorporated, and it remained but a community for many years (see section V).

EL DORADO

The Felsenthals became a part of the history of El Dorado in Union County as well. The town, incorporated in 1870, was aptly named, as oil was discovered near there some fifty years later.[34] The Felsenthals, Ike and Sidney, were associated with the Carson Dry Goods Company's branch store at El Dorado until 1921, when oil was discovered in the area. They sold the dry goods store and became pioneers in the oil business. After the big gusher came in on 10 January 1921, the town of El Dorado had an influx of more than five thousand people within a few days. It grew from a population of less than four thousand in 1910 to more than sixteen thousand in 1921.[35] The Felsenthals joined Col. T. H. Barton and G. W. Jones in 1926 to found the Exchange Realty Company, which built the Exchange Building, El Dorado's largest office structure at the time. Ike Felsenthal was instrumental in establishing the city's Chamber of Commerce and was also interested in bettering farming conditions, serving as acting chairman of the farm bureau. He introduced the velvet bean to Union County and initiated home demonstration work in the county. Sidney Felsenthal was active in civic organizations as well; he served fifty years on the Salvation Army Board.[36]

With the prospects for business so good in El Dorado, a number of Jewish merchants flocked to the area along with other fortune seekers. Among these were Isadore Berk, Samuel Baum, and E. J. Stein. Isadore Berk (1895–1969) was the son of German-born Ben Berk, a watchmaker. Isadore, an optometrist, opened a jewelry store in El Dorado in 1925, sold it to his brother, then practiced optometry. He married Rose Burd of Forrest City.[37] Samuel Baum also had a jewelry store and was active in local civic organizations.[38] E. J. Stein came to El Dorado with his family in

1932; his son, Floyd, became a well-known attorney there.[39] In 1937 the city directory of El Dorado listed more than thirty Jewish families, with occupations ranging from oil field suppliers to the usual dry goods New York Store.[40]

When oil was discovered near El Dorado at the community of Smackover, that little town grew from a population of some one hundred to around ten thousand in 1922.[41] Although Jewish stores are known to have operated at Smackover, they were temporary (the owners of which have not been traced).

TEXARKANA

The city of Texarkana, situated squarely on the border of Arkansas and Texas, was laid out as a town in 1873, but the Arkansas municipality, located in Miller County, was not incorporated until 1880. Lying among timbered lands and farming communities, it was a perfect distribution point when the railroads came through.[42] It was here that Joseph Deutschmann (1828–1897) settled in the early 1870s and helped transform the community from a primitive settlement to a thriving town. He bought some undesirable land called the "sand flat" in the area, drained it, and developed it into a black residential site. When a spring flood hit in 1874, the land was flooded along with other low areas of the town. Deutschmann's tenants were marooned, and one drowned. Having had some engineering training, he built a canal that not only drained his property, but others as well. Known as "Deutschmann's Canal," it became an annual reminder of his contribution to the town.[43]

Louis Heilbron (1869–1949), a member of the Heilbron family that settled in Texarkana, headed the Heilbron Investment Company of that city; he served as president of the Arkansas Real Estate Association in the 1920s.[44]

Prussian-born Louis Josephs (1874–1957) was a turn-of-the-century settler in Texarkana. An attorney, he served three terms as a state representative from Miller County, beginning in 1913, and he was elected municipal judge in 1925 and served ten years.[45] Josephs had come to America in 1892 after attending an academy in Dublin. He was in the U.S. Army from 1894 to 1899, serving in the Spanish-American War. He then settled in Arkansas, where he studied law at the University of Arkansas, Fayetteville. Josephs was deeply committed to his faith and to its ideals. At one point in his career he defended a black person who had shot and killed a white man in self-defense. When racist language was used by the opposing attorney, Josephs pleaded for justice, mercy, and racial understanding, quoting "profusely and cogently" from both the Jewish and Christian Bibles, showing that it was the people of Texarkana who were on trial, not the defendant. When the verdict of "not guilty" was returned the next day, even Josephs was so stunned that he fainted. Judge Josephs was considered a miracle worker among the black community, and they often sought his assistance.[46]

Some pioneer settlers in southwest Arkansas settled in small towns like Fulton, Hope, Ashdown, Washington, Prescott, Center Point, and Mena.

FULTON, HOPE

Several members of the Rosenberg family from Meisenheim am Glan, Germany, settled at Fulton and Hope in Hempstead County. The Rosenberg brothers, Joseph and Gus, opened a small store at Fulton in 1874 and by 1877 were doing a considerable amount of trade in their new home.[47] They also had business ventures at nearby Hope, where they bought land and established a credit business and became prominent. They were later joined by other family members—brother George and sisters Regina, Carolina, and Helena "Lena." (Lena married Adolph Goldsmith [1860–1942] of Texarkana, and they established a store at Ashdown.) The Rosenberg's nephew, Leopold "Lee" (1881–1960), at age thirteen joined his uncles in their venture at Hope and in 1900 brought his parents, Ferdinand and Rosalie, to America. George Rosenberg (1859–1911) began dealing in cotton, and by the time of his death, he was said to be one of the richest men in Arkansas. He was a member of the Little Rock Board of Trade and the Cotton Exchanges of Memphis and New Orleans. In national cotton circles, he was said to have been from one season to another the largest individual holder of spot cotton in the world.[48] After George died, most of the family moved elsewhere; Joseph and Lee opened a store at Kennett, Missouri, then later moved it to Manila, Arkansas.

William Fried (1850–1908) was a pioneer settler at Fulton, where he became one of the town's most prominent merchants. When he was murdered at his store in 1908, there was talk of lynching the felon who did it.[49]

WASHINGTON

At Washington, less than ten miles north of Hope, Abraham Block had established a store in the 1820s that had prospered and had drawn trade from a wide area in Arkansas, Texas, and Louisiana, and the firm was continued by his sons after Abraham's death in 1857. The town had reached its peak around 1860, with some one thousand permanent residents.[50] The temporary influx of citizens during the Civil War, when Arkansas's confederate seat of government was temporarily located there, dropped off by war's end, and Reconstruction times brought ruin to many. Planters who had prospered under slavery faced bankruptcy, and the stores of the town were deeply affected. The town's commercial district experienced two fires, and a further blow came when the Missouri Pacific Railway, the main traffic artery, bypassed the town.[51] David Block (1823–1865) died at the end of the war, and his brother and partner, Virginius (1828–1871), was left "poor and embarrassed by debt." The latter followed the Texas Central Railroad into Texas, attempting to start anew, but he died in October 1871. Local friends at Washington remembered him for his "integrity" and "generous liberality to the poor and unfortunate."[52] He preceded his mother, Fanny Block (1796–1871), in death by one month. She was remembered for her "kindness, prudence, and gentle charity."[53] Through the years, descendants of the Block family continued to be prominent in the state's history.[54] A few Jewish merchants settled at Washington at various times, but none remained permanently.

ASHDOWN

Samuel J. Meyer (1885–1960), son of Charles Meyer of Newport, settled with his family at Ashdown, located in Little River County. He conducted a business there for many years. His family members included the Salingers of Brinkley and the Rosenzweigs of Lake Village. Other Ashdown merchants included Adolph Goldsmith (noted above) and J. L. Levinson.[55]

PRESCOTT

Max Simon (1847–1916) was one of the earliest merchants in Prescott, Nevada County, less than forty miles northeast of Texarkana. He had stores at Camden and at Junction City at various times. Moses Winter also had stores at Camden and Prescott.[56]

CENTER POINT

Nathan Levi (1826–1907), who had settled in Arkansas in 1848 (see section I), had stores in several southwest Arkansas locations and was identified with the progress of the area. He had businesses variously at Washington and Camden and at Nashville and Center Point in Sevier County. He was involved with mail contracts, the livery business, and horses. He also built a two-story building at Center Point, where he was elected city treasurer in 1870 and as town marshal in 1890.[57]

MENA

Mena, located in Polk County in the breathtakingly beautiful Ouachita Mountains, was incorporated as the county seat in 1896.[58] It was here that Sam Badt and his family settled when the town was born. Sam had come to America from Germany in the 1880s and had peddled in Oklahoma Territory. According to family members, he did business with the Dalton Gang and Jesse James and even named one of his sons Jesse. The Badts had a mercantile store and millinery shop. Jesse worked in the Badt store, his brother Arnold operated a popular confectionary store, and brother Mendel, who was a graduate of the University of Arkansas with a pharmacy degree, worked in a Mena drugstore. (Arnold Badt lost an eye when he was shot in the face by an excited spectator during the showing of an early western movie, which was presented outside. He slowly lost sight in the other eye as well.) Jesse married Sybil Lyons of Little Rock, and their son, Ernest J., was Mena's first Jewish baby. (Some curious local citizens asked if the child had horns.) When the Klan became active in the 1920s, the drugstore at which Mendel worked was boycotted because he was Jewish, and the Badt family moved to Michigan.[59]

When diamonds were discovered at Murfreesboro in Pike County in 1906, several Little Rock Jewish businessmen—jeweler Charles Stifft and merchants M. M. Cohn and Ike Kempner—became involved with attempts to mine the stones. They abandoned their efforts around 1910, however. (After many years of attempts by various companies at mining, the state purchased the site in 1972 and established the Crater of Diamonds State Park.)[60]

HOT SPRINGS

Hot Springs, located in Garland County, was set aside by the U.S. Government in 1832 for preservation as a natural resource land (Hot Springs Reservation). The natural hot springs had drawn the sick for centuries, but the town of Hot Springs was not officially platted until 1877.[61] Jewish pioneers were known to have been there since the 1840s (see section I), and one of the first merchants to open for business after the Civil

War was pioneer Jacob Kempner (1838–1910). He operated stores at Hot Springs and Little Rock and accumulated "considerable" property at both places.[62] He married Fannie Murphy of Hot Springs, and they had three children, Joe, Isaac "Ike," and Alice. Alice married Simon Blumensteil (1865–1939), a Hot Springs wholesale and retail cigar manufacturer who also was co-owner of the Princess Theater.[63]

Emanuel Burgauer (1838–1916) was a pioneer of Hot Springs who came to Arkansas from Germany as a youth with his brothers Moses and Isaac and peddled around the state during the 1850s (see section I). The brothers tried stores at Rockport, Dover, and Mount Ida before serving in the Civil War, during which Isaac was killed.[64] Emanuel settled at Hot Springs in the 1860s, locating his store where the Arlington Hotel was later built.[65] He married Babette Guggenheim, whom he had met when she visited the spa with her family, and they had five children.

Babette's sister Fannie was married to German-born Henry Fellheimer (1850–1936), who joined Emanuel in establishing one of Hot Springs' first furniture stores. Henry also had a real estate firm and was active in the cultural, civic, and religious life of the community, while Fannie was involved as a board member and treasurer for the public library.[66]

David "Dave" Burgauer (1873–1959), the only son among Emanuel and Babette's five offspring, attended college in Virginia and then returned to Hot Springs and entered the banking business. He served as president of the Arkansas Trust Company and was associated with the Morrison and Belding Insurance Company. He served on numerous civic boards of the city, including the Business Men's League, the Y.M.C.A., the Garland County Development Corporation, and the Leo N. Levi Hospital Board. It was said of him that his "vocation was banking, his avocation was humanity."[67]

Although a number of Jews became prominent in the business and civic life of Hot Springs, relatively few served in public office. Those who did included Henry Cohn, J. C. Wolf, Bernard Gross, Nathan Schoenfeld, and Ernest Klein.

Henry Cohn (1844–1904), United States Commissioner from 1898 to 1904, served as a justice of the peace. He became well known as Judge Cohn, and he was a prominent businessman as well.[68] J. C. Wolf, a business partner of Sam Blumensteil in operating the Princess Theater, served as an alderman.[69]

Bernard "Billy" Gross (1854–1919), a well-known Jewish pioneer in Hot Springs, served on the city council. He first came to the town in 1881 and opened a dry goods store; then he joined J. B. McCafferty in an undertaking business. In 1866 Gross became full owner of the firm, which grew to become one of the largest in the area. He later served as president of the Arkansas Funeral Directors Association. Gross, affectionately called "Billy," organized the first volunteer fire department in Hot Springs and served as its chief. Cited as "one who never forgot a friend," he personally pensioned the fire department's first members when they became old or needed help.[70]

Nathan L. Schoenfeld, born in 1913 to S. L. and Lulu (Cohn) Schoenfeld, was a Harvard Law School graduate and a major in the Army Air Force in World War II. He received an Air Medal with two clusters as well as a Presidential Citation for his actions in service. After returning to Hot Springs in 1946, he practiced law with Sid McMath (who later became the state's governor) and was a state representative from Garland County. He joined the Catholic Church and became active in the Catholic Men's Club.[71]

Ernest F. Klein, a graduate of the Cincinnati College of Pharmacy, established a drugstore at Hot Springs in 1884. He served on the Hot Springs School Board and was vitally active in the pubic school system. He also owned the Park Hotel and served as the superintendent of its bath house. He was an officer of the Arkansas National Bank and of the State Board of Pharmacy.[72]

Ludwig "Louis" Benedikt (1875–1946), a relative of Bernard "Billy" Gross, came to Hot Springs with his brother Frank Benedikt in the 1890s. After Louis served in the army in the Spanish-American War, he returned to Hot Springs and opened one of the town's first bakeries. During the 1930s, the family brought two cousins from Nazi Germany, Dr. Alexander Benedikt (1900–1983), who practiced at Hot Springs, and Stefan Benedikt, who settled in Dallas, Texas.[73]

Italian-born Robert Nordlinger (1841–1921) migrated to Hot Springs after coming to America in 1866. He and his son Selmar were merchants in Hot Springs; Selmar also had interests in a furniture and household storage business in Little Rock.[74] Selmar and his wife, Clara (Levy) Nordlinger, had a daughter, Helen, and a son, Percy (1902–1981). The latter was an honor graduate of the University of Tennessee Dental School in Memphis in 1923; he became a prominent dentist in Little Rock, where he practiced for fifty-six years (see section V).

The Mendel brothers, Mose (1847–1934) and Simon (1851–1937), came to Hot Springs in 1877 and their brother Albert (1869–1948) came in 1882. They were partners for a time, then established separate dry goods stores.[75] Members of the Mendel family became well known in Hot

Springs' civic and business circles for more than a hundred years. Mose's daughter married Ike Kempner of Little Rock.

Jacob Geschmay (1857–1933) immigrated to America as a young boy and later opened a men's clothing store on Hot Springs' Central Avenue. He married Emma Lazarus of Camden in 1902, and their three daughters—Mrs. Al (Hannah) Lasky, Mrs. Norton (Caroline) Perry, and Mrs. Phil (Frances) Levin—remained in Hot Springs. In the mid-1880s Simon Meyer (1861–1935) settled at Hot Springs, where he established the S. Meyer, Clothier store. Flora Meyer, daughter of Simon and his wife, Rosa, married David Lockwood in 1906, and they had six children. Members of the Lockwood family continued businesses in Arkansas for more than eighty years. In the 1870s Carl and Rosalie Gersman settled in Hot Springs, where he was a merchant. Their daughter Bertha married merchant Samuel Newman.[76]

J. Herman Traxler (1850–1900) came to Hot Springs around 1880 and became a partner in the Roth, Traxler and Roth dry goods firm and the Southern Palace Store. Traxler was also a partner with Isaac Dreyfus of Pine Bluff.[77] Simon Samuel (1843–1935) and his brother were tailors who operated a dry goods store.[78] Morris H. Guggenheim (1856–1937) came in the mid-1870s and practiced as a masseur for more than fifty years. Elias M. Cohen (1874–1938), son of Bernard and Rebecca (Navra) Cohen of Little Rock and husband of Leah (Pollock) Cohen, was a Hot Springs insurance and real estate agent who became known for his philanthropy and civic work.[79] Dr. Samuel D. Weil Sr. (1870–1953) moved to Hot Springs in 1903, where he practiced medicine for a number of years. He married Stella Fellheimer, daughter of prominent Hot Springs merchant, Henry Fellheimer, mentioned above. (Fellheimer's daughter Carrie married Sidney Weil of Pine Bluff, and another daughter, Bernice, married Hubert Mendel of Hot Springs.)[80]

Other families, such as Mayer, Kaufman, Baer, Seckbeck, Goodman, Raphael, Dinkelspiel, Levy, Cohn, and many others settled at Hot Springs as well. The Hot Springs Rotary Club was chartered in July 1916 with fifteen charter members, four of whom were Jewish: Dave Burgauer, Arthur Katz, Joseph Klyman, and Albert Mendel.[81]

MALVERN

Malvern, located in Hot Springs County some twenty miles southeast of the city of Hot Springs, was incorporated in 1876 and became the county seat in 1879. Sitting in the midst of great lumber interests, the town was laid out by a railroad company in 1873.[82] The Berger brothers, Henry (1858–1926) and Benjamin, members of the Berger family of Jonesboro, established a trading post in Clay County in 1874, then moved to Malvern in 1878 and formed the B. and H. Berger mercantile and farm supply store. Before they helped establish the Bank of Malvern in the 1870s, their store was a depository for a number of Malvern citizens. During the business recession of the early 1890s, the Bergers lost their Malvern firm and Henry began studying law.[83] He was admitted to the Arkansas bar in 1903 and formed a partnership with Col. N. P. Richmond of Malvern. Henry became an advisor to several railway companies and the Acme Brick Company. He served four terms as Malvern's city attorney, and a street there was named for him. He was cited as being one of the best-read lawyers in the state. Henry married Carrie Ottenheimer, daughter of Phillip Ottenheimer of Little Rock.[84] Lawrence Berger, son of Henry and Carrie, became a well-known North Little Rock attorney (see chapter 7, this section).

Around the turn of the century Adelbert Strauss (?–1927), son of German immigrants Theodore (1820–1884) and Emilie Strauss, settled at Malvern and became prominently associated with the area's lumber industry. He was president of the Malvern Lumber Company and served as president of the Arkansas Forest Protection Association. When the state's forestry commission was originated in 1931, Strauss was appointed its chairman by Governor J. M. Futrell.[85] His son, Albert L. Strauss (1886–1939), also served as president of the Malvern Lumber Company and as chairman of the State Forestry Commission. He was considered "a great asset to the state" through his activities with the Forestry Commission.[86]

Two Jewish businessmen who established stores at Malvern were Sigmund Eisman (married to an Ottenheimer), who had a shoe and clothing store, and another merchant, a Mr. Hess.[87]

Northwest Arkansas

FORT SMITH

Fort Smith in Sebastian County is located at the gateway to the great southwest and lies in the foothills of two mountain ranges, the Ouachitas and the Ozarks. Situated on the border between Arkansas and Oklahoma, it remained a frontier town for years until the Oklahoma Territory was opened in 1889 and settlers could move west through Fort Smith. The town was incorporated in 1842, and its history is intertwined with such notables as Gen. Sam Houston, Zachary Taylor, Albert Pike, and the mixed-ancestry Cherokee, Sequoyah. The population grew slowly at first, with 964 in 1850 and 3,099 in 1880. By 1930 it had a population of 31,434, making it the second largest city in Arkansas.[88] Jews had migrated to the area as early as the 1840s (see section I), and by 1881 about one hundred Jewish merchants were listed in the city directory.[89] This probably represented a Jewish population of at least four hundred. With the population of Fort Smith at the time standing at 3,099, some 13 percent were Jewish. Except during the 1920s, when Fort Smith had a "pretty good-sized" Klan membership whose influence hurt some of the Jewish-owned stores, such settlers found the population of the town to be broadminded, and there was little anti-Semitism.[90]

Fort Smith had alternated between the Federal and Confederate occupation during the Civil War, but they had wreaked less havoc than did the outlaws who roamed Arkansas and the Indian Territory. The beginnings of law and order were brought to the area when Judge Isaac Parker arrived in 1875. Parker, who became known as "Hanging Judge Parker," was stern and inflexible toward criminals, some ten thousand of whom faced him during his tenure, and one hundred sixty-eight were hanged. But he was known as a kind and gentle person socially.[91] He became friends with Jewish merchants in Fort Smith, particularly Isaac Cohn (1847–1899). Cohn, a German immigrant, had opened a store in Pine Bluff in the early 1870s and had done well, although some of his customers were said to be "undesirables" [that is, blacks].[92] When his store in Pine Bluff burned, he settled at Fort Smith, where he established a rapport with the Indians. He became known as a "prudent, hard-working" person.[93] His friend Judge Parker performed the wedding ceremony when Cohn married Fannie Silverberg in 1883. The two men developed a loosely formed business relationship.

Cohn also developed a close friendship with a young Choctaw Indian, Green McCurtain. A number of Choctaws often dined at the Cohn house in Fort Smith, and McCurtain would stay in their home during these visits.[94] Green McCurtain served the Choctaw Nation as sheriff of Skuyllyville County, as a member of its house of representatives, as a school trustee, and in 1896 was elected chief of the tribe—the last Choctaw chief. In 1882 McCurtain served as district attorney and treasurer of the Choctaw Nation. He served in this capacity for nine years, and during his last year paid to the tribe a million and a half dollars of a "leased district fund."[95] Evidently the loose business relationship Cohn had with Judge Parker included McCurtain as well. When the Indians received their government checks, Cohn provided cash for them and also merchandise for sale. The friendships of Cohn were helpful in building up his fortune, which amounted to millions by the time he died in 1899.[96] Cohn brought over some of his relatives from Europe to work in his store, and one of them, Benno Stein, opened a store at Fort Smith in 1892 and a wholesale dry goods firm in 1901.[97]

Another Jewish Indian trader was Prussian-born pioneer settler Edward Czarnikow (1820–1892), who had come to Fort Smith in the 1840s (see section I). Known affectionately as "General," he was one of the most successful Indian traders, and a number of Indians named their children after him.[98] Czarnikow married Rose Happek of Little Rock, who outlived him by thirty-five years. Residing in their large Victorian home in Fort Smith, she became a gracious hostess of the city, giving elegant parties for the Jewish women of the community and graciously entertaining visiting dignitaries in her home.[99]

Mark Stuart Cohn (1849–1930), also an Indian trader, became known as one of the most colorful and prominent men of that area, especially in Indian circles. (It is not known if Mark Cohn and Isaac Cohn were related.) He was connected with several industries that interlocked Fort Smith with the Indian Territory, such as cattle, cotton, and gravel. Cohn and an Indian partner bought a ranch on the Massard Prairie, a portion of land near Fort Smith, where they discovered a large gravel deposit. At great expense to himself, Cohn built a short rail line to the quarry and supplied gravel for the Frisco Railroad Company when it was extended into Fort Smith, for the tunnel near the border town of Jenson, and for the Van Buren–Fort Smith bridge across the Arkansas River.[100] He had several trading posts; one was located on the site that became the town of Shawnee, Oklahoma, and two of his ranches were located where the towns of Spiro and Poteau were established. He served as an intermediary in tribal affairs and was one of those responsible for merging the Indian Territory and the Oklahoma Territory for statehood. He was said to be the first homesteader in Oklahoma, his claim being filed at Guthrie, Oklahoma.[101]

Mark Cohn owned several general merchandise stores as well as trading posts. When building his store on Garrison Avenue in Fort Smith, he brought expensive, imported brick from Belgium. One of his customers was Belle Starr, who bought boots and a hat for her boyfriend.[102] Mark and Henrietta Cohn had five sons, only two of whom, Sol C. and Will V., remained in Fort Smith. (The Mark Cohns also had two daughters, Mrs. Nathan (Agnes) Stein and Marguerite.) Will V. Cohn (1876–1937) was manager of his father's gravel company; he married Rae Berman, and their daughter Henrietta married Sam Peck, who was later a Little Rock hotel owner. Sol C. Cohn (1877–1940) began his career in Indian trade with his father, then opened a clothing store that began specializing in men's better clothing, such as Hart Shaffner and Marx.[103]

Sol C. Cohn married Minnie Isaacson, the daughter of Isaac Isaacson (1852–1921), who was a licensed Indian trader and who had served as postmaster of Cache, Oklahoma Territory. In 1886 German-born Isaacson established a store that developed into a large retail and jobbing firm and farm supply store. He served as president of the Home Building and Loan Association for nineteen years, during which time he built a number of houses in the Fort Smith area. He married Henrietta Spiro and had a cotton gin in the town of Spiro, Oklahoma (named for his wife's family).[104] Cohn, who served as a commissioner of elections in Arkansas, was one of Fort Smith's leading merchants.[105]

One of Fort Smith's most outstanding Jewish pioneers was Bernhard Baer (1836–1886), a cousin of Samuel Adler (the Adlers had settled in the 1850s at Van Buren, located just across the Arkansas River from Fort Smith [see section I]).[106] Baer entered the Third Arkansas Regiment as a private in 1861 and was mustered out as an officer in 1865. After he returned to Fort Smith, he established a grocery firm and, together with Col. Logan H. Roots and R. C. Kerens, established the National Bank of western Arkansas in 1871. He also joined the two men and several others in financing the railroads into western Arkansas.[107] His grocery trade extended some two hundred miles west into Indian Territory and fifty miles out from Fort Smith in other directions. Joining him as partners were relatives Samuel Baer (1842–1908) and H. Baer and his brother-in-law, Moses Joel (1840–1917). By the 1880s their firm was doing a half million dollars of business a year.[108]

Bernhard Baer was well educated and proficient in six languages. Known for his charity and kindness, he served several years as a Fort Smith alderman, beginning in 1873. He was an honored member of the Fort Smith Masonic Lodge, and when the organization's large, new temple was built in 1889, three years after his death, it was named for him. (Col. Logan H. Roots delivered the temple's dedicatory address, in which he lauded B. Baer's charitable deeds and entreated that "through all time the memory of the good deeds of Brother Baer" be recalled.)[109] Baer's partners continued the grocery firm for several years after his death, and by 1900 there were ten adult Baer family members living in Fort Smith.[110] Bernhard's brother-in-law, Joseph Adler (1834–1909), was in the banking and dry goods business in Fort Smith for more than twenty-five years.[111]

It was under the inspiration of Bernhard Baer and through his financial help that his young relatives, Julius Baer and Sigmund Baer, together with Aaron Fuller, began the Boston Store, which became one of the largest mercantile stores in the Southwest for the next one hundred years. After the young men came to Arkansas, Bernhard advanced $350 to Julius and Sigmund to open a store at Magazine in Logan County and $500 to Aaron Fuller and Ike Apple to open a store at Witcherville, about fifteen miles south of Fort Smith. The stores prospered, and in 1881 the young Baers and Fuller combined their efforts at Fort Smith and bought out Betty Fitchenor's millinery store, changing its name to the Boston Store.[112] The store grew so quickly that it opened branches at nearby Van Buren and later at Dardanelle and Fayetteville and at Springfield, Missouri. The men took wives in the mid-1880s; Aaron Fuller married his partners' sister Frieda, Julius married Freda Adler, and Sigmund married Mary Pappenheimer. By 1892 the store had grown to such size that it would either have had to expand or the partnership be dissolved. That same year, one of the largest department stores in St. Louis burned, and the Baers and Fuller were assisted by the financier C. A. Stix to secure an option on the site. Thus was born the Stix, Baer and Fuller firm, later known as The Grand-Leader. The three families moved to St. Louis in the 1890s and left the Boston Store at Fort Smith in the hands of Rudolph Ney.[113]

German-born Rudolph Ney (1860–1936) had joined his brother in Leadville, Colorado, in the mid-1870s and began his career as a traveling salesman. Stopping to rest in Fort Smith from the tedious travel of the period, he was welcomed by the Jewish community and spotted by Julius and Sigmund Baer as an excellent prospect for their sister Marie. He did indeed marry her and became a partner in the Boston Store. By the time the other partners moved to St. Louis, Ney had grown to love Fort Smith and wanted to raise his family there. Over the years, he slowly bought out his partners' shares in the firm. The Boston Store continued to grow and prosper. By the time it celebrated its thirty-seventh anniversary in 1929, its sales were totaling a million and a half dollars a week.[114] The firm continued solidly through the 1930s and in 1936 bought the Rosenthal store at Beaumont, Texas. It later bought two other stores there as well—the White House and the Gus Mayer store.[115] Through the years, Ney used the store to benefit the community in other ways besides goods. He brought the 1894 World's Fair to his customers in the form of a pictorial book. He also brought cultural events in the form of artifacts from Italy, China, and other countries and displayed what local clientele would never have seen otherwise.[116] Ney presented plays and parties at his home that benefitted orphanages and service organizations of the area. Many of the Boston Store's workers became veteran employees, and their loyalty and expertise drew customers from as far away as a hundred miles.[117] The store continued for 107 years before it was sold in 1986 (see section V).

Rudolph Ney's daughter, Elizabeth, married Louis Cohen (1889–1960), who had come to Fort Smith as a young man of sixteen. Louis began his career as the first paper carrier for the *Southwest American* and was made circulation manager of the newspaper at age seventeen. In 1919 he opened his own store, the Fort Smith Office and Supply Company, and became involved in the city's civic life. He served as president of the Lions Club and helped raise funds for a number of civic and charitable causes. As chairman of the disaster committee of the local Red Cross, he helped raise ten thousand dollars for the 1927 flood victims. He served as president of the Fort Smith Advertising Club and was an officer in the Chamber of Commerce and the Community Chest.[118] He was also active in the religious affairs of the Jewish community (see section IV).

Ludwig L. Langfelder (1870–1953) settled at Fort Smith around 1899 and became prominent in the business, civic, and religious life of the city. He worked for the Boston Store at first, then established a successful insurance business. He married Blanche Heymann, whose father had settled in Arkansas after the Civil War and had operated a store at Booneville (see below). Blanche was active in the women's clubs of Fort Smith, and one of the Langfelder daughters, Maxine, was a public school teacher in Fort Smith (see Distaff Side below).[119]

The Wolf family of Fort Smith became vitally intertwined in the city's history. German–born Moritz "Morris" Wolf (1835–1923) had settled there before the Civil War and had resumed his business after its conclusion. Other members of his family moved to Chicago, but his brother Ben (1847–1916) joined him after the Chicago fire. Morris moved his store to McAlester, Oklahoma, and in 1876 Ben and his brother-in-law, Abe Mayer, (1842–1906) opened the Mayer and Wolf store in Fort Smith. It became one of the largest in the city, drawing mostly Indian trade from miles around. Abe Mayer, senior member of the Wolf store, became one of the most prominent men in Fort Smith. He was also a strong leader in the Jewish religious community.[120] After Mayer died in 1906, Ben Wolf operated the store under his own name until 1912, when he was joined in partnership with his brother-in-law, Al Pollock (1871–1931), who had married Mae Wolf. It was then called the Wolf-Pollock store. Ben served as a director of the Peoples Building and Loan Association. He was known

as a "kindly courteous . . . honorable" person who held the "deserved confidence" of the Fort Smith area for half a century.[121] Ben had married
Zippie Oppenheimer, and they had one child, a son, Herbert (1885–
1926). After Ben died in 1916, Herbert worked diligently to improve the
store and changed it from a country supply house into one of the city's
largest department stores, the Wolf-Pollock Dry Goods Company. The
store continued under the direction of Al Pollock for a short while after
the death of Herbert Wolf in 1926.[122]

During the Federal occupation of Fort Smith during the Civil War,
one of the soldiers stationed there was Louis Tilles (1830–1875) of St.
Louis. Considering Fort Smith a better location for rearing his family, he
brought them there at war's end, and he built a homey cottage at 400
North Eighth Street.[123] The Tilleses had five children, George (1859–
1929), Emanuel (1862–1881), Cap Andrew (1865–1951), Hannah (Mrs.
Ike Apple), and Carrie (Mrs. Chauncy Lick). Louis was interested in the
civic affairs of the town, particularly education, and served on the school
board. His wife, Rosalie, died in 1872 at age thirty-five, becoming the first
known Jewish person to be buried in Fort Smith. Louis remarried two
years later, and when he died suddenly in 1875, his new wife put the five
Tilles children in a Catholic orphanage in Fort Smith and returned to her
home in Chicago. Concerned Jewish families of the community took the
children in and cared for them. When his father died, George Tilles at age
sixteen began his business career, starting out as a cigar manufacturer.
When he married Ella Wormser of Little Rock in 1882, the couple took
George's three siblings (Emanuel had died in 1881) to raise.[124]

George Tilles was a self-made man with a varied career: after his business was destroyed by fire in 1882, he opened the first telephone exchange
in the city, which he sold to the Bell Telephone Company. He had a franchise for distributing garbage boxes to four Arkansas cities; he was secretary-treasurer and city editor of the Fort Smith *Tribune*; and he managed
the Fort Smith Opera House for several years.[125] A Republican, he ran
unsuccessfully for state senator; he remained an outspoken party member,
however.[126] George Tilles was a student of history as well as of current
events. It was said of him that there was "no better-informed man in Fort
Smith on local and state and national events."[127] He established the Fort
Smith Pioneer Club to keep the old settlers together. He wrote a history
of the city from the 1860s to the 1890s and intended to write more, but a
local newspaper editor rejected his article as too lengthy for his readers'
interest. Such shortsightedness robbed succeeding generations of "the rest
of the story," which later had to be pieced together without Tilles's color-

ful anecdotes. Career-wise, George became so prominently known in his insurance business that, at one time, he received an out-of-state letter addressed to "George Tilles, Arkansas."[128]

As were most Jewish men of the day, George Tilles was an active Mason. He was one of a committee of seven Masons who sponsored and campaigned statewide for funds to erect a children's building at the State Tuberculosis Sanatarium at Booneville. The needed funds were collected in three years, and the state received the building debt free.[129] George visited the children often at the sanatarium, and at Christmas he made sure that every child had a gift.[130] (Two of the regular contributors to the children at the tuberculosis sanatarium were nationally prominent Cyrus Adler and his mother, Mrs. S. J. Adler. The Adlers sent numerous gifts for books and holiday treats until 1940, when Cyrus Adler died. After the death of both Adlers, the young tuberculosis patients were said to have lost "two friends who had contributed since the building was established.")[131]

George's brother Cap moved to St. Louis, where he prospered greatly; his love for his Arkansas home never left him however. In 1912 George, Cap, and their two sisters established in memory of their mother the Rosalie Tilles Children's Home for orphaned children of the area. It was built and maintained by a trust fund set up by the Tilles family.[132] In 1924 Cap Tilles also established a twelve-acre Tilles Park for children in Fort Smith; it was later made into a city park.[133] A public school and a street in Fort Smith were named for the Tilles family.

Samuel Tilles (1864–1923), a cousin of George Tilles, had a women's clothing store in Fort Smith named The Fair. After his death in 1923, it was renamed Tilles and was continued by his son Alvin (1894–1978), who had been the first young man in Fort Smith to volunteer in World War I.[134] In the 1930s Nicol Wintory came with his parents, a brother, and two sisters as refugees from Nazi Germany. Nicol later bought the Tilles ladies' ready-to-wear store.[135]

Relatively few of the early Jewish citizens of Fort Smith entered into politics. Except for Bernhard Baer and the Tilleses noted above, only two others are known—Henry Kaufman (1870–1943) and Jacob Baer. Kaufman was elected twice as a state representative from Sebastian County, serving from 1931 to 1935. He had been brought as a boy to Charleston in western Arkansas by his parents. When he grew older, he moved to Fort Smith and entered business with Louis Samter (1846–1924), then established his own brokerage firm.[136] (Samter came to Arkansas in the 1860s and had stores in several of its western towns before settling at Fort Smith.

The Samter's daughter, Thyra Samter Winslow [see Distaff Side below], became a nationally known writer.)[137] Jacob Baer served as Sebastian County treasurer in the 1870s.[138] Although a number of Baers settled originally at Fort Smith, they all eventually moved elsewhere.

Several Jewish professional men distinguished themselves at Fort Smith, including Dr. Davis W. Goldstein, Dr. Irvin Marcus Sternberg, Dr. Sidney J. Wolferman, and attorney Ben Kimpel Sr.

Dr. Goldstein (1888–1980), a native of Greenville, Mississippi, was a graduate of Tulane University and the University of Tennessee Medical School. He studied dermatology at Vienna, London, and Philadelphia before coming to Fort Smith in 1913. He served as regimental surgeon to the U.S. Army 328th Combat Infantry in World War I, and during that time became acquainted with Sergeant Alvin York. He returned to Fort Smith after the war and was a founding member of the Cooper Clinic, which grew to serve a large area of western Arkansas and eastern Oklahoma. He led in treating venereal disease and cancer, and he was advisor to the local health department and nearby Camp Chaffee in control of venereal diseases. He helped organize the Sebastian County and the Arkansas chapters of the American Cancer Society. He held free clinics in western Arkansas and was an advisor to many small communities when they established hospitals. He was magnanimous in spirit and for many years personally underwrote the expenses for Christmas gifts for children in Fort Smith's lower income district. He was often called to handle indigent patients.[139]

Dr. Davis Goldstein's father, Marx Goldstein (1857–1927), was a native of Birmingham, England. He emigrated to New Orleans, then conducted a store at Greenville, Mississippi. He and his wife, Rosa (Woolf) Goldstein, joined their son at Fort Smith in 1912.[140] Other members of the Goldstein family settled at Little Rock, including Edgar L. Goldstein, Miss Florette Goldstein, and Mrs. L. A. Sanders.

Dr. Irvin M. Sternberg (1882–1958), one of the first dentists in Fort Smith, was the son of Mark and Sarah (Oppenheimer) Sternberg, who had settled at Ozark, Franklin County, in 1875. The Sternbergs and their four children moved to Fort Smith in 1881, where Mark (1844–1923) conducted a commission business, dealing in poultry and cotton. (Mark and Sarah's son Henry [1872–1957] was a Fort Smith merchant, and their other son, Silvey [1877–1928], became a prominent cotton broker at Blytheville; they also had a daughter, Alice Holberg.) Irvin, the youngest child, was a 1907 graduate of the Washington University Dental School in St. Louis. He soon built up the largest dental practice in Fort Smith and served as president of the Arkansas State Dental Association from 1908 to 1911. He organized both the Fort Smith and northwest Arkansas dental societies and served as president of the organizations. He married Bertha Levinson, daughter of Newton P. and Minnie (Harris) Levinson. In 1913 the Levinsons had come from Cincinnati to Fort Smith, where Newton (1854–1921) opened a furniture store. Bertha was a musician, teaching piano and serving as head of the Columbia Concert Club, for which she brought artists to perform at Fort Smith.[141] The Irvin Sternbergs had three daughters, Sidney and twins Ione and Leone, and a son, Irvin. Ione married Jerome Ney, who later succeeded his father, Rudolph Ney, as owner of the Boston Store.

Dr. Sidney J. Wolferman, one of the organizers and original partners in the Cooper Clinic of Fort Smith, came to the city in 1913. He served as a member of the Army Medical Corps in World War I, then returned to Fort Smith. A graduate of the University of Wisconsin and of the Northwestern University School of Medicine, he specialized in plastic surgery. He served as president of the Sebastian County Medical Society and the Arkansas Medical Society.[142] Although he was born to Jewish parents, he intermarried and did not identify with Judaism.[143] He died in 1945.

Ben Drew Kimpel (1883–1918), son of pioneer Dermott settler Dave Kimpel, became one of Fort Smith's most promising attorneys after he settled there in 1906. He was a graduate of the University of Arkansas, Fayetteville, and of Columbia University Law School. He had then studied law at Fort Smith under Col. T. P. Winchester and W. R. Martin, and had later established the firm of Kimpel and [Harry P.] Dally. Kimpel dedicated his time and talents to community interests and became generally liked by local officials. He served as chairman of the United War Work Campaign for Sebastian County in 1918 and represented the group at an October meeting held that year in Little Rock. While there, he contracted the dreaded Spanish flu and died a short time later. Fort Smith mourned his passing, and statements of regret were given at his funeral by Mayor Arch Monro, Judge Joseph M. Hill, Colonel Winchester, and several others.[144] Like Dr. Wolferman, Kimpel did not identify with the Jewish faith. He was survived by his wife, Gladys (Crane) Kimpel, a non-Jew, and a young son, Ben Kimpel Jr., who became a legendary English professor at the University of Arkansas, Fayetteville (see section V).

By mid-1890s there were 118 Jewish business men and women found in the Fort Smith City Directory. They were listed as attorneys, auctioneers, book binders, brokers, carpet and matting store owners, cigar manufacturers, china-glass-queensware sellers, commission merchants, dyers and scourers, grocers, livery stable owners, tailors, saloon keepers, meat market owners, printers, newspapermen, and dealers in hides, wool, and hardware.[145] Some of these pioneer merchants included David Jacobs (1853–1919), who had a popular eatery called the Farmers' Eating House. He was open twenty-four hours a day, and his services included lodging (at fifteen cents and twenty-five cents a night), meals at any hour, and groceries.[146] Those with mercantile stores included Pincus Berman (1839–1910), who came virtually penniless and "amassed a large fortune through hard work and diligence";[147] N. Nathan (1839–1914), who had a line of clothing stores at Fort Smith, Texarkana, and Springfield, Missouri;[148] Mendel Hopp (1827–1900), an 1890s settler;[149] Isadore Moses (1871–1958), a sixty-five-year resident of Fort Smith;[150] William E. Marks (1877–1949), owner of Marks' Store on Garrison Avenue;[151] and Jacob Pappenheimer, who had a furniture business in Fort Smith in the 1870s and 1880s.[152] Joe Rosenstiel (1873–1939) was an independent cotton broker, and his brother Albert (1879–1958) was a Fort Smith businessmen.[153]

Jacob Goldman, who had first settled in Jacksonport in the 1870s, became associated not only with the cotton trade in Arkansas and some of the railroads into the state, but also with the Goldman Hotel of Fort Smith. The hotel became that city's most prestigious meeting place for some thirty years. Construction of the hotel, located at Garrison Avenue and North Thirteenth Street, began in 1908, but funds were depleted after only two floors were built. A new company, the Southwestern Hotel Company, was formed with seven directors, one of whom was Rudolph Ney, owner of the Boston Store. Ney contacted Jacob Goldman, who supplied needed funds to complete the hotel, and it was named for him. From the time it opened until it closed after World War II, it became the focal point of Fort Smith society. Its grand service was unmatched, and notables who visited it included Bob Burns, Will Rogers, Susan Hayward, Mickey Mantle, Dizzy Dean, President and Mrs. Harry Truman, and Rosalind Russell. A reception for Mrs. Eleanor Roosevelt also was held there.[154]

BOONEVILLE, CHARLESTON, WITCHERVILLE, MAGAZINE, AND PARIS

Northwest Arkansas was much less populated than the other three quadrants of the state, probably because it included the beautiful but hard-to-travel (and hard-to-farm) terrain of the Ozark Mountains. Still, a number of towns in this area, including Booneville, Charleston, Witcherville, Magazine, and Paris, saw Jewish merchants settle there between the Civil

War and the turn of the century. (Almost all later moved their stores to Fort Smith, and some moved to other states.) Maximillion Heymann (1839–1884) established a store in Booneville with partner Joseph Joel (1841–1888); Joel later moved to Fort Smith, but Heymann remained in Booneville until his death in 1884. (Joseph's brother, M. Joel, married the sister of Bernhard Baer.) Simon Joel (1846–1915) and a Baer family member established the Baer and Joel firm at Charleston in 1873. Simon Joel dissolved his partnership and opened a store called The Beehive.[155] Aaron Fuller and Ike Apple had a store at Witcherville (see above on the Boston Store); Isaac Kaufman (1846–1924) opened a store at Charleston, and after several years opened a meat market at Fort Smith, where he became known for his sense of humor and keen wit.[156]

Israel H. Oppenheimer (1846–1916) settled in the Fort Smith area in 1876, and Isaac Oppenheimer (1854–1907) established a store at Paris in Logan County in 1891. The latter had a farm supply store and was an agent for the Lesser-Goldman Cotton Company. On Sundays, Isaac, his wife, Emma (Lederer) Oppenheimer, and their three children, Harry, Brunette, and Karl, would ride in their buggy over winding mountain roads to Magazine, some thirty miles away, to visit other Jewish settlers. Although the Oppenheimer family moved from Arkansas to St. Louis in 1899, they kept close ties with the state. Harry Oppenheimer (1891–1989) worked his way through college in St. Louis, became associated with the Lesser-Goldman Cotton Company, and later joined the S. D. Leidesdorf Certified Public Accountant firm as a partner, heading its Chicago office. During the Depression, he heard that some of his relatives in Little Rock had no jobs, and he brought six of them to Chicago and helped to reestablish them.[157] The Oppenheimer family intertwined with a number of other Arkansas Jewish families, including those of Wolf, Sternberg, Thalheimer, Siesel, Krone, Lewis, Reubel, Hirsch, Kastor, Friedman, Stifft, Weinstein, Pollock, Mendel, Ehrman, Weinberger, Levinson, Ney, Davidson, Fox, and Billstein.[158]

FAYETTEVILLE

Fayetteville in Washington County, located in the northwestern corner of the state, became home of the University of Arkansas in 1870, when the the city and county outbid other sections of the state to secure the institution. At that time, the population of Fayetteville was 955.[159] Six years before this occurred, in 1864, the Baum brothers, Leopold, Joseph, and Moses, had peddled out from St. Louis into the northwest Arkansas area and judged that Fayetteville would be a good place to settle. They began in a small former blacksmith's shop, becoming the second store to open at Fayetteville after the Civil War.[160] Their store grew to become the largest farm supply store in northwest Arkansas; after surviving a cyclone, hailstorm, fire, and panic, it remained a leader in the mercantile business for some fifty years, into the early 1930s.[161]

Leopold Baum, known affectionately as "Uncle Lee," was a charter stockholder in the city's electric light and power company, and he gave liberally toward education for the area's youth. Moses Baum (1845–1934) married Julia Heller and they had eight children. Julia was a prominent member of club and social circles in the city and worked in a number of charitable organizations, particularly the City Hospital.[162] Although the Baums were the only Jewish family in the area until 1919 and had no formal place of worship, they retained their Jewishness (and closed their store on High Holidays) and all but two of their children married within their faith. (When daughter Leah "ran off" and married a University of Arkansas professor, the Baums were "as mad as you know what" that she had married a non-Jew.) The family experienced little anti-Semitism; one daughter could remember only a single incident—that of being called a "sheeny."[163] At one time, one of the Baums' granddaughters was asked by a local friend when she was leaving. "To go where?" she asked. "To Palestine; all Jews have to go back there," was the reply.[164]

In 1919 the Baum family was finally joined at Fayetteville by another Jewish family, the Silvermans, who opened a jewelry store. Louis Silverman (1876–1948) was joined in the business by his son Bernard (1908–1961). After Louis died in the 1940s, Bernard and his mother, Dorothy Silverman, ran a women's specialty shop.[165]

Julian Seesel Waterman (1891–1943), son of Gus Waterman, a prominent pioneer settler of Dumas, became closely associated with the University of Arkansas in Fayetteville. A graduate of Tulane University, the University of Michigan, and an honor graduate of the University of Chicago Law School, he started teaching for the University of Arkansas Department of Economics in 1914. After serving as a first lieutenant in the U.S. Army in World War I, he returned to Fayetteville. Waterman did a feasibility study on having a law department for the university in 1923 and headed the one established a year later. The first faculty member to join Waterman was Claude D. Pepper, who later distinguished himself as a senator and congressman from Florida. The University of Arkansas School of Law was established in 1926, with Waterman as dean. As a result of his Herculean efforts, the school was accredited as a member of the Association of American Law Schools just one year later. (Only eleven other schools in the South had received such accreditation at the time.)

Waterman enlisted Robert A. Leflar as a law faculty member in 1927. During Leflar's leave of absence in 1936, Waterman invited his friend J. W. Fulbright to fill in the term. Fulbright taught until 1939, when University of Arkansas President John C. Futrall was killed in an auto accident. Waterman was vice-president of the university at the time, but he "was not about to become president," and convinced Governor Carl Bailey to appoint Fulbright to the position. (J. W. Fulbright was later removed from his position as University of Arkansas president by Homer M. Adkins, who had won the governorship from Carl Bailey. Fulbright then ran for the position of U.S. senator from Arkansas and was elected; thus began his long and illustrious career in politics.)[166]

Waterman had no taste for politics or the necessary wrangling for University of Arkansas funds. A dedicated pedagogue and writer, he declined an appointment to the Arkansas Supreme Court, preferring to teach and to continue his prolific writing; he was a frequent contributor to law journals. Waterman died of a ruptured appendix in 1943. It was said of him at the time that few individuals had exerted as much influence in the fields of law and higher education in Arkansas as he had, and his death was viewed as "an irreparable loss to the University" by its then president, Dr. A. M. Harding.[167]

MARSHALL

Marshall, county seat of Searcy County, also located in the beautiful Ozark Mountains, was incorporated in 1884, although it was little more than a hamlet at the time.[168] To this little village, which had been known as Burrowville prior to its incorporation, came the Federal Civil War veteran Max Dampf (1848–1914). Dampf, born in Bavaria to Samuel and Matilda (Apple) Dampf, had immigrated to America in 1866 and had joined the Federal army. He was sent to Little Rock, where he was honorably discharged in 1869. He moved to the Ozarks and married non-Jew Sarah C. Hollis in 1870. They lived at Bear Creek that year; Dampf listed himself as a "professor" (teacher).[169] He also farmed and had a store at Marshall. A local paper noted in 1898 that his "talking machine" (undescribed as to its exact nature) was drawing large crowds.[170] He became known as a "fine penman and excellent accountant" and served as county tax assessor, 1878–1880, and as county clerk, 1884–1886; he served a number of years as deputy clerk. Dampf, who attended Jewish services at Little Rock, accumulated a host of friends in the Marshall area. He was said to be a man of "exceptionally good moral character" whose influence was "for good."[171] Max and Sarah Dampf had twelve children, and their descendants scattered across Arkansas and into other states.[172]

PERRYVILLE

What drew the Jewish pioneers, particularly the well-educated ones, to Arkansas's remote communities can only be surmised. Austrian-born David Herstein (1850–1934), a graduate in literature and theology who had committed the Talmud to memory, is material for such surmise. He came to Arkansas in 1876, peddled over its northern region, and in 1878 settled at Perryville, a small village incorporated that year less than forty miles northwest of Little Rock. There he established the general mercantile firm of Herstein and Mondschein. His honest business practice was said to have helped him develop a large trade. An active member in local civic and fraternal organizations, he was said to have helped in every effort for the public welfare. He married Lena Lasker of Cincinnati; Benjamin, the oldest of their children, was the first Jewish child born in Perry County.[173]

MORRILTON

At Morrilton, less than twenty miles north of Perryville, in Conway County, the German-born Frank brothers, Al (1891–1979), and Karl (1894–1979), opened what became one of the larger, privately owned dry goods stores of the town. The store was established in 1922 and continued for forty-four years. Al and his wife, Bertha, (see Distaff Side below) had one son, Gordon, who became an ophthalmologist and moved to Dallas. Karl and his wife, Rosalind, had a daughter, Karlyn. These were the only Jewish families in town, and they were welcomed freely into every club and every other organization, with no sense of prejudice.[174]

CONWAY, HEBER SPRINGS

What became one of the most successful farm supply stores in the state, Frauenthal and Schwarz, had a quite modest beginning in 1872 at Conway, located in Faulkner County less than twenty-five miles northwest of Little Rock. It was founded in a small frame building by Maximillian "Max" Frauenthal (1836–1914), an unsung Civil War hero (see section I) who came to Conway Station in 1871 with a railroad crew.[175] Frauenthal's store grew, and he sent for his cousin Joseph "Jo" Frauenthal (1858–1944) in Louisville, Kentucky. The store was then known as M. and J. Frauenthal. It prospered as a supply store, and riders were hired to visit farmers and give credit on the worth of their crops. They opened stores at Atkins and Clarksville as well. Other Frauenthals, whose family hailed from Marianthal, Germany, were brought to Conway, including Joseph's parents, Jacob and Yetta Frauenthal, and his brothers, Samuel (1862–1935), Isaac "Ike" (1865–1891), Maurice (1868–1901), Henry, Charles (1871–1929), and his sister, Cora (1869–?).[176] When Max needed more help, he visited Germany with Gus Blass of Little Rock and Mr. Lowenstein of Memphis, and Max brought back a cousin, Leopold "Lee" Schwarz (1854–1928). The Frauenthal brothers, Jo and Charles, and Lee Schwarz, who had married their sister, Cora, took over the supply business, and it became known as the Frauenthal and Schwarz store. The Frauenthal family was involved in a number of enterprises that benefitted farmers and helped build up the city of Conway.[177]

Jo Frauenthal, who was known as the "dean of Conway merchants," became a member of the city council, served as president of the school board, and became a member of almost every committee that built churches, schools, or colleges in Conway. For some twenty-five years he headed the Conway Chamber of Commerce, and his farsightedness helped bring improvements of water, sewerage, electricity, and the building and paving of county roads. He was active in politics, helping others to become elected; he was most pleased with the election of George W. Donaghey of Conway to the office of governor of Arkansas in 1908. With limited formal schooling, he was self-educated and described as a "profound scholar."[178] He was a collector of classics and accumulated one of the finest and most valuable private libraries in the state. He enlarged the Frauenthal and Schwarz store and constructed a large, two-story brick building, the second floor of which was used for a social hall. All social functions of the town took place there—balls, dances, skating, and elaborate events that at times included an orchestra from Little Rock and for which participants would send to Memphis for rental costumes.[179] Jo Frauenthal and Opie Read, an Arkansas newsman, briefly published a paper, the "Spyglass," that was to cater to the "cultured moderns" of the town.[180] He married Ida Baridon of New York, and they built one of the city's most palatial houses, located on several acres where Governor Donaghey's home had stood before it burned. (Ida Frauenthal became known statewide, serving as president of the state's Federation of Women's

Clubs and as a member of the state Defense Board and a committee to select a state flag for Arkansas. A residence hall at Arkansas State Teachers College [now University of Central Arkansas] was named Baridon Hall as was a street in Conway, both in recognition of Ida's civic efforts.[181] She and Jo had no children.)

In the 1920s Mayer F. Gates (1892–1966), son of Ferdinand Gates of Lonoke, who had married Gladys Frauenthal, daughter of Charles Frauenthal, took over the Conway firm and continued it for almost twenty years. He, Harvey C. Couch, and several others helped organize the First National Bank of Conway.[182]

After selling his interest in the store he founded at Conway, Max Frauenthal spent his energy on new developments. He was a small man (about five feet four inches) with a big heart; he was also ingenious and farsighted. His interest was piqued after hearing of healing springs located some forty-plus miles northeast of Conway. For many years John T. Jones had held the land on which the springs were found, but he had done nothing significant with the property. After visiting the area and seeing the beautiful hills and scenic wonderland, Max saw it as a challenge. In 1881 he bought from Jones and his wife 360 acres, which included the springs and surrounding land. He then formed a land development company and incorporated the town of Sugar Loaf, which was named the county seat of a new county, Cleburne, formed in 1883. Through his advanced business ability, he was able to purchase back the land that he had sold to the development company. He then donated land for a courthouse, which he built, and for a school; he also donated the acreage on which the springs were located, naming it Spring Park. The town rightfully should have been named Frauenthal after the mover and shaker that had brought it into existence, but it was first named Sugar Loaf (for the unique mountain peak to its east). The name Heber was later chosen; it honored Dr. Heber Jones, son of the property's former owner, John T. Jones, and also Frauenthal's people, the Hebrews.[183] Max moved his wife, Sallie (Jacobs), and family to Heber Springs, where he built a thirteen-room house and a twenty-six-room hotel (both eventually burned). Max became known as the "Father of Heber Springs and Cleburne County"; his picture was placed in the courthouse rotunda by a Circuit Court order, and it hung there for many years. By 1920 the town's population was 1,675.[184]

Only six of Max and Sallie's thirteen children lived to adulthood, three girls and three boys. Only two of these married Jewish: Theresa married Isadore Friedman of McGehee, and Ruth married Lucian Krone of St. Louis. A third daughter, Cora, married Dr. Foster G. Richardson, and their daughter, Irene Richardson, became well known as the librarian at Fort Smith Junior High School. Max and Sallie's son Mortimer (1871–1936), a Heber Springs attorney, served as mayor of the town for two terms and was manager of the Heber Springs townsite, which covered some 680 acres. The Frauenthal's son Clarence operated several businesses in Heber Springs, including a recreation hall, two theaters (one named The Clarece for his wife, Clara, who operated a beauty salon and gift shop), two soda fountains, and a grocery store. Their son Arthur was an optician and jeweler in Heber Springs and Conway before he retired for health reasons to Phoenix, Arizona, where he owned and operated Westward Lodge.[185]

Samuel "Sam" Frauenthal, brother of Jo, Henry, Charles, and Cora (Schwarz), served as an associate justice of the Arkansas Supreme Court in the years 1909–1913. He was appointed to the office by Governor George Donaghey to fill the unexpired term of Judge Edgar A. McCulloch, who was appointed chief justice when Judge Joseph M. Hill resigned. A deeply conscientious person, Sam brooded over the decisions the Court made, and although he was encouraged to run for the office when the term expired in 1913, he did not. He chose to help others quietly rather than engage in a public campaign.[186] Sam Frauenthal lived at Conway, where he practiced law and was a member of the Conway Fire Company. In 1898 he and Robert Fones established a plant to produce metal harrows; the company helped sustain a new power plant until a sufficient demand for electricity arose to make the power plant self-sustaining.[187]

Other pioneer West European Jews who settled in Conway included Sam Heiligers (1848–1921), who came to America from Rotterdam with his parents. Both parents died in the yellow fever epidemic of 1879, and Sam moved to Conway and opened a grocery store. Although he had a number of business reverses, he overcame all and grew to be known as one of the "most energetic" Conway men ever engaged in business.[188] He married Minnie Merriman, who had been the first white girl born in Conway. Her mother, Matilda Menkus, was Jewish,[189] but her father, Judge E. M. Merriman (Conway's second mayor and a judge of Faulkner County), was a Gentile. After marrying Sam, Minnie became the first president of Conway's School Improvement Association.[190] Sam Heiligers' brothers, Jake and Isaac, lived at Little Rock, but Jake later moved to Newport.

Joseph Van Ronkle, also from Holland and brother-in-law of Sam Heiligers', established a dry goods store at Conway; he served as president of the town's school district. The silk hat he wore and the gold-headed cane he used gave such a striking appearance that it was rumored he "belonged to nobility somewhere."[191]

Leo Hamberg (1887–?), another Jewish settler at Conway, served as a city alderman. He also had roots in Holland; his father, Alphonse Hamberg of Lonoke, was born there. Leo was associated with S. G. Smith of Conway and also with the Lesser-Goldman Cotton Company. He owned a two-thousand-acre cotton plantation and in 1920 went into business under his own name and bought, sold, and merchandized cotton to world markets. Active in a number of civic and fraternal organizations, he was cited as one who had aided materially in Conway's civic growth.[192] Leo's brother Alphonse "Alph" Hamberg Jr. (1899–1984) was also a Conway resident and served as the city's mayor in the early 1940s. He had a store at Conway that sold cotton muslin by the bolt, and windows in homes, churches, and businesses statewide sported curtains made of the durable fabric. The Hambergs had two other brothers, Walter of Lonoke and Edwin of Pine Bluff. They also had a sister, Julia Payne of Oklahoma City.[193]

The Distaff Side

Four Jewish women from the western section of Arkansas are noted here: Thyra Winslow, Ella Falk, and Maxine Chapman, all of Fort Smith, and Bertha Frank of Morrilton.

Writer Thyra (Samter) Winslow (1893–1961), daughter of Louis and Sarah Samter, was listed in the 1978 *World Almanac as* one of eleven famous Arkansans, although by that time few people in Arkansas remembered who she was.[194] At age fourteen, Thyra, who had become repulsed by the sweet stereotypical phrasings in the local newspaper society columns, began writing a column for the Fort Smith *Southwest American*. In the column, called "The Lady Clerk," she would impale local citizens in tongue-in-cheek caricatures with the "sharp pin of her keen-witted insight." Although she became less than popular in her hometown, her column began to compete with front page news. After graduation from high school at Fort Smith, she studied at the University of Missouri, the Cincinnati Art Academy, and Columbia University. Her writings caught the eye of noted newspaperman H. L. Mencken, who supervised her first book, *Picture Frames*. She wrote several books and a motion picture scenario for Columbia Studios that was taken from her short story, "She Married Her Boss." The film starred Claudette Colbert. She also wrote the dialogue for the Warner Brothers film, "Four Daughters." She lived at New York, where she became well known among such celebrities as Dorothy Gish, Dashiell Hammett, Sam Hellman, Nunnally Johnson, and dozens of others.[195]

It was not until fifteen years after Thyra Winslow left Fort Smith that she revisited her home town. At that time, she made light of it, comparing it with New York. As she became older, however, she began to appreciate Arkansas, and in the 1950s she made a two-week tour of the state to collect data for a book that would extol the state's industry, recreational facilities, and points of interest. (She unfortunately did not live to complete the book.) She was writing it, she said, because "no one seems to know anything about Arkansas except a few rude jokes." Arkansas, she noted, appeared to be "an unknown state." Thyra Winslow credited her desire to write to two of her grade school teachers at Belle Grove School in Fort Smith, a Mr. Parker, who gave her a feeling for words, and B. W. Torreyson.[196]

Mrs. George (Ella Tilles) Falk, granddaughter of one of Fort Smith's pioneer Jewish settlers, Louis Tilles, was born to Louis's son George in 1902. From her father, she learned to appreciate education, history, and culture. She was a graduate of the University of Chicago and while in that city served as social secretary to the portrait painter Julian Lamar. After returning to Fort Smith, she married George Falk, an insurance agent; the couple had no children. Ella entered the civic life of the city and was tireless in her efforts. She organized or helped organize the Family Service Agency, the Home Makers Service, the American Association for University Women (Fort Smith chapter), Operation Head Start, the Fort Smith Little Theatre, the Broadway Theatre League, the Republican Women's Club, and the Sparks Hospital Women's Board. During World War II she was active in almost every organization in Fort Smith pertaining to the war effort. Over the years she collected more than thirteen hundred dolls, and thousands of individuals, including Girl Scouts, Sunday School classes, public and parochial school classes, Y Teens, student nurses, and adult groups came to view the collection.[197] (Ella made Fort Smith her lifelong home, continuing to live there into the 1990s.)

Mrs. Arch (Maxine Langfelder) Chapman was born at Fort Smith in 1908 to L. L. Langfelder and Wilheminia "Minna" Heymann, whose family had settled at Booneville after the Civil War. An appreciation for education was also instilled in her, and she was a graduate of the National College of Education at Evanston, Illinois. Maxine returned to Fort Smith after college and taught third grade at Bellepoint Elementary School in Fort Smith for thirty-seven years. In 1964 she was chosen as Teacher of the Year in Arkansas. She served on the national board of the Classroom Teachers Association, a subsidiary of the National Education Association (NEA) and served as an NEA director for Arkansas for six years. She helped organize the State Childhood Education Association and helped form the State League of Women Voters. She married Dr. Arch H. Chapman, and they had one son, Arch.[198] (Like Ella Falk, Maxine's lifelong home was in Fort Smith; she continued to live there into the 1990s.)

Bertha (Levine) Frank (1898–1988), a native of Bonham, Texas, was brought to Pine Bluff as a child with her three sisters by her mother, Susan (Levy) Levine (1866–1942), after the death of her father, Max Levine. Her two brothers, Jay and Sam, had preceded them to Arkansas. Bertha was educated at Peabody College in Nashville, the University of Chicago, and a music school at Chautauqua, New York. She taught three years at Pine Bluff, then married Al Frank, who established a store at Morrilton. In her new location, Bertha became a leader in civic affairs. She served as chairman of the State Library Board and of the Conway County Library Board and served on the board of the Parent-Teacher Association, and on boards on parks, safety, city planning, women's groups, book clubs, and as president of the United Daughters of the Confederacy (her maternal grandfather, Bernard Levy, had served as a lieutenant in the Confederate army). She also served as president of the state's Federation of Women's Clubs. She was chairman of the Conway County Rationing Board during World War II, and she taught a class for adults and teachers through the PTA. She remained active in Morrilton affairs until the Frank store was closed in the mid-1960s and she and her husband moved to Little Rock, where she served as president of the Bayview Club (for book reviews, lectures, etc.) and was active in other civic and social organizations.[199]

Mrs. Noland (Isabel) Blass Sr., Little Rock, ca. 1940. (Photo courtesy of Gus Blass)

Wolff-Goldman Mercantile Store, Newport; center: Sigmund Wolff, seated with legs crossed (hatless); to his right: Isaac Goldman. (Photo courtesy of Tom Wolff)

Adler-Hirsch stagecoach, Batesville, 4 July 1861. Among the passengers were Albert Carter, Lazarus Hirsch, Israel and Simon Adler, Sam Earnheart, Sam Hirsch, Jeff Stone, Dick Hayden, Jeff Massey (on horse at right), *and driver John McBride.* (Photo courtesy of Marie Adler Kessel)

Harold Sternberg, (right), 1920s, Blytheville. (Photo courtesy of Helen [Sternberg] Stern)

Ferdinand Gates Store, Lonoke, 1889; left to right: Frank Bennett, Jim Lassiter, Ike May, William Wilkenson, Albert Hester, Dave Gates, M. W. Bizzell. (Photo courtesy of David Bizzell)

Judge Jacob Trieber from Helena, first Jewish Federal judge in America. (Photo courtesy of J. Marshall Trieber)

Solomon family of Helena; top row, left to right: Meyer Cook, Ella Solomon Cook, Lafe Solomon, Henry Solomon, Sophie Solomon, Joe Solomon; middle row: Dave Solomon Sr., Sarah Solomon; seated: Louis Solomon, Ruth Cook, Pauline Solomon (mother), Myrtle Solomon, Phillip Solomon; portrait, Moses Solomon (father). (Photo courtesy of David Solomon Jr.)

Solomon brothers in front of Helena's "skyscraper," the Solomon Building, five stories high (now Helena National Bank Building); back seat, left to right: Lafe, Henry; middle seat: Joe, Dave; front seat: Phillip, Louis. (Photo courtesy of David Solomon Jr.)

"Col." Louis Altheimer, cofounder with his brother Joseph of the town of Altheimer, Arkansas. (Photo courtesy of Alan J. Altheimer)

Jimmy and Betty Lou Sachs, Altheimer, Arkansas, 1930s. (Photo courtesy of Betty Sachs Prousnitzer)

Charles Weil family of Pine Bluff; clockwise from lower left: Charles Weil (father), Ben, Claudia (Oppenheimer), May (Strauss), Burton, Sidney, Sayda (Franklin), Amelia (mother), David; center, Harry. (Photo courtesy of Ernest P. Weil)

Children of Pine Bluff pioneer settlers Sol and Goldina Franklin; standing, left to right: Dave, Sam, Bennie; seated: James, Hattye (Prousnitzer), Joe, Miriam (Eisman). (Photo courtesy of George Franklin)

Front row, *David Felsenthal* (*white-bearded man*), *early pioneer Camden citizen;
his family: front row, left to right: Beatrice (Heller) Masur, Marie (Heller)
Sugar, Eva (Mrs. David Felsenthal), Sonell Felsenthal, Dorothy (Heller)
Goldman, Corrine (Mrs. Jake Felsenthal), Nora Felsenthal; second row: Ike
Felsenthal, Eva (Felsenthal) Heller, Gertrude (Mrs. Ike Felsenthal), Blanche
(Felsenthal) Levy, Sidney Felsenthal, Jake Felsenthal; top row: Adolph Felsenthal,
Lee Felsenthal, Arthur Levy, Henry Heller. (Sonell is Ike and Gertrude's son;
Beatrice, Marie, and Dorothy are Eva and Henry Heller's daughters.) (Photo cour-
tesy of Martha Felsenthal Hainsfurther)*

Meyer-Lockwood wedding, Hot Springs. (Photo courtesy of Susi Rosenzweig)

Meyer brothers (front seat) *and Alfred Blumenstiel of Hot Springs. (Photo courtesy of Susi Rosenzweig)*

Bernice and Lewis Goltz (center), *Hot Springs, 1930s. (Photo courtesy of Bernice Goltz)*

Moses and Julia Baum, 1860s settlers at Fayetteville. (Photo courtesy of Gustine Lorich Weber)

Portrait of Julian Waterman, first dean of the University of Arkansas Law School.

Max Frauenthal, 1870s settler at Conway and founder of Heber Springs, Arkansas. (Photo courtesy of Julian Frauenthal)

Joseph Itzkowitz (left), ca. 1915, member of the Little Rock banana cooperative, with his wagon. (Photo courtesy of Bob Itzkowitz)

Fiftieth wedding anniversary of Abraham and Dora Sanders, Little Rock, with their eight daughters and one son; top row: Esther Cooper, Bess Greenstein, Rose Waldman, Bill, Adele, Tillie, Sophie Cohen; bottom row: Becky (Rebecca), Dora, Abraham, Jennie Loket. (Photo courtesy of Jennie S. Loket)

*Lena Latkin, assistant super-
intendent of the Pulaski County
Public Schools, 1920s–1930s.
(Photo courtesy of
Gertrude Latkin)*

*Louis "Uncle Louie" and Minnie Meyer (couple seated on second tier, far left,
Minnie in white hat), Rector, around the turn of the century. (Photo courtesy of
Rosalind Sarason)*

Jerry Cohen (left), Samuel Joseph Cohen, and Luba Cohen of Blytheville. (Photo courtesy of Marcie A. Cohen)

Mike Drexler family of Wynne; top row, left to right: Mike, Dora, Mitchell, Lena, Bess; front row: Ben, Lee, Rose, David, Manuel. (Photo courtesy of David Drexler)

Tiger family, Luxora, 1904; back row, left to right: Abe, Esidor, Ethel, Bessie; front row: Lillian, Rebecca, Louis, Helen. (Photo courtesy of M. Gordon Tiger)

Jake Tupper, peddler and later store owner at Earle, ca. 1930. (Photo courtesy of Lena Tupper Bursk)

The Boston Store in Earle, ca. 1920; left to right: customer and owners Dave and Claudia (Erber) Schwartz. (Photo courtesy of Joe Erber)

Ciener's dry cleaning shop, Helena, 1908. (Photo courtesy of Sam Ciener Jr.)

"Buster Brown" (center, on platform) promoting Buster Brown shoes in front of Rosenzweig's store, Lake Village, 1930s. (Photo courtesy of Joe Rosenzweig)

Marks family, Fort Smith, ca. 1937; front row, left to right: *Morton B. Marks Jr.,
Ruth Frauenthal Marks, Morton B. Marks Sr., A. M. Marks*; back row, *Jeanette
Marks, Pearle Marks Pansy, Merle Marks, Iras Marks Mendel. (Photo courtesy of
Morton B. Marks Jr.)*

Yaffe family, Fort Smith, 1925; seated, left to right: Simon, Helen, Rae, Lena; standing: Dorothy, William, Joseph, Adele, and Ben. (Photo courtesy of Dorothy Yaffe Miller)

Iser H. Nakdimen (right) *as a successful businessman, Fort Smith, ca. 1905.*
(Photo courtesy of Rae Stern)

Louis and Sarah Kasten, Fort Smith settlers, 1918. (Photo courtesy of Sarah Kasten)

East European Migration in Central Arkansas

Pulaski County

LITTLE ROCK

The new Jewish immigrants from East Europe, most of whom left their native country because of persecution, were ill prepared for life in a foreign country. Familiar with ghetto life, literate in Yiddish, few were in professions that required formal education. Most were craftsmen, skilled as tailors, cobblers, bakers, carpenters, jewelers, printers, and in other such trades. It was a gigantic task for their already established brethren from West Europe to help absorb them in America, but help they did. Local committees, usually composed of spiritual leaders and prominent Jewish businessmen, helped place the immigrants nationwide. In Little Rock, Rabbi Wolsey of Congregation B'nai Israel worked on such a committee, assisted by Mark M. Cohn, Jacob Blass, L. M. Levy, M. Salinger, C. T. Abeles, Max Heiman, C. S. Stifft, Louis Volmer, and Arthur Pfeifer.[1] Although relatively few of the East Europeans came to Arkansas, those who did made a positive contribution to the state's economic progress, and their ethical lives reflected a deep allegiance to their faith. Within one generation, most families could boast of economic success for their children, who had been well educated through means provided by the parents' hard work. Enough East European Jews did come to Arkansas to make a mark on the state's history, and their story, in part, is told here.

It is not possible to tell just how many of those sent to Arkansas by the Jewish immigrant aid societies remained there, nor how many sent to other states found their way into Arkansas. For example, when Louis "Louie" Rubin (1878–1952) came from Russia to America shortly after the turn of the century, the Hebrew Immigrant Aid Society (HIAS) sent him to eastern Oklahoma to help build the Kansas City Southern Railway. He and other immigrants—Jews, Irishmen, Poles—slept in boxcars. Hearing there were Jews in Fort Smith, Rubin went there with his small savings and was set up as a peddler by Joseph Itzkowitz, owner of a small dry goods store. Later, both men moved to Little Rock, where Rubin boarded at the home of Joseph's uncle, Max Itzkowitz (1866–1924). After opening his own small store in North Little Rock, Rubin sent for his wife and family in Russia. He remained in Arkansas until his death.[2]

The East European Jews who came to Arkansas after the turn of the century found that a few others had preceded them. A handful had settled in Pulaski County between the late 1860s and the 1890s, and some of these included members of the Back, Green, Meisner, Stern, Storthz, Stiel, and Tenenbaum families.

Abraham "Abe" Back came from East Europe to Little Rock in the 1860s and opened a small Surprise Store. His brother Pincus (1830–1898) and sister Minnie and her husband, Marcus Green (1853–1904), later joined him. Pincus Back's sons, Joseph D. (1857–1911) and William (1866–1950), established the Joe D. Back and Bro. department store in 1883.[3] William Back helped establish the Retail Merchants Association of Little Rock (later Chamber of Commerce), and during a business recession, helped establish the "Buy A Bale" cotton selling campaign. He was cited for his activities in the selling of War Bonds during World War I.[4] The Joe Back store became well known in Little Rock, and it was continued by family members until the bank failures of 1930s.[5]

Phillip G. Back (1902–1979), son of William and Sophia (Goldstein) Back, was educated at Harvard University and studied topographical drafting, photography, and aerial reconnaissance with the U.S. Corps of Engineers. He was active in Civil Defense work during World War II and served as a lieutenant colonel in the state's wing command of the Civil Air Patrol, which he helped organize. He was a department store merchant and laundry manager until 1945, when he opened an advertising agency. The firm coordinated the political advertising for eighty-four campaigns, including those of Senator John L. McClellan, U.S. representatives Wilbur D. Mills and Brooks Hays, and state governors Sid McMath, Francis Cherry, and Carl Bailey. He was a partner in a number of Little Rock businesses and was a founder and president of several advertising clubs. He served as a justice of the peace and promoted the use of voting machines. He also was active in religious affairs (see section V).[6]

The East Europeans who came before the great wave that began around the turn of the century were more quickly absorbed into the mainstream of business and community life than those who came later. Polish-born David "Dave" Meisner (1839–1927) established a mercantile store in Little Rock in the 1870s and became well known, serving as a justice of the peace for many years. He became known as "the marrying justice," for during his career he united more than fifteen hundred couples. He and his German-born wife, Bertha (Stern) Meisner (1857–1912), were known for their generosity in giving the orphans of Little Rock annual Thanksgiving and Christmas banquets, which Bertha prepared and Dave hosted. He performed marriages free on Christmas Day, and Bertha served meals to the newlyweds.[7] David's brother, Ike Meisner (1855–1939), had a clothing store at Seventh and Spring streets. A lifelong bachelor, his store was a "hangout" for local Orthodox Jews, and daily minyans were held there.[8] Emanuel Stern (1862–1924), who clerked for his brother-in-law, Dave Meisner, also was elected justice of the peace. (Stern was struck by a streetcar in January 1924 and died of the injuries.)[9]

The Polish-born Storthz brothers, Levi (1852–1932) and Samuel (1858–1946), came to Little Rock in 1886. Sam was a merchant, but Levi, who opened a pawn shop, was also interested in mining. He eventually accumulated fifteen hundred acres in Pulaski and Saline Counties that contained bauxite. After selling part of that land in the 1890s, he bought thousands of acres in seventeen counties in northern Arkansas, where he had mining and timber interests. He later engaged in real estate and investments.[10]

Levi Storthz's sons Sam Jonas (1885–1948) and Joseph "Joe" (1883–1952) were partners in the mercantile business; they established the Interstate Jobbing Company and opened twenty-nine department stores in small Arkansas towns. They also owned the Crescent Jewelry Company and the Storthz Bros. Investment Company in Little Rock. Sam Storthz, a mining engineer, was prominently noted for development of mineral resources in Arkansas, and he continued to hold much of the land owned by the family in northern Arkansas.[11] Joe Storthz Sr.'s son Herbert (1921–1991) became a Little Rock real estate developer. Joe Storthz Jr. (1911–1990) was left a small sum by his grandfather, and with it he began the Standard Luggage Store, which handled quality luggage and accessories. (The store he rented for his enterprise had been the Standard Liquor Store; his dad suggested he simply change the middle word, which he did.)[12] Standard Luggage became known as one of the finer such stores in Central Arkansas.

In 1888 Nachman Stiel (1852–1905) immigrated to Little Rock with his family. He was associated with the *Arkansas Gazette* and was editor and publisher of a German newspaper, *The Freie Presse*. He had just started his own publication, *The Jewish Press*, when he died as the first issue was to be printed.[13] One of his sons, Barney Stiel (1878–1911), served as a sergeant major in the Spanish-American War. On his return to Little Rock, Barney worked as an *Arkansas Gazette* reporter and from 1900 to 1911 served as deputy sheriff of Pulaski County. In September 1911 he formed part of a posse headed by Desha County Sheriff William Preston. The two criminals being sought were located near Dumas, Desha County. A shoot-out occurred, during which Barney killed one felon, but both Barney and Sheriff Preston were killed in turn.[14] (Barney Stiel's sisters, Mrs. Charles Dante and Mrs. Herman Marcus, lived at Dumas.)

Most of the new immigrants who settled in Arkansas had little or no money. They were enterprising, however. Some became junk peddlers, buying and recycling discards long before such action became popularly promoted. Having been relegated to menial occupations in their native countries, in America they did not eschew such work as collecting scrap, peddling fruit, repairing or making clothes, dealing in fur pelts, bones, pecans, used furniture or clothing, and junk of any sort. Whatever they attempted, they did so with zeal, thankful to be in a country that offered so much freedom and limitless opportunities. Some who went into the scrap and fur business in Little Rock included Abraham Tenenbaum, Abraham Sanders, Charles Alman, Louis B. Siegel, Sam Barg, Isaac Bennett, and A. J. Goldman.

By far, the most successful of all the scrap dealers was A. "Abe" Tenenbaum (1869–1952). Coming to Little Rock from Russia in his midteens, he had his own small business by 1890, dealing in hides, furs, wool, beeswax, burlap bags, scrap iron, and metals. His business grew, and he was able to give jobs to other needy immigrants, including his nephew, Julius Tenenbaum (1886–1965). The firm prospered and became the largest of its kind in the state (see section V).[15]

Abraham Sanders (1867–1946), known as "Honest Abe," became a junk dealer and formed his own company around 1901. He and his wife, Dora, had a son, William (see below), and eight daughters. Abe's son-in-law, Herman Loket, joined the Sanders firm, which became known as the Loket-Sanders Company.[16]

Charles Alman (1883–1943), a native of Zaclaw, Russia, came to America as a child and in 1905 settled at Little Rock, where he founded the Charles Alman Waste Material Company. He married Gussie Gilman, who came to Little Rock with her brother Will Gilman (see below). Alman was joined in his company by Charles Schlosberg in 1928. Sol Alman, son of Charles and Gussie, later joined the company.[17] Sidney Rosenberg (1912–1969), who had served with the British Royal Air Force, was associated with the Alman Company.[18] The firm continues into the 1990s.

The Siegel brothers, Charles (1857–1935) and David (1861–1935), emigrated from Poland to Little Rock around the turn of the century. One of David's sons, Louis B. Siegel (1892–1939), established a scrap company, which grew to be one of the largest such dealers in Arkansas.[19]

During World War I, Sam Barg came to Little Rock, where he established a scrap company. Several relatives worked with him, and his nephew, Saul Goodman (1917–1977), became a partner; the firm was then known as Goodman and Barg Scrap Company.[20]

The Bennett brothers, Max and Isaac "Ike" (1865–1949), came to Little Rock in the 1870s and opened a dry goods store and a scrap iron and paper business. Max later went west, but Ike remained. He conducted the I. Bennett Iron and Metal Company that grew to "immense proportions" by 1908, covering a half block at 315 West Seventh Street.[21] The family owned a chain of general merchandise stores throughout Arkansas and Louisiana during the 1930s and 1940s. They also established a military supply store at Third and Main streets (see section V).[22]

A. J. Goldman (1894–1975) went into the waste paper business after trying other ventures, such as selling efficiency gasoline (forerunner of ethyl gasoline) in Arkansas. (When he attempted to sell the gasoline, he set up headquarters in Little Rock in 1920 and hired twenty salesmen, only to find there were no more than seven thousand cars or trucks in the entire state at the time.) He then worked for the post office, where he organized the first American Federation of Labor (AFL) Union of Post Office Clerks—Local No. 189. In 1925 he established a waste paper processing plant, Goldman and Company, which graded and processed waste paper for industrial concerns. His son-in-law, Lee Kretchmar (1907–1976) later joined him in the firm.[23]

Some immigrants ventured into pawn shops as Levi Storthz had done, but most, as he also did, later branched out into other businesses. The

Jewish-owned pawn shops of Greater Little Rock that are best known or remembered in the last half of the twentieth century were not established until the late 1930s or early 1940s. Four of these were the Square Deal Pawn Shop, Maxie's Reliable Pawn Shop, Doc's Trading Post, and the National Pawn Shop. The Square Deal store was begun originally as a dry goods business by Joseph Itzkowitz. He had come from Russia at age sixteen to Little Rock, where his uncle Max Itzkowitz lived. Joseph first peddled bananas, then lived and worked in Fort Smith for a time (as well as at Joplin, Missouri, where he met and married widow Rose Zarik), then moved back to Little Rock and there had the Square Deal dry goods store. He later moved it to North Little Rock. His son Robert attempted to join him in the store in 1934, during the depths of the Depression. As business was so bad, Robert suggested they open a pawn shop, which they did, keeping the "Square Deal" name. Robert's brother, Leon (1920–1960), later became a partner in the store, and the Square Deal Pawn Shop prospered over the years, continuing into the 1990s.[24] Maxie's Pawn Shop was owned by Max Itzkowitz (1912–1988), a half brother of Robert's, who, as a Golden Gloves boxing champion, was nicknamed "Slapsie Maxie." The small, wiry man became a colorful figure in Little Rock, and his shop became well known for its "going out of business" sales, which began shortly after he opened the store in 1945. Sam Levine (1900–1963) owned the pawn shop, Doc's Trading Post, located on Main Street in Little Rock and on Asher Avenue (his brother Harry was a Little Rock pharmacist).[25] In 1913 Meyer Lulky came to Little Rock through Galveston from Russia, where he had served in the Russian army. A blacksmith, Meyer opened a shoe repair business in Little Rock, then moved it to North Little Rock. It was in that city that his son, Morris "Mo" Lulky, established the National Pawn Shop after World War II.[26] It also continues into the 1990s.

Hyman Schlesinger (1870–1918), a native Russian who fled to Poland and then to America, was a cobbler. He opened the Little Rock Shoemaking Shop on Louisiana Street after the turn of the century (his brother William settled at Hot Springs). Hyman's son Morris (1898–1976) was associated with the Rephan's Department Store in Little Rock. Morris married Minnie Razaper of Little Rock. (Minnie's sister Birdie married Julius Tenenbaum, above). The Schlesingers also married into the Marcot and Schweig families.[27]

At times, circumstances determined what business the East Europeans would pursue. Samuel Breier (1869–1947), for example, came to Little Rock from Hungary in 1895, and he and his wife, Bertha (1879–1967), opened a retail fruit business on East Markham Street. The building they purchased had an old exterior sign that gave it the appearance of a restaurant. When people began coming in and asking for meals, the Breiers abandoned their original intention and opened an eatery. In 1916 they moved to 124 West Markham Street near the newly erected Marion Hotel. Their establishment, dubbed Breier's Fine Old Restaurant Since 1901, became one of Little Rock's finest eating places and was visited by famous show personnel who performed at the nearby Robinson Auditorium. The restaurant, which closed on the High Holy Days, was known for its striking Venetian glass mirror, marble floors, huge baroque backbar, and its German cuisine.[28] Sam and Bertha's children, Edith and Matthews (1902–1978), and Matthews' wife, Nancy, later continued the business.

Other East Europeans who had restaurants in the Little Rock area included Sam Narkinsky and Max Granoff. Sam Narkinsky (1861–1925) left his native Russia to escape the draft (to be a Jew in the Russian army was, at times, almost a death sentence, and expediency prompted the emigration of many young Jewish boys on that account). Landing first at New York, he began peddling and drifted to Little Rock, where he opened a fold-out store (similar to a large steamer trunk) at Fifth and Main streets. In 1910 he opened Sam's Chili Parlor, which became famous for its main entree. He was very patriotic and attended several presidential inaugurations. Sam brought over other relatives, including Adam and Mary Latkin (see below). Sam and his wife, Rebecca (Ginsburg) Narkinsky, had four sons and three daughters. After their son Charles, an army captain in World War I, was killed in battle in France in 1918, both Sam and Rebecca mourned grievously until they both died within four days of each other in 1925.[29]

Max Granoff (1914–1963), son of immigrants Morris (1883–1951) and Bessie Granoff (1884–1942), established a fine restaurant at Tenth and Main streets and another one on the old Hot Springs Highway going west out of Little Rock. At the time, the restaurants were among the finest eating places in Central Arkansas. Morris Granoff was a Little Rock merchant, having settled there in 1905. His other son, Edward M. (1900–1963), served as president of the Little Rock City Employees Local 153 and as deputy revenue collector for the city.[30]

Just as the Breiers had converted their original business to one more profitable, so also did the Besser brothers. They began in the clothing business but later made their mark in the hardware trade in Little Rock. Lippman (1855–1937) and Leopold Besser (1866–1927) came to Arkansas around 1909, opened clothing stores, and branched out into a hardware business on Center Street. When sales of the latter eclipsed clothing sales, they concentrated on the hardware line. The Besser name became a household word in the hardware business of the Little Rock area. Lippman's son Joseph (1886–1967) operated a pawn shop on Center Street. His sons Ben (1894–?) and Isadore "Izzy" (1895–1974) opened hardware stores just across the street from each other on Asher Avenue in West Little Rock. Isadore, who married Rose Ruff, had a catchy sign, "Keep Izzy Busy," which became a familiar sight along the avenue for many years.[31] The Bessers married within a number of other East European families, such as Weinberg, Weintraub, Kassoff, Siegel, Filion, Walberg, Gordon, and Goodman.

As East European Jews moved into Little Rock, a few became familiar sights as they peddled their pushcarts of bananas and vegetables through the streets, as some had done in their native countries. One of the first to begin making a living this way was Russian-born Sam Bernhard (1882–1943). He came to Little Rock around 1897 and soon became known as "Sam the Banana Man" as he peddled his produce from door to door. He established a regular route and used wagons for years until he purchased a truck.

Sam Bernhard, along with several other Orthodox immigrants (and one Gentile, John Seaser), formed a "banana cooperative." Other members included Joseph Kosten (1887–1946), who had come to Little Rock through Galveston; Morris Kluglose (1888–1958), a cabinetmaker who had been sent by HIAS to work in the Charles Abeles furniture mill (but found he could make more by peddling on his own); Max Snyderman (1879–1932); Samuel Barg (who later went into the scrap business); William Gilman (1884–1933); and Aaron Kossover (1895–1943). Being part of the cooperative allowed the men to purchase bananas by carload lots at lower prices. Some of the members formed a wholesale grocery firm, first known as Snyderman and Kosten. When Snyderman formed his own business, the former company became known as Gilman and Kosten. (Will Gilman, one of the partners, was shot and killed in May 1933 by a huckster from Conway, W. H. Walker, who had been Gilman's former partner and who owed Gilman money. Although Gilman was unarmed, a grand jury dismissed charges against Walker, saying he acted in self defense.)[32] Others were associated with the wholesale produce coop from time to time, such as Samuel Lebovitz and Meyer Weiner.[33] The Gilman and Kosten Company later became a wholesale institutional food business.

As the older members of the original banana cooperative began to retire or die (from the 1920s to the 1940s), some of their children contin-ued their fathers' businesses; these included Louis Snyderman, Dorothy (Kosten) Geller and her husband, Phillip Geller, Jake Kossover, and Ben Kluglose. Charles Kluglose, brother of Ben, formed the K Quality Bag Company of Little Rock. (As had Maxie Itzkowitz, Charles Kluglose took up boxing and became an Amateur Athlete Union [AAU] featherweight champion; his name appeared in many local sports columns in the 1930s.)[34] Joe Bernhard, son of Sam, and his wife Evelyn established Joe's Hobby Shop (see section V).

Solomon Ruff was another fruit peddler, having first begun at Hot Springs before moving his business to Little Rock. He married Ella Snyder, sister of E. Snyder of the Forrest City scrap company, and they had eight children. (When Solomon Ruff settled in Little Rock in 1918, his twelve-year-old son, Leo, began spending a great deal of time at Camp Pike, a military base not far from Little Rock. When some soldiers who had befriended Leo were moved out, he managed to hide aboard their troop ship headed for Europe. When discovered, he told the captain he was sev-enteen; he may have been the youngest soldier to serve in World War I. He was considered a mascot by the other servicemen, who called him "Ruff Stuff." Another son of Solomon Ruff, David, served as a bugler in the Marines and was in the battle of Belleau Wood in France. He received five citations for bravery, plus the French medal of bravery.)[35] When Solomon Ruff died, his widow married Sam Barg of the Goodman and Barg scrap company, and they had three children.

The East European Jews followed the same pattern of settlement as that of the German Jews when they had first come to America. Most of them began their business careers as peddlers or blue collar workers, but in a short while they saved enough to branch out on their own. The R. Baum and Company, founded by the Baum family, and the Charles T. Abeles Company were two firms that cooperated with Jewish immigrant aid societies, such as HIAS and the Industrial Removal Office (IRO), to bring Jewish immigrants to Little Rock. The new workers generally saved their funds until they could begin their own modest businesses. Some, such as Jacob S. Frank and Ben Besser, stayed with the host company until they died. Frank (1857–1942), sent by an immigrant aid society to the Baum company, remained a loyal employee there until his death.[36] Ben (1876–1910), a brother of Leopold and Lippman Besser, was sent by HIAS to the Charles Abeles Company, where he remained as an employee.[37]

Some East Europeans opened department stores, and the most success-ful of these were the Grundfest brothers, Sam (1893–1955) and David

"Dave" (1901–1974). Born in Cary, Mississippi, to immigrant parents Morris and Molly (Bernstein) Grundfest, the brothers came to Arkansas after Sam returned from military service in World War I. They began opening variety stores, called Sterling Stores, in southern Arkansas, beginning at El Dorado. By 1932 they had established seventy stores throughout Arkansas and neighboring states. The Depression cut these back to a total of twenty-seven, but by 1941 the company had sixty-five stores and a wholesale house in Little Rock. Annual retail volume at the time was twelve million dollars.[38] At the suggestion of Hugo Kahn, Sam joined the Storthz brothers, Joe and Sam, in establishing the Interstate Jobbing Company. The Grundfest brothers founded the first garment factory in Little Rock (Hewitt Manufacturing Company), which made women's and children's dresses for the Sterling Store chain. Sam was one of the first white men to serve on the board of Philander Smith College, a black school.[39] Sam and his wife, Mable (Feld) Grundfest, had two daughters, Janet and Loris. Sam became ill in 1941 and retired. Dave Grundfest served on a number of business and civic boards. He helped found the Grundfest Foundation, used primarily to aid needy students. He married Maurine Frauenthal, daughter of Charles Frauenthal, who was part of the well-established Arkansas German-Jewish family of Conway.[40] Dave and Maurine Grundfest had two children, Dave Grundfest Jr. and Barbara (Bauman) (see section V).

Other East Europeans who established department stores included Jacob Rephan, Abraham N. Nossek, and Barney Levin. Their stores, generally found off the main streets except in the smaller towns, became successful, serving mostly the country trade. Jacob Rephan (1871–1925) opened a mercantile store at England, twenty-five miles southeast of Little Rock. He later moved to Little Rock and began branching out with a chain of stores scattered around the state. Relatives headed these branches: his sister Tillie and her husband, Louis Festinger (1894–1935), ran the branch at Conway; another sister and her husband, Max Reich (1872–1945), ran the branch at Morrilton; and his brother Henry (1901–1969), a graduate of Washington University in St. Louis, ran the branch at El Dorado. Another brother, Edward I. Rephan, also established Rephan department stores in Arkansas (see chapter 6, this section). After Louis Festinger worked in Rephan's Conway store for some ten years, he moved to Little Rock and opened his own "New York" store. He later had shops at Hot Springs and at Altheimer as well.[41] Abraham Nossek (1881–1946) came to Little Rock in 1906 and worked for the Pfeifers' department store. In 1918 he established the Famous Store, a department store with the motto "The Customer Is Always Right." He had stores on Center Street in Little Rock and on Second and Main in North Little Rock. He developed elaborate plans for a chain of stores across the state, but the effort was curtailed by the Depression.[42] Russian native Barney Levin (1872–1920) came to Arkansas in the 1890s, opened a department store in North Little Rock, then moved his store to 515–517 Center Street in Little Rock. His son Daniel "Chink" Levin (1908–1963) owned the Standard Automatic Distributing Company, which distributed Wurlitzer juke boxes in Arkansas.[43]

A few of the East Europeans opened clothing stores in Little Rock, and this included Ellis Yout (1855–1911) of Russia. He had come from East Europe with his family to Chicago in 1887 and in 1891 settled at Little Rock, where he opened The Hub men's clothing store on Main Street. He sold this to Henry Marx and established the United Clothing Company. Ellis and his wife, Rose (Ochs) Yout, had a large home on Ringo Street and took in boarders. When Charles and Toney Dante (who became prominent citizens of Dumas) first married, they stayed a short while with the Youts. Ellis was joined in the clothing business by his sons, Louis (1885–1950) and Mike (1886–1958). Lou married Hattie Feinstein of Little Rock, and Mike married Rose Sonnenschein of Pine Bluff. Mike and Rose's daughter Rosa Belle married Martin Dreyfus, whose family settled at McGehee. Hattie (Feinstein) Yout's father, J. Feinstein, had come in 1911 with his family to Little Rock, where his son Howard Feinstein (1891–1969) later established a ladies' ready-to-wear store (see section V).[44]

Other types of businesses that the East Europeans entered included electrical supply, furrier, furniture, hat, and jewelry companies. Jack Tenzel and Albert I. Korenblat (1906–1956) established the T and K Electric company in the 1920s. Albert assumed sole ownership in 1920 and named it I. K. Electric Company (Jack later moved to Nashville with his wife, Dr. Pauline [Korenblat] Tenzel, see Distaff Side below). Albert's brother Maurice (1907–1962) joined him in the firm, which became an established name among Little Rock's electrical suppliers and contractors.[45] Zusman Bensky (1903–1993) came from Poland via New York to Little Rock, and in his adopted city bought a bankrupt fur store. Little by little he built it up, along with an impeccable reputation for quality and honesty, and Bensky Furs became the most prestigious name in the furrier business in Arkansas. He helped one of his employees, Ben Spector, establish his own fur store, and Spector Furs also became a respected, well-known firm.[46] Edgar Schweig (1888–1962), son of East-European immigrant Charles Schweig (1854–1931), was a Little Rock furniture dealer.

The Schweigs married into several East European families, including those of Schlesinger, Bernhard, Itzkowitz, Koenig, and Gross.[47] Polish-born Israel Safferstone (1872–1941), who settled at Little Rock in 1909, established a wholesale hat company with his brother-in-law, Harry Dreeben (1884–1951). (Israel had begun his career in Little Rock by establishing the Pilsor Carriage Company, but when offered an automobile franchise, he refused, thinking there was no future in it.)[48] After Israel's death, his son Marion "Mooch" continued the Safferstone Hat Company when he returned from military service in World War II.

Several East Europeans were involved in the jewelry business, including Harry Scher, Sam Backel, and Joseph Goetz. Harry Scher (1888–1950) opened Scher's Jewelers at 208 Main Street in Little Rock in 1914, and it became a successful store for some fifty years. (His father, David Louis Scher [1855–1914], and his father's brother Morris [1874–1939] emigrated from East Europe to America in 1884 and to Arkansas in the 1890s. Deeply religious, David helped organize the Agudath Achim Synagogue [see section II]. Morris operated a clothing store.) Harry's son David L. (1920–1952) and his daughter Elsie (1917–1957) and her husband, Louis Lane (1911–1971), were associated with the Scher jewelry firm.[49] Rumanian-born Sam Backel (1888–1966) came to Little Rock in 1916 and engaged in the jewelry business. He married Sayde Simon of Pine Bluff.[50] Joseph Goetz (1862–1952), who came from an area of what later became Czechoslovakia to Little Rock in 1893, conducted a jewelry business from a portable outdoor jewelry stand in front of any building that happened to be empty on West Second Street between Main and Louisiana. An avid sportsman, he would close his stand when the Arkansas Traveler baseball team was in town (so that his "help" could attend the games). He died of a heart attack at Travelers' Field during a game in June 1952.[51]

Early East European immigrants of the Erber family, who had come to Little Rock by 1880, began bringing members of their family to Arkansas, and these in turn married and brought their relatives. Their descendants later married into the families of Wexner, Rosen, Lofton, Hill, Weintraub, Scher, Gruner, Kroll, Freeman, Burta, Schweig, Loebner, Riff, Levy, Besser, Kossover, Schwartz, Shainberg, Layman, Stein, Lesser, Brandeis, and others. Many of these in turn opened small stores in a number of Arkansas towns. Most succeeded in modest ways, but the family also had its share of disaster. Jacob Erber (1846–1885), whose business did not do well in 1885, threw himself into the Arkansas River and drowned in July of that year after trying to win money at shooting dice and losing his last fifty dollars.[52]

At almost the same location in 1904, the river claimed another Erber. Thirteen-year-old Abe Erber (1891–1904) was drawn with other boys his age to the river bank when the steamboat *Lucile Nowland* blasted its whistle on its arrival on 24 June 1904. The young boys began playing, jumping from the *Nowland* to the steamer *Henry Sheldon* docked alongside. Abe, who could not swim, fell in and drowned.[53] Rosa Erber (1874–1972) came from Poland and married Polish-native Isaac Rosen (1874–1908), and they had five children. When Isaac died at age 36, Rosa had to send the two youngest children, Marcus, age four, and Louis, age three, to the Jewish Children's Home in New Orleans.[54] Another calamity befell the Erber family in 1920, when Joe Erber (1860–1920), a policeman and the father of Abe, who had drowned, was killed in line of duty when he tried to arrest a felon on Lincoln Avenue near the Arkansas River in Little Rock. Erber, who had joined the Police Department in 1893, was well thought of and the City Council appropriated special payment to his family.[55]

Other East Europeans besides the Erbers found they had escaped the horror of persecution in their native countries only to find sorrow and misfortune in their adopted land. These included the Levinson, Unger, Kassoff, Dante, Sanders, and Arber families. Joseph Levinson (1873–1913), who came to Little Rock via New York after the turn of the century and opened an electrical supply shop on Main Street, became well known for his helpfulness. When a group of teenaged boys cut the wire used to lower the street arc light at Sixth and Cross streets on Halloween night in 1913, the light fell and broke. Levinson quickly attempted to cut the power line. Although an experienced electrician, he used uninsulated pliers and was electrocuted. It was thought that in his concern for others he neglected to protect himself.[56] Another ill-fated family was that of Ralph Unger (1880–1937), who worked for years as a hoseman for the Little Rock Fire Department. In 1932, within a few hours of the marriage of his daughter Goldie to Morris Katrovitz of Memphis, the nineteen-year old bride was killed in a car accident just east of Memphis.[57] Five years later, Ralph himself, who was off duty at the time and was substituting for a fellow worker, was killed in a fire. He had been known for his willingness to fill in for coworkers.[58] Lena Kassoff (1868–1936) was killed when she touched a highly charged radio aerial running from her home at 3402 Mary Street to a chicken barn in the rear yard.[59]

One of the worst and most moving disasters to befall the East European Jewish community of Arkansas involved two of the Dante brothers of Pine Bluff—Joseph (1875–1897) and Jacob (1878–1897)—and their fiancés, teenagers Joan Sanders and Mary Arber, both of Little Rock. On the night of 4 July 1897, the two young Jewish couples were among hundreds who had flocked to the Arkansas River to watch the fireworks display that evening. All four drowned when they were swept into the dark water after a pleasure barge collided with the skiff on which they were sitting. They were the only casualties.[60]

As East European Jews became established, they, like the German Jews before them, occasionally entered politics. This occurred in the larger cities as well as the small towns. St. Louis-born William B. Sanders (1891–1972), son of East European immigrants, settled at Little Rock, where he was graduated from the Arkansas Law School at Little Rock. He met and was associated with Justin Matthews Sr. when the latter was chairman of the Arkansas Highway Commission and influential in state affairs. Sanders was elected to the Little Rock City Council and in that position exerted such influence that one Little Rock mayor called him "the boss of Little Rock."[61] He worked with the Little Rock Improvement District when bridges were built over the Arkansas River on Broadway and on Main Street. He also was elected to the Board of Public Affairs, where he served sixteen years.

Joseph H. Schneider (1891–1966), also a lawyer, was campaign manager for Governors John E. Martineau and Homer M. Adkins; he served as executive secretary to the former. Schneider, who held positions that required preparation of legislation and coordination of state agencies' functions, also served as city attorney for North Little Rock. He served as referee in bankruptcy and general counsel for the Motor Carriers Claims Commission.[62] Joseph's brother, Charles Schneider (1860–1916), came from Russia to America in the 1880s and to North Little Rock in 1904. He established what became a highly successful tailoring business. He was later joined in the firm by his son, Harry (1884–1964), who married Esther Besser (1895–1968), daughter of Morris Besser.[63]

David Goldberg (1881–1922), son of Harris J. Goldberg, an organizer of Agudath Achim Congregation, became well known in North Little Rock, where he worked for school betterment and was elected to the city's school board. Edward Bennett (1903–1971), born to Little Rock pioneer Ike Bennett, was a graduate of the Arkansas Law School in Little Rock. He was active in the Democratic Party and served on the Democratic Committee for forty-three years. He ran unsuccessfully for the state senate in 1931. Known for his satirical wit, he helped organize the Hotel Marion Breakfast Club, which was an aggregation of politicians, businessmen, professionals, and civic workers. He was noted to be a valuable citizen of Pulaski County.[64]

From the family of Hungarian native Moritz "Morris" Spitzberg (1817–1910) and his wife Tonie (Taube Erber) (1842–1907) sprang several well-known Little Rock men. In 1889 the family settled at Little Rock, where Morris and Tonie conducted a mercantile store, The Leader, on East Markham. Their son Leon (1876–1958) continued the store, while another son, Joe (1875–1929), opened a ladies' clothing store on Capitol Avenue. Joe was fiercely loyal to America, which he felt was a land of boundless freedom and opportunity. During World War I, he placed a sign in his store that read:

> This an American house. You earn a better living here than you ever did before. Do not criticize our president, our government, and our allies. If you do not like the way we run our government, go back to your own country. If you are a natural rebel . . . go to hell![65]

Sam Spitzberg (1871–1943), another son of Morris and Tonie, was in the grocery business. He joined the Little Rock Police Department in 1912 and served there ten years. Among his duties as a patrolman were interpreting languages (he was multilingual) and escorting to the city limits long-haired wandering preachers, who called themselves "Israelites."[66] Sam served as a justice of the peace in the 1920s and 1930s, during which time he became a well-known courthouse figure, marrying more than six thousand couples.[67] Sam and his wife, Jennie (Seifter) Spitzberg, had fourteen children, only six of whom lived to adulthood. A son, Jacob (1899–1921), a postal clerk, died at age twenty-one, but his twin brother, Irving (1899–1989), became a well-known Little Rock pediatrician and gynecologist. Irving served in World War I and was active in the American Legion, serving as Chef De Gare in the Forty and Eight. He was a professor of pediatrics at the University of Arkansas Medical School in the 1920s and 1930s, and he also specialized in diseases that afflict women.[68]

Henry Spitzberg (1902–1990), another son of Sam and Jennie, became a prominent, respected Little Rock attorney. He was a graduate of the Arkansas Law School at Little Rock and passed the bar in 1922, a year before he graduated in 1923. He began his career in the office of Judge W. H. Donham during the active Klan days of the 1920s. Judge Donham was invited to join the Klan if he would put Henry out of his office, but the Judge told Klan members frankly to "go straight to hell." When Henry supported Judge Donham's nephew (a Klan member) for prosecuting attorney, he was criticized by the Jewish community. Spitzberg said he knew the nephew had joined the Klan for political expediency only. Henry later ran for the office of prosecuting attorney, but, as a virtual unknown at the time, he lost to the popular Sam Robinson. Some of Henry Spitzberg's better-known cases involved twenty million to thirty million dollar lawsuits against a Dr. Brinkley, who gained wide-spread notoriety by promising a returned virility to susceptible men.[69] (See section V for more data on the Spitzberg family.)

Attorney Louis Tarlowski (1901–1980) served as a special judge in the Sixth Judicial District of Arkansas. He also served with a committee that helped draft the state's first sales tax law. Tarlowski, who was born of immigrant parents in Brooklyn, New York, was a graduate of the University of Virginia and began practicing law in Little Rock in 1922. He became known for his work in Interstate Commerce Commission cases. Tarlowski served as president of the National Motor Carrier Lawyers Association and as a member of the Little Rock Planning Commission.[70]

Charles C. "Rube" Rubenstein (1882–1958) became a well-known figure in the political life of Little Rock. He was state chairman of the Privilege Tax Commission and was considered a "vice mayor" under several Little Rock mayors, including Mayor Sam M. Wassell, who served in the period 1947–1952. Rube was born at Muscatine, Iowa, of immigrant parents, and grew up an avid sports fan. Rather small of stature, he managed a semi-pro baseball team by age eighteen. He moved to Ruston, Louisiana, where he managed a men's clothing store and developed the innovative idea of advertising on the sports page in the local paper. He joined the army in World War I and was stationed at Camp Pike near Little Rock. Pfeifer's Department Store had a camp store there, which Rube managed. He had been a scout for the Louisiana State University sports program before the war and resumed those activities at Texas Christian University after the war. In 1922 he accepted an offer by Harry Pfeifer to become buyer and manager of Pfeifer's Men's Department. In 1932 Rube and his brother-in-law, Walter L. Scott (1888–1943), opened a men's clothing store, Rube and Scott, which became one of the city's most popular such stores. Rube introduced the installment payment plan for clothing, which helped customers during the Depression. He was active in numerous civic organizations. Although he and his wife had no children, they helped raise several and assisted a number in attending college.[71] (Leonard Scott [1914–   ], son of Walter L. Scott, whose family hailed from Poland, was a graduate of Vanderbilt University and Harvard Law School. He began a law practice in Little Rock in 1937 that has continued more than fifty years.)[72]

Other East Europeans and their descendants who were in mercantile related businesses included Jack Fine (1893–1951), who came to Little

Rock from El Dorado in 1924 and opened the Palais Royal. The store featured quality ladies' ready-to-wear and millinery. He later founded the Town and Country Women's Dress Shop and Mrs. Jack Fine's Dress Shop. His stores became well known as places of high fashion.[73] Others in the mercantile business were Samuel Rosenbloom (1879–1926); Charles Cohen (1894–1973), who was also an employee of Arkansas Power and Light Company; Leon Kassoff (1856–1931); and Hyman Yeszin (1896–1972). Russian native Adam Latkin (1860–1916), who had been brought to Little Rock by his wife's relative Sam Narkinsky, conducted business from the small fold-out street stand that had belonged to Sam. Adam operated it at 102 West Capitol Avenue in the 1890s, and when an ordinance was passed by the city council to ban such stands, local merchants circulated a petition on his behalf, and he was allowed to continue.[74] Adam and his wife, Mary, had six children: four girls, who never married, and two sons. Two of the Latkin daughters, Lena and Annie, became well known in the educational circles of Pulaski County (see Distaff Side below). Adam's son, Herbert, a graduate of the University of Illinois, served as editor of the *Union Labor Bulletin* in Little Rock for some thirty years and also established the *Jefferson County Progress* at Pine Bluff in 1930.[75]

Some East Europeans became established in other parts of America before finally settling in Arkansas. Joseph Shrader (1870–1946) was trained as a skilled portrait photographer in his home at Orel, Russia, before migrating to New York. He had studios in several states before moving to St. Joseph, Missouri, in 1900. He married Bertha Frank, and they had one son, Gustave Joseph "Buddy" Shrader. In 1910 the family visited Hot Springs, attempting to cure a chemical burn on one of the elder Shrader's hands. Falling in love with Arkansas, they bought a small photography studio in Little Rock and renamed it Shrader's. The family was so skillful at portrait photography that their studio became the most prestigious of its kind in the state. Beginning in 1911, Shrader's Studio photographed members of the Arkansas House of Representatives and Senate individually and compositely for more than fifty years. In Oklahoma City in 1925, Bertha Shrader became the first woman to address an American photographic convention.[76]

Several of the immigrants could be found in a variety of other occupations—some exciting; some intriguing; some mundane but necessary. William S. "Billy" Kramer (1891–1982) came to Arkansas in 1917 and promoted boxing at Camp Pike. After the war, he was persuaded by the Little Rock Boathouse Club to become a physical education instructor there. In 1920 he opened a private gym on East Seventh Street, and during World War II he served as a physical education instructor in the Little Rock public schools.[77]

S. S. Seligman (1894–?) began his career as an auctioneer at age eleven by working after school at an auction house in Monroe, Louisiana. He later owned the Federal Auction Company and came to Little Rock in 1930, where he was appointed by Judge John E. Martineau as official auctioneer for the U.S. District Court for eastern Arkansas (he was later reappointed by Judge Thomas C. Trimble). He was one of nine Federal Court auctioneers in America at the time. After World War I, he auctioned off military installations that included the U.S. Cavalry posts, airfields at Camden, Helena, Pine Bluff, and the WAC School at Russellville. The French flying cadet training base at Orangeburg, South Carolina, was the largest auction he held. He was a showman as well as an auctioneer, performing with twenty-seven entertainers overseas for six months during World War I.[78]

Mark Lipman, born in Philadelphia of Lithuanian immigrants, came to Little Rock in 1935 with his wife, Belle (Ackerman) Lipman. He was just passing through the city on his way to Houston, when he stopped at Little Rock, liked it, settled there, and opened a private investigation business, the Mark Lipman Service. He was assisted in his small operation by his son, Ira (1940–   ), by the time the youngster was eight years old. Over the years, Mark became an expert at interrogating dishonest employees. With a twinkle in his eyes as he would peer over his glasses, he became deceptively perceptive. After a misunderstanding occurred at the synagogue where Mark and Belle attended, the family moved to Memphis (see section V).[79]

Samuel "Cooney" Young (1866–1946) became well known in Pulaski County, serving as custodian for the Eagles Club of Little Rock for forty-two years.[80]

NORTH LITTLE ROCK

Several East European Jews located their small shops in North Little Rock. Some of these included Abraham "Abe" J. Kroner (1883–1943), a mercantile store; S. Lewis "Lew" Berger (1890–1928) and Louis B. Goldberg (1898–1952), dry goods stores; and Louis Sklar (1888–1949). Hyman Burta (1882–1965), who emigrated from Europe to Mississippi and became a cotton farmer and merchant, moved to England, Arkansas, after World War I. He opened a store at North Little Rock as well.[81] Other

Jewish-owned firms of that city were headed by members of the Weintraub, David, Freeman, Schweig, Loebner, Levy, Gross, Riff, Wexner, Rubin, Lion, Linz, Zwirn, Kossover, Sanders, and Eisenberg families.

The Distaff Side

The women among East European immigrants usually had more to overcome than did their German counterparts. They had to find acceptance not only from the general population, but also from their German coreligionists, some of whom viewed them as poor stepchildren. Despite social obstacles, some of them went on to excel in various ways. Seven are mentioned here as examples of these stalwart women.

Lena Latkin (1886–1933), oldest of Adam and Mary Latkin's six children, came as a child with her family to Arkansas from Russia. After being graduated from Little Rock High School, she had further training at the University of Arkansas, the University of Chicago, and at Columbia University. She was a primary teacher at Rightsell School and at Peabody School in Little Rock from 1901 to 1919. From 1924 to 1933 she served as assistant superintendent of the Pulaski County elementary schools, where she became known and loved among its pupils and teachers. She assisted deserving students in acquiring student loans for higher education.[82] She provided leadership for the consolidation and upgrading of county schools during her tenure. She wrote a number of articles for educational journals and was a program speaker in several southern states. She coauthored the book, *Bible Stories*, which was used in the state's public schools. She pushed for improvements in the city library and helped establish the bookmobile program, which made library books available to rural students of Pulaski County. After she died in 1933, a Lena Latkin Memorial Room was established in her memory at the Little Rock Public Library. (She also served as superintendent of Congregation B'nai Israel's Sabbath School for many years.)[83] Lena's sister, Annie Latkin, educated at the University of Chicago and the University of California, served as a teacher in the Little Rock school system for forty-two years.[84]

The Green sisters, Teanie and Gertrude, were daughters of Marcus and Minnie (Back) Green. The parents had come to Arkansas when Minnie's brothers, Joe, William, Morris, and Louis, had settled there in the 1870s (see above). Teanie Green (1882–1975) served as office manager in the Joe D. Back and Bro. Department Store for many years and also worked with the Block Realty Company. She was secretary to Rabbi Ira Sanders and was active in both the Temple and Synagogue affairs. She was a leader in the women's suffrage movement around the time of World War I and helped spearhead a march in downtown Little Rock during the struggle to ratify the Nineteenth Amendment. She had been graduated from the Peabody High School in 1898 and served as class secretary from the time of graduation until 1971. She assisted in organizing class reunions until her ninetieth birthday.[85] Gertrude Green (1884–1970) also was a Peabody High School graduate. She served as a secretary for the Rock Island Railroad and for the Arkansas Highway Department in the period 1913–1915. During World War I she served with the Volunteer Services of the American Red Cross in France, and she was in Paris for the signing of the Armistice. While in France, she served on the staff of the Episcopal Bishop of New York, de Wolf Perry. She later became a national representative of the Women's Overseas Service League and traveled nationwide on the organization's behalf. She and C. Hamilton Moses formed the staff for Governor Charles H. Brough during his term, 1917–1921.[86] Teanie and Gertrude, both of whom never married, were active in the Little Rock Chapter of Hadassah, a women's Zionist organization, after it was formed in the mid-1940s.

Mary Hellen Herr (1882–1942), daughter of Rabbi Meyer Herr of Ponewez, Lithuania, left her native land alone as a young girl of twenty to visit her maternal aunt, Mrs. Nathan (Rosemary) Harris, who lived in Little Rock. When Mary first saw America, she said it seemed her heart "would burst with new hopes for a better life." In Little Rock she fell in love with and married "Sam the Banana Man" Bernhard. She was awed that the citizens of America were not cowed and afraid, "like in Russia." In her native home, she had been taught to appreciate education and culture, and in Little Rock she attended almost every cultural event offered. She learned English and began writing letters to the editors of local newspapers, telling of her life in Russia and contrasting it with the freedoms and opportunities found in the United States. She also wrote a history of her early life in Russia for her two sons, Ely and Joseph "Joe," so that they would not "lose sight of [their] origin" in generations to come. Her civic and charitable works, such as her diligent service for the Red Cross and the selling of War Bonds, were almost without number.[87]

Perla "Pauline" Korenblat (1900–1980), born to Jacob and Rachel Korenblat in the village of Bender (Bendery), Russia, yearned as a young girl to be a doctor. Through much monetary sacrifice, her parents sent her to study medicine at the University of Kausenberg in Cluj, Rumania, in 1919. Pauline's cousin, Jack Tenzel, who had emigrated to Little Rock, had fallen in love with her before he left Russia. Jack's immediate family had joined him in Arkansas in 1920, some of them settling at De Witt. Jack saved enough funds to bring Pauline and her brother, Albert, to Little Rock in August 1921. He and Pauline were married that month by Rabbi Aaron Colatz at Synagogue Agudath Achim.

While Jack and Albert became partners in the T and K Electric company, Pauline was allowed to enroll at the University of Arkansas Medical School in Little Rock for the September 1921 term (despite the fact that her transcripts from the European university never arrived). Although she was fluent in Russian, Rumanian, French, and German, Pauline knew little English, yet she excelled in her studies. An article about her appeared on the first page of the society section in the 11 March 1922 *Arkansas Democrat,* entitled "Romanian Girl Brightest Student in Arkansas Medical School Here." She was graduated in June 1927. During her academic years she had borne a son, Meron, who died at age three months in 1923.

Pauline's internship was completed at Women's Medical College Hospital in Pennsylvania. Her husband, Jack, had moved there with her and while there had become seriously ill with tuberculosis. In 1929 they moved back to Little Rock, where Jack received excellent care from Dr. A. C. Shipp, director of the Arkansas Tuberculosis Association. Pauline began practicing pediatric medicine, opening an office in the Donaghey Building at Seventh and Main streets in Little Rock. She later added obstetrics to her practice.

In 1932 Jack, who by then was fully recovered and was associated with the Metropolitan Life Insurance Company, was transferred to Nashville, Tennessee, and he and Pauline and their two children, Richard, four, and Doris, six months, made their home at Nashville. There, Pauline became a well-known and respected physician, and for many years she was the only woman obstetrician in that city. Jack, who had a weak heart, died in 1953. Pauline continued a long and distinguished career until her death in 1980. Their son, Richard, became an internationally known ophthalmologist, and other members of the Korenblat and Tenzel families entered the medical field.[88]

Adele Sanders (1905–1989) was a second generation American, the daughter of "Honest Abe" Sanders, who had established a scrap business in Little Rock (see above). Adele, one of nine children (eight sisters and one brother) and who never married, was an adventuresome person from her youth. She spent ten years as secretary-treasurer for Charles DeLeuw and Company, a Chicago firm of consulting engineers. She worked both at the Pine Bluff Arsenal and in administrative work at the Rocky Mountain Arsenal in Denver, and she served a number of years as secretary with the

Department of Indian Affairs' Bureau of Land Management in Phoenix. During World War II she worked at the Fort Logan Reception Center Headquarters, Denver, then joined the Women's Army Air Corps and was stationed in California and Arizona. She later returned and remained with her family in Little Rock until her death.[89]

East European Migration in Eastern Arkansas

Eastern Arkansas

Near the turn of the century, specific needs were being created that affected two groups of peoples half a world apart. In Russia and East Europe, the Jews were undergoing severe persecution; they needed a safe haven and a place to establish homes and livelihoods. At the same time, in America's rural south, the farming community was proliferating with farms and families that needed supplies and goods. These two needs would be met when numerous Jewish families found their ways into the South and began opening small specialty stores. Although only a comparatively few Jewish immigrants migrated to the South, there were enough such settlers to make an impact on the region as a whole. Although some of the East European Jews who came to the South settled in urban areas, most found greater opportunities in the rural communities. In Arkansas this was especially so in the rich farming country of the Delta in the state's eastern section.

The lives of these new immigrants were anything but easy. They worked hard and spent long hours trying to make a livelihood for their families. They had learned such struggle in their East European homes and had become "experts at the postponement of pleasure in order to achieve a better life later on . . . better for their children, seldom for themselves."[1] For an insight into this history, the lives of some of the Jewish merchants and their families who settled in east Arkansas are chronicled here. The narrative follows a somewhat clockwise fashion, beginning at Newport.

NEWPORT

Owners of the previously established Jewish-owned stores at Newport did their part in helping to absorb their persecuted brethren by giving them jobs as clerks. As had the German Jews before them, however, these industrious newcomers soon saved enough to open their own stores. Some of them who came to Newport included S. Grossman, Jake Lebovitch, and H. Salenfriend, and the families of Schneider and Wolf.[2] Enough Jews came to the area that they joined together and a congregation functioned there for a short while (see section II). At that time, Newport was a thriving river town, conducive to merchant activity. By the 1930s and 1940s, however, only a few Jewish families remained.

Russian natives Mordecai and Jenny (Schwartz) Beisan came to Newport in the early 1880s and tried their hand at farming. Adverse conditions soon forced them to leave, and they moved to St. Louis. The Beisans came about the time that a farming colony for Russo-Polish Jews was attempted at Newport (see section II). They may have been drawn to the area with the same group. Their son, Joseph Beisman, became a physician and surgeon of distinction in Detroit, Michigan. He was the first Jewish physician of East European origin to practice medicine in that city.[3]

Members of the Brownstein family established businesses in Newport before World War II. Gus Brownstein (1897–1985) and his brother Mose, sons of Russian-born Ben and Sarah Brownstein, established a salvage business and bought several thousand acres of land in the Newport-Amagon area of Jackson County. Their sister Annie married Jake Lebovitch, who operated Mr. Jake's Store at Newport for many years.[4]

WALNUT RIDGE

Sam Levit (1884–1943), who had come from Russia to America as a teenager, established a store at Walnut Ridge in Lawrence County in 1910. His general mercantile store operated on the town's Main Street until his death. He and his wife, Yetta, had one child, a son, Ervin (1919–1981), who grew to be six-feet-four-inches tall. Ervin excelled in basketball and track in high school, where he was known as "poetry in motion." Ervin was editor of the school's Bobcat Scream and leader of the local town orchestra. He was graduated as one of the "most versatile and active students" ever to attend the school. He married Jean Grossman of Joiner.

After serving in World War II, Ervin received a law degree and moved to Memphis, where he served as a special probate court judge.[5]

TUCKERMAN

Arthur S. Riegler (1892–1991) operated a store briefly at Walnut Ridge, where he met and married Rose Smith. The couple moved to Tuckerman in Jackson County in 1913 and opened a grocery and dry goods store. Riegler was well accepted and became known as a "tremendous asset to the community."[6] He was active in fraternal and civic organizations, serving as a city councilman, president of the Chamber of Commerce, and board member of the Bank of Tuckerman. During the Depression, while facing possible financial ruin himself, he not only struggled to regain solvency, but he also helped to keep others from going under as well. "Without this man's kindness and generosity," one of his patrons said, "we would never have made it." A World War I veteran, he was known for his honesty and his help to any needy person.[7]

CORNING

Polish-born Joe Steinberg and his wife, Minnie Steinberg, settled at Corning, Clay County, on the Missouri border in 1914, where Joe opened a store and bought cotton. He had a gin in Cardwell, Missouri. The Steinbergs had five sons: Nathan and Jake, who oversaw the Corning store, Simon, who was a Corning merchant, Harry, who became an attorney in El Dorado, and Sol, who was a cotton buyer at Paragould. Jake married Mildred Bondi, daughter of the prominent Clarendon family. (Sol and Simon married non-Jews.) Russian-born Gordon and Fannie (Froma Solomon) Graber established a store at Corning in 1914. Their daughter Sarah married Nathan Steinberg. The Steinbergs and Grabers were well accepted in the town.[8]

PARAGOULD

Other members of the Graber family established a chain of stores that eventually numbered thirty; they were located in towns in several southern states, including the Arkansas towns of Jonesboro, Paragould, Helena, Blytheville, and Pine Bluff. The warehouse for the chain was located at Paragould. Abraham Graber was patriarch of the family, and his family of six sons and a daughter helped run the stores. Three of the sons, Sam, Louis, and Max, lived in Missouri; Meyer Graber ran the Blytheville store, and Dave and Joe ran the warehouse at Paragould. Abraham's daughter, Bena, married Ewing Friedman, who ran the Paragould store.[9]

Isaac Goldstein established a tailoring store in Paragould that became popular in a multi-state area. Polish-born, he had emigrated to America in 1891 and worked in his brother's store at Murfreesboro, Tennessee, until he was offered a job in Jonesboro by merchants Less and Frank, owners of the Star Clothing House. After opening his tailor shop, he built up a trade that included state Governor John E. Martineau and Senator T. H. Caraway, and a number of officials of two large St. Louis companies. He also supplied uniforms for the Cotton Belt and Frisco Railroad. Known as one of the "most artistic merchant tailors" in the state, he employed as many as thirty tailors at a time.[10] Although he had never attended school or learned to read and write, he could remember his customers' measurements. He was later joined in the tailoring business by his son Harry, who married Velma Lazarus of Pine Bluff. Isaac also had a branch store at Jonesboro. He and his wife, Ethel (Finkel), had six children who lived to adulthood. Only one of them, a daughter, married non-Jewish. His son, Jaime, a tailor and manager of the Palace Theater at Jonesboro, served as Jonesboro's city treasurer.[11]

JONESBORO AREA

By the early 1890s there were enough East Europeans (mostly Lithuanians) at Jonesboro to compose a fair-sized Orthodox community, and a shul was formed (see section II). One of its members, Nathan Blecker, established a dry goods store at Jonesboro with branches at Lake City and Monette. Many of the Orthodox families moved to Memphis, including the Bleckers. Nathan opened another store at Turrell, about twenty-five miles northwest of Memphis, where he became familiarly known as "Judge." He lived there and his family visited him on weekends.[12]

At Lake City, some thirteen miles east of Jonesboro, Maurice S. Rubenstein (1910–1979), whose family had settled at Osceola in 1908 (see below), helped found the Farmers' State Bank. The bank later moved to Jonesboro, where it merged with the Citizens' Bank. Rubenstein, who was co-owner of a mercantile store in Lake City, served on the city's school board. He later moved to Jonesboro, where he was a leader in the drive for a stadium at Arkansas State University at Jonesboro.[13]

Lithuanian-born Charles Grossman (1877–1952) immigrated to America in 1893 and began peddling in southeast Missouri and northeast

Arkansas with a horse named "Maude." In 1905 he established a store at Jonesboro, where he married Bessie Berger. He brought from Europe his parents, Abraham and Bessie Grossman, and siblings Jake, Sarah, Rose, Hyman, and Jesse. Jake opened a ladies' clothing store at Jonesboro, Sarah and her husband, Louie Berger, had a store at Harrisburg; Rose and her husband, Monte Fallek, and Jesse Grossman had stores at Trumann. Jesse became well known in the area as a basketball player called "Chickie."[14]

Perry Cooperman (1892–198?) came from Russia to Arkansas as a teenager with his siblings and widowed mother. He began peddling across the state with a horse and wagon, then lived at Little Rock for several years. While there, he worked for Charles Abeles and learned the window-glazing trade. He helped install the windows in the new state Capitol building at Little Rock. He moved to Jonesboro, where he met and married Mary Friedman. He also had a hide and fur business at Paragould.[15]

BLYTHEVILLE

The growth of the northeast corner of the state after the turn of the century can almost be written by chronicling the history of the Jewish merchants and developers who helped build up the area (these included both German and East European Jews). By the 1930s there were more than two dozen Jewish-owned businesses in Blytheville. Some of the men who helped make Blytheville a center for buying and selling cotton were Adolph and Max Meyer, Lee Rosenberg, Silvey Sternberg and his son Harold, Milton Sternberg, and the Jiedel brothers, Siegbert "Zeke" (1902–1955) and Richard (a third brother, Jake Jiedel, settled at Helena). Others opened general mercantile, dry goods, or hardware stores, some of which became the largest in the area. These merchants included A. M. Weiner, Louis Lansky, Henry Reidan, Morris Zellner, Sam Florman, Meyer Graber, Sam Joseph, and H. Kleban.[16]

Wolf Arian (?–1954) was one of Blytheville's earliest merchants. He had settled there in 1905 after having tried his hand at business in Oklahoma, where he had been made an honorary chief of one of the Indian tribes. He married Jessie Berkowvitz, and their daughter Florence married Philip Feinberg (1900–1945), who opened the "Feinberg's Fashion Shop" in 1930 that remained a family business in Blytheville for thirty-two years.[17]

Samuel J. Cohen came to Arkansas as a graduate engineer from Russia; he worked with the firm of Pride and Fairley in Blytheville and helped construct drainage canals throughout northeast Arkansas. He also worked on highway construction and levees. Samuel's wife, Luba, a registered nurse, was from Odessa, Russia, where she had attended the city's only Zionist school, taught by Mrs. Kopp, sister of Zionist leader Vladimir Jabotinsky.[18]

Members of the Rosenthal family, Ike, P. H. and Walter, were Blytheville merchants. Walter Rosenthal (1886–1975), a spiffy-dressing young man from St. Louis, settled there in 1909 and eventually opened what became a fashionable and popular ladies' clothing store. He married Lillie Weinberg of Osceola, daughter of the matriarch Annie Weinberg (see section II). The Rosenthals had a son, Harold (1921–   ), who grew up perplexed and confused by the snobbery of some of the Jews toward his family and the fact that the Rosenthal's best friends turned out to be a Catholic priest and a Baptist minister rather than members of their Jewish community. During the days of the Klan, crosses were burned on the Rosenthal lawn, and the family as well as a nearby Catholic family hid in the Rosenthal home.[19] A feeling of "unJewishness" never left Harold in later life, and it left a residue of bitterness. He compiled his perceptions in an insightful, humorous, and slightly irreverent Weinberg family history. Ike Rosenthal lost a great deal when the First National Bank of Blytheville failed in the 1930s. His daughter married Dr. Maja Skaller, who practiced medicine in Blytheville for many years.[20]

Joe Isaacs was a merchant, banker, and cotton buyer of Blytheville who had begun as a peddler in northeast Arkansas at the turn of the century. He had built one of the town's first brick buildings and had helped establish the First National Bank. He became one of the town's most prosperous businessmen and served on every board that promoted the area's welfare. He built a large home and entertained his local friends in grand style. His parties would include an orchestra, dances in his home's lavish ballroom, and midnight suppers. The events would be talked about for weeks afterward. Joe was a hunter, and his trophy room sported the heads of Arkansas black bears, wolves, and birds. Described as a "lovable character," he was interested in sports and assisted the local athletic teams.[21] His son Louis also was a Blytheville merchant.

Jack Applebaum (1898–1938), who opened a ladies' clothing store at Blytheville in the early 1920s, became identified there with civic, municipal, and religious affairs. He was head of the town's Chamber of Commerce and was active in promoting the Boy Scouts. His brothers Joe and Phillip had stores at Blytheville, and his brother Louis was in the cotton trade at Osceola.[22]

MANILA

Some sixteen miles west of Blytheville lies the little town of Manila. It was here that members of the Tiger and Levine families opened a general store. Nathan Tiger (1869–1959) had emigrated from Russia (Latvia) in 1888 and settled near Luxora, where he peddled with a horse and wagon. He was joined in 1897 by his brother Esidor (1867–1961), who had left a wife and two children in Russia. Esidor sent for his family, and seven more children were born to him and his wife, Bessie (Garfinkel), in Arkansas. Annie Winer, Bessie's sister, and her husband settled at Blytheville, where they had a dry goods store. In 1901 the Tiger brothers (the name had been Tager in Russia, but was changed at Ellis Island) became partners with Ike Levine in establishing the Tiger-Levine store at Manila. The store's motto was "From the Cradle to the Grave," and it furnished clothes, groceries, farming supplies, and caskets (there was no undertaker, and families handled their own funerals). In 1908 all the Tigers moved to St. Louis, and the Manila store was sold to Ike Levine.[23] Ike married Esther Borowsky, and they made their home at Jonesboro some thirty miles away because of the crude living conditions in Manila at the time. Ike commuted by train to his store. In 1911 Esther visited her native Poland and brought back two of her brothers, Max and Boris. Max joined them in the Manila store, while Boris and his family opened a store at Pocahontas. (Boris's wife later died, and he moved out of state.) Another Borowsky brother, William "Bill" dreamed of becoming an accountant when he first came to work at the Tiger-Levine Store in the 1920s. (There were fourteen Borowsky children in all, half of whom came to America.) Intending to stay only a short time, Bill was caught by the Depression and remained on in order to make a living, and his dream of being an accountant never materialized. The Borowskys were deeply religious; Max and his wife, Leona (who had two children), and Bill and his wife, Pearl (who had four children) kept observant homes all during the years they lived at Manila. Kosher meat was sent by rail from Memphis or St. Louis.[24]

Another Jewish-owned store of Manila was that of Abraham "Alfred" Fendler (1885–1948), who was born in Cracow, Poland. (Austria ruled Poland when Fendler was born there in 1885). From an Orthodox background but considering himself a "German Jew," he felt rather superior to the mainly Russian Jews who had settled in the northeast corner of the state; he had little association with them. His nickname in Manila was "Germany" until World War I, when Germany fell out of favor in America.[25] Abraham and his wife, Rebecca, had four children, only one of whom, Oscar, remained in Arkansas. (The Fendler children who left Arkansas were Mrs. Ben [Frances] Schneider, who moved to Indianapolis; Benjamin, who became a physician in Alexandria, Louisiana; and R. E., who became an Atlanta attorney.) The childhood of the Fendler children was rather normal until World War I. Young Oscar, who headed the town's "German" group, clashed one night in 1918 with a local jokester, and a half-drunken group of anti-Germans became violent. Fearing to go home, the Fendler family spent the night in the home of a local Lebanese family. Racial slurs were so common that the Fendler children became accustomed to them, and Oscar only fought over them on occasion. During the active days of the Klan in the 1920s, almost every man in Manila was a member, but the Jews were not taunted or harassed; Klan activity was mostly rhetorical.[26] Oscar was a graduate of the University of Arkansas and of Harvard Law School. He began practicing law at Blytheville in 1933 with a partner, Cecil Shane, and he married Patricia, Shane's daughter. The Fendlers had a daughter, Frances, (Fendler also had a stepson, T. P. Wright III). Oscar Fendler became a prominent attorney, well known statewide (see section V).

Guy "Cotton" Rubenstein (1912–), whose family had settled at Osceola in 1908 (see below), had a store at Manila. He was active in civic organizations, such as the Lions Club and Chamber of Commerce.[27]

OSCEOLA

Osceola, located sixteen miles south of Blytheville on the Mississippi River, was the largest town in that section of the state after the turn of the century; by 1912 it had about twenty-five hundred residents. Eleven East European Jewish families had settled there at the time. The first Jewish person to come was Israel "Louie" Harwarg (1864–1943), who had left the Ukraine in order to escape the Russian military draft. (According to Louie, "to be in the Russian army was like being in hell; to be a Jew in the Russian army was like being in hell with your back broken.")[28] He immigrated to Memphis, where he met and married Tillie Shatsky, a piano teacher (Louie was known as a fine singer, himself). They established a dry goods and tailoring shop at Osceola in the early 1890s, while the town was still quite primitive. Just a few years before, panthers had roamed the area, and bear meat sold for ten cents a pound. The railroads did not reach the town until 1899.[29] Harwarg, who felt his first duty was to his Maker and his second to the country that now sheltered him, was well received. The Harwargs always felt they were a part of the community, not separate from it. The townspeople of Osceola told the family, "Now our town is complete—we have a Jew."[30] After completing school in Cleveland, Louie Harwarg's son Kohath joined his father in the Osceola business.

Ike Miller was the second Jewish settler in Osceola. He had begun as a peddler and eventually established several successful stores. Lithuanian-born Max Rubenstein (1874–1940) also began as a peddler but was not materially successful, although he was well appreciated for his contributions as a lay reader for Temple Israel that later formed in Blytheville. He and his wife, Lena (Brenner), had four sons. Two of them, Lewis and Abe, were cotton brokers in Osceola. Son Maurice settled at Lake City (later at Jonesboro) and son Guy at Manila. Their daughter Rose married a Memphis dentist, Herman Levitch.[31] Polish-born Morris Silverfield (1894–1958) migrated to Osceola in 1916 and operated a clothing store. His son, Lionel (1932–   ), continued the family business.[32]

Russian-born William Nickol (1885–1940), a shoemaker who had been sent by the Hebrew Immigrant Aid Society to Memphis, settled at Osceola in 1913 and established a dry goods and shoe store. He was quite civic minded and contributed generously to the town's public schools. One of his seven children, Abe, was killed while serving in the U.S. military in France in World War II. William's son Ben worked in the Osceola store and continued its operation. Another son, Morris (1909–   ), was a 1931 graduate of the University of Tennessee Dental School and practiced at Osceola. Morris served as president of the northeast Arkansas Dental Association and was active in local civic organizations.[33]

Louis Lapides (1899–1981) settled first in Mississippi, then moved to Osceola in 1922, opening "Little Lap's" general store. He was later joined in the family business by his son Melvin (1915–   ), who served in the U.S. Army in World War II. Melvin became one of the city's most outstanding citizens (see section V).[34]

The Weinberg family of Osceola was a vital part of that city's business community for many years. (See section II for more data on the Weinberg family.) Some of the other Jewish families of Mississippi County in the 1920s included those of Dave Dinkelspiel, Ben H. Levy, Dave Silverblatt, Herman Hess, C. E. Coulter, Abe Liverant, Henry Loberg, Ed Weiss, Hyman Kurtz, Louis Lansky, and E. M. Joffe.[35]

WEST MEMPHIS AREA

The small town of Joiner in south Mississippi County had several dry goods stores owned by Jews, including Jesse and Jeanette Evensky, Sam and Esther Weiss, Meyer Silberstein, and Jack Grossman. Grossman (1877–1971), who was not part of the Grossman family of Jonesboro, and his wife, Dora, settled there in 1919, then opened a store at Turrell for Jack's sister Sadie and one at Tyronza for his brother Frank. The stores continued into the 1950s. (A daughter of the Jack Grossman's, Jean, married Ervin Levit of Walnut Ridge.)[36] Luxora, a small town near Joiner, also had Jewish merchants, one of whom was Julius Burfield, noted as a good tailor. Those merchants who settled in eastern Arkansas tended to be dedicated to their Orthodox religion, and many were members of the Traditional Baron Hirsch Synagogue of Memphis.[37]

Some of the towns in Poinsett County that saw Jewish-owned stores established around the turn of the century included Marked Tree, Trumann, Harrisburg, and Lepanto. Jacob L. "Jake" Schonberger (1883–1945) conducted business at Marked Tree for almost sixty years, beginning in 1904. He had come with his parents to Jonesboro at age eleven, then opened his own business at age twenty-one. He was a charter member of Marked Tree's Rotary Club and active in the Chamber of Commerce.[38]

LEPANTO

After coming to America, Rumanian-born Meyer Bindursky (1864–1953) settled with his wife, Minnie, at Drew, Mississippi, where their four children, A. B., Albert, Herman, and Esther, were born. In 1922 the family moved to Lepanto and established a dry goods store. A. B. Bindursky (1898–1960) later opened a clothing store in Lepanto. Albert (1901–1984) and Herman (1906–1969) were owners of a men's clothing store in Lepanto, and their sister, Esther, became editor of the town's newspaper (see Distaff Side below). The family experienced some anti-Semitism in the town ("when push came to shove, they let you know you were Jewish"), and the Bindurskys attributed it to prejudice and ignorance.[39] Albert Bindursky experienced some anti-Semitism, but found good in others also.[40] The Bindursky children felt that they led two lives while growing up, one in Lepanto and one in Memphis, where they attended services. The Lepanto friends of Herman Bindursky's daughter, Eve, never mentioned that she was Jewish; "the subject was taboo." She said she experienced "more prejudice from Jewish kids [in Memphis] than from non-Jewish ones [in Lepanto]." She was well accepted in high school, serving as a cheerleader, as student council president, and as a member of Girl's State. Milton Bernard Bindursky, son of A. B. Bindursky, sang with the Boy Scouts statewide.[41]

McCRORY

Heyman Arnof and his wife, Fannie (Shapiro), came from Russia via Memphis and settled at McCrory, a small town in Woodruff County with a population of about 225 at the time. Heyman opened a clothing store and in 1903 helped organize the Bank of McCrory. When grown, only two of the Arnof's seven children, sons Nathan "Nudy" and Ellis, stayed in Arkansas (Nudy [1901–1986] remained in McCrory until his death). Nudy sold the Arnof mercantile store in the 1940s to employees, and the business branched into three separate stores—men's clothing, women's clothing, and a shoe shop. Nudy then worked in the bank full time; he became its president in 1934 and later served as chairman of the board and chief executive officer. He served on the town council and helped promote the area's growth (see section V).[42] Nudy married Lucille Picard of Memphis in 1934, and their two children, Ann and Ian, both remained Jewish, although they did not have spiritual concourse with other Jewish children or families. Their training, they said, came from the examples set before them by their parents.[43]

AUGUSTA, COTTON PLANT

Other Jews settled in the small towns of Augusta and Cotton Plant in Woodruff County. Lithuanian–born Morris Wilenzick (1862–?) had come to America in the early 1880s, peddled around Boston, then drifted to the Arkansas delta about 1890. He married Irene Goldblatt, and they settled at Augusta, where Morris established a mercantile store, prospered, and served on the town's school board and city council. The Wilenzicks had eight children. When their daughter Gladys wed Joe Dante of Dermott, the town of Augusta saw its first rabbi (Rabbi Fineshriber of Memphis), who married the couple. The wedding was also attended by Arkansas Governor Harvey Parnell, a family friend, and Jewish relatives and friends from Dermott, Dumas, England, Earle, Trumann, Foreman, Forrest City, Wynne, Memphis, and Washington, D.C. After the arrival of the boll weevil in the early 1920s and the devastation of the 1927 flood, the Wilenzick family moved in 1929 to Monroe, Louisiana.[44]

Louis Blumberg peddled in Arkansas after the turn of the century and met and married Rose Davis, whose family was associated with the Levy Department Store of Forrest City. Louis eventually opened a store at Cotton Plant, where he became vice-president of the local bank and purchased a motion picture theater. (The Blumberg's had five children, and when son Ralph was born, no mohel [ritual circumciser] would come from Memphis. Rabbi Jerome Marks of Helena agreed to come; however, he missed the train at Brinkley. In desperation, he went part of the way to Cotton Plant in a railway handcar.) The Blumberg's experienced some anti-Semitism from schoolmates, being called "sheeny," "kike," and "Jew-baby." (David "Dave," one of the Blumberg sons, remembered in first grade that a minister led the class in prayer and asked if anyone wanted to accept Jesus as Saviour. When Dave started forward, his teacher said she didn't think he would want to do that, and he did not.[45] In later years, Dave Blumberg was associated closely with both national and international leadership in B'nai B'rith (see section V).

WYNNE

Wynne, in Cross County, which had been home to Jewish citizens since its inception (see chapter 9, this section), saw the opening of a number of stores by Jewish immigrants between 1905 and 1920. Owners of these stores included the families of Drexler, Steinberg, Reagler, Saripkin, Goldberg, Greenfield, Speil, and Bornstein. Latvian-born Mike Drexler (1863–1935) established a store in Wynne around 1901, and over the next thirty years the business grew to become one of the town's largest. He became one of the most widely known merchants on Crowley's Ridge.[46] Mike Drexler married Dora Glass, and they had eight children. A son, David (1903–), worked in the Drexler store until 1928, then bought The Candy Shop from the Reaglers and Bornsteins and expanded it into a restaurant. After serving in the military in World War II, David established the Wynne Insurance and Loan Company. He was active in several civic organizations (see section V).[47]

Polish-born Hyman Steinberg (1875–1958), another Wynne settler, first made his home in Little Rock in 1910, where he opened a bakery at Seventh and Center that offered challah (Sabbath braided bread) and other specialty items. After his health failed in 1920, he moved with his family to Wynne, where he became a pillar of the community. Hoping to improve that agricultural area, he furnished farmers with necessities and provided a ready market for their crops. He joined others to create the Merchants and Farmers Gin Company, served as a director of the Cross County Bank, and helped finance the industrialization of the area. Extremely generous, he would help anyone in need. He married Tillie Smuloff, and they had four children. Sons Isadore (1905–) and Morris (1913–) remained with the family business in Wynne; daughter Sadie married Arthur Evensky, who had a mercantile store at Parkin; son Jake moved to St. Louis (see also section V).[48]

Lithuanian-born Morris Reagler (1887–1977) had a confectionary store at Wynne and was joined by Russian-born Herman Bornstein (1872–1945) as a partner in 1916. They both later opened their own dry goods stores. Reagler and his wife, Rachel, both of whom had no more than sixth grade educations, had three children. Bornstein and his wife, Cecile, sister of Little Rock junk dealer A. J. Goldman, had two daughters. Both families were typical of the East European Jews who brought to their adopted country a self-denial that was centuries old.[49] The parents worked long hours six days a week, determined to make a better life for their children. There were no babysitters for the youngsters, who stayed close to their parents' stores and often slept in the back corners or on counters on Saturday evenings. As the children grew, they helped in the stores, but their parents insisted they take advantage of the culture that was available—music and dancing—and go to college.[50]

Most Jewish families felt well accepted in Wynne, and some, such as the Drexlers, Reaglers, and Steinbergs, were members of the local country club. The Sharpes and Bargs of Forrest City also joined the country club at Wynne after World War II.[51]

TURRELL, CLARKEDALE

Small towns in Crittenden County, which borders the Mississippi River, saw a number of stores opened by Jewish immigrants. One of these immigrants, Polish-born Nathan Baer (1892–1970) immigrated to Memphis in 1908, following his brother Max Baer, who had come earlier. (Max later had a store at Hughes in St. Francis County, which he and his son Morris operated.) Nathan Baer prospered at Memphis, owning three stores, some thirty houses, and a two-hundred-acre farm. The 1929 crash left him with only a single truck, and he began selling produce in eastern Arkansas. He settled at Turrell, where he eventually opened six stores, dealing in such goods as auto parts, groceries, dry goods, and furniture. He and his wife, Ruth (Levitch) Baer, had six children, and they and some fifteen other employees kept the stores going. A bell system was set up to alert family and employees to the store needing the most help. Nathan Baer, who had a sense of humor and prankishness about him, was well liked. The family heard numerous anti-Semitic remarks, however, and they attributed these to less prosperous individuals who seemed to resent the Baer family's success and achievements. The Baer children were not allowed to date non-Jews, but the boys were popular with non-Jewish girls. The Baer youngsters were sent by bus to Memphis each Friday to attend Hebrew school. The family kept a kosher home, obtaining their meat and supplies from Memphis. Nathan's son Herman served as mayor of Turrell (see section V).[52]

Others who had stores at Turrell included Louis and Joe Friedberg, H. A. Furst, Jerry Reisman, and Nathan Blecker. Blecker's son, Dr. Abe L. Blecker, practiced briefly at Turrell, then moved to Memphis, where he served as chief of staff at St. Joseph Hospital. Max Friedman established a store at the small town of Clarkedale, just south of Turrell, around 1920.[53]

MARION

Russian native Isador Brick (1889–1948) came to Memphis around 1910 and opened a secondhand store. About ten years later, he settled at Marion in Crittenden County, where he opened a trading store, prospered, and built up a reputation as a helper of those in need; he later served on the Marion City Council. Isador and Rose (Mirsky) Brick had three children, Jake and Meyer (both of whom served in World War II) and Virginia. Although the family was well accepted in the small town, the Brick children often heard the racial slurs of "kike" and "Jew-baby."[54]

EARLE

Russian-born Jake Tupper (1881–1966) began his career out of Memphis as a peddler in east Arkansas. When his wife died in 1927, he moved the family to Earle, where he operated a grocery store until he retired in 1953. Tupper remarried, and his stepson, Sol Bursk (who also became his son-in-law; Bursk married Jake's daughter Lena), served in the military in World War II. Sol then returned to Earle, where he first peddled and then opened the Bursk Department Store and was involved in other businesses (see section V).[55]

William H. Harris (1899–1954) and his wife, Dora, opened a store in Earle, the "People's Bargain Store," with fifty dollars given to them as a wedding present by Dora's father, Jacob Speil. (Jacob owned a store at Tyronza, Poinsett County.) The Harris store at Earle prospered, and William eventually opened a chain of thirteen department stores scattered across Arkansas, Tennessee, and Missouri.[56]

Sol Stein and his wife, Irene Erber (daughter of Joe Erber, a Little Rock policeman who was killed in the line of duty), settled at Earle, where Stein was partner in a liquor store with his brother-in-law, Dave Schwartz (who was married to Irene's sister, Claudia; another sister,

Johnnie Erber, married Mendel Shainberg, who had a chain of Shainberg ladies' ready-to-wear shops in the South). Sol and Irene had two sons, George and Raymond, both of whom were popular in high school, excellent as students, and were two of the "greatest athletes ever developed at Earle High School." George Stein, who married a non-Jew, opened a grocery store at Earle in the 1940s.[57]

CRAWFORDSVILLE, WEST MEMPHIS

Joe Warshaw (1891–1960), born in St. Louis to immigrant parents from Poland, established a store at Crawfordsville in Crittenden County, where he served as alderman and as school board member, and later served as mayor from 1925 to 1950. During his tenure as mayor, he went to Washington, D.C., with Senator Hattie Caraway to generate funds for Crawfordsville's waterworks, sewers, and paved streets. With a loan from Washington, a deep well was drilled for water. Joe managed the plant so well that the bond indebtedness was retired before it was due, and new bonds were acquired for paved streets. His management skills made it possible for the city services to operate without the levying of a property tax—an almost unheard of achievement.[58] With only a sixth-grade education, self-taught Joe Warshaw worked to add the twelfth grade to the town's high school, so it could be accredited. As a school board member, he also promoted the establishment of a school for blacks locally. (After the school was built, Joe was dismayed that the school was not properly cared for: "They were given a whole new school, and now they're wrecking it," he said; but he continued to work for the betterment of the conditions of the blacks.)[59] Although he was criticized at times for his diligence in civic affairs, he continued to do good for the town "when no one cared."[60] Joe had begun his career as a peddler in southern Missouri and northern Arkansas with his father. He later opened a store at Joiner, where he used his musical talents and organized a civic band.

When Joe Warshaw and his wife Fannie (Burfield), and daughters Ethyl and Dorothy first settled at Crawfordsville, the daughters experienced "raw anti-Semitism" when they started to school in the small town. They were pelted with gravel and called "sheeny." After they became better known, they were well accepted and in later years remembered the citizens of the town as being "very aristocratic" and friendly. For the High Holidays the family went to Fannie's family, the Julius Burfields, at Luxora and celebrated the events with a number of other Jewish families in the Osceola area. Joe also took his family to concerts in Memphis and to the opera in St. Louis.[61]

Russian native Joe Levitch (1884–1952) came to Crawfordsville around 1923 and established a mercantile store. He had first immigrated to Memphis in 1908 and begun peddling food and wares in Arkansas's Crittenden County with his "rolling store" in a wagon. He would alert customers of his approach by ringing a bell. Four mules pulled his wagon, and two relief mules were led behind. Occasionally, he would take his young sons, Mike, Louis, and Ben, with him. In order to stay warm in the cold of winter, the boys would snuggle under the straw that protected the bananas. In summer the mosquitos were so bad that they had to pull a potato sack over themselves to keep the pests off. During those years Crawfordsville was thriving with customers; at times, the streets were full of people, making it difficult to walk. In 1937 Joe, called "Dago Joe" because of his Italian appearance, opened a branch store on Main Street in West Memphis and made his son Mike (1901–198?) its manager. After World War II the store dealt in military supplies.

The Levitch family was religious, keeping "one hundred percent kosher," and Joe's business life was permeated with his religious ethics. He was well thought of by both blacks and whites for his honesty. During the Depression, he gave to any hungry person who came into his store. During the flood of 1937 when livestock owners at West Memphis were selling their stock quickly, Joe took almost a hundred head of his customers' cattle to his lot at Crawfordsville for safety and returned them to their grateful owners after the flood waters receded.[62]

Several other East European immigrants and their families settled at West Memphis. Among them was Ukrainian native Harry Weisburd, who came to Arkansas via St. Louis and lived in several small Arkansas towns. He clerked for Jewish stores at Holly Grove, Marvell, and Clarendon, opening his own store at the latter. He married Aimee Johnson, granddaughter of Charles Weil of Pine Bluff. Weisburd family members had a store at Blytheville (The Grand Leader) from 1923 to 1934; the store was then moved to West Memphis, where it continued almost fifty years. Harry's son Jerrold (1911–), a graduate of Washington University, continued the business, and his other son, Everard (1913–), a graduate of the University of Arkansas, Fayetteville, became a West Memphis attorney.[63] Other Jewish attorneys in West Memphis were Bernard Goldstein and Alvin Fink; the latter moved to Clarksdale, Mississippi. Max Levy bought Harry's Department Store at West Memphis and continued it under that name for some fifty years. Dr. Milton Lubin, who began his medical practice at Turrell, moved it to West Memphis, where he became a prominent physician.[64]

COLT

One of the earliest Jewish settlers in St. Francis County was M. Davidson, who had emigrated from a border town in Poland to America in 1882. He peddled south from Indianapolis and wandered into Arkansas, settling in 1892 at the small community of Colt (formerly Taylor's Creek). He began his career there as a common laborer and "without a dollar." Although he was opposed by some local citizens in his efforts to have the Central Manufacturing Company of Kansas City establish an axe handle factory at Colt, he was successful, and the factory added to the economy of the area. He later established his own such factory, which continued to improve the area's revenues. Davidson, who married Bell Simon and had seven children, purchased a home and farmland.[65]

FORREST CITY

By 1920 there were forty-nine Jews, ten of whom were children, living in the bustling town of Forrest City in St. Francis County.[66] Among those who settled there were the families of Warshavsky, Snyder, Barg, Sharpe, Cohn, Cohen, and Burd.

Harry Jacob Warshavsky and his family settled in Forrest City in 1906. It had been a long trek for Harry to find a safe home. Born in Russia in the 1860s, he was conscripted into the Russian army at age twenty-one. After seeing a Russian officer beat his Jewish companion to death, Harry escaped in a load of hay and eventually made his way to St. Louis, where he arrived with $1.50. He peddled and saved until he could send for his beloved, Miriam Elizabeth "Lizzie" Shapiro, whom he married. In 1898 Harry opened a store in a lumber community in north Arkansas. When a block of frame stores burned, including Harry's, someone yelled, "Throw the Jew in the fire, he started it for the insurance money." The local insurance agent assured the crowd that Harry had no effective insurance, and thus saved him from harm. Undaunted, Harry returned to St. Louis, saved, and opened another store at Pocahontas in Randolph County but later relocated at Forrest City.

Harry and Lizzie Warshavsky had four children, two of whom died before 1906. Their two surviving children, Jeannette "Jean" and Sarah, grew up in Forrest City, where they were given lessons in voice, elocution, and piano. Their comfortable home sat on a quarter of a block, on which they had a vegetable garden, a cow, a horse, a dog, chickens, and geese. They had a cook and housemaid, for Lizzie worked in the store. Harry ran a second store at nearby Madison. Clerks and customers called Lizzie "Mother," and the family, the only Jews there for several years, became part and parcel of the town. The Warshavsky daughters fondly remembered their days at Forrest City.[67] When the oil boom hit the town of El Dorado in the 1920s, Harry and Lizzie moved, opening a store there and also a store at nearby Smackover and Norphlet.

Lithuanian native Esrael Snyder immigrated to Cincinnati at age eighteen, then moved to Little Rock when he heard it was a good place to settle. He peddled junk from there out into the state and found he did well at Forrest City, where he settled in 1913. He married Rebecca Cohen, and their two older sons, Charlie and Reuben, kept the Forrest City business when their father moved to Memphis in 1928. After the 1929 crash, Esrael and Rebecca moved back to Forrest City, where they built a lovely home. Charlie died, and Reuben and his family moved north. Esrael's daughter, Gertrude, and her husband, Louis Barg, continued the Snyder business, later changing the company name to Barg's.[68] Louis and Gertrude were active in the affairs of Forrest City (see section V).

Russian native Samuel "Sam" Sharpe (1889–1962) came to America in 1906 to escape the pogroms in his native country. A tailor, he settled first at Memphis and went occasionally to Forrest City to take measurements for suits. He liked the city and he, his wife Sarah, and their son, Raymond, settled there in 1914 (where they had two more children, Harold and Estelle). Sam was quite active in the Masons at Forrest City, and the Masonic Temple there was later named the Sam Sharpe Memorial Temple. Sam's son Harold (1914–   ), a graduate of the University of Arkansas Law School and a postgraduate student at George Washington University Law School, began practicing law at Forrest City in 1938. After serving in the military in World War II, during which time he worked for government agencies in Washington, D.C., Harold set up his own practice at Forrest City. The country club there did not allow Jewish members for many years, but Harold was permitted to buy a golf membership in it.[69]

Sol Cohn (1898–1974), also from Russia, came to Forrest City via Galveston and Memphis. He began working at Swift Meat Packing House in Memphis, saved his money, and with one hundred dollars opened Cohn's Penny Store in Forrest City. He opened four other such stores in nearby towns, then sold all of them and bought the Forrest City Wholesale Grocery Company. The firm grew through the years, and after Sol died, its management was continued by his children, William, Sylvia, and Freda (see section V).[70]

Russian-born Max Cohen (1909–　) came with his parents to Minneapolis, where he finished high school and also took pre-med courses. In the late 1920s he visited his brother, Maurice Cohen, at Pine Bluff, where the latter worked in the Siegel-King Department Store. Max worked in stores at Eudora and Dermott before opening his own store at Forrest City in 1933. Max married Elouise Reagler, daughter of the Morris Reaglers of Wynne. The Cohens' son, Barry Alan, later took over the Cohen store. Max Cohen was active in a number of civic organizations of Forrest City.[71]

Tailor Sam W. Burd and his wife, Cynthia Freeman Burd, a seamstress, came from Lithuania to Memphis around the turn of the century. They later bought stock from a bankrupt merchant and with it opened a mercantile store at Forrest City. They had two daughters, Rose and Sadie, who were provided with voice and piano lessons. Sadie moved to St. Louis, and Rose married Isadore Berk, owner of an El Dorado jewelry store.[72]

HUGHES

Some twenty-five miles east of Forrest City lies the small town of Hughes, also in St. Francis County. Several East European Jews opened stores here as well. Abe Zuckerman (?–1946) of Russo-Poland came to America in 1905 and served in the military in World War I. At the close of the war he opened a store at Hughes, where he built up a busy dry goods trade and was considered a pioneer of the town. In 1923 his brother, Max Zuckerman (1890–1968), settled there, where he "devoted all his time to his business and the service of the people."[73] Max and his wife, Annie (Goldberg), had four children, one girl and three boys. The sons, Marshall, Theodore, and Joseph, served in the military. Joseph became a physician in Chattanooga, and only Theodore (1920–　) remained in Arkansas. Some of the other Jewish-owned stores at Hughes were those of Julius and Libby Reisman, Mervin Reisman, and the Weintraub family.[74]

ENGLAND

Several East European Jews settled at England, Lonoke County, and helped in the production of the prosperity of that area of the state. One of these was Leon Sakon (1863–1920), whose honesty helped him get a start in America. While in the Peabody Hotel in Memphis, he found a billfold that contained thousands of dollars and returned it to its owner, a grateful Dr. Brooks. The latter helped him get established in business in

Tennessee. In 1907 Leon settled at England, Arkansas, and opened what became one of the town's largest dry goods stores. After Leon died, his widow married Marcus Adler (1864–1947), of German forebears, who continued the Sakon store. Leon's son, Robert Sakon (1904–1987), an adventuresome sort, tried his hand as a traveling salesman, as a writer for the Associated Press, and as a "flunky" for Paramount Studios in Hollywood. After his stepfather was injured in 1935, Robert returned to England, where he conducted the family store for more than forty years. A bachelor who became well noted for his philanthropy, he speculated in the stock market and made and lost millions.[75]

A number of other Jewish people had stores at England, which was a thriving agricultural town for many years. These included Sam Wexman, who settled there about the same time as Leon Sakon. He built up a large trade and had a modern brick store. He was boycotted during the active days of the Klan in the 1920s and lost the store.[76] Frank Wexman (1901–1965) had a store at England until the end of World War II. Abraham Lindenberg (1873–1955), who married Sarah Dante, sister of Charles Dante of Dumas and Eli Dante of Dermott, conducted a successful mercantile store at England. Other families with stores there included the Weintraubs, Reutlingers, Burtas, Krolls, and Rephans. The Weintraub store was later bought by A. Abroms of Dermott, and it was managed by Maurice Zimmerman.[77]

DE WITT, STUTTGART

East European Jews opened stores in other Lonoke County towns. Louis Riff (1856–1917) and his wife, Rachel, had a store at De Witt before World War I, and Harry Lipman had a store there in the 1930s. The Lipmans were related to the Sklar family of Little Rock and Texarkana.[78] Russian native Solomon Bilsky (1862–1935) settled at Stuttgart in Lonoke County in 1918 and opened the Chicago Hide and Fur Company. He and his first wife had three sons, William, Max, and Charles, all born in Russia. Bilsky's second wife, Jeanette Adler (sister of Marcus Adler of England), had six children. Five of Bilsky's children lived at Stuttgart— Miss Fretha, Mrs. Sam (Beatrice) Friedman, and Mrs. Morris (Essie) Bloomfield, and sons Maurice and Dr. Isaac Bilsky. The latter was a dentist who practiced at Stuttgart, Forrest City, and later at Memphis. William Bilsky (1892–1959), a furrier, and Miss Hannah Bilsky lived at Pine Bluff; Solomon's other sons, Max and Charles, lived at Memphis.[79]

LONOKE

Early German-Jewish settler Ferdinand Gates of Lonoke, who had accumulated huge land holdings in Lonoke County, brought some East Europeans to Arkansas and offered them land for farming. Unfortunately, those whom he sought to help knew nothing of farming, and they settled elsewhere.[80]

Southeast Arkansas

Shortly after the turn of the century, Marianna in Lee County became one of the state's many flourishing little towns in the Delta. Photos of that period show the public square filled with horses and wagons and also show the new railroad lines being laid between Marianna and Memphis.[81] With more farmers needing household and agricultural goods, merchants began opening new stores in this area, and the earlier German-Jewish merchants were joined by the Jews from East Europe, which included the Lewis, Cohen, Cohn, Nathan, and Shoemaker families.

One of the largest Jewish-owned businesses in Marianna was established by Lithuanian-born Morris Lewis (1869–1937). He had first settled in the 1890s at Dardanelle in Yell County, where he and his wife Mary and their three children, Lillian, Leon, and Naomi, lived in the back of his small store. He had a number of reverses and moved to Booneville in Logan County, where sons Bernie, Max, and Julius were born. Around 1910 the family moved to Marianna, where they prospered. During the family's hard times, Morris told his children that "the worst in this great country would be heaven under Russian rule."[82] Leon and Julius continued the family business at Marianna.

The Jewish community of Marianna was significantly affected by the Depression; some merchants retired and others moved away. But still other Jewish merchants came in behind them and established more stores. Over the years these included Dave Alperin, Morris Nathan, Jesse Isaacs, Leonard and Roberta Strasberg (two stores), the Panicks, the Bishins, the Silversteins, the Spitzers, the Shankmans, the Shainbergs, and the O'Mells.[83]

MARVELL

Several members of the Davidson family settled at Marvell in Phillips County. Russian natives Isaac Davidson (1850–1925) and Samuel J.

"Sam" Davidson had come to Memphis after the turn of the century. Sam and his wife, Fannie (Bernstein), settled first at Clarendon in Monroe County before moving to Marvell prior to World War I. Sam was joined by Isaac, and they operated general mercantile stores and began investing in land. Three sons of Sam and Fannie, Abe J., Saul, and Ely, remained in Marvell. Abe (1895–1984) married Sarah Rankin, a native of Russellville, and they had two daughters, Edith and Dorothy. Ely "Sonny" (1899–1952) was a cotton buyer and merchant, and in the 1940s he had a store at Forrest City. Another son, Dr. J. S. Davidson, practiced at Forrest City. One daughter, Mrs. L. D. Rutstein, lived at Stuttgart, and another daughter, Mrs. William C. Biskin, lived at Memphis. On part of the Davidson's land was located the base point for all surveying that was done for the property bought from Napoleon in 1803, known as the Louisiana Purchase. A marker was erected at that base point in 1926.[84]

HELENA

Several East European Jewish families settled at Helena in Phillips County. They were drawn there by other Jewish merchants, some of whom cooperated with the Jewish immigrant aid societies. Examples of these new migrants include the Feldman, Ciener, Levine, Hyman, Kaplan, and Cohen families.

Rumanian native David Feldman was the first of his family to come to Arkansas, where he peddled fruit in Little Rock in the 1890s. His son Herman (1874–1940) came to Little Rock with his wife, and they moved to Helena; David returned to Rumania. Herman, a short, stocky man who spoke broken English, became a familiar sight in Helena as he peddled produce from a horse-drawn wagon. He opened a small produce store and formed a commission company; he built a cold storage plant in 1918. Extremely generous and affable, he was noted to be an example of the American success story of the immigrant who came to America and "through hard work and honest dealings rose to great success as a businessman."[85] Herman had three sons, Adolph (1900–1978), Simon (1902–1974), and Solomon (1907–   ), all of whom joined him in the Feldman Commission Company. Solomon "Solly" was a graduate of the University of Chicago.[86]

Hungarian native Samuel F. Ciener Sr. (1882–1962) happened by chance to settle at Helena. His brother Joe, a traveling salesman for the Headlight Overall Company, became stranded at Helena when his company reneged on payment of a commission owed to him. Joe noticed the town needed a cleaner, and he opened "Ciener the Cleaner." (The sign painter misspelled it as "Ciener the Cleanser," and Joe didn't have funds to change the sign.) Joe invited his brother Sam to join him, which he did. The cleaning shop, which used gasoline at the time, later blew up, and Joe opened a wholesale dry goods company; Sam established "The Stag," a young men's clothing store. Sam was active in civic affairs, serving on the Helena school board for twelve years; he sponsored a baseball team, was a member of the Helena Hospital Board, and was president of a local savings and loan company. He was proud of his membership card in the Helena Country Club, which allowed Jewish members from its inception in 1916. (Sam proudly displayed his card in his store's front window.) He married Stella Ball. Their son, Sam "Sonny", continued the family business, and their daughter married Jack Cohen of Helena.[87]

Samuel Levine (1883–1974) emigrated from Minsk, Russia, to Helena in 1915, where he established his own company; he was later joined by his son, Irvin.[88] John Irwin Hyman (1895–1972), who came to America and served in World War I, settled at Helena shortly after that conflict. He established what became one of Helena's finest ladies' shops and became active in civic affairs.[89] Samuel Kaplan (1875–1946), a Russian emigré, established a grocery store at Helena. He had four daughters, Misses Miriam and Freda, Mrs. Harry Cohen of Helena, and Mrs. A. B. Bindursky of Lepanto.[90] Harry Cohen (1897–1965) and Nathan Cohen (1904–1976) conducted the Cohen Salvage Company. Nathan was particularly well known, serving as a director of the Helena Terminal Company and the Ophelia Polk Home.[91]

ARKANSAS CITY

Several East Europeans found Arkansas City in Desha County to be an opportune place to open stores. Among them were the Abowitz, Roby, and Raphael families. Samuel Abowitz, a native of Vilna, Russia, came to America before World War I and settled at Arkansas City, where he established a furniture store. He and his wife, Molly, born in pre-Israel Palestine, became well loved in the community; he was known as "Papa Sam" and she as "Mama Molly." The Abowitzes would attend local churches with their friends, and they felt a comfortable acceptance. Sam served on the city council and school board. He continued his store until the 1930s, when he began work on the levees in Arkansas and Louisiana. He accumulated some twenty-four-hundred acres of land, began farming cotton, and established a gin. He also raised cattle and was a fur buyer. He and Molly had a daughter, Shirley (who married William Sherman of Pine Bluff), and two sons, Herbert (1913–1945), who was killed in Italy during World War II, and Maurice (1920–   ). The latter served in the Army Air Force in World War II, then returned to Arkansas City, where he married Joan Scholem of Pine Bluff and continued the family farming enterprises. Maurice was a member of the Equalization Board of Desha County and of the Federal Appeals Board for eastern Arkansas.[92]

Molly Abowitz's brother, Max Roby, a graduate of an agricultural school in Palestine, worked for Eli Dante of Dermott, then moved to Arkansas City, where his brother Harry had opened a store. Max's son, Irving, was killed in service in World War II. Ralph Raphael, who married Molly's sister Anna, had a clothing store at Arkansas City. He had a pot-bellied stove in the rear of his store that became a local gathering place for men to chat.[93]

McGEHEE

After the devastating flood of 1927, Arkansas City began losing its population to nearby McGehee. The latter town grew from a dozen residents in 1905 to almost thirty-five hundred by 1930.[94] Among the East European Jewish families that settled at McGehee were the Wolchanskys, Fleisigs, and Meyers.

Sam Wolchansky (1874–1953), born in Suwalki, Poland, came as a lad of fourteen to New York, then wended his way to southern Arkansas. He established a general store at McGehee, becoming one of its pioneer merchants. He later became a cotton broker and ginner, eventually establishing three cotton gins; he also bought land. He had some twenty-five-hundred acres near McGehee and five thousand acres, called the Redfork Plantation, near Watson. "Mr. Sam," as Wolchansky became affectionately known in McGehee, married Vera Friedman, a Pine Bluff native, and they had two sons, Howard (1906–   ) and Roy (1908–   ), and a daughter, Helen, who married Bernard Sabin (1910–1961); Sabin joined the Wolchansky enterprises in 1939. (During World War I, Sam moved his family to Little Rock so their three children could attend better schools; Sam commuted to McGehee at the time.) Mr. Sam was a charitable person; one of his donations included land on which to build a temple at McGehee. During the devastating 1927 flood, the Redfork Plantation was inundated and left in an irreparable state. Sam and others of the area lost their holdings there. Howard Wolchansky married Louise Goldstein of Paragould, and they lived for a time in McGehee. In the 1930s they began seeking a place with more advantages for their children and moved to New Orleans in 1938. Roy also moved there and established Security Van Lines.[95]

The Fleisig family that became a part of McGehee's business, civic, and religious communities began with Charles Fleisig (1881–1963), who came to America after the turn of the century. He married Mollie Rephan and managed the Rephan store at Conway at first, then established the New York Bargain Store at De Witt, which lasted from 1916 to 1925. He moved to Little Rock, where he had a millinery store on East Markham, and opened five stores over the state, called Fleisig's. After the Depression began, he moved to McGehee in 1932, where he conducted the New York Store until his death. Seymour Fleisig (1916–1993), son of Charles, was a high school graduate in 1932 when his dad moved to McGehee. He remained in Little Rock, attended Little Rock Junior College, worked a short while, then joined the U.S. Army. During service he met and married Edith Lipsey of Rhode Island, who was serving as a sergeant in the Women's Army Corps. The two returned to McGehee after the war, where Seymour joined his father in the mercantile store and became active in the town's civic affairs. A student of religion, he also taught Sunday School and confirmation classes for the local congregation. Charles Fleisig's daughter married Mendel Pinkus of Dermott.[96]

Several members of the Lithuanian-born Meyer family settled in several southeast Arkansas towns, as had members of the German-born Meyer family some twenty years earlier. Mayer and Malke Meyer, relatives of William and Morris Rosenzweig (see below), had seven children born in Europe: Morris, Dave, Abe, Zippie, Bertha, Lena, and Sarah. Beginning in 1902, members of the family began migrating to America, and when possible, these would send for other members. By 1907 all had come to Arkansas. Their oldest son, Morris, moved to St. Louis, but his son, Sol F., settled at Eudora, where he established a store; Sol married Fannie Pinkus of Dermott.[97] Dave Meyer managed the Rosenzweig store at McGehee, then opened his own store and became one of the town's most successful businessmen.[98] After working at the Rosenzweig store in Pine Bluff, Abe Meyer established a men's store in that city that catered mostly to blacks; he married Anna Reinberger of Pine Bluff. Zippie married Mayer Marcus, and Sarah married Mayer's brother, Isadore. In 1933 Isadore Marcus established a store at McGehee. Lena Meyer married Ben Sandstein, and they established a store at Gould.[99]

A number of other Jewish people had stores at McGehee; some of whom had first established their businesses at Arkansas City. These merchants included Melvin Rappaport, Victor Grober, I. Silverman, Morris Cooper, Ben and Dave Marcowitz, A. L. Ruskin, Bernard Tanenbaum, Abe Zeno, Bernard Cohen, Joe Selz, Morris and Sam Dessent (who had a hotel and furniture store), and the Shach brothers, Mike, Phillip, Irving, and Joe (who had a clothing store and funeral home). Isadore Small bought the Morris R. Dessent dry goods store in 1947 and continued it for thirty years.[100] Although the Grand Dragon of the Ku Klux Klan lived at McGehee during the 1920s, there was "no commotion," and Jews faced "no real problems."[101]

DERMOTT

Dermott, just ten miles south of McGehee, had its share of Jewish-owned stores, especially after the East Europeans began establishing businesses there. At one time there were some eight Jewish-owned dry goods stores in the small town. Occasionally a light feud would spring up among the Jewish merchants, but their bond was stronger than their differences. As did other Arkansas Jewish merchants until the 1940s, they closed their stores on the High Holy Days.[102]

One prominent Jewish merchant of Dermott was Eli Dante. He and his brother Charles (who were brothers of the young Dante boys who drowned at Little Rock in 1897 [see chapter 10]) peddled goods in southern Arkansas for William Rosenzweig of Pine Bluff. Eli saved enough to open his own store at Dermott, seventy-two miles south of Pine Bluff. (During his days as a peddler, Eli traveled through Lonoke, and on his trips there stayed in the home of Joseph T. Robinson, who later became one of Arkansas's most well-known senators.) Eli prospered in Dermott, where he served as an alderman and was active in civic and fraternal affairs. Eli had studied to be a rabbi in his native Russo-Poland, and in 1905 he founded an Orthodox congregation at Dermott (see chapter 6).[103]

Other Jews who settled at Dermott after the turn of the century included Joseph Weisman, Isadore Pinkus, Abe Abroms, and Joseph Cohen. Rumanian native Joseph Weisman (1887–1951), who had come to Pine Bluff in 1906, moved to Dermott in 1912, opened a dry goods store, and became a prominent merchant of the town. He married Stella Fink of Pine Bluff, and they had two daughters. One of the daughters, Bernice, married William Sherman of Pine Bluff, and their son, Robert "Bob" Sherman, became a Little Rock artist. The Weisman's other daughter, Louise, married Bernard Levi of Pine Bluff, son of Sam and Henrietta (Vogel) Levi. After Joseph Weisman's death, Bernard took over the

Weisman store at Dermott, where he became active in civic affairs, serving on the County Equalization Board and as president of the Rotary Club.[104]

Isadore Pinkus (1870–1959) of Russo-Poland came to America and began peddling in Connecticut and wended his way on foot to Pine Bluff. He peddled south from there, opening a store at Parkdale. When the lights were shot out of his store one Saturday night, he moved to Dermott. (Isadore told his son that no malice was intended by the vandalism, that someone was just having fun; many of his Gentile friends urged him to stay at Parkdale.) Besides his store, Pinkus built up a hide and fur trade, traveling regularly within a fifty-mile radius of Dermott to pick up pelts. Extremely religious, the Pinkus family would keep a kosher home during Passover, but found it impossible to do so on a regular basis. When minyans (a group of ten men) were needed for yahrzeits (observance of the anniversary of a loved one's death), men would come from Arkansas City and McGehee and stay in the Pinkus home. Isadore's son Mendel married Beulah Fleisig, who was active in local school affairs and worked on a committee that helped keep the schools open at a time when operating funds were depleted.[105]

Abraham "Abe" Abroms (1896–1979), son of Russian immigrants, came to Dermott during World War I and opened a retail clothing store. This grew to become a large mercantile store. Civic-minded and charitable, he helped build a hospital in Dermott and was instrumental in getting the Wells LaMont Glove Manufacturing Company and Davis Industry to locate in Dermott. He had four branch stores at one time at England and Benton in Arkansas, at Oak Grove in Louisiana, and at Shaw in Mississippi. He also had a wholesale distributorship for ladies' wear. He married Ruth Koppel, and they had four children. Abe also helped bring the Goodyear Mid-South Distributing Company to Dermott. Michael Seligson headed the enterprise, which was a distributorship for rubber footwear. Abe Abroms nephew, Joseph "Joe" Goldstein, worked with the Abroms enterprises at Dermott and was a founder of the First National Bank of Dermott. He became active in the town's civic affairs, serving as president of the Chamber of Commerce and helping in the building of a public swimming pool. He moved to Cleveland, Mississippi, in 1965 to work in another Abroms store.[106]

Joseph Cohen (1865–1946) came to Dermott after the turn of the century and opened a dry goods and notions store. His daughter married Sam Nussbaum (1895–1968), who also established a store there. Other stores were established by E. Schnelz, H. Greenberg, and Nathan Semack.[107]

LAKE VILLAGE

At Lake Village, less than twenty-five miles below McGehee in Chicot County, several East European Jews established stores. One of these was Sam Epstein (1875–1944), who came from Russia around 1900 and peddled in south Arkansas. He opened a small store at Lake Village and slept on its counter at night.[108] His business, as well as the area, prospered, and he became one of the incorporators of the town. He loved the land and at one time had accumulated some ten thousand acres. He was elected as a member of the Chicot County Central Committee and was active in the development of the Mississippi River Levee System, serving as a member of the Chicot County Drainage Board. He also served as president of the Lake Village School Board for a number of years. It was said that he was illiterate, but his "scratchings" were not recognized as Yiddish by the local citizens.[109] He was known for his generosity, and in the 1920s lent fifty dollars to H. L. Hunt (who called Sam "my Jewish pal"); Hunt used it to buy land at El Dorado, where he struck oil and became wealthy.[110]

Lithuanian native Morris Rosenzweig (1876–1950) was brought to Arkansas by his brother, William, who had established a mercantile and farm supply store at Pine Bluff (see below). Morris was sent by his brother as a peddler into south Arkansas and eventually opened a store at Lake Village. (He had first attempted to open a store at Winchester in Drew County, but a rock was thrown through his window with a note that read, "Jew, get out of town.") The store at Lake Village prospered, and Morris opened a chain of five other stores in Arkansas. He served on the Lake Village city council and on its school board. He married Clara Meyer, daughter of Charles Meyer of Newport, and they had two sons, Joseph "Joe" and Jack. Joe was president of his public school class "eleven out of twelve grades," and president of the student body in high school and captain of both the football and basketball teams. Both boys were valedictorians of their senior classes, and both served in World War II, Joe as a lieutenant (j.g.) medical officer in the Navy and Jack, as a captain and bombardier-navigator in the Air Force. After the war, Joe became a prominent doctor in Hot Springs, and Jack, who had a journalism degree, became a merchant.[111]

Louis Bloom established a drug store at Lake Village in the early 1920s. (He had attempted to open a store at Monticello in Drew County but was told Jews were not welcome there.)[112] His store motto, which was "Help Us Bloom," was printed on all advertisements, including an ad on the auditorium curtain of St. Mary's Catholic School. Louis was killed at a hunting camp in Chicot County in 1929; his family was told he had been thrown from a horse, but Klan involvement was suspected.[113]

The David Markowitz family had a laundry in Lake Village for a number of years, beginning in the early 1920s, and a Mr. Grossman was a local tailor. Nathan "Mr. Freedie" Friedman served as a constable in Lake Village and as a deputy sheriff in Chicot County. He was remembered as zooming around Lake Village on his motorcycle, with motorcycle cap pulled firmly down on his head, ear flaps flying in the wind.[114]

EUDORA

At Eudora, seventeen miles below Lake Village, more than a half dozen East Europeans established stores alongside those owned by people with German-Jewish backgrounds. There were so many Jewish merchants and their families at Eudora at one time, that the Jewish community jokingly called it "Jewdora."[115] The new settlers included Dave Cornblatt, N. Abrams, Sol F. Meyer (who had stores at McGehee and Dermott as well), and Sol Levy. Most established dry goods and mercantile stores.[116]

In 1926 Rumanian native Max H. Hart came to Arkansas, hoping to escape the flood waters and boll weevils of Louisiana, where he had first settled (he later commented that the plagues followed him to Arkansas). In Eudora he bought the M. Schwartz dry goods store. He and his wife, Mary (Sloss), had three children, Anna Ruth (Warfield) and sons Leon and Harold. Both sons were captains in the military in World War II. Leon later became a prominent New Orleans physician; Harold continued the family clothing store in Eudora and entered the town's civic life. The Hart family experienced some anti-Semitism, which "is impossible to get away from," but Harold was well accepted in school. He was captain of the high school football and basketball teams and was valedictorian of his senior class. He was so well accepted that he was even invited to join the Klan. (His father also had been invited to join the Klan in Louisiana; both Harts declined.)[117]

DUMAS

Eighteen miles north of McGehee on Highway 65 is the town of Dumas. It was here that the German-Jewish settler, Gus Waterman, established a store and pioneered the area. In the 1890s he was joined by Polish immigrant Charles Dante (1877–1967), brother of Eli of Dermott. Charles married Antoinette "Toney" Stiel of Little Rock, and they and their family became the builders and developers *par excellence* of southeast Arkansas (see Distaff Side below). Charles came almost penniless to

America and began his career at Pine Bluff by peddling matches and novelty items throughout south Arkansas. He managed temporary stores at Parkdale and Portland for William Rosenzweig of Pine Bluff. He saved five hundred dollars and in 1897 rented a store at Dumas for seven dollars a month and opened The Globe Cash Store. Dumas had only eight white families at the time, and the Dante's worked alongside the other pioneers and helped build the community into a thriving town.

Charles Dante's store prospered, and he became involved in the town's civic life, serving as mayor, president of the school board, president of the Chamber of Commerce, and chairman of the Dumas Water and Light Commission, helping bring utilities to the town. When his store burned in 1925, a nearby neighbor, R. A. Pickens Sr. helped him financially and reaffirmed Charles's faith in America, which he saw as a bountiful new homeland and which he never took for granted. He rebuilt and opened a twenty-thousand-square-foot store—the largest in that section of the state. He loved the land and bought up thousands of acres for investment and farming. A deeply religious man who found himself outside the umbrella of a Jewish community (the closest congregation was at Pine Bluff, and the impossible road conditions for years prohibited attendance there), he taught his own family, conducting the holiday services in their home. He later generously supported a Reform congregation established at McGehee, some eighteen miles south of Dumas.[118]

The Dante's had a son, Jack Stiel (1900–1977), and two daughters, Helen and Naomi. In 1920 Jack joined the family business and followed his father's footsteps in civic and charitable contributions. Jack served on the Dumas School Board for ten years and on the Desha County Hospital board for twenty-five. For more than fifty years he was at the forefront of every civic drive in Dumas, and he became known for his extensive philanthropies. He was an aggressive chairman of the city's Industrial Foundation and pushed for soybean storage facilities when none existed; soybeans later became the area's number one crop. Jack worked for better libraries, improved drainage, and he helped churches and other charitable institutions. (Jack Dante married Rose Mae Herrman, and they had a son, Charles H., who joined the family enterprise at Dumas, and a daughter, Mrs. Dave [Julianne "Judy"] Grundfest.)[119]

Naomi Dante married Bernard Jerome Tanenbaum (1904–1981), an enterprising young man whose family had operated stores at Harrisburg and Dermott. He moved to Dumas in 1932 and joined the Dante enterprises. Bernard and Naomi had one son, Bernard Jerome "Jerry", who also became a member of the Dante-Tanenbaum enterprises.[120]

Charles Dante helped a number of Jews escape from Europe after Hitler came to power. One of these was his nephew, Harry Phillips (1916–1993), who came to England, Arkansas, and stayed with his aunt, Sarah (Dante) Lindenberg, then moved to Dumas, where he was associated with the Charles Dante enterprises. He served in World War II, during which time he was wounded and received the Purple Heart. (Harry's parents and a brother died in the concentration camp at Treblinka.) In 1946 Harry married Elsie Hamburger, who had been brought from Germany to McGehee by family members in 1936. Harry managed the Dante-Tanenbaum store in Dumas and later was the district manager for the United Dollar Stores.[121]

The Rumanian-born Wolff brothers, William, Leo, and Samuel, came to Dumas in 1911 after first trying their luck on the Panama Canal. (After Sam got yellow fever there and almost died, they took their accumulated savings and returned to the States. William lost their savings while shooting dice on the return boat trip, and they returned as destitute as they had been when they had left.) After working in New York and Pennsylvania, they migrated south to Natchez, then to Dumas, where they opened the Wolff Brothers Dry Goods Store. Sam Wolff (1885–1947) operated a branch store in Tillar; Leo operated another Wolff store at McGehee. Sam married Sadie Rosenberg, and they had two sons, Mercer and Haskell, and a daughter, Grace. Mercer (1915–1970) was a graduate of the University of Arkansas and Harvard Law School. After serving in the Army Air Force in World War II, he operated the Wolff store at McGehee. Grace married Michael "Mike" Seligson of Dermott, and Haskell married Elaine Waldman of Little Rock. Haskell "Hack" (1918–   ) operated the Dumas store and became involved in the town's civic life. He served for a number of years on the city council and was president of the Chamber of Commerce, Lions Club, hospital board, and the city's Industrial Foundation.[122]

PINE BLUFF

The already relatively large Jewish community of Pine Bluff in Jefferson County grew considerably as East European immigrants began arriving, some as early as the 1880s. Two of the first to arrive were Polish-born Harris Bram (1866–1950) and his brother Barnett (1871–1949). They began as peddlers in the 1880s, traveling across southern Arkansas. When they passed through Lonoke, they were the invited guests at the hospitable Joe T. Robinson's home.[123]

Lithuanian native William Rosenzweig (1871–1949) came in 1889 and established The Good Luck Store, which became one of the area's largest mercantile and farm supply firms. Deeply religious, he served as treasurer of Temple Anshe Emeth and of the Jewish Federated Charities and was president of the B'nai B'rith Lodge at Pine Bluff. He was known as a man with a big heart, considerate of employees, and highly esteemed in the community. He brought from Europe several relatives, including his brothers Morris (noted above) and Sigmund (1881–1922); the latter was associated with the Pine Bluff store. William promoted Pine Bluff at every opportunity. On the back of his business stationery were photos of the city's banks, library, business section, and other notable areas, along with facts about the city and Arkansas.

William Rosenzweig married Pauline Sarason, whose brother Sam was a partner with William for a short period before establishing his own store at Conway (see chapter 13). William and Pauline had two daughters, Irene and Sylvia (Schloss). Irene was a graduate of Bryn Mawr who received a doctorate from the American Academy in Rome. She taught in private schools in the Washington, D.C., area, and her pupils included the nieces of President Franklin D. Roosevelt. Sylvia, a graduate of Washington University in St. Louis, established the Rosenzweig-Schloss Foundation in Pine Bluff, which benefitted the city's charities and area Jewish philanthropies.[124]

Around 1900 Rumanian native Ben "Jake" Riesenberg (1871–1938) came to Pine Bluff. He married Bertha Wiseman, and they had seven sons, five of whom remained in Pine Bluff. Their son Sol (1905–1976) had a bakery business; Itsy (1906–), Harry (1908–1981), Louie (1909–1981), and Ottie (1910–) had clothing or mercantile stores. (Sons Joe and Mannie had a scrap metal business at Memphis.) Samuel Baer Baim (1875–1956), from Russo-Poland, also came around 1900 and migrated to Pine Bluff. He bought an existing clothing store and renamed it Baim's. He married Sarah Fink, and they had six children, all of whom remained in Pine Bluff. Their daughter Adah (1899–1989) married Milford "Buddy" Sonnenschein (1895–1971), and they had The Sunshine Shop in the Hotel Pines. Son Gene Baim (1908–1979) was a Pine Bluff attorney. The other sons of Sam and Sarah Baim were Charles (1902–1960), who had the Hot Springs Baim store, and Aaron (1904–1956), Leo (1907–1976), and Bennie, who helped run the Pine Bluff store.[125]

The Russian-born Soltz family also settled at Pine Bluff. Theirs was a most poignant migration to America. Samuel Soltz (1858–1942) and his wife, Malky (1861–1920), were natives of Vilna, Russia, where they had six children. Samuel came to the United States first, hoping to save enough to bring his family over. He found work in St. Louis, but his earnings were so meager that he could only send for one family member at a time. It took twelve years before the last one came—his wife, Malky.[126] Sam later brought his family to Pine Bluff, where he established the Pine Bluff Scrap Iron and Metal Company, which later became known as Soltz Machinery and Supply Company. After Sam's death, the company was continued by his son, Hyman (1887–1954), and other family members.

Russian-born tailor Max Schlosberg (1876–1951) also came to Pine Bluff via St. Louis around 1900. He worked for Henry Marx, then went with the large Kastor-Bluthenthal firm. In 1907 he opened a tailor shop, which he continued for a number of years. Max married Bessie Nichols, and they had seven children, three of whom remained in Pine Bluff. Their son Burton opened a men's store in 1935, and their daughter Zelda married Harry Riesenberg and with him opened a small shop called "Zelda's."[127]

Russian native Aaron Goldweber (1881–1973) came to Pine Bluff around 1906 and operated a furrier and tailoring business. Hungarian-born Louis Englander (1836–1917) migrated to Pine Bluff at about the same time and conducted a mercantile business for a number of years.[128] Andrew Kahn (1889–1968), also from Hungary, came to Pine Bluff around 1910 and opened a watchmaking business. He also was an optometrist and sold glasses and jewelry. The store became so popular that it was often open until midnight. The local farmers worked until sundown, then would drop by and shop at night or just come by to talk with Dr. Kahn. His family continued the business.[129]

Latvian native Jacob Eli Smulian (1870–1943) settled first at Stroud, Oklahoma, where he became the town's mayor, before migrating to Pine Bluff. (His daughter Fay married E. M. Pfeifer Jr. of Little Rock.) When his brothers-in-law Louis and Abe Froug came to Pine Bluff in 1909, he joined them in opening the Froug Department Store, which grew to be one of the largest and most successful in southern Arkansas. They also opened several branch stores in Arkansas and three at Tulsa, Oklahoma.[130]

Russian native Maurice Cohen (1900–198?), brother of Max Cohen of Forrest City, came to Pine Bluff in the 1920s. He had first settled at Minneapolis with his family at age twelve. His mother, Bessie, had a boarding house, and one renter was Russian-born Joe King. When Joe almost died, Bessie nursed him back to health. Joe later settled at Hot Springs, and in appreciation for what Bessie had done for him, offered her son Maurice a job. Maurice settled at Pine Bluff in 1924 and managed the Siegel-King mercantile store, then later bought it when the owners' partnership dissolved. Maurice began with an almost empty building, selling

Army surplus and women's work clothes. He built it up into a good-sized department store and also opened a fashionable ladies' clothing store. In 1926 he was able to bring his mother (1877–1928), who had dreaded the cold Minnesota winters, to Arkansas; she enjoyed the South for two years before she died. Maurice continued his Pine Bluff businesses for some sixty years.[131]

There were numerous other East Europeans who settled at Pine Bluff, and these included merchants Abe (1894–1974) and Samuel Barre (1917–1950); James "Jake" Marcus (1881–1974); Abraham (1870–1933), Nathan (1899–1965), and Joe Udes (1902–1967); Jacob (1872–1949), Henry (1875–1939), and Charles Rutstein (1905–1984); Abe Baer; and Morris (1882–1938), Harry, and Jacob "Jake" Levine (1906–1973). Harry and Jake had a men's clothing store; Jake (who married Henrietta Rutstein) also joined Hubert Eisenkramer in 1947 to found the W. Morris Company. The Levines were the sons of Morris and Esther (Bram) Levine.[132]

The Distaff Side

The lives of the three women noted here reflect a devotion to home and community which matched that of their male counterparts. These women are Mrs. Charles (Antoinette "Toney" Stiel) Dante of Dumas, Esther Bindursky of Lepanto, and Selma Schloss of Pine Bluff—all children of East European immigrants.

Antoinette "Toney" Stiel (1882–1976), who married Charles Dante and settled with him at Dumas, is an example of the hardy, dedicated women who were wives and mothers and community leaders in some of Arkansas's small towns. She was born in Newark, New Jersey, to Nachman and Fanny (Fischer) Stiel and moved with her parents to Arkansas at age six. On her eighteenth birthday, 6 February 1900, she married twenty-two-year-old Charles Dante, who had a "one boy store" at Dumas, a village located in virgin swamp and wilderness seventy-six miles below Little Rock. The newlyweds rode the train to Dumas. When Toney arrived at what was to be her home for the next seventy-six years, she found but eight white families in town, three stores (two were Jewish owned, her husband's and Gus Waterman's), and a required walk of two blocks just to obtain water. Chickens and cows provided eggs and milk, and a wagon coming by once a week provided beef, but there was no ice to keep it fresh. Loaves of bread were not for sale at the time, and no ready-made clothes were available. The first modern convenience came in 1905 in the form of one long-distance telephone that served the whole community.

Running water from a deep well came in 1908, and electric service began in 1917. Toney Dante took it all in good grace, for she loved her husband and the community he had selected.

Toney became a town leader and helped found the first public library. For several years she and two other women grew a small field of cotton, which they picked themselves, and used the proceeds for the library. After she and Charles had three children, Jack, Helen, and Naomi, Toney became vitally associated with the schools of the area. She was a founding member of the School Improvement Association (forerunner of the Parent-Teacher Association) and served as its president. Her philosophy and that of her husband was, "If you don't have good schools and good churches in a town, you are going to have to have a big jail."[133] She was part and parcel of Dumas, being a charter member of the Highway Garden Club and Circle 2 of the Methodist Women; she cared for people regardless of race or creed. During World Wars I and II, she organized a sewing room and led in its efforts. She often worked side by side with her husband in their store, where she became a beloved figure. When Charles and Toney died, they were buried at Walnut Lake Cemetery at Dumas, near the community they loved and served so well. And their children and grandchildren, who remained practicing Jews, continued the legacy of service left to them by this dedicated couple (see section V).[134]

Esther Bindursky (1906–1971), who had no formal training in journalism, in 1937 became the one-woman editorial and advertising staff for the weekly *Lepanto News Record,* and she continued the job with superior results for almost thirty-four years. Her father, Meyer Bindursky, was from Bessarabia, and her mother, Minnie Iskiwitch, was from Poland. The family migrated to Drew, Mississippi, in 1895 and opened a mercantile store. Three sons (see above) and Esther were born to them there. In 1922 the family moved to the small town of Lepanto, Arkansas, where they established stores. In 1937 Guy Graves, who was publisher of the Marked Tree *Tribune* and the Trumann *Democrat,* asked Esther to head a newspaper, the *News Record,* which he was establishing at Lepanto. With only a little experience as an occasional writer and a love of words and literature she had inherited from her father, she tackled the job with zeal and went on to excel in the field of journalism. She won more than two hundred awards from the National Editorial Association, the Arkansas Press Association, and the Arkansas Press Women. She helped found the latter organization and served as its president. Some of her articles appeared in the *Saturday Evening Post, The New York Times Magazine,* and other magazines. She was a correspondent for the *Memphis Commercial Appeal* and the *Arkansas Gazette*. In 1960 she was selected as Woman of the Year in Lepanto, and the townsfolk collected $1,575 to send her with a group of American journalists to Europe and Russia. Until her death in 1971, she continued the necessary grueling pace required to keep the citizens of her town and county informed of local, regional, and world events.[135]

Selma Schloss (1895–1966), a Pine Bluff native, became one of the first women in Arkansas to own her own jewelry store. She was the daughter of Julius Schloss (1860–1922), a Pine Bluff merchant who had settled there in the 1890s. After graduating from high school at age fifteen, Selma began working in the R. H. Stern Jewelry Store. When Mr. Stern died in 1923, she bought the store's merchandise and opened the "Selma Schloss Jewelry Store." At the time, she was the only woman jeweler in the state with her own business. Her store became quite successful, and her motto was, "Selma Schloss, all gold and no dross." She was a member of the board of the Arkansas Retail Jewelers Association. She moved the store to a new Pine Bluff location in 1951 and continued working in the store until her death.[136]

CHAPTER 12

East European Migration in Western Arkansas

Southwest Arkansas

Relatively few East Europeans migrated to western Arkansas, and these people located mostly at Hot Springs, Texarkana, and Fort Smith. Some were scattered in other small towns as well. Examples of those who settled in this section of the state are noted here, beginning at Camden.

CAMDEN

Frank and Yetta (Lipschitz) Phillips fled from Czarist Russia in 1903 and established a small dry goods store at Camden, Ouachita County. Frank had begun his career in southwest Arkansas driving a Watkins wagon, selling spices and specialty items throughout Ouachita County. The Phillipses had come with their son, Sam, their daughter, Bessie, and their niece, Dora Shapiro, and they had five more children born at Camden. The Phillipses had little formal schooling of their own, but they scrimped and were able to educate their children, some of whom became successful professionals. Sam, for example, became a prominent Little Rock pediatrician, and their daughter Daisy (Mrs. Abe Arnoff) became president of the Southern Region of Hadassah and authored a children's book. Frank and Yetta's grandchildren became professionals in the fields of medicine, education, and business. The Phillipses lost their store in Camden during the Depression and moved to Memphis.[1]

Mose and Ida Zavelo opened a ladies' clothing store at Camden in the 1920s that was later continued by their son Burton. The Zavelos had come to Arkansas after Mose's brother, Sam Zavelo, who was stationed at Camp Robinson in North Little Rock during World War II, married Wilma Froug and settled at El Dorado. Froug family members had a department store in Camden and stores in several other Arkansas towns.[2]

EL DORADO

The oil boom in El Dorado sounded promising to many East Europeans who were looking for job opportunities around that time. One of these was J. Benjamin "Ben" Miller (1895–1970), who immigrated to New York with his parents around 1905, served in the U.S. Army in World War I, then settled in the mid-1920s at El Dorado, where he became an insurance agent. He married Goldie Packman and had a daughter, Marjorie. He was vitally active in the American Legion Post at El Dorado. Well taught in Hebrew and Orthodox Judaism, Ben became lay leader of the El Dorado Jewish community (see chapter 6).[3]

Morris Lewis (1901–1980), son of immigrants Abraham and Rachel (Packman) Lewis, was invited to the town by Hyman Packman, an earlier settler. In 1932 Morris opened the New York Store, a ladies' ready-to-wear, and continued in business for the next forty-two years.[4]

The Warshavskys of Forrest City (see chapter 11) had moved to El Dorado after the oil boom began, and they were joined by their daughters, Mrs. Moe (Sarah "Selma") Steinberg and Mrs. Martin (Jeannette "Jean") Bernstein. The two sons-in-law opened businesses at Norphlet in 1924, but mosquitos and the threat of typhoid fever drove them back to El Dorado to live. Martin Bernstein, an accomplished violinist, played for many groups in El Dorado. A World War I veteran, he became American Legion Commander and president of the Lions Club. In 1932 he sold his store, and he and his wife, Jean, opened the El Dorado Conservatory of Fine Arts. He headed the violin department, and she headed the speech department and Junior Little Theatre. They hired instructors in dance, band, and art. The Bernstein's came to love and appreciate the pre–oil-boom settlers of the area and considered them gracious people, interested in the arts. Martin also resumed his law studies and began practicing law. Family responsibilities at Cheyenne, Wyoming, in 1936 prompted them to leave Arkansas, and they did not return.[5]

Irving Leon "Izzy" Pesses (1900–1976), a New Orleans native and a civil engineering graduate of Tulane University, settled at El Dorado in

1932. He helped establish and served as president of the Pesses and Marks Pipe and Supply Company and was vice-president of the El Dorado Paper Bag Company. He was quite active in civic affairs and later served as El Dorado's mayor for nine years (see section V).[6]

Ben Berk (1870–1959) and his son Isadore "Issy" Berk (1895–1969) both established jewelry stores in El Dorado in the 1920s. Issy also was a practicing optometrist, and when a state law was passed prohibiting a combined jewelry and optometry business, he sold the jewelry store. He had enlisted in World War I at age seventeen and served overseas during most of the conflict. Isadore married Rose Burd of Forrest City, whose family had come from Lithuania. Ben Berk, who was deaf, did a large trade in repairing watches for railroad men. Ben's other son, Joe Berk, established a dry goods store at nearby Magnolia; it continued until 1944.[7]

Others who had businesses at El Dorado included Joseph Goodkin (1881–1952), a merchant and oil man, and Mike and Sara (1876–1938) Goodman. Their daughter Rose was married to Carl Kramer, a Rock Island Railway employee.[8]

PRESCOTT

Edward I. Rephan settled in Arkansas after World War I and in 1922 opened a department and clothing store at Prescott. Over the years a chain of such stores developed, and by the mid-1970s there were sixteen Rephan Department Stores in Arkansas and one in Oklahoma. They continued to be family owned and run until the last one closed in 1992 (see section V).[9]

TEXARKANA

One of the first East European Jewish families to settle at the border town of Texarkana was the Kosminskys. They left Russia in the 1870s, prior to the severe persecutions that broke out in the next decade. Joseph and Marks Kosminsky opened a store in Texarkana in 1876 and dealt in cotton; many of their customers were blacks. Leonce J. Kosminsky (1877–?), a graduate of the University of Paris, the Northwestern University School of Pharmacy in Chicago, and the University of Maryland Medical School, had been the first Jewish child born in Texarkana.[10] He was a practicing pharmacist who later served several years as a staff surgeon for the Missouri Pacific Hospital at Texarkana. He also was a teacher and writer. He was a captain in the Army Medical Corps in World War I and was later active in the American Legion, serving as national commander of the Forty and Eight. His wife, Nettie (Friede), was a published writer as well.[11]

The Scherer family emigrated from Poland to Texarkana in the mid-1880s. Julius Scherer (1870–1953) went first to Louisiana in 1883 to join an uncle, then moved to Texarkana and opened a store in 1886. He married Ada Marx of that city. A relative, Max Scherer (1879–1938), came to Texarkana through Galveston in 1898 to join his brother Isadore. They were partners in a store until 1904, when Max established what became one of the leading ladies' clothing stores in town; it continued for some forty years. Isadore moved to St. Louis, but two of his other brothers, Alex (1889–1957) and Jack (1873–1945), became Texarkana merchants.[12]

Jake Eldridge (1866–1929) and his wife Bessie settled at Texarkana around the turn of the century and established a mercantile store. In 1904 they were joined by Zalmin (Salomon) Wexler, who had left Russia to escape conscription into the Russian army and had migrated through Galveston to Texarkana. Salomon's wife, Naomi (Kardamon) Wexler, and their five children, Max (1897–   ), Lena, Fannie, Bessie, and Miriam, joined him in 1909. Another daughter, Yetta, was born to them in Arkansas. Salomon opened a dry goods store, and his children were enrolled in the local schools. Son Max began the first grade at age twelve, and he was teased and taunted by the other students. He attended school three years and business school for seven months and then went out on his own.

Max Wexler tried several jobs—working as a collection agent, smoking meat for Swift, Inc., and treating hides—before settling in with Four State Grocery Company, where he stayed for almost thirty years. In 1944 he opened a dry goods store with a partner, Vasco McCoy, and the firm Wexler-McCoy was born. They made the company profitable for their employees with bonus arrangements and profit sharing.[13] Yetta Wexler, a talented musician, trained in Chicago. Her parents, Salomon and Naomi, moved there to be near her. She served in the Women's Army Corps during World War II and married David Schmidt of New York.[14]

Russian native David Kusin (1895–1938) came to America in 1917 and served with the U.S. Army in France. After the conflict he worked briefly for his brother at Monroe, Louisiana, then opened a secondhand furniture and harness store in Texarkana. It grew to become one of the city's first-class furniture stores and one of its important commercial firms.[15] A second store was opened at Hope as well. David married Anne Brody of Denver, and they had three children, Melvin, Sherman, and Gloria. After David died, his family continued the firms. Anne's brother Ralph (1904–1986), who lived at Boulder, Colorado, with his wife, Billie, and daughter Eileen, moved to Texarkana and joined the Kusin firm after banks nationwide began closing in 1933.[16]

Other immigrants and their families who settled at Texarkana included Leo Krouse (1873–1926), who owned the Texarkana Casket Company, which manufactured caskets and made bedroom and dining room furniture; Isaac "Ike" Schwartz (1861–1928), who owned a large department store; Harry Grossman (1880–1943), who owned Texarkana Iron and Metal Company; Louis Heilbron (1869–1949), a real estate agent who served as president of the Arkansas Real Estate Association; Benjamin Fane (1857–1935), who had a tailoring shop; and Solomon Erlich (1846–1891), an attorney.[17]

FOREMAN

Sam Seligson (1892–1951) and Isadore Marcus (1896–1979) settled at Foreman in Little River County in 1919 and opened the People's Store. When Isadore later moved, Sam's brother Julius joined him as a partner. Sam was well received in the area, and he served in the state House of Representatives from 1939 to 1941 and from 1943 to 1945. Another Jewish merchant of Foreman was Joseph Shafter, who had the J. B. Department Store.[18]

DE QUEEN

Hungarian native Joseph Greenwald (1850–?), who migrated to Hope, Hempstead County, in the 1890s, settled at De Queen in Sevier County in 1898. He established a dry goods store and acquired large real estate holdings in that area.[19]

HOT SPRINGS

East European Jews began filtering into Hot Springs, Garland County, in the 1890s. Those who came before the turn of the century included Simon Meyer, Peter Gartenberg, Peter Brockman, Morris Moscowitz, Morris Zucker, Clemons Welcher, and the Gilbert-Kallsnick family. In 1890 Simon Meyer (1861–1935) came from Poland to Hot Springs, where he established a men's clothing store that continued until his death.[20] Peter Gartenberg (1866–1941) migrated to America in 1889 to escape conscription into the Russian army. He went first to San Francisco, did not like it, and came through Hot Springs on his way back to New York. He liked the Arkansas town and opened a dry goods store there in 1893. It grew, and his son Leonard "Leo" (1899–1955) joined him. Leo served in World War I, then returned to Hot Springs. Leo's son Robert (1929–   ) joined the family business, which grew to become a large department store. During his public school years in Hot Springs, Robert and other Jewish children formed their own groups when they were excluded from the high school sororities and fraternities.[21] Peter Brockman (1859–1926) migrated to America in the 1880s and peddled in Oklahoma, where he briefly had a store, then settled in Hot Springs in 1894 and opened a small store that continued until his death. He married Clara Moscowitz, and they had a son, Sidney, and a daughter, Bess. Sidney (1907–1981) had a shoe store in Hot Springs, and Bess (1904–1983) married Ewell Weinberg (1898–1966) of Osceola, who had stores at Eudora and Hot Springs.[22]

Hot Springs was the birthplace of the second Jewish Federal judge to serve in the United States. (Jacob Trieber of Helena was the first such judge [see chapter 8].) Grover M. Moscowitz (1885–1947), born in Hot Springs to Morris and Bertha (Less) Moskowitz, was a graduate of New York University Law School in 1906. In the period 1909–10 he served as a special attorney general to prosecute election-fraud cases in Brooklyn. He served in that position again in 1922 and in 1925. In the latter year, he was appointed to the U.S. District Court in Brooklyn, New York, by President Calvin Coolidge. Grover Moscowitz, forty years old at the time of his appointment, was the youngest person to serve on the Federal bench at that time; he served until his death. He was active in Jewish philanthropic work and was a Zionist. He was a member and past president of Beth Elohim Congregation of Brooklyn, which he helped to organize.[23]

Grover Moscowitz's father, Morris (1867–1928), and his father's partner, Morris Zucker (1868–1938), had migrated to Hot Springs in 1895 and opened a haberdashery and men's clothing store. (Morris Zucker also was associated with Dave Lockwood in a ladies' dress shop, the Palais Royal.) Morris Moscowitz's other sons, Isadore "Izy" (1898–1942) and Leo (1900–1934), continued the family business. The Moscowitz businessmen were said to be among the best-known and most highly regarded merchants in Hot Springs.[24] Morris Moscowitz's daughter Rebecca (1896–1975) married Himes Schwartz, and another daughter, Hannah, married Arthur Welcher.

Clemons Welcher (1870–1942) of Poland settled at Hot Springs in 1890 and conducted a toggery shop for more than fifty years. Several of his brothers remained in Poland and one, Adolph, came to Hot Springs as a Displaced Person after World War II.[25]

Iman Gilbert (1878–1938) and his wife, Esther Kallsnick Gilbert (1878–1935), settled on a farm on the Arkadelphia Highway near Hot

Springs in the 1890s. In 1899 they were joined by Esther's brother Aaron (1877–1939) from Russo-Poland. Aaron bought a fifteen-acre plot next to the Gilberts and established one of Garland County's first dairies, which featured the latest equipment of that period. Aaron and his wife, Ethyl (1877–1956), had five sons, Dave, Joseph, Abe, Sam, and Maurice, and a daughter, Sarah. When Aaron died, his son Sam (1913–1948) continued the dairy; when Sam died, the equipment, cows, and land were sold.[26] Abe (1909–1950) was a partner in the Petty Brothers Lumber Company. He married Elizabeth King (see below). Maurice (1916–1965) opened "Maurice's" shoe store in Hot Springs in 1940, and David (1904–1931) operated a store at Camden.[27]

Isaac Moretsky (1880–1934) migrated to Hot Springs around 1900 and conducted a mercantile business on Ouachita Avenue. A quiet, unassuming person, he became known for his promotion of the city's welfare and for his charity to the poor.[28] Isaac's nephew, Ben J. King, fled to Hot Springs from Russia, where he had been imprisoned and was scheduled to go into the Russian army. Ben served in the U.S. Army in World War I, then returned to Hot Springs and entered a scrap iron business with Louis B. Siegel. In 1927 he opened King's Cut Rate Store at Camden, which prospered, and he opened several more branches in southwest Arkansas. He married Henrietta Weitzman of New York, and she was active in his business in Camden. She served as president of the Camden Business and Professional Women's Club. Ben King was active in civic work as well, serving on several boards and as president of the Camden's Lions Club.[29]

Ben's brother, Joseph "Joe" King (1878–1944), came to America shortly before World War I, hoping to earn enough to send for his family. Taking a job in Minneapolis, he boarded in the home of Bessie Cohen, who later nursed him through an almost fatal illness. When World War I broke out, Joe lost contact with his family—wife Anna and son Louis and daughter Elizabeth. It was through an ad in the *Jewish Daily Forward* seven years later that he was able to contact them in Russia and send passage money. It then took his wife and children another two years before they could surreptitiously leave the country. The family later settled at Hot Springs.[30] Joe King was so grateful for the care given him by Bessie Cohen that he sent for her two sons, Maurice and Max, and brought them to Arkansas to work in his branch stores. They each in turn opened their own stores, Maurice in Pine Bluff and Max in Forrest City. Joe King's son, Louis, became a Little Rock merchant, and his daughter, Elizabeth, married Aaron Kallsnick.[31]

Another King brother, Leon (1908–1942), came to America in 1923 and was graduated from the University of Arkansas Medical School in 1929. He practiced in Hot Springs, specializing in rheumatic diseases. He died tragically while on a fishing trip in 1942.[32]

Samuel Simon (1843–1935) settled at Hot Springs in 1900 and became a leading tailor in the community for thirty-five years. Louis Schlessinger (1872–1939) migrated to Hot Springs in 1906 and established a shoe store, which he continued until his death.[33] The Klymans—Mose (1878–1956), Abe (1879–1949), and Joseph (1886–1931)—had the Craighead Laundry in Hot Springs. Krakow natives Morris (1858–1920) and Samuel (1886–1974) Schudmak Sr. had a jewelry store in Hot Springs for sixty years, beginning in 1912. Hungarian-born Jacob Falk (1884–1941) married Ella Rutman, and the couple came to Hot Springs in 1937 and established a scrap business, then opened a wholesale plumbing house. Only one of their three children, Helen, remained in Arkansas (daughter Sandra married Sam Schudmak Jr., and daughter Margaret married Irving Gladstein; both of these families moved out of state). Helen married attorney Walter Kleinman, who associated with the Falk plumbing firm. The Kleinman's son, Louis, later joined the company (their daughter Janet married architect Dennis Daniel and moved out of state).[34] Some of the others who had stores at Hot Springs were Louis Festinger, James Glass, Joseph Gurdin, I. Greenberg, L. Cohen, J. Karatofsky, C. Kerstein, Abe Krokow, P. Walkowitz, M. E. Weinberger, and Harry Lax, and the families of Shiff, Alexander, and Wexler. Most of these people operated small shops—dry goods stores, mercantile firms, tailor shops, or secondhand stores. The Leibers had a candy manufacturing plant (see section V).[35]

Hot Springs saw several hotels and kosher (and kosher-style) restaurants opened by East Europeans over the years. It was a bustling spa city, and beginning in the 1890s, numbers of Orthodox were drawn to the baths. In the 1920s Isadore Schulman and Miss Clara Zach established and operated the Balfour Hotel. The food served in the hotel's dining room was strictly kosher, and there was a chapel for weekly services so that patrons would not have to ride on the Sabbath. Clara Zach died in the mid-1940s, but Isadore continued the facilities until the early 1960s.[36] The Metropolitan Hotel was owned and operated by Eli and Eve Miller in the 1920s, and they operated a kosher dining room in the Eastman Hotel. They later conducted a restaurant and catering business at 610 Central Avenue until after World War II. Their customers included Broadway celebrities. Louis Darch (1878–1949), his son Sol (1904–1981), and their wives ran a kosher hotel and dining room.[37] Several restaurants featured kosher-style cuisine, and two of the most popular and well known of these were the "Mayflower" and "Molly's." (The latter continues into the 1990s [see section V].)

BENTON

Before World War I, Louis and Freida Wolchansky established a dry goods store at Benton in Saline County; they later moved to Shreveport. Another Jewish-owned store was conducted by the Reed family, and in the early 1940s, Jacob Martin Koppel established a mercantile store at Benton. Jacob had first come to Arkansas in the 1920s to help his brother-in-law, Abe Abroms of Dermott. Jacob opened a store at Warren (Abroms was a partner) in 1935 that lasted about six years. Jacob married Frances Zimmerman in 1936, and they opened the Benton store six years later. It was called "Jay's Department Store" and continued for many years.[38]

Northwest Arkansas

COAL HILL

Coal Hill, Johnson County, in western Arkansas, was a thriving coal-mining town around the turn of the century. Several Jews were involved with mining operations there (see chapter 7). An East European Jewish immigrant, R. J. Werschky, settled at Coal Hill in the 1890s and established a general store. He was a generous man, and during a coal strike in 1898 gave credit to the miners and carried them through the difficult time.[39] Werschky continued his store there for a number of years.

FORT SMITH

Some of the East European Jewish immigrants who came to Fort Smith before the turn of the century quickly made their mark and rose to significant heights. Hungarian-born Lewis Friedman (1873–1944) came to Fort Smith in 1893 and worked as a bookkeeper for the Mayer-Wolf Company. He married Leah Spiro of Oklahoma and opened his own business in Indian Territory where the town of Spiro later developed. He accumulated large property holdings and went into real estate. He and his brother-in-law, Arthur Mincer, built a block of buildings on Garrison Avenue, including the Mincer-Friedman building. Appointed postmaster at Fort Smith by Congressman Ben Cravens, Lewis served from 1933 to

1944. He and his wife had a son, Myles, who became a well-known Fort Smith attorney.[40] The Lewis Friedman family included members of the Isaacson and Mendel families of Fort Smith.

Iser Hiram Nakdimen (1869–1943), a native of Grodno, Russia, could be classified as a Jewish peddler who became a merchant prince. Immigrating to America at age fourteen with fourteen cents in his pocket, he attempted all sorts of jobs before finding a place to settle. He cut ice on the Hudson River as a day laborer, worked in a brick yard, peddled tinware, clerked in a Chicago store, then wended his way south to Fort Smith in 1894. There he opened an overall factory. As it prospered, he shared his profits with employees; in 1901, he doubled their wages.[41] He attempted his hand at banking, and by 1914 had founded sixteen banks in Oklahoma and three in Arkansas (at Fort Smith, Greenwood, and Hartford). When some banks began closing during the panic of 1907, Iser lent hard-pressed farmers cash on their cotton, which he stored until prices went up, much to the delight and advantage of his customers. By 1911 he was so successful that he was able to come to the rescue of the State of Oklahoma by purchasing $1.75 million in building bonds that had been issued for the completion of public buildings in Oklahoma, including the Eastern Oklahoma Hospital at Vinita. Oklahoma officials had tried unsuccessfully for eighteen months to find a buyer for the bonds.[42] He was a religious man and a Zionist, and he bought trees on occasion to be planted in Israel. His philosophy was:

> In order to be a good man or woman, always remember there is a God above us and a Sabbath to be observed. If you want to be satisfied, always look upon the man who is below you instead of above you and who has less than you have, and when you do, you will always be satisfied.[43]

During World Wars I and II, it was the policy of Iser Nakdimen to lend money to servicemen on their word only. (The City National Bank of Fort Smith, which Nakdimen founded and owned, later said that not a cent was lost on such loans.)[44] He treated all peoples fairly and showed respect and concern for the Indians, often encouraging them to save their money and let it draw interest. He turned away no needy person and often helped students with funds for higher education. He had a great dignity about him; senators and congressmen were often his dinner guests.[45] Nakdimen was sternly opposed to monopoly and used the *Fort Smith Tribune*, which he owned, as a forum for his stinging editorials on the subject. He was a "master of satire and invective," and U.S. senators and congressmen would use his editorials in their fight against monopoly.[46]

Iser Nakdimen married Celia Spiro in 1899, and they had a son, Hiram, and a daughter, Pauline. Pauline (1899–1953) married Ernest Mendel of Fort Smith, and they had a daughter, Joanne, who married Ben Pollock, who, with his brother Alfred, operated a dry cleaning business. Hiram (1901–1955) married a non-Jew, and they had one son.[47] Hiram, a graduate of the University of Arkansas, was associated with the KWHN Broadcasting Company. He was president of the City National Bank and had extensive real estate holdings.[48] Iser Nakdimen's brother Velvel (1855–1942) was killed by the Nazis in Poland; other family members settled in Brooklyn, New York.[49]

Shortly after the turn of the century, Polish native Louis Feenberg came to America, peddled out West, then settled at Fort Smith and opened a junk business with David Sugarman (1870–1932). Louis married Esther Siegel, and their two sons, Eugene "Gene" (1906–1977) and Ben (1911–), were born in Fort Smith, where Gene finished high school. Louis did not encourage Gene to go to college, suggesting he go into business instead. Louis branched out into steel fabrication, then in 1925 sold out to Sugarman and moved with his family to Dallas. Gene worked and saved his money for college; he was a 1929 graduate of the University of Texas and received a fellowship at Harvard University. While at the latter, he twice received the Parker Traveling Fellowship to Europe. While in Europe in 1933, he was incensed at the treatment of the Jews by the Nazis and the Jews' acceptance of their lot. He proposed that the German export trade be destroyed by a quiet and efficient boycott.[50] (See chapter 18 for more information on Gene Feenberg.)

Russian-born Sander Katzer (1895–1956), a self-taught engineer, had a junk business in Fort Smith for about ten years before he established the Fort Smith Structural Steel Company in 1924. Katzer married Rose Sugarman.[51]

After the turn of the century, Simon Yaffe (1884–1938) emigrated from Lithuania to Little Rock, where he joined a banana co-op. He frugally saved enough to purchase a blind horse, which he hitched to a wagon load of produce and led horse and wagon along the Arkansas River to as far away as Fort Smith. Yaffe collected junk on his way back to Little Rock and found he made more money on the return trips. He and Sam Sugarman (1906–1982), son of David Sugarman of Fort Smith, who also tried his hand as a Little Rock banana peddler, became partners and opened a junk business, the Yaffe Iron and Metal Corporation, in Fort Smith.[52] Sam's brother Barney (1908–1946) joined the business and also was owner and operator of the Capitol Trailer Company.[53]

Charles Miller (1868–1922) migrated to Fort Smith in 1905 and established the Eagle Clothing Store. He had come with his wife, Mamie, and their two sons, Hugo (1896–1929) and Charles Miller Jr. (1888–1970). Hugo conducted the store after his father's death; at Hugo's death, Charles and his family continued it.[54] Charles Jr. was a charter member of the Fort Smith Lions Club, and he and Dr. Fred Krock established the Albert Pike Numismatic Club of Fort Smith.[55]

Lithuanian native Morton B. Marks (1869–1959) was a pioneer merchant in Oklahoma Territory at Drumright in the 1890s. He came to Fort Smith around 1905 and opened The Leader Department Store on Garrison Avenue that continued for more than fifty years. He married Ruth Frauenthal, daughter of Abraham and Jeannette Frauenthal (distant relatives of the Frauenthal family of Conway and Heber Springs), and they had four daughters, Iras, Jeannette, and twins, Merle and Perle, and two sons, Armand and Morton B. "Mort" Marks Jr. (1914–   ). Morton Marks Sr. opened another store, the Supply Syndicate, which Armand (1905–1971) helped manage. After World War II, Armand and Mort Marks Jr. combined the stores as the Leader Army Store. The Marks clan included members of other Fort Smith Jewish families, such as Eisen, Mendel, Sugarman, Marks (another family), and Pansy. Mort Marks Jr., who married Isabel Lappin of Fort Smith, became one of the main leaders of the United Hebrew Congregation and remained its primary historian. Although Jews were not allowed in the local Hardscrabble County Club until around 1960, there was little anti-Semitism in the Fort Smith area. However, almost all Jewish children heard the slur, "Jew baby," from time to time while attending public schools.[56]

Joseph Lappin (1883–1950), a tailor, was brought from St. Louis by Rudolph Ney to work in the Boston Store. He made Fort Smith his home, and there he and his wife, Rea (Levy), raised their two sons, Israel and Bernard, and a niece, Isabel. Bernard Lappin later became a buyer with the Boston Store at Fort Smith and at Fayetteville.[57]

Isaac "Ike" Pahotski (1863–1926) came to Fort Smith around 1905 and established a store. The Pahotskis became part of a small but growing group of Orthodox families. They valued education, and their daughter Minnie (1882–1968) was educated at the University of Chicago, where she received a master's degree in education. She taught in the Fort Smith public schools for more than fifty years, during which time she served as supervisor of the primary grades and as principal of Belle Grove School.[58] The Pahotskis' daughter Florence married Dr. Davis W. Goldstein of Fort Smith. Some of the others who joined this East European conclave were

Leon Eisen, David and Emanuel Schlesinger, Isadore Moses, Simon Goldman, and Lucian and Lehman Kahn.[59]

In 1910 the Hebrew Immigrant Aid Society sent Isadore Kasten of Russia and his wife, Mary, to Van Buren (just across the Arkansas River from Fort Smith), where they opened a small dry goods store. They built a modest house, for which they initially could not afford indoor plumbing. They kept a strictly traditional home; Mary would go to Oklahoma for kosher products. They planted fruit trees, grapevines, vegetables, flowers (including a rose garden), and raised chickens. Isadore sent for his brothers, Sussman and Louis, and as they married and had children, family get-togethers became delightful and memorable. The Kastens joined other newcomers who worked with the immigrant societies to help absorb new arrivals, wanting to share with their coreligionists the joy of living in a free country. Sussman wrote plays and presented them to help raise funds for Jewish immigrants, even though he was ill from tuberculosis that he had contracted while working in a New York shirt factory. As more newcomers trickled in, the Kastens joined with other Orthodox families of the Fort Smith area and in 1913 formed an Orthodox congregation, B'nai Israel (see chapter 6). Isadore and Mary, with their two daughters, lived in Van Buren from 1910 to 1924, then moved away. Mary remembered most fondly her life in Van Buren to the end of her ninety-eight years; there she had "felt fulfilled," being so close to the land—planting it and reaping from it.[60]

The Kasten family history in Russia was fraught with poignancy. They lived in one-room quarters at Bobrusk in the state of Minsk; their name in Russia was Kustonovitch. The family consisted of the parents and five sons. The older boys, Isadore, Zussman, and Abe, came to America in the years 1908–09. Back in Minsk the younger sons, Louis and Pinia, slept on two boards placed on two straight chairs; the father, a cap maker, slept on the floor, and the mother on the one small bed. The children attended a Jewish parochial school, where they received lunch. Louis and Pinia later emigrated to America; the latter was killed in service in World War I. The other four boys saved funds to send for their parents, who were under severe persecution (for example, the father's beard was set on fire one day as he was selling caps). To the sons' sorrow, both parents died of starvation before they could leave Russia.[61]

All of the Kastens settled elsewhere except Louis and his wife, Sarah (see Distaff Side below), who remained in Fort Smith and reared their children, Reba, Anne, and Maurice. Louis (1897–1976) opened the New York Bargain Store, and when it failed in the 1930s, he joined the

Metropolitan Life Insurance Company. All three of his children were graduates of eastern universities. They remembered very little anti-Semitism while growing up in Fort Smith. (Maurice recalled an incident that revealed the mystique surrounding Jewish religious customs in Gentile eyes. While he was in grade school, a fellow student told him that she had passed the Jewish temple and had seen everyone wearing black, down on their knees. He knew she had made it up; even the Orthodox would not do that!)[62] The Kasten children were struck deeply by the class contempt shown them and other East European Jews by the well-established German-Jewish community of Fort Smith. Maurice grew up with a "powerful prejudice" against the German Jews.[63]

Joseph Glick came to Fort Smith shortly after World War I and established a large dry cleaning business. He liked the area so well that he expanded in 1922 and built a quarter-of-a-million-dollar plant. Several Jewish residents of Fort Smith worked with him.[64]

Born in Odessa, Russia, David Soifer (1891–1970) emigrated to Chicago, then answered an advertisement in a trade magazine placed by Glick's Cleaners of Fort Smith. He had been trained in a hat factory in Russia, and after working at Glick's for a short while, he opened the Soifer Hat Works. David was schooled in Hebrew and in Torah and often led the Orthodox congregation that formed in Fort Smith in 1913 (see chapter 6). Although he was crushed when on occasion he was called a "damned Jew," what affected him most deeply was the high-handed way the German Jews treated the East European Jews. David was married twice, the second time to non-Jew Verna Soifer, a writer for a local newspaper.[65]

Irving J. Friedman (1889–1964), a native of Kovno, Lithuania, was one of the early Jewish attorneys in Fort Smith. He was brought there by a chance meeting with Alvin Tilles while the two men were serving in the U.S. Army during World War I. Alvin invited Irving for a visit, during which the latter met Elizabeth Stein (daughter of Benno Stein; she was engaged to Leonard Ney at the time). Irving and Elizabeth fell in love, married, and Irving made Fort Smith his home. He was an astute man of integrity, and the local population was counting on him to be "a latter-day Ben Drew Kimpel" (see chapter 9). Irving was active in civic work, helping to organize the Fort Smith Kiwanis Club and serving as department commander of the Arkansas Veterans of Foreign Wars (he had received a battlefield promotion to captain in World War I). He became best known for his work in helping needy veterans and their families. He was also deeply religious and schooled in Hebrew and Torah. He conducted services when no rabbi was available and taught confirmation classes. He was an early active Zionist and was involved in the Arkansas Jewish Assembly during the 1930s and 1940s. He and his wife had five children, none of whom remained in Fort Smith. One of their sons, J. Fred Friedman, became a well-known criminal attorney in Memphis.[66]

The Abe Bogoslavsky family migrated to Fort Smith in the 1930s and opened a scrap business. They had come from Russia to America around 1900 and had first settled in Chicago. Abe married Rose Gampol, and they had two sons, Leonard and Gerald, both of whom served in World War II.[67]

FAYETTEVILLE

Very few Jews, whether German or East European, settled at Fayetteville. The Baums, who came in the 1860s (see chapter 9) welcomed the few who did come. On occasion a few were found as professors at the University of Arkansas. One of the most illustrious of these was Dr. Barnett Sure (1891–1960), an international authority in nutrition who discovered vitamin E while doing extensive work on amino acids. Dr. Sure was a native of Vilkomir, Lithuania, and had come with his family to America in 1908. His early education was at Cape Town, Union of South Africa, and he received his Ph.D. from the University of Wisconsin. He taught at Johns Hopkins University before joining the Chemistry Department at the University of Arkansas in 1920; in 1927 he became a full professor and department chairman. As a result of his experimental work, vitamin B was routinely fed to infants by specialists in children's diseases. During World War II, Dr. Sure sought alternative sources of protein that would be cheaper and more available than meat. Through his research, he developed a low-cost milk product composed of milk solids that were supplemented with fat, food yeast, vitamins, and minerals. In powder form it could be prepared in a variety of ways. It was called "Sure Food," and his discovery led to the use of food additives to supplement the diet of the undernourished. He was an avid music enthusiast and played in the symphony orchestras in Capetown, South Africa, in Wisconsin, and at Fayetteville. His extensive collection of classical music records was donated to the U of A Music Department when he died.[68]

SILOAM SPRINGS

In 1905 East Europeans A. H. Marshall and his brother-in-law, Isaac Sussman, settled at Siloam Springs, Benton County, in Arkansas's northwest corner. A. H. had a dry goods store, and contiguous to it was a grocery store run by Isaac. They closed their stores on High Holy Days and also kept kosher homes, having meat sent from Joplin, Missouri. Isaac and his wife, Lena (Marshall), had two children, son Phillip and daughter Tamar. The families were well received by the local populace, and Mrs. Sussman shared special Jewish foods with her neighbors. After Isaac died around 1920, the Sussman and Marshall families moved away.[69]

A few other towns in the state's northwest section saw East European Jewish settlers, and these included Eureka Springs, Dardanelle, Plumerville, and Conway.

EUREKA SPRINGS

Eureka Springs in Carroll County lies northeast of Fayetteville in the beautiful Ozark Mountains. Healthful springs were discovered there in 1858, but a town was not incorporated at the site until 1880.[70] B. J. Rosewater (1857–1943), who had emigrated from Eastern Europe at age twelve to visit relatives in Chicago, wandered down to Cairo, Illinois, and in 1882 visited Eureka Springs for his health. When he arrived there, the living conditions were "most primitive": the wealthy families preferred tents to living in local shacks, the accommodations were few, and "the inconveniences many."[71] In spite of these negatives and the fact that there was discord over land ownership, Rosewater decided to settle there. He aligned himself with Gen. Powell Clayton in a movement to improve the town. Rosewater's first effort was to raise funds to fence and beautify the Basin Spring reservation. He also served as director of the Interstate Summer Normal and Educational Assembly, and during his three year tenure, the three thousand seat auditorium at times was filled to capacity for both afternoon and evening performances. (The Frisco Railway had regular excursions scheduled into the town at the time.)[72]

B. J. Rosewater was among the leaders who sought a grant from the Andrew Carnegie Fund to build a public library at Eureka Springs.[73] The effort was successful, and Rosewater, who was elected president for life of the library board, oversaw its construction. He helped organize the Commercial Club, predecessor of the Chamber of Commerce, and served as its president and secretary. He ran for the office of postmaster in 1898, and during the campaign, his opponent listed several reasons why Rosewater should not be elected; "first, he is a Jew, and has all the charac-teristics of the tricky Jew . . ."[74] Despite the diatribes, Rosewater's character spoke for itself; he was elected and served twelve years. During his tenure, he established both city and rural delivery; he also joined a Dr. Ellis in constructing a building, part of which was used for the post office and was equipped "with the finest of fixtures."[75] Rosewater, who headed a local firm that manufactured a health food product, married non-Jew Gertrude M. Britts, daughter of Civil War veteran Capt. S. H. Britts. Their son Jerome and daughter Jeanette (Bullock) remained in Eureka Springs and also were active in its civic affairs.

DARDANELLE, PLUMERVILLE

Morris Saiewitz, a veterinarian, settled at Dardanelle with his wife, Jennie (Bloom), and their family after World War I. Jennie's family was living at Lake Village at the time.[76] Saul and Ida Friedman moved to Plumerville, Conway County, before the turn of the century and established a store that continued a number of years. They had two children, Judith and Arnold, both of whom moved from Arkansas.[77]

CONWAY

Members of the East European Sarason-Prensky family that settled at Conway, Faulkner County, would later have a significant influence on General Motors in Detroit. The family's sojourn in Arkansas began with red-headed Sam Sarason's (1869–?) migration from Kovno, Lithuania, to St. Louis in 1885. There he boarded with his sister, who, with her family, had a dairy. Sam began peddling throughout Illinois, Arkansas, and Louisiana. He established a store briefly at Dermott, Desha County, and then formed a partnership with William Rosenzweig of Pine Bluff. On a trip to St. Louis in 1894, Sam met Freyda Leah "Lizzie" Prensky, a boarder in his sister's home, and he and Lizzie married the next year. After William Rosenzweig married Sam's sister Pauline, Sam opened his own store at Conway in 1897.

The Sarason family, which eventually had eight children (Pauline, Arthur, Sara, Harry, Isaac, Roy, Burton, and Kenneth) joined the Orthodox synagogue in Little Rock, and they kept a traditional home. Other East European Jews that located at Conway at the time the Sarasons lived there included the Maddens, Blackmans, Rosens, and Weinmanns.[78]

At the turn of the century, Lizzie Sarason's brother, Meyer Prensky, came to work in the Sarason store. When his father, Samuel, died in 1903, Meyer, the Prensky family's oldest son, returned to St. Louis. After attending business school and working as a bookkeeper for the Laclede Gas Company, Meyer joined General Motors of Detroit in 1911. In 1919 he became treasurer of the company and held the post for some forty years.[79]

Lizzie Sarason became ill in 1912, and that, coupled with the fact that the older Sarason children were beginning to date non-Jews, prompted Sam to move his family to St. Louis; he kept the store in Conway and commuted. In 1914, Sam's oldest son, J. Arthur "Art," joined him in Conway and enrolled at Hendrix College, where he played on its football team. Art was a 1922 graduate of Washington University in St. Louis, after which he joined General Motors, where he was responsible for the company's consolidated financial statements for thirty years. In his position, he hired, among others, Thomas A. Murphy and Roger B. Smith, both of whom subsequently became GM chairmen.[80]

Although Sam sold his store at Conway around 1920 and joined his family in St. Louis, his four older children remembered fondly their childhood days in Conway, where they lived across the street from the Faulkner County Courthouse; they enthusiastically wrote of those days some sixty to seventy years later.[81] The Sarason's fourth child, Harry (1902–1991), wrote a poem in 1984, expressing his feelings about his childhood town. It reads in part:

> I left part of my heart in Conway,
> That's where I got my start, in Conway,
> Those Southern folks are gentle
> That's why I'm sentimental
> That's why I left my heart, the sentimental part,
> In Conway.
> The courthouse lawn held wonderlands,
> Acorns and flowers for my childish hands,
> The oak trees reached the sky,
> Now they're only sixty feet high . . .
> That's why I left my heart,
> The sentimental part,
> The boyhood wonder part,
> In Conway.[82]

The Distaff Side

The lives of two Fort Smith women, Sarah Kasten and Rose Weinberger, both of whom were born in 1899, are contrasted here. Both expended their lives for others, but in totally different ways.

Sarah (Churgin) Kasten was a native of Hlusk, Russia. Her father and an older sister emigrated to America around 1905, but Sarah, her mother, and a young brother remained in Russia, detained because of the young brother's chronic nephritis. The problem was solved in a tragic way when the young boy was killed after falling into a vat of chemicals while playing near a candle factory. After coming to America, Sarah visited her half sister Mary in Van Buren, where Sarah met Louis Kasten, brother of Mary's husband. Sarah and Louis were married in 1919.

The Kastens became part of an Orthodox group that formed in the Fort Smith area, and Sarah was active in events that centered around her home and children (Maurice, Reba, and Anne), family picnics and get-togethers, and religious festivals. A quiet, unassuming person, she was cheerful and friendly and expended her efforts away from the limelight of public scrutiny. She remained in Fort Smith all her life, quietly helping others and working conscientiously with religious affairs. She continued there into the 1990s.[83]

Rose (Sherman) Weinberger (1899–1986) was as caring a person as Sarah, yet she expended much of her energy toward the general public while raising four children. Like Sarah, her guiding principle was "Godliness is helping others." Born at Harrisburg, Pennsylvania, she came to Fort Smith with her husband Louis in 1931, where they had four children, daughters Dorothy and Susan and sons Robert and Richard.

Upon arrival in Fort Smith, Rose almost immediately began a life of service to the community. She became the first Jewish member of the YWCA Board of that city; her initial responsibility with the group was in helping young women find jobs. She provided clothes for some of them and contacted local businessmen for jobs, scholarships, and references. Her concern for minorities prompted her to help establish a YWCA branch for black women and a nursery for black children. When she found that blacks were not admitted to the two local hospitals, she worked with Dr. Charles Holt to found the Twin City Hospital for them. She helped establish a library for blacks at Lincoln High School since they were not allowed in the city's public library at the time. She encouraged the collection of food, toys, and clothing for blacks, particularly during the Christmas season.

Rose cared for the the disabled and helpless as well. She helped initiate the Roger Bost School for mentally retarded and developmentally disabled children and adults (the school grew to become the state's largest community-based system for this group of citizens). She worked with Governor Ben Laney toward the establishment of the Arkansas School of Nursing. She founded the Fort Smith Junior Civil League in 1942 while serving as president of the local United Service Organizations (USO). An ardent political worker, she assisted in forming county and state Democratic women's clubs. She was a member of United Hebrew

Congregation and was active in the Arkansas Jewish Assembly during the 1930s and 1940s. She received a number of awards for her civic and humanitarian efforts. Until shortly before her death in 1986, she was still active in Fort Smith's Project Compassion, which entailed visiting elderly residents of a local nursing home.[84]

Strengthening the Threads

1930s–1950s

THE ARKANSAS

JEWISH ASSEMBLY

YEARS

The Arkansas "Kehillah," 1930s

The 1931 to 1951 period was a time of great change, both for the United States and for the world at large. And the changes occurring then affected the Jews of Arkansas as it did other American Jews, particularly those in the southern states. But the history of Arkansas Jewry during that period is unique compared to that of most other states, for during those tempestuous times, the Jews of Arkansas created and diligently maintained an organization, the Arkansas Jewish Assembly, whose specific purpose was to promote the preservation of Jewish identity and brotherhood statewide. Except for a hiatus during World War II, which drew Assembly leaders into the military, the Arkansas organization flourished from 1931 to 1951.[1]

Such an organization as the Arkansas Jewish Assembly could not have been born at a more unfavorable time. At the close of the 1920s, the South was just recovering somewhat from the devastating flood of 1927 when the New York stock market broke in 1929, and this was followed in 1930 by one of the worst droughts in history. These events were particularly hard on an agricultural state such as Arkansas, and merchants (most of the Jewish businessmen were in this category) suffered financially along with the farmers. The beginning of the 1930s saw the Arkansas farmer unable to pay his debts and being delinquent on payments on almost a third of the state's rural land. More than half of the state's manufacturing concerns closed between 1929 and 1933, and almost 150 banks failed. Some 245,000

Arkansans were unemployed by 1933, a 10 percent increase from 1928. The needs of Arkansans were so great that local governments and private charities were soon depleted. The state's efforts to help farmers failed because loans to farmers could not be repaid. Federal aid helped ameliorate the situation, and by 1937 the state's relief programs had received 59 million dollars in Federal grants.[2]

The hardships Arkansans faced during the Great Depression were exacerbated in most of the state's rural areas by the fact that little progress had been made in the way of utilities. Only one-tenth of the farm homes had electricity and running water in 1930, and most of these did not have telephone service until after World War II.[3] During these unusually hard times, the Christian community, at least, could find solace for their troubles in many of the churches available to them, but the comparatively small Jewish population of the state that lived in scattered communities and towns did not have this privilege. In many instances, these isolated Jews were left spiritually stranded without the encouragement of a congregation.

There was at least one man in Arkansas who was acutely aware of the plight of these Jews who were isolated from their own community of faith. This man, Rabbi A. B. Rhine of Hot Springs, was executive secretary of the Leo N. Levi Hospital Board. He had worked hard to see the establishment of the hospital and then traveled intermittently throughout the state for some twenty years (1914–34) to seek funds for its continued support. In the course of his travels, he had become acquainted with almost every Jewish individual, family, community, and congregation statewide. His heart was touched, he later observed, when he encountered the gladness with which his fellow Jews welcomed him on his rare visits. Their enthusiasm led him to believe that they would gladly retain their identity and loyalty to Judaism under more favorable conditions. He was disturbed that many Jewish names were found on the membership lists of Christian churches—names that were a credit to any group but would, if nourished in Judaism, grace the lists of Jewish congregations. He was particularly concerned for the Jewish youth and looked for some way to stem the process of assimilation.[4]

In 1931 Rabbi Rhine called a meeting of the Jews of Arkansas to Hot Springs to discuss the problems he had encountered. Almost three hundred attended the meeting, and such a large number indicated to him that he had gauged interest in the matter correctly. Steeped in European Jewish history, he spoke to the group about the fact that, although traditionally each Jewish congregation is autonomous and free from outside interferences, there had always been a "kehillah," a voluntary federation of Jewish communities, that looked after the interests of Jewry of a particular country or section. He noted the number of national bodies in the United States that stimulated the life of American Jewry in its various manifestations. He considered the number of congregations in Arkansas as not too small, not too large, "to make a real union of communities practical."[5] A temporary association was formed that year, which called for a convention to be held in 1932.

On 24 April 1932 the Arkansas Jewish Assembly became an official organization, voted into being by the 135 delegates attending that year. Rabbi Rhine was appreciative of the cooperation of the state's five other Reform rabbis toward his idea and acknowledged them as cofounders of the Assembly.[6] These included Ira Sanders of Little Rock's Congregation B'nai Israel, Samuel Teitelbaum of Fort Smith's United Hebrew Congregation, Morris Clark of Pine Bluff's Temple Anshe Emeth, Carl Miller of Helena's Beth El Congregation, and David P. Alpert of Texarkana's Mount Sinai Temple.

At its first convention the Assembly created an eleven-member board and ruled that one of the vice-presidents must be a woman. The first officers, composed of some of the state's most outstanding Jewish citizens, were Rabbi Rhine, president; Louis Cohen of Fort Smith, first vice-president; Mrs. Jesse Heiman of Little Rock, second vice-president; and I. J. Friedman of Fort Smith, secretary-treasurer. Board of directors members were: William Rosenzweig and H. Y. Marx, Pine Bluff; Mrs. Seelig Mundt, Helena; Judge Louis Josephs, Texarkana; Harry B. Solmson Sr., Little Rock; Adolph Felsenthal, Camden; and Dave Burgauer, Hot Springs.[7] More than half of these committed workers, together with the state's rabbis, became the foundation on which the organization rested for many years.

The Assembly's Constitution was not presented until April 1933 at its second annual convention, and its preamble stated the organization's raison d'etre:

> The purpose of this Association is to assist in and promote the activities of all Jewish organizations in the State of Arkansas now affiliated or hereafter to become affiliated with this Association in accordance with the highest purpose and spirit of Judaism and on the broadcast principles of humanity, and to bring about a closer acquaintance, friendship, and brother-hood between the members of all Jewish organizations within the State of Arkansas.[8]

Also at their first convention, Assembly members enthusiastically began to define needed programs, most of which centered on two areas:

Jewish education for youth and adults, and reaching unorganized communities and isolated individuals.[9] In order to determine the exact needs of Arkansas Jewry, the Assembly divided the state into four zones at its 1933 convention. Committee members and their zones were: Harry B. Solmson Sr. of Little Rock—El Dorado, Camden, England, Morrilton, and Arkadelphia; Rabbi Clark of Pine Bluff—Dumas, McGehee, Lake Village, Eudora, Stuttgart, De Witt, Arkansas City, and Altheimer; Rabbi Miller—Forrest City, Blytheville, Jonesboro, Holly Grove, and Paragould; and Rabbi Alpert of Texarkana—Wynne, Ashdown, Foreman, Hope, Nashville, Lewisville, and Magnolia. The University of Arkansas campus at Fayetteville was assigned to Rabbi Teitelbaum. Also, it was determined that each leading community should organize a Federation of Jewish Charities, and these would coalesce under a state federation.[10] (From time to time it was reported that local federations had been established.)[11]

In 1934 the Assembly sent out a census letter together with an invitation to individuals and groups to join the organization, which would in turn assist in any needs of spiritual work, congregational activities, and religious schools.[12] No doubt there was some surprise at the results of the census, which tallied in at "3,000 Jewish souls" scattered in seventeen different areas, including twenty-five people in the miscellaneous category.[13] It was assumed that another one thousand had not been reached, which put the total at about four thousand. Before the census, it had been estimated that there were some eight thousand Arkansas Jewish citizens.[14] (Rabbi Sanders of Little Rock, who worked closely with the Assembly, said in 1983 as he recounted his knowledge of Arkansas Jewry that he felt there were never more than some four to six thousand Jews in Arkansas at any one time, even though the American Jewish Yearbook at times estimated many more.)[15]

The contribution files of the Jewish Children's Home in New Orleans from 1918 to 1977 give some insight into the demographics of Arkansas Jewry during the 1930s period. The files contain data from 366 Arkansas Jewish individuals or families located in fifty-six towns in thirty-one counties. Most of these were merchants who lived in the central and Delta sections of the state. Between 1918 and 1930 there were 188 who began their contributions to the home; between 1931 and 1939, only 60; and after 1940, 118. Families or individuals who stopped giving to the Home between 1918 and 1930 numbered 52; between 1931 and 1939, 117 stopped donating; and between 1940 and 1977, 237 dropped out (as the federations grew after World War II, most donors gave directly to them, which in turn distributed funds to charities, such as the Jewish Children's Home).

Some 60 contributors died during the 1930s. Only a handful of donors moved out of the state during that period (some had already left after the devastating flood of 1927); there was more movement within the state itself. Contributions dropped considerably during the Depression, but most were made on a periodic basis and consisted of a dollar or less per donation.[16]

The fact that Arkansas contained about half the number of Jews that the Assembly felt it would be ministering to did not cause it to swerve from its goals. To the contrary, it seemed to rally members all the more, believing that "our little handful of Jews within the borders of the great state of Arkansas" could accomplish "great good."[17] Ministering to such a small number over such a large territory (Arkansas encompasses more than 53,000 square miles) required strong dedication to meeting Assembly goals. Just getting to the convention each year and attending board meetings could prove hazardous to one's health. Road conditions in Arkansas before the late 1940s and the 1950s were often primitive, and many towns did not have paved streets. The state highway system consisted of seven thousand miles in 1923, and only a fourth of these were hard surfaced by 1936. Most Arkansas roads were crooked, narrow, and worn out.[18] Assembly minutes and correspondence are sprinkled with tales of car accidents of members traveling to and from Assembly events.[19]

Although a great deal of the Assembly's efforts were expended during the 1930s when the Depression was at its worst, it is interesting that such hard times are barely mentioned in Assembly records. Very little of what was going on outside the world of Judaism in Arkansas crept into Assembly files, but it was noted that bleak financial times almost caused the postponement of its 1933 convention scheduled at Little Rock. The funds for the convention that year had been impounded by Little Rock banks. The banks reopened five weeks before the April 21 meeting, which was held on schedule for the "wholesome effects" it would have on delegates.[20] Annual dues to the Assembly in the 1930s were quite modest—ten dollars per congregation, and five dollars for other groups, such as B'nai B'rith lodges and Sisterhoods. As modest as the dues were, however, getting payment for them entailed constant reminders during those tight financial years. Rabbi Miller of Helena may have summed up his congregation's nonpayment when he wrote Rabbi Teitelbaum in response to a dun. Miller noted that his congregation had to be "persuaded or blackjacked" into payment of dues because his secretary was an "alte koker" [sic] who opposed any expenditures not connected with local work. ("Alter kocker" is a vulgarism, meaning a "crotchety, fussy, ineffectual old man.")[21]

During the Great Depression the needs of Arkansans, both Jews and Gentiles, were so great that Assembly members as well as many other Jewish citizens worked diligently to help ameliorate the situation. The Little Rock School of Social Work established by Rabbi Sanders in the late 1920s provided help for the common good; it had trained many social workers needed for the social and charity programs that sprang up during the 1930s. Mrs. Ora P. Nix, who took nine sociology courses under Rabbi Sanders, served as director of the Pulaski County Office of Public Welfare. When the Federal government insisted in 1935 that the state establish an official Board of Welfare to assume the responsibility for public assistance, the state legislature was slow to do this. Within an hour or so of its adjournment that year, Mrs. Nix was alarmed to learn that it had done nothing to meet the responsibility. She immediately called Rabbi Sanders, who, with other members of the Pulaski County Board of Public Welfare, rushed to the state Capitol. The rabbi made an impassioned plea to the legislators, who resumed the session long enough to pass relief measures.[22] Mrs. Nix was named director of the subsequently established State Social Welfare Office.[23]

After Mrs. Nix assumed her new duties, she found that many needy individuals and families came to her attention whose cases did not fall into the categories allotted by government funding. In the early 1930s she had worked with the Red Cross and during that time, she later said, had come to know and appreciate the Jewish leadership in the community. The Gus Blass family gave "great help" to the family agency that was "trying to carry the load in those years." She often turned to Temple B'nai Israel's charity fund, which at the time was administered by Elsa Rosenthal. Mrs. Nix said she would not have stayed in public welfare had she not had that group to call on. Mrs. Noland (Isabel) Blass and Mrs. Maxwell (Salene) Lyons promoted and led in organizing the establishment of a Family Service Agency. Mrs. Nix said the two women also wore out much shoe leather, walking the streets of Little Rock to solicit charitable donations from businessmen.[24] Helen Lockwood (Mrs. Charles Eichenbaum), who had studied for grand opera and the concert stage in New York, gave a concert in Little Rock to raise funds for underprivileged children during the Depression.[25] Mrs. Nix also recalled the generosity of Morris Schlesinger of Little Rock, who gave clothes at Christmastime but who also could be called upon in emergency situations at any time of the year. Members of other Jewish families—the Stiffts, Cohns, Pfeifers, and many others—were active on welfare boards and in charity organizations. "The Jewish people in our state made great contributions to it," Mrs. Nix later recounted in admitted admiration.[26]

Several Sisterhood members of Little Rock's B'nai Israel Congregation planned and set up a community center on the city's east side. The women, Mrs. Salene Lyons, Mrs. Herbert (Gertrude) Latkin, and Mrs. Arthur (Miriam) Phillips, surveyed the city and selected the most needy area. Three groups of children were served: preschool, intermediate, and older ones. Scraps donated by the Ottenheimer Brothers Manufacturing Company provided material to be made into quilts by mothers who were involved in the center. The City of Little Rock paid the center's utility bills as well as the salary of its director. Dave and Sam Grundfest, Gus and Leonard Ottenheimer, and Maxwell Lyons purchased the property for the center. Prenatal classes were held, and several doctors donated their services. The Sisterhood women received a letter from Mrs. W. P. McDermott, juvenile court judge in the 1930s, saying their efforts with the children's center considerably reduced juvenile delinquency.[27]

Some of the male members of Congregation B'nai Israel offered considerable help to the unfortunate, especially in the early days of the Depression before government welfare programs were started. At that time, hundreds of people with no jobs or money came to Little Rock from around the state. Harry Lasker and Sam Louchheim of Little Rock helped turn the vacant Abeles plant at Third and Scott streets into a mission. The large facility, equipped with cots and a soup kitchen, provided food and shelter for 150 to 200 people daily.[28]

Other male members of the various Jewish congregations in Arkansas were generous in their contributions to charity during those dark financial days, but the men of Congregation B'nai Israel of Little Rock offered something more—a unique diversion from the hard times being experienced. In 1930 the Temple Men's Club was organized, and one of its main functions was an annual Institute on Judaism that was presented for religious educators, Christian clergymen, and the general public. The club, under its first president, S. Lasker Ehrman, started its lecture series with a bang: Rabbi Sanders debated the nationally known lawyer Clarence Darrow. The debate was held on 3 November 1930 in the Little Rock High School (later known as Central High School) auditorium. An estimated twenty-four hundred people crowded into the hall as the two men debated the subject "Is Man Immortal?" Although no winner was declared, the audience generally gave the debate to Rabbi Sanders, who had approached the subject from a broad, philosophical way; Darrow had contended from a personal and emotional angle.[29] Those who attended the lecture remembered it for years afterward.[30] The Temple Men's Club lecture series continued to bring distinguished speakers from various fields and was for many years Little Rock's only forum for presentations on the arts and sciences. Lecturers included Will Durant, Abram Leon Sachar, Dr. Jacob Marcus, H. V. Kaltenborn, Lewis Browne, John Mason Brown, John Haynes Holmes, S. Parkes Cadman, and many others.[31]

While many Assembly members at large were engaged in general welfare and social work, the purview of the organization itself centered on helping Jews only. The Assembly shared its meager dues with the Leo N. Levi Hospital, the Jewish Children's Home in New Orleans, the B'nai B'rith Home for the Aged in Memphis, and other Jewish charities.[32] It also found another expense—its own publication, the *Arkansas Assembly Bulletin*. Members were glad to underwrite the *Bulletin* because it fulfilled two purposes: to keep the constituents of the Assembly informed of its activities and to help promote one of the group's major concerns, Jewish education. The publication was filled with articles on local, state, and national Jewish history, and it was sent to Assembly members as well as to leaders in the Christian community statewide.[33]

The Assembly did not confine its efforts to helping Reform Jews only but also sought to reach and to help the Orthodox within the state. In March 1935 Rabbi Teitelbaum wrote to Rabbi Joseph Shapiro, spiritual leader of the state's only functioning Orthodox congregation, Agudath Achim of Little Rock, inviting him to affiliate with the Assembly.[34] Teitelbaum assured Shapiro that the Assembly was making a special effort to unite all of the state's Jews. Rabbi Shapiro replied that he would bring the matter up with his congregation and that he would attend the 1935 conference at Fort Smith.[35] Although Rabbi Shapiro attended some of the meetings and showed an interest in the organization, his congregation operated from its own matrix, and the Assembly had little effect on it. But Orthodox Jews scattered throughout the state were strengthened by the Assembly, and many ultimately joined the Reform congregations that sprang from its efforts.[36]

From its outset, the Assembly was concerned with its youth. The keynote speech at the organization's first convention, delivered by prominent Little Rock attorney Henry Spitzberg, was on "Jewish Adolescent Youth and the Synagogue."[37] At the second convention, delegates organized a Junior Congregation, which may have spawned another similar but larger Jewish youth organization, the Southern Jewish Youth Assembly that formed at a Little Rock convention held in April 1934. Membership of the latter group included Jewish youth from Arkansas, Texas, Tennessee, Missouri, and Louisiana.[38] The Assembly also had a Youth Welfare Committee that was given the task of investigating the needs and opportunities for work among Jewish youth in the unorganized communities. The Assembly's Youth Group promoted the establishment of other such groups when possible. By 1938 there were three Assembly-sponsored Junior Congregations in Arkansas, at Little Rock, at Fort Smith, and at Helena, and others were being planned.[39]

Over the years, the Assembly's youth work centered on its Junior Congregations and its efforts with the students at the University of Arkansas, Fayetteville. Jewish youth of Arkansas found one of its most dedicated and indefatigable workers on its behalf to be Rabbi Teitelbaum of Fort Smith. Born in Galicia in 1900, he came with his family to St. Louis in 1908. He was educated in public and Hebrew schools, graduating cum laude from Harvard in 1922. After a year in medical school and further studies at the Jewish Institute of Religion in New York, he became spiritual head of Fort Smith's United Hebrew Congregation in 1927. He served there until he entered the U.S. Army as a chaplain in 1942.

When Rabbi Teitelbaum first came to Fort Smith, his immediate concern was the Jewish youth of the city. He was also interested in social action for blacks and working people of the area. He tried to make social action a project of the Arkansas Jewish Assembly but was unsuccessful. His efforts in helping relief workers when their wages were cut during the Depression caused such a public furor that he escaped being ousted by his own congregation "by a hair."[40]

The work which the Assembly did in the 1930s for University of Arkansas students was built on efforts that Rabbi Teitelbaum had started in 1928. Several University of Arkansas students attended the High Holy Day services at United Hebrew Congregation in Fort Smith that year, and they expressed to Teitelbaum their strong desire for a Jewish student organization on campus. Familiar with the Intercollegiate Menorah Association in New York, Teitelbaum and his wife helped organize a Menorah Society at Fayetteville (some sixty miles north of Fort Smith) at the home of the Moses Baum family, one of two Jewish families living there at the time.[41]

The Menorah Society grew under the leadership of its early officers: Ralph Uhrmacher, president; Milton Baim, vice-president; Oscar Fendler, secretary; Bernard Silverman, treasurer; Gerald Steinberg, librarian; and Daisy Phillips of Camden (its first secretary).[42] The fledgling group sought to become an official one on campus so that all would know "that a

Menorah is here and what its purpose is." The society had its own official stationery printed, and programs by Milton Baim of Pine Bluff "fired up" the interest of the members. It was hoped that word of the society would spread throughout the state in order to increase the number of Jewish students at the University of Arkansas.[43]

The work the society did was impressive: it presented Jewish educational programs, promoted interfaith understanding (members attended local Christian churches, and ministers of these reciprocated by attending Menorah meetings), and encouraged attendance at services at Fort Smith's Temple. Oscar Fendler of Blytheville, who served as secretary and as president of Menorah (and who later became a well-known Arkansas attorney), undertook a task of no small size. He wrote to superintendents at fifty Arkansas high schools to acquire a list of prospective Jewish students and then wrote to the students, hoping to double Jewish enrollment at the University of Arkansas.[44]

During the early 1930s a gradual influx of Jewish students from northeastern states came to the Fayetteville campus. As the Menorah Society gained members, it expanded its activities with the help of Moses Baum, Dr. Gregson of the YMCA, University of Arkansas professors Virgil Jones and Barnett Sure, and University of Arkansas Law School dean, Julian Waterman.[45] But, while the Fayetteville group continued to grow, the national Menorah Association began to founder and was not able to give guidance as before. Rabbi Teitelbaum then wrote to Abram Sachar, director of the B'nai B'rith Hillel Foundation, asking if an organization under Hillel's auspices could be established at the University of Arkansas. This was done, and later, when the Arkansas Jewish Assembly was founded, the Hillel Society affiliated with it. As more Jewish students arrived in the 1930s, other Jewish groups began to form, such as the Tau Kappa chapter of Tau Epsilon Phi. This fraternity cooperated with Hillel to further Jewish life scholastically and spiritually. Seders (Passover meals) and prayer services for all holidays were conducted as a result of this joint effort.[46]

By 1934 a viable Hillel Society was functioning at Fayetteville under the able leadership of Max Schwartz of the Bronx, New York. Other leaders included Harold Schwartz, James Izenberg, Ted Sylvan, Joe Born, Ben Ginsberg, and Mannie Riesenberg. Meetings were usually held in the campus YMCA building.[47] The Assembly worked closely with the young men. Besides Rabbi Teitelbaum, University of Arkansas Jewish students found Louis Cohen of Fort Smith to be an "energetic super-salesman for Hillel."[48] Cohen served as Assembly president in 1934 and as editor of the organization's *Assembly Bulletin* for many years.[49] He served on the national executive committee of the B'nai B'rith Hillel Foundation. He was particularly interested in young people, having started his own climb to business success at the early age of sixteen. He had come to Fort Smith in 1915 and had gotten a job as a paper carrier. At age seventeen he was made circulation manager over sixty-five other carriers for the *Fort Smith Times-Record*.[50] By 1919 he had opened his own store, the Fort Smith Office and Supply Company, and had prospered. As an ardent worker in Fort Smith's Lions Club, he had organized Boys' Clubs in at least eight towns in the area surrounding Fort Smith. Active in almost every civic organization in his adopted city, he also served as president of B'nai B'rith's Southern Region and as president of United Hebrew Congregation for fifteen years.[51] Cohen married Elizabeth Ney, daughter of Rudolph Ney, owner of the famous Boston Store of Fort Smith. Their daughter, Marie, was active in the Assembly's Junior Congregation and attended Hillel meetings at Fayetteville. (Through a friend in Little Rock whom she had met in the Assembly's Junior Congregation, she came to know Joe Storthz Jr. of Little Rock, and the two later married. Such unions were a side benefit of the Junior Congregations.)[52]

There were about sixty Jewish students in the University of Arkansas Hillel in 1934, most of whom were from the northeastern states, where anti-Jewish prejudice had precluded them from being accepted into their region's schools. Some two dozen young people from Fort Smith attended the University of Arkansas Hillel meetings.[53] A disagreement arose that year among the northeastern students as to whether Hillel's Friday night services should be Orthodox or Reform. Rabbi Clark of Pine Bluff's Anshe Emeth helped bridge the gap. From an Orthodox background himself, yet having been trained as a Reform rabbi, he reawakened a "quiescent spirit" in a number of students.[54] Rabbi Teitelbaum coordinated Assembly efforts in having the state's rabbis address the Hillel group on a regular basis (expenses for which were underwritten by the local B'nai B'rith lodges).[55] By 1937 Jewish enrollment had reached more than 150 at the University of Arkansas. This large number was somewhat of a strain on the sparse Jewish population of the area. There was only one Jewish family left in Fayetteville at the time, and Fort Smith could accommodate only a limited number of students for socials, High Holy Days, and other events.[56] But even with the larger membership, University of Arkansas Hillel remained a society; it never grew large enough to entitle it to a Hillel Foundation status.[57] The Assembly made several attempts to establish at the University of Arkansas Medical School at Little Rock a group similar to the Hillel Society at Fayetteville. When it was found that the medical students had no time for outside activities, the efforts were dropped.[58]

Hillel Society members recognized the work Arkansas Jewry did in their behalf. They noted that the Assembly's efforts drew Jewish students to Hillel and made them realize that it was "more than a way of getting their picture put in the Razorback."[59] In a fervent talk given to Hillel in 1938, one of its members related how much the group owed to the state's rabbis; to the Fort Smith congregation; to the Arkansas Jewish Assembly; to Mrs. Will Marks, sponsor of Hillel functions in Fort Smith; to Mrs. Louis Weinberger, sponsor of Hillel on campus; and to Louis Cohen.[60]

Another successful Assembly project undertaken for its young people was a scholarship fund set up in 1934 for needy Arkansas Jewish students.[61] The fund was named the Annette B. Rhine Scholarship Fund when Rabbi Rhine's beloved wife died in September 1934. Established in the midst of the Depression, the fund was maintained by the Assembly's Sisterhood members. The scholarships supplied a definite need, and after just one year it was stated that if the Assembly had no other virtue to justify its existence "the Annette B. Rhine Fund would do so."[62]

While the Assembly's efforts for its young people were never lacking, it pursued many other projects as well. Some of its greatest efforts were expended in reaching the unorganized communities. A circuit rabbi idea was proposed, and such a prospect was bandied about with various degrees of earnestness. One of the unorganized communities was willing to pay as much as one thousand dollars a year toward such a project, and several others offered from three hundred to four hundred dollars annually.[63] The circuit rabbi concept succeeded in some ways beyond what the Assembly could have hoped. Just the thought of having a part-time rabbi inspired the Blytheville community to engage the services of a full-time leader. The community, located in northeast Arkansas, had seen a number of new Jewish stores open even during the throes of the Great Depression. Almost every small town in the area, including southeast Missouri and eastern Tennessee, had from one to a half-dozen Jewish merchants. Siegbert Jiedel, an active member of the Arkansas Jewish Assembly, was a member of the Blytheville community, and he and his brother, Richard, became a driving force in the establishment of a congregation at Blytheville. Rabbi Maurice Lyons, a promising member of the Hebrew Union Class of 1936, assumed his duties at Blytheville's Temple Israel in the fall of that year.[64] The next year, he led the congregation in officially joining the Assembly.

Although some Assembly members continued to pursue the circuit rabbi idea, it lost support about the time of the Assembly's census. Finding there were fewer Jews in the state than was imagined may have prompted another look at the idea. The state's rabbis and qualified laymen were encouraged to offer their services to the unorganized communities, and this proved quite successful.[65] Rabbi Morton Cohn, regional representative of the Union of American Hebrew Congregations, helped in this endeavor. He and Rabbi David Max Eichhorn, who by then was serving the Texarkana congregation, organized monthly services at Camden and El Dorado, and Rabbi Clark had monthly meetings at Eudora and McGehee. It often took dedication for such effort. Rabbi Clark and his wife drove regularly on Sunday afternoons, covering the 101 miles over roads described as "more like a corkscrew than a highway."[66] Camden and El Dorado were large enough and financially able to hire a Hebrew Union College student to conduct services on the High Holy Days while Assembly laymen went to the smaller communities, such as Wynne, Forrest City, Eudora, and McGehee, to hold such services.[67] Rabbi Lyons served the Jonesboro congregation on biweekly visits. By 1937 the good news that the unorganized communities were being covered in fact, not just in theory, was announced at the Assembly convention in April at Texarkana.[68]

The success of the Assembly's efforts in the smaller communities at times hinged on the interest of a few dedicated workers in the communities themselves. Sometimes it rested on one lone individual. An example of this was the unflagging efforts of Camden's Henry Berg. Born at Camden in 1869 to Meyer and Gette Berg, Henry began his business career at age fourteen when his father died. Berg saved his small income and bought property. Not only did he prosper, but he was also quite generous with the fruits of his success. All of Camden's churches benefited from his generosity, especially the black congregations.[69] Berg attended both Assembly conventions and its board meetings. By 1937 he was expressing his optimism that his city could soon have a spiritual leader for its small flock.[70] In April 1938 Berg told the Assembly Board that his community was planning to pay the expenses and honoraria for a monthly speaker and either to purchase a building to be used as a temple or to erect one.[71] By the time of the Assembly's April 1938 convention, Berg reported that the few Jews in Camden, who were trying to do all they could to preserve Judaism there, had purchased a building site.[72] A contract for construction of the edifice was awarded to J. S. Johnson of Hot Springs in October 1938.[73] Berg was called the "guiding light" in its being built; after its completion in 1939, it was said that the little temple "would be a reminder of the work and faith of this one man."[74]

When Jonesboro's Temple Israel joined the Assembly in 1938, all of the state's standing Jewish organizations were by then part of the Assembly, including existing congregations, sisterhoods, youth groups, and B'nai B'rith Lodges. At that time, lodges were located at Hot Springs, Wynne, Helena, Lake Village, Texarkana, Pine Bluff, Blytheville, Camden, El Dorado, and Little Rock. A lodge was formed at Jonesboro in 1938.[75] The enthusiasm generated by having the Jews of Arkansas meet and become acquainted made closer ties even more desirable. Plans were made for the exchange of pulpits for the rabbis and for lay speakers and workers.[76] As it developed, the lay membership of the Assembly was far more anxious for a pulpit exchange than were the rabbis, and the project met with only moderate success.[77] When it developed that there were not enough funds in the Assembly treasury to cover expenses of the pulpit exchange, its limited funds were used to provide speakers to the small unorganized communities instead.[78]

One task the Assembly took upon itself regarding the state's rabbis was to make sure one of them was available in the state during the summer months for emergencies. (Traditionally, rabbis take from one to three months off in the summer for vacation, travel, or educational purposes.) It seemed impossible for the Assembly to coordinate such a service, and Rabbi Miller of Helena, who was in charge of making rabbis available, said in a moment of frustration, "Suppose we pass a law against death and marriage of Jews during July."[79]

National organizations became aware of the Arkansas Jewish Assembly shortly after it formed. In 1934 Oscar Leonard, executive secretary of the American Jewish Congress of New York, wrote Rabbi Teitelbaum inquiring about the organization and its purposes.[80] Teitelbaum expressed hope that the Assembly would join the Congress and approached the Assembly's board on the subject in 1935.[81] Because of the differences between the Congress, which leaned toward Zionism, and the American Jewish Committee, which emphasized Americanism and eschewed a "Jewish Commonwealth," it was decided that the purposes of both organizations would be presented at an open Assembly meeting. (Both the Congress and the Committee sought to create a central authoritative representation for American Jewry.)[82] Rabbi Clark presented the aims and functions of both national organizations at an Assembly Board meeting held in April 1935, and he encouraged delegates at the assembly's fourth convention to study the two groups.[83] Affiliation with either group was not introduced for fear that Congress or Committee advocates might split the convention and the Assembly, and the Arkansas organization was thought to be "too young to withstand a division in its ranks."[84] Although the Assembly voted in 1936 to take a neutral stand toward the Congress, it heartily endorsed the fund-raising activities of the Joint Distribution Committee (a national Jewish relief organization) and the United Palestine Appeal, urging its member communities to make their contributions as large as possible for the "eminently worthy organizations."[85] Although several of the state's congregations—Helena, Pine Bluff, and Fort Smith—supported the Congress with fairly generous contributions,[86] the Assembly never joined the group.

Jewish education was one of the Assembly's most ambitious goals. As part of its earliest plans, the Assembly appointed Rabbis Alpert, Sanders, and Teitelbaum to prepare a curriculum for the state's religious schools.[87] When Rabbi Alpert was succeeded by Rabbi David Max Eichhorn, the latter immediately began an adult student class for his Texarkana congregation.[88] He sought to capitalize on southern ways and had Jewish "revivals" to acquaint Gentiles with the place of the Jews in civilization; he encouraged the Assembly to hold similar meetings in all the state's organized Jewish communities.[89] Rabbi Sanders, a scholar par excellence, continually drilled education into Assembly consciousness. Concerned that the Jews in the state's small communities did not subscribe to Jewish periodicals, he admonished the Assembly to take on a broad educational program that would reach all citizens, not just Jews. He stressed this particularly in the late 1930s, when "forces of hatred were rampant against the Jew."[90]

One of the most interesting insights to be gained by studying the records of the Arkansas Jewish Assembly can be found in examining its seemingly small concern at the onset of the developing catastrophe in Europe in the 1930s and tracing its awareness of the situation's gravity. At the Assembly's 1933 convention in Little Rock, attended by some two hundred of the state's Jewish leaders, members voted on but failed to pass the following proposal:

> The Jewish people of Arkansas in Convention assembled, express their sympathy with their brethren in Germany in their plight, and deplore the resurgence of forces of darkness in that land, and pray that the spirit of brotherhood will soon reign supreme again.[91]

Why this simple statement of support was defeated is puzzling. Perhaps the delegates did not grasp the extreme seriousness of the situation in Germany at the time, or maybe they thought that their relatively small group could do no good. Just one year later, however, a change had come about. Of the six resolutions passed at the Assembly's 1934 convention, three of them had to do with the plight of German Jews. One resolution called for a statewide appeal for German-Jewish relief, one called for a boycott of Germany, and one was an endorsement of the above resolution that had failed to pass in 1933. The latter not only passed, but it was voted that copies of the resolution be widely distributed and sent to the U.S. president and vice-president, to the state's political leaders, and to the U.S. Senate's Foreign Relations Committee. A letter was to be sent to the latter as well, urging the Committee to adopt the "Tydings Resolution," which protested the persecutions in Germany.[92]

Arkansas's Jewish citizens continued to grow more concerned about the European situation, but none could envisage the magnitude of what would arise. At the time, charity and concern and a riding out of a bad situation seemed to be the only solutions.[93] When Rabbi and Mrs. Sanders planned a summer vacation in Europe in 1934, he contacted U.S. Senator Joe T. Robinson of Arkansas, then chairman of the Conference of the Majority, and requested a letter of introduction to Italian dictator Benito Mussolini. Rabbi Sanders wanted to meet the dictator to urge him to "use his influence to dissuade Hitler from his 'Juden rein' campaign against the German Jews."[94] Robinson granted the letter, which described Rabbi Sanders as an "ardent student of sociological and political problems . . . an outstanding citizen [of Arkansas, who enjoyed] the high esteem and respect of those with whom he is acquainted . . ."[95] But whether a Sanders-Mussolini visit would have made a difference in history will never be known. When Rabbi and Mrs. Sanders called at Italy's State Office in Naples, Mussolini was in Germany conferring with Adolph Hitler, and Rabbi Sanders did not have an opportunity to see Italy's dictator.[96]

An element of naivete regarding the intentions of Adolph Hitler still pervaded the thinking of some Assembly members as late as 1935. Rabbi Samuel S. Mayerberg of Kansas City, keynote speaker for the convention, held that year April 5 through 7 at Fort Smith, pleaded "with a high degree of force, oratory, and emotion" for the demobilization of the military mind in order to demobilize the nation's military. To some Assembly members, his talk reached its high point when he stated that if the country were invaded, he would defend it with his life, but he would rather go to jail than participate in an aggressive war.[97] At that Assembly convention, a professionally printed flyer was distributed entitled *The Assembly Blah!* On it were bold headlines that stated "Hitler Joins B'nai B'rith," with the subtitle "Appointed Chairman of the Anti-Defamation League." The tongue-in-cheek article that accompanied the headlines had a Berlin dateline and reported that the Assembly secretary had climaxed his "triumphant tour of

Germany" with the "sensational announcement that Adolf Hitler, Feuhrer of the Nazis, had defied all precedent." Using his "extraordinary diplomatic skill," the secretary "succeeded in having Hitler initiated into the mysteries of the Independent Order of B'nai B'rith" and subsequently "appointed chairman of the Anti-Defamation League." The "inimitable" secretary was quoted as saying, "Hitler's success in the past leads me to say that he will be a riot in his new job. He has just been misunderstood."[98]

Rabbi Mayerberg was again the keynote speaker at the 1936 Assembly convention, held at Helena April 24 through 26. (After Mayerberg's visit with the Assembly at its 1935 convention, it was reported in June 1935, he was so impressed by the organization's role in Arkansas Jewry that he wanted to attempt a similar organization in Kansas.)[99] Both he and the Assembly had made some changes in their thinking by 1936. Mayerberg, who spoke on "The Eternal People," stirred his audience with a plea for aid to the oppressed Jewry in Europe. He also asked for an "understanding and appreciation of participation in the great work in Palestine." The Assembly's executive committee that year was instructed to send a strong letter of protest to the Polish ambassador to the United States, to the U.S. State Department, and to many state newspapers, seeking to offset the possibility that Poland's Jews "experience the same cruel fate which has befallen our German brethren."[100]

As the condition of European Jews worsened, the Assembly sought ways to offset the rising anti-Semitism found on its own doorstep. One particularly disturbing incident occurred in 1937 when Senator Hal Smith of Clarendon made disparaging remarks on the floor of the Arkansas Senate concerning the Jews of Arkansas. Smith had coauthored the Smith-Coleman liquor bill that would have outlawed liquor in Arkansas, and in his plea to have it passed, stated that "eighty-five percent of the wholesale liquor dealers of Arkansas are Jews." He asked his assembled peers, "Are you going to continue to make a bunch of Jews millionaires in Arkansas, or are you going to carry out your pledge to the old folks back home . . . ?"[101] Dr. L. J. Kosminsky of Texarkana, Assembly president at the time, called Smith down for defaming the character of a religious group that had given ample evidence of "its loyalty and devotion to the best interests of the state of Arkansas." He told Smith that it was a well-known fact that the "overwhelming majority of the Jews of Arkansas" had nothing to do with the liquor business. To condemn the whole group because of a grudge harbored against a few individual members of that group was a sure indication that the person guilty of such prejudice was not worthy of public trust or support.[102]

While there had been no reported anti-Semitism at the University of Arkansas campus at Fayetteville in the 1920s, Assembly members became particularly concerned about such incidents experienced by Jewish students in the 1930s. One of these occurred during the fall of 1937 when several evenings in a row some Gentile students stood in front of the Tau Epsilon Phi house, where a number of Jewish students were living, and "cursed them outrageously" and asked them to come out and fight.[103] After the incidents, school authorities and two Fayetteville Christian ministers, Rev. James W. Workman of Central Methodist Church and Rev. Royal Humbert of First Christian Church, sought to handle the affair. Rabbi Teitelbaum was called as a special speaker in the churches on three occasions.[104] Although the Jewish students referred to the above incidents as "rather minor and unimportant," the events did make the campus aware of its Jewish students and inspire the Fayetteville clergy to continue to preach on the need for a greater amount of tolerance.[105] When word of the trouble at Fayetteville reached Assembly members, they began sending in funds to help disseminate information. Some $170 was received and was used to purchase a number of specially chosen books that were placed in the University library.[106] Interest in the events at Fayetteville ran so high among Assembly members statewide that the entire January 1938 issue of the *Assembly Bulletin* was devoted to the Hillel Society. A thousand copies of the issue were sent to Jews statewide.[107]

The Hillel-donated books were well received by University officials, and a placard was placed above them on the library shelves that read "Given by the Hillel Organization." A Jewish student writing for the *Assembly Bulletin* commented that there had "always been a good deal of anti-Semitism on the Arkansas campus" and he hoped the books would help eliminate the ill feeling. He lamented that "we [Jews] have tried many things in order to gain the friendship of the Gentile boy," but such efforts bore little success. "Like our ancestors," he wrote, "we do not recognize defeat. If this method fails, we will try another."[108]

As the Assembly became more concerned about anti-Semitism in the state, particularly at the University of Arkansas, it explored ways of uniting action with non-Jewish groups in Arkansas on such issues as peace, anti-Fascism, social betterment, civil liberties, and race relations. When it was suggested that the Assembly join such national organizations as the National Religion and Labor Foundation, the American Civil Liberties Union, the National Conference of Christians and Jews, and the American League for Peace and Democracy, Assembly members voted to affiliate with the latter two only.[109]

At the Assembly's seventh annual convention, held at Hot Springs 24 April 1938, the keynote speaker, Dr. Felix Levy of Chicago, emphasized how serious the situation was in Europe and spoke on the needed role of Palestine and Zionism. At that meeting the Assembly endorsed the work of the Assembly's Sisterhood Committee, headed by Mrs. Jesse Heiman of Little Rock, in cooperating with national work aimed at resettling German-Jewish immigrants in the state. It was also announced that Little Rock's Jewish Federation planned to help settle German Jews on farms in Arkansas.[110]

Resolutions expressing horror and condemnation of the practices of the powers of Germany and the Nazis were passed at the 1938 convention. The Assembly viewed President Franklin D. Roosevelt as a great humanitarian and voted to send an expression of its appreciation to him and his Secretary of State, Cordell Hull. It noted the two "illustrious leaders" had expended their efforts to "perpetuate American traditions" by calling on other nations to join America in "offering hope to thousands of refugees fleeing from the horrors of Nazi persecution."[111] Roosevelt sent a platitude to the Assembly regarding the celebration of Rosh Hashanah in 1938, which was printed in the *Assembly Bulletin*. In it he said he hoped that "the path which we now but dimly perceive soon will be found to be a real road to world peace and world justice."[112] Rabbi Clark, who was an Assembly delegate to the national meeting of the American Jewish Congress in 1938, was more skeptical of such platitudes than many Assembly members. He noted that Dr. Stephen S. Wise, American Jewish Congress founder and president, had "a hard road to travel" regarding actions to prevent a further deterioration of the Jewish status in Europe. Clark observed that there was a "large percentage of Jews in America who were 'chickenhearted' and feared 'Ma yomru hagoim?'" (what will the Gentiles say).[113]

On 11 November 1938 Arkansas Jews were astonished and dismayed along with their kinsmen worldwide after hearing of Kristallnacht (the night of broken glass) in Germany, at which time a "wave of destruction, looting and incendiarism unparalleled in Germany since the Thirty Years' War" destroyed Jewish shops, offices, and synagogues.[114] The destruction was initiated as supposed revenge for the murder of Ernst vom Rath, a young German Christian who was serving as third secretary of the Germany embassy in Paris.[115] After this devastating incident, the Synagogue Council of America issued a mandate calling for both Jewish and Christian congregations throughout the country to assemble in their houses of worship on Sunday, 20 November 1938, and intercede with God on behalf of German Jewry.[116] As in other synagogues and temples nation-wide, those of Arkansas were filled to capacity. After the service at crowded Temple B'nai Israel in Little Rock, none left the service dry-eyed.[117]

Mrs. Gus Blass served as general chairman of the Federation of Jewish Charities in 1938, and the organization's goal of fifteen thousand dollars was used to aid both Jews and non-Jews. It also joined forces with other American Jews in seeking aid for the millions of their oppressed coreligionists in Poland and Germany.[118]

In November 1938 Harry B. Solmson Sr. of Little Rock succeeded Rabbi Sanders as chairman of the State Refugee Aid Committee. A more dedicated person could not have been chosen for the task. Solmson, born at Dyersburg, Tennessee, in December 1876, had grown up at Pine Bluff, where he had moved with his parents in 1880. He subsequently married Gertrude Myar, daughter of one of Camden's earliest and most successful businessmen, Henry Myar. Solmson moved with his family to Little Rock around 1920 and was successful in real estate and in the insurance firm of Malony and Solmson. The interest both he and his wife had in civic and religious affairs knew no bounds. The many offices he held included chair-man of the Arkansas chapter of the Joint Distribution Committee, presi-dent of Congregation B'nai Israel from 1936 to 1939, and Assembly Board member and president in 1937.[119] He served as chairman of the Assembly's Circuit Rabbi Committee, and he himself was lay speaker for several of the state's unorganized communities, particularly at Jonesboro and Blytheville.[120] During the Depression, Solmson was particularly interested in the plight of poor minorities. In 1933 he formed the Arkansas Farm Homes, Inc., a limited dividend corporation in which he planned to use five thousand acres of the Henry Myar estate west of Camden to create a modern farm colony for blacks.[121] One hundred farms were to be located on fifty-acre tracts, each having a house, barn, and woven wire fence. Annual payment would have been $125, which would have included pay-ment on principal, interest, insurance, and taxes. Although the project was accepted by the State Housing Board and the Federal government, lack of funds during the Depression prohibited its implementation.[122]

When Solmson was named head of the Assembly's Refugee Aid Committee, he immediately enlisted the help of Louis Cohen of Fort Smith and Henry Berg of Camden. The three men began to devise ways of opening up cooperative industries in Arkansas for some of the expected flood of refugees into America.[123] Solmson saw three problems facing world

Jewry: providing food, shelter, and physical safety for more than five million Jewish refugees; preserving democracy; and finding solutions to worldwide anti-Semitism.[124] At that time, he could not have foreseen that the more than five million souls he had estimated as needing refuge would not live to find it.

World War II–the Perspective Changes, 1940s

B y 1940 members of the Arkansas Jewish Assembly could look back proudly at its efforts during the past decade. When Charles Dante of Dumas reported to the Assembly Board in December 1940 that the Jewish families of southeast Arkansas had coalesced as one community and would join the organization, all the Jewish groups of the state were then affiliated with it. The unorganized communities were sending delegates regularly to all Assembly meetings and presenting their needs, which were met when possible. Rabbi Miller of Helena reported that he had visited Forrest City and Wynne on occasion, and it was his conviction that organizing the two groups as one congregation would be impossible because the Wynne group was Orthodox and the one at Forrest City was Reform. It was noted that the completed Beth El Emeth Temple at Camden was dedicated by Rabbi Sanders that year.[1]

The Assembly's Youth Congregation had been inactive for a time in the late 1930s but was reorganized with a flourish in 1940 under the leadership of Blanche Schlosberg. A meeting held that year was attended by youth from Little Rock, the host city, and from Osceola, Pine Bluff, Hot Springs, Fort Smith, and Helena. The group had taken a census of the state's Jewish youth (the results of which were not recorded). Young Blanche announced at the meeting that the National Federation of Temple Youth had "now come into the picture" and was the "last member of the family that the Union of American Hebrew Congregations" had established.[2] The benefits of Assembly efforts for Arkansas Jewish youth were attested to on occasion. Isabel Lappin of Fort Smith saw the Assembly as a way to keep in touch with other Jewish youth throughout the state, and it met a need to "preserve our race" in order to "present a united front to other peoples." Without such encouragement as provided by the Junior Congregation, it was felt that the Jews as a religious group "would soon disappear or diminish to a large extent . . . "[3] Other Jewish youth had benefitted monetarily from the Assembly's scholarship fund. By 1940 some twelve hundred dollars had been dispersed to "worthy students."[4]

Not all of the Assembly's projects were progressing at the beginning of its second decade. The pride the Assembly had exhibited in its work with the University of Arkansas Hillel was deflated in 1940 when in December of that year Rabbi Teitelbaum presented its board with a very gloomy report. Hillel was "practically extinct," he said, with only twelve Jewish students enrolled at the U of A that fall. Reasons cited for such a drop included a tuition increase, extra restrictions on out-of-state students for medical school, and a current of anti-Semitic feeling still felt among the student body.[5] The small number of Jewish students, encouraged by Rabbi Teitelbaum and Dr. Barnett Sure, head of the U of A Agricultural Chemistry Department, continued monthly meetings until 1942, when the group disbanded after Rabbi Teitelbaum entered the U.S. Army as a chaplain.[6] (A Hillel group would not form again at the U of A until 1964 [see section V].)[7]

The Assembly suffered from the death of some of its most devoted workers during the 1939–41 period. Harry Solmson Sr., a past Assembly president, died in 1939. He had been an indefatigable lay worker in efforts to reach the unorganized communities and in promoting Assembly goals.

Assembly treasurer Rue Abramson of Holly Grove died in November 1940. Active in his own local civic affairs, he had also shown a keen interest in Arkansas's scattered Jews and was a key anchor person for the Assembly in the east southeast section of the state.[8]

The Assembly felt a stunning blow at the death of its beloved founder, Rabbi A. B. Rhine, on 8 August 1941. A state newspaper, the *Arkansas Gazette*, editorialized that his death was more than a loss to his congregation, city, and state: "It is a loss to education, to religion, and to humanity."[9] Rabbi Sanders eulogized the rabbi's outstanding leadership at the 1941 Assembly convention.[10]

As the 1940s had begun, the Assembly had taken its serious "business as usual" attitude toward its projects within the state. It soon began emphasizing a more outward look, however, which focused on work with

European refugees. Mrs. James Kempner, Assembly president for the period 1940–41, chided members at a board meeting at Little Rock in December 1940 for the fact that not more was being done to help relieve the refugee problem. She was told by Mrs. Leo Baim of Pine Bluff, Refugee Committee chairman, that refugees who had been contacted were not particularly interested in coming to the Arkansas towns that had indicated a desire to assist them.[11] Refugees did begin to trickle into the state, most of whom were brought by relatives who worked tirelessly to get them out of Europe. Charles Dante of Dumas was an example of many who wrote numerous letters and signed documents for a number of refugees, regardless of whether they were his relatives.[12] One of the refugees he brought to Arkansas was his nephew, Harry Phillips, who later married Elsie Hamburger of McGehee.[13] Other refugees included the Edmund Frenkel family, brought to Arkansas by Mrs. Frenkel's brothers, T. M. and Gus Loeb of De Witt (son Herbert Frenkel married Ruth Hamburger of McGehee; he became a pharmacist in Little Rock and Conway);[14] the Wintory family of Fort Smith (young son Nicol, who later purchased the Tilles ladies' clothing store, began a long service to Fort Smith Jewry when he served as president of the Fort Smith Junior Congregation in 1941);[15] the Selz family was brought to McGehee (son Freddie later moved to Little Rock, where he came to be known as "one of the deans" of Little Rock real estate);[16] Eric Nussbaum came from Germany to Little Rock as a youth in the late 1930s and entered the U.S. Army in 1942, where he served with distinction;[17] Karl and Yetta Rhein were brought to Eudora by relative Jacob Rexinger (they later moved to Little Rock with sons Louis and Edwin and a daughter, Mrs. Edward Strauss, and their families; Edwin developed a successful necktie factory in Little Rock).[18] Mr. and Mrs. Joseph Spitzer and Mr. and Mrs. Abraham Jacubowicz survived the death camps and came to Arkansas after the war. The Spitzers settled at Hot Springs, where they opened a kosher meat market, and the Jacubowicz family settled at Little Rock.[19] A number of other refugees came as well, and all became a credit to the Arkansas Jewish community. Assembly members were disappointed at how few refugees the organization was privileged to assist.[20]

The 1941 Assembly convention was held on 7 December at Fort Smith. It was at this conference, the theme of which was "Jewish Faith— For Living," that the startling news of the bombing of Pearl Harbor was announced. To mention the Assembly a half century later to any delegate who was at the 1941 meeting elicits an immediate recall that "the Assembly was in session when World War II began for the United States."[21]

The war effort and the plight of European Jewry quickly became the focus of the Assembly after Pearl Harbor. Dave Grundfest, state chairman of the United Jewish Appeal (UJA) in the early 1940s, made a strong plea to Arkansas Jewry through the Assembly for support of needs of both the UJA and the Joint Distribution Committee.[22] The 1942 Assembly convention was scheduled to be held in Helena, but incoming president Simon "Sammy" Feldman, who joined "Uncle Sam's Army," concluded that the "best thing . . . is to forget the Assembly for the duration." He had talked to several Assembly members, none of whom could attend either conventions or board meetings because of gasoline rationing.[23] Louis Cohen of Fort Smith concurred with Feldman, noting that after the war the Assembly could "start again with a bang."[24]

Although the Assembly did not function during the war years, its members and many other Arkansas Jews expended a great deal of effort toward America's war effort. As many as six hundred Jewish servicemen from across Arkansas served in the U.S. Armed Forces in World War II. One hundred forty of these were from the membership of Temple B'nai Israel of Little Rock.[25]

Mrs. Herbert (Gertrude) Latkin, president of Little Rock's B'nai Israel Sisterhood in the early 1940s, is an example of those who served selflessly during the war years. She was also president of the Little Rock section of the National Council of Jewish Women. She served as a member of the boards of the United Service Organizations (USO), the Pulaski County Mental Health Association, and the Arkansas Chapter of the American Red Cross. She supervised bandage meetings for the latter and was part of a delegation that regularly met planes and trains at all hours of the day and night with refreshments for military personnel, both the wounded and the well. Sisterhood women would take food to the Jewish soldiers at nearby Camp Robinson on Friday nights for the Sabbath services there.[26] Members of both the Reform and Orthodox congregations of Little Rock invited Jewish servicemen into their homes for the holidays, particularly for Passover.[27] A community center had been established in the 1930s by members of Little Rock's Council of Jewish Women, and it was converted into a day-care center for the many mothers who had entered the work force during the war.[28] The center's founders included Adele Bluthenthal and Gertrude (Myar) Solmson. Mrs. Richard (Gertrude Remmel) Butler also was active in the work.[29]

Presidents who served the Assembly in the 1940s were Mrs. James Kempner, 1940; Maurice Cohen, 1941; Bernard Moretsky, 1942; Simon

Feldman, 1946–47; Mrs. Leo Baim, 1948; Mrs. R. C. Kory, 1949; and Jack Botnick, 1950. Others who served on the executive committee of the Assembly during the 1940s included Charles A. Rutstein, Siegbert Jiedel, Mrs. David Menkus Jr., Louis A. Cohen, Henry Spitzberg, Sol Klarberg, Ralph Abramson, Mrs. Simon Feldman, Adolph Laytin, and David Solomon.[30]

In 1944 two Little Rock Jewish women, Mrs. Louis (Dorothy) Goldberg and Mrs. Isador (Sarah) Scrinopski, established a chapter of Hadassah, which was a national Jewish women's Zionist organization that had been founded by Henrietta Szold in 1912 in New York.[31] The initial meeting of the Little Rock group was well attended, and most of the participants became members. Membership cards, which bore the notation that Hadassah was a Zionist organization, were sent to those who had joined. Zionism was not popular among the Reform movement at the time, and many from the Reform community who had joined Hadassah (evidently not realizing its Zionistic thrust) not only resigned from the group but also openly opposed it. Sarah Scrinopski, who had been elected its first president, turned to Rabbi Sanders for consolation. He told her that she was on the right track and would win out in the end.[32] Sarah's devoted husband, Isador, became as interested in Hadassah as his wife, and he gave generously to its causes and underwrote life memberships for some of its ardent workers. He was later called the "patron saint" of Little Rock Hadassah, and it was said that all the adulation that could be heaped upon him "would not be too much."[33] Although men could not be members of Hadassah, they were allowed to become Associates for a onetime fee; Isador was Little Rock's first Hadassah Associate.

Zionism spawned a controversy among American Reform rabbis during the early part of the war, and in 1942 ninety-two rabbis, including seventeen from the South, met in Atlantic City to adopt "A Statement of Principles by Non-Zionist Rabbis." A lay organization was proposed "for a righteous onslaught on Jewish nationalism." It was felt that if Americanism was its focus, an anti-Zionist group could succeed; it was therefore named the American Council for Judaism. Southern Reform Jews were confronted in 1943 with the Council's main statement of purpose:

> We oppose the effort to establish a National Jewish State in Palestine or anywhere else, as a philosophy of defeatism and one which does not offer a practical solution to the Jewish problem. We dissent from all those related doctrines that stress the racialism, the nationalism, and theoretical homelessness of the Jews. We oppose such doctrines as inimical to the welfare of the Jews in Palestine, in America, and wherever Jews may dwell.[34]

The American Council for Judaism gained a few adherents in Little Rock, and a group functioned there for a while.[35] Although it did not grow significantly either locally or nationally, the Zionist organization of Hadassah did: it became the largest women's organization in the world.

As the full import of the disaster faced by European Jewry began to unfold toward the end of the war, the cause of creating a homeland for the Jewish people took on an imperative nature. The Holocaust became more real to the Little Rock Jewish community when one of its members, Nathan Steppach, who served as a pharmacist in the Army Medical Corps, wrote home about his experience in helping to liberate Dachau, one of the infamous concentration camps. In a letter dated 4 May 1945, Nathan wrote to his wife, Anne (Ehrenberg) Steppach:

> Be on the lookout . . . for pictures about Germany's worst concentration camp . . . The scenes are by no means faked . . . If every person in the whole wide world would be made to march single file around the area where we are now, the German race would be wiped off the map to the last man . . . If you and others could get across to the American people what we've seen in the past three days . . . if it could be shouted from the house tops . . . if these poor peoples' bodies could be stacked up in the cities over there, like they are . . . here for people to squirm and puke at the sight and stench . . . then maybe by some miracle . . . there would be no more wars. The Pharoahs, the Czars, and the other madmen in history were pikers compared to these sons-of-bitches.[36]

With such knowledge and impetus, Arkansas Jewish Assembly president Sammy Feldman called a meeting of the organization's board shortly upon his return home from service in 1946. Some of the board were surprised to find themselves still members after almost four years, and members were pleased that the Assembly was reorganizing.[37]

The Jewish communities at Blytheville, McGehee, and El Dorado, which had been vital concerns to the Assembly, had continued to be strengthened from within themselves during the 1940s. A building fund committee was established in 1942 at Blytheville that included Siegbert Jiedel, Max Meyers, L. K. Harwarg, and E. M. Jaffe. Although necessary funds were raised, a building permit was not issued by the War Production Board in Little Rock until 1945. Materials were not available at that time, and the congregation, which had sold its small community house in 1942, rented the Blytheville Women's Club facilities four times a month and for a three-day period for the High Holy Days. Services were conducted by lay persons (usually Siegbert or Richard Jiedel, or Max or Bill Borowsky of Manila). Rabbi Albert Vise became leader of the congregation in 1945. The membership of Temple Israel, drawn from seven Arkansas towns and four in Missouri, were mostly of East European descent and traditional backgrounds, and the temple was viewed as Conservative by some even though it had joined Reform Judaism's Union of American Hebrew Congregations in 1939.[38] Non-Jews supported Temple Israel's building fund drive, prompted by their appreciation of its members. Herman Alston, proprietor of a drug store in Manila, was impressed by the lives of the Borowsky brothers, Max and Bill. The Borowskys had supported every "worthwhile cause, whether civic or religious," and had been outspoken as Jews, living their religion before the community. He admired them, Alston said, and donated one hundred dollars to the temple's building fund, trusting that it would "in some measure" express his feelings toward the Borowskys and the religion by which they lived.[39]

Temple Israel's house of worship was finally completed and dedicated in September 1947. Several Arkansas Jewish Assembly members participated in the ceremony. The Gothic-style structure had six thousand square feet, eight large stained glass memorial windows, 150-seat capacity, and an educational unit with classrooms, study, recreational hall, and modern kitchen. It was considered one of the most impressive temples in the state.[40] Several other Jewish organizations were established at Blytheville during the 1940s: a Federation of Jewish Welfare in Mississippi County, the Annie Weinberg Women's Chapter of B'nai B'rith, and a chapter of the American Zionist Association.[41]

The Jews of southeast Arkansas were served by Rabbi Clark after he was contacted by Mrs. William (Joan) Hamburger of McGehee. The rabbi held services at McGehee on Sunday afternoons and also conducted a Sunday School for children. When gasoline rationing made this no longer possible, the Meyer brothers, Dave and Sol, served as lay leaders. By 1946, Dave Meyer was encouraging the building of a temple at McGehee, and Charles Dante and William Hamburger, both liaison members to the Assembly, served on the building committee that was formed. The committee, headed by Hamburger and Sam Wolchansky, also included Isadore Marcus, Sam Abowitz, and Joseph Weisman. Wolchansky was overseer of the actual construction. The temple was to be named Beath Chym in honor of Dave Meyer, but the name was changed to Meir Chayim in memory of Sergeant Herbert M. Abowitz, son of Sam and Mollie Abowitz of Arkansas City, who was killed in action in Italy at the close of World War II. The temple, also built on Gothic lines, contained thirty-two hundred square feet, with a 150-seat auditorium. It had ten identical stained glass memorial windows. Rabbi Sanders of Little Rock gave the dedicatory address of the temple on 1 May 1949. Other Assembly members who participated in the program included Rabbis Walter Kaelter of Hot Springs, Ernest Grey of Fort Smith, and Morris Clark of Pine Bluff. The latter was the principal speaker at a banquet held that evening at the Greystone Hotel.[42]

While the Jewish community of Camden had been declining, the one at El Dorado, thirty-two miles south, had more than thirty families in 1946 (many others who had come in the first flurry after oil was discovered had moved away). A congregation, called Beth Israel, was established. Its meetings were held in rented space on the second floor of a building on North Washington Street. Members partitioned off a long narrow space and placed a stage at one end. J. B. Miller served as lay leader, conducting services each Friday evening. An active Council of Jewish Women was founded, which helped with fund raising. (The congregation belonged briefly to the Union of American Hebrew Congregations in the 1960s.) Although some of the members were Orthodox, the temple remained Reform.[43]

The rabbis who served in the state during the 1940s continued to be a source of strength to the Assembly. Sammy Feldman, Assembly president, found Rabbi Alfred Vise of Blytheville to be an avid worker. Vise, who had served as associate rabbi of the Jewish Temple Association in Hamburg, Germany (the oldest and one of the largest liberal congregations in Europe), had been imprisoned in a German concentration camp when the temple he served was destroyed on Kristallnacht in November 1938. Through intervention of the U.S. State Department, he had been allowed to answer a call from Temple Beth El in Clarksville, Tennessee, where he served from 1939 to 1945.[44] Vise served the Blytheville and Jonesboro congregations until his death in 1957.

The Assembly was older and wiser by the time it resumed its efforts in 1946. It no longer hesitated to speak out on issues that involved the American government or others in authority. At its tenth annual convention, held in Hot Springs in October 1946, Dr. W. Gunther Plaut, rabbi of Washington Boulevard Temple, Chicago, was the keynote speaker. He let his vulnerability show when he spoke on "The Wondering Jew" and asked if there were any persons at the meeting who did not wonder at one time or another "Why doesn't this world love us a little better?" and, "What have they got against us?" Did any feel at times a twinge of regret that he was a Jew? he queried. He spoke boldly against the government, saying that the Jews "did not have the guts" to point a finger at the government, to say that it had "forsaken the tradition of our country." The immigration laws of the 1920s were a public disgrace and a "slap in the face of every tradition" that the country stood for, he said. He asserted that the Jews needed more knowledge of themselves, for "we are a people of heroes, of men of law . . . of musicians, a people that is creative, a people . . . we might well love." The Assembly resoundingly supported the board's recommendation that the U.S. president, senators, and representatives be contacted and every effort exerted to relax the U.S. immigration laws.[45]

While the Assembly had been hesitant to join either the American Jewish Congress or the American Jewish Committee prior to the war, it joined, without fanfare, the American Jewish Conference after the Holocaust.[46] The Conference had been called in New York in 1943, prompted by a desire shared with the American Jewish Congress: to see a Jewish commonwealth established in Palestine.[47] Two Assembly delegates—Rabbi Kaelter of Hot Springs and Rabbi Ernest Grey of Fort Smith—attended the 1947 American Jewish Conference Convention.[48]

Interfaith understanding became a priority project for the Assembly after the war. Each community was encouraged to hold annual interfaith meetings, usually during Brotherhood Week. As a former concentration camp prisoner, Rabbi Vise of Blytheville particularly saw the need for greater understanding between peoples. He was lauded in his efforts and was said to have brought about "a great forward step . . . in bringing the different faiths together."[49] Governor Sid McMath, governor of Arkansas in the period 1949–53, supported efforts to establish an Arkansas office of the National Conference of Christians and Jews (NCCJ).[50] (Although such efforts were begun in 1939, an Arkansas office of NCCJ was not established until 1964.) Rabbi Martin M. Weitz and George Sackville, both of Hot Springs, were commended by the NCCJ Dallas office for some twelve meetings they had organized in Hot Springs during Brotherhood Week in 1950.[51]

The role the church had played—or had not played—in the Holocaust came under attack by Dr. Ernest Grey of Fort Smith's United Hebrew Congregation in 1948. In an *Assembly Bulletin* article entitled "The World Council of Churches and the Jewish People," he noted that the church would not be able to "maintain its moral authority any longer if it condones any form of prejudice and discrimination." He said it was not in vain that the New Testament mentioned "wickedness in high places," adding that it was easy to point to highly placed persons, "who with their one hand supported the churches and with the other shook the hand of the devil himself, who was incorporated in Hitler and his ilk."[52]

Assembly members continued to counter any anti-Semitic acts and enlisted the help of Fred Grossman, associate director of the Southwest

Office of B'nai B'rith's Anti-Defamation League (ADL). Grossman said he was encouraged that the "great churches of the South," the Baptist and Methodist, were battling against discrimination "with increasing vigor" and were availing themselves of ADL literature to educate their members toward better human relationships. Grossman was glad to report that the prompt indignation of one Arkansas community toward a property owner who had listed his land for sale to "Gentiles Only" made the "bigot" withdraw his ad. He also cited a writer in a religious publication in Arkansas who was using the problems of the State of Israel as a "point of departure for expressing animosity towards Jews." Grossman added, "Happily, such incidents have been few in Arkansas."[53]

Rabbi Sanders, who had advocated and had worked for a deeper understanding between Jew and non-Jew since he had come to Little Rock in 1926, was at the forefront in Assembly efforts in education. He advocated that an executive be paid from Assembly funds to organize an educational program that would reach all of Arkansas's citizens. He insisted that more educational material be published in the *Assembly Bulletin*; this was carried out, and Christian and secular leaders throughout the state were added to the *Bulletin*'s mailing list.[54] As chairman of the Harry B. Solmson Sr. Educational Fund (established in memory of the dedicated Assembly worker), Rabbi Sanders became a one-man educational fount. In 1948 he mailed out some five thousand pieces of literature on American Jewish history to the small Jewish communities in the state, placed thirty-seven books in the state's public libraries, and had a Chanukkah ceremony by him and B'nai Israel's choir recorded and broadcast over radio stations in Arkansas's four largest cities.[55]

The Assembly conducted another census in 1946, and the results showed 2037 Jewish citizens in eleven communities.[56] (Additional data regarding citizens of small towns, which was to be printed later, is not extant.) In 1948 Helena's new rabbi, H. Cerf Strauss, warned the Assembly that, if it was to fulfill its purpose, it should not just collect Jewish names in the state but go out to them and instill in them an interest in Jewish affairs.[57] The Assembly planned a summer camp for children that year as well as a Sunday School teachers' training course, and it appointed field workers for small communities.[58]

The Assembly-sponsored youth congregations entered the 1950s decade by electing a full slate of officers, which included president Melvyn Kossover, vice-president Hazel Thalheimer, secretary Rita Rosenbloom (all of Little Rock), treasurer Leonard Rutstein of Stuttgart, historian Dena Schneider of North Little Rock, chaplain Lillian Cohen of Helena, and sergeant-at-arms Betty Ann Brown of Hot Springs. The youth group had begun publishing its own quarterly bulletin, entitled the *Schmoose*.[59]

In November 1950 the Assembly, prompted by Rabbi's Sanders' push for Jewish education, held one of the most successful events in its history —a statewide conference on education. Dr. Samuel Blumenfield, president of the College of Jewish Studies and school superintendent of the Board of Jewish Education in Chicago, led the conference in Little Rock. It was well attended and received such positive results that it was being considered as an annual Assembly event.[60] Rabbi Sanders, who helped conduct the conference, had observed that there was on the national level a resurgence of Jewish learning in Jewish schools, and only a "few barren places" existed in this "bright picture of Jewish education resurgence." He confessed that Arkansas was one of those barren places. He proposed that courses in Jewish life and history be sent to Jews in rural areas of the state and that trained laymen and rabbinical leaders conduct follow-up classes. He suggested a rental library as well as a series of lecturers and artists to visit the outlying communities.[61] He noted that a Passover radio broadcast he had initiated was so successful that he planned Sabbath and High Holy Day radio programs to be aired statewide in 1951 with the goal of reaching a million listeners.[62]

Rabbi Samuel Fox, who served Orthodox Congregation Agudath Achim of Little Rock in the late 1940s and early 1950s and who supported the Assembly's efforts, agreed with Rabbi Sanders' assessment of Jewish education in Arkansas. Rabbi Fox observed that the level of religious training was at such a low ebb in Arkansas in 1950 that

> . . . our vast and rich culture hangs on a bare thread. Even a small wind blowing our way threatens to sever this threadbare attachment to a vacillating and seemingly lifeless Judaism.

To help remedy the lack in his own congregation, Rabbi Fox had formed two daily children's classes, covering Hebrew, Bible, and Jewish history, and established an adult education class. He considered the educational task as a "long and fierce struggle" with Jewish illiteracy.[63]

Under the able leadership of Jack Botnick, the Assembly seemed more ready than ever to serve Arkansas Jewry for the coming 1950s decade. Botnick had moved from his home in Newark, New Jersey, to Hot Springs in 1939 as representative of the Little Rock Paper Company. A gregarious person deeply dedicated to Judaism, he taught Sunday School for Hot Springs' House of Israel Congregation. In 1951 he became vice-president of the paper company and moved his family to Little Rock. Vitally enthusiastic about whatever he undertook, he began his year as Assembly president with zeal.[64] The readers of the Assembly's November–December 1950 *Assembly Bulletin* were notified of the 1951 convention, scheduled for mid-April in Pine Bluff. Also included in the same *Assembly Bulletin* was a letter from President Botnick in which he promised that the Assembly would become a model workshop in Jewish values—that it would be "A blockhouse for defense, a schoolhouse for learning, and a lighthouse for living." The publication included data on a series of statewide "talk tours" that were scheduled that year, which would include lectures by Botnick, Rabbi Sanders, Rabbi Weitz of Hot Springs, and Arkansas Jewish youth leaders Melvyn Kossover and Sara Lois Brown.

But Jack Botnick fell ill and died at age forty-eight on 18 May 1951, and with him died the Assembly. There was no 1951 convention, and no one rose up to take charge of the organization's affairs.

It has been difficult to determine why the Assembly could fail so quickly. Some individuals who could have helped to answer the question are gone. Explanations offered years later by former Assembly members attribute its demise to several factors. Some have said that it died of its own success; many of its original goals had been reached and it was no longer needed. Formerly unorganized communities had coalesced over time and began using the services of Hebrew Union College students. Also, most of those who lived in very small communities had died or had moved away as the communities themselves were disappearing. Another explanation of the Assembly's demise included the observation that, because the various Jewish communities had become so organized, efforts to that effect may have worked against the need for an overall group. The January 1948 *Assembly Bulletin* listed all the Jewish organizations in the state, which totaled forty-three. Officers were needed for all these local groups, which drew leadership potential away from the state level.[65]

It has also been observed that the Assembly's demise may have been helped along by the reverberations of World War II events. After that conflict the Jews worldwide had their sights lifted above and beyond their local, state, and national scenes. The Holocaust had led to a keen awareness of the need for a homeland for their persecuted brethren, and this—together with the rebirth of the State of Israel—provided a cohesiveness that took precedence over more provincial efforts.[66]

It is certain that the Assembly did not fail from lack of goals. In its last published *Assembly Bulletin*, ten viable projects were listed for the association to work toward, and four of them pertained to education. It also listed eight of the Assembly's accomplishments: annual conventions, *Assembly Bulletin* publications, the Youth Group, the "Message of Israel" radio series, annual sponsorship of two Jewish summer youth camps, quarterly board meetings for exchange of ideas between rabbis and laymen, talk tour series to small communities, and the Institute of Jewish Education (planned to be an annual event). It noted that the Assembly attempted to serve the state's Jewry in the same way that each congregation served its own Jewish community.[67]

It is of interest to note that the principal speaker at the Assembly's last convention, held in April 1950, was Dr. Jacob R. Marcus, founder and director of the American Jewish Archives, who spoke on "Jewry at Mid-Century—Its Romance and Its Reality." In his address he told the delegates that

> This Assembly may serve as a model of how American Jewry can best bridge differences among its variety of units and serve as a bridge between various communities and between religious and secular organizations. If you show all of us how to do this well, you give us the very model we are looking for throughout the country.[68]

But just as all the attempts have failed at the national level to create a cohesive American Jewish community, so Arkansas Jewry's attempt at the state level faltered and came to an end after some nineteen years.

Those involved in the Assembly could look back with pride on their efforts, even after it had long ceased to be. Many results remain into the 1990s. The congregations that arose from the state's smaller Jewish communities, such as McGehee, Blytheville, and El Dorado, give testimony to the Assembly's existence. All of the state's congregations were strengthened by its efforts. Because of the Assembly's scholarship fund, many young Jews received college educations through the 1930s and 1940s and went on to become successful in business and the professions. Other youths were strengthened in their faith through the work with Hillel and the junior congregations and were and are a credit to Judaism. And young people were brought together through Assembly youth work who later married.

The Assembly's efforts did not go unnoticed by a new generation in the 1980s. When a Jewish Identity Group sponsored by the Jewish Federation of Little Rock (later known as the Jewish Federation of Arkansas) learned of the Assembly and its work, several group members were inspired to revive the organization. They too sought to draw Arkansas Jewry together, but under a different format from that of the earlier Assembly. Initiated by the Federation in 1986, the New Arkansas Jewish Assembly consisted of a Jewish cultural series of three events each fall and spring. These have included entertainment as well as serious lectures, and all have been well attended.

The Warp and the Woof

1940s–1990s

MERGING OF

GERMAN AND

EAST EUROPEAN

B y the end of World War II, the state of Arkansas was in the midst of numerous changes. The natural disasters of the 1920s, the Great Depression of the 1930s, and the effects of World War II and its aftermath had changed rural Arkansas for all time. During the 1940s many left the land to join the armed forces, and others left it for the more lucrative jobs in wartime factories. While in 1935 the number of Arkansas farms stood at some 253,000, these had decreased to 95,000 by 1959.[1] The steady decline in farms continued: by 1978 there were fewer than 52,000, and by 1987 there were just over 48,000.[2] The state remained a leading cotton grower; farms simply became larger as the number of them declined. Whereas 63 percent of the state's farmers were tenants in 1930, only 24 percent were such in 1959. And by 1960 about half of the cotton crop was harvested mechanically, replacing the work that was almost totally done by hand just ten years earlier.[3]

As Arkansas saw a movement away from the land by many of its small farmers, the cities began to grow, and by 1960 half the state's population lived in urban areas (four-fifths of the population had lived on farms in 1940). Few who had left the land during World War II returned to it, and more left during the Korean War in the 1950s, seeking higher-paying jobs in other states and in war plants. By 1960 Arkansas saw a 9 percent loss of population from its 1940 census.[4]

To offset the change from a mostly rural citizenry and an agricultural economy to industrialization, the state began establishing councils and organizations in the 1940s to address the problems of balancing agriculture with new industry. Some of these organizations included the Arkansas Economic Council, which later merged with the State Chamber of Commerce, and the Arkansas Resources and Development Commission (created by the General Assembly in 1945). In 1955 the Arkansas Industrial Development Commission was created by the General Assembly, and

Winthrop Rockefeller, a Republican who had made Arkansas his home, was appointed as head of the new agency by Governor Orval E. Faubus (Rockefeller later served as governor in the period 1967–71).

While the state's leaders were gearing up to bring industrialization to Arkansas, changes at the grass roots level were having a deep effect on the state's Jewry. The move away from the land meant the slow death of once-bustling small-town Arkansas. It was in this small-town environment that many of the Jewish merchants, particularly those from East Europe, had flourished. Fewer farms meant fewer people to need consumer goods. And with the rise of mechanization in the fields, there was a drop in the number of field hands and tenant farmers who needed goods. Another factor that had a direct effect on the local merchants of small towns was that, beginning in the 1950s, Arkansas roads were finally receiving the attention they needed. While less than 25 percent of the state's roads were hard-surfaced in the 1930s, by 1969 this proportion had grown to 87 percent. And the state highway system doubled from seven thousand miles in 1923 to fourteen thousand miles in 1968.[5] By 1990 it had grown to include more than sixteen thousand miles in the state highway system and almost five hundred fifty miles in the interstate system.[6] With good roads, better cars, and unrationed gasoline, those in rural Arkansas could breeze into larger towns to purchase their needed goods for generally lower prices and thereby bypass the local merchants. Another reason for the departure of Jews from the towns and small cities was the emphasis parents placed on education for their youth. After going away to college, the young people simply did not want to come back to the stores established by their families and chose better opportunities elsewhere. (This was true of both Jewish and non-Jewish youth.)

Over the forty-five-year period subsequent to World War II, the prominence of Jewish influence on society was diminished considerably by the deaths of some of the state's most outstanding and well-respected Jewish citizens. For example, as the older owners of the large Jewish-owned stores passed away, their firms were either sold or closed. Jewish names, such as Blass, Pfeifer, and Kempner in Little Rock and other names throughout the state that had been seen every day in newspaper ads and heard on everyone's lips became but a memory. However, several prominent Jewish citizens who died left legacies that insured that their names would not be forgotten. These included members of the Ottenheimer family of Little Rock—Gus and Leonard and their sister, Gladys Hirsch, and her husband, Joe Hirsch—and Robert Sakon of England. The estates left by these citizens were such that they would benefit Arkansas for years to come. This was true also of Leah (Cohn) Arndt, the last survivor of Fort Smith pioneer Isaac Cohn, who left most of the Cohn Estate to the Fort Smith Public Library. The Ben J. Altheimer Foundation also continued to benefit the state into the 1990s.

Arkansas saw little overt anti-Semitism over the years, and it was almost ironic that Gerald Lyman Kenneth Smith, a known anti-Semite, should establish several "sacred projects" at Eureka Springs during the 1960s. His coming eventually drew other extremist groups to the northern and western sections of the state (see chapter 18).

During the last half of the twentieth century, there has been a merging of the Jews into the warp and woof of Arkansas life, which has included a merging of the East European Jews (also referred to as Russian Jews) and the German Jews. Although the latter had felt ashamed of the East Europeans, who were mostly Orthodox, when they first came to America, the Russian Jews won admiration in the long run. Within a generation the Russian Jews had begun turning Judaism in America back to a more traditional mode. They worked hard to educate their children, and many of those second-generation citizens, who soon dominated the German Jews in numbers, became their peers educationally, culturally, professionally, and economically. Coming to America virtually penniless, the Russian Jews had considered no honest job too low for them to take. They worked long and hard at menial tasks in order to raise the quality of life for their children and for themselves. "The pushcarts and sweatshops were rungs by which [they] raised themselves into manufacturing and the professions."[7] This was true generally in America and in Arkansas as well.

Members of the Orthodox and Reform branches in Arkansas began working together in common causes, such as Bonds for Israel drives, Hadassah, B'nai B'rith, and the Jewish Federation. They also began marrying without distinction between the branches (except in certain families). Whereas intermarriage with non-Jews had previously been fairly rare and at times had even generated front page news,[8] by the 1960s to the 1990s it had become commonplace among the Reform (which followed a national trend). The Jews also slowly became more accepted in social circles as old prejudices fell by the wayside. The downside to the history of this period was in the continuing loss in the number of Jews found in the state in all areas except Little Rock and northwest Arkansas. As can be seen from the following text, the small-town Jewish merchant practically disappeared over this forty-five-year period. By the 1990s there were about two thousand Jews in the state out of a general population of 2.3 million.

This section covers the changes in the state's congregations (chapter 5) and then follows some of the individuals and businesses found in section III. Chapters 16 through 18 cover the state in that section's fashion—central, eastern, and western Arkansas.

CHAPTER 15

Congregational Histories

W̱ith the exhilaration and reunions with loved ones in service brought about by the end of World War II and the impetus afforded by the rekindling of the Arkansas Jewish Assembly, the Jewish communities of Arkansas were in full swing by the beginning of the 1950s decade. Although the Assembly did not survive, it had served as a springboard for the state's Jewry, particularly in the smaller communities. During the three decades following World War II, eleven new Jewish houses of worship were built in nine cities. Seven of these replaced prior edifices. Blytheville, McGehee, and El Dorado saw their first Jewish temples, and an Orthodox synagogue was built at Hot Springs for the first time. Below are given some of the highlights of congregational histories in Arkansas during the more than forty-five years since World War II.

Little Rock

CONGREGATION B'NAI ISRAEL

Having the largest congregation in Arkansas and being led by the venerable scholar, Rabbi Ira E. Sanders, Congregation B'nai Israel of Little Rock stood head and shoulders above the other Jewish communities of the state. In 1949 B'nai Israel built an educational plant adjacent to its temple at 421 Broadway. A memorial library was opened, followed by an art gallery that connected the Educational Building with the temple. When "Uncle" Joe Goetz died in 1952 at his favorite spot in Little Rock, Travelers Field, the small savings he left to B'nai Israel were matched by others and a chapel was added to the temple.[1] The temple itself was remodeled during the period 1953–54; by the late 1950s its membership included 313 families.[2]

The respect Rabbi Sanders had generated in the 1920s and 1930s in his founding and directing of the Little Rock School of Social Work was compounded in the 1950s by his stand on the school integration crises in Little Rock (see chapter 16). He spoke out in his pulpit in support of the 1954 Supreme Court ruling. And although he was sympathetic toward Zionism, he did not espouse it in his Reform pulpit. After the Holocaust, however, the congregation realized that, because the nations of the world did not open their gates to persecuted Jews, a Jewish state was necessary. At that time the temple began to support the establishment of the State of Israel.[3]

After thirty-seven years in the pulpit, Rabbi Sanders retired from B'nai Israel in 1963 and assumed the position of rabbi emeritus, which he continued until his death in 1985. Rabbi Elijah E. Palnick, a Canadian native and Hebrew Union College graduate who had served congregations in Alabama and Florida, assumed the leadership of B'nai Israel in the fall of 1963. He came at a time when Little Rock was still feeling the after-effects of the integration crisis, and he quickly entered into the religious and civic life of the city and state. He assumed a leadership role in the Committee on Race and Religion, serving with such men as Disciples of Christ minister Rev. Colbert Cartwright and United Methodist minister Rev. William Gentry. One of Rabbi Palnick's first efforts was to host at Temple B'nai Israel a Committee's interfaith, interracial report session; some four hundred church leaders attended the meeting. (The Committee became known as the Greater Little Rock Conference on Religion and Human Relations.)[4]

Rabbi Palnick served as state chairman of the Arkansas Council on Human Relations, traveling statewide with ACHR executive director Elijah Coleman. He also served as chairman of the Interfaith Denominational Executive Roundtable and was a member of the Little Rock Committee on Foreign Relations, the Citizens Committee on Human Affairs, and the Pulaski County Office of Economic Opportunity. He represented Arkansas at the White House Conference on Children, served as president of the Southwest Region Association of Reform Rabbis, and was a member of the

Union of American Hebrew Congregations' Social Action Commission. He served on the executive board of the Central Conference of American Rabbis. He taught Bible and religion both at the University of Alabama and, later, at the University of Arkansas at Little Rock. As had Rabbi Sanders before him, he received the National Conference of Christians and Jews' National Humanitarian Award from the NCCJ's Arkansas Council on Brotherhood. He was also honored by several of Little Rock's African-American churches. After a Jewish congregation formed at Fayetteville in 1981, Rabbi Palnick assisted in its congregational life.

Within the context of interfaith marriages, Rabbi Palnick broke with tradition and performed such ceremonies. In this, he followed the trend found at the time in religious groups, such as Catholic, Protestant, and others. (Most of the couples of the interfaith marriages he conducted between Jews and non-Jews chose to raise their children in the Jewish faith.)[5] Rabbi Palnick—who, with his wife, the former Irene Melton, had two children, a son Lazar and a daughter Rachelle—served Congregation B'nai Israel through 1986.

When a multi-story building was planned at Fifth and Broadway streets in Little Rock, a momentous decision was made by members of Congregation B'nai Israel to vacate the beautiful old temple and build a new house of worship in West Little Rock. The temple was destroyed, but its lovely furnishings were transferred to a modern, commodious edifice built at 3700 Rodney Parham Road; the old temple's exterior carved stones were sold to its members and to the Little Rock community. At the new temple's dedication in May 1975, 342 families were listed as members in its dedication program. (Jewish congregations count memberships by families, rather than by individuals.)

During the years subsequent to World War II and with the increased interest in Zionism, the Reform movement nationwide, which included Arkansas, began to make a slow but steady return to a more traditional worship service. Those of B'nai Israel who were older and had been raised in Reform's services, which had been conducted almost entirely in English, saw any changes as spurious. During the fall 1977 High Holiday Services, one of the temple's members, prominent Little Rock attorney Phil Kaplan, acted as cantor and gave the Haftorah portion in Hebrew while wearing a tallit (prayer shawl) and yarmulke (skullcap). After the High Holidays, temple president Eugene Weinstein received a number of letters protesting such a turn from the historically Reform stand. Petitions of protest also were circulated, which contained some fifty signatures. He also received ten letters, generally from younger members, that viewed the service favorably.[6] Other changes were moving B'nai Israel into a more traditional stance; for example, by the 1980s many of its young members were becoming bar mitzvah and bat mitzvah as well as confirmed.

In 1987 Rabbi Eugene Levy, a native of San Antonio, Texas, and also a Hebrew Union College graduate, became leader of Congregation B'nai Israel. When he had been a senior at HUC, his class had been told that if they wanted to "make anything of [their] rabbinate, [they] would have to go east of the Mississippi and north of the Ohio River."[7] Rabbi Levy had done the opposite, serving for twelve years at the Reform congregation in Tyler, Texas, and three years as director of the Hillel Foundation at the University of Oklahoma. A gracious, caring, and knowledgeable person, he was well received in Little Rock among both the Jewish and the non-Jewish communities. By the end of the 1980s, B'nai Israel had about four hundred families as members. (While about half of the members of B'nai Israel who married during the period from the 1960s to the 1980s were united with non-Jews, the non-Jewish spouses, for the most part, either converted or agreed to raise any children of their unions in the Jewish faith.)[8]

Those who served as presidents of B'nai Israel from the 1940s to the 1990s were S. Lasker Ehrman, Leo Pfeifer, Roy Harris, Louis Rosen, Harry Lasker, Dr. Jerome S. Levy, Sol F. Klarberg, Henry Spitzberg, Phillip Back, Arnold Mayersohn, James B. Pfeifer Sr., Max Heiman, Arnold Goodman, Gene Weinstein, Arthur Pfeifer, Dr. Wilma Diner, Allen Mendel, Dave Grundfest Jr., Joseph Kaufman, Mrs. Dale Ronnel, Dr. Richard Lewis, and Leonard Hasson.[9]

SYNAGOGUE AGUDATH ACHIM

Changes were also occurring after World War II in Little Rock's other Jewish congregation, the Orthodox Agudath Achim. Its members decided to tear down its old synagogue, constructed in the 1880s, and build a new edifice at the same location at Eighth and Louisiana Streets. One of the most popular rabbis ever to serve the congregation, Rabbi Samuel Fox, came in 1949 and helped promote the new building. A. J. Goldman chaired the building committee, and dedication of the new synagogue was held 14 December 1952. Mark Lipman, a Little Rock private detective and congregational president at the time, wrote at the dedication, "When men dream of things that men can do . . . they accomplish what men can do, but when men dream dreams of what G-d can do, they build for eternity."[10] A Sunday School for the congregation's children was inaugurated.

A cheder (Hebrew class) was also inaugurated, which was held four afternoons a week.

Although new and accommodating, the Little Rock Orthodox synagogue's location presented several problems: it was situated on a busy downtown street, parking was difficult, and most of its members lived at least seven miles away (the congregation's rabbis who lived away from downtown had to register in a nearby hotel each Shabbat in order not to walk farther than their religious law would allow). In 1965 property was purchased at 7901 West Fifth Street, and several temporary buildings were used for classrooms and worship until a new synagogue at that location was completed and dedicated in May 1976.

Rabbi Fox left in 1954, and the congregation was headed by several leaders from the 1950s to the 1970s. These included Rabbis Irwin Groner, Aaron Shapiro, Weisenfeld, Sheldon Stauber, Seymour Atlas, and Sheldon Kilimnick, who was serving when the new synagogue was erected and dedicated. Rabbi Seymour Weller, who was given the title of "rabbi for life," joined the synagogue as leader in 1977. An astute scholar and educator, he was well received among the Jewish and non-Jewish communities of Little Rock. He served as auxiliary chaplain at Little Rock Air Force Base and the two Veterans Administration Hospitals in the Greater Little Rock area and on a number of civic boards. By the end of the 1980s, the Orthodox synagogue had some 150 family members, some of whom also belonged to the Reform temple. After the furor that had come about when Phil Kaplan had been cantor in the Reform temple, several of B'nai Israel families joined the synagogue and became active members.

Those who have served the synagogue as presidents since the 1940s are Ben Kluglose, Mark Lipman, Albert Korenblat, Sol Alman, Bob Itzkowitz, Z. Bensky, Herman Loket, Ben Spector, Marvin Cohen, Maurice Besser, Charles Kluglose, Dr. Gary Weisbly, Dr. Irving Kuperman, Sheldon Taxer, Eric Nussbaum, David Greenbaum, Jeff Baskin, Dr. Glenn Lowitz, Dr. James Aronson, and Dr. Sam Goldstein.[11]

Concordia, the Jewish social club, had sold its building before World War II, and a Jewish country club, Westridge, was established in Southwest Little Rock. Interest in the club waned after World War II, and the facilities were sold.

Over the forty-five-year period between World War II and the 1990s, the Reform and Orthodox communities were slowly drawn together as they had never been before. One of the strongest common denominators was the State of Israel. Leaders for the Israel Bonds drive in Little Rock were found in both groups. Phillip Back, who headed Israel Bonds campaigns for a number of years and whose family originally came from an Orthodox background, was active in the Reform temple, and he served as a bridge between the Jewish communities.

JEWISH FEDERATION OF LITTLE ROCK

The Jewish Federation of Little Rock also was a common meeting ground for the Orthodox and Reform. It had been organized as a charity in 1912, and by World War II it was known as the Federation of Jewish Charities and Jewish Welfare Fund. At that time, Elsa K. Rosenthal served ably as executive director. She inaugurated the *Welfare News*, which was sent to the local Jewish community as well as to its men in military service. Subsequently, the office was conducted by Isabel Cooper, a quiet, reserved person. In the mid-1970s the Jewish Welfare Agency was replaced by the Jewish Federation of Little Rock.

The Little Rock Jewish community considered it their good fortune when Nanci Goldman, who moved to Little Rock with her husband, Stephen and her family in 1968, was hired as the Federation's director in September 1977. Nanci proved to be the driving force behind the organization's growth from a small, one-room office to large facilities in the Little Rock area (it was housed in several locations). Its purview reached out beyond charity to include a multifaceted education program. The Federation began making data on Jewish culture available in the state's schools, conducting classes on Holocaust studies, providing volunteer speakers for churches and civic groups, and working as a clearing house for local and state Jewish events. By the mid-1980s the Federation's budget had reached $245,000. After Nanci resigned as Federation head in 1988, she served as president of the Little Rock Chapter of Hadassah. She was succeeded at the Federation office by Ariel B. Imber, who promoted it into a statewide organization—the Jewish Federation of Arkansas. Imber was succeeded by Harvey Luber in March 1993.

Had the leaders of the original Arkansas Jewish Assembly—who had sought to bring together the Jews of Arkansas into one umbrella group—lived to see the 1990s, they would no doubt have been pleased that their goal was coming to pass. The Jewish Federation of Arkansas also became involved in camp scholarships, the Our House Shelter for the Homeless, the Voluntary Organizations Active in Disaster, the Arkansas Interfaith Conference, the Ati' Day Yisroel Nursery School (located at Temple B'nai Israel, Little Rock), the University of Arkansas Hillel Foundation, the New Arkansas Jewish Assembly (a culturally oriented organization), the

B'nai B'rith Home for the Aged (Memphis), the Leo N. Levi Hospital (Hot Springs), the Israeli Youth Delegation, and the Israeli Scouts. It also was helping Russian Jewish immigrant families to settle in Little Rock.[12]

The Jewish Federation cooperated closely with the Arkansas Council on Brotherhood of the National Conference of Christians and Jews. Ron Lanoue, a member of Congregation B'nai Israel who had served for more than eleven years as director of planning for the University of Arkansas for Medical Sciences, was named director of the Arkansas Council on Brotherhood of the NCCJ in 1985. He was the third executive director of the NCCJ's Arkansas unit, which was formed in the mid-1960s. In the 1980s the Arkansas Council on Brotherhood of the NCCJ began sponsoring "Anytown Arkansas," which involved students of Arkansas's high schools in a one-week camping program. The purpose of the camp was to help the delegates learn respect for those with diverse cultural, ethnic, and religious backgrounds.

HADASSAH

The Little Rock Chapter of Hadassah, composed mostly of women from the Orthodox community in its early years, saw its membership grow in the Reform community over the decades. In the 1960s Little Rock Hadassah began sponsoring a Young Judaea chapter, which emphasized education for Jewish youth regarding the State of Israel. (One of its early leaders, Melanie Bernhard, headed the regional Young Judaea program. She was assisted in Little Rock by Robin LeMaster. Melanie later married Stephen Rosenberg of Long Island, New York, and in the mid-1970s the couple made their home in Israel, where Melanie became a well-known writer and journalist. Robin, who became a nurse, lived in Israel several years, and while working at Hadassah Hospital in Jerusalem, she met and later married cardiologist Dr. Joe L. Rod.) Little Rock Hadassah grew significantly under Nanci Goldman's presidency in the 1980s, drawing members statewide, and it became known as the Arkansas Chapter of Hadassah. Besides Nanci, several of its members served on Hadassah's regional board, including Velma Block, Bella Levy, and Susie Balkin. Arkansas Hadassah began holding joint meetings with the Sisterhoods of both Temple B'nai Israel and Synagogue Agudath Achim.

ATI' DAY SCHOOL

In 1973 the Jewish community of Little Rock saw the need for a nursery school for its children. The Ati' ("Our Future") Day School was opened in

September 1973 with six students and one teacher and one hundred dollars in its checking account. Other programs were later added to the school, such as day care and summer day camps. By 1988, the school had grown to include some forty students, a principal (Gail Schwartz), three preschool teachers, three assistant teachers, afternoon day-care teachers, and several other assistants.[13] In 1992 Terry Heard was principal of the school, which had about fifty students, five teachers, five assistants, and several helpers.

Little Rock's Elias Navra Lodge of B'nai B'rith had a resurgence of interest in the early 1980s. The organization became involved with the American Red Cross programs, sponsored political speeches, and established an ongoing education program. In November 1988 Drs. Ray Biondo and Gerald Weiss of Little Rock helped establish Arkansas Post 436 of the Jewish War Veterans of the United States. Dr. Weiss served as the first acting commander of the group, which became almost immediately one of Little Rock's most active Jewish organizations.

In 1992 a branch of the Hasidic sect of Judaism known as Lubavitch was opened in Little Rock, headed by Rabbi Pinchus Ciment and his wife, Esther Hadassah. (The Lubavitch movement was originally brought from Russia to America in 1940 by Rabbi Joseph Isaac Schneersohn.)[14] The thrust of the group's worship centers on Chabad (a Hebrew acronym meaning knowledge, wisdom, understanding), which teaches that all aspects of life should be translated into service for God. The Little Rock Lubavitch branch was one of two hundred such centers nationwide.

Pine Bluff

Congregation Anshe Emeth, which had formed shortly before B'nai Israel of Little Rock in the 1860s, began its post–World War II years with a flourish. By the 1960s, however, membership stood at 230 families, and the number was steadily dropping. As agriculture became mechanized, the multitude of farmers that had at one time surrounded Pine Bluff began to wane, and the future looked bleak for the once-thriving stores. The congregation's large temple, which at one time had been packed on High Holy Days, became rather roomy; in addition, its location in a residential area that was declining in value did not help the situation. In 1961 the congregation followed the residential trend to the southwest section of the city and purchased two and one-half acres at Fortieth and Hickory Streets. A new building was completed in September 1967. The congregation had decreased so much since its large temple was built in 1902, at which time it was the second largest temple in the state (after Little Rock's B'nai Israel's), that the one built in the 1960s was one of the state's smallest Jewish houses of worship.

Since Rabbi Morris Clark left the congregation in 1949, subsequent leaders have been Rabbis Henry Sandman, Solomon Herbst, Hyman Solomon, Herbert J. Weiss, Solomon Kaplan, S. Howard Schwartz, and Alvin Sugarman. Rabbi Leslie Sirtes served the congregation from 1970 until the mid-1980s, after which Hebrew Union College students were engaged for the High Holy Days and for monthly visits. Lay members began leading services between the rabbis' visits. By 1992 there were about forty individual members of the temple.[15]

Those who have served as president of Anshe Emeth from the 1940s to 1990s include William Rosenzweig, Charles Dante, Henry Marx, Hubert Eisenkramer, Jerome "Jerry" Glatstein, Harold Morris, Sam Levine, Leonard Selig, William Sherman, David Bram, Merritt Fruhman, Morris Rosen, Sam Goldweber, Lou Siegel, Maurice Cohen, Paul Greenberg, Robert Banks, Joe and Charlotte Webberman, Susie Marx, Sheldon Blau, Ira Gershner, Henry Levi, Louis Siegel, Kenneth Baim, Robert Rosen, and Stanley Maas.[16]

Helena

Congregation Beth El's temple at Helena is the oldest Jewish house of worship in the state that continues with a Jewish congregation. (The temple built by Anshe Emeth of Pine Bluff in 1902 still stands, but it was sold in the 1960s; in the 1980s a black Baptist congregation owned it.) Helena's temple was remodeled at one time, but in the 1970s it was restored to its former beauty.

Rabbis who served the congregation after World War II were Nathan Barasch, William B. Schwartz, and Samuel R. Shillman. Subsequently, retired Rabbi James A. Wax of Memphis visited the congregation on High Holy Days and on monthly visits. An astute leader, he endeared himself to the community. By 1967 the congregation's membership was sixty-eight families; by the 1980s it had dropped to forty-two families and was on a steady decline. Presidents of the congregation subsequent to World War II have been Solomon Feldman, John Hyman, Bertram M. Solomon, Aubrey Solomon, David Solomon, Abe Danziger, Alvin Solomon, Irvin Levine, and M. Gradus.[17]

Camden

The Jewish community of Camden might be likened, on a very small scale, to the Jewish community of Newport, Rhode Island, which was one of the first thriving Jewish settlements in America. As did the one in Rhode Island, the Camden Jewish community flourished, and its members became prominent in the business and civic life of the town. They contributed generously to the town's growth. But, just as Newport Jewry became a "nostalgic memory" and was remembered by Henry Longfellow and Emma Lazarus in poems that cited, of all things, its cemetery, all that remains of the Camden Jewish community's illustrious past in the 1990s (except for one lone Jewish family), is its cemetery. As Longfellow said, "Gone are the living, but the dead remain . . ."[18]

Henry Berg, who had been so vitally interested in the Arkansas Jewish Assembly and who had, with the organization's encouragement, built a small Jewish temple at Camden, died in 1950. (The building was sold and made into a private residence in the 1980s.) In the 1960s and 1970s Harry B. Solmson Jr. of Memphis and Evelyn (Levy) Rosenbaum of St. Louis, whose family relatives were buried at Camden, contacted surviving members of those buried at Camden, and a substantial trust was established to care for the Jewish cemetery in perpetuity. In 1989 a gift of one thousand dollars was given from the cemetery fund to the Camden Area United Way fund. Edwin Horton, president of Camden's First National Bank, which administers Beth El Emeth's trust fund, was "very moved" when Harry Solmson and Evelyn Rosenbaum made the contribution; he cited Camden's Jewish citizens as being "really . . . prominent leaders" in the 1800s and early 1900s.[19]

El Dorado

The Jewish community in El Dorado, thirty-two miles southeast of Camden, was more fortunate than the Jewish community of the latter city in that it still had some thirty Jewish families at the close of World War II. Encouraged by the Arkansas Jewish Assembly, the El Dorado Jewish community met regularly in rented quarters on North Washington Street. The Jewish community was also fortunate in having J. B. Miller, a trained Hebrew scholar, as lay leader.

In the 1950s a building project was initiated, and citizens and businesses in El Dorado gave generously to it. Jack Prince, a singer who had appeared in the Broadway show *Guys and Dolls* and was a nephew of a couple in nearby Calion, gave a benefit concert in the old El Dorado High School auditorium to help raise building funds. I. L. Pesses, a congregation member who later became mayor of El Dorado, was owner of a construction company at the time and erected the temple. It was completed with no mortgage on it. J. B. Miller continued as leader until his death in 1970. A Hebrew Union College rabbinical student served on High Holy Days. When the congregation sought deeper instruction in Judaism, Rabbi Joseph Levine of Texarkana came once a month during the 1960s and 1970s. He held services on Friday evenings, had a discussion group and dinner on Saturday evenings, and assisted with the religious school on Sunday mornings. He did not drive a car but rode the bus to El Dorado. As he did in Texarkana, he enjoyed walking the streets of El Dorado and visiting with those he met; he was beloved by all who knew him.

By the 1980s only a half dozen Jewish families remained in the city, and a Christian group rented the temple, which helped with its upkeep. Only a Sunday School functioned by the 1980s, taught by Janet Stuart.[20]

Hot Springs

Membership of Congregation House of Israel at Hot Springs grew after World War II, and the city bustled again as a spa, drawing tourists nationwide. Toward the end of the 1950s, the old temple built in 1905 was torn down, and a building known as Burgauer Hall was erected and used for worship until a new auditorium was completed in 1965. The new temple's interior architecture, which symbolized Judaism and its history, was unique in comparison with any other of the state's Jewish houses of worship.[21]

House of Israel continued its good fortune in the quality of spiritual leaders who served it. Rabbi W. Kaelter, who served from 1945 to 1949, was elected president of the Hot Springs Symphony Society. Rabbi Martin M. Weitz, who served from 1949 to 1951, a prolific writer, compiled a history of Hot Springs and the city's Reform Jewish congregation (*Diamond Jubilee Bibilog . . . Temple Beth Israel, May 1950* (Hot Springs; Ark.: M.P., 1950). He was active in civic work as well, serving on the board of the Hot Springs Civic Improvement Association. Rabbi Samson A. Shain, who served from 1951 to 1956, a graduate of Harvard University and the Jewish Institute of Religion, had done graduate work at Columbia and at Hebrew University in Jerusalem. He was active in the Garland County Boy Scout Council. Rabbi Albert A. Michels followed Rabbi Shain, serving from 1956 until the mid-1970s. During his tenure he served as president of the Hot Springs Ministerial Alliance. Having served with distinction as a World War II chaplain, Michels became a popular lecturer throughout the Southeast.

Rabbi Selvyn Goldberg, of Manchester, England, who served from 1974 to 1981, became one of House of Israel's most respected leaders. He endeared himself to his congregants and to the community at large. It was he who conceived of an apartment complex for the elderly that was later built adjacent to the Levi Hospital. (The apartment building was called Levi Towers.) After he died suddenly in October 1981, his friend, Rev. Doug Dickens, pastor of the First Baptist Church of Hot Springs, delivered the Yom Kippur (Day of Atonement) sermon at House of Israel.

Leaders who served House of Israel subsequent to Rabbi Goldberg have included Rabbis Tom Friedmann, J. Heyman (a Little Rock native), Angela Grayboys (who was the first female rabbi to serve full time in an Arkansas pulpit), and Matthew Friedman. (Friedman had served as a student rabbi at both Texarkana and Fort Smith before joining the Hot Springs congregation.) By the 1980s some eighty families were associated with House of Israel. Its membership held rather steady over the years, as Hot Springs, with its multiple lakes, museums, amusement parks, and lovely scenery, remained one of the state's most popular areas for tourists. By the late 1980s Hot Springs' House of Israel was the only congregation in the state outside Little Rock that maintained a full-time rabbi. This was made possible in part by the fact that the local rabbi also served as a chaplain to the Levi Hospital, which underwrote part of the rabbi's salary.

House of Israel members who served as president of the congregation subsequent to World War II were Dr. Alex Benedikt, Paul Forshberg, Robert Gartenberg, Lewis Goltz, Walter Kleinman, Louis Kleinman, Harry Kupperman, Dr. Hal Koppel, Harold Krane, Dr. Martin Lax, Jay Leiber, Hubert Mendel, Ed Rephan, Bernard Rephan, Dr. J. L. Rosenzweig, Bernard Silverman, Howard Schlesinger, Martin Fleishner, Mark Fleishner, Irving Greenberg, Steve Kirsch, Arthur Stone, Leo Gartenberg, Al Lasky, and Gary Lax.[22]

BETH JACOB

In 1950 the Orthodox Jewish community of Hot Springs erected a modest synagogue, Beth Jacob, at 200 Quapaw Street, just one block down from the Reform House of Israel and directly across the street from the Leo N. Levi Hospital. Numbers of Orthodox Jewish tourists had been drawn to the city through the years, and after World War II, about thirty or more were permanent residents of Hot Springs. The group had, at first, converted a second-floor apartment in a downtown Central Avenue building (which was later torn down) and used it as a small synagogue. Members of the group included Morris Ostrow, Morris Frank, S. A. Long, A. Ritter, Abe Miller, Jack M. Miller, Max Isken, I. Berland, Samuel Rochefsky, Samuel H. Kirsch, Meyer Weiss, Murray Forshberg, Henry Gottlieb, and Joe Spitzer. Both Ostrow and Kirsch are known to have served as presidents of the congregation. Morris Ehrenberg was architect for the building.

Samuel Kirsch was typical of the Orthodox group. Born in Russia in 1897 and brought to New York at age six, he had moved to Hot Springs around 1940. Deeply religious, he became involved in the city's Orthodox community. In the 1980s his son Eugene "Gene" Kirsch was serving as overseer of Beth Jacob. Services were held on High Holy Days, and a cantor hired for the event. The synagogue also was available for special occasions. Some of Beth Jacob's members also affiliated with the Reform House of Israel.[23]

LEO N. LEVI HOSPITAL

By 1951 an administrative crisis at Leo N. Levi Hospital at Hot Springs had placed the facility in financial straits, and B'nai B'rith's Supreme Lodge Executive Committee as well as a number of interested individuals helped rescue it from closing. Dave Grundfest of Little Rock was one of the individuals who helped, as was (former Arkansan) David Blumberg of Knoxville, Tennessee. The facility was closed as a general hospital in 1952 and was devoted exclusively to arthritis treatment. Several new facilities were added through the years—the Gladys M. Harrison Pavilion in 1966, the Jack R. Linsky Pavilion in 1969, and the McLaughlin Wing in 1972. From 1976 to 1978 there was a major renovation of all patient care areas, and two additional floors were added to the Harrison Wing during the period.

After Regina Kaplan retired as administrator, Fannie (Benedikt) McLaughlin served in that capacity from 1950 to 1970. Administrators who followed her were Warner Kass, Harry A. Rosenzweig, Richard Bluestein, Dale E. Wagoner, and Pat McCabe. The name of the hospital was shortened to Levi Hospital in the 1980s.[24]

Texarkana

In 1947 Texarkana's Mt. Sinai Congregation sold its property, located on the Arkansas side of the city, and bought new property at 1310 Walnut

Street on the Texas side. At that time the congregation was composed of about forty Texarkana families and seven families from the surrounding area. During construction of the new temple, the congregation used a room in the Miller County Courthouse for regular meetings; High Holy Day services were held at the nearby Congregational Church. The new temple, of modern architecture and low-pitched roof, was dedicated in March 1949. Additional classrooms were needed within five years, and several were added in 1956.

Spiritual leaders who served the temple subsequent to World War II were Rabbis Moses M. Landau from 1946 to 1950, Avery J. Grossfield from 1951 to 1954, Harry B. Ettinger from 1954 to 1956, and Joseph Levine from 1958 to 1981.

Rabbi Levine, Mt. Sinai's last full-time spiritual head, became an outstanding leader in Texarkana's religious and civic life. During his twenty-three years in the city, his scholarly teachings and his warm, loving personality were poured out on his adopted community. Son of an Orthodox rabbi and the youngest of thirteen children, he had espoused Reform Judaism and its liberal teachings. He was a popular speaker and his frequent lectures were well received, as evidenced when he was given a prolonged standing ovation after a talk to the Texarkana American Legion Post in 1971. His speech was described as "one of the most masterful addresses ever to be heard" within the city.[25] His concern for the citizens of Texarkana did not go unnoticed. A full-page article in the *Texarkana Gazette* on Easter Sunday (April 4) in 1974 was headlined "Brotherhood: Rabbi Joseph Levine Spreads His Love." It was noted that the rabbi had displayed brotherhood "equal to no other" in the city's area. After his death, the Greater Texarkana Ministerial Alliance honored him by dedicating its 1981 Brotherhood Service award to him.

After Rabbi Levine's death in 1981, the congregation was served by students from Hebrew Union College. Between the students' visits, Leo Walkow served as lay leader and prepared youngsters for their bar mitzvahs or bat mitzvahs. His services were given permanent honor when the temple's social hall was rededicated as the "Leo A. Walkow Hall."[26]

Dedicated individuals served as Mt. Sinai's president through the years, including Max Wexler, Leo Walkow, Jeff Steinhart, Joe Ruskin, Ed Pearlman, Jake Meyers, Sherman Kusin, Melvin Kusin, Henry Kaufman, John Hearn, Mordecai Glick, Howard Glick, Ruben Gilden, Leon Friedman, Harry Friedman, Don Friedman, Ralph Brody, Leo Bishkin, and Leon Arnold. In 1987 the congregation elected its first woman president, Mrs. Leo Bishkin. B'nai B'rith Women of Texarkana, which was established in 1947, continued through the years, meeting on the same night as the men's B'nai B'rith lodge.[27]

Ralph Brody, a pillar of strength among Mt. Sinai's membership, promoted the development and transformation of the congregation's cemetery from a somewhat neglected condition to a beautiful memorial park (it was renamed "Mt. Sinai Memorial Park" in 1974.) He was assisted by Leon Friedman in landscaping the area. They were both, along with the entire congregation, grieved when twenty-seven monuments were vandalized in 1980. Brody himself was laid to rest in his beloved park in October 1986.

Membership in Mt. Sinai has remained static through the years, but its numbers are declining by age and relocations. About forty families, located in Texarkana and the surrounding area, were members in the late 1980s.[28]

Fort Smith

By 1950 the Jewish community of Fort Smith was in full swing. All its activity centered around the temple and the local B'nai B'rith lodge. United Hebrew Congregation's Sunday School had five trained teachers. The Sisterhood was active and had a number of circles; combined, they would sponsor entertaining and profitable affairs, such as square dances, turkey suppers, and canasta tournaments. In 1950 a "Supper Club" was established, which included discussions, led at the time by Rabbi S. Kleinberg.[29]

In 1955 UHC sold its house of worship at 422 North Eleventh Street to the First Evangelical Lutheran Church. A new temple with modern, straight lines was erected at 126 North Forty-Seventh Street and dedicated on 29 April 1956. Rabbi Sanders of Little Rock, the dedication speaker, said of the ceremony, "This is no dedication of bricks and steel, but a dedication of dutism and Americanism for our coming generations."[30] The membership of UHC at the time was sixty-five families.

Except for a short period during the war, Rabbi Samuel Teitelbaum served UHC from 1927 until 1946. Spiritual leaders subsequent to him were Rabbis S. Kleinberg, M. Mann, Albert Friedlander, Maurice Feuer, H. Richard White, and Sol Kaplan. From 1968 to 1974 Rabbi Kaplan, who lived in Dallas and was director of the Southwest region of the Union of American Hebrew Congregations, served UHC twenty-two times a year, including the High Holy Days. Since that time, the congregation has been served by Hebrew Union College students.

The mortgage on UHC's new temple was burned in September 1968 by Alvin Tilles. The building sustained damage from a fire in 1970, and the congregation met in the First United Methodist Church and the Salvation Army building while it was being repaired. UHC celebrated its centennial year in 1986 with a gala dinner.

As were other small congregations in Arkansas, the temple was fortunate in having strong lay leaders through the years. Newsy bulletins entitled *The Temple Tablet* have kept members informed of congregational life. The temple parking lot was resurfaced in 1985. Community seders (Passover meals) are offered; eighty members and guests attended the event in 1986. Members also started a museum fund in 1987. Weekly services were still being held in the 1990s, with an HUC rabbinical student visiting twice monthly and lay leaders Mort Marks and Felix Pansy conducting the services on the other Friday evenings. At the beginning of the 1990s, membership included some thirty-nine families, most of whom were over age sixty. Religious school was composed of three or four children; only occasionally did new families move into the area.

Members of UHC who served as its president subsequent to World War II were Louis Cohen, Dr. E. A. Mendelsohn, M. B. Marks Jr., A. E. Laytin, Newton Pollock, Sam Goodkin, Gerald Bogoslavsky, Nicol L. Wintory, Mrs. Sue Sherman, Robert S. Blatt, Felix E. Pansy, and Mrs. Ted Miller.

Jonesboro

With the impetus given by the Arkansas Jewish Assembly during the 1930s and 1940s, Jonesboro's Temple Israel saw a resurgence of interest. A B'nai B'rith's Women's Group was formed in the 1940s, known as the Elise Schoenberg Chapter. Congregation members were active in various civic drives, and annual brotherhood services were held with local Christians. Temple Israel celebrated its sixtieth anniversary in 1958 with a gala event. Four of its original members were present: Hugo Sachs, Mrs. M. Stonefield, Mrs. Rosa Rosenfield, and Jake Schoenberger.

As membership increased after World War II, a larger facility was needed, and in 1959 the temple was sold to the First Baptist Church. (At that time, the building was the oldest house of worship in Jonesboro as well as one of the oldest in eastern Arkansas.) The new temple was built in a residential area at Oak and Madison streets, and its contemporary structure was a far cry from the synagogue type of design of the old edifice. The new facility had almost four thousand square feet of floor space, about twice that of the first building. Congregants were drawn not only from Jonesboro, but also Lake City, Marked Tree, and Paragould.[31]

Temple Israel's Sisterhood was active through the years, and it was quite successful in raising funds from its annual sale of Holland bulbs. In 1957 it was recognized by the National Federation of Temple Sisterhoods for contributing the largest per capita amounts to the Youth, Education, and Scholarship Fund. The membership of Temple Israel in the 1980s was thirty-three families, with congregants coming from Paragould, Corning, Amagon, and Marked Tree in Arkansas, and from Cardwell and Poplar Bluff in Missouri. At least a dozen members were from single families.

A 1980s newcomer to the Jonesboro area, who had come from a northern congregation with a membership of about three hundred families, said she suffered a culture shock after moving to Jonesboro, where she found about a dozen active Jewish families. After adjusting to the change, however, she said she would not want to live in the North again. She was pleased with the rapport she found among the city's Jewish citizens.[32]

Temple Israel could not support a full-time rabbi, and it shared the cost of one with Temple Israel at Blytheville. Rabbi Alfred Vise, a German refugee, was the last such spiritual leader to serve the two congregations. He served the groups from 1945 until his death in 1957. By 1990 the congregation had fewer than two dozen member families, and a student rabbi was serving twice annually.

Members who served as its president subsequent to World War II include Julius Jacobs, Aaron Modelevsky, Morris Rubenstein, Sam Levitt, Abe Blindman, Stuart Frankel, Bernard Samuels, Sam Buchman, Joe Blindman, Simon Nisenbaum, Charles Katz, Mel Freed, Marty Buchman, Herb Hahn, and Joe Heinemann. Temple Israel had a bright spot in the beginning of the 1990s decade: the congregation saw its first Brith Milah (circumcision ceremony) in thirty years on 5 October 1991.[33]

Blytheville

Although there was a surge of interest in Jewish congregational life in Blytheville in the 1940s that culminated in the building of a temple whose mortgage was paid off by 1950, the numbers needed to sustain it financially dropped sharply in the 1950s. The city had been a major cotton-producing and cotton-handling area, but the changes in the farming community in Arkansas had a tremendous effect on local merchants and businessmen. By 1955 Blytheville's Temple Israel was down to twenty-seven member families, and more members were planning to move. The congregation mourned the passing of their beloved Rabbi Vise in 1957. He was loved not only by his own congregation and the local community, but he also had become "like a father" to the men at nearby Blytheville Air Force Base.[34]

During Temple Israel's busiest years, from 1947 to 1972, seventy children had been instructed in its religious school; twenty bar mitzvahs and five bat mitzvahs had been held, and fifteen youngsters had been confirmed. There were twenty-six children enrolled in 1972, the silver anniversary year of the temple's building. Family seders were held on the second night of Passover. The home built for Rabbi Vise in 1951 was debt free shortly after it was constructed, and it was dedicated for educational purposes in 1967. The temple's sanctuary was also dedicated that year to the memory of Siegbert Jiedel as a lasting reminder of his efforts in its construction. Temple Israel had devoted women members, such as Mrs. Jerry (Huddy) Cohen, temple organist, who organized a youth choir (she was elected Blytheville's "Woman of the Year" in 1954). One of the Temple's Sisterhood presidents, Mrs. George (Norma) Fisher, served as president of the National Federation of Temple Sisterhoods, District 16, for the 1972–74 term.[35]

The memberships of the temple in 1947 and 1972 were compared at that time. The 1947 list included one hundred nine adults, eighty-one of whom were from seven Arkansas towns and twenty-eight of whom were from seven Missouri towns. In 1972 there were thirty-two adults from four Arkansas towns and thirty-nine adults from five Missouri towns.[36] The temple's 1980–81 membership list showed thirty-five adults from four Arkansas towns and thirty-one from six Missouri towns. By the end of the 1980s, only three Jewish families were left in Blytheville. Most of the membership of Temple Israel was drawn from southeastern Missouri and western Tennessee.[37]

Temple Israel presidents who served from the 1940s to the 1970s included (from Arkansas) William Borowsky, Jerry Cohen, George Fisher, Richard Jiedel, Siegbert Jiedel, Hyman Weinberg, Nathan Weinberg, and Arthur Bass. Those given particular credit for temple activities at the Silver Anniversary Celebration were Walter Rosenthal, Kohath Harwarg, George Fisher, Arthur Bass, and Huddy Cohen.[38]

McGehee

By the mid-1980s the membership at Meir Chayim had slipped to twenty families, and four of these were associate members. A Hebrew Union College student was engaged for monthly visits. The congregation did not maintain a Sunday School; the four children of its members attended such services at Greenville, Mississippi. The congregation realistically contemplated a trust fund to care for its building when a sustaining membership no longer existed.[39] Meir Chayim profited greatly from the services of Hebrew Union College rabbinical students, as did most of Arkansas's small Jewish congregations. The students served Meir Chayim for some forty years, and in 1991 the student rabbi was Jeffrey Astrachan, whose father, Rabbi George Astrachan, had served the same congregation twenty-seven years previously. One of Meir Chayim's associate members, B. J. Tanenbaum Jr., served as vice-chairman of the Union of American Hebrew Congregations and as a vice-president of the World Union for Progressive Judaism; he also was a member of the Hebrew Union College Board of Governors.

The Dave Meyer Lodge of B'nai B'rith at McGehee, with twelve members in the 1990s, continued to be active. Meir Chayim members who served as its presidents subsequent to World War II were William Hamburger, A. L. Ruskin, Bernard Cohen, Joe Goldstein, Martin Dreyfus, Mercer Wolff, Seymour Fleisig, Haskell Wolff, Jay R. Lewis, Harry Phillips, Bernard Levi, B. J. Tanenbaum Jr., Leo Levi, J. H. Slager Jr., Robert J. Heiman, Charles H. Dante, Barry Brunner, Patricia W. Tanenbaum, and Lester and Linda Pinkus.[40]

Fayetteville

Over the years only a few Jews settled in Fayetteville, the home of the University of Arkansas and the Razorback sports program. In the 1950s Dr. Barnett Sure (see section III) was joined by Drs. Jacob and Wilma Sacks. Dr. Sure had helped with the work of Hillel from the 1930s until it ceased in the 1940s. Hillel was revived in the mid-1960s by the efforts of U of A students Harry L. Ehrenberg Jr., Jerry Glatstein, Nan Selz Brown, and Robert "Bud" Brown. U of A professors also helped with its reestablishment, including Jerome Rappaport, Dr. Mort and Norma Gitelman (who served as Hillel advisors), and the two Dr. Sacks (Dr. Sure had died in 1957).

Beginning in the 1960s the Northwest corner of the state began rapid development of industry. This included companies such as Hudson Foods, Tyson's (chicken and food products), Wal-Mart, Jones Truck Lines, and others. With this growth, new workers were needed as well as professional managers. This brought Jewish families into the area (several towns profited from this trade boom, including Rogers, Springdale, Bentonville, and the retirement community of Bella Vista). In addition, the U of A generally had several Jewish professors. By the early 1980s there were about three dozen Jewish families in the Fayetteville area, and the closest services for them to attend were either at Fort Smith, some sixty-three miles south, or Tulsa, some one hundred twenty miles west. Because of the distance, most Jewish life in the area centered around the Hillel house.

Because of the growing need for Jewish community life, it was inevitable that a congregation should develop. In early 1981 a meeting was held in the home of Dr. and Mrs. Gerald Halpern of Fayetteville, and a new congregation, to be known as Temple Shalom, was formed.[41] Participants came from Fayetteville and the surrounding towns. A meeting was held 25 February 1981 at the home of Dr. and Mrs. Barry Brown, and the congregation's first officers were elected. They were Jay Lewis, president; Jeremy Hess, vice-president; Daniel Levine, treasurer; and Marcia Keyserling, secretary. Consecration services for Temple Shalom were held on 25 April 1981. Having no facilities of their own, the congregation rented a room at the Unitarian Church, 902 West Cleveland Street, Fayetteville. They had a small ark that enclosed one Torah, which had come from the defunct temple at Camden. Rabbi Norbert L. Rosenthal, rabbi emeritus of Temple Israel in Tulsa, conducted the services. He subsequently served the congregation as its first rabbi and conducted biweekly visits. On the alternate Fridays without the rabbi, services were held at the Hillel House at 607 Storer Street, Fayetteville. One year later a mailing list was drawn up that included members and prospective members in the area that totaled some seventy-five families.

By the mid-1980s fifteen Ph.D.s were included in the more than thirty-five families participating in Temple Shalom's congregational life. There were twenty-two children in Sunday School. Blytheville's Temple Israel, which had no children by that time, donated their Sunday School material to the fast-growing Temple Shalom. In 1986 Dr. Michael Lieber, U of A professor of physics, became president of Temple Shalom. His three children, son Ken and daughters Laura and Debbie, received their bar mitzvah and bat mitzvahs at Temple Shalom. For several years Rabbi Elijah E. Palnick of Little Rock taught Hebrew to the children of Temple Shalom and prepared them for their bar mitzvahs and bat mitzvahs.

The work of the U of A Hillel was aided by the establishment of Temple Shalom. The new congregation began supporting Hillel's work, as did the Jewish Federation of Little Rock (later known as the Jewish Federation of Arkansas) and the Arkansas B'nai B'rith State Association. The house at 607 Storer Street was purchased and was formally dedicated as the Sam Barg Hillel Jewish Student Center on 1 November 1983 (the center was named for the father of Louis Barg of Forrest City). In 1989 U of A Hillel, which numbered twenty-five members at the time, began sending out a newsletter.[42]

In 1990 Rabbi Wolfgang Hamburger of St. Joseph, Missouri, served the congregation, which had one hundred twenty-two (individual) members drawn from a thirty-five mile radius of Fayetteville.[43]

By 1992 the Fayetteville area was the only location in Arkansas outside of Little Rock that had a thriving, growing Jewish community. And Temple Shalom's prospects of continued growth were very bright.

Rabbi Abraham Benedict Rhine of Hot Springs House of Israel Congregation, originator and founder of the Arkansas Jewish Assembly.

Members of the Rhein family in Germany, some of whom fled the country during the 1930s, were some of the few refugees of Nazi Germany who settled in Arkansas. Back row, left to right: Karl Rhein, Pauline Rexinger Rhein, Yetta Rhein; front row: Louis Rhein, Arthur Metzger (cousin), and Lena Rhein (who was killed by the Nazis before the family escaped). (Photo courtesy of Louis Rhein)

Rabbi Elijah E. Palnick (left) of Congregation B'nai Israel, Little Rock, with Rabbi Nathan Falk of Nashville, Tennessee; the latter, a native of Little Rock, was a former member of B'nai Israel. (Photo by Carolyn Gray LeMaster)

Rabbi Seymour Weller of Synagogue Agudath Achim, spiritual leader since 1977 of Arkansas's only active Orthodox congregation. (Photo courtesy of Rabbi Seymour Weller)

Harry Solmson Sr., a successful Little Rock insurance executive, was an active worker in the Arkansas Jewish Assembly and served as one of its presidents.

Nanci Goldman, director of the Little Rock Federation, during one of its annual Holocaust memorial ceremonies held in the Capitol rotunda, Little Rock. (Photo by Carolyn Gray LeMaster)

Margaret Ann Schneider (left), president of Little Rock Hadassah, at a reception for Mrs. Anwar (Jehan) Sadat (right), given by Governor Bill Clinton at the governor's mansion, Little Rock. (Photo courtesy of Margaret Ann Schneider)

Rabbi Ira Sanders served as spiritual head of Congregation B'nai Israel of Little Rock from 1926 to 1963 and as rabbi emeritus from 1963 until his death in 1985. He was known statewide as an astute orator and leader.

Several Little Rock Jewish men became
highly successful. Harry B. Solmson Jr.,
an executive of Plough, Inc. (later
Shering-Plough), helped bring a large
Maybelline plant to North Little Rock.
(Photo by Carolyn Gray LeMaster)

Richard Thalheimer is founder and
president of The Sharper Image.
(Photo courtesy of Richard
Thalheimer)

Ira Lipman is founder and president of Guardsmark, Inc., of Memphis, Tennessee.
(Photo by Carolyn Gray LeMaster)

Members of the Grundfest family (owners of the Sterling Stores chain), Little Rock, ca. 1950; standing, left to right: Dave, Jack, Bill Klaus, Jake Stein, Morris Sebulsky, Sam, Mabel, Sinai Brownstein, Jean, Ike; seated: Maurine, Sadye Klaus, Kate Sebulsky, Mollie, Dorothy, Hattie Brownstein, Freda Stein. (Photo courtesy of Janet G. Mayersohn)

Descendants of the early pioneer Little Rock Jewish families such as Pfeifer, Levy, and Loeb also include the Jacobson family; on a family picnic in the mid-1980s. (Photo courtesy of Mrs. E. G. Levy)

Bernard Tanenbaum of Dumas,
active in civic and business
progress of the city. (Photo
courtesy of Jerry Tanenbaum)

Walter Rosenthal in
his New York Store,
Blytheville, early
1960s. (Photo
courtesy of
Norma
Neaderthal)

CHAPTER 16

Central Arkansas

As the state's capital city, Little Rock had bustled and thrived during World War II. It had profited greatly from trade generated from nearby Camp Robinson, a U.S. Army encampment that had included at its height some forty-eight thousand officers and enlisted men.[1] (Camp Pike had been located on the site during World War I.) Little Rock continued to prosper after the war; downtown merchants saw a postwar boom as scarce commodities became available again and as returning servicemen began establishing new households. By the 1950s, however, shopping centers began to spring up in the city's western section, and in March 1959 Downtown Little Rock Unlimited was incorporated to help offset the inroads of such centers. The organization was headed by Sam Strauss Jr., whose family owned the Pfeifers of Arkansas department stores. By July 1960 Downtown Little Rock Unlimited had one hundred sixty members and was composed of retail merchants and owners of other businesses. Merchants were busily remodeling their stores: the prestigious M. M. Cohn department store at 510 Main Street expanded its facilities by 60 percent, Pulaski Federal Savings and Loan Association built a new building, Lou Hoffman remodeled a building at Fourth and Louisiana streets that would house a young men's and boys' clothing store, and Southwestern Bell Telephone Company spent more than one and one-half million dollars expanding its facilities for the metropolitan area's needed increase in phone service.

Sam Strauss Jr. optimistically commended Little Rock's efforts, saying they were done in time to ensure that the downtown would remain the center for metropolitan shopping as well as continue to be the state's largest financial and business area. He compared the still-thriving downtown to Beaumont, Texas, which at the same time (1960) had fifty-two empty stores in its downtown area.[2]

Pulaski County and Central Arkansas received a tremendous boost in 1955 when Little Rock Air Force Base was established at Jacksonville. A campaign by a "Committee of 100," composed of the area's businessmen, had been mounted to raise funds to purchase land for the base. The drive was headed by Arthur N. Phillips, husband of Miriam "Mimi" (Cohn) Phillips, whose family had established and owned the M. M. Cohn Company. A number of Jewish business and professional men were active in the campaign as well, such as Sam Strauss Sr., James M. Kempner, Harry Pfeifer Jr., James B. Pfeifer Sr., Lou Hoffman, and Harry Ehrenberg Sr. (The Committee raised more than one million dollars in four weeks; funds left over after purchasing the air base land were used to benefit the urban area.)[3] By 1960 LRAFB was pumping thirty-six million dollars annually into Pulaski County. Most of the funds were in payroll, which was spent in Central Arkansas.[4]

1957 School Integration Crisis

As delighted as Central Arkansans were over the establishment of the air base, Little Rock itself received a negative blow, beginning in 1957, that would be included in historical annals for all time. What became known as the "crisis of Central High School" over the integration of nine black students in Little Rock was preceded by the U.S. Supreme Court's ruling in May 1954 that racial segregation must end in public schools. After the ruling, several school districts in Arkansas began quietly integrating their students. In 1955 trouble over integration began to develop in some Arkansas counties, such as Lawrence and Crawford counties. By 1956 political resistance to integration began to mount in the state.

In February 1957 the state legislature met to consider four bills that were intended to ensure segregated schools. A Senate hearing on the bills, which were passed in the House 88-1, was held 18 February, and Rabbi Ira Sanders of Little Rock was one of several persons who spoke in opposition to the bills. He made an impassioned plea, appealing to the moral law based on Judeo-Christian concepts, asking that the measures be defeated in order to keep the state's good name unsullied. He reminded the legislators that, if they passed the laws, which were aimed at circumventing the legal authority of the Supreme Court, future generations reading the Arkansas statute books would be compelled to pray for them the words Jesus spoke from the cross, "Father, forgive them, for they know not what they do."[5] Rabbi Sanders received commendations from notables state- and nationwide on his courage and on his speech, parts of which were reprinted in national newspapers and magazines.[6] (Despite the opposition by Rabbi Sanders and many others, the bills passed handily, and Governor Faubus signed them into law.)[7]

The gradual integration planned by the Little Rock School Board was to begin at Central High School in the fall 1957 with nine black students. On 2 September, avowing that he was acting in a measure to keep the peace, Governor Orval E. Faubus called in armed National Guardsmen, who were instructed to stop the blacks from entering Central High. Governor Faubus removed the Guard on 21 September, and after a mob formed, President Dwight D. Eisenhower placed the Arkansas National Guard under Federal control and sent the 101st Airborne Division of the U.S. Army to Little Rock to help control the situation. He also called for a day of prayer. Rabbi Sanders joined a group of Arkansas leaders, headed by Episcopal Bishop Robert R. Brown, that proposed a Columbus Day prayer rally, called a "ministry of reconciliation."[8] Congregation B'nai Israel joined in the event, along with forty-five other houses of worship. Some five thousand people prayed about the situation, and about five hundred of these met at the temple.[9] When the temple received a bomb threat against a Sunday morning class, Rabbi Sanders refused to be intimi- dated, and he held Sunday School as usual. A few brave mothers brought their children to the services, which proved to be uneventful.[10]

Rabbi Sanders, as a Jew, was not alone in his involvement in the Little Rock school crisis. Attorney Henry Spitzberg of Little Rock and many of the city's Jewish women joined with many other concerned citizens in helping to find solutions resulting in a peaceful integration of the schools. Spitzberg, who had begun practicing law in Little Rock in the early 1920s, was one of the attorneys engaged by Little Rock school superintendent Virgil Blossom during the integration crisis. Spitzberg strongly supported the Supreme Court decision and trusted that implications of the ruling would change race relations in the South. He fought for the schools, both in the legal field and with action groups that arose.[11]

After Governor Faubus closed the city's high schools in September 1958, many of the city's civic and religious leaders sought ways to reopen them. During this time Rabbi Sanders met openly as well as in secret with like-minded people in the community; together they helped lay the strategy that would reopen the schools.[12]

Soon after the schools had been closed, the Women's Emergency committee to Open Our Schools (WEC) was formed. It was composed of a group of some one thousand women, most of whom were wives of young business and professional leaders. A substantial number of Reform Jewish women became strong workers in the organization's campaign. Among others, these included Josephine Menkus, Jane Mendel, Alice Back, Rosa Lasker, Carolyn Tenenbaum, and Irene Samuel. The latter, wife of Dr. John M. Samuel, served as WEC's executive director and was considered the group's "organizational genius."[13] She later said that, had it not been for the help of the Jewish women, the organization would not have been as effectual. Many of the women worked behind the scenes, such as Marilyn Siegel, who, dying of cancer, raised financial support for WEC from her sick bed.[14]

After the contracts of forty-four teachers and employees of the Little Rock school system were not renewed in the spring of 1959 because they did not support segregation, an action group called Stop This Outrageous Purge (STOP) was initiated by several professional and business men of the city. The organization drew support from a cross section of Little Rock citizens. For the most part, the businessmen who actively worked in STOP were the second rank executives. The economic power center of the city supported the movement both financially and by giving its tacit permission to its younger executives to become involved. STOP efforts were successful, and the contracts of all purged teachers and employees were confirmed. In June 1959 a Federal court ruled that the school closings were illegal, and the high schools were reopened that fall. Officers of the STOP campaign conceded that the group's success was due to the work of WEC members. STOP members changed the organization's name to the Committee for the Peaceful Operations of the Public Schools, and Irene Samuel was appointed as one of its four leaders.

Josephine Menkus served as an active volunteer for WEC and as a member of the Council on Human Relations and People for the American Way. She also was president and treasurer of the Council of Jewish Women and Temple B'nai Israel Sisterhood. (She and Irene Samuel were cofounders of the Jet Letter Service in Little Rock.) Alice (Lasker) Back was one of many Jewish women who was active in both WEC and the STOP campaign. She was also cochairman of the Bonds for Israel Campaign with her husband, Phil, for fifteen years (during which time they made numerous trips to Israel). She served as president of the Temple Sisterhood and the local Hadassah chapter.

Phil Back, who headed the Anti-Defamation League of B'nai B'rith in Arkansas, was a moderate leader during the school crisis years. Most of the support from the business community in Little Rock for school integration was done behind the scenes because a boycott list was being circulated. The city's Jewish businessmen followed the trend in the South at the time, "quietly working with the good Christians" toward school integration, yet letting few know of their efforts.[15] A group of prominent Jewish business-man and professionals set themselves up as an "advisory" committee for consultation to the Jewish community as a whole. Actually, in essence it was seen to be a censorship group "to keep certain things out of the press." Although it did not view itself in a censorship capacity, "its mere exis-tence had a silencing effect on many members of the Jewish community."[16] Rabbi Sanders, in referring to such response to the crisis, said that "the Jewish people have always been lackadaisical when confronted with a social problem." They followed the trend of other community leaders, he said, and "were committed to the status quo."[17]

There could be adverse consequences for those who chose to stand for social justice during that tumultuous time. For example, the medical prac-tice of Dr. John Samuel, whose wife, Irene, was in the forefront of the WEC campaign, suffered greatly. Dr. Samuel had resumed his practice in Little Rock after serving in the U.S. Army in World War II (during which time he had received a Bronze Star) and continued his custom of an inte-grated patient waiting room. Due to emphasis on segregation that was pro-mulgated at the time, some of Dr. Samuel's patients protested at having to share his waiting room area with "niggers." He lost so much of his practice that he considered leaving Little Rock.[18]

Dr. Samuel was not alone in bearing severe consequences for his actions during the school crisis. Pine Bluff attorney Sam Levine was outspoken and paid dearly for his stand. Levine served in both the state house of rep-resentatives and the state senate, beginning in the 1930s. He again served in the senate during the crucial years of 1957 and 1959. One of the out-standing moments of his career came in 1959 on the closing day of the general assembly. He filibustered for thirty-three minutes and thereby killed an administration bill that would have packed the Little Rock School Board with supporters of Governor Faubus. This was but one of the few defeats of a Faubus-supported bill in the state legislature. Although Levine had distinguished himself during his long legal career, this incident, which was said to have saved Arkansans "from [their] fevered selves and from [their] politicians," ended his political role in the state.[19] Levine, who was said to have the biggest vocabulary in Pine Bluff and the poorest clients, was ahead of his time, for during that crisis period, Faubus-following segregationists were in popular demand. Levine did not run for the legislature again, but did run for a chancery judgeship that became vacant in Jefferson County. Although the lawyers of the county backed him, his opponent used anti-Semitic tactics, even painting swastikas on his posters. Levine lost in a primary runoff by ten votes, but in the general election he quietly backed another opponent, who won the race.[20]

In 1963 the Committee on Race and Religion was formed, and members of different races and religions met to try and bring the groups together. That year, the Panel of Americans was established, which succeeded the Women's Emergency Committee. Members of the organization included Catholic, Protestant, Jewish, Oriental, and black individuals. These formed groups of five, one from each background, that spoke at churches, schools, and civic gatherings and gave five-minute summations of the ways they had encountered prejudice. It was the first such panel in the South and was well received by all its audiences.[21]

When Rabbi Sanders retired in 1963 and assumed the position of rabbi emeritus, he was succeeded that fall by Rabbi Elijah E. Palnick. The latter came at a time when the city and state were still adjusting to the integration crisis, and Rabbi Palnick quickly put his full weight behind efforts to bring peoples of various races and religions together (see chapter 15).

Even after the initial furor of the integration crisis subsided, Little Rock's Jewish women continued to help the public schools. For example, when more than fifty Little Rock school teachers requested help in 1971 to ensure a smooth transition to crosstown busing that had been begun, Jane Mendel founded the Volunteers in Public Schools (VIPS) program, which began with sixty-seven participants. Fifteen years later, the organization had grown to more than three thousand workers. In 1983 the Little Rock School Board and the VIPS board established the Jane Mendel Award to be given annually to an outstanding volunteer. She was named "Woman of the Year" by the *Arkansas Democrat* in 1973. She was instrumental in forming the Interfaith Sensitivity Council on the Holocaust in 1979 and was active in numerous civic causes.[22]

Although the Jewish community of Little Rock as an organized group did not adopt an official position on integration during the crisis years, the fact that Rabbi Sanders was considered the recognized leader among them and campaigned to adhere to and enforce the law of the land, plus the fact that so many Jewish women were active in supporting the Supreme Court decision, presumably caused the non-Jewish population to feel that the Jews did take sides.[23]

Merchants

BUSINESS

The business community of downtown Little Rock had other worries and concerns in addition to the school problems. With the continued erection of more and better shopping malls in both Little Rock and North Little Rock, the trend away from downtown steadily continued. In the 1970s a drastic measure was taken when Metrocentre Mall was built, which closed off several blocks on Main Street. An attractive pedestrian area with shrubs, benches, and a fountain was developed in the closed area. In the 1980s the buildings on the east side of Main between Fifth and Sixth streets were converted into a mall, the MainStreet Market, which housed numerous shops and restaurants, and the Repertory Theatre remodeled the Galloway Building at Seventh and Main streets. The positive effects of all such efforts were short lived, however, and by 1990, almost all the shops in MainStreet Market had closed along with all the large downtown department stores and many specialty shops. Main Street was eventually reopened to vehicular traffic.

About one-fourth of the members of Downtown Little Rock Unlimited had been Jewish merchants and business owners, and almost all of these had either closed their stores and retired or had moved to the area's malls by the end of the 1980s. Below is a review of some of Little Rock's Jewish businesses, individuals, and professionals during the forty-five-year period after World War II.

DEPARTMENT STORES

Four of the most prominent Jewish business names in Arkansas by the 1950s were those of Pfeifer, Blass, Kempner, and Cohn. All were associated with large, prestigious department stores, some of which branched out to other cities in Arkansas. The Pfeifer department store expanded after the war and opened a large home center at 601 Main Street. A branch was opened at Hot Springs, and the name was changed to Pfeifers of Arkansas. In 1952 Pfeifers established a sporting goods store and toyland at Seventh and Main streets. Two years later three stories and a basement annex were built next to Pfeifer's main store between Fifth and Sixth streets on Main. A year-round toyland was opened in 1959, and a service building was opened at Third and Rock streets. But four years later, the family-owned Pfeifers of Arkansas was sold to William Dillard, owner of Dillard Department Stores.

From the 1930s until it was sold, the Pfeifers' company had been headed by Sam B. Strauss Sr., a Columbus, Indiana, native who in 1923 had married Eleanor Pfeifer, daughter of Leo Pfeifer and granddaughter of the company's founder, Joseph Pfeifer. Strauss was active in civic affairs, serving as chairman of the Chamber of Commerce Industrial Committee that helped bring a Westinghouse Electric Corporation manufacturing plant to Little Rock. He was chairman of Metroplan and a founder of Downtown Little Rock Unlimited. He served as president of the Little Rock Boys Club and founded Pfeifer Youth Center, later known as Campus Inn, at Central High School. He was a major contributor to the Arkansas Arts Center and served on the boards of several companies.[24]

The Joseph Pfeifer name was still being remembered in the 1990s, kept alive by the Kiwanis Camp named for him at Ferndale in west Pulaski County. The Joseph Pfeifer Kiwanis Camp, established in 1929, was used for a number of programs in the 1980s and 1990s, such as the Alternative Classroom Experience that was established to help troubled city children, and Anytown Arkansas, a multicultural program sponsored by the Arkansas Council on Brotherhood of the National Conference of Christians and Jews.[25]

The Gus Blass Company that had originated in Little Rock in the 1860s (see chapter 7) continued as a family-owned store by the Blass-Heiman families. In 1950 Noland Blass Sr., son of Gus Blass, retired as president and was succeeded by Hugo Heiman. Heiman, who became chairman of the board in 1960, served as a director of Downtown Little Rock Unlimited and of the Urban Progress Association. Others who were involved in the management of the Blass company included Julian Blass Jr., Gus Blass II, and Max A. Heiman, all grandsons of the original founders. In 1961 a branch store was opened at Pine Bluff, and in 1963 the Blass Company became the first major store in Little Rock to announce plans to establish a branch at the Park Plaza Shopping Center, west of downtown. In 1964 Julian G. Blass Jr. resigned as president, and the company was sold to Dillard's Department Stores. Leonard F. Levy was then named president of the stores, which Dillard combined under the name of Pfeifer-Blass; later they were given the Dillard name.[26]

In 1966 Pine Bluff native David S. Bluthenthal, who had served as sales and merchandising manager for several Little Rock department stores, was named vice-president of Dillard Department Stores and general manager of the company's Arkansas division, which included six Pfeifer-Blass stores. In 1969 Bluthenthal resigned from that position and opened an office as a consultant to retail store managements and became director of local and regional sales and creative services for the television station, KTHV. He died in 1971.

In 1956, Gus "Buddy" Blass II, who had served in the U.S. Army in World War II as a first lieutenant and had been awarded a Purple Heart, was chosen by the Little Rock Junior Chamber of Commerce as the city's Outstanding Young Man of the Year. He left the Blass Company and in 1962 became president and managing officer of the Capitol Savings and Loan Association. He was active in the Chamber of Commerce, Downtown Little Rock Unlimited, Urban Progress, Boy Scouts of America, Salvation Army, United Fund, American Red Cross, and the Family Service Agency and served on the boards of several Little Rock businesses. In the early 1990s he was named as chairman of "Project 2000," a private group that proposed the Diamond Center, a major project of more than one hundred million dollars in new construction, including a multipurpose event arena and the enhancement of the downtown area. (The Project was put to the ballot and was defeated.) Noland Blass Jr., brother of Gus Blass II, became a prominent Little Rock architect (see below).

Kempner's, a specialty store that emphasized fashion and quality, particularly in footwear, had a level of name recognition similar to that of the Pfeifer and Blass stores. James Mendel Kempner, son of the store's founder, Ike Kempner, was associated with the firm from 1925 until his death in 1973. Ike's brothers, Abe, Dave, and Melvin, also were members of the firm. The Kempners saw the company grow until it had one of the highest sales volumes for a retail shoe firm in America, and it drew customers in all fifty states and in some foreign countries.[27] The store was remodeled several times, the last of which was in 1962 at a cost of some four hundred thousand dollars. It opened branches at Park Plaza in Little Rock, McCain Mall in North Little Rock, and at Hot Springs. But the downtown store closed in the 1970s, and by the mid-1980s all its branch stores had closed as well. The Kempners were also active in civic affairs; James M. Kempner, for example, who served in the U.S. Army Air Force as a major in World War II, was a founder of the Little Rock Urban Progress Association and was associated with a number of business and civic organizations.

The M. M. Cohn Company also specialized in high fashion and quality and viewed itself in the same category as Saks Fifth Avenue, I. Magnin, and Neiman-Marcus.[28] After World War II it grew significantly and the store on Main Street was remodeled and expanded. After Albert Cohn died in 1934, the company was continued by Arthur Phillips, husband of Albert's daughter Miriam "Mimi." Albert Cohn's other daughter, Raida, married Harry W. Pfeifer Jr., a grandson of Joseph Pfeifer, founder of the Pfeifer department store. After serving as a captain in the U.S. Marines during World War II, Harry Pfeifer Jr. joined the M. M. Cohn Company. He also was active in civic organizations, serving as president of the Chamber of Commerce, director of the Urban Progress Association, and helping organize and head the United Way of Pulaski County. He was active in Rotary and Boy Scout work and was a member of the Arkansas Arts Center Foundation. (His wife, Raida, also was civic minded, serving on the boards of the Girl Scouts Council, Visiting Nurses Association, Red Cross, and the Parent-Teacher Association. Much of her effort, however, was centered on the Arkansas Arts Center.)

By the mid-1980s, the M. M. Cohn Company of Little Rock and the Boston Store of Fort Smith were the last two large Jewish family-owned department stores in Arkansas. M. M. Cohn expanded under the leadership of Dan Phillips, son of Arthur and Mimi Phillips. After he became president in 1969, the company grew from one to eleven stores by 1985. He also was involved in other companies, such as Skyways airline, which he bought in the early 1970s and later sold to Air Midwest. M. M. Cohn also had in the 1980s a subsidiary firm, Retail Data Systems, which did data processing for stores nationwide.[29] After Fort Smith's Boston Store closed in 1986 (see chapter 18), M. M. Cohn became the last store of its kind in Arkansas, but it too was sold in April 1989. It was bought by the Dunlap Company of Fort Worth, Texas. The downtown Cohn store was closed, but the stores at Park Plaza in Little Rock and McCain Mall in North Little Rock continued under the M. M. Cohn name. By 1991 only Don Pfeifer, son of Harry Pfeifer Jr. and Raida Pfeifer, continued with the firm, serving as executive vice-president and general merchandiser.

The Sterling Department Stores chain, which was originated in Arkansas in the 1920s by Sam Grundfest and his brother Dave, had grown to sixty-five stores in four states by the 1940s. After Sam retired in 1941, Dave became head of the company. It continued to expand, and by 1965 it had eighty-five stores in six states, with a retail volume of eighteen million dollars annually.

Dave Grundfest married Maurine Frauenthal, and they had two children, Dave Grundfest Jr. and Barbara (Mrs. Stanley Bauman Jr.). Dave Grundfest Sr. was active in civic affairs and represented the U.S. Department of Commerce as an emissary on Trade Missions to Europe in 1957 and 1959 and represented Arkansas in 1966.[30] Dave Grundfest Sr. wanted the continuity of the business firms that he and his brother had established (which included Cash Wholesale Company as well as the Sterling Stores) to be unbroken to provide security for those who had helped in their success.[31] Dave Grundfest Jr. was associated with his father and became president and chief executive officer of Sterling Stores, Inc., in 1991. The chain continued to grow, and by the early 1980s it had one hundred variety stores, three Sterling Department Stores, and forty-seven Magic Mart discount stores in six states. Dave Grundfest Jr. was married to Julianne "Judy" Dante of Dumas. A former U.S. Air Force fighter pilot who served in the Arkansas Air National Guard from 1956 to 1963, he also served on the Little Rock Regional Airport Commission and in other civic organizations. He was killed in an air crash in July 1987 at the age of fifty-one while flying in an aircraft he had built.

Arnold Mayersohn, who had married Sam Grundfest's daughter Janet, became manager of Cash Wholesale Company, a subsidiary of Sterling Stores. In 1983 the Sterling Stores Company of Little Rock was sold to Duckwall-Alco of Abilene, Kansas.

Another department store chain, Rephan's, continued to expand after World War II. Although it thrived for several decades, it also succumbed, and the last store closed in 1992 (see Hot Springs, chapter 18). In the 1940s Isaac Salinger, a native of Brinkley, opened his own department store in Little Rock that continued for more than twenty years before closing.

SPECIALTY CLOTHING

Little Rock had a number of Jewish-owned specialty clothing stores that continued or were established after the war. The men's clothing store of Rube and Scott continued into the late 1950s; Charles C. "Rube" Rubenstein died in 1958. After serving in the U.S. Army in World War II, Howard R. Cohn opened Howard Cohn's Men's Store, which featured men's better clothing. It continued into the 1970s. Jack Fine served in the military in World War II and returned to Little Rock, where he founded the Town and Country Women's Dress Shop and Mrs. Jack Fine's Dress Shop, which became well known as a place for high fashion. Bauman's, the men's clothing store established by Simon Bauman in 1919, was sold in 1958, and the new (non-Jewish) owners retained the Bauman name.

The company, which opened a branch store in west Little Rock, continued into the 1990s.

What became one of Little Rock's most fashionable ladies' clothing stores, Feinstein's, was founded in 1957 as Feinstein's California Casuals by Howard and Nancy Feinstein after Howard retired as merchandising manager for Pfeifers of Arkansas.[32] Nancy (Pfeifer) Feinstein was the daughter of Preston and Ruth (Levy) Pfeifer and the granddaughter of department store magnate Joseph Pfeifer. The Feinstein's daughter, Ann Williams, continued the ladies' specialty store under the name of "Feinstein's" into the 1990s.

Max Gold came to Little Rock in 1962 and bought out a ladies' ready-to-wear shop that had originated with Eugenie (Stifft) Frank in the 1920s. Max doubled its volume within one year. He established Gold's House of Fashions at 317 Main Street in 1964 and opened two branches by 1973. He was active in Downtown Little Rock Unlimited and fought to save landmarks in the area. He helped organize the Downtown Farmers Market, which functioned during the summer months into the 1990s. Max and his wife, Sarah, retired in 1979, and their son Donald continued the family business. The latter served as president of Little Rock Unlimited Progress. He and James A. Moses bought the Rose Building at 307–11 Main Street from Dave Grundfest Jr. and restored it to its former beauty. Gold's had six outlets by the late 1980s, and plans were underway for a number of others.[33]

A Stein Mart branch, part of a chain that originated from a store owned by Jake Stein in Greenville, Mississippi, was opened in Little Rock in the 1980s. Located on Cantrell Road in west Little Rock, the store drew a large clientele.[34] Sheldon L. Rand from Atlanta established a ladies' clothing store in Little Rock in the 1970s that continued for some fifteen years. It boasted a "Shelly Rand" look for its patrons and appealed to the younger set.

In the 1980s the Lockwood family of Hot Springs began opening branches of Lockwood's Sportsmart in the greater Little Rock area. By 1988, five of the sports supply stores had been opened, including the initial one, which was founded at Hot Springs by Gene Lockwood in the early 1970s.

The tailoring shop founded by Charles Schneider in North Little Rock was continued by his son, Harry, who died in 1964. The company was sold by Harry's son, Charles Schneider, in 1970 to the shop's manager, Dan Acord, and his nephew, Bill Acord. It continued under the founder's name into the 1990s.

Bennett's Military Supplies thrived on Little Rock's Main Street after World War II. It was run by Meyer and Fannie (Bennett) Kaufman. After Meyer died in 1973, his son Joe, an engineer, helped his mother run the store. Joe opened a branch store in southwest Little Rock in 1987 and planned a military museum next door to the downtown store. He served as chairman of the Pulaski County Planning Board for twenty-five years, beginning in the late 1960s.[35]

Bensky Furs, the company established by Zusman Bensky in the late 1920s, was sold when Bensky retired in the 1970s. He had endowed his work with such prestige that his name was continued by the company's new owners. The same was true of Spector Furs, founded in North Little Rock by Ben Spector, when the store was sold in the 1980s. (Milton Green, another Little Rock furrier, was a founder of the Arkansas Hall of Fame and served as vice-president of the organization until his death in 1975.)

Dave Grundfest Sr. helped several young men establish businesses after World War II. Lou Hoffman, who had been stationed at Camp Robinson during the war, decided to remain in Little Rock. With Grundfest's help, Hoffman first opened the Krystal Kiddie Shop, which sold quality children's clothes, then later went into men's and boys' wear. He opened several branches in Arkansas; his popular stores continued until his retirement in the 1980s.

Theodore D. Abeles Jr., grandson of the lumber magnate, Charles Abeles, served in World War II, and upon his return from the military, became co-owner with his father of the United Shoe Store in Little Rock and the Famous Brand Shoe Store in Texarkana. Theo Abeles Jr. died in 1968. The Abeles name continued to make news in the late 1980s. The elegant apartment complex built by Charles Abeles in 1911 at 1403 Louisiana Street was one of fifty development restoration projects undertaken in downtown Little Rock in 1988 by Charles Marratt, a property developer. The apartments had been the city's first luxury complex.[36]

LUMBER, CONSTRUCTION, HARDWARE

The descendants of Philip Pfeifer, brother of Joseph Pfeifer, became well known in the lumber and plumbing businesses in Central Arkansas. Philip's son Eugene "Gene" Pfeifer, who had bought Mechanics Lumber Company from Charles Abeles, remained as its president until 1962. He was also president of the Arkansas State Lumbermen's Association. Eugene M. "Blue" Pfeifer Jr. succeeded his father as president and expanded the company into three retail-wholesale outlets in the metropolitan area. He also established a custom millwork division and had a wholesale distribution yard in North Little Rock. He was involved in several civic and business organizations.[37] After Blue Pfeifer's death, his son Eugene M. Pfeifer III continued the company as well as its expansion. He bought Arkmo Lumber and Supply in North Little Rock in 1989, opened a fourth outlet at Maumelle in North Little Rock in 1990, and merged the company with May Supply Company in 1992, making it the largest locally owned building supply company in Central Arkansas.[38] James B. Pfeifer, grandson of Philip Pfeifer, joined Mechanics Lumber Company in 1936 and became one of its partners. He served as president of the North Little Rock Chamber of Commerce in 1955, as board chairman of the North Little Rock Salvation Army, as vice-president of the United Fund, and was a founder of the North Little Rock Chapter of the (University of Arkansas) Razorback Club. He served as executive vice-president of Mechanics Lumber Company into the 1990s. Emmanuel G. Levy Jr. also was a partner in Mechanics Lumber Company (the company's name was changed to "One Source Home and Building Center" in the 1990s). He married Elizabeth Pfeifer, daughter of Eugene M. Pfeifer and granddaughter of Philip Pfeifer; the couple became well known for their volunteer work with civic organizations, hospitals, and charities.

Arthur H. Pfeifer, also a son of Philip Pfeifer, established a plumbing company that later grew to become Pfeifer Plumbing and Heating Company. Arthur J. "Art" Pfeifer, son of Arthur H., continued the company until 1988, when he sold it to Arkansas Mechanical Contractors of North Little Rock. He then joined the firm of Cromwell Architects Engineers as a vice-president of planning and development. In the 1980s Art Pfeifer served as president of the Little Rock Rotary Club, and at that time he challenged the group to provide the needed leadership for Little Rock schools.[39] Subsequently, the Business Committee for Public Education was formed, which included 101 businessmen. Five were Jewish: Art Pfeifer, Dan Phillips, Sam Strauss Jr., Noland Blass Jr., and Arthur Korenblat.[40]

The Tri-States Construction Company, established by Edward D. Elias in the 1940s and which built the governor's mansion and other prominent commercial and industrial structures, closed in 1960. Edward's sons, Charles and Barney, who had worked with their father in the business, continued in general construction into the 1980s and 1990s. Barney's son Edward K. and Charles's son Charles E. followed their forebears with careers in the building industry.[41]

Charles E. Joseph, son of Sam Joseph of Blytheville, was an electrical engineering graduate of the University of Arkansas, and in 1946 he joined the Peterson-McFadyen Construction Company of Little Rock. After Charles bought into the company, it was known as Joseph and Daugherty, Inc. In Little Rock the company built Barton Coliseum, the Blue Cross–Blue Shield Building, and the state Game and Fish Commission Building, as well as industrial plants and military bases nationwide. Later, after retiring from the company, Charles was involved in real estate.[42]

Besser Hardware continued to be one of the best-known businesses in that line in Little Rock. The store on Center Street was continued by Lippman Besser's daughter, Aileen, and her husband, Jack C. Walberg. It was sold shortly after the war to George Lorenz, who continued it under the respected Besser name. Isadore Besser's hardware store on Asher Avenue eventually closed; he died in 1974. The Besser hardware store just across from him on Asher was continued into the 1990s by Besser family members.

P. C. Hardware and Machine Company, which was established by Philip C. Prousnitzer Jr., a World War II veteran, served a wide radius in the Little Rock area. P. C. Prousnitzer Jr. married Betty Sachs, daughter of Altheimer merchant Irvin H. Sachs, and their son, Paul C. "Chuck" Prousnitzer, continued the firm after his father died in 1983. The business expanded in the 1980s with a branch store in west Little Rock.

FOOD SUPPLY, EATERIES

Two sons of Max Mayer of the Scott-Mayer Commission Company, Theodore and Jacob, had the Black and White Food Stores before World War II. (Jacob died in 1940.) Theodore "Teddy" and Nicholas "Nick" (also a son of Max Mayer) both served in the military during the war, and both rose to the rank of major. Teddy returned to Little Rock after the war and continued as head of the Black and White food stores, which closed around 1960. The Scott-Mayer Commission Company closed after the war.

Sam Morris Vogel, who had been employed by the Scott-Mayer Commission Company before serving in World War II (during which time he flew fifty-two bombing missions in the South Pacific), returned to Little Rock after the war and established Vogel's, Inc., which pioneered in the frozen food industry. He was appointed by President Dwight Eisenhower to serve on the Advisory Committee of the U.S. Department of Agriculture for frozen food and refrigerated products. He was a founder of the Frosty Acres Brands, Inc., in Atlanta and served as an honorary member of its board of directors. He continued as manager of the Vogel company when it was sold in 1963; it was later owned by Borden Food Company. Dan Schwartz, who married Sam Vogel's sister Rose, was part owner of the Vogel company; he established the Dan Schwartz [food] Brokerage Company in the 1960s, sold it after some twenty-five years, and then opened the Super Sales Brokerage Company in the late 1980s.[43]

Gilman and Kosten, the produce company that was started in the 1930s by members of the early banana cooperative (see chapter 10), continued to grow after the war. Members of the Gilman and Kosten families, as well as Louis Snyderman, whose father had been a member of the cooperative, continued the firm. It had fourteen salesmen by 1974, when it was sold to Kimbell and Company of Texas.[44]

Jewish-owned eateries that continued after World War II included Breier's Fine Old Restaurant, which was operated by Breier family members. The restaurant's location on Markham Street was taken over by Urban Renewal, and in 1964 it was closed. Even a bill introduced in the state legislature failed to save the building, and the restaurant moved to Old Cantrell Road, where it continued until 1970. After World War II Morris Granoff continued his restaurants, located on Main Street and on the Hot Springs Highway 5 west of Little Rock, until his death in the 1950s. Phillip and Dorothy (Kosten) Geller operated a small restaurant, The Purple Cow, on Broadway that continued for a number of years.

After serving in the U.S. Army Air Force in World War II, Edward "Ed" Back, younger brother of Phillip Back, continued his association with Capitol Distributing Company, a wholesale specialty and gourmet food distributing business. Ed married the daughter of Laurence Rudolph; the latter had purchased the company in 1940.

Jack Grundfest, son of Dave Grundfest Jr., acquired the local franchise from the yogurt company, Freshens, of Atlanta and opened several outlets in the Greater Little Rock area in the late 1980s.

JEWELRY

The successful jewelry firm of Stifft's, founded by Charles Stifft and his father, Michael, was the oldest such business in the state when it was sold in the 1940s to Max M. Moses. A New York City native who was raised in Fort Worth, Texas, Moses entered Little Rock business and civic life with zeal and was honored in both 1966 and 1980 for his devotion to his country, his community, and his people. He sold the Stifft Jewelry to Arkansas Fine Jewelers Guild, and the company was continued under the Stifft name.[45]

Selwyn and Rose (Heiman) Loeb also were Little Rock jewelers. Selwyn had been stationed at Camp Robinson in World War II and had met and married Rose. He later leased the Dillard jewelry departments, beginning in the 1960s, and also those of fifty Magic Mart stores. In the 1980s the Loebs had a jewelry store in Pulaski Heights in west Little Rock.[46]

PAWN SHOPS

Several Jewish-owned pawn shops and a night club were opened or continued after World War II. Sam Levine, who owned Doc's Trading Post, died in 1963. Doc's Trading Post was incorporated by other owners in 1971. Barney Levine (no relation to Sam Levine) owned and operated the Westwood Club in Little Rock, located on the old Hot Springs Highway. A veteran of World War II, he was well known and appreciated as a charitable person. He developed notoriety, however, when on a number of occasions he overstepped the boundaries of legality by violating state gambling laws at his club. He died in 1970, and the club was closed.[47]

Max "Maxie" Itzkowitz, who served in the U.S. Army Air Force in World War II, ran a pawn shop on Main Street from 1945 until he died in 1989. His "going out of business" signs were plastered on his windows for years and all rhymed, such as "Maxie will be through in 1972," and "Over 40 years, I don't mean maybe, Maxie will be through in 1980." Small, wiry Maxie was well known to the Little Rock police as a "good old boy"; he would pass on to them key information on pawned objects.[48] After he died, his large home at Ninth and Rock streets in Little Rock was donated to the Historic Preservation Alliance of Arkansas.[49]

After serving in the military in World War II, Maxie's half brother, Robert "Bob" Itzkowitz, returned to his Square Deal Pawn Shop, located in North Little Rock. He married Ruth Schweig and was later joined in the family business by their children, Marvin and Judy. Morris "Mo" Lulky opened the National Pawn Shop across the street from Robert Itzkowitz's store after World War II. He and his wife, Geline, had a son, William, who later joined in the family business.

According to an Arkansas farmer-businessman, the Jewish pawn brokers, whom he described as "first class," provided many services that banks did not, such as providing quick money during economic downturns. They also provided fine investment quality jewelry at good savings, he said, and they were "extremely fair" in their dealings.[50]

REALTY

The Block Realty Company of Little Rock grew apace after World War II, with the need for land and housing at a premium high for returning servicemen. The children of founders Lewis and Raymond Block entered the family business, with Lewis Block Jr. serving as vice-president of the company. He also was president of Little Rock Builders, Inc. Mark J. Block, son of Raymond and Helene (Eisenkramer) Block, left Block Realty in 1955 and formed Block-Meeks Realty Company with partner William R. Meeks Jr. Mark, who was a World War II fighter pilot in the U.S. Army Air Force and who received four decorations while on combat duty, was a civic leader and interested in political affairs. His brother Raymond continued with the Block Realty Company. After being a household name in central Arkansas real estate circles for more than sixty years, the company was sold in 1984 to the Independence Corporation, a holding company that owned Independence Federal Bank (at Batesville) and Independence Federal Life Insurance Company.[51]

Jewish-owned real estate companies that were established in Little Rock subsequent to World War II included the Cooke-Sanders Realty Company and the Selz Realty Company. The former was founded by William B. Sanders and E. V. Cooke. Sanders, who had helped develop Park Hill in North Little Rock with the Justin Matthews Company, left that firm in 1946 to establish the one with Cooke; he continued with the company until his death in 1972.[52]

Fred "Freddie" Selz, a survivor of Nazi Germany who came to America in 1938 at age fifteen, first worked with horses and mules with an uncle at McGehee. He later joined the Reinman and Wolfert horse and mule barn in North Little Rock. By the time the war ended, there was little future in such trade, and Freddie joined the Block Realty Company's farm division. He continued this until 1957, when he opened his own realty company with partners Floyd Fulkerson and Sam Reynolds. Freddie Selz became the exclusive agent for Winrock (a Winthrop Rockefeller enterprise) in the development of Pleasant Valley, which became Little Rock's most prestigious housing development in the 1970s and 1980s. Selz grew to love Arkansas and became an avid promoter of the state. He felt there were "no finer people anywhere" than in Arkansas, and he sought ways to do good for the state that had done so much for him. His son Joe, who became president of Selz Realty, was named a member of the Little Rock Planning Commission in 1990.[53]

Some Storthz family members continued their business involvement in real estate. After serving in the U.S. Army in World War II, Sam Storthz Jr. established Sam's Investment Company, which dealt primarily in real estate rentals for offices and store buildings. The family also retained real estate holdings in north Arkansas. Sam's brother, Lewis Storthz, was also involved in real estate. He had a small delicatessen in Park Plaza Mall for a number of years. Sam Storthz III also was in realty; he became a Little Rock real estate appraiser. (Lewis's son Larry became a photographer in the city.)[54]

James "Jim" Moses Jr. established the dual firm of AMR Real Estate and AMR Architects in Little Rock with several partners.[55] Jim had been one of the owners of the Moses Melody Shop on Main Street, which was sold in 1977. He married Jeanne Kahn, daughter of Alfred Kahn Sr.

MANUFACTURING, MACHINERY

The ladies' garment manufacturing company established by the Ottenheimer brothers, Gus and Leonard, in the 1930s was sold to Sears, Roebuck in 1955. The Ottenheimers then built an industrial complex in southwest Little Rock and leased the plant to Kellwood (a subsidiary of Sears). They also developed Cloverdale, a four-hundred-house project in the area. They donated a park, "Ottenheimer Park," as part of the project. Although the brothers sought to retire in the late 1950s, they—especially Gus—became involved in higher education in Little Rock. Gus was elected president of Little Rock University Foundation, Inc., in 1961, after having headed a group that supported Little Rock Junior College's efforts to become a four-year institution. (The foundation was composed of more than 130 members, including Arnold Mayersohn, Eugene M. Pfeifer Jr., and Louis Rosen.) Gus was elected chairman of the Little Rock University Board of Trustees in 1962. He also headed the committee that recommended the merger of Little Rock University with the University of Arkansas, Fayetteville. This proposed merger was enacted by the state legislature in 1969. Gus was awarded an honorary Doctor of Laws degree by the University of Arkansas at Little Rock in 1978. In the fall of 1980 Gus and Leonard established the Ottenheimer Tuition scholarships, enabling ten students a year to continue their studies at UALR and the UALR Law School. Leonard Ottenheimer died in 1984, and Gus died a year later.

The philanthropy of the Ottenheimer brothers was continued after their deaths. In 1985 E. Charles Eichenbaum, head of the Ottenheimer Foundation Board, donated one million dollars from the foundation to the UALR Engineering Technology and Applied Science Building. The library at UALR was named the Ottenheimer Library that year in memory of the brothers and their longtime support of the school. In 1988 the Ottenheimer Foundation pledged fifty thousand dollars to create a special collection of management books and materials at UALR. The philanthropy also extended to the field of medicine, and a half-million dollars was given by the foundation to the Arkansas Cancer Research Center, which underwrote a wing on the center that was designated as the Ottenheimer Cancer Education Center. (Neither Gus nor Leonard Ottenheimer ever married. Their sister Gladys married Joe B. Hirsch—the couple had no children—and the four lived in the Ottenheimer home in Pulaski Heights. Gladys and Joe Hirsch also supported the family's philanthropy, although they did not become so well known. Another Ottenheimer sister, Ruth, married Dr. Nat M. Cohen; the couple had one son and five grandchildren, none of whom made their homes in Arkansas.) When Gus Ottenheimer died, Arkansas historian Richard B. Dixon commented that not many members of prominent families had contributed as much to Little Rock as had Gus Ottenheimer, his brother Leonard, and their sister, Gladys Hirsch. The city lost a "premier citizen . . . and a friend and benefactor of higher education" when Gus died, Dixon said.[56]

A survivor of a concentration camp in Nazi Germany, Edwin Rhein, who made Little Rock his home, developed his own necktie company. Almost all members of the Rhein family fled to America in 1937 after Karl Rhein, who headed the family, was arrested in Germany by the Gestapo. The Rheins lived briefly at Eudora with family member Jacob Rexinger, then moved to Little Rock, where Edwin and his wife, Betty, started a small necktie factory in their home. He peddled them on a bicycle, selling them to individuals and to stores. Dave Grundfest Sr. lent him a thousand dollars, and he and his wife opened a factory in the city's industrial area. The business prospered, and the neckties were distributed nationally. The firm, known as the Edwin Rhein Neckwear Manufacturing Company, grew to employ from forty to forty-five people. In 1969 the Rheins opened the Rhynecliffe Factory Outlet Store adjacent to the necktie factory (Rhynecliffe was the trade name for the neckties). After Edwin died in 1972, his wife sold the manufacturing plant but kept the outlet store. When the plant later went into bankruptcy, she bought back the company, and, managed by her daughter and son-in-law, Liane "Lee" and Bill Humble, it was reestablished as a successful business. Renamed Le-Bil's Manufacturing Company, it grew to employ as many as seventy workers. In 1986 the plant was sold to Tandy Brands Accessories of Dallas; Lee and Bill Humble continued as its managers as well as as owners of the outlet store. In 1973 Betty Rhein's other daughter and son-in-law, Bettye Lou and George Yakoubian, opened a men's clothing store in west Little Rock called Rhynecliffe Men's Wear that continues into the 1990s.[57] (Edwin's brother Louis worked as a supervisor with the Silbernagel Distributing Company for forty-five years. The Rheins and Silbernagels were distant cousins.)

Maxwell J. Lyons, who had been one of the U.S. Marines' most decorated men in World War I, continued in the Lyons Machinery Company until his death in 1978. He was active in the Red Cross and served as president of the Family Service Agency. He was a founder of the Senior Citizens Activities Today (SCAT) and served on the board of the state Chamber of Commerce.[58] Samuel Lyons, Maxwell's brother, and the latter's son, Maxwell Lyons II, continued the Lyons Machinery Company until it was sold in the early 1980s. Both Samuel and Maxwell Lyons II were vitally involved in the city's civic and charitable organizations. Samuel served on the Salvation Army advisory board and worked in several volunteer activities after his retirement. Maxwell Lyons II joined the L. Darragh Company Construction and Industrial Sales and Service Division in 1983. He served as chairman of the Industrial Services Commission, as president of the Arkansas Association Equipment Distributors, the Little Rock City Board of Adjustment, and the Arkansas Junior Chamber of Commerce. He was active in the Rotary and Red Cross Organizations.

LAUNDRY AND CLEANING

Jewish-owned laundry and cleaning businesses in the greater Little Rock area had been prominent before the war, but only one remained in the 1990s—the Levinson Cleaners. It had been established by William B. Levinson and was continued by his daughter, Edna L. Roberts. She incorporated the firm in the 1960s with a (non-Jewish) partner, Bill Rambo. It grew to include the original plant plus two branches. The other such firms had been sold or closed. L. Julian Alexander, owner of Majestic Laundry and Cleaners, sold his firm when he retired in 1967. Harry Lasker Jr., vice-president of the Little Rock Laundry and Cleaners, was later president of the Imported Car Center. He retired and moved out of state in 1969. Joseph and Lillian Morris came to Little Rock during World War II, drawn there by their son, Dr. Harold J. Morris, who was stationed at Camp Robinson. The Morris family opened a shoeshine and cleaning and pressing business on Capitol Avenue between Main and Louisiana, which drew numerous patrons from the army base. Morris Cleaners later moved to

Main Street, and the couple was joined in the business by their son Sheppard; the shop continued into the 1960s, when it was moved by the family to Memphis. (Another son, Edward "Eddy" Morris, had a small cafe in Little Rock. Dr. Harold Morris became a well-known Pine Bluff physician.)

HOTELS

Two major Little Rock hotels associated with Jewish owners met different fates during the 1970–80 decade. The Hotel Marion, the grand hotel promoted and built by Herman Kahn, was destroyed by implosion in February 1980 to make way for the new Excelsior Hotel and the Statehouse Convention Center. The Sam Peck Hotel at 625 West Capitol Avenue continued under the management of Sam and Henrietta Peck. During the Central High School crisis of the late 1950s, the hotel was used by a number of national journalists, including Harry Reasoner of the Columbia Broadcasting System (CBS). Reasoner found the professionalism of the hotel and the homey atmosphere created by its owners to be such that, when he once ended a network special on hotels, he noted that his favorite one was the Sam Peck at Little Rock.[59] When Winthrop Rockefeller moved to Arkansas in the 1950s, he made the Sam Peck his home for a year. In 1959 the Pecks added a motel section onto the hotel's south side. Sam Peck died in 1967, and the hotel was sold in 1972. The name of the facility was then changed to the Legacy Hotel, and in 1986 it became part of the Radisson chain, owned by Carlson Companies, Inc.

SCRAP AND METALS

Only two of the scrap companies that were established in the Little Rock area by East European Jewish settlers were continued by family members into the 1990s. These were the A. Tenenbaum Company and the Sol Alman Company. Tenenbaum's became not only the largest such company in Arkansas but also the largest Jewish family-owned business in the state by 1990. Having been established by Abe Tenenbaum in 1890 with two or three employees, the company had grown to almost two hundred workers in the 1980s and had expanded to three divisions. These consisted of a metal processing warehouse that included an automobile shredder—the only one in Central Arkansas; a supply yard for wrecking railroad cars and handling heavier separation loads; and a third division, Arkansas Aluminum Alloys, Inc., at Hot Springs, a processing plant that took aluminum scrap and made specification aluminum alloy for the die-casting industry. (By 1987 the Tenenbaum Company was producing some five thousand tons of iron nuggets a month, a million pounds of copper, brass, and iron, and some three hundred thousand pounds of aluminum scrap.)[60]

After Abe Tenenbaum died in 1952, the company was bought by his nephew, Julius Tenenbaum, who served as president of the company until his death in 1965. Julius's son Joe continued as head of the company and promoted its expansion. (Joe's brother, Harold Norman Tenenbaum, was killed in service during World War II.) Joe married Carolyn Summerfield, and their son Harold continued the business into the 1990s. Several Jewish men were associated with the Tenenbaum Company, including William A. Bushman, who served as company president, Irvin "Buddy" Schweig, and Abe Greenbaum.

The Alman scrap company, which had been founded in 1905 by Charles Alman, continued through three generations to the 1990s. After Charles Alman died in 1943, the company was continued by his son Sol, who gave his name to the business. (Sol also was a talented musician and performed locally.) After he retired in 1982, the company passed to his two sons, Charles and Larry. In 1983 an aluminum can recycling center was established by the company and a facility to produce one-thousand-pound aluminum ingots was constructed. The Alman's also installed a powerful new shearing machine to cut scrap metal. In 1988 the company began redeeming container glass for recycling.

The Siesel scrap company, which had been established by M. J. Siesel in the 1870s, was sold after World War II to a Dallas Company. The Goodman and Barg scrap company was dissolved after Sam Barg retired in the early 1960s. The Sanders Junk Company, founded by Abe Sanders in 1901, became the Loket-Sanders Company when Abe's son-in-law, Herman Loket, joined the company. After Abe died in 1946, the company, which became known as Loket Scrap Processors, was sold by family members in the mid-1970s to Soloco, Inc.

The Goldman scrap company, established in 1925 by A. J. Goldman as a waste paper processing plant, was continued by Goldman's son-in-law, Lee Kretchmar, after 1962, when the founder retired. After Kretchmar died in 1976, his widow, Ruth (Goldman) Kretchmar, and A. J.'s widow, Augusta, sold the business in 1978 to Fenley Enterprise of Arkansas, which retained the Goldman name. (Ruth G. Kretchmar became a well-known artist, exhibiting in juried shows in watercolors in several southern states. She served on several state and national boards, and was listed in *Who's Who in the South and Southwest, 1980–1981* and in *American Artists of Renown, 1981–1982.*)

ADVERTISING

The S. M. Brooks Advertising Agency, founded in 1911 as the first such company in Arkansas by Harvard graduate Sidney M. Brooks, was, from the 1920s, the largest advertising agency in the state for almost forty years. Brooks was a founder of the Little Rock Rotary Club and served as its secretary for thirty-eight years. He established Rotary Clubs in a number of Arkansas cities. Brooks managed the advertising agency until he retired in 1965 (he died at age 98 in 1985). Three officers of the agency, Earl Saunders, Don Burkhart, and A. Hall Allen, continued the company. Bob Wimberly joined the agency in 1969 and served as president and general manager. Wimberly later bought the company; in 1979 he closed all but its public relations section and formed Bob Wimberly Public Relations, Inc.[61]

Several other Jews have played important roles in the advertising or public relations fields in Little Rock. George W. Dickinson, who married Miriam Sanders of Little Rock, served as director of the Arkansas Free Enterprise Association from 1959 until his death in 1980. The agency, which defended the state's "right to work law," was formed in 1946 to protect and promote the Arkansas business community through the advocating of free enterprise. Dickinson also was in advertising and sales promotion work and was an organizer of the Razorback Football and Basketball radio networks.

Richard Stein, a victim of cerebral palsy, came to Little Rock in 1971 at the invitation of Little Rock newspaper editor Robert McCord. Stein worked in public relations with various companies until 1973, when he formed his own agency. His handicap did not hamper his business success, but his career was cut short when he was killed in an automobile accident at age thirty-five in 1983.

Chester Storthz, son of Herbert and Charlotte Storthz and grandson of Joe Storthz Sr., was with the Brooks-Pollard advertising agency for several years before establishing Chester Storthz Advertising in Little Rock in the mid-1980s.[62] Storthz's agency won an award of excellence from the American Advertising Federation's Tenth District competition in 1987.[63]

Phil Back, who was an outspoken proponent of peaceful integration of Little Rock schools in the late 1950s, had opened an advertising agency after World War II and also had founded Superior Attractions for Theatrical Entertainment. He later started the Broadway Theater Series, bringing numerous productions to Little Rock, including *Hello Dolly* with Carol Channing in 1966. After he died in 1979, Superior Attractions was continued by his daughter Marilyn and her husband, Gene Weinstein.[64] The company brought other Broadway productions to Little Rock, including *Applause, Evita, Chorus Line, Cats,* and *Les Miserables.* For an average show, people came from some one hundred towns statewide and from neighboring states. Phil Back also was a partner in several Little Rock businesses, including two companies, Little Rock Engraving and Southern Association Manufacturing, with partner Milton Loeb. Loeb married Phil's other daughter, Mimi, and the Milton Loebs established Speedee Print company in the 1980s.

Nathan Steppach, who had helped liberate the infamous concentration camp, Dachau, while serving as a pharmacist in the U.S. Army Medical Corps during World War II, worked with several advertising agencies in Little Rock upon his return home. He headed the advertising for Sterling Stores and the Magic Mart stores from 1966 to 1977. He then worked with his son, Nathan Steppach Jr., who had established S and W Chemical Sales.

BANKING

There was little Jewish involvement in Arkansas banking during the second half of the twentieth century. Two of the few exceptions included Gus Blass II (noted above) and Alfred Kahn Sr. The latter had been associated with Union Trust Company (later Union National Bank) in Little Rock since 1907. Known as the dean of Little Rock bankers, Kahn remained as president of Union Bank from 1933, when it was chartered, until 1950, when he became board chairman and chief executive officer. He retained ownership of the Rose City Cotton Oil Company until 1954. He was president of the Arkansas Bankers Association, the Little Rock Chamber of Commerce, Little Rock Rotary, and both the Arkansas and the Interstate Cottonseed Crushers associations. Both Alfred Kahn Sr. and his brother Sidney continued their promotion of Little Rock until their deaths in 1976 and 1972, respectively.

MISCELLANEOUS BUSINESSES AND BUSINESSMEN

A variety of other Jewish businesses were in operation in Little Rock after the war. Henry Posner, son of Louis and Mary (Goldberg) Posner and a World War II veteran, established the Dixie Home Modernizers in Little Rock, which he continued until his death in 1974. William "Billy" Kramer, who operated a gymnasium on East Seventh Street, served as a physical education instructor in the Little Rock public schools; he advocated physical fitness programs until his death in 1982. Erwin Gartenberg had a stamp and supplies firm in Little Rock; he died in 1977. Nelbert Meyer, president of Midwest Beauty Supply Company, died in 1962. Sidney T. Koenig, a pharmacist and owner of Magic Mart Pharmacy, retired in the 1980s and died in 1991. I. K. Electric Company, founded by Albert I. Korenblat in 1919, was continued by his son Arthur and his grandson Scott. The company was sold to JWP, Inc., of Purchase, New York, in 1989, but Korenblat family members continued its management into the 1990s. (Robert Korenblat, son of Maurice Korenblat, a brother of Albert of the electric company, became a Little Rock pharmacist.)

Several Jewish men were involved with the Strauss Distributors company of Little Rock, including Sam Strauss Sr. and Sam Strauss Jr. David S. Sherman was a cofounder of the company and served as its president. Sherman also was founder and chairman of the board of David S. Sherman Corporation of St. Louis, board chairman of Paramount Liquor Company of St. Louis and Cape Girardeau, Missouri, and board chairman of the Mid-Continent Distributors in Kansas City, Kansas.[65]

Shrader Studio at 117 West Sixth in Little Rock continued as one of the most prestigious photography studios in the state for a number of years after the war. When founder Joseph Shrader died in 1946, the studio was continued by his wife, Bertha (Frank) Shrader, and their son, Gustave J. "Buddy" Shrader. Bertha Shrader died in 1959, and the studio was sold in the mid-1960s. Although it continued into the 1990s under the Shrader name, by that time it had lost the prestige it once had.[66]

Eric Nussbaum, a survivor of Nazi Germany, worked for the Little Rock Paper Company for forty-two years. He married Betty Heiligers of Conway and was active on a number of religious boards.

Sally (pronounced Solly) Cohn, a law graduate of the universities of Berlin and Breslau who had practiced law at Brandenburg, Germany, also was a survivor of Nazi Germany. He came to Little Rock at age sixty-two in 1941, and he and his wife, Grete Zwirn Cohn, opened a rooming house on State Street. Cohn became well known in Little Rock for his short essays, booklets, and letters that he had published. He was affectionately called "Uncle Sally" and was helpful to other immigrants in their legal matters dealing with various countries of Europe.

After serving as a captain in the U.S. Army in World War II, Harry Ehrenberg Sr. became involved with the insurance business that had passed from his grandfather, Herman Ehrenberg, to his uncle, Mannie. Harry Ehrenberg Sr., who married Joyce Schneider of North Little Rock, was joined in the business in the 1980s by Harry Ehrenberg Jr., making it a four-generation insurance agency. (Harry Ehrenberg Sr.'s father, Morris Ehrenberg, continued to work with Mechanics Lumber Company until his death in 1953. A widower, Morris had met and married Minnie Solovey, an Army nurse stationed at Camp Robinson during World War II. He became interested in Zionism through her and became president of the Little Rock chapter of the Zionist Organization of America.)

After serving with the Quartermaster General's office in Washington, D.C., during World War II, Joseph Bernhard, son of produce merchant Sam Bernhard, bought Holman Hobby House at 2719 Kavanaugh Boulevard in 1948 and changed the name to Joe's Hobby Shop. Joe married Evelyn Rosch of Pennsylvania, whose brother, a dentist, was stationed at Camp Robinson during World War II. Evelyn joined her husband in running the hobby shop, and they, and later their two daughters, Melanie and Susie, became well known to hobbyists throughout central Arkansas. (When she first came to Little Rock, Evelyn, from an Orthodox background, found the area to be a wasteland, so far as keeping kashrut [the Jewish dietary laws] was concerned. She formed a pool among the Orthodox women, and the group had kosher meat sent from Memphis.) Joe and Evelyn were ardent workers at the synagogue and in Zionist organizations. Their whole family became involved with Hadassah's Young Judaea group when daughters Melanie and Susie headed it in the 1960s. (After Melanie married Stephen Rosenberg and the couple moved to Israel to live, she became a writer and helped establish a public relations company. She contributed a number of articles on conditions in Israel to the *Arkansas Gazette* during the Desert Storm operation against Iraq in 1991.) Joe's Hobby Shop closed in 1983 when the Bernhards retired.

New York native Myrna Taxer, whose family later settled in Dallas, Texas, joined the Weight Watchers program in 1967. In 1969 she and her husband, Shep Taxer, acquired the Arkansas franchise of the company and moved to Little Rock. By the late 1980s their enterprise had grown to three offices in the greater Little Rock area and one each in Pine Bluff, Hot Springs, and Fayetteville.

Lt. Col. Sidney A. Kegeles, who retired from the U.S. Air Force after serving as deputy commander of the Little Rock Air Force Base, was appointed state purchasing director under Governor Rockefeller. In that position, he established fair bidding measures on government contracts. (Kegeles had served as a pilot in the U.S. Army Air Corps in World War II. After flying two hundred war missions in Europe, he received the Distinguished Flying Cross with Oak Leaf Cluster and the Silver Star. He was knighted by the president of Bolivia for saving the lives of some one thousand Bolivian citizens in a rescue mission.) Kegeles, who married Mayna (Bloom) Fish of Little Rock, died in 1988.

The Professions

A number of descendants of Arkansas Jews distinguished themselves in the professions both before and after World War II. Other newcomers later joined their ranks.

MEDICINE

Dr. Jerome S. Levy, whose father had been a Hot Springs merchant, began his practice in Little Rock in 1929 and continued it until his death in 1978. He was a faculty member of the University of Arkansas for Medical Sciences, specializing in internal medicine and gastroenterology. After serving in the U.S. Army Medical Corps in World War II, he retired as a lieutenant colonel. He was president of the Arkansas Tuberculosis Association and was head of a number of medical organizations. Five months after the death of the much-honored doctor, a Levy Chair in Gastroenterology was established by the UAMS Board of Trustees in his memory; it was the fourth chair at the institution.[67]

A number of Jewish doctors have been associated with the University of Arkansas for Medical Sciences since World War II. Examples of these include Dr. Wilma Diner, who joined UAMS in 1956 as an assistant professor of radiology and rose to full professor. Her husband, Jack Diner, was a medical illustrator, sculptor, and instructor at UAMS. He was a member of the Association of Medical Illustrators and editor of its newsletter. He died in 1988. Dr. Fay Sloan joined UAMS as an associate professor of anesthesiology in 1954. She went into private practice in 1966 and served as chief of anesthesia at Baptist Medical Center from 1983 to 1987. She assisted in the first kidney transplant in Arkansas and was a pioneer in open heart anesthesia in the state. Dr. Albert E. Kalderon served as professor of pathology at UAMS in the 1970s and 1980s (he died in 1983). Dr. Howard Quittner served during that period as associate professor of pathology at UAMS and also at University Hospital of Arkansas. Dr. Milton Waner, an internationally known otolaryngologist (ear, nose, and throat specialist), joined UAMS in the late 1980s. A native of the Union of South Africa who had practiced in Australia, Waner developed a successful treatment for removing unsightly birthmarks using laser treatments. Others who joined UAMS include Drs. Howard Barnhard, radiology; Victor Biton, neurology; Michael Frais, cardiology; Arthur Haut, hematology; David Vesole, oncology; and Glenn Weitzman, obstetrics and gynecology. Dr. Suzanne Kleimberg, a surgeon and breast cancer specialist, joined the Arkansas Cancer Research Center at UAMS.

Several Jewish people with Ph.D.s who have served with UAMS include Dr. Sidney J. Fields, associate professor of psychiatry from 1952 to 1981. He was one of the first five psychologists licensed for private practice in Arkansas. Dr. Jerry Sherman, professor of anatomy at UAMS since 1959, became known for his volunteer work, and in 1991 he was the first recipient of the newly established UAMS Faculty Volunteer Service Award. Both he and Dr. Almen Barron, chairman of the Department of Microbiology and Immunology, received the UAMS College of Medicine's Distinguished Faculty Award. Other Ph.D.s include Alan Elbein, chairman of the Department of Biochemistry; Joshua Epstein, oncology; Harold Resnick, biochemistry; and Joseph Stone, pharmacology. Daryl B. Matthews, a member of the UAMS faculty who holds both M.D. and Ph.D. degrees, joined the Arkansas State Hospital as chairman of forensic psychiatry. Dr. Michael Simon became associated with Arkansas State Hospital as a clinical psychologist in the 1980s. Dr. Bradley Diner, a psychiatrist and a son of Jack and Wilma Diner, joined the Arkansas Psychiatric Clinic in Little Rock in 1989 and became associated with Baptist Medical Center, Bridgeway Hospital, and Rebsamen Regional Medical Center.

There have been several Jewish psychiatrists who have practiced in the greater Little Rock area. Dr. Leopold N. Judah and Dr. Arthur D. Rosenthal, both veterans of World War II, worked at the North Little Rock Veterans Administration facility until their deaths, Dr. Rosenthal in 1967 and Dr. Judah in 1971. Dr. Henry Griffenhagen was associated with the VA Hospital in Little Rock in the 1960s. Dr. Oscar Kozberg served as psychiatric specialist supervisor at the Arkansas State Hospital from 1946 until his retirement in 1978. (His wife, Mary Kozberg, was active in civic affairs and served several years as president of the Little Rock Chapter of Hadassah.) Dr. Morris Levy served as a psychiatrist with the North Little Rock VA Hospital until his retirement in the 1990s.

Dr. Bertram L. Levy, a member of the UAMS faculty, served as chief of medicine at the Little Rock VA Hospital from 1958 to 1966. Dr. David A. Lipschitz joined the VA Hospital in 1979 as director of the Geriatric Research, Education, and Clinical Center (GRECC), and Dr. Samuel Goldstein joined GRECC as assistant director in 1981. (Both Lipschitz and Goldstein serve as professors of medicine at UAMS, Lipschitz also serves as director of the UAMS Division on Aging.) Dr. Harold J. White served as chief of pathology at the Little Rock VA Hospital, and Dr. Stefan Bracha joined the Department of Psychiatry. Since the early 1980s, Dr. Jay Marks has been an emergency room physician at both the Little Rock VA Hospital and Rebsamen Regional Medical Center in Jacksonville (his wife, Becky Marks, joined UAMS as a nurse practitioner). Several people with Ph.D.s who serve with the VA hospitals in greater Little Rock into the 1990s are Bernard Soloff, administrative officer of research and development since 1965; Daniel Rodell, social worker; and Kenneth Heard, audiologist.

Dr. Gerald Weiss joined the VA hospital in North Little Rock as chief of the surgery department in 1984. He had served as a lieutenant colonel in the U.S. Air Force before coming to Arkansas. He began private practice in Little Rock in 1986 and then served as medical director of Plasma Alliance, a division of Rhone-Poulenc-Rorer pharmaceutical company, beginning in 1989. (His wife, Elaine Weiss, a registered nurse, served as president of the Little Rock Chapter of Hadassah and worked in media modeling in central Arkansas.)

Dr. Weiss and Dr. Raymond V. Biondo helped organize Arkansas Post No. 436 of the Jewish War Veterans of the United States. Dr. Biondo, a native of New Jersey, was a UAMS graduate who made Little Rock his home. He conducted a private practice in dermatology until his retirement in 1990. Devoted to Judaism, he served on the boards of almost every Jewish organization in central Arkansas.

Dr. Alfred Kahn Jr., son of banker, businessman, and land developer Alfred Kahn Sr. of Little Rock, was a 1941 graduate of Harvard Medical School. After serving in the U.S. Army Medical Corps from 1942 to 1945, he became a Little Rock physician, specializing in internal medicine. He served as chief of staff at Baptist Medical Center and St. Vincent's Infirmary and was editor of the journal of the Arkansas Medical Society. He served on numerous boards, including that of the George W. Donaghey Foundation and the Little Rock Boys Club. He married non-Jew Redith Aline White and attended the Presbyterian church. By 1986 he had limited his practice to diagnosis and consultation.[68]

Dr. Irving J. Spitzberg, brother of prominent Little Rock attorney Henry Spitzberg, specialized in diseases that afflict women. Through the years he donated his time and practice to help the less fortunate and minorities at Arkansas Children's Hospital. He served as a member of the Staff of Polio Pioneers, contributing to the proving of and the success of the Salk vaccine. He was also active in the Boy Scouts and in baseball programs. He died in 1989.[69] Other prominent Little Rock physicians have included Dr. Howard Schwander, surgeon, and Dr. S. William Ross, a specialist in hematology and oncology. Dr. Irving Kuperman settled in Little Rock subsequent to World War II and became a well-known gynecologist.

Dr. Norman N. Fein, a native of Milwaukee, Wisconsin, became a prominent Little Rock ear, nose, and throat specialist after serving in the U.S. Navy in World War II (during which time he received a battlefield promotion to commander). He was first associated in Little Rock with Trinity Hospital Clinic on Main Street before opening a private practice in the 1950s. He also served as a faculty member at UAMS. He died in 1976.

Dr. Alvin Weil Strauss of Little Rock was joined in his practice in the mid-1940s by his son, A. W. Strauss Jr. The younger Dr. Strauss, a World War II veteran of the U.S. Army Medical Corps, was a colonel in the Medical Battalion of the Arkansas National Guard. He served as chairman of the Arkansas National Guard Association and as president of the Arkansas Academy of Family Practice. He was later joined in his practice by his son, Mark A. Strauss, who continued his practice into the 1990s. (Another son, Stanton, became an elementary school principal with the Little Rock school system.) Dr. A. W. Strauss Sr. died in 1955 and Dr. A. W. Strauss Jr. in 1989. (Dr. John Maurice Samuel, mentioned earlier regarding the 1950s school integration crisis, was a cousin of Dr. A. W. Strauss Jr. Dr. Samuel's sister, Claire, married architect Herbert S. Levy, a native of Monroe, Louisiana, who, after retiring to Little Rock in 1975, became associated with the Erhart Eichenbaum Rauch and Blass architectural firm.) Other Little Rock area Jewish physicians in private practice in the 1980s and 1990s include Drs. Frederick Levin, pediatrician, and Edward Loebl, cardiovascular and thoracic surgeon. Little Rock has several clinical psychologists, including Ralph Hyman, Glenn Lowitz, and Sheri Simon.

Dr. Jacob Amir, a hematology and oncology specialist, joined the Little Rock Diagnostic Clinic in 1977 and became well known in his field. Several physicians joined Arkansas Children's Hospital during the past fifteen years, including Dr. Gerald Bushman, an anesthesiologist (and son of Mr. and Mrs. W. A. Bushman of Little Rock); Dr. James Aronson, a pediatric orthopedic surgeon; and Dr. Chris Cunniff, a geneticist. Dr. Marvin Leibovich joined Baptist Medical Center, serving as an emergency room physician. Dr. David C. Bauman, son of Stanley and Barbara (Grundfest) Bauman Jr., joined the Little Rock Cardiology Clinic in the mid-1980s.

Dr. Charles Barg, son of Louis and Gertrude Barg of Forrest City, became a family and general practice physician in Little Rock. Dr. Jack

Sternberg, an oncologist, began his practice in Little Rock in 1977. He and Dr. Barg caused some stir in the Jewish community of Little Rock when they converted to Christianity in the late 1970s. Dr. Lawrence "Larry" Mendelsohn, son of Dr. Ernest Mendelsohn of Forth Smith, joined the Hematology-Oncology Associates in Little Rock in the 1980s. He too accepted Christianity.

Dr. Benjamin "Ben" Saltzman, born to Orthodox Jewish parents in Brooklyn, New York, became one of Arkansas's most well known doctors. As a young man, Saltzman had turned from the strictness he had found in his parents' religion, and he chose to attend a medical school in Portland, Oregon—a place as far away from the hub of Orthodoxy in Brooklyn as he could find. He served in the U.S. Army Medical Corps in the Panama Canal Zone during World War II and reached the rank of captain. After the war he joined Dr. E. M. Gray, a leading doctor of northwest Arkansas, in his practice at Mountain Home. Dr. Saltzman's efforts in improving health care in rural Arkansas did not go unnoticed. In 1981 he was named director of the state Department of Health and served in that capacity until 1987, when he became director of the Pulaski County Health Department. (He retired as its director in 1991.) He served as president of the Arkansas Medical Society as well as of several other medical organizations. Dr. Saltzman married a non-Jew and joined the Unitarian Church. He observed that, had he been familiar with Reform Judaism, he might have identified with it, as he found it to be similar to Unitarianism.[70]

Two Arkansas families saw their sons enter the field of dentistry in Little Rock. Dr. Percy C. Nordlinger, son of Selmar and Clara (Levy) Nordlinger of Hot Springs, had begun practicing dentistry in Little Rock in 1925 and continued until his death in 1981. Dr. Nordlinger developed a new method of making gold dental caps that would ensure a precise fit; he later applied the same process to less expensive stainless steel caps. (His son, Dr. Charles D. Nordlinger, began a practice in San Francisco.) Dr. Sam D. Nickol, son of Osceola dentist Dr. Morris Nickol, began practicing dentistry in Little Rock in the 1970s. He and his wife, Bonnie, spent a month on an Israeli kibbutz near Haifa in 1982 under a program organized by the American Dental Volunteers for Israel.[71]

Dr. Maurice J. Friedman, born at Chicago, Illinois, practiced dentistry in Chicago before serving in the U.S. Army during the period 1942–46. While stationed at Camp Robinson, he was encouraged by Lester Marks of Little Rock to make Arkansas his home, which he did. While serving as state president of B'nai B'rith, he met Jewish groups statewide, finding them to be friendly and close knit; he was impressed at the openness and warmth they experienced with their Christian neighbors.[72] Dr. Friedman practiced general dentistry in Little Rock from 1946 to 1967, at which time he limited his practice to endodontics. He served as an officer in a number of dental societies and was president of the Arkansas State Dental Association in the 1960s. A founder of the Pulaski County Dental Society, he retired in the late 1980s. Drs. Gary Weisbly and Richard Lewis practiced dentistry in Little Rock in the 1980s and 1990s.

Little Rock has had several Jewish podiatrists. Dr. Marvin F. Cohen, son of Charles Cohen of Little Rock, became head of the Little Rock Foot Clinic. Both he and his wife, the former Leaine Selz, became well known for their volunteer work, especially with the Red Cross. Other Little Rock podiatrists of the 1980s and 1990s include Drs. Terri Cohen, Richard Bronfman, and Allen Gold.

Several Jewish veterinarians have practiced in the greater Little Rock area, including Drs. Lance Bogoslavsky; Martin Fish; Larry Nafe and his wife, Joan Nafe; Saul Shemin; and Susan Weinstein. Dr. Fish began his practice in Lake Village in 1945 and was for many years the only graduate veterinarian in southeast Arkansas. He moved to Little Rock in 1964 and continued his practice there until his retirement in the 1980s. Dr. Shemin, a New York native, came to Little Rock in 1950. He served as president of the Young Businessmen's Association and Synagogue Agudath Achim Men's Club. He was a board member of the Salvation Army. He died in 1974. New York native Susan Weinstein came in the 1980s with her husband, Jeffery Baskin, who joined UAMS as associate librarian. (Baskin was named director of the William F. Laman Library of North Little Rock in 1987.)[73]

Other Jews, such as A. Allen Weintraub, were associated with the medical field in other ways. A native of Philadelphia, he served in the Medical Administration Corps in World War II and later retired as a colonel from the U.S. Army Reserves. During World War II he was stationed at Camp Robinson, at which time he met and married Mildred Strauss, daughter of Dr. Alvin Strauss Sr. After the war he became a partner in Central Surgical Company with Melvin Spear and (silent partner) Dave Grundfest Sr. He left that firm and in 1954 joined St. Vincent's Infirmary, a Catholic hospital, as assistant administrator; he was named administrator in 1967. (It was observed at the time that he was probably the only Jewish administrator of a Roman Catholic hospital.)[74] In 1974 he was promoted to assistant to the president. Weintraub served on a multitude of civic boards, but his most lasting contribution to Arkansas was his cofounding (with Blue Cross–Blue Shield president Samuel M. Butler Sr.)

of the Central Arkansas Radiation Therapy Institute (CARTI). He died in 1974, having seen the finalization of the plans for the institute. It was noted that, had death taken him a year earlier, it would have been doubtful that the concept of such a center would have been realized. It was his "determined leadership, perseverance, and negotiating skills" that brought it to fruition.[75] By October 1991 more than 28,500 patients statewide had received treatment there.[76]

Melvin Spear and his father, Henry, together with Harry Ehrenberg Sr. and Dave Grundfest Sr., founded Central Surgical Company in 1946. Allen Weintraub later bought out Harry's share; the company was sold to Cummings X-Ray Company, Inc., in the 1960s. Melvin served as president of the Pulaski County Humane Society and was known for his efforts in reopening the Humane Society's animal shelter after it closed for lack of funds.[77] His cousin, Marion "Mooch" Safferstone, a Little Rock native whose family had established the Safferstone Hat Company, closed out the family firm in 1942 when he entered the U.S. Navy. He operated the hat company briefly after the war and then became a partner in Central Surgical Company from 1951 to 1956. He became purchasing agent for UAMS, where he remained until his retirement in 1977. He served one year as state purchasing director during the administration of Gov. Winthrop Rockefeller.[78]

JURISPRUDENCE

The field of law in Little Rock has included noted Jewish attorneys, including Henry Spitzberg (mentioned earlier with the 1957 school integration crisis), Lasker Ehrman, and E. Charles Eichenbaum. Ehrman continued with the prestigious law firm he had established with Grover T. Owens until his death in 1946. For many years Ehrman had served as chairman of the Examining Board of the U.S. District Court.

Charles Eichenbaum, who began practicing law in Little Rock in the late 1920s and who became one of the city's best-known attorneys, was continuing his practice into the 1990s with twenty lawyers associated with his firm, Eichenbaum Scott Miller Liles and Heister. Active in civic and educational affairs, Eichenbaum was given an honorary Doctor of Laws degree from UALR in 1990 for his "outstanding service to the University, the legal profession, and the state."[79] His clients and his firm established the E. Charles Eichenbaum Scholarship Fund—the Arkansas Bar Association's largest single scholarship endowment. One of the lawyers with the Eichenbaum firm in the 1990s was Leonard Scott, son of

Walter Scott, who, with C. C. Rubenstein, had established the well-known "Rube and Scott" men's clothing store. Steve Bauman (brother of Dr. David Bauman) joined the firm in 1979.

Another Jewish lawyer practicing in the Little Rock area into the 1990s was John Selig, son of Leonard and Elsie (Jacobs) Selig of Pine Bluff and great-grandson of Joseph Altheimer. John Selig established a private law practice in Little Rock after serving as a captain in the U.S. Army in World War II; he rose to the rank of colonel in the Army Reserve. He and Lee Thalheimer, also a Little Rock attorney and a great-grandson of pioneer Jewish settler Ben Thalheimer, served as State Securities Commissioners. David Greenbaum, a son of Abram and Nellie Greenbaum of Little Rock, was appointed an administrative law judge for the State of Arkansas in 1978. Other Little Rock attorneys in the 1980s and 1990s include Bettina Brownstein, Jo-Ann Goldman (daughter of Stephen and Nanci Goldman of Little Rock), Alan J. Nussbaum, and Jeff Rosenzweig. The latter was a son of Dr. and Mrs. Joe Rosenzweig of Hot Springs (whose other son, Kenneth, was a graduate of UAMS [see chapter 18]). Jeff Rosenzweig, who began practicing criminal law in Little Rock, married Frances Fendler, also a lawyer and daughter of noted Blytheville attorney, Oscar Fendler.

Philip Kaplan, who, with his wife, Ruthe, and two children, moved to Little Rock in 1968, became one of the best-known Jewish lawyers in central Arkansas. He was active in religious and civic affairs of the city, serving as president of the Jewish Federation of Little Rock, the Little Rock National Conference of Christians and Jews, and radio station KLRE. He also served as a board member of Synagogue Agudath Achim, Temple B'nai Israel, the Council of Jewish Federations, and the Pulaski County Bar Association. He became best known, however, when he served as lead attorney for the Little Rock School District during the controversy over desegregation orders given by Federal Judge Henry Woods in the mid-1980s. Kaplan also served as a lecturer for the UALR School of Law. Ruthe Kaplan was active in Temple B'nai Israel and in civic affairs. She served as president of the Arkansas chapter of the National Association of Social Workers and was a board member of the Youth Home of Little Rock. She was director of social services of Bridgeway Hospital into the 1990s.

Two men with law degrees who did not practice law were Sol Thalheimer Jr., who served with the U.S. Army Air Force until his retirement as a lieutenant colonel, and Louis Rosen, who was associated with the Williams and Rosen, Inc., insurance firm. Rosen, who was a lieutenant colonel in the U.S. Army Air Transport Command in World War II, served as president and business manager of the insurance company until 1970, when he sold his interest. He was active in a number of civic affairs and served as head of the Arkansas Children's Hospital Board of Trustees, Little Rock Planning Commission, and Little Rock Rotary. Having lived at the Jewish Children's Home in New Orleans as a small child, he said one of the highlights of his career came when he presented a check to the Home in the amount of what had been expended on him. He married Vivian Brooks, daughter of advertising magnate Sidney M. Brooks. (Rosen's son, Brooks Rosen, married Lollie Meyer of Eudora, who had been born to a Jewish father, Alvin Meyer, and a Catholic mother, who had raised her children Catholic. Lollie converted to Judaism at her marriage.)[80]

Annabelle Clinton, a Little Rock attorney, was appointed as a chancery judge and was later elected to the position. She converted to Judaism and joined Congregation B'nai Israel; she later married Ariel Imber, executive director of the Jewish Federation of Arkansas.

OTHER PROFESSIONALS

Another Jewish professional in Little Rock in the 1980s and 1990s was Leonard Hasson, a certified public accountant. Two Ph.D.s, Andrew Scallet and George Wolff, serve with the National Center for Toxicological Research, Scallet in neurochemistry research and Wolff in genetics and cancer research. (William Rubenstein of Pine Bluff serves on the administrative staff at NCTR.)

POLITICS

Following the trend that had been in existence since the turn of the century, few Little Rock Jews ran for political office in the years subsequent to World War II. Texarkana native Jake Sklar, who had moved to Little Rock in 1935, was defeated when he ran for a position in the state house of representatives in 1968. After serving as a sergeant in the U.S. Army during the war, Sklar had become a leader in the treatment of the mentally retarded in Arkansas. In 1957 he had helped to found and was president of the Arkansas Association for Retarded Children and was appointed by Governor Orval Faubus as chairman of the Governor's Advisory Committee on Mental Retardation. Sklar died in 1969.[81] Attorney Mark Ross moved to Little Rock in 1979 to join his father, Joe Ross, in a law practice. Mark ran for the position of City Director No. 3 in 1984 and ran fourth in a race of five contestants. Little Rock dentist

Martin Zoldessy won the election for a position on the Pulaski County Special School District Board in 1987.

From the 1960s to the 1980s, Little Rock lost three Jewish attorneys who had been active in politics and government. Joseph H. Schneider died in 1966, Edward Bennett in 1971, and Louis Tarlowski in 1980. (For more data on these men, see section III.)

EDUCATION

The University of Arkansas at Little Rock has had a small number of Jewish professors through the years, including, Allan Glubok, professor of economics and finance; Michael Gilbert and William Jacobson, professors of education; Lester J. Bilsky, history department chairman; Richard S. Fischer, professor of music; Jerry Flanzer, associate professor, Graduate School of Social Work; Sally M. Flanzer, lecturer in sociology, anthropology, and gerontology; and Erich Franken, assistant professor of business and marketing. Alan Marks served ten years on the Governor's Advisory Council on Aging. German-born Erich Franken, who came to Little Rock in 1953 and was president of Herbert Cox Correct Shoes, Inc., died in Bonn in 1966 while completing his doctoral degree.

Dr. James W. Spears has served for a number of years as a professor of law at the University of Arkansas at Little Rock Law School, and Dr. Howard Eisenberg was named dean of the Law School in July 1991.

ARCHITECTURE.

Howard Eichenbaum, brother of attorney Charles Eichenbaum, became one of central Arkansas's most prominent architects. A resident of North Little Rock's Park Hill section, Howard served as head of the North Little Rock Planning Commission as well as as head of those of Little Rock and of the Pulaski County Metropolitan Area. At the time of his death in 1973, he was the only person to have chaired all three commissions. He was invited to join the International Institute of Arts and Letters, headquartered in Switzerland, in 1961. Others invited that year included Thornton Wilder and Aldous Huxley. He was president of the Quapaw Area Council of the Boy Scouts of America and served on numerous civic and religious boards. His firm designed a number of Little Rock's noted structures, including Baptist Medical Center, St. Vincent's Infirmary, the Veterans Administration Hospital on Roosevelt Road, and Worthen Bank and Trust Company.

Noland Blass Jr., grandson of Gus Blass, joined the Erhart and

Eichenbaum firm in 1946. The company evolved into Blass Chilcote Carter Lanford and Wilcox Architect and Engineer Professional Firm by the 1980s, headed by Noland Blass Jr. Blass received honors for his projects, which included the Worthen Bank building, Metrocentre Mall, Horace Mann School, the (Arkansas) Justice Building, Veterans Medical Center, UAMS, and Temple B'nai Israel. He became associated with several business-related organizations as well as serving as president of the Arkansas Arts Center and the Arkansas Symphony Orchestra Society and as director of the Mid-America Arts Alliance.[82] His wife, Betsy, became prominently known as president of the UAMS Cancer Research Center, for which she headed a four-year drive that raised seven million dollars in private gifts for the facility. She served as head of the UAMS Education Endowment Fund and as a board member of a number of institutions and organizations that spanned a wide range of fields, such as health care, research, education, arts, and human services. She personally funded a "Garden of Exploration" for the Arkansas School for the Blind that was used as a model for other schools for the blind both nationally and internationally. She was selected as "Arkansas Volunteer of the Year" in 1986 by the National Society of Fundraising Executives, and she received the UAMS Chancellor's Award in 1989.[83]

Eugene Pfeifer "Gene" Levy, son of E. G. and Elizabeth (Pfeifer) Levy of Little Rock, became a well-known architect with the Cromwell Truemper Levy Thompson Woodsmall architectural firm. He married Trudy Cromwell, and one of their three sons, Ed, also became an architect. (Their son Stewart was a UAMS medical student.) Gene Levy's building designs included the Plaza West Office Building, the Camelot Hotel, Convention Plaza, the Arkansas Bar Center, the Plough-Maybelline factory, and the National Investors Life Building. His design was selected for a belvedere (a gazebo-like structure) to commemorate the state's Sesquicentennial in 1986, and the trellised, pyramid-shaped building was constructed east of the Main Street Bridge in Little Rock's Riverfront Park.[84] James B. Pfeifer Jr. also became a Little Rock architect. While associated with the prominent Cromwell architectural firm, he headed the remodeling of the historic Capital Hotel. He later joined the U.S. Army Corps of Engineers.

MUSIC

Some Jewish newcomers to Arkansas during the postwar period distinguished themselves in the field of music. Martin D. "Marty" Rosen, a native of Chicago who was stationed at Camp Robinson during World

War II, remained in Little Rock after the war and established the Rosen Music Company. He also founded Romco Drums, Inc., a musical instrument repair and custom percussion company. In 1965 the University of Arkansas Band made a special request for a drum ten feet across and three feet deep; it was played at the U of A and University of Texas football game that year. Marty also played drums for a band that he founded. He served as State Fair parade marshal and led the Rodeo Band for more than thirty-two years. He began a band program at Catholic High School and organized and directed the Mount St. Mary's Academy Band. He was active in a number of civic organizations. He died in 1984.[85]

New York native Harold J. Geiler was the founder, music director, and conductor of the Pops Orchestra of Arkansas. He had been a French horn scholarship student at Juilliard School of Music and, after serving in World War II, studied at the Cherubim Conservatory at Florence, Italy. During the Korean War, he was stationed at Camp Chaffee at Fort Smith, where he led the 189th Army Band. He also reorganized the Fort Smith Symphony Orchestra and conducted it until 1960, when he moved to Little Rock and formed the Pops Orchestra. The Pops' summer concerts under his direction featured Arkansas talent as soloists; for his work with the orchestra, he was called the "Arthur Fiedler of Arkansas."[86] He died in 1979.

Dr. Richard S. Fischer, UALR professor of music, served as principal viola in the Arkansas Symphony Orchestra in the 1970s and 1980s. His wife, Ruth (Krug) Fischer, was an accomplished cellist.

Outstanding Former Arkansans

A number of Jewish Arkansas natives moved from the state and distinguished themselves in signal ways in other locales. Some did not forget their Arkansas roots and continued to benefit the state from their new locations. Three of these people from Little Rock are mentioned here: Harry B. Solmson Jr., Ira Lipman, and Richard Thalheimer.

Harry B. Solmson Jr., son of Harry and Gertrude (Myar) Solmson of Little Rock, a graduate of the University of Chicago Law School, practiced law for five years in the 1930s with the Little Rock firm of Robinson, House and Moses. He married Harriet Sternberger of Memphis and joined the firm of Plough, Inc., of that city, becoming executive vice-president. He served in the U.S. Army Air Force in World War II, reaching the rank of captain, and then rejoined Plough, Inc., after the war. The firm became Schering-Plough after its 1971 merger with the Schering Corporation, and Solmson became president of Plough and senior vice-president and director of the parent company. He retired in 1975 and became counsel to the Memphis law firm of McDonnell, Boyd, Smith and Solmson. Harry and Harriet Solmson had three sons: Harry III (deceased), who had farming interests in St. Francis and Cross Counties in Arkansas; William, an attorney with the McDonnell law firm; and Robert, president of Realty and Financial Services of Memphis, developers of shopping centers.

"Harry B.," as Harry Solmson became affectionately known to his friends, never forgot his Arkansas roots. His grandfather, Henry Myar of Camden, had done untold good for that area of the state, and his concerns for Arkansas and for his fellow man were continued by his posterity. Harry B. Solmson Jr. was active in civic affairs both at Memphis and at Longboat Key, Florida, where he later became a resident. While he was president of Plough in 1974, it was decided that the Maybelline company, which had been purchased by Plough in 1969, should have a single facility in the United States. Several southern locations were considered, and a consultant firm was engaged. Harry B. Solmson was helpful in bringing the plant to Arkansas.[87] The 775,000-square-foot facility, located on Interstate 40 east of North Little Rock, was completed in 1975 and became the only manufacturing and distribution center for Maybelline cosmetics. By 1988 some twelve hundred employees worked at the plant, which had an annual payroll of twenty-five million dollars at the time.[88] (In 1990 Schering-Plough sold the Maybelline company to the Wasserstein Perella Group, Inc., a New York investment firm.)[89]

In 1961 Harry Solmson donated one of the world's finest collections of Confederate money to the Arkansas History Commission. The collection, consisting of more than twenty-five hundred notes and bonds, was donated in memory of Henry Myar, a Confederate veteran. Harry B. continued his interest in Arkansas into the 1990s, still involved in more than a thousand acres of farming lands in eastern Arkansas.

Ira Ackerman Lipman, born in Little Rock in 1940 to Orthodox parents Mark and Belle Lipman, founded the security services company, Guardsmark, Inc., in Memphis in 1963. It grew to become the fifth largest of some thirteen thousand companies operating in the United States in that field. Ira began working with his dad's investigating company, Mark Lipman Service, in Little Rock at age eight. Mature beyond his years, the young Ira was keenly observant and excelled at his school work. At Central High School, his speech teacher, Marguerite Metcalf, and journalism teacher, Mrs. Williams, encouraged his progress. He was greatly influenced in his youth by his parents, Jewish youth organizations, and

Rabbi Samuel Fox, who prepared him for his bar mitzvah. Ira helped establish Little Rock youth branches of the American Zionist Association and B'nai B'rith (the latter was named for Harold Tenenbaum, a Little Rock Jewish youth killed in action in World War II).

After the family moved to Memphis in 1958, Ira attended Ohio Wesleyan University but also continued to help his father. Young Ira noticed that a number of requests were for guards, and in 1963 he started his own security company and added his father's first name; thus Guardsmark was born. By the 1990s the company had eighty-six branch offices in the United States, served organizations in more than four hundred cities, employed about eight thousand workers, and had annual revenues in the range of $150 million. One of the company's branches was in Little Rock (with a substation at Ashdown) that employed 213 workers in parts of four states. A prolific writer of articles, Ira Lipman also authored the book *How to Protect Yourself from Crime* (published in its third edition in 1990 by Contemporary Books), and he had numerous articles published. Both religious- and civic-minded, Ira Lipman was involved in a number of organizations and received a number of awards, such as "Best Corporate Chief Executive of Achievement" in 1974 by the Gallagher Presidents' Report; "Security Person of the Year," by Security Letter, 1988; and "Outstanding Young Men of America," award in 1970. Ira married Barbara Couch, and they had three sons, Gustave, Joshua, and Benjamin. The family maintained residences at Memphis and New York.[90] Ira's father joined Guardsmark and was often hired as an expert at interrogating dishonest employees. He authored the book, *Stealing*.[91]

One of the greatest latter-day successes by an Arkansas Jewish native came from one of its oldest families. Richard Thalheimer, great-grandson of Ben S. Thalheimer, a pioneer settler to the state, began the Sharper Image catalog company in 1977. Described as a "Toys 'R' Us" designer products playpen for yuppies, by 1989 it had grown into a retail business with two hundred million dollars in sales.[92] A Yale Law School graduate, Thalheimer practiced law in San Francisco. He then began a new venture by advertising a twenty-nine-dollar stopwatch in a running magazine. The effort was successful, and he began putting out a color catalog, and the Sharper Image company came into being. He then began opening retail outlets and by 1989 had sixty-six stores in the United States and six abroad. Richard's father, Alan R. Thalheimer, who had bought out the Irma Dumas chain of dress shops in Arkansas, sold them in 1980 to help in his son's firm.[93] By 1989 the advertising budget of Sharper Image was twenty-five million dollars annually. (Richard had sought to go into advertising after finishing law school and had applied to a large Boston advertising agency. He was told that only Catholics and Irish could succeed in the Boston advertising world. After his company's amazing success through advertising, he noted that things had come full circle, in that he still was not Catholic or Irish.)[94] Based in San Francisco, the Sharper Image began reevaluating its focus by 1991, and its three distribution centers were consolidated into one, a one-hundred-thousand-square-foot facility located at Little Rock. The company had some one thousand employees in its various locations by that time.[95]

CHAPTER 17

Eastern Arkansas

Northeast Arkansas

During the forty-five years subsequent to World War II, the greatest changes in Jewish life in America occurred in the small towns and rural areas. In Arkansas, a mostly rural state, numbers of Jewish stores closed in that period of time, which reflected the general decrease in population outside the urban areas. Below are examples of what occurred with some of the Jewish individuals, families, and their businesses during this time.

BATESVILLE, NEWPORT, POCAHONTAS

Rose Jacobs, daughter of early Batesville merchant Michael Jacobs, died in March 1976. She was the last member of the Jewish families of Batesville. Members of the Brownstein and Salenfriend families were the only Jews left in Newport into the 1980s. Edith Dodson, a descendant of pioneer Jewish settler Isaac Hirst of Pocahontas, remained in that town into the 1980s. Neither she nor descendants of A. Z. Schnabaum (an early Jewish settler in Pocahontas), who located in several Arkansas towns, identified with Judaism.

PARAGOULD

At Paragould, members of the Samuels family did remain Jewish, and their family business was continued into the 1990s. William and Fannie (Sorkin)

Samuels, who established the Samuels Hide and Metal Company in the 1930s, had three sons, Bernard, David, and Alvin. All three served in the military in World War II. Bernard, who had risen to the rank of captain in the U.S. Army, returned to the family business after the war. (David also was associated with the company until he moved to St. Louis in 1960.) Bernard also was a partner in the Arrow Auto Parts store in Paragould. He became one of the town's leaders, serving as president of the Chamber of Commerce and also serving as chairman of the organization's Industrial Committee. He helped organize the Lions Club and served as its president. He was a musician as well. Bernard married Barbara Turkow, and their three children, Daniel, Edward, and Stephen, became professionals and practiced outside of Arkansas. When Bernard retired in 1981, a nephew, Martin "Marty" Buchman, son of Samuel and Selma (Samuels) Buchman, continued the Samuels company.[1] Alvin B. Samuel, whose father settled at Paragould in 1900, intermarried and did not identify with Judaism. He remained active in the business and civic life of the city into the 1990s.

The Graber family moved their large distribution center for their Graber store chain from Paragould to Memphis after World War II. Their department stores, which grew to number thirty, five of which were in Arkansas, were closed by the mid-1960s. Al and Roslyn "Rose" Weisberger, who had come to Paragould to work for the Graber enterprise (Al served as advertising manager), opened their own business in the 1940s, a women's dress shop named Roslyn's. After Al's death, the store was continued into the 1980s by Rose; she joined the Baptist church at Paragould in the late 1970s.[2]

JONESBORO

Jewish involvement in Jonesboro's business and civic life underwent a number of changes after World War II. By the mid-1980s there were no Jewish-owned retail stores in the city. George Heinemann, who had worked with Heinemann's Department Store until entering service in World War II, found the firm had been sold when he returned. He then opened Joseph's Footwear, which continued until his retirement in 1980. His son, Joe, established a marketing firm, HCH, Inc., with two partners, and the company marketed Jonesboro area products. Joe Heinemann served as president of the Jonesboro University Rotary Club in 1982. Phil Banks, owner of a Jonesboro department store, died in 1944. His brother Jesse then closed his own business at Wynne and moved to Jonesboro and continued Phil's store until his own death in 1961.[3] The mercantile store established by Ben Schoenfield in the 1890s was sold in 1974 by Ben's son, Morris "Bud" Schoenfield. Bud was active in civic affairs, serving on a number of the city's boards. The Schoenfield store was continued by its new owners under its original name until 1982.[4] Dr. A. C. "Model" Modelevsky, after serving in the U.S. Army, settled at Jonesboro after the war and worked with the state Health Department. He was active in local civic and temple affairs.

Although the Berger brothers, Ben and Alec, had been instrumental in establishing the Mercantile Bank of Jonesboro in the 1930s, a brochure published by the bank in 1968 made no mention of the leadership efforts of the men. Nor did it mention that Ben Berger had served as president of the bank for many years and that Alec had served as chairman of the board. Rather, it stated that "the efforts of local leaders, civic clubs, etc." had brought about the founding of the bank.[5] Nathan Deutsch, who had started with the bank when it first opened, continued there until his death in 1968. In 1982 his widow, Hazel (Johnson) Deutsch, donated fifteen thousand dollars to Arkansas State University, establishing the Nathan Deutsch Faculty Development Fund.[6] Maurice Rubenstein, who had served as executive vice-president of the Citizens' Bank of Jonesboro, died in 1979. Two of his children remained in Arkansas; his son Robert was associated with the state's rehabilitation program at Jonesboro, and son William worked at the Pine Bluff Arsenal.[7]

Several Hummelstein men of Jonesboro served in World War II—Sam B. and his brother Abe's sons, Lee and Louis. The Jonesboro Hide and Fur Company, established by Abe Hummelstein in 1907, became the Hummelstein Iron and Metal Company in 1974. It was continued by Lee Hummelstein, who married Victoria Wiggins, daughter of a Methodist minister. He was later joined in the firm by their children Lee Ann, who married John Sloan, and Sam, who married Marilyn McCracken. (Lee also had another daughter, Victoria.) Abe's brother Sam, who had worked with the Hummelstein firm and had served as its president, left the company in the 1950s and established Arkansas Metal Company, which refined and reclaimed cadmium. He became widely known in his field and held offices in several national scrap metal organizations; he served as a member of the President's Advisory Commission on Strategic Metals. The Arkansas Metal Company closed in 1980. In the 1980s Lee Hummelstein's son, Sam, served as a director of Simmons First Bank of Jonesboro and as president and treasurer of the Jonesboro Fine Arts Council. He and his wife, Marilyn, cochaired the Greater Jonesboro

United Way campaign in 1986. The Hummelstein company continued into the 1990s.[8]

In January 1945 Jonesboro businessmen and professionals raised funds to remodel a building that would be the temporary home of a new footwear factory that Harry Alberstein of St. Louis intended to establish in their city. Alberstein was not a newcomer to the locale; he had been born at Jonesboro in 1911, but his family had moved to St. Louis when he was about five years old. He had worked with a shoe factory while in college, had later run such a company, and then had made plans to start his own. Business and professional leaders of Jonesboro formed Jonesboro Industries, Inc., and erected a permanent building for Alberstein's company, known as Frolic Footwear.[9] The company was the first major-size manufacturing plant built in the city. It grew over the years and eventually employed eighteen hundred workers at its height. The plant was expanded to Walnut Ridge in 1966, to Monette in 1969, and to Fisher in 1973.[10]

Harry Alberstein had loved sports and had always wanted to be a coach. In 1951 he started the Frolic All Stars basketball team, which he and Willard Tilley managed. Alberstein bought the uniforms and a nine-passenger DeSoto, and for ten years the team traveled the mid-South, playing college and semi-pro teams, such as Ole Miss, the University of Arkansas freshmen, Arkansas College, and the Phillips Oilers. The team won two mid-South tournaments and one Amateur Athletic Union (AAU) state tournament, and it competed at Denver in the AAU National Championship tournament in 1952. The city of Jonesboro became well known in athletic circles through its Frolic All Stars.[11]

Alberstein sold his shoe company to Wolverine Worldwide in 1970 and became Frolic's executive vice-president. He died in 1976. The company continued to expand after his death, and in 1979 a plant was opened at Russellville with 250 employees. The Frolic Division of Wolverine also had plants in Little Falls, New York, and Monterey, Mexico, into the 1990s. When Frolic came to Jonesboro, the only other industrial employer was a basket factory, which closed. Frolic grew to become one of the leading industries of northeast Arkansas. With it began the rise of an industrial boom in Jonesboro; other plants followed and made the city a major industrial center. Alberstein was remembered as a person "who contributed heavily" to the area's progress. In the mid-1980s Frolic had more than a thousand employees, had sales of $28.6 million, and had a payroll of $12 million.[12]

The Blindman brothers, Abe and Joe, and their brother-in-law, Sam Levitt (who had married Anne Blindman), owners of a factory in

Minneapolis, Minnesota, that manufactured industrial boxes and crates, established the Southern Wooden Box Company in Jonesboro in 1954, which manufactured soft drink cases. The company employed some thirty-five people at first, but the plant grew to two hundred employees by the 1960s. Jonesboro proved to be an excellent site for the company, as much of the lumber in its operation came from Arkansas. Also, Jews were allowed into the local country club, and the Blindmans were avid golfers. The Blindmans entered the civic life of the city, finding Arkansas to be readily open to its Jewish settlers. (Jews were not allowed in civic organizations in Minneapolis in the 1940s and 1950s.)

After soft drinks began being bottled in plastic and aluminum containers, the wooden case industry declined, and the Blindmans sold their company in 1984. Joe retired and moved out of state, but Abe remained in Jonesboro, where he continued his interest in civic affairs and politics. He and his wife, Marna, became participants in plays offered by Jonesboro's Fine Arts Council.[13]

WALNUT RIDGE

The Sam Levit store of Walnut Ridge, the only Jewish store in town for many years, continued until 1954; family members then moved to Memphis. A few miles south at Tuckerman, Arthur Riegler remained a prominent citizen until his death in 1991 at age ninety-nine. His help and advice were valued by the community even during his later years. Although he had intermarried, he remained true to his faith and was buried in Mount Zion Cemetery in St. Louis.[14]

MANILA

Shortly after World War II, Abraham "Alfred" Fendler of Manila died. His wife, Rebecca, continued their store for several years and then moved to Memphis.[15] The Tiger-Levine Company of Manila was continued by the Borowsky brothers, Max and Bill, but in 1952 Bill bought out Max's interest. Bill continued his devotion to the town and its civic causes. Deeply religious and trained in Judaism, he prepared his three sons, Colman, Benjamin, and Leslie, for their bar mitzvahs and his daughter, Fruma, for her bat mitzvah. He and his family were committed to Temple Israel at Blytheville and went to every service if possible. Twice, when the St. Francis River between Manila and Blytheville flooded the highway, the family, including all four children, crossed afoot on the railroad trestle and were met by friends on the other side on their way to the temple. The

Borowsky children were well educated; none settled in Arkansas. In June 1982 the Tiger-Levine Store was sold, and the Borowskys, the town's last remaining Jewish citizens, moved to St. Louis to be near their sons. Both Bill and his wife, Pearl, had passed away by 1991.[16]

BLYTHEVILLE

Jerry Cohen, son of S. J. and Luba Cohen of Blytheville, was an honors graduate in engineering from Cornell University. He returned to Blytheville to work with his father (also an engineer) in constructing highways, levees, canals, and other structures. He and his wife, Huddy, were active in both the religious and civic life of Blytheville. Jerry's returning to his hometown was an exception; most of the young people who went away to school settled elsewhere. The Jewish community of Blytheville, which had been so vibrant immediately after World War II, steadily lost its Jewish citizens by death, retirement, and relocation. The Jerry Cohens moved to Memphis when they retired in the late 1980s. (In 1991 the Cohen's daughter Marcie was named project director of the Museum of the Southern Jewish Experience at Utica, Mississippi.) By the 1990s only three Jewish families were left in the city.[17]

Jewish newcomers had appeared occasionally in Blytheville after World War II. George and Norma Fisher worked with the Arkansas Industrial Development Commission (AIDC) in the early 1970s, seeking a suitable place to open a garment factory. (A major requirement was that a Jewish house of worship be nearby, and Temple Israel of Blytheville filled that need.) They opened the factory, called Anngeo Company, at Manila, and then moved it to Blytheville. George had come to America from Poland by way of Palestine in the late 1930s. He was imprisoned by the British on his first attempt to enter Palestine, but he later succeeded and joined the Irgun Zvi Leumi, a resistance group that sought to take Palestine from the British. It was headed by Vladimir Jabotinsky, who, after he was killed, was replaced by Menachem Begin, who subsequently served as Israel's prime minister. George joined the U.S. Army after coming to America and later served as an interpreter in prisoner-of-war camps. The Fishers sold their Blytheville company in the 1980s and moved to Memphis.[18]

Although Blytheville lost one Jewish family when the Philip Feinberg ladies' dress shop was sold in 1962 and the family moved to Memphis, a Jewish couple from Dumas, Robert and Hattie Heiman, moved there in the 1970s and operated a ladies' clothing store that handled a fine line of ready-to-wear. Robert, grandson of Max Heiman, who had helped to found the Gus Blass Store in Little Rock, had worked several years in Little Rock after serving in the Navy in World War II. He was associated with the United Dollar Stores at Dumas for twelve years before moving to Blytheville.[19] The Heimans lived there until their retirement in the late 1980s, when they moved back to Dumas.

One person who remained a constant in the Blytheville Jewish community was attorney Oscar Fendler, son of Abraham Fendler of Manila. Oscar Fendler was outspoken in his efforts on prison reform—he assisted in closing down the Mississippi County Penal Farm, the Phillips County Penal Farm at Helena, and helped clean up the administration that ran the St. Francis County jail. He worked with the Arkansas Bar Association and the American Bar Association, helping to improve the system of jurisprudence throughout America. Feeling that dishonest judges should be punished, he needled the state legislature on judicial reform. In 1963 a Little Rock newspaper said that some Arkansans, including legislators, had "tiptoed" up to the subject of judicial reform, while Fendler, then president of the Arkansas Bar Association, had "galloped up in a cloud of dust" on the subject.[20] Although he was described as being flamboyant and as a gadfly, he was pleased with the changes he had helped bring about over a fifty-year period.[21] He was just as tireless in his efforts to help the Blytheville area as he was in fighting hate, prejudice, dishonest judges, and inhumane treatment of criminals. On two separate occasions, he was instrumental in the reactivation of the Air Force base at Blytheville, spending considerable time and money on such efforts (the Base did close, however, in December 1992). Fendler expressed his love for Arkansas, saying that no more loyal Americans than its Jewish citizens could be found in the state.[22] His daughter, Frances, also a lawyer, married attorney Jeff Rosenzweig, son of Dr. Joe and Susi Rosenzweig of Hot Springs, and both practiced law at Little Rock into the 1990s.

OSCEOLA

Lionel Silverfield, son of Morris and Edythe (Bisno) Silverfield, was one of only a handful of young Jews who returned to Osceola after completing his education. He was a graduate of the University of Alabama and served in the Army Medical Corps from 1955 to 1957. He continued the family's clothing store and was active in local civic affairs, serving on the boards of the Chamber of Commerce, City Planning Commission, Kiwanis, Retail Merchants group, and several charity organizations. He and his wife had three children.[23]

Two Osceola merchants, brothers Nathan and Hyman "Hymie" Weinberg, who were sons of the dedicated Annie Weinberg (see chapter 6), remained lifelong residents of the city even after their retirement in the 1970s. Melvin Lapides, son of Louis Lapides, also remained in the city and became one of its most successful businessmen. Unassuming, yet friendly in appearance, he became an influential citizen, helping local churches and promoting state and local politicians, such as President Bill Clinton, U.S. Representative Bill Alexander, and U.S. Senator Dale Bumpers.

In 1960, when founder and president of the American Greetings firm, Jacob Sapirstein, drove through east Arkansas, he stopped at Melvin Lapides' general mercantile store and asked him how Jews were treated in the area. When Lapides told him, "Just fine," Sapirstein said he was considering putting a small factory near the town.[24] The small factory turned out to be a facility that covered twelve and one-half acres initially; then it grew to be the seventh largest employer in Arkansas by 1988. By November 1990 American Greetings of Arkansas reported a net income for the third quarter of 1990 at almost $31 million.[25] According to Lapides and Osceola mayor, Richard "Dick" Prewitt, the city did not have a hint of anti-Semitism; Jews and Gentiles were all viewed as people, without discrimination.

JOINER, MARION

At Joiner, in Mississippi County, the stores of the Evenskys, Weisses, Silversteins, and Grossmans continued into the 1950s through the 1970s and then closed as family members died or retired and moved elsewhere. Their stores constituted almost all of the town's business district, and their closing was a considerable loss to the area.

At Marion, in Crittenden County, the store established by Isador Brick was continued by his son Meyer after Isador became ill and died. Meyer (1919–) gave up a career as an engineer to return and continue the small family business. He was active in civic affairs and was elected to two terms on the county court. Meyer and his wife, Virginia, had two sons, Steve and Phil. Jewish students were not allowed in high school fraternities at Marion while the boys were growing up, and a friend of Phil's resigned from a fraternity in protest of such discrimination. Meyer's brother Jake became an attorney in West Memphis. Both men served in the military during World War II.[26]

LEPANTO

Albert and Herman Bindursky also served in the war and returned to Lepanto, continuing the family store for a number of years. Another brother, A. B., a World War I veteran and a Lepanto merchant, married Addie Kaplan, who became involved in almost every activity that helped the town. The Bindursky's sister Esther continued her dedicated work as editor of the *Lepanto News Record* (see chapter 11) into the 1970s. After thirty-four years as an editor, during which time she won more than two hundred journalism awards, Esther Bindursky died in 1971.[27] Only Albert, a lifelong bachelor who retired in the 1970s, remained in Lepanto until his death in the mid-1980s.

McCRORY

I. N. "Nudy" Arnof continued to be an infuential citizen of McCrory in Woodruff County until his death in 1986. He was the original organizer of the Woodruff County Industrial Corporation and helped bring to the county the Royal Shoe Company and a branch of the American Greetings firm. His interests in and contributions to the schools of McCrory were without equal. He donated the I. N. Arnof Library to the McCrory school system, raised funds for the town's Walter Raney Memorial Park, and served on every civic and cultural board that had to do with McCrory's progress. In 1974 he received the Exceptional Accomplishment Award for community leadership from the Arkansas Development Program. He served a number of years as a town council member, and the council designated 30 April 1978 as "Nudy's Day" in recognition of his outstanding, dedicated leadership. After Arnof died, John Eldridge, a Woodruff County attorney, said that the results of Arnof's labors had left a number of monuments that were important to the lives of McCrory's citizens; Eldridge could not remember many civic projects of the county to which Arnof had not generously contributed.[28]

COTTON PLANT

At Cotton Plant, also in Woodruff County, Sol Nathan continued his store for a number of years after the war. Dave Blumberg, who was born at Forrest City in 1911 and spent part of his childhood in Cotton Plant when his father, Louis Blumberg, ran a store there, remained in the South in his adult years. He had moved with his family to St. Louis and after college lived in Knoxville, Tennessee, where he became identified with the struggle for equal opportunity for blacks. He was vitally active in B'nai B'rith; he served District Seven as president, served two three-year terms as an international vice-president, and was international president from 1971 to 1978. He worked closely with the B'nai B'rith–sponsored Levi Hospital in Hot Springs until his death in 1989.[29]

WYNNE

Several sons of the early Jewish merchants in Wynne, Cross County, remained in the city and helped it grow. Most of them served in World War II and then returned to family-owned businesses or established new ones. David Drexler returned after the war and conducted his restaurant, David's, for a short while. He sold it and established the Wynne Insurance and Loan Company, Inc., with a partner to whom he sold the business in 1967. Drexler served as president and director of the Wynne Federal Savings and Loan Company, was a director of Cross County Bank, a member of the Chamber of Commerce, and chairman of the Wynne Planning Commission.[30]

Benjamin Meyer, a grandson of Solomon Block, whose family had set-tled at Wittsburg and, later, at Wynne, continued as a cattle farmer at Wynne after serving in World War II. He was on the board of the Eastern Arkansas Livestock Association and the Cross County Conservation District.[31] Raphael Holt "Rafe" Andrews, a descendant of Raphael Block of the pioneer Block family of Wittsburg, was associated with the Cross County Bank at Wynne in the 1980s. His family had intermarried and was no longer Jewish.[32]

David Reagler, son of Morris Reagler of Wynne, served in World War II and returned to Wynne after receiving a business degree at Louisiana State University. He felt obligated to return in order to help his parents. He was active in the town's civic affairs.[33]

The three sons of Hyman Steinberg, Isadore "Izzy," Morris, and Jacob "Jake," continued as active partners in the Wynne family business, which consisted of a store and farmlands. Izzy was head of the Merchants and Farmers Cotton Gin and was a member of the Chamber of Commerce and the Wynne Industrial Park Board. All three Steinbergs were active in Wynne's civic life and the local B'nai B'rith lodge. Izzy married Pearl Milstein and had two children, Alvin and Elaine; Morris, who served in the Navy in World War II, married a non-Jew, Edie, and they had two sons, Ron and Harold; Jake did not marry. The Steinbergs all remained Jewish and attended Baron Hirsch in Memphis or Agudath Achim in Little Rock.[34] Hyman Steinberg's daughter, Sadie, married Arthur Evensky, a merchant at Parkin. The Evenskys had two daughters, Bette and Marcia. Bette (Greene) became an author and wrote several children's books, all of which had their settings in Arkansas. One of them, *Summer of My German Soldier*, was made into a movie.[35] After Hyman Steinberg died in 1958, family members donated some of their downtown property to the city of Wynne, and the Hyman Steinberg Park was established on the site.

EARLE

The store begun by William H. Harris at Earle continued to operate after the war, and he eventually had a chain of thirteen stores. When Harris died in 1954, he had only seven stores, five of which were in Arkansas. His daughter Irmazell married Stanley Lee of Memphis; the Arkansas stores eventually closed.[36]

After serving in the U.S. Army in World War II, Sol Bursk returned to Earle, where he and his wife, Lena, opened the Bursk Department Store. They closed it in 1962 when they bought the Western Auto Store at Earle and enlarged its facilities. In 1973 Sol bought the American Chair Manufacturing Company with two partners, Max Elms and Tom Fournier. By the 1980s they had sixty-five employees, were distributing to twenty-eight states, and had about $3 million in annual sales volume.[37]

George Erber Stein, son of Saul and Irene (Erber) Stein, returned to Earle after serving in the U.S. Army in the 1940s. He married Jessie Smith, a non-Jew, and their son, George Raymond Stein, continued into the 1980s with the family grocery store.[38]

TURRELL

Herman Baer continued the family businesses at Turrell after serving on the U.S. Navy battleship *West Virginia* as a gunner in World War II (his brothers also served in the military—Robert, Navy; Jake, Army; and Isadore, Air Force). Herman served as Turrell's mayor for more than twenty years; a street in the town was named in his honor. He retired in the late 1970s and moved to Horseshoe Lake near West Memphis. His son Ronald operated a men's clothing store in West Memphis in the 1980s.[39] Dr. Milton Lubin, who began his medical practice in Turrell in a rented store that formerly belonged to the Friedberg family, moved to West Memphis and became a prominent doctor there. He bought up large farms around Turrell, which were operated by his son in the 1980s.[40]

FORREST CITY

At Forrest City, Sol Cohn's children, William, Sylvia, and Freda, continued the family wholesale grocery company. William headed the firm and expanded the company, building a large warehouse in 1963, which was doubled in size in 1977. The company grew to become one of the state's largest in that type of business. William was active in civic affairs in Forrest City. He married Suzanne Bronstein of New York, and two of their four children had joined in the family business in the 1980s. Freda (Cohn) Brode moved to Memphis, where she became active in Hadassah and later served as president of its Southern Region. Sylvia (Cohn Gruner) Walters also was active in Hadassah and B'nai B'rith; she served as Arkansas president of the latter.[41]

Harold Sharpe returned to Forrest City after serving in World War II and continued his law practice. In 1962 he helped found another country club in Forrest City, one that allowed Jewish members. (He considered it ironic that after two of the three men who were instrumental in banning Jews from the first country club died, he was asked to handle their estates.) Mr. and Mrs. Harold Sharpe were both active in civic life of Forrest City.[42]

Max Cohen's store at Forrest City was continued after the war and its size was expanded. He retired in 1980 and sold his interest to his son, Barry, who had joined the firm after graduating from college. Both Max and Barry were active in the civic life of the city.[43]

After serving in the U.S. Marines in World War II, Louis Barg returned to Forrest City and went into used, new, and surplus steel and then became a new steel distributor by 1951. In 1974 he formed the Barg Steel and Pipe Company, with locations at Little Rock, West Memphis, Osceola, and Forrest City. He had some sixty employees and sales of from six to seven million dollars annually by the early 1980s. He entered the civic life of Forrest City with zeal, helping the drive for an airport, and then serving as chairman of the airport committee for ten years. He was chairman of the Red Cross, the March of Dimes, Lions Club warehouse broom sales (for thirteen years), and helped in developing a horse show grounds, which was used to raise funds to aid crippled children. He served as a justice of the peace for two years. From an Orthodox background, he and his wife, Gertrude, drove the 120-mile round trip to Memphis each Sunday to take their two children, Barbara and Charles, for Jewish training. Louis served as head of B'nai B'rith in Arkansas and of District Seven. He also served as an international vice-president. (For many years, Jewish life in Forrest City centered around the B'nai B'rith lodge; members came from miles around each month, bringing their families.)[44] The Barg's son, Charles, became a Little Rock physician. The Louis Bargs moved to Memphis in the late 1980s.

BRINKLEY

At Brinkley, Louis Salinger, son of Charles and Zerlena (Meyer) Salinger, whose forebears were pioneer settlers of that section of the state, continued the family store in Brinkley after serving in the U.S. Army Air Force in World War II. He was active in the town's civic affairs and served as president of the Rotary Club. He moved to Little Rock in the 1980s.[45]

Dr. Evelyn Harberg, an optometrist, settled in Brinkley in 1956. She was the daughter of Dr. Hyman Harberg, who had practiced medicine at Jonesboro before joining the staff of the Veterans Administration Hospital in Little Rock. Dr. Evelyn Harberg was one of the first single persons in the state to adopt a child, a daughter, Sarah. After Evelyn's mother, Sarah, died in the 1970s, Dr. Hyman Harberg moved to Brinkley to help raise the child. (Dr. Hyman Harberg said that, during his practice at Jonesboro, he had made several house calls where the patients would rub his forehead to see if he had horns.)[46] The Harberg family moved to Little Rock in the late 1980s. Young Sarah became a lawyer and joined the state attorney general's office in 1990. Dr. Hyman Harberg died in 1991.

WEST MEMPHIS

Several Jewish stores continued to operate at West Memphis after the war; some of their owners lived at Memphis. The Weisburd store, which had operated at Clarendon and Blytheville before moving to West Memphis, closed in 1981. Mike and Sadie Levitch continued their army surplus store on Broadway in the 1980s. The Kaplan's operated Kay's Furniture Store, and the Levys had Harry's Department Store. Most of these stores had closed by the mid-1980s.

Mildred "Mickey" Reagler of Wynne married Edward J. Rubens, and they made their home at West Memphis. Rubens, an attorney, became municipal judge, serving from 1950 to 1970. Originally from Bridgeport, Connecticut, Rubens had a warm, friendly manner and adapted well to Southern hospitality; he served as president of the Lions, Rotary, and the Chamber of Commerce. Mickey Rubens was chairman of the Library Board, president of the 20-Club (for college scholarships), and president of the Parent-Teacher Association. Their son Kent, also an attorney, served as a state representative from Crittenden County from 1974 to

1980. While in the state legislature, he helped to locate the Vocational-Technical School at West Memphis.[47]

HUGHES

Hughes, in St. Francis County, had a few Jewish stores that continued after World War II. The men's clothing store established by Abe and Max Zuckerman was continued by the latter after Abe died. The store thronged with customers for many years, and in the 1960s Max retired to Florida and left the store with his son Theodore. By that time trade had slowed considerably, and by the 1980s Theodore was buying lottery tickets through a friend in Missouri, hoping he could win and move away from the seemingly dying town. The stores run by Mervin Reisman, Julius Reisman, and the Levy family had closed some years before. Although the Zuckerman children had no formal religious training and the parents had no time to train them at home, all remained Jewish; two married non-Jews, but the spouses converted to Judaism.[48]

Southeast Arkansas

The Jewish merchants of Marianna continued their stores after the war, and most of them did quite well until a boycott by blacks of white-owned businesses began in July 1971 and continued until August 1972.[49] Many of the boycotted stores closed, and by the late 1970s the only Jewish-owned stores remaining were those of the Lewis family and the O'Mells.

The Lewis store in Marianna was continued by Peggy (Lewis) Young after the death of her father, Leon, in 1969. The store closed in the mid-1980s. Leon's younger brother, Julius, remained in Marianna until his death in 1980. Both brothers were friends to all races and were known for their honesty. Max O'Mell came to Marianna after World War II and opened a car dealership with his brother-in-law, Nate Silverstein. After O'Mell died in 1956, his widow, Dorothy, married Julius Lewis. The O'Mell's sons, Ron and Steve, opened Five Dollar Stores in four Arkansas locations and in one location in Mississippi that continued into the 1990s. Ron served as president of the Marianna Rotary Club and was active in other civic organizations.[50]

HELENA

Helena, in Phillips County, continued to flourish after World War II, but the general changes in the agricultural life of the South made continuing inroads into the population through the next four decades. After Abe Goldsmith died in the 1940s, his wife, Louise (Hurst) Goldsmith, continued to operate their store until the 1960s. Lafe Solomon continued operating his large farming interests until his death in 1949. His nephews, George Goldsmith and David Solomon Jr., formed the Solomon-Goldsmith Cotton Company to oversee the operation. George Goldsmith died in 1960 and left David Solomon Jr. to handle the business, which he did into the 1990s.[51] The Feldman Commission Company, a produce and cold storage business, was liquidated by Solomon Feldman Jr. in 1975. The Ciener clothing store was continued into the 1980s by Sam "Sonny" Ciener Jr. The Grauman family, one of Helena's early Jewish families, ontinued in the city in the 1980s, with Edward Grauman serving as municipal judge.

Helena's downtown section underwent remodeling efforts in the 1980s to spruce up the business section, and an annual King Biscuit Blues Festival was inaugurated in 1986. It was drawing thousands of visitors to the city from as far away as Great Britain by 1991.[52] A Delta Cultural Center was established at Helena in 1990. The Jewish population of the city continued to be diminished by death, however, and its young people did not return.

David Solomon Jr., an attorney, made Helena his lifelong home, and he became one of the most prominent men in eastern Arkansas. After serving in the Army in World War II, he resumed his law practice and his civic involvement at Helena. He served on the Helena–West Helena School Board, served as one of fourteen members of the Arkansas State Advisory Committee on Public Education under President Richard Nixon, served a ten-year term on the State Highway Commission and was commission chairman in 1984, served as city attorney in Helena, and served as president of the Helena–West Helena Industrial Development Corporation and the Helena Cotton Oil Company. He was commissioner and chairman of the White River Drainage District of Phillips and Desha counties, president of the Phillips County Chamber of Commerce, and a member of the executive committee of the Lower Mississippi Valley Flood Control Association. He received the Arkansas Bar Association's "Outstanding Lawyer-Citizen" award in 1982. He became well known statewide, and it was said that he probably would have gained national stature had he not chosen to live in a portion of the state that was "perceived by many as backward."[53] Dressed impeccably with the bow ties he favored, he was known for his modest demeanor, sincerity, and honesty, coupled with his amazing legal and business acumen. He always had time for people who needed him.[54] Solomon and his wife, Miriam (Rayman), had three sons, David, Rayman, and Lafe (none of whom returned to Arkansas after college).

Although Josephine "Miss Josie" (Krow) Mundt died in 1943, her legacy continued through her efforts with the Helena Civic Music Association. (The Association disbanded after the Warfield Concerts were established; Samuel Drake Warfield died in 1967 and left his estate to fund free concerts at Helena.) She also continued her legacy through her daughters, Rosalind and Vera. Rosalind became an accomplished violinist until a recurring problem in her left hand ended her ability to play. She returned to Helena, where she married Aubrey Solomon and was active in musical affairs, engaging in activities such as directing choirs. Those who sang under her professional, authoritative direction remembered long afterwards her ability to "pull the voice out of you."[55] After Rosalind died in 1980, a special concert was presented in her memory at Helena by the New Orleans Philharmonic Orchestra.

Vera Mundt, who married Fred Miller of Helena, was a graduate of Louisiana State University. She began teaching senior English at Helena's Central High School in 1963. She was highly thought of by her students, and when she died in 1982, a flower garden was built in front of the high school and a tapestry placed in the school's library in her memory. Many of her students wrote to the local paper, recounting the positive impact her teaching had on their lives. Steve Phifer wrote that he credited his success in dealing with the world of ideas to "the best classroom teacher I ever had, Vera Miller."[56] Several years after her death, a former student wrote of her, saying that she prepared her students to go into any field they wanted. The student said that "nothing before or since" had prepared him for the loss of this "magnificent lady."[57]

MARVELL

At nearby Marvell, the Davidson family continued to accumulate land holdings, owning some seven thousand acres in the state in 1985, six thousand of which were under cultivation. A piece of their land was donated to the state for the Louisiana Purchase Historic State Park.[58] Abe Davidson served as state commander of the Arkansas American Legion—possibly the only Jew ever elected to the post. He was active in civic affairs and was an avid athlete. He was a semipro baseball player and won medals in the low hurdles. One of his six grandchildren, David Berger (son of his daughter Dorothy), followed his grandfather's athletic bent and became part of the Israeli weightlifting team that competed in the 1972 Olympic Games in Munich. David Berger was one of eleven hostages taken by Arab terrorists and killed.[59] He had moved to Israel in 1970 and held dual American and Israeli citizenships. Some of the Davidson sons, Joe, Buddy, and Sol, continued to live in Marvell into the 1980s. Joe established a catfish farm there.[60]

Ludwig Hirsch and Ira Krow, longtime merchants of Marvell, both died in 1951. An editorial at the time noted that the two men were instrumental in the agricultural growth of Phillips County for fifty years. Through good times and bad, the two had never lost faith in the area's future, it said. It also noted that the younger generation, which was more interested in success than in helping others, would do well to learn from Krow and Hirsch in such matters.[61] Edmund Hirsch died in 1974. There were a few other Jewish-owned stores in Marvell, operated by the Baers, Mosses, and Tubas, and all closed subsequent to World War II.[62]

HOLLY GROVE

Members of the Abramson family continued to live in and to lend support to the area of Holly Grove down through the fourth generation. Ralph Abramson, grandson of pioneer settler Rudolph Abramson, served as mayor of Holly Grove from 1948 to 1958. He was active in Rotary, the Boy Scouts, and the Cotton Ginner's Association and served on the city council in the 1980s. At that time the family owned some fifteen hundred acres of land, which were managed by Ralph's son, Ralph Abramson Jr. The latter's wife, Linda Abramson, was head of the White River Nature Center and was instrumental in the establishment of the 204-acre Hardwood Wetlands Nature Reserve in Monroe County in 1987. (The land was donated by L. E. Thompson of Pine Bluff.) Ralph Abramson Sr.'s other son, Raymond, practiced law at Clarendon and was city attorney for Holly Grove in the 1980s. Janice (Abramson) Feldman, Ralph Abramson's sister, continued to live in the large Abramson home into the 1980s. She was active in local affairs also, holding local and regional offices in the American Legion Auxiliary, serving with all charity drives, and working with the Parent-Teacher Association.[63]

CLARENDON

Only the large two-story red brick building with the Bondi name at the top, located at 104 Madison Street in Clarendon, remains as a memorial to the once-thriving business conducted by the Bondi brothers. Edward and Ike Bondi, who ran the store, died in 1942. The Jewish presence in Clarendon was continued, however, by Leonard Kern Jr., who continued into the 1990s the store established by his father in 1935. Leonard Kern Jr. and his wife, Sally (Freedman), added a photography studio to the general store. Kern was active in civic affairs, serving as president of the Lion's Club, the Chamber of Commerce, and the Arkansas Professional Photographers organization.[64]

LAKE VILLAGE

Members of the Sam Epstein family remained in Lake Village into the 1990s. Sam's daughter Sylvia married Ben Angel of Memphis; the couple lived at Lake Village and was active in the family business. Ben served as vice-president and board member of the Bank of Lake Village; he received the city's first "Man of the Year" award in 1963. He served on the city council, the Lakeside School Board, as a commissioner of the Chicot County Drainage District, and as a commissioner of the Lake Village Planning Commission. He also was a trustee of the Ben Epstein Scholarship Trust Fund and of the Morris and Clara Rosenzweig Trust Fund.[65] The Angels had two sons, Sam Epstein and Rodney. Sam married Jan Hallmark, who converted to Judaism; their two children were raised Jewish. Sam was appointed to the Southeast Arkansas Levee District in 1979; he was the second man from Arkansas to serve on it and the only Jewish person ever to be appointed to the position.[66] Sam Angel succeeded his father in the Epstein enterprise after the latter died in 1968. Rodney Angel was active in almost every local civic group and was particularly involved in politics as an avid supporter of the Democratic Party. He died at age forty-four in 1991.

Melvyn Epstein, another daughter of Sam Epstein, married Ed Festinger, whose family operated stores at Conway and Hot Springs. After serving in the military in World War II, Festinger and his wife lived at Lake Village, where he operated the Lake Village Implement Company, later known as the Epstein-Festinger White Land Company.[67] (A third daughter of Sam Epstein, Helen, married Harold Kantor and moved out of state.) After Sam Epstein died in the 1940s, the intent of his will was debated by family members in numerous court appearances for decades before it was settled in the 1980s.

Nathan "Mr. Freedie" Friedman continued as a constable for the city of Lake Village until his death in the late 1950s. Michael "Mike" Rankin, son of James and Geraldine (Minsky) Rankin of Lake Village, served as a state mental health commissioner in Arkansas in the 1970s; he moved to California in the 1980s.[68]

EUDORA

The numerous Jewish-owned stores at Eudora had all but ceased by the 1980s. After serving as a captain in the U.S. Army in World War II, Harold Hart returned to Eudora and continued the clothing store established by his father, Max, in the 1920s. (Harold's brother, Leon, served as a captain in the U.S. Army Air Force during the war.) Harold served on the Eudora City Council for a number of years, was president of the Chamber of Commerce, and served on the Democratic Central Committee. His wife, Lucille (Mathis) Hart, served as city recorder, city clerk, and on the local school board.

Carroll Meyer Sr. also remained in Eudora, where he continued to serve on the city council until 1958. He retired from business in 1965 and died in 1988. His son, Carrol Meyer Jr., served in the U.S. Army in World War II, and his younger son, Charles, was in the U.S. Army Infantry during the Korean War. Charles later joined the U.S. Air Force Reserve and reached the grade of captain. He left Eudora in 1956, and both he and his brother eventually settled at San Antonio, Texas.[69] A cousin of the Meyers, Alvin Meyer Jr., remained at Eudora, where he continued his family's extensive farming enterprise. He was selected as chairman of a political lobbying group, "Farmers for America," that was organized in 1984 by Arkansas farmers.[70]

CROSSETT

Julian F. Haas, a journalist and broadcaster who had settled at Little Rock in 1936, moved to Crossett in 1952 and bought the radio station KAGH. During its first year the station went from one hundred to two hundred fifty watts, and Haas later added KAGH-FM. When he died at age seventy in 1974, the Arkansas Broadcasting Association lauded him in a resolution, noting that he was highly thought of in his field; he was an "erudite person whose quality of expression was held in high esteem by those who knew him."[71] Haas also was a founder and first president of the Ashley County Historical Society.

DERMOTT

Bernard Levi of Pine Bluff married Louise Weisman of Dermott. After serving in the U.S. Army in World War II, he returned to Dermott, where he worked in the Weisman store. He and his wife became its owners after Joseph Weisman died, and they continued the store into the 1980s.

Bernard was president of the Dermott Rotary Club, a member of the County Equalization Board, and a member of the board of directors of the Dermott bank. He was active in the Boy Scouts and in a number of other civic causes as well. [72] Mendel and Beulah Pinkus continued the Pinkus store at Dermott until their retirement. They remained in Dermott into the 1990s. Abe Abroms and his wife retired to Florida in the 1970s. In 1972 they sold their large department store in Dermott to their great-niece and her husband, Marjorie and Barry Brunner,[73] who sold it in the mid-1980s.

McGEHEE

The Jewish-owned stores at McGehee followed the pattern of those in other small Arkansas towns. Isadore Marcus, who owned the Eagle Store at McGehee, was joined in the business by his daughter Faye and her husband, Jay Lewis, in 1954. They stayed with the store until it closed in 1966. Jay worked with the United Dollar Stores at Dumas, and when they were sold, joined Wal-Mart in northwest Arkansas and moved to Bella Vista. The Dreyfus Company of McGehee continued into the mid-1980s, when it was sold. Maurice Abowitz, son of Sam Abowitz of Arkansas City, continued the family farming enterprise into the 1990s and was joined by his son Stephen "Steve." Isadore Small, who, with his wife, Ella (Dessent) Small, had the Morris R. Dessent Dry Goods Store, closed the store and left McGehee after he was robbed in 1978 (his wife had died in 1976).[74] Sam Wolchansky, a pillar in the religious community, remained in McGehee until his death in 1953. William and Joan Hamburger continued their cotton and cattle business in McGehee until their retirement in the 1970s; they moved to Memphis, where he died at age ninety-four in 1984.

Seymour Fleisig—son of Charles Fleisig, who had established a clothing store at McGehee in 1932—served in the U.S. Army five years. He married Edith Lipsey, a graduate of Brown University and the Rhode Island School of Design; in 1942 she was the fourth woman in the state of Rhode Island to enlist in the Women's Army Auxiliary Corps (WAAC) (it was later shortened to Women's Army Corps [WAC]). Her family was deeply religious, and her brother was a rabbi. She sang in the WAAC choir and was also an artist. After the war, Seymour and Edith continued the Fleisig New York Store. They had three children, all of whom were artists. Edith wrote a column for a local newspaper, and she became recognized for her art work, some of which was placed in Meir Chayim Temple.

Seymour and Edith continued to make McGehee their home after the Fleisig store closed in 1982; the Fleisig children moved out of state.[75]

DUMAS

Dante-Tanenbaum family members continued their enterprises at Dumas during and after World War II. They did well and were generous in giving back to their beloved community. The family established a student loan program so that any young person desiring to attend college could do so. They gave the seed fund of one thousand dollars that brought about a twenty-one-acre park for the city in 1953 and gave the same amount to start the fund for a city pool. Bernard Tanenbaum established the United Dollar Stores in 1957, using the original Dante store as a pilot. The chain grew to 278 stores by 1976. When the firm was sold to the Dollar General Corporation in 1977, it was one of the largest companies in the South. Bernard had started an industry in Dumas after the town's only industry burned in a mill fire. He began in 1955 with eighteen sewing machines in the rear of the Dante store and named it Dantan for the Dante and Tanenbaum families. It grew into a sportswear manufacturing plant, which still operated in the 1990s (by then it had been sold by the Tanenbaum family). Bernard was active in civic affairs and was prominent in getting the streets of Dumas paved and in raising funds for sidewalks. He was active in every aspect of Dumas life that promoted the good of the city. Arkansas Jaycees made him the first recipient of the Bernard J. Tanenbaum Humanitarian Award, established in his honor in 1960. The United Dollar Stores became one of the first firms in southeast Arkansas to give job advancement opportunities to blacks; the company also built a modern housing development for blacks that included some seventy homes, apartments, and a park.[76]

Charles Dante's son Jack was an active partner in the Dante enterprises, and he also was at the forefront of every civic drive in Dumas. He served as chairman of the Chamber of Commerce Industrial Foundation that was begun in the mid-1950s. He served on the city's school board—three years as president—and on the Drainage District No. 5 board. He assumed the management of the farming properties of the Dante enterprise as well as of the Dante gin. Jack's son, Charles H. Dante, was graduated from Tulane University and served as a first lieutenant in the U.S. Army. As did his father, he also worked with the farming operations and the gin, serving as president of Charles Dante and Son, Inc. He held a number of civic positions in Dumas. He married Jo Ann Meyers, and they had three children, daughters Toni and Camille and son Charles. Jack Dante died in 1977.[77]

The older Charles Dante died in 1967, but the philanthropy he had begun was continued by the Dante-Tanenbaum families in helping the community. They donated a forty-acre site for a new school complex in 1975 and donated sites for several churches. They gave more than three acres of valuable highway frontage land to the city on which to build a museum. When a segregated library was built by the city in the 1950s that was open only to whites, the Tanenbaum family built one for blacks and duplicated the white library's holdings. The Dante-Tanenbaum families gave land to build a center for handicapped children. When Bernard Tanenbaum Sr. died in 1981, he was working on another park for the city. It was said of him at the time that he was always working on something good, "something to be shared, like his ideas . . ."[78]

Bernard "Jerry" Tanenbaum Jr., also a graduate of Tulane University, joined the Dantan Company in 1955 and helped organize the United Dollar Stores (UDS), Inc., serving as its chief executive officer for fifteen years. He was active in a number of civic organizations of Dumas. He received the "Boss of the Year" award from the state Jaycees in 1970, was named one of the Ten Outstanding Young Men in Arkansas by the Jaycees in 1971, and received the "Distinguished Arkansan Award" from the Jaycees in 1974. He was president of the Southwest Council of the Union of American Hebrew Congregations from 1980 to 1984. His wife, Patricia "Pat" (Wise), was also active in civic and religious work. She served as president of the Dumas Jaycettes, of the Arkansas Jaycettes, and of District 16 of the National Federation of Temple Sisterhoods. She was named in the National Register of Prominent Americans in 1970. Jerry and Pat retired to Hot Springs in the late 1980s. They had two sons, B. J. "Jay" Tanenbaum III and Albert Wise Tanenbaum.[79]

Haskell Wolff continued the Wolff Department Store at Dumas into the 1990s. He also was civic minded and served as an alderman, as a member of the Dumas Water and Sewer Commission, and on the street committee of the city council; he also was a member of the board of the Dumas Agricultural Association. He served as president of the Dumas Chamber of Commerce and of the Lions Club. While Chamber of Commerce president, he helped establish the Industrial Foundation.[80]

Harry Phillips, who had escaped from Poland to America in 1938, returned to Dumas after serving in the U.S. Army in France during World War II, at which time he was wounded and was awarded a Purple Heart. He joined the Dante-Tanenbaum enterprise at Dumas and later worked with the United Dollar Stores. He and his wife Elsie (Hamburger), were active in local fraternal, civic, and religious organizations.[81]

Several Jewish citizens of Dumas received the "Outstanding Citizen Award" from the Chamber of Commerce. These included Charles Dante, Jack Dante, Mrs. Jack (Rose Mae) Dante, Elsie Phillips, B. J. Tanenbaum Sr., Pat Tanenbaum, Elaine Wolff, and Charles H. Dante (son of Jack Dante).

PINE BLUFF

Pine Bluff was Arkansas's fourth largest city in the 1980s. By that time most of the city's early Jewish pioneer families had either died or moved away. Some had intermarried, particularly after the 1940s, and their descendants were no longer Jewish. For those who remained in Pine Bluff during the decades following World War II, their dedication to their city and state continued. For example, when Harry Hanf, whose forebears had settled in Pine Bluff in the 1860s, visited New York with his wife in the 1940s, he ran an advertisement on his own initiative in the *New York Times*, inviting inquiries from industries interested in moving to a "charming Southern city." Sam and Jean Larkin responded to the ad and moved their plant, Larkin Lectro Products, Inc., to Pine Bluff. Larkin was considered a genius in his field, with some two hundred patents to his credit in such diverse fields as electronics, metalworking, and conventional machines. Several Jewish families came with the company, including E. Geiringer, a prominent European industrialist and former assistant finance minister of Austria who had fled Hitler's regime. Mrs. Geiringer had been a portrait photographer, and Albert Einstein was among her clients. After the Larkins returned to New York, the company continued under other management and became Central Transformer Corporation, a major industry in Pine Bluff.[82] Harry Hanf died in 1950, before he could see the full results of his efforts.

Pine Bluff lost one of its noted attorneys in 1960 when Maurice Reinberger died. He had taken as a partner R. A. Eilbott Jr. after World War II, and Eilbott continued the firm. In the 1980s it was known as Eilbott Smith Eilbott and Humphries.

Attorney Sam Levine, who served both in the state house of representatives and in the state senate beginning in the 1930s, was again elected to the Senate in 1956 and in 1958. His overt stand in upholding the Supreme Court's 1954 decision on school integration during the Little Rock Central High School integration crisis of the late 1950s and early

1960s cost him his political career (see chapter 16). His hurt over his political loss had somewhat mended by the time he died at age seventy-four in 1965.[83] Sam's brother, Jay Levine, who had established the Levine Cotton Company in Pine Bluff, continued with the firm until 1968; he died in 1969.

The F. M. Altschul Company, which in 1951 was considered Pine Bluff's oldest wholesale or retail business in continuous operation by the same family, was liquidated in the 1960s. Julius Lester, a descendant of Adolph Altschul, an early Pine Bluff pioneer who had married a mulatto, Maggie Carson, was the son of a black Methodist minister. Julius converted to Judaism in 1980 and published his life story in *Lovesong, Becoming a Jew*.[84] Lester served as a member of the Department of Afro-American Studies at the University of Massachusetts at Amherst. By the 1990s the only Altschuls in Pine Bluff were of the Christian faith.

Ira Bloom, son of early Pine Bluff pioneers, began his own company, Arkansas Collection Service, in the 1960s. He had worked with the Pfeifers of Arkansas company until it was sold. Bloom died in 1967. Dolf Kastor, who had been a featured soloist in the vaudeville Al G. Field Minstrel Show, died at age ninety-five in 1988. Harry and Zelda (Schlosberg) Riesenberg ran Harry's Department Store until Zelda's death in 1975. Harry died in 1981.

The Silbernagel wholesale produce company, which grew to serve a large area of southern Arkansas and northern Louisiana, later became a wholesale liquor firm, Silbernagel Company, Inc., which continued into the 1980s. Burt Schlosberg's men's store continued until the building burned in 1965. He then operated a small men's store with a partner until his retirement in the 1980s. Morris H. Rosen, owner of the Reed-Collier Drug Store, served as president of the Arkansas Pharmacy Association; he died in 1985. The store was continued by his son Robert. The Soltz Machinery and Supply Company, established by Hyman Soltz, was continued by Hyman's nephew, Gene Sherman, and later by Joe Webberman.[85]

Maurice Cohen continued his department store into the 1980s and also opened a ladies' dress shop, The Fashion. The stores were sold when he retired in the mid-1980s; both had closed by the 1990s. Jerome N. "Jerry" Glatstein's department store was continued by him and his wife, Geraldine, into the 1980s. He died in 1987 at age fifty-nine. Glatstein served somewhat as a shammas (sexton or caretaker) of Temple Anshe Emeth. He was active in civic affairs as well and served as president of the Preservation and Redevelopment of the Urban District of Pine Bluff.

The Baim Department Store (known originally as the Eagle Store), founded by Samuel "Sam" Baim around 1906, was continued by his sons Leo, Aaron, and Bennie. Sam's son Charles operated a branch store at Hot Springs. Aaron Baim died in 1956 and Leo in 1976. After Bennie retired, his daughter and son-in-law, Kay and David Shapiro, continued the store into the 1990s. Sam Baim's son Eugene "Gene" became a Pine Bluff attorney; Gene's son Kenneth followed in his father's profession. Sam's daughter Adah married Milford "Buddy" Sonnenschein, and they operated the Sunshine Shop at the Hotel Pines; the shop closed in 1962 when the hotel ceased to function. Adah died at age ninety in 1989.[86]

The Kahn jewelry store in Pine Bluff, established by optometrist Andrew Kahn in 1910, was continued after his death in 1968 by his wife, Bess; when she retired, their son, Stanley "Stan," assumed the business. One of Stan's four children, Adrianne, became a gemologist, completing studies at the Gemology Institute of America at Santa Monica, California, in 1976. She opened her own jewelry store at the Hot Springs mall in 1982.[87]

The Henry Marx men's wear company was continued into the 1990s by Henry F. Marx, grandson of Henry Marx, who had established the store in the 1880s. Henry F. married Susan Menzoff of St. Louis, and she became a well-known civic activist in Pine Bluff. She was assistant coordinator of the school district's Volunteers in Public Schools program, president of the Pine Bluff Junior League, and was associated with the Junior Auxiliary, the Easter Seal Society, and the southeast Arkansas Arts and Science Center. She served as chairman of the city's Reading is Fundamental Steering Committee and served on numerous boards. After she died at age forty-four in 1987, she was awarded posthumously the Ella Hunn Payne Award by the Pine Bluff Junior League. She and her husband had two sons. (Henry F. Marx's brother, Sydney, married non-Jew Sandra Willis, and they did not affiliate with the Jewish temple.)[88]

Dr. Harold Morris, who had been stationed at Camp Robinson in Little Rock during World War II, settled at Pine Bluff after the war and became well known in the area. Another prominent physician to settle there was Dr. Howard Stern, son of noted Little Rock architect Eugene J. Stern. Howard Stern married Jane Ellenbogen of Little Rock, who was descended from one of its pioneer Jewish families. Jane Stern became known for her interest in environmental problems and in 1963 helped develop the Jefferson County Audubon Society, in which she held a number of offices. Her interests covered the state, and she was active in saving the Buffalo River from developers and was responsible for preventing the Bayou Meto channelization. She received the Arkansas Wildlife

Federation's "Water Conservationist of the Year" award in 1971 and received the federation's highest award, the "Conservationist of the Year," in 1978.[89] She died at age seventy in 1989.

Some of the other Jewish people involved in the business life of Pine Bluff in the 1980s included Louis Siegel, a chemist with the Pine Bluff Arsenal; Mr. and Mrs. Daniel Stein, accountants; Mrs. Jimmy Collier and Mrs. Allen Goldman, who ran Zelda's, a clothing store; and Mr. and Mrs. Myron Abrams, who ran a jewelry store. Simon S. Joseph, son of Blytheville merchant Sam Joseph, joined the McNew Insurance Agency in Pine Bluff in 1944. He continued with the company into the 1990s, serving as vice-president and general manager.[90] Dr. Sheldon Blau, a veterinarian and a native of New York, settled in Pine Bluff in the 1950s and practiced there until his death in 1980.

No other transplanted Jewish person ever became so well known in Pine Bluff and the state as did Paul Greenberg, who came to Arkansas in 1962 as an editorial writer for the *Pine Bluff Commercial*. A native of Shreveport, Louisiana, who had done postgraduate work at Columbia University, Greenberg began winning prizes for his editorials and in 1969 won the coveted Pulitzer Prize for editorial writing. His work received Pulitzer recognition again in 1978, and he served as a Pulitzer Prize juror in the years 1984–85. He won numerous other awards, including the Scripps-Howard Foundation's Walker Stone Award in 1986 and the H. L. Mencken Award of the National Press Club in 1987. Because his writing reflected a sophisticated and confident manner and because of his Jewishness, he was often viewed as a "foreigner from the North."[91] His syndicated column appeared in newspapers nationwide by the 1980s and 1990s. In 1990 he was referred to by John Robert Starr, a well-known Arkansas journalist, as the best writer associated with Arkansas newspapers at the time.[92] In March 1992 Greenberg joined the statewide newspaper, the *Arkansas Democrat-Gazette*, as editorial page editor.

ALTHEIMER

At Altheimer, the town that was started after the Civil War with such hopes and dreams by the Altheimer brothers, Louis and Joseph, there was nothing Jewish about the town but the name after Jewish merchants left in the years after World War II. As did other rural towns in the state that saw progressive decline as farms grew larger and mechanization took over, Altheimer slipped into the byways. It was visited in 1980 by Donald R. Katz, great-great-grandson of Louis Altheimer, during a fast trip through

Arkansas. His observations of Altheimer and the state were an irreverent, outsider's view of the area; he saw almost nothing but the rehashed country bumpkin stereotype of the state and its citizens.[93] The antithesis of Katz's impression of Arkansas and Altheimer's citizens was found in the person of his great-uncle, Ben J. Altheimer, son of Joseph and Matilda Altheimer. Ben J. had returned to Arkansas in the 1930s and bought up much of the land originally owned by his family. When he died in 1946, the Ben J. Altheimer Foundation was established and did untold good for the town of Altheimer and for the state.

At Altheimer, the Ben J. Altheimer Foundation funds built a clerical and machine trades school, a technical school building, and a Boy and Girl Scouts building; it has provided college scholarships annually for two top Altheimer high school students as well as granting extensive funds to Altheimer public schools and churches. Arkansas educational institutions are its beneficiaries as well. In 1951, 1968, and 1974 it endowed faculty chairs at the University of Arkansas, Fayetteville, which covered cotton research and development, soybean research, and weed science. By 1986 the foundation had donated $3 million to the campus. In 1983 it donated more than fifty-two acres of land east of downtown North Little Rock to UAMS in Little Rock. The land was appraised at some $135 thousand.[94] The foundation also funded a lecture series at the UALR Law School as well as the Ben J. Altheimer Law Library at the Jefferson County Courthouse. The foundation's funds, which come from the farming of the extensive lands accumulated by Ben J. Altheimer, continue to benefit Arkansas charities and educational projects into the 1990s.

ENGLAND

Robert Sakon of England also was an outstanding benefactor of the state. He continued the family business in England until he retired in 1980. All the other Jewish-owned stores of the town had long since closed. Until his death in 1987, Sakon was a benefactor of a number of civic, charitable, and religious groups. And in his will he left two million dollars to seventeen Arkansas charities. His favorite charity, the Arkansas Enterprises for the Blind, received $300 thousand. Other recipients were Synagogue Agudath Achim, Temple B'nai Israel (both of Little Rock), the American Cancer Society, the American Diabetes Association, the American Heart Association, the Little Rock Chapter of Hadassah, and others.[95]

CHAPTER 18

Western Arkansas

Southwest Arkansas

CAMDEN

Between 1945 and the 1990s, all the Jewish citizens of Camden moved away or died with the exception of members of the Berg family. Judge Leonard Stern, prominent in civic and judicial affairs of the city, died in 1951. His son, Leonard Stern Jr., served in the U.S. Navy during World War II, returned briefly to Camden, then moved out of state. (He retired to Little Rock in the 1980s.) Harold Shyer Lazarus, a well-known south Arkansas plumbing and heating contractor who was a descendant of a pioneer Jewish settler, died in 1952. The ladies' clothing store established by Mose and Ida Zavelo was continued by their son Burton until 1964, when the latter moved to Little Rock.

Henry Berg, who had held the torch of Judaism high in the Camden community, died in 1950. Henry Myar "Mike" Berg, son of Leo Berg (Henry Berg's brother), married Helen DeFrance of Little Rock; she was a member of Temple B'nai Israel. Mike Berg continued the family enterprises in Camden with zeal and was active in the city's civic life. He was a director of the Merchants and Planters Bank, a member of the Arkansas State Police Commission (for twenty-one years), and was on the Ouachita

Hospital board for fourteen years. He continued his interest in the fire department as well. During his lifetime, Mike Berg expanded his family-owned financial empire, which included large land holdings in some six or seven counties. When he died in 1974 at age sixty-five, a local paper said that he could be counted on in backing important civic projects, that he was a good family man, and that he was a good citizen.[1]

Helen, Mike Berg's widow, continued her association with the Berg enterprises after his death. She was active in a number of civic organizations, including the building program for the Teen Town Center and the Camden Boys' Club. She was selected as Camden's Outstanding Woman of the Year twice by the Lions Club; she died at age sixty-nine in 1990.

Two of the three children of Mike and Helen Berg, H. M. Berg Jr., and Mrs. E. D. (Elaine Berg) Eckert, remained at Camden and continued with the Berg enterprises into the 1990s. In the 1980s and 1990s, the Eckerts drove the 196-mile round trip to Little Rock each Sunday to bring their children for instruction at Temple B'nai Israel; Elaine also taught Sunday School there.

EL DORADO

El Dorado's Jewish community, which stood at some thirty families in 1946, slowly diminished over the years. Some members of these families include Joseph Goodkin of the Oil Field Supply and Metal Company, who died in 1952; Benjamin and Isadore Berk, who continued their jewelry store into the 1960s (Ben died in 1959 and Isadore in 1969); J. B. Miller, insurance agent and lay leader of Temple Beth Israel, who died in 1970; and tailor Michael Fry, who died in 1976. Morris Lewis continued his New York Store, a ladies' ready-to-wear, until his retirement in 1974. Prominently known for his civic work, he died in 1980.

Irving Leon "Izzy" Pesses, who served as president of Pesses and Marks Pipe and Supply Company and vice-president of the El Dorado Paper Bag Company, established the Arkansas Steel Company as well. He continued his civic work in El Dorado and was elected by a landslide vote as mayor of the city in 1967. He served until his death in 1976. Known as a dynamic father figure and having been trained as an engineer, he made a number of improvements in El Dorado, such as straightening streets and building bridges. He also served as president of the El Dorado Kiwanis Club, the Chamber of Commerce, and the city's Industrial Development Corporation. He served on the Arkansas Crime Commission under Governor Winthrop Rockefeller and was a member of the executive board of the

Arkansas Municipal League. He was active in the Jewish community and served as president of Temple Beth Israel.[2]

After the war, El Dorado saw several newcomers who stayed and made the city their home. Jules Feinberg came to El Dorado in 1952 and opened his own engine and pump company, selling mostly water and sewer pumping for municipalities in seven mid-South states. As he traveled throughout the area, he observed the numbers of empty Jewish stores still standing. In many towns he was the only Jew the people there had ever met, and he was often expected to be an expert on the Bible (he was embarrassed that he knew so little). He married non-Jew Johanna Pellizzari, who converted to Judaism, and they had three children. From an Orthodox background, Feinberg occasionally took his family to the synagogue in Little Rock for worship.[3]

Joseph "Joe" and Janet Stuart, natives of Memphis, Tennessee, also came to El Dorado shortly after the war and established an office supply store that branched out to nearby Magnolia. They were active in Temple Beth Israel of El Dorado. Other newcomers to El Dorado included Ralph and Bluma Ginsburg, who came in 1948; Ralph managed the pipe department of Arkansas Pipe and Supply Company. Attorney Harry Steinberg, a native of Corning who handled mostly civil cases, settled at El Dorado. A lifelong bachelor, he had a country-boy appearance and a natural inclination toward helping anyone in need. He died in the 1970s.[4] Robert Koppel, son of Jacob and Frances Koppel of Benton, served as associate administrator of the Warner Brown Hospital at El Dorado in the 1960s and 1970s.[5]

The country club of El Dorado excluded Jewish members until the mid-1970s, when the club publicly acknowledged the existence of the rule and discontinued it. Every Jewish person in town received a personal apology and was invited to join the club. Three did—Izzy Pesses, his son, Arnold Pesses, and Joseph Stuart. Stuart was invited from four to eight times a year to speak on Judaism in Christian churches at El Dorado. He said he felt that anti-Semitism came from uninformed people who did not know Jews personally.[6]

FELSENTHAL

The town of Felsenthal, which had been established with such enthusiasm by the Felsenthal brothers around the turn of the century but had slowly ebbed away by the 1920s, received a new breath of life in 1978 with its reincorporation. Its resurgence came about when the sixty-five-thousand-acre Felsenthal Wildlife Refuge was established in Union, Bradley, and Ashley counties. The Refuge was located in the Felsenthal basin, an extensive natural depression crisscrossed by a system of lakes, sloughs, and bayous that are home to some endangered species of wildlife. When a lock-and-dam system was installed on the Ouachita River in the mid-1980s, it added to the system begun in 1915 that had been promoted so vigorously by Adolph Felsenthal and others of the area. The name Felsenthal was given to the lock and dam that opened near the town of Felsenthal in 1984. The town itself experienced a growth in sportsmen's cabins. A new sewer system was installed, costing more than $780 thousand. Two hundred ten people had signed up for connection to the system by the 1980s. The Felsenthal [family] Estate still owned some sixteen hundred lots in the town in the 1980s. By 1987 the town had one hundred fifty permanent residences, with an increase of twelve hundred people on weekends. It became a fishing and sporting paradise in southern Arkansas.[7]

TEXARKANA

Texarkana lost one of its most prominent Jewish citizens when Judge Louis Josephs died at age eighty-three in 1957.[8] Several other Jewish attorneys practiced there during the latter half of the twentieth century, including Harry Friedman and his sons Errol and Michael and his nephew, Don Friedman. The furniture store established by David Kusin was continued by his widow, Anne (Brody) Kusin, who married Louis Gold in 1969. Anne's son, Mel Kusin, later continued the business and also had Mel's Casual Furniture Store. He was active in the community civic life and received the city's "Man of the Year" award in 1956. Anne's daughter Gloria married Leo Bishkin, and they opened a bowling alley in Texarkana in 1959. Anne's son Sherman returned to Texarkana after serving in the U.S. Air Force in the 1950s and practiced law with Harry Friedman. Early settler Max Wexler sold his interest in his wholesale dry goods company, Wexler-McCoy, to employees when he retired in 1977. He and his wife, Marguerite, moved to Denver, Colorado, in 1985 to be near their children.

A number of Jewish newcomers settled in the border city subsequent to World War II. These included Mordecai "Morde" and Betty Glick, who established the Tri-State Iron and Metal Company in 1947. Their son Howard later joined in the business. In 1948 Ruben and Jeannette Gilden, together with cousins Arthur and Minette Vener, bought out a men's clothing store in Texarkana. The Veners later moved to Dallas, but the Gildens remained, and the men's shop continued until their retirement in 1980. Leon Friedman, son of early settler Benjamin Friedman, returned to Texarkana in 1960 and established the Friedman Steel Sales company. Joe Ruskin from McGehee married Rebecca Walkow of Texarkana and set up practice there as a pharmacist. (Rebecca's parents, Leo and Madelyn Walkow, were longtime residents of Texarkana and active in Mount Sinai Temple.) Sam and Marjorie Weisman, who came in 1964, were in the construction business; Sam built the Carver Terrace subdivision. Ed and Hedy Pearlman came in 1969 and opened the Ark-La-Tex Medical Rentals business. Betty Feir, a clinical psychologist, established a private practice in Texarkana in 1978 and also taught at East Texas State University in the city. Jim and Charlotte Ottinger came in 1980; Jim served as president of the Tex-Ark Joist Company in Hope, Arkansas.

In 1982, after Phillip Shuman had worked for the Offenhauser Company in Texarkana for fifty years, the company set up a scholarship fund in his honor. Shuman was active in civic work, serving as Optimist Club president; he received the C. E. Palmer Award for his services to the city.

ASHDOWN

The feed store in Ashdown established by Henry Kaufman in the 1940s continued to grow until it became one of the largest industries in the town. Kaufman became an authority for southwest Arkansas on feeds and built the company into an international seed firm, importing and exporting seed worldwide. He had several local warehouses for the seed, much of which he bought, cleaned, and resold. In the 1950s he was appointed to the State Plant Board and also served as president of the Arkansas Seed Dealers Association. Active in local civic affairs, he served on the city council for nineteen years during the 1950s and 1960s. He served as a director of the First National Bank of Ashdown for many years and continued to serve as a director into the 1990s. His wife, Ellen (Zacharias), served as a Little River County health nurse for nineteen years and also was active in civic affairs. They had two daughters, Laura and Joanne. The family affiliated with Mount Sinai Temple in Texarkana, sixteen miles south of Ashdown. Henry Kaufman was joined by a partner, John Hearn, in the 1970s. Hearn, a Methodist, married Phyllis Ruskin (sister of Texarkana's Joe Ruskin) and converted to Judaism; they had three children. Kaufman retired in 1990 and sold the company to Hearn.[9]

FOREMAN

Sam Seligson of Foreman, who had served three terms in the state house of representatives, died in 1951. A rabbi with a delegation came to Foreman for the funeral services; Seligson was buried in the Jewish cemetery at Pine Bluff.[10]

Although there had been no Jewish presence in Old Washington, Arkansas, in more than a century, the two-story home built in the 1820s–1830s period by the state's first documented Jewish settler, Abraham Block, was restored in the 1980s and stands as a monument to his presence. In the mid-1980s Skip Stewart-Abernathy directed extensive archeological studies at the Block home (known by then as the Block-Catts Home), and an exhibit of artifacts was presented at the Old State House Museum in Little Rock in the 1980s. A great-great-grandson of Abraham Block, Monsignor Claiborne Lafferty, died in Little Rock at age eighty-four in 1986. Claiborne was ordained a Catholic priest in 1935 and later served on the faculty of St. John's Seminary in Little Rock and at the Pontifical Seminary in Rome.[11]

HOT SPRINGS

Hot Springs was almost an exception to what was occurring in the Jewish communities in other parts of the state outside central Arkansas. As a spa city, its main resource was tourism, and thousands came yearly for the baths. The brisk business helped keep the city's economy stable. A decrease in tourism came about by increments, however. The use of modern medicines, such as antibiotics and steroids, brought about a reduction in the large numbers of people who had once sought cures from the hot waters. The large Army and Navy Hospital assured a goodly influx of people for many years until it was closed in April 1960 (it was then converted into a state rehabilitation center). Also, some tourism was affected in the 1960s when antigambling laws were enforced by Governor Winthrop Rockefeller through the use of the state police. (Illegal gambling had flourished in Hot Springs prior to that time.)[12]

Still, many Jewish businesses flourished in Hot Springs into the 1970s. Some of the most popular to remain were restaurants on Central Avenue, such as Molly's and the Mayflower. Murray Forshberg, Molly's husband, died in 1955, but Molly continued the business with growing success. When the restaurant partially burned in 1977, it was moved to Grand Avenue. Molly became ill shortly after that, and her son Paul managed the business until his death in the mid-1980s; his wife, Betty, then became manager.

Molly Forshberg's nephew, Gene Kirsch, served as shammas (sexton or caretaker) of the Orthodox Beth Jacob Synagogue in Hot Springs. His sister, Laura Fleishner, and her husband, H. Mark Fleishner, were owners of Lauray's jewelry store, known as the Diamond Center of Arkansas. It was one of the popular stores on Central Avenue into the 1990s. Mark Fleishner served as president of the Arkansas Jewelers' Association, as a state board member of the Better Business Bureau, as vice-president of the Hot Springs Chamber of Commerce, and was active in the Rotary and the Jaycees of Hot Springs.

The Mayflower restaurant on Central Avenue was bought by Herman and Jean Kahn in 1947 after the couple visited the city for the baths. They owned a resort hotel in Sharon Springs, New York, that was mainly a summer business, and they wanted a place in which to live and work in the winter. When their New York hotel was destroyed by fire in the 1950s, they settled permanently in Hot Springs. All the bath houses were flourishing at the time, and business was excellent. Herman managed the front part of the restaurant, and Jean supervised the kitchen, which served "kosher-style" food. Herman died in 1963, and Jean continued the business until 1970. She remained in Hot Springs, enamored of its cleanness, the magnolias on Central Avenue, and the lovely promenade in the springtime. The Kahn's son, Roger, married Rosalind Buchman from Paragould, and the two moved out of state.[13]

Hot Springs lost one of its most devoted citizens when Dave Burgauer died in 1959. The Burgauers had paid off the mortgage on Congregation House of Israel's new hall and library on Dave's eighty-fourth birthday, two years prior to his death. The Mendels, one of the city's early families, lost Albert Mendel in 1948, and his wife died in 1955. Only Hubert Mendel remained in Hot Springs by the 1980s, during which time he passed away; he had retired from his clothing store in the 1960s. The store established by Peter Gartenberg in 1892 was continued on Central Avenue by his grandson, Robert Gartenberg. He later expanded the business and opened a store at the Hot Springs Mall, which was built in the 1980s. The last Rephan's department store closed in Hot Springs in November 1992. A chain of such stores had been established when Edward I. Rephan opened his first store at Prescott in 1922. The chain grew to include seventeen stores, all but one of which were in Arkansas, and four were at Hot Springs. Bernard Rephan, Edward's son, had ceased expanding the chain when it became evident that none of his three children wished to continue the stores. The Lockwood clothing store was continued in downtown Hot Springs by family members, and a Sportsmart was established on Highway 270 in west Hot Springs that was managed by Lewis Goltz, who had married Bernice Lockwood. (Branches of the Lockwood's Sportsmart were later established in Little Rock.)

Phillip Levy, who had conducted a luggage business in Hot Springs for several years, died in 1952. Alfred M. Cohen died in 1962, and his son Lewis continued the family's clothing store. The men's clothing store, Welcher's Toggery, was continued by Arthur Welcher until his death in 1963. The store was sold to Pfeifer's of Arkansas. Welcher's widow, Hannah (Moscowitz), died at age eighty-eight in 1991. Moritz Roth, a shoe store owner, died in 1954, and Charles Singer, a Hot Springs tailor for forty-seven years, died in 1958.

After Regina Kaplan retired as administrator of the Leo N. Levi Hospital, she was succeeded by Fannie Benedikt McLaughlin, daughter of one of Hot Springs' early Jewish settlers. Fannie served as hospital administrator from 1950 to 1970. Dr. Alex Benedikt, a cousin of Fannie McLaughlin, who fled from Germany in the 1930s and settled in Hot Springs, continued his practice until his illness and death in 1983 (he had specialized in obstetrics and gynecology, but had mostly treated arthritics after moving to Hot Springs). He loved music and had helped establish a symphony society as well as a tennis club in Hot Springs. Joseph "Joe" and Anna Spitzer, survivors of the Nazi regime in Germany who had settled in Hot Springs, established a kosher meat market in 1955. Anna supervised the kosher preparation of food at Levi Hospital. Joe died in the mid-1980s and Anna died a few years later.

Besides the Herman Kahns noted above, other Jewish visitors to Hot Springs eventually settled there. Some of these who did so after World War II included Harold Gottlieb and Charles and Victoria Lieber. Harold "Hank" Gottlieb visited the spa in 1946 and liked it so well that he liquidated five businesses in Savannah, Georgia, and moved there with his wife. Their six children were born at Hot Springs. Gottlieb went into real estate sales, and by the 1980s he was one of the oldest members of the Real Estate Board of Hot Springs. From an Orthodox background, he became one of the lay leaders of Congregation House of Israel.[14] Charles and Victoria Leiber came to Hot Springs after Victoria's father had begun selling pecans there and had prospered. The Leibers opened a candy manufacturing business known as the London Candy Company; they also sold "Mammy Liza" candies. The firm was sold in 1969, and Charles died in 1972.[15] Bradley and Elaine Wolken established the Turf Catering service, which catered to Oaklawn Racetrack in the 1980s and 1990s, and Imy and Harriet Marcus opened the Toy Chest, which carried a large line of children's toys, on Central Avenue in the 1980s.

Hot Springs has had a number of Jewish professionals in the medical field, including Dr. Joseph "Joe" Rosenzweig, who was born and raised at Lake Village. After serving in the U.S. Navy during World War II, he began practicing pediatric medicine in Hot Springs in 1949 (he also served in the Korean Conflict). In 1977 he became supervisor of the Medical Service at the Hot Springs Rehabilitation Center and served in that capacity until he retired in the mid-1980s. During his career, Dr. Rosenzweig served as an assistant professor in pediatrics at the University of Arkansas for Medical Sciences (UAMS), as a board member of the Arkansas Children's Colony at Conway, and was named in 1985 to the Arkansas Advisory Committee to the U.S. Commission on Civil Rights.[16]

Dr. Erwin Lax was also a Hot Springs physician who continued his practice in the 1980s and 1990s. His brother, Dr. Martin Lax, was a Hot Springs dentist who served as president of the Garland County Dental Society and was on a number of dental boards. He was a co-founder of the Garland County Industrial Development Commission and was active in several civic and community organizations. He died in 1989. Dr. Harold "Hal" Koppel, son of Jacob and Frances Koppel of Benton, became an orthodontist and practiced at Hot Springs into the 1990s.

Northwest Arkansas

FORT SMITH

Like water slowly leaking from a vessel, the Jewish community of Fort Smith followed the trend across Arkansas (and the South) in experiencing a slow decline in population subsequent to World War II. Some of its most dedicated civic and religious citizens passed away, such as Louis Cohen, who died in 1960. (The office supply company Cohen established continued into the 1990s under non-Jewish ownership.) I. J. Friedman, who with Cohen had been an ardent worker in the Arkansas Jewish Assembly, died in 1964. Friedman had served as lay reader for the Fort Smith congregation and had prepared its young people for confirmation. He and his wife, Elizabeth (Stein), were founders of the Fort Smith Art Center; she was active in Project Compassion (she died in 1981).

Louis Kasten, a founder of the Orthodox congregation established in Fort Smith, had joined United Hebrew Congregation after a Traditional minyan could not be maintained. Also a dedicated UHC worker, he continued his insurance business until his death in 1976. By the 1990s his widow, Sarah Kasten, was the last surviving member of the early Orthodox group.

Several of the early Jewish-owned stores of Fort Smith continued into the 1980s and 1990s. The largest and best known in western Arkansas, the Boston Store, continued for 107 years until it closed in 1986. It had grown after World War II under the leadership of Jerome Ney, son of Marie (Baer) Ney, sister of one of the store's early founders, and her husband, Rudolph Ney. Jerome was later joined in the firm's operation by his two sons, Randolph "Randy" Ney and Jerome "Jerry" Ney Jr. Over the years they purchased three stores at Beaumont, Texas—the Rosenthal, the White House, and the Gus Mayer Store. They bought a store at Lake Charles, Louisiana, and established a branch of the Boston Store at Port Arthur, Texas, and continued one at Fayetteville. The Garrison Avenue store was closed in 1973 after the firm moved to Fort Smith's Central Mall, which had opened in 1971. It was the largest mall located between Little Rock and Tulsa, Oklahoma.

With the drop in oil prices in the 1980s, the economies of Texas and Oklahoma affected businesses based in Fort Smith. Although the city was known as having the broadest manufacturing base of any city in Arkansas, the problems afflicting the rest of the Southwest were felt in Fort Smith as well. By 1986 retail sales, real estate, and construction were down. The Fort Smith and Port Arthur Boston Stores were sold to Warmack and Company and the Fayetteville store was sold to Beall-Ladymon (the Ney sons retained the stores at Beaumont and Lake Charles). Jerome Ney, who headed the Boston Store enterprises for sixty years, was owner of the Universal Travel Service when he died in 1988.[17]

Nicol Wintory continued the Tilles ladies' clothing store established by Alvin Tilles and moved it to Central Mall. (Tilles, supposedly a confirmed bachelor, married Bertha Sternberg when both were in their seventies; Tilles died in 1978 at age eighty-four.) Alfred "Al" Cohn continued the men's clothing store established by his father, Sol Cohn. Al owned the Arcade Men's Store and the Poise-N-Ivy ladies' clothing store until his death in the mid-1980s. After Morton "Mort" Marks Jr. returned from military service in World War II, he and his brother Armand continued the family-owned military supply store. Mort established his own men's clothing store, Mr. Vic's, in 1957, which continued into the 1990s.

J. H. "Jerry" Friedman established the Fort Smith Tobacco and Candy Company with his brother-in-law, Maurice Bershoff, after World War II.

Their company had several branches, one of which was located at North Little Rock and known as Mid-Continent Wholesale Company. The North Little Rock branch closed in the 1960s; the Fort Smith company continued into the 1980s.

The large dry cleaning company established by Joseph Glick was bought by Bernhard "Ben" and Alfred Pollock. (Ben was a major in the U.S. Army, serving in World War II and the Korean War.) The cleaning company continued until 1968, when it was closed. Ben S. Pollock Jr. became a copy editor and journalist for the *Arkansas Democrat* newspaper in Little Rock in the 1980s.

Businessman Harry N. Pollock established the Newton House in Fort Smith as a recreational center for senior citizens. For his efforts in this area, he was appointed in 1960 to the White House Conference on the Aging; actress Mary Pickford also was a member of the Conference. After the government began sponsoring senior citizen centers, the Newton House on Grand Avenue became headquarters for the Retired Senior Volunteer Program (RSVP).[18]

The Cooper Clinic continued to grow after World War II, and a number of Jewish doctors were associated with it over the years. Dr. Davis Woolf Goldstein, a founding member of the clinic, became a "father advisor" to many of the young Fort Smith medical men. He received the "Golden Deeds Award" in 1954 from the Fort Smith Exchange Club. His life was guided by Judaism's ethics and precepts, and those who knew him said that a spirit of love permeated his life.[19] After his first wife died in 1973, he married Leona Heilbron, a longtime family friend. (The Heilbron family had established a jewelry store in Fort Smith but had moved to California during the Depression; they had kept in touch with the Goldsteins over the years. Heilbron's son, Jerome, practiced law in Fort Smith from 1950 to 1961.) Dr. Goldstein died in 1980 at age ninety-one.

Dr. Carl L. Wilson, who had joined the Holt-Krock Clinic in 1940, rejoined the facility after serving in the U.S. Army Medical Corps in World War II. In 1953 he was joined at the Clinic by his brother, Dr. Morton W. Wilson, and in 1974 by his son Steven. All three men were urologists. Dr. Carl Wilson served as chief of staff at Sparks Regional Medical Center six times. He was president of several medical societies, including the Sebastian County Medical Society, and was a consultant in urology at various medical institutions in Arkansas and Oklahoma. He died in 1983. Dr. Morton Wilson, a graduate of Harvard University and the University of Virginia Medical School, served as chief of staff at Crawford County Memorial Hospital and Sparks Regional Medical Center.

He prepared six scientific exhibits with his brother, Dr. Carl Wilson, and they received four awards.[20] Dr. Steven Karl Wilson and his wife, Arlene (Drescher), restored several historical homes in Fort Smith.

Dr. Ernest A. Mendelsohn, who had joined Holt-Krock in 1941, served as chief of radiology there and at Sparks Regional Medical Center. In 1962 he became associate clinical professor of radiology at UAMS, Little Rock. His hobby was music, and he was a board member of the Fort Smith Symphony Association and the Fort Smith Fine Arts Center. He was active in United Hebrew Congregation and in the local B'nai B'rith lodge. He died in 1979. His son, Dr. Lawrence "Larry" Mendelsohn, began practicing with the Hematology-Oncology Associates in Little Rock in the 1980s.

Dr. Kenneth M. Rosenzweig, an orthopedic surgeon and son of Dr. Joseph and Susi Rosenzweig of Hot Springs, joined the Cooper Clinic in Fort Smith in 1988. He had married Carolyn Long, a television newscaster, in 1982. (She had joined KARK-TV in Little Rock in 1978 and had become one of Arkansas's best-loved newscasters. In 1983 she received the *Arkansas Democrat's* Woman of the Year Award and was named Outstanding Young Arkansan by the Arkansas Jaycettes.)

The Fort Smith Structural Steel Company, founded by Sander Katzer, was continued by him and family members until his death in 1956, when it was sold (the company continued into the 1990s). A subsidiary of the company, the Searcy Steel Company, which was run by Ben Katzer, also was sold. Sander Katzer's daughter, Dorothy "Dot," became an instructor of philosophy and psychology at Westark Community College at Fort Smith, serving there into the 1990s. She married Myron "Bubba" Rappaport, who worked with the steel company until it was sold; he then became sales manager for a Sallisaw, Oklahoma, company. The Rappaport's son, Dr. Stephen A. Rappaport, was a graduate of Tulane Dental School and became a Fort Smith orthodontist.

The Yaffe Iron and Metal Company, established by Simon Yaffe, continued into the 1990s under his grandson, Richard Yaffe. The company also included the Rogers Iron and Metal Company of Rogers. One of Simon Yaffe's daughters, Dorothy, married Theodore "Ted" Miller, whose grandfather, Charles Miller, had owned the Eagle Clothing Store at Fort Smith since 1909. Ted Miller continued the company, which later specialized in Western clothes and boots, until he retired in 1981.

The grand old Goldman Hotel, which had been Fort Smith's focal point for civic, social, and political events for many years, lost its luster after World War II and was closed. The building was purchased by a local group in 1978, but it still sat forlornly empty in 1991. The Rosalie Tilles Children's Home was continued until August 1960, when the foster-home system made its services unnecessary. The building later housed the Family and Children's Service Center and a day-care center. The Roger Bost School began operating in the home until new facilities were built (the Bost school was for mentally retarded and developmentally disabled children and adults).

All of the original Tilles family members of Fort Smith intermarried and left the faith, with the exception of Ella (Tilles) Falk, who continued to make the city her home into the 1990s. Many reminders of the Tilles family also continued, such as Tilles Park, Tilles Elementary School, Tilles Street, and the Roger-Tilles home, all of which give evidence of the efforts and concern of this Jewish family for its community. Rose Weinberger continued to make Fort Smith her home and was given the 1983 Golden Deeds award for her contributions to the community. She died in in 1986. Maxine (Langfelder) Chapman, a Fort Smith schoolteacher for many years, continued to live in the city after she retired.

One of Arkansas's most notable Jewish native sons was Eugene "Gene" Feenberg, son of a former Fort Smith scrap metal dealer, Louis Feenberg. Gene Feenberg, a Harvard University graduate, taught at several universities before 1946, when he accepted a faculty position at Washington University in St. Louis, where he served as Wayman Crow Professor of Physics until his death in 1977. He was well loved and respected by his students, who remembered him for his astuteness as well as for his deep concern for individuals and their rights.[21]

In his research, Gene Feenberg made fundamental contributions to the theory of quantum fluids, nuclear theory, and approximation methods. He was a pioneer in the application methods and the theory of quantum mechanics to nuclear structure. In 1950 he wrote an original paper in which the basis for much of modern nuclear shell theory was laid. Two other papers were published on the same subject by Maria Goeppert-Mayer and by Hans D. Jensen. The latter two received the Nobel Prize for physics in 1963; Feenberg did not. Although his lack of such recognition bothered others, Feenberg said that his life was a quest for knowledge, not human acknowledgment.[22] He was elected to the National Academy of Sciences in 1975. A two-day Eugene Feenberg Symposium was held that year; one hundred eminent physicists gathered at Washington University to pay him homage. After Feenberg's death, the International Conference, held in 1978 at Trieste, Italy, was dedicated to his memory. The April 1979 issue of the international journal *Nuclear Physics* also was dedicated to him. A new international prize, the Eugene Feenberg Memorial Medal, was established in his memory and was to be given for outstanding contributions in the field of physics theory at two-year intervals at successive International Conferences.[23]

When Leah (Cohn) Arndt, the last member of the family of Isaac Cohn, early pioneer settler of Fort Smith, died in October 1990, she left the bulk of the Cohn family's multimillion-dollar estate to the Fort Smith Library. All but one hundred thousand dollars of the estimated three-million-dollar estate was designated for the institution.[24] Leah Arndt and her bachelor brother, Josh Cohn, lived at Oklahoma City for more than fifty years but retained property holdings in Fort Smith. Josh became known for his eccentric looks and ways. (He was once about to be arrested by a police officer after he was found on top of the J. C. Penney store at Fort Smith. Wearing an old overcoat that was fastened with a safety pin, he assured the officer that he was inspecting the building, which he owned. Not until the Penney's manager confirmed that he was indeed the owner was Cohn released. Josh was often seen driving around the town in old, beaten-up vehicles, wearing sloppy and disheveled clothing. Called a "living, breathing eccentric," he would sleep in his vehicles rather than pay for a hotel bill.)[25]

In the early 1980s a group of some three hundred Hmong immigrants, refugees from Southeast Asia, settled in the Fort Smith area. The leader of the group, Chang Xiong, refused to accept help from the local populace, saying that the Hmong took care of their own. Jack Moseley, editor of the *Southwest Times-Record* of Fort Smith, likened the Hmong to the early Jewish settlers. Both had a distinct culture that they wanted to preserve, he said, and they banded together to help one another. Moseley said the Jews had helped Fort Smith in a number of civic ways, such as the Ney family's heading the United Way drives. And they added significantly to the culture of the area. He said the Boston Store emulated Neiman Marcus with their Fortnight programs, such as its Irish and Italian Fortnights. The store sent Moseley to Italy to see how merchandise was made, and the foreign-made items brought to Fort Smith by the the Neys were generally seen only in such stores as Neiman Marcus. He said the venture was more than a public relations or prestige event; it was a cultural contribution. They made available to people of the area such displays that they would never have seen otherwise. "The Jews have added significantly to this area," he said, not only in business, but with their civic-mindedness and in culture.[26]

FAYETTEVILLE

The jewelry store established at Fayetteville in 1919 by Louis Silverman was continued until his death in 1948. Silverman's widow, Dorothy (Slovich), and their son Bernard then opened a women's specialty shop, which they continued until it was sold in 1960. The Silvermans moved out of state.[27]

Jewish involvement in the northwest corner of the state centered for years at the University of Arkansas. Waterman Hall, a law school building erected at the University of Arkansas in 1951, was named for Julian Waterman, first dean of the U of A Law School; it was expanded in 1975. Years after Waterman's death in 1943, he and Robert Leflar (who served with Waterman as a law faculty member) were remembered by a former student as the "brightest stars in the firmament" in teaching law.[28]

Another building on campus was named for the son of Ben Drew Kimpel Sr., who had served with signal prominence as a Fort Smith attorney. Ben D. Kimpel Jr. (who did not identify with Judaism and whose mother was non-Jewish) served as a professor of English at the U of A from 1952 until his death in 1983. He was chairman of the U of A Department of English in the 1970s. Kimpel had served as an interpreter for the U.S. Army in Europe in World War II and was a secretary to the U.S. diplomatic delegation to Vienna from 1946 to 1950. Multilingual, he spoke Italian, French, and German and had a reading knowledge of Spanish, Greek, and Chinese. Kimpel became interested in the work of American poet Ezra Pound because of Pound's knowledge of the above languages and the use of them in his poems. Kimpel authored several scholarly works and some fifty articles on authors such as Pound and Samuel Richardson. He received the Distinguished Faculty Award from the University of Arkansas in 1961, and after he died, the campus building in which he taught was renamed Kimpel Hall in his memory. Kimpel was described by many of his peers at the University of Arkansas as having had "the finest mind on campus."[29] Miller Williams, a Fayetteville poet and Kimpel's longtime friend, said "What luster the University has, we owe to a few top-ranked people like Ben Kimpel."[30]

Drs. Jacob and Wilma Sacks came in 1952 to Fayetteville, where Dr. Jacob Sacks served as a professor in the U of A Department of Chemistry until 1972. He then served as professor emeritus until his death in 1978. He wrote two books, *The Atom at Work* (New York: Ronald Press Company, 1952) and *Isotopic Tracers in Biochemistry and Physiology* (New

York: McGraw-Hill, 1953). Dr. Wilma Sacks served as medical director of the Health Department of Washington, Madison, and Benton counties for seven years and then ran family planning clinics in Washington and Madison counties. She was president of the Regional Mental Health Association twice and served on the board of the American Association of University Women. She served on local and state boards of the League of Women Voters; she was president of the Washington County League for four years and was selected their Woman of the Year in 1982. Wilma Sacks was a prolific writer, having a number of articles published, and she wrote a column for a local Fayetteville newspaper. She died in the mid-1980s.

Nutritionist Dr. Barnett Sure, who joined the U of A in 1920 and served as head of the Department of Agricultural Chemistry and who had helped to strengthen Judaism in northwest Arkansas (see chapter 12), died in 1960. His wife, Ethel (Estes), and their daughter, Mrs. Daniel (Charmain) Rane, moved out of state. Through the years after World War II, a number of Jewish professionals joined the U of A faculty. Examples of these are Drs. Barry Brown, David Epstein, Elliot M. Fielstein, Joel Freund, Morton Gitelman, Gerald Halpern, Michael Lieber, Daniel Levine, L. J. Rosenberg, Ben Sacks, Boris Schein, Stephen Strausberg, and Kurt Tweraser. Such newcomers to the area helped make possible the establishment of a congregation in Fayetteville in 1981 (see chapter 15).

EUREKA SPRINGS

Jerome Rosewater, son of early Eureka Springs Jewish pioneer Ben J. Rosewater, continued to live in the city his father had helped develop until he died in the late 1980s. On his eighty-fifth birthday, 2 June 1986, Jerome was honored for his dedicated activities to the community through the years and was made "Mayor for the Day." He had served as an officer with the Chamber of Commerce for several years and was active in the town's civic endeavors.[31] Ben Rosewater's daughter, Mrs. Jeanette Bullock, and her family continued to live in Eureka Springs into the 1990s.

None of the Rosewater family members identified with Judaism, and it was many years before Eureka Springs saw another Jewish settler. Crescent Dragonwagon, daughter of Maurice Zolotow of Los Angeles, came from New York in 1971 to Eureka Springs, where she opened the Ozark area's first bed and breakfast inn, the Dairy Hollow House. Dragonwagon, who married Ned Shank, authored several books, some of which were cookbooks.[32] Zolotow was a Hollywood biographer who profiled celebrities such as Marilyn Monroe, John Wayne, and Billy Wilder and wrote numerous magazine articles. He died in 1991 while planning to portray himself in a September performance of "Who Killed Marilyn Monroe?" at Dragonwagon's Dairy Hollow House.

Although Arkansas had seen little overt anti-Semitism over the years, it could be considered ironic that Gerald Lyman Kenneth Smith, one of the most notorious anti-Semites in America, should establish "sacred projects" at Eureka Springs. (Smith had been a cohort of Huey Long of Louisiana and had pronounced Long's eulogy after the latter was shot in 1935.[33] Smith published and promoted anti-Semitic literature nationwide.) In 1964 Smith bought acreage in the Ozark town and subsequently built a giant seven-story statue called the "Christ of the Ozarks." In 1968 Smith opened at Eureka Springs his version of the Passion Play, which covered Jesus' final week on Earth and his crucifixion. The site for the play was located on one of the Smith Foundation's three mountaintops, which was renamed Mount Oberammergau (after the Bavarian village which had staged the play in 1634 and has continued it thereafter every ten years). The citizens of Eureka Springs, pleased with the financial gains Smith's "sacred projects" brought in, were oblivious of or were willing to overlook Smith's anti-Semitic diatribes that often appeared in his publication, *The Cross and the Flag*.

Gerald L. K. Smith died in April 1976 and was buried at the base of the "Christ of the Ozarks" statue. The Passion Play continues to be presented annually for about one hundred performances from May through October, and it uses the Oberammergau version. This includes the inflammatory words, "His blood be upon us and our children," found in Matthew's account of the crucifixion and which perpetuated the portraying of the Jews as "Christ-killers." Seven members from the Arkansas Interfaith Conference reviewed the Passion Play during the 1990 season and issued a statement opposing the insensitivity to Christian scripture used in the play. Conference members concurred that "when religion is used to breed contempt toward an individual or group, the foundation of the Judeo-Christian faith tradition is betrayed."[34]

The presence of the Elna M. Smith (the wife of Gerald L. K. Smith) Foundation's projects in northwest Arkansas drew other anti-Semitic groups to the area. Members of The Covenant, The Sword and The Arm of the Lord (CSA), a militaristic white-supremacist group, began operating on several hundred acres in northern Marion County by the 1980s, and Thom Robb, grand wizard of the Knights of the Ku Klux Klan and former associate of politician David Duke of Louisiana, established a new headquarters at Zinc (Boone County) in the summer of 1991. Robb felt that the more central location in Arkansas rather than in Pulaski, Tennessee, would make it easier to organize Klan events.[35]

MORRILTON

Except for the Fayetteville area, few Jews were found in other sections of northwest Arkansas. Al and Bertha Frank of Morrilton operated their store until 1966. Bertha continued her civic work in Conway County and in 1965 was one of thirteen local residents to be included in John L. Ferguson's book, *Arkansas Lives: The Opportunity Land Who's Who*.[36] After the Franks retired, they moved to Little Rock, where Bertha was active in both civic and cultural affairs. Al died in 1979 and Bertha died in 1988.

RUSSELLVILLE

Lena Rexinger, who was born and raised in Eudora, received her master's degree from Columbia University and subsequently taught in Arkansas, Louisiana, South Carolina, and Michigan. From 1949 to 1970, she served as head of the Department of Elementary Education at Arkansas Tech University, Russellville.

CONWAY

Mayer Gates, who had married Gladys Frauenthal, continued the large Frauenthal and Schwarz, Inc., company of Conway until 1952, when the eighty-year-old firm was closed. At the time, a local newspaper article noted that Conway had "appreciated the fine position the firm . . . has occupied in this community and county" for more than three-quarters of a century."[37] (The company's building remained into the 1990s and was placed on the National Register of Historic Places in 1992.) Mayer Gates remained as a director of the First National Bank of Conway until he retired in 1963. He died in 1966. Max Frauenthal's granddaughter, Irene Richardson, continued as librarian at Fort Smith Junior High School until her retirement. Members of the Frauenthal family still lived in Arkansas in the 1990s, including Max Frauenthal of Little Rock, the great-grandson of the original Conway settler. None of those who carried the Frauenthal name in Arkansas had remained Jewish, although others of his descendants had done so.

Charles "Charley" Heiligers, son of Sam and Minnie Heiligers of Conway, bought a small book store in the 1940s for his son Bill and called it "a plaything for Bill" (Bill had a congenital deformity and was wheelchair bound all his life). The store grew unexpectedly and developed into the Conway Book and Office Supply Store. When both Charley and his wife became ill in the 1960s, they sold all but the books and greeting card section of the store in 1965 and kept the latter for Bill, which he continued until his death in 1987. Bill did not identify with Judaism, but his sister, Betty Nussbaum of Little Rock, did.[38]

BENTON

Jay's Department Store in Benton, which was established in the 1940s by Jacob and Frances Koppel, was continued until 1973, when it was sold to the Rephan Department Store chain. (The Rephan stores were later closed.)[39]

During the last three decades (1970s–1990s), a few Jewish newcomers could be found scattered around the state in some of the smaller cities and towns. Most of these newcomers were older Jewish couples from the North who were drawn to Arkansas for its relatively mild climate; some settled in the retirement communities located in the lovely Ozark Mountains.

EPILOGUE

Although there had never before been a statewide attempt by Arkansas's Jewry to promote a political candidate, an exception occurred in 1992 when the state's governor, Bill Clinton, ran for president. While many Arkansas Jewish citizens were already serving as volunteers in his campaign, a group formed that sought to elicit statewide backing from Arkansas Jewry for Clinton. The committee, composed of Phillip E. Kaplan, Jane Mendel, and Joe Selz from Little Rock, Dr. Joe Rosenzweig and Pat Tanenbaum from Hot Springs, and David Solomon from Helena, formed a temporary group called "Arkansas Jewry to Elect a President." Their aim was to have as many members of the Arkansas Jewish community as possible sign their names to an advertisement promoting Clinton. The ad, which showed a picture of a smiling Governor Clinton, stated: "Arkansas Jewish Travelers Urge You to Join Us in Voting for the 'Dream Ticket,' Vote Clinton/Gore November 3rd." The ad was to be placed in Jewish publications nationwide to apprise readers of the support Clinton had among the state's Jewish citizens.

The letter to Arkansas Jewry soliciting such support went out in early September. In it was noted the fact that Bill Clinton was "the candidate who has unwaveringly supported our social agenda as well as the State of Israel." Replies to the inquiry were due back by 25 September so the ad could be placed before the election. The ad, signed by more than 225 Arkansas Jewish citizens, appeared in ten national Jewish publications. More than a thousand letters had gone out, and fewer than a half dozen replies were negative (and three of these writers of negative replies signed the ad). Some who did not answer before the deadline later said they regretted not getting their response back in time. According to Jane Mendel, members of the Arkansas Jewry to Elect a President Committee were pleased with the response to what they called their last-minute efforts to help elect Clinton. Also, both Rabbi Eugene "Gene" Levy of Little Rock and Rabbi Matthew Friedman of Hot Springs sent letters to their colleagues nationwide urging other rabbis to support Clinton. Rabbi

Seymour Weller of the Orthodox Agudath Achim Synagogue of Little Rock also strongly promoted Clinton's candidacy.

There was not a consensus among Arkansas Jewry over the issue, however. One of the most notable non-endorsements of Bill Clinton was expressed 28 October 1992 by Pulitzer Prize–winning editorialist Paul Greenberg, member of the local synagogue and temple and editorial page editor of the statewide newspaper, the *Arkansas Democrat-Gazette*. Greenberg faulted Governor Clinton for being "a great theorist of how government should operate, not a great practitioner." He wrote that the administrations of former Arkansas governors Winthrop Rockefeller, Dale Bumpers, and David Pryor "showed more gumption when it came to basic reforms in government" than Governor Clinton's. He wrote that Arkansas had progressed [under Clinton's administration], but "not nearly so much as it would have if Bill Clinton had been the Bill Clinton of the campaign ads."

A number of Arkansas Jews attended Bill Clinton's inauguration on 20 January 1993. President-elect Clinton began the day with a prayer service at downtown Washington's historic Metropolitan African Methodist Episcopal Church. As part of the service, Rabbi Levy of Congregation B'nai Israel of Little Rock was asked to give "An American Challenge." In this, he asked, "Bill Clinton with Al Gore . . . We offer you this challenge to unify our individual souls . . . Bring us together, we pray." (Rabbi Levy had also given the benediction at the last inaugural of Clinton as governor.) At receptions during the Arkansas and New York inaugural festivities, tables of kosher food were made available through the encouragement of Rabbi Weller (who designated himself as "the president's rabbi").

During the time Bill Clinton was governor of Arkansas, he visited both the Jewish temple and synagogue on various occasions. His wife, Hillary Rodham Clinton, in one of her many efforts to improve Arkansas education, brought the Home Instruction Program for Preschool Youngsters (HIPPY) to the state. She first introduced it—a Hebrew university-created program for disadvantaged families—at an appearance at Temple B'nai Israel.

Just how much influence was exerted for or against Bill Clinton by Arkansas Jews will probably never be known. Governor Clinton carried his home state with 54 percent of the vote and carried the nation with 43 percent. But the attempt among Arkansas Jewry in a statewide effort to help promote the election of a political candidate was a change in its own right.

Abbreviations used in notes

AHC Arkansas History Commission
AHQ Arkansas Historical Quarterly
AJA American Jewish ARCHIVES [Journal]
AJA American Jewish Archives, Cincinnati, Ohio
AJH American Jewish History
AJHQ American Jewish Historical Quarterly
AJHS American Jewish Historical Society, Waltham, Mass.
BIA Congregation B'nai Israel Archives, Little Rock, Ark.
CAL Central Arkansas Library, Little Rock, Ark.
FSPL Fort Smith, Ark., Public Library
PAJHS Publications of American Jewish Historical Society (predecessor of AJH)
PBPL Pine Bluff, Ark., Public Library
PCHQ Phillips County Historical Quarterly
PCHR Pulaski County Historical Review
PCPL Phillips County, Ark., Public Library
SARA Southwest Arkansas Regional Archives, Washington, Ark.
TIAB Temple Israel Archives, Blytheville, Ark.
TIAJ Temple Israel Archives, Jonesboro, Ark.
UofA University of Arkansas, Fayetteville
UALR University of Arkansas at Little Rock
UHCA United Hebrew Congregation Archives, Fort Smith, Ark.

CHAPTER I
Abraham Comes to Arkansas, 1820s–1830s

1. Various dates have been given as to the exact year Block first came to
Arkansas, ranging from 1820 to 1827. After comparing all data, it would seem
that he was there by 1823, the date given in his obituary in *The Occident* 15: 2
(May 1857): 106–08, AJA. He is listed in the Hempstead County Tax Record
Book in 1825. See Hempstead County Tax Record Book, 1826–1832, 13, SARA;
Biographical and Historical Memoirs of Southern Arkansas (Chicago: The Goodspeed
Publishing Company, 1890), 419 (hereafter cited as *Southern Arkansas*);
Washington Telegraph, 18 November 1871.

2. Gravestone, Dispersed of Judah Cemetery, New Orleans, La.

3. *Southern Arkansas*, 419; Myron Berman, *Richmond's Jewry, 1769–1976: Shabbat in Shockoe* (Charlottesville: University Press of Virginia, 1979), 4.

4. Pauline Booker Carter, "Genealogical Memoranda of Abraham Block," Block File, SARA (hereafter cited as "Abraham Block"). According to cemetery records, however, Fanny would have been sixteen when she married. (*Record of Interments, Cemetery, Dispersed of Judah*, Touro Synagogue File 224, vol. 2, Special Collections, Tulane University Library.

5. Berman, *Richmond's Jewry*, 3; Isaacs Family Folder, Beth Ahabah Archives, Richmond, Va.

6. Herbert T. Ezekiel and Gaston Lichtenstein, *The History of the Jews of Richmond from 1769 to 1917* (Richmond, Va.: Herbert T. Ezekiel, 1917), 15.

7. I. Harold Sharfman, *Jews on the Frontier* (Chicago: Henry Regnery Company, 1977), 83.

8. Berman, *Richmond's Jewry*, 7.

9. Ezekiel and Lichtenstein, *Jews of Richmond*, 14.

10. Berman, *Richmond's Jewry*, 349.

11. Ezekiel and Lichtenstein, *Jews of Richmond*, 327.

12. See Carter, "Abraham Block," chap. 1, n. 4.

13. Nancy E. Willner, "A Brief History of the Jewish Community in Charlottesville and Albemarle," *The Magazine of Albemarle County History* 40 (1982): 2.

14. Ezekiel and Lichtenstein, *Jews of Richmond*, 327, 328.

15. Sharfman, *Jews on the Frontier*, 179.

16. Ezekiel and Lichtenstein, *Jews of Richmond*, 73.

17. Ibid., 39.

18. Sharfman, *Jews on the Frontier*, 179.

19. Grant Foreman, *Indians and Pioneers* (Norman: University of Oklahoma Press, 1974).

20. According to his obituary, published in *The Occident* 15: 2 (May 1857): 106–08. It is stated that Abraham Block appeared before the Justice of the Peace on 5 November 1825 and swore out a complaint against John Hinmon, who was indebted to Block for a sum "not exceeding $100" (Hempstead County Tax Record Book, 1826–1832, 13, SARA).

21. *Arkansas Gazette*, 13 September 1887.

22. Obituary of Virginius Block, *Washington Telegraph*, 18 November 1871.

23. In the 1990s, the house that Abraham Block built still stands in Old Washington State Park, Ark. It has been restored and is known as the Block-Catts House. It is one of the oldest two-story homes in the state.

24. Mary Medearis, *Washington, Arkansas: History on the Southwest Trail* (Hope, Ark.: Etter Printing Company, 1976), 3.

25. Charlean Moss Williams, *Washington Hempstead County Arkansas: The Old Town Speaks* (Houston: Anson Jones Press, 1951), 231.

26. David Y. Thomas, ed., *Arkansas and Its People*, vol. 2 (New York: American Historical Society, Inc., 1930), 712; Medearis, *Washington, Arkansas*, 30; Francis Irby Gwaltney, "A Survey of Historic Washington, Arkansas," *AHQ* 17:4 (1958): 350–59.

27. Medearis, *Washington, Arkansas*, 3, 5–9.

28. *Washington Telegraph*, 4 May 1842, 31 May 1848.

29. Ibid., 28 April 1847.

30. Bertram Wallace Korn, *The Early Jews of New Orleans* (Waltham, Mass.: AJHS, 1969), 198.

31. Abraham Block's Obituary, *The Occident* 15: 2 (May 1857): 107. *The Occident* was the first national Jewish periodical in America, edited by Isaac Leeser, leader of Mikveh Israel Synagogue, Philadelphia.

32. Leslie Stewart-Abernathy and Barbara Ruff, "A Good Man in Israel: Zooarcheology and Assimilation in Antebellum Washington, Arkansas," December 1985, courtesy Leslie Stewart-Abernathy.

33. *Arkansas Gazette*, 6 July 1831.

34. Ibid. For more information on the Red River Raft, see Muriel H. Wright, "Early Navigation and Commerce Along the Arkansas and Red Rivers in Oklahoma," *Chronicles of Oklahoma* 8 (March 1930):65–88.

35. Ibid.

36. *Southern Arkansas*, 216.

37. Ibid., 350; *Arkansas Gazette*, 6 February 1839.

38. Sevier County Court Records, Sevier County, Ark.; W. D. Lee, "A Historical Sketch of Center Point," *AHQ* 12:3 (1953): 264, 265.

39. Farrar Newberry, "The Grand Old Roman," *AHQ* 18: 1(1959):30.

40. Donald Ray Montgomery, "Simon T. Sanders: Public Servant," *AHQ* 39:2 (1980): 163n.

41. *Arkansas Gazette*, 10 September 1830.

42. John L. Ferguson and J. H. Atkinson, *Historic Arkansas* (Little Rock: AHC, 1966), 26–27, 48.

43. *Little Rock Board of Trade 12th Annual Report, 1900–1901*, 71.

44. Ferguson and Atkinson, *Historic Arkansas*, 48.

45. George A. Kohut, "Arkansas," *PAJHS* 6 (1897): 158.

46. *Arkansas Gazette*, 22 May 1833.

47. Ibid.

48. Ibid., 9 May 1976.

49. Ibid.

50. Kohut, "Arkansas," 158.

51. *Acts of the Eighth Session of the General Assembly of the Territory of Arkansas, 8 November 1833*, sec. I, 113.

52. Fannie Benedikt McLaughlin, interview with author, Hot Springs, Ark., 20 April 1982.

53. Harry L. Golden, *Our Southern Landsmen* (New York: G. P. Putnam, 1974), 131.

54. Frederick Gerstaecker, *Wild Sports in the Far West* (Durham, N.C.: Duke University Press, 1968), 83.

55. Ibid., 213.

56. Evan Burr Bukey, "Frederick Gerstaecker and Arkansas," *AHQ* 31: 1 (1972): 6.

CHAPTER 2

The Search for a Safe Home, 1840s

1. George A. Kohut, "Arkansas," *PAJHS* 6 (1897): 158.

2. *Arkansas Gazette*, 13 April 1846.

3. Ibid., 24 May 1846.

4. Ibid., 19 June 1847, 8 June 1848, 24 May 1849.

5. "Life at the Arkansas Springs," "Bally," *New Orleans Daily Picayune*, 22 July 1849; James R. Masterson, *Arkansas Folklore* (Little Rock: Rose Publishing Company, 1974), 139.

6. Masterson, *Arkansas Folklore*, 139.

7. Kohut, "Arkansas," 158.

8. *Little Rock Board of Trade 12th Annual Report, 1900–1901*, 71.

9. U.S. Bureau of the Census, *Ninth Census of the United States, The Statistics of the Population of the United States, vol.* 1 (Washington, D.C.: Government Printing Office, 1872), 13.

10. *Arkansas Gazette*, 19 May 1841.

11. Margaret Ross, *Arkansas Gazette, The Early Years 1819–1866* (Little Rock: Gazette Foundation, 1969), 180.

12. "A Sketch of Congregation B'Nai Israel," Board of Directors Meeting, 4 May 1880, Ladies Temple Aid Society Folder, Little Rock, Ark., Box X–38, AJA.

13. Gordon N. Peay served as Little Rock's mayor during the years 1859–60, and William E. Ashley served from 1861 to 1863. From 1863 to 1866, Little Rock was under military occupation after Federal troops took the city (James W. Bell, *The Little Rock Handbook* [Little Rock: James W. Bell, 1980], 51–52). For two accounts listing Levy as mayor, see Bernard Postal and Lionel Koppman, *American Jewish Landmarks: A Travel Guide and History, vol.* 2, *The South and Southwest* (New York: Fleet Press Corporation, 1979), 57; Rabbi Samson A. Shain, "The Story of Arkansas Jewry, 1836–1953," 3, Arkansas Folder, Histories File, AJA.

14. *Arkansas Gazette*, 3 June 1907.

15. Ibid., 11 April 1850.

16. Ibid., 5 June 1902.

17. Ibid., 7 November 1931.

18. "Arkansas 1840s–1870s" 2: 42, R. G. Dun & Co. Collection, Baker Library, Harvard University Graduate School of Business Administration (hereafter cited as R. G. Dun & Co., "Arkansas").

19. *Arkansas Gazette*, 3 November 1859.

20. R. G. Dun & Co., "Arkansas" 2: 42.

21. Mary Ann Rapp (Jacobi's great-great-granddaughter), letter to author, Baton Rouge, La., 17 March 1986.

22. R. G. Dun & Co., "Arkansas" 2: 135.

23. *Arkansas Gazette*, 29 September 1845; R. G. Dun & Co., "Arkansas" 2: 270.

24. *Fort Smith Elevator*, 26 February 1892.

25. Edward Czarnikow tombstone, House of Life Cemetery, Fort Smith, Ark.; *Fort Smith Elevator*, 26 February 1892.

26. "History of the Jews of Fort Smith," *Reform Advocate*, 10 January 1914.

27. George Tilles, "A History of Fort Smith," courtesy of Ella Tilles Falk, Fort Smith, Ark., 13.

28. *Fort Smith Elevator*, 26 February 1892.

29. *Biographical and Historical Memoirs of Southern Arkansas* (Chicago: The Goodspeed Publishing Company, 1890), 247 (hereafter cited as *Southern Arkansas*).

30. Ibid., 247, 280. Although it is mentioned twice in *Southern Arkansas* that Nathan Levi named the town of Center Point, W. D. Lee, in an article, "A Historical Sketch of Center Point," *AHQ* 12 (1953): 265, mentions that the honor of naming the town was claimed by two men, Levi and Rev. John H. Propps.

31. *Southern Arkansas*, 247.

32. Ibid., 279–80. Levi died in 1907 and is buried in the City Cemetery at Nashville, Ark.

33. R. G. Dun & Co., "Arkansas" 4: 2.

34. Ibid.

35. Ibid., 3, 69.

36. Ibid., 2: 3, 7.

37. Ibid.

38. *Arkansas Gazette*, 8 March 1936.

39. R. G. Dun & Co., "Arkansas" 2: 3.

40. M. L. Griffin, "A Social History of Camden, Arkansas, 1824–1860," a paper submitted in partial fulfillment for the degree of master of arts in the School of Political Science and Philosophy of Columbia University, 6, Camden, Ark., Public Library.

41. Dallas T. Herndon, *Annals of Arkansas, vol. 2* (Hopkinsville, Ky.: The Historical Record Association, 1947), 830.

42. See sec. II, chap. 5, n. 2.

43. Adolph Felsenthal, "Nearly Threescore and Ten," part 2, *Arkansas Gazette*, magazine section (1934): 3 (full citation unavailable), Camden, Ark., Nearprint File, AJA; Max B. May, *Isaac Mayer Wise* (New York: G. P. Putnam's Sons, 1916), 37, 38, 42.

44. Felsenthal, "Nearly Threescore."

45. According to Block's tombstone in Beth El Emeth Cemetery, Camden, Ark., he was born in 1826; in the Marriage Book of Hempstead County, he is listed as being thirty-five years old in 1846, and Mary is listed as being seventeen (Marriage Book of Hempstead County, A–245, SARA).

46. Felsenthal, "Nearly Threescore."

47. R. G. Dun & Co., "Arkansas" 10: 21.

48. Ibid., 4: 108.

49. Ibid., 7: 5.

50. Ibid., 243–81.

51. On 29 August 1843, Jonas Levy swore on oath in the County Clerk's office that he had acted for several years as minister of the Jewish Church; his credentials were noted to have been in the Jewish language and could not be translated. (Pulaski County Marriage Book B, 66, 67, AHC).

52. On 13 October 1843, James (Jonas) Levy united in marriage Edward Barinds of Malvern and Charlotte Levy of Little Rock (Pulaski County Marriage

Book B, 87, 88). Why Levy was allowed to perform the marriage ceremony is not known. The Arkansas legislature had passed a statute on 20 February 1838, limiting the performance of the marriage ceremony to Christian ministers only. This statute was not changed until 21 January 1873, when it was amended to read "religious" instead of "Christian."

53. Kohut, "Arkansas," 158.

54. *Arkansas Gazette*, 28 February 1869. Subtracting thirty years from 1869 would put the congregation back to 1839, which is much too early. The Mitchells, and perhaps Jonas Levy, were the only recorded Jews living in Little Rock at the time; the other Levy family members and the Kempners had not yet made their appearances in Arkansas. Congregation B'nai Israel, which formed in 1866, was without a "priest" from 1868 to 1872 (Ira E. Sanders and Elijah E. Palnick, comps. and eds., *One Hundred Years, Congregation B'nai Israel 1866–1966* [Little Rock: n.p., 1966], 83).

55. "Trailblazers of the Trans-Mississippi West," AJA 8: 2 (October 1856): 69.

56. Jacob Rader Marcus, *The American Jewish Woman, 1654–1980* (New York: KTAV Publishing House, Inc., 1981), 2.

57. R. G. Dun & Co., "Arkansas" 3: 304; 6: 304; 12: 14, 17.

58. Ibid., 1: 3; 3: 304; 2: 270.

CHAPTER 3
A Persistence Greater than Prejudice, 1850s

1. John L. Ferguson and J. H. Atkinson, *Historic Arkansas* (Little Rock: AHC, 1966), 84, 101–04.

2. Ibid., 103.

3. *Little Rock Board of Trade 12th Annual Report, 1900–1901*, 71.

4. Based on information collected from the R. G. Dun & Co. (forerunner to Dun & Bradstreet) records for Arkansas, newspaper articles and advertisements, data on tombstones in the Jewish cemeteries of Arkansas, obituaries, and other research material pertaining to Arkansas Jewry.

5. See n. 4 above.

6. "Arkansas, 1840s–1870s" 10: 21, R. G. Dun & Co. Collection, Baker Library, Harvard University Graduate School of Business Administration (hereafter cited as R. G. Dun & Co., "Arkansas").

7. *Biographical and Historical Memoirs of Eastern Arkansas* (Chicago: The Goodspeed Publishing Company, 1890), 337 (hereafter cited as *Eastern Arkansas*).

8. Ibid., 338.

9. *Arkansas Gazette*, 6 November 1870, 5 March 1967.

10. R. G. Dun & Co., "Arkansas" 11: 137–279.

11. Based on information in the R. G. Dun & Co. records pertaining to Arkansas from 1840 to 1878, almost half of the Jewish-owned stores in the state failed at least once, and sometimes as often as three or four times. This almost always occurred after a bad harvest. It was occasionally noted—and in a deroga-

tory manner—regarding Jewish merchants whose businesses failed that they had tended to extend credit to minorities, to the detriment of the merchants.

12. R. G. Dun & Co., "Arkansas" 11: 152, 153.

13. "A Sketch of Congregation B'nai Israel," Board of Directors Meeting, 4 May 1880, Ladies Temple Aid Society Folder, Little Rock, Ark., Box X–38, AJA.

14. R. G. Dun & Co., "Arkansas" 11: 148.

15. Ibid., 185, 238, 278.

16. *Arkansas Gazette*, 2 December 1892; R. G. Dun & Co., "Arkansas" 11: 147.

17. *Arkansas Gazette*, 9 September 1883; *Arkansas Democrat*, 21 November 1901.

18. *Arkansas Democrat*, 23 December 1922.

19. R. G. Dun & Co., "Arkansas" 11: 138–274.

20. Ibid., 270.

21. *Arkansas Democrat*, 18 January 1940.

22. R. G. Dun & Co., "Arkansas" 6: 304.

23. Bernard Postal and Lionel Koppman, *American Jewish Landmarks: A Travel Guide and History*, vol. 2, *The South and Southwest* (New York: Fleet Press Corporation, 1979), 55.

24. Cyrus Adler, *I Have Considered the Days* (Philadelphia: Jewish Publication Society of America, 1945), 4 (hereafter cited as *Days*).

25. Ibid., 4, 5.

26. Rabbi Raphael Goldenstein, comp. and ed., "History and Activities of Congregation Anshe Emeth, 1867–1917" (1917), 25, Anshe Emeth Archives, Pine Bluff.

27. *Arkansas Gazette*, 13 December 1908.

28. R. G. Dun & Co., "Arkansas" 7: 178.

29. Dorothy Stanley, ed., *The Autobiography of Sir Henry Morton Stanley* (Boston: Houghton Mifflin Company, 1909), 5–125; See also Ian Anstruther, *Dr. Livingstone, I Presume* (New York: E. P. Dutton & Company, 1957), 8–29.

30. Data courtesy Rabbi Leo Turitz, Laguna Hills, Calif.

31. *Pine Bluff Daily Graphic*, 4 December 1917.

32. *Pocahontas Star Herald Centennial Edition*, 20 September 1956.

33. Ibid.; *Biographical and Historical Memoirs of Northeast Arkansas* (Chicago: The Goodspeed Publishing Company, 1889), 396 (hereafter cited as *Northeast Arkansas*).

34. David Y. Thomas, ed., *Arkansas and Its People*, vol. 2 (New York: American Historical Society, Inc., 1930), 709; Vivian Hansbrough, "The Crowleys of Crowley's Ridge," *AHQ* 13:1 (1954): 58.

35. *Pocahontas Star Herald Centennial Edition*, 20 September, 1956.

36. *Helena World Souvenir Edition*, 11 May 1904.

37. *Helena Weekly World*, 28 May 1899; *Eastern Arkansas*, 790.

38. *Northeast Arkansas*, 870.

39. *Arkansas Gazette*, 24 February 1916, 1 March 1936; Gus Ottenheimer, interview with author, Little Rock, Ark., 7 March 1984.

40. Sifford's Scrapbook no. 4, Camden, Ark., Public Library.

41. Adolph Felsenthal, "Nearly Threescore and Ten," part 2, *Arkansas Gazette*, magazine section (1934): 3 (full citation unavailable), Camden, Ark., Nearprint

File, AJA; Beth El Emeth; Camden, Ark., Folder, AJA; Data to author courtesy Harry B. Solmson Jr., Memphis, Tenn., 8 February 1983.

42. R. G. Dun & Co., "Arkansas" 13: 90, 96, 98, 100, 188.

43. *Arkansas Gazette,* 20 February 1949.

44. *Arkansas Democrat,* 17 April 1914.

45. R. G. Dun & Co., "Arkansas" 5: 2–84.

46. Ibid., 6: 287.

47. Ibid., 3, 254–304; E. M. Dreidel, "Temple Meir Chayim: A Century Old Need," *Programs of the Desha County Historical Society* (1978): 29.

48. Adler, *Days,* 5.

49. R. G. Dun & Co., "Arkansas" 4: 121, 138.

50. Ibid., 12: 51; 2: 115, 58; 8: 38; 6: 227; 10: 58; 2: 55, 59.

51. Richard Gates (grandson of Ferdinand and Sally [Mayer] Gates and son of Victor Gates), "Gates Family History," courtesy Louise Dickerson, Hot Springs, Ark.

52. *Eastern Arkansas,* 555.

53. *Northeast Arkansas,* 898. The fact that Shoffner was Jewish was discovered by a great-granddaughter, Julia Shoffner Phelps of Little Rock. She had been raised as a Christian but, after learning of her forebear's faith, converted to Orthodox Judaism (Julia [Shoffner] Phelps, interview with author, Little Rock, Ark., 2 November 1982).

54. *The Occident* 15: 2 (May 1857): 106–08.

55. Letter from Mrs. Jacob M. Carter, descendant of Abraham and Fanny Block, 4 February 1967, SARA.

56. *The Occident and American Jewish Advocate* 2: 1 (January 1845), quoted in "Trail Blazers of the Trans-Mississippi West" 8: 2 AJA (October 1956): 61.

57. *The Occident* 12: 2 (May 1854): 17; 15 (1857): 106–08.

58. Ibid., 10: 9 (December 1852): 27.

59. Ibid., 418–19.

60. Ibid., 14: 9 (December 1856): 409–11.

61. Ibid., 412.

62. *The Occident Advertiser* 17: 13 (June 1859): 2a.

63. *The Occident* 17: 15 (July 1859): 88–89.

Chapter 4
Loyalty to a New Land, 1860–1865

1. John L. Ferguson and J. H. Atkinson, *Historic Arkansas* (Little Rock: AHC, 1966), 113.

2. *Little Rock Board of Trade 12th Annual Report, 1900–1901,* 71.

3. Ferguson and Atkinson, *Historic Arkansas,* 84.

4. Jonathan J. Wolfe, "The Peopling of Pulaski, Pulaski County Population Sources and Composition, 1830–1860," *PCHR* 21 (September 1973): 54.

5. Ibid., 85.

6. Ferguson and Atkinson, *Historic Arkansas,* 86.

7. Ibid., 88.

8. Ibid., 90.

9. Ibid., 91.

10. Ibid., 94–96.

11. Ibid., 98, 99.

12. "A Sketch of Congregation B'nai Israel," Board of Directors Meeting 1880, Ladies Temple Aid Society Folder, Little Rock, Ark., Box X–38, AJA; *The Occident* (1860): 190.

13. *Arkansas Gazette*, 9 June 1903. According to an earlier article, the club was founded in 1871 with twenty-eight members; this may have been when it changed from the Little Rock Club to the Concordia Association (*Arkansas Gazette*, 18 April 1899).

14. Mary Medearis, ed., *Sam Williams: Printer's Devil* (Hope, Ark.: Etter Printing Company, 1980), 77.

15. *The Biographical and Historical Memoirs of Southern Arkansas* (Chicago: The Goodspeed Publishing Company, 1890), 380, 381.

16. *Washington Telegraph*, 24 September 1862; 1 October 1862.

17. Medearis, *Sam Williams*, 78.

18. "Arkansas, 1840s–1870s" 6: 225, R. G. Dun & Co. Collection, Baker Library, Harvard University Graduate School of Business Administration (hereafter cited as R. G. Dun & Co., "Arkansas").

19. Fay Hempstead, *Historical Review of Arkansas, vol.* 3 (Chicago: The Lewis Publishing Company, 1911), 1597, 1598. The Jetts had thirteen children, and many of these as well as their descendants became prominent Arkansas citizens.

20. One of the sons of Edwin and Rosina Block Brittin became head of a leading cotton firm in New Orleans and served three terms as president of the New Orleans Cotton Exchange (*Chambers' Historical Society* 2 [1925], Abraham Block File, SARA).

21. Charlean Moss Williams, *Washington Hampstead County Arkansas: The Old Town Speaks* (Houston: Anson Jones Press, 1951), 231; David Y. Thomas, ed., *Arkansas and Its People*, vol. 1 (New York: American Historical Society, Inc., 1930), 131; *Biographical Directory of the U.S. Congress, 1774–1989* (Washington, D.C.: U.S. Government Printing Office, 1989), 1511.

22. *Pine Bluff Weekly Commercial*, 5 April 1902.

23. Hempstead, *Historical Review of Arkansas* 2: 795.

24. *Arkansas Democrat*, 21 February 1887; *Pine Bluff Graphic*, 12 April 1895.

25. R. G. Dun & Co., "Arkansas" 7: 212.

26. *Arkansas Gazette*, 21 January 1903.

27. *Helena Weekly World*, 15 April 1896.

28. Ted R. Worley, "Early History of Des Arc and Its People," *White River Journal* (March 1956–March 1957): 1–80.

29. R. G. Dun & Co., "Arkansas" 13: 104.

30. Adolph Felsenthal, "Nearly Threescore and Ten," part 2, *Arkansas Gazette* magazine section (1934) (full citation unavailable), Camden, Ark., Nearprint File, AJA.

31. R. G. Dun & Co., "Arkansas" 13: 150; 13: 92, 124, 169; 13: 110.

32. Harry B. Solmson Jr. (grandson of Henry Myar), interview with author, Memphis, Tenn., 9 May 1983.

33. R. G. Dun & Co., "Arkansas" 2: 59; 6: 287; 5: 107; 7: 128; 10: 64, 285, 64.

34. Ibid., 12: 105. The Dun Records are sprinkled with anti-Semitic slurs.

35. Ibid., 113b.

36. Ibid., 4: 21.

37. *Arkansas Gazette*, 1 April 1911, 3 April 1923.

38. R. G. Dun & Co., "Arkansas" 11:172, 267, 167, 181, 291, 213.

39. Ferguson and Atkinson, *Historic Arkansas*, 115, 116.

40. *Washington Telegraph*, 16 July 1846.

41. *Washington Telegraph*, 4 March 1863; 2 September 1863.

42. Little Robert E. Lee Block lived only one year; he was buried beside his grandfather, Abraham Block. (*Record of Interments, Cemetery, Dispersed of Judah*, Touro Synagogue File 224, vol. 2, Special Collections, Tulane University Library.)

43. Emma Jett married Capt. John Morgan, and their daughter Mabel married Thomas Lafferty, a devout Catholic and a prominent Little Rock businessman. Some of the Block family papers were handed down through this line of the family and remained in the possession of the Laffertys' children, Rose and Claiborne. The latter became a monsignor of the Roman Catholic Church and taught in the North American College at Rome and at St. John's Seminary in Little Rock. The Block papers are now in the possession of the Laffertys' nephew, Thomas L. Boone, who is a great-great-great grandson of Abraham and Fanny Block. Some information on the Block history is taken from these papers, including the portion regarding Emma Jett's speech.

44. Jacob Rader Marcus, ed., *Memoirs of American Jews, 1775–1865*, vol. 2 (Philadelphia: The Jewish Publication Society of America, 1955), 141.

45. Ibid., 138–44.

46. Sifford's Scrapbook no. 4, Camden, Ark., Public Library; Dallas T. Herndon, *Centennial History of Arkansas*, vol. 2 (Chicago–Little Rock: The S. J. Clarke Publishing Company, 1922), 984.

47. *Arkansas Gazette*, 17 April 1914, 16 November 1914.

48. *Biographical and Historical Memoirs of Eastern Arkansas* (Chicago: The Goodspeed Publishing Company, 1890), 699 (hereafter cited as *Eastern Arkansas*).

49. Harry B. Solmson Jr. interview.

50. *Biographical and Historical Memoir of Central Arkansas* (Chicago: The Goodspeed Publishing Company, 1889, 483).

51. *Biographical and Historical Memoirs of Northeast Arkansas* (Chicago: The Goodspeed Publishing Company, 1889), 396 (hereafter cited as *Northeast Arkansas*).

52. *Arkansas Gazette*, 6 November 1870, 24 February 1916.

53. *Eastern Arkansas*, 555.

54. AHC, Department of Archives and History, Little Rock, Ark., letter to E. M. Dreidel, 17 January 1960, which includes Emanuel Hoover's service record in the War Between the States, courtesy E. M. Dreidel.

55. Hempstead, *Historical Review of Arkansas* 2: 795.

56. "Mary Lee Chapter #87 United Daughters of the Confederacy," 153, Small Manuscript Collection, AHC.

57. Felsenthal, "Nearly Threescore," part 2: 3.

58. Rev. Henry Cohen, "A Modern Maccabean," *PAJHS* 6 (1897): 31–37.

59. *Arkansas Gazette*, 2 December 1892.

60. Ibid., 19 July 1905.

61. *Pine Bluff Daily Graphic*, 12 December 1908; *Arkansas Gazette*, 13 December 1908.

62. *Eastern Arkansas*, 337–38.

63. Marcus, *Memoirs*: 2 165–213; Harry Simonhoff, *Jewish Participants in the Civil War* (New York: Arco Publishing Company, 1963), 29–35 (hereafter cited as *Participants*).

64. Marcus, *Memoirs*: 2 207.

65. Simonhoff, *Participants*, 34.

66. *Arkansas Gazette*, 16 September 1934.

67. Simon Wolf, *The American Jew as Patriot, Soldier, and Citizen* (Philadelphia: The Levytype Company, 1895), 123, 124 (hereafter cited as *Patriot*); *Arkansas Gazette*, 21 March 1900, 19 November 1903.

68. William S. Speer and John Henry Brown, eds., *The Encyclopedia of the New West* (Marshall, Tex.: The United States Biographical Publishing Company, 1881), 250.

69. Cyrus Adler, *I Have Considered the Days* (Philadelphia: Jewish Publication Society of America, 1945), 3–8, 297–99.

70. *Northeast Arkansas*, 899.

71. *Arkansas Gazette*, 14 September 1909.

72. *Marshall Mountain Wave*, 22 August 1914.

73. Felsenthal, "Nearly Threescore," part 2: 3.

74. Arkansans found on Simon Wolf's list who are not included here are: E. Burgauer, Henry Baum, Wolf Cohn, David Daniel, Marcus Dryfus [Dreyfus], Theo. Dryfus [Dreyfus], Jacob Erb, S. Erb, Isaac Frank, Samuel Franklin, W. Fox, E. Feds [Fels], I. Frank, Herman Goodman, Henry Hirschfield, M. L. Hineman, Henry Heilbroner, Jacob Kempner (listed twice), S. Kalischer, Abraham Klein, Sigismund Kuhn, L. Lewis, Gabriel Meyer, Moses Mock, Samuel Mook, Myer Newman, Abraham Ottenheimer, Philip Pfeifer (listed also as Philip Pfarffer), Abraham Pollock, M. Pollock, Leo Pollock, Rudolph Rich, Jacob Simmons, Solomon Stern, J. Samuels, Harvey Simmons, Louis Vollener [Volmer], Moses Winters. Wolf erroneously lists Capt. J. G. Fletcher (partner of Peter Hotze of Little Rock) among the Jewish Arkansans. See Wolf, *Patriot*, 123, 124.

75. R. G. Dun & Co., "Arkansas" 7: 286, 293; Wolf, *Patriot*, 124.

CHAPTER 5
The German Migration, 1865–1930

1. According to Dr. Jacob R. Marcus, considered the dean of American Jewish history, as quoted in Leonard Dinnerstein and Mary Dale Palsson, eds., *Jews in the South* (Baton Rouge: Louisiana State University Press, 1973), 26.

2. A reform movement in Judaism began slowly in Germany in the nineteenth century that sought to bring the religion into more modern worship. This effort is associated with such European Jews as Samuel Holdheim, Abraham Geiger, and

Zachariah Frankel. As German Jews migrated to America, a few brought with them the idea of reform. While the reform movement in Germany affected only a small percentage of the country's Jewry, it was more readily received in America. One of the better-known leaders in the American Reform movement was Isaac Mayer Wise. A German-educated rabbi, Wise immigrated in 1846 to America, where he began introducing changes. He modified the traditional Jewish worship ritual for diverse American Jewry, and this prayer book, entitled *The Minhag America* (The American Ritual), was published in 1856. Wise joined others in bringing about the Union of American Hebrew Congregations, formed in 1873. From this organization a rabbinical school, Hebrew Union College, was established in 1875. Wise served as its first president. Although Reform Judaism did not accomplish the task of bringing all the Jews of America together as a cohesive group, it succeeded in strengthening Judaism in America and was particularly helpful to the scattered communities in the South and West. For more data on Orthodox and Reform Judaism, see Leo Trepp, *A History of the Jewish Experience* (New York: Behrman House, Inc., 1973) and James G. Heller, *Isaac M. Wise—His Life, Work and Thought* (New York: Union of American Hebrew Congregations, 1965).

3. Cyrus Adler, ed., *The American Jewish Year Book, 1899–1900* (Philadelphia: Jewish Publication Society of America, 1900).

4. Dan Durning, "Attracting the German Immigrant," *PCHR* 28 (1980): 2. Louis E. Brister, "The Image of Arkansas in the Early German Emigrant Guidebook: Notes On Immigration," *AHQ* 36: 3 (1977): 338–45.

5. John L. Ferguson and J. H. Atkinson, *Historic Arkansas* (Little Rock: AHC, 1966), 158, 159, 191. Foreigners made up only a fraction of Arkansas's population by 1880. Out of a total of 802,525 citizens, only 10,350 were foreigners. *Biographical and Historical Memoirs of Southern Arkansas* (Chicago: The Goodspeed Publishing Company, 1890), 10.

6. *Arkansas Gazette*, 3 May 1875; Jonathan J. Wolfe, part 1 "Background of German Immigration," *AHQ* 25: 2 (Summer 1966): 151–82 (hereafter cited as "German Immigration").

7. The history of the Concordia Club was given at the dedication of its own building on 8 June 1903 by Morris M. Cohn, a prominent Little Rock attorney. His account was printed in two local newspapers. One, the *Arkansas Democrat* (10 June 1903) said the club began with eleven charter members; the *Arkansas Gazette* (9 June 1903) reported it had one hundred charter members. Although either number was possible at the time, it is more likely that the *Democrat* report was correct.

8. *Arkansas Gazette*, 31 January 1880.

9. *Arkansas Democrat*, 10 June 1903.

10. Ibid., 16 April 1880.

11. *Arkansas Gazette*, 31 January 1880.

12. Wolfe, "German Immigration," 166; *Arkansas Gazette*, 12 March 1897.

13. The exact number can only be speculated upon. In cities such as Helena and Fort Smith, it seems that two congregations formed shortly after the Civil War, but the two groups in each city later merged. Data for congregational histories are taken from Works Progress Administration (WPA) Churches and Synagogues Historical Records Survey, Arkansas, Box 434, Folders 1 and 2, Box

453, Folder 26, Special Collections, UofA Library (hereafter cited as WPA Records); Arkansas Jewish congregational histories; Jewish publications and records, AJA; personal interviews.

14. *Pine Bluff Commercial,* 22 April 1873; *Pine Bluff Dispatch,* 27 October 1866. Although High Holy Day services were held in the synagogue in 1867, poor economic conditions of the Reconstruction era delayed the building's completion until 1869. (See James W. Leslie, "History of Congregation Anshe Emeth, 1867–1977," Anshe Emeth Archives, Pine Bluff, Ark. [hereafter cited as "Congregation Anshe Emeth"])

15. *Acts of Arkansas 1866–1867,* 427.

16. Rabbi Raphael Goldenstein, comp. and ed., "History and Activities of Congregation Anshe Emeth, 1867–1917," (1917), 18, Anshe Emeth Archives, Pine Bluff, Ark. (hereafter cited as "Anshe Emeth").

17. *Biographical and Historical Memoirs of Central Arkansas* (Chicago: The Goodspeed Publishing Company, 1889), 146 (hereafter cited as *Central Arkansas*); *Pine Bluff Press Eagle,* 8 January 1883; *Arkansas Gazette,* 13 December 1908.

18. *This Is B'nai B'rith* (1979 brochure), B'nai B'rith International Archives, Washington, D.C. (For information on early IOBB lodges in the South, see Michael Neiditch, "Watering the Desert: The Role of B'nai B'rith International in the Development of the Jewish Communities in the South, 1850–1880" [paper presented at the Southern Jewish Historical Society's Fifteenth Annual Conference, Jackson, Miss., 4 November 1990].)

19. The Levi Lodge and the Pine Bluff Lodge no longer exist. The first three B'nai B'rith lodges to form in Arkansas, Nos. 88, 158, and 159, belonged to District No. 2 until 1873; Arkansas then became part of District No. 7. (B'nai B'rith International Archives, Washington, D.C.)

20. Goldenstein, "Anshe Emeth," 28.

21. *Pine Bluff Weekly Press,* 8 December 1870.

22. Ibid., 5 December 1872.

23. Ibid., 21 April 1872.

24. Ibid., 1 April 1875.

25. *Pine Bluff Commercial,* 14 April 1887.

26. *Pine Bluff Graphic,* Special Edition, August 1896.

27. Goldenstein, "Anshe Emeth," 28; *American Israelite,* 21 January 1876.

28. "Arkansas 1840s–1870s," 7: 2430, R. G. Dun & Co. Collection, Baker Library, Harvard University Graduate School of Business Administration (hereafter cited as R. G. Dun & Co., "Arkansas").

29. *Pine Bluff Weekly Commercial,* 24 December 1885.

30. *Pine Bluff Weekly Press,* 23 September 1880.

31. Goldenstein, "Anshe Emeth," 43.

32. Ibid., 41, 42.

33. Ibid., 29.

34. *Pine Bluff Weekly Commercial,* 25 May 1901; Jefferson County Land Records, Deed Book 44, 69; Leslie, "Congregation Anshe Emeth," 9.

35. Goldenstein, "Anshe Emeth," 36, 37.

36. *Pine Bluff Weekly Press,* 9 November 1876, 16 November 1876; *Pine Bluff Semi-Weekly Graphic,* 5 January 1898, 20 October 1901.

37. Herbert Friedenwald, ed., *The American Jewish Year Book, 1909–1910* (Philadelphia: Jewish Publication Society of America, 1909), 57. X. O. Pindall was one of several men who served as acting governor after the collapse of Gov. John S. Little in 1907. (See David Y. Thomas, ed., *Arkansas and Its People*, vol. 1 [New York: American Historical Society, Inc., 1930], 281, 282.)

38. *Pine Bluff Commercial*, 3 May 1911; *Pine Bluff Graphic*, 3 May 1911; *Pine Bluff Herald*, 3 June 1911. For more information on Isaac Fisher, see Elizabeth L. Wheeler, "Isaac Fisher: The Frustrations of a Negro Educator at Branch Normal College, 1902–1911," *AHQ* 41: 1 (Spring 1982): 3–50.

39. Isaac Landman, ed., *The Universal Jewish Encyclopedia*, vol. 4 (New York: Universal Jewish Encyclopedia Company, Inc., 1948), 461.

40. Goldenstein "Anshe Emeth," 37.

41. Ibid., 29.

42. *New Orleans Jewish Ledger*, 13 April 1923.

43. Ibid.

44. *Pine Bluff Commercial*, 27 September 1921; Leslie, "Congregation Anshe Emeth," 11.

45. *New Orleans Jewish Ledger*, 13 April 1923.

46. Dallas T. Herndon, *Centennial History of Arkansas* vol. 2 (Chicago–Little Rock: The S. J. Clarke Publishing Company, 1922), 331. The Harmony Club was a Jewish social club that had originated under the name "Bluff City Club." (*New Orleans Jewish Ledger*, 13 April 1923.)

47. Herndon, *Centennial History* 2: 538, 539; *Pine Bluff Commercial*, 21 April 1923; Leslie "Congregation Anshe Emeth," 11.

48. *Pine Bluff Commercial*, 23 April 1925; Leslie, "Congregation Anshe Emeth," 11.

49. Anshe Emeth Archives, Pine Bluff, Ark.

50. "A Sketch of Congregation B'nai Israel," Board of Directors' Meeting (1880), Ladies Temple Aid Society Folder, Little Rock, Ark., Box X-38, AJA. This and subsequent data through 1876, except where noted differently, are taken from this brief sketch of B'nai Israel's early history.

51. Ira E. Sanders and Elijah E. Palnick, comps. and eds., *One Hundred Years, Congregation B'nai Israel 1866–1966* (Little Rock: n.p., 1966), 16 (hereafter cited as *One Hundred Years*).

52. Fay Hempstead, *A Pictorial History of Arkansas* (New York: N. D. Thompson Publishing Company, 1890), 757.

53. *Arkansas Gazette*, 10 December 1869.

54. *Central Arkansas*, 415.

55. Sanders and Palnick, *One Hundred Years*, 30.

56. Ibid., 31

57. Wolfe, "German Immigration," 169. In Traditional Judaism, holidays are celebrated for two days.

58. Sanders and Palnick, *One Hundred Years*, 31.

59. *Arkansas Democrat*, 18 September 1879.

60. *Jewish Spectator* article (full citation unavailable), Rabbi Ira E. Sanders Papers, BIA.

61. Sanders and Palnick, *One Hundred Years*, 30.

62. *Reform Judaism* (September 1973).

63. Union of American Hebrew Congregations, letter to author, 31 January 1986; "B'nai Israel Minutes," 1873, 1880, BIA.

64. David Menkus, interview with author, Little Rock, Ark., 22 April 1985; Dr. B. D. Auerbach, *Berith Abraham* (Frankfurt, Germany: Berlag von Kauffmann, 1880).

65. Of the fifteen full-time rabbis who have served B'nai Israel from its inception until 1990, eight have been Hebrew Union College graduates. The others received their training abroad before coming to America.

66. The Pittsburgh Platform was a document characterized by rationality, ethics, and social justice. A belief in the restoration of a homeland in Palestine for the Jews was sharply denied. The Jew was seen as a promulgator of universal ethics and, as such, was destined to be scattered among the peoples of the world. It was not until the Nazi threats of the 1930s that the Pittsburg Platform was superseded in 1937 by the Columbus Platform, at which time the peoplehood of Israel was emphasized and a Zionistic work in Palestine was deemed significant. (See Steven Bayme and Gary Rubin, comps., *American Jewry and Judaism in the Twentieth Century* [New York: Hadassah, The Women's Zionist Organization of America, Inc., 1980], 39–42.)

67. Hempstead, *Pictorial History*, 757; *Arkansas Democrat*, 18 September 1879.

68. The data from this paragraph are contained in a letter dated 9 February 1937 from Rabbi Stolz to Rabbi Sanders, sent on the occasion of B'nai Israel's seventieth anniversary celebration. Stolz was unable to attend in person. (Sanders Papers, BIA)

69. *Arkansas Gazette*, 28 August 1891, 2 April 1890.

70. "Assessments of All Members of the Congregation, September 1, 1889, to September 1, 1890," BIA; *Guide to Little Rock, 1890* (n.p., n.d.), 61.

71. *Guide to Little Rock*, 20, 25.

72. *Arkansas Gazette*, 8 May 1897, 9 May 1897.

73. B'nai Israel Ladies Aid Society Folder, Temple B'nai Israel, Little Rock, Ark., Folder, AJA; Sanders and Palnick, *One Hundred Years*, 23, 43.

74. *American Hebrew*, 9 January 1903; Sanders and Palnick, *One Hundred Years*, 45; *Arkansas Democrat*, 5 March 1953.

75. Joseph Stolz Collection, Nearprint File, AJA; *The Jewish Review of Cleveland*, 28 May 1948; *Arkansas Democrat*, 10 February 1925.

76. *Arkansas Democrat*, 19 January 1906.

77. *Little Rock Board of Trade 17th Annual Report, 1906*, 146.

78. *Little Rock–Hot Springs Blue Book* vol. 1 (Little Rock–Chicago: The Blue Book Publishing Company, 1901), 55–86.

79. "Annals of Arkansas 1866–1903," gleaned from various sources, WPA Project 6715, 236, AHC.

80. Rufus Learsi, *The Jews in America: A History* (New York: KTAV Publishing House, Inc., 1972), 133.

81. B'nai Israel Ladies Aid Society Folder, Temple B'nai Israel, Little Rock, Ark., Folder, AJA.

82. *Arkansas Democrat*, 7 October 1879.

83. Ibid., 14 March 1898.

84. Mrs. W. E. Wilson, "The Changing Face of Social Work" (paper given in 1951), Graduate School of Social Work File, UALR.

85. Ibid.; *Arkansas Gazette*, 28 January 1912.

86. *Arkansas Democrat*, 18 May 1912; *Arkansas Gazette*, 18 May 1912.

87. *Arkansas Gazette*, 23 January 1877, 2 May 1916, 3 May 1916.

88. Ibid., 4 December 1924.

89. Rabbi Ira E. Sanders, "The Journal of a Southern Rabbi," courtesy Rabbi Ira E. Sanders.

90. Rabbi Ira E. Sanders, interview with author, Little Rock, Ark., 23 March 1983; Sanders, "The Journal of a Southern Rabbi."

91. Sanders interview.

92. Sadye Allen Thompson, interview with author, Little Rock, Ark., 9 March 1982. Mrs. Thompson was one of the two blacks who initially enrolled in Rabbi Sanders' class (the other student dropped out almost immediately). Rabbi Sanders encouraged her to stay, she said, and he did all within his power to make it possible; however, school officials enforced the segregation policy. Years later, she still appreciated the Rabbi's concern for her.

93. Sanders and Palnick, *One Hundred Years*, 83.

94. R. G. Dun & Co., "Arkansas" 9: 249–93.

95. "Centennial Celebration of Congregation Beth El, Helena, Arkansas, 1867–1967," Churches Folder, PCPL, Helena, Ark.

96. B. M. Solomon, "Jewry in Helena Dates From 1867," *Arkansas Assembly Bulletin* 16(April 1950):7.

97. *American Israelite*, 2 June 1873.

98. *Helena World*, 26 September 1926.

99. "The Churches of Helena," *Helena World*, 11 November 1923.

100. *American Israelite*, 18 March 1880.

101. *Helena World*, 26 September 1926.

102. Ibid. Jews who had died previous to November 1875 had been buried in a section west of the city. After grounds for a Jewish cemetery were purchased (located next to the Catholic and Protestant cemeteries), the dead were transferred there (David Solomon Jr., interview with author, Helena, Ark., 29 June 1982).

103. *Helena World*, 26 September 1926.

104. "Centennial Celebration of Congregation Beth El."

105. Solomon, "Jewry in Helena,"7.

106. Ibid.; George E. N. deMan, comp. and ed., *Helena: The Ridge, the River, the Romance* (Little Rock: Pioneer Press, 1978), 107.

107. "The Churches of Helena," *Helena World*, 11 November 1923; "Combined Directory of the Churches of Helena, Arkansas," 1 June 1926, Churches Folder, PCPL.

108. E. G. Green, "A Brief History of West Helena," *PCHQ* 3 (June 1965): 20–23.

109. "Twentieth Century Club Easter Edition," *Helena World*, 20 April 1930.

110. deMan, *Helena*.

111. R. G. Dun & Co., "Arkansas."

112. *Arkansas Gazette*, 23 July 1869.

113. Adolph Felsenthal, "Nearly Threescore and Ten," part 1, *Arkansas Gazette*, magazine section (1934) (full citation unavailable), Camden, Ark., Nearprint File, AJA (hereafter cited as "Nearly Threescore").

114. "Razing of Synagogue Marks Passing of Landmark," Camden newspaper clipping, Sifford's Scrapbook no. 6, Camden, Ark., Public Library.

115. *American Israelite*, 24 October 1873.

116. "Razing of Synagogue"; Felsenthal, "Nearly Threescore."

117. "Razing of Synagogue."

118. *American Israelite*, 5 November 1875.

119. Rabbi Martin M. Weitz, *Diamond Jubilee Bibilog . . . Temple Beth Israel, May 1950* (Hot Springs, Ark.: n.p., 1950), 13 (hereafter cited as *Jubilee*).

120. Ibid.; Hoffstadt Tombstone, Jewish Rest Cemetery, Hot Springs, Ark.

121. Weitz, *Jubilee*, 12, 13.

122. Ibid.

123. *Arkansas Democrat*, 22 September 1900.

124. Weitz, *Jubilee*, 7, 20.

125. "Proceedings of the 1902 and 1903 Conventions, District Grand Lodge No. 7," B'nai B'rith International Archives, Washington, D.C.

126. Ibid.; Dr. Joseph Rosenzweig, "The Story of Leo N. Levi Memorial Hospital," *Hospital Heartbeat* (Levi Hospital publication) (1951): 6, Hot Springs, Nearprint File, Misc. Collection, AJA (hereafter cited as "Levi").

127. *American Hebrew*, 8 September 1911.

128. Ibid.; *B'nai B'rith's Levi Arthritis Hospital, A Heritage of Caring* (Levi Hospital brochure, n.d.), 2.

129. Rosenzweig, "Levi," 8.

130. Weitz, *Jubilee*, 7.

131. Mrs. Joseph Rosenzweig, "House of Israel," *The Record* (1970 Year Book of the Hot Springs–Garland County Historical Society) 11 (1970): 68; Dr. and Mrs. J. L. Rosenzweig, letter to author, 28 September 1991.

132. W. H. Arnold Sr., "Historical Statement of Texarkana, Arkansas, to 7 February 1917," *AHQ* 5: 4 (1946): 341.

133. Rabbi David Max Eichhorn, "History of the Jews of Texarkana" in Charles Grossman, comp. and ed., *Mount Sinai Jubilee* (Texarkana, Ark.: n.p., 1935), Mt. Sinai Archives, Texarkana, Ark. (hereafter cited as "Texarkana").

134. Ibid.

135. *Texarkana Democrat*, as quoted by Rabbi David Max Eichhorn in his book, *Joys of Jewish Folklore: A Journey from New Amsterdam to Beverly Hills* (Middle Village, N.Y.: Jonathan David Pubs., Inc., 1981). Rabbi Eichhorn served as spiritual leader of Mt. Sinai Congregation in Texarkana during the years 1935–38.

136. W. A. McCartney, Sr., "The Story of Dr. Charles Goldberg, 1820–1890," AJA (hereafter cited as "Goldberg").

137. *American Israelite*, 8 October 1876.

138. Letter of Charles Wessolowsky, representative of *The Jewish South* newspaper and of B'nai B'rith, quoted in Louis Schmier, ed., *Reflections of Southern Jewry: The Letters of Charles Wessolowsky 1878–1879* (Atlanta: Mercer University Press, 1982), 123, 124.

139. McCartney, "Goldberg."

140. Eichhorn, "Texarkana."

141. Barbara Glick, ed., *Centennial Journal of Mount Sinai Congregation, 1885–1985* (Texarkana, Ark.: n.p., 1985), 21, 22.

142. Eichhorn, "Texarkana."

143. Ibid.

144. Ibid.

145. Ibid.

146. Warranty Deed of the United Hebrew Congregation's Cemetery Association's Incorporation, 3 October 1887. UHCA.

147. *Fort Smith Times-Record*, 14 November 1915.

148. William S. Speer and John Henry Brown, eds., *The Encyclopedia of the New West* (Marshall, Tex.: The United States Biographical Publishing Company, 1881), 251.

149. *American Israelite*, 22 April 1881.

150. *United Hebrew Temple*, (printed history of United Hebrew Congregation) (n.p., n.d.), UHCA.

151. Warranty Deed of the United Hebrew Congregation's Cemetery Association's Incorporation, 3 October 1887, UHCA.

152. *Fort Smith Times–Record*, 27 February 1914.

153. Unidentified newspaper article, ca. 1919 (full citation unavailable), Rabbi Charles Latz Folder, File 1628, AJA.

154. *Fort Smith Southwest American*, 12 September 1912.

155. "Fort Smith, Arkansas, B'nai B'rith 75th Anniversary, 1878–1953," 28 November 1953 brochure, UHCA.

156. UHC Judaica Exhibit Paper (1982), 2, UHCA; "Program of Dedication, 18 September 1892," UHCA.

157. *Reform Advocate*, 10 January 1914.

158. *Fort Smith News Record*, 17 July 1902.

159. UHCA.

160. Data provided by R. H. Meyer and Mrs. Babette Berger, charter members of Jonesboro's Temple Israel, WPA Records.

161. Sam Levitt, "A History of Temple Israel, Jonesboro, Ark.," *The Craighead County Historical Quarterly* 3 (1965): 8 (hereafter cited as "Temple Israel").

162. "Dedication Programme of Temple Israel of Jonesboro, Arkansas, Held Sunday, January 2, 1898," TIAJ. The original written speech and the rose worn by Rosa Schoenberger Rosenfield are housed in the TIAJ.

163. *Jonesboro Enterprise* (full citation unavailable).

164. WPA Records; "Dedication Programme of Temple Israel of Jonesboro, Arkansas, Held Sunday, January 2, 1898."

165. Levitt, "Temple Israel," 9, 10.

166. Ibid.; *Arkansas Gazette*, 29 December 1907.

167. "Sixtieth Anniversary Services of Temple Israel, Jonesboro, Arkansas, 1898–1958," TIAJ.

168. Levitt, "Temple Israel," 9.

169. Morris Schoenfield, "Talk by Morris Schoenfield on the Occasion of the 75th Anniversary Celebration of Temple Israel, Jonesboro, Arkansas" (14 December 1973, Jonesboro, Ark.), Temple Israel Folder, Misc. File, AJA; Levitt, "Temple Israel," 9.

CHAPTER 6
The East European Migration, 1880–1930

1. Rufus Learsi, *The Jews in America: A History* (New York: KTAV Publishing House, Inc., 1972), 124–28 (hereafter cited as *Jews in America*); Leo Trepp, *A History of the Jewish Experience* (New York: Behrman House, Inc., 1973), 260–63 (hereafter cited as *Jewish Experience*); Max I. Dimont, *The Jews in America* (New York: Simon & Schuster, 1978), 147–61 (hereafter cited as *The Jews in America*).

2. The Orthodox often referred to their meeting places as "shuls," which is taken from the German *Schule* (Greek *schola*). It is a Yiddish word, and in the East European communities the local shul was the center of Jewish communal life. The word is used synonymously with the word *synagogue*. (Leo Rosten, *The Joys of Yiddish* [New York: Pocket Books, 1968], 379.)

3. Learsi, *Jews in America*, 127, 134, 135.

4. Samuel Joseph, *History of the Baron de Hirsch Fund: The Americanization of the Jewish Immigrant* (Philadelphia: Printed for Baron de Hirsch Fund by the Jewish Publication Society, 1935), 289.

5. Rabbi M. Cahan, Fort Smith, Ark., letter to Industrial Removal Office, New York, 1905, Industrial Removal Office (IRO) Papers, Arkansas, 1–91, Box 29, AJHS (hereafter cited as IRO Papers).

6. Dimont, *The Jews in America*, 162.

7. IRO Papers (see note 5).

8. Rabbi Raphael Goldenstein, comp. and ed., "History and Activities of Congregation Anshe Emeth, 1867–1917" (1917), 19, Anshe Emeth Archives, Pine Bluff, Ark.

9. Quoted by Abraham J. Karp, *Haven and Home: A History of the Jews in America* (New York: Schocken Books, 1985), 183–84.

10. Gabriel Davidson, *Our Jewish Farmers and the Story of the Jewish Agriculture Society* (New York: L. B. Fischer, 1943), 195; see also, Leo Shpall, "Jewish Agricultural Colonies in the United States," *Agricultural History* 24 (1950): 120–46.

11. "Newspaper Report," *Allgemeine Zeitung des Judenthums* 47 (1883): 536, 537.

12. As reported in the *Batesville Guard*, 23 February 1883.

13. Davidson, *Our Jewish Farmers*, 209.

14. Ibid., 208, 213.

15. Dimont, *The Jews in America*, 175; for more information on Cyrus Adler, see sec. I chap. 3.

16. Conservative Judaism had its beginnings in Germany with the teachings of Zachariah Frankel (1801–1875). Italian Rabbi Sabato Morais (1823–1897), who succeeded well-known Jewish leader Isaac Leeser (1806–1868) at Mikveh Israel congregation in Philadelphia in 1851, is considered a chief founder of Conservative Judaism in America. Later, it became well established under the leadership of Rumanian-born Rabbi Solomon Schecter (1847–1915), who had taught Talmudics at Cambridge University. Conservative Judaism, which professed allegiance to the rabbinical code but actually disregarded almost "all laws and customs which are out of joint with the times," eventually became the largest

branch of Judaism in the U.S. (See Jacob Rader Marcus, *The American Jewish Woman, 1654–1980* [New York: KTAV Publishing House, Inc., 1981], 12; Learsi, *Jews in America*, 120, 205–06; Trepp, *Jewish Experience*, 302–06, 393–96.)

17. Based on Works Progress Administration (WPA) Churches and Synagogues Historical Records Survey, Arkansas, Box 434, Folders 1 and 2, Box 453, Folder 26, Special Collections, UofA Library (hereafter cited as WPA Records); Arkansas Jewish congregational histories; records and journals, AJA; personal interviews.

18. Morris Schoenfield, "Talk by Morris Schoenfield on the Occasion of the 75th Anniversary Celebration of Temple Israel, Jonesboro, Arkansas" (14 December 1973, Jonesboro, Ark.), 1, Temple Israel Folder, Misc. File, AJA.

19. Pearl Hummelstein interview with author, Jonesboro, Ark., 9 November 1982.

20. Lena Mae (Wainman) Rubenstein (granddaughter of Nathan Blecker), interview with author, Memphis, Tenn., 11 May 1983.

21. Lee Hummelstein, interview with author, Jonesboro, Ark., 9 November 1982. The Orthodox congregation, Beth Jacob, of Hot Springs, established its own cemetery in the 1950s.

22. Sam Levitt, "A History of Temple Israel, Jonesboro, Arkansas," *The Craighead County Historical Quarterly* 3 (1965); B'nai B'rith International Archives, Washington, D.C.

23. *Arkansas Democrat*, 2 October 1903.

24. *Arkansas Gazette*, 9 September 1904.

25. "Our Dreams Fulfilled" (Dedication Program of Congregation Agudath Achim, Little Rock, April–May 1976), 3; Charles Elias, interview with author, Little Rock, Ark., 17 February 1982; Dorothy Goldberg, interview with author, Little Rock, Ark., 24 July 1982; and Charles Kluglose, interview with author, Little Rock, Ark., 17 December 1985.

26. "Our Dreams Fulfilled."

27. "Short History of Second Baptist Church, Little Rock," Second Baptist Church Archives.

28. Dorothy Goldberg, interview with author, Little Rock, Ark., 29 July 1982.

29. *American Hebrew*, 23 May 1913.

30. Based on newspaper articles of the time, 1920–30.

31. Joe Bernhard, interview with author, Little Rock, Ark., 16 March 1983.

32. Edith Breier, interview with author, Little Rock, Ark., 11 March 1983.

33. Charles Kluglose, interview with author, Little Rock, Ark., 2 December 1985.

34. Joe Dante (son of Eli Dante), telephone interview with author, Winnsboro, La., 12 April 1984.

35. Joe Dante, letter to author, 4 August 1984.

36. Robert and Hattie Heiman, interview with author, Blytheville, Ark., 25 June 1982; Mrs. William (Joan) Hamburger, interview with author, Memphis, Tenn., 10 May 1983; Roy Wolchansky, letter to author, 20 November 1982; B'nai B'rith International Archives, Washington, D.C.

37. *American Israelite*, 13 June 1873.

38. WPA Records; Nancy Britton, interview with author, Batesville, Ark.,

12 November 1982. James Logan Morgan, *Centennial History of Newport* (Newport, Ark.: Jackson County Historical Society, 1975), 35.

39. "Arkansas-Oklahoma Report," (January 1909): 135, 136, R. G. Dun & Co. Collection, Baker Library, Harvard University Graduate School of Business Administration; *Golden City Messenger*, November 1925, Jewish Children's Home Collection—180, Sec. 8, Special Collections, Tulane University Library.

40. Nancy Zilbergeld and Nancy Britton, "The Jewish Community in Batesville, Arkansas, 1853–1977," *The Independence County Chronicle* 21: 3 (April 1980): 1–32.

41. Information on Pine Bluff's B'nai Israel congregation is taken from Burton Schlosberg and Louis Bram, interviews with author, Pine Bluff, Ark., 24 April 1982; WPA Records; *Arkansas Democrat*, 2 October 1921.

42. Bram interview.

43. Schlosberg interview. Orthodox services cannot be held without at least ten men (a minyan) in attendance.

44. *Arkansas Democrat*, 2 October 1921; Bram interview.

45. WPA Records.

46. Ibid.; Elizabeth (King) Kallsnick, interview with author, Hot Springs, Ark., 21 April 1982.

47. Eugene "Gene" Kirsch, interview with author, Hot Springs, Ark., 6 April 1982.

48. *American Israelite*, 20 April 1911.

49. Lena Rexinger (daughter of Jacob Rexinger), interview with author, Russellville, Ark., 1 June 1983.

50. Ibid.; *American Israelite*, 20 April 1911.

51. Maurice Cohen, interview with author, Forrest City, Ark., 22 June 1982.

52. Rexinger interview.

53. *American Israelite*, 18 July 1912.

54. Norma Goldner Neaderthal (granddaughter of Annie Weinberg), letter to author, 5 April 1982; Hal Rand (born Harold Rosenthal, grandson of Annie Weinberg), "Weinberg Family History," New York, N.Y., 28 July 1980, courtesy Carrol S. Meyer Jr., San Antonio, Tex.

55. B'nai B'rith International Archives, Washington, D.C.

56. "Dedication Services of the New Temple Israel, Blytheville, Arkansas," 7 September 1947, TIAB.

57. Mrs. Siegbert (Eva) Jiedel, interview with author, Blytheville, Ark., 25 June 1982; William "Bill" Borowsky, interview with author, Manila, Ark., 27 June 1982.

58. Jiedel interview.

59. *Hebrew Standard*, 17 October 1913.

60. Sarah Kasten and son Maurice Kasten, interview with author, Fort Smith, Ark., 18 August 1982.

61. Ibid.; Morton B. Marks, Jr., interview with author, Fort Smith, Ark., 19 August 1982; Reba (Kasten) Nosoff, letter to author, 23 August 1991.

62. Jeannette (Warshavsky) Bernstein "A Grateful Thread, A Family Journal," 4 January 1957, Arkansas, Jeannette Bernstein Folder, Box 1784, AJA (hereafter cited as "Thread").

63. *Hebrew Standard*, 17 April 1914.

64. *American Israelite*, 15 January 1920.

65. Harold Sharpe, interview with author, Forrest City, Ark., 22 June 1982; *Golden City Messenger*, 1925–38.

66. Sharpe interview.

67. Ibid.

68. Richard L. Hartness, Sr., *Wittsburg, Arkansas: Crowley's Ridge Steamboat Riverport, 1848–1890* (Little Rock: Rose Publishing Company, 1979), 109.

69. WPA Records.

70. Ibid.; David Drexler, interview with author, Wynne, Ark., 23 June 1982; David Drexler, letters to author, 7 October 1982, 23 January 1986; Robert W. Chowning, *History of Cross County* (Wynne, Ark.: *Wynne Progress*, 1955), 88; John L. Ferguson, *Arkansas Lives: The Opportunity Land Who's Who* (Hopkinsville, Ky.: Historical Record Association, 1965), 130, 131.

71. Bernstein, "Thread."

72. Drexler interview.

73. U.S. Bureau of the Census, *Fourteenth Census of the United States, 1920* (Washington, D.C.: Government Printing Office, 1923).

74. *American Israelite*, 15 January 1920.

75. Ibid.

76. Barbara Glick, ed., *Centennial Journal of Mount Sinai Congregation, 1885–1985* (Texarkana, Ark.: 1985), 13; Ralph Brody interview with author, Texarkana, Ark., 27 October 1982.

77. WPA Records.

78. Marjorie (Miller) Miron (daughter of Ben Miller), letter to author, 19 November 1985.

79. *Golden City Messenger*, December 1923, November 1925.

80. This observation is based on research of Arkansas congregational histories and on numerous interviews with Jews and non-Jews in Arkansas.

81. This was true in other parts of the South as well (see Leonard Dinnerstein and Mary Dale Palsson, eds., *Jews in the South* (Baton Rouge: Louisiana State University Press, 1973), 12 (hereafter cited as *South*).

82. For insight into how some Jews viewed attendance at Christian churches and perceived Christian doctrine, see Eli N. Evans, *The Provincials: A Personal History of Jews in the South* (New York: Atheneum, 1976), 120–39

83. These observations came from author's interviews with a number of older East European Jewish citizens of Arkansas and correspondence with them and their offspring. See secs. III, IV, and V for further data on anti-Semitism in Arkansas.

84. Based on interviews conducted by author.

85. Ibid.

86. Dinnerstein and Palsson, *South*, 7.

87. Robert Itzkowitz, interview with author, North Little Rock, Ark., 4 April 1983.

88. Maurice Kasten, interview with author, Fort Smith, Ark., 18 August 1982.

89. Based on interviews and correspondence by author with Maurice Kasten and a number of offspring of East European Jews who settled in Arkansas.

Section III Introduction

1. Part of a letter written in 1877 by Sol Rosenberg of Pine Bluff and addressed to a future generation. The letter was found sealed in a bottle and placed in the foundation of a building being constructed that year by him and his partners, the Altheimer brothers, Joseph and Louis. The bottle was discovered in 1948 when the foundation for another building was being excavated. (Undesignated Pine Bluff newspaper article, 1948 [full citation unavailable], courtesy Mrs. Carl [Dorothy Jacobs] Frankel, granddaughter of Joseph Altheimer, Toronto, Canada.)

2. This was true for the Southern Jewish community as a whole. See Elliott Ashkenazi, *The Business of Jews in Louisiana, 1840–1875,* (Tuscaloosa: University of Alabama Press, 1988), 16, 158.

3. This observation, noted in Ashkenazi, *Business,* 168, is based on research of Jewish business practices found in the R. G. Dun & Co. records of Louisiana. What Ashkenazi notes regarding the Jewish businessmen of that state can also be said of their counterparts in Arkansas, based on the R. G. Dun & Co. records of Arkansas.

4. Thomas D. Clark, "The Post–Civil War Economy in the South," *AJHQ* 55 (June 1966).

5. Ibid., 16, 160–67.

6. From information collected for this book, which includes data on Arkansas Jewry from the AJA; AJHS; "Arkansas 1840s–70s," R. G. Dun & Co. Collection, Baker Library, Harvard University Graduate School of Business Administration (hereafter cited as R. G. Dun & Co., "Arkansas"); other archival material; data from all stones in Jewish cemeteries in Arkansas; more than fifteen hundred obituaries on Arkansas Jews; personal letters and data from dozens of present or former Arkansas Jewish citizens; some four hundred oral interviews, mostly with present or former Arkansas Jewish citizens; material from Arkansas Jewish congregational histories, biographical histories of Arkansans; newspaper and journal articles from the 1840s to the 1990s; census and court records, and other data collected over a ten-year period of research on Arkansas Jewry (hereafter cited as "Jews of Arkansas" Research Data).

7. "Jews of Arkansas" Research Data.

8. R. G. Dun & Co., "Arkansas." It may be noted that 72 percent of those who were rated as bad or poor on their business evaluations were also rated bad as Jews (their ratings included racial slurs), while 28 percent who were rated with good business evaluations were viewed negatively as Jews.

9. R. G. Dun & Co., "Arkansas." Because the Jew tended to use innovative business methods and risk the loss of his assets in any venture he undertook, he chose his associates carefully. As an immigrant and a newcomer, he would naturally choose partners he knew, which usually entailed family members or other Jews. (See Ashkenazi, *Business,* 162.)

10. Clark, "Post–Civil War," 162, 168–69.

11. Ibid., 168.

12. Hal Bridges, "The Robber Baron Concept in American History," in Abraham Seldin Eisenstadt, ed., *American History: Recent Interpretations,* vol. 2 (New York: Thomas Y. Crowell Company, 1962), 58.

13. Theodore Saloutos, "The Agricultural Problem and Nineteenth Century Industrialism," in Abraham Seldin Eisenstadt, ed., *American History: Recent Interpretations*, vol. 2 (New York: Thomas Y. Crowell Company, 1962), 125.

14. Based on "Jews of Arkansas" Research Data.

15. Abraham D. Lavender, ed., *A Coat of Many Colors: Jewish Subcommunities in the United States* (Westport, Conn.: Greenwood Press, 1977), 7.

16. John L. Ferguson and J. H. Atkinson, *Historic Arkansas* (Little Rock: AHC, 1966), 233.

17. Although there was some increase in land use, for the most part, the farms simply became smaller. While the average farm size had been 245 acres in 1860, it shrank to 75 acres by 1920. (David Y. Thomas, ed., *Arkansas and Its People*, vol. 2 [New York: The American Historical Society, Inc., 1930], 394.)

18. Hundreds of obituaries and editorial comments written at the deaths of Arkansas Jewish businessmen carried this commendation.

19. *Pine Bluff Graphic*, 18 October 1889. In the article, the Jews are described as "the most wonderful people the world ever produced, their history and achievements largely entitle them to the claim of superiority."

20. Ferguson and Atkinson, *Historic Arkansas*, 176; Dallas T. Herndon, ed., *Centennial History of Arkansas*, vol. 2 (Chicago–Little Rock: The S. J. Clarke Publishing Company, 1922), 23–24; Diann Sutherlin Smith, *The Arkansas Handbook* (Little Rock: Emerald City Press, 1984), 313, 314.

21. Quoted by Leonard Dinnerstein and Mary Dale Palsson, eds., *Jews in the South* (Baton Rouge: Louisiana State University Press, 1973), 13.

22. See Leonard Dinnerstein, *The Leo Frank Case* (New York: Columbia University Press, 1968; reprint, Athens: University of Georgia Press, 1987); Dale Schwartz, "Justice Delayed, Justice Denied: The Case of Leo Frank" (paper delivered at the Southern Jewish Historical Society Conference, Richmond, Va., 4 November 1984).

23. Ferguson and Atkinson, *Historic Arkansas*, 265–69.

24. Clark, "Post–Civil War," 166.

25. Ibid., 169.

26. See Eli N. Evans, *The Provincials: A Personal History of Jews in the South* (New York: Atheneum, 1976), 69.

27. "Jews of Arkansas" Research Data.

28. Thomas, *Arkansas and its People* 3: 272.

CHAPTER 7

German Migration in Central Arkansas

1. *Arkansas Gazette*, 29 July 1865; see Ira Don Richards, "Little Rock on the Road to Reunion, 1865–1880," *AHQ* 25: 4 (1966): 313 (hereafter cited as "Reunion").

2. U.S. Bureau of the Census, *Compendium of the Ninth Census* (Washington, D.C.: Government Printing Office, 1872; reprint, New York: Arno Press, 1976), 26.

3. *Arkansas Gazette*, 18 February 1868.

4. Richards, "Reunion," 319.

5. *Arkansas Gazette*, 9 August 1870, 9 November 1870.

6. John L. Ferguson and J. H. Atkinson, *Historic Arkansas* (Little Rock: AHC, 1966), 167.

7. Richards, "Reunion," 323.

8. Ibid., 324; Thomas S. Staples, *Reconstruction in Arkansas, 1862–1874* (New York: Columbia University, 1923), 420–21.

9. *Arkansas Gazette*, 7 May 1874, 8 May 1875.

10. "Arkansas, 1840s–1870s" 11: 192, R. G. Dun & Co. Collection, Baker Library, Harvard University Graduate School of Business Administration (hereafter cited as R. G. Dun & Co., "Arkansas").

11. Richards, "Reunion," 325, 326.

12. David Y. Thomas, ed., *Arkansas and Its People*, vol. 3 (New York: American Historical Society, Inc., 1930), 71.

13. R. G. Dun & Co., "Arkansas" 11: 250.

14. *Little Rock Board of Trade 18th Annual Report, 1907*, 98–99.

15. *Arkansas Gazette*, 10 July 1988.

16. Ibid., 4 March 1929.

17. Ibid.

18. Thomas, *Arkansas and Its People* 3: 71–72; *Arkansas Gazette*, 20 August 1972.

19. Thomas, *Arkansas and Its People* 3: 72–73; *Arkansas Gazette*, 12 April 1932, 7 December 1976.

20. In the 1840s some of the state's real estate bonds had been acquired by James Holford and Company, a London banking house. These bonds, which the state said were acquired illegally, were a financial albatross to Arkansas for years, and in 1884 the state finally reneged on any further payment on them (see Ferguson and Atkinson, *Historic Arkansas*, 70–74).

21. Ibid., 242.

22. Ibid., 243.

23. *Arkansas Gazette*, 11 November 1933.

24. Ibid., 15 September 1885, 15 May 1887.

25. Ibid., 1 March 1908.

26. Information provided by Perry Cooperman, a former Abeles employee who helped install the sashes, doors, and windows of the Arkansas State Capitol, interview with author, Steele, Mo., 26 June 1982.

27. *Arkansas Democrat*, 31 August 1918.

28. Thomas, *Arkansas and Its People* 4: 662–63.

29. *Arkansas Gazette* editorial included by Thomas, *Arkansas and Its People* 4: 663.

30. *Quapaw Quarter Chronicle* (Little Rock) 15 (October–November 1988): 1.

31. *Arkansas Gazette*, 6 September 1929.

32. Ibid., 7 February 1927.

33. Ibid., 5 April 1918.

34. Thomas, *Arkansas and Its People* 3: 243. Charles T. Abeles married nineteen-year-old Delia Ringelhaupt in 1882; she died after their son, Theodore D. Abeles, was born in November 1883. Charles married one of Delia's sisters, Rose Ringelhaupt, in 1889, and he and Rose had one child, a son, Charles T. Abeles Jr. After leaving Little Rock for college, the latter did not return to Arkansas to make his home.

35. Harry Ehrenberg Sr., interview with author, Little Rock, Ark., 29 July 1982; *Arkansas Gazette*, 7 November 1921, 6 January 1940, 6 November 1953.

36. *Arkansas Democrat*, 16 July 1913; Ehrenberg interview.

37. George Franklin, Shreveport, La., letter to author, 14 March 1983.

38. *Arkansas Gazette*, 28 April 1906; *Little Rock Board of Trade 23rd Annual Report, 1912*, 113; Fay Hempstead, *A Pictorial History of Arkansas* (New York: N. D. Thompson Publishing Company, 1890), 798.

39. *Arkansas Gazette*, 31 January 1877, 23 October 1877, 19 January 1929.

40. *Little Rock Board of Trade 23rd Annual Report, 1912*, 155.

41. *Arkansas Gazette*, 30 November 1946.

42. Ibid., 1 November 1900.

43. Robert J. Brown, *Romance of the City of Roses* (Little Rock: n.p. , n.d.), 49; *Arkansas Gazette*, 15 September 1885.

44. Ferguson and Atkinson, *Historic Arkansas*, 244.

45. *Arkansas Gazette*, 15 September 1885, 16 April 1909, 26 August 1913, 27 August 1913.

46. *Little Rock Board of Trade 23rd Annual Report, 1912*, 83, 84; *Arkansas Democrat*, 31 August 1918, 27 July 1936; *Who's Who in Little Rock, 1921* (Little Rock: Who's Who Publishers, 1921), 68; Fay Hempstead, *Historical Review of Arkansas*, vol. 2 (Chicago: The Lewis Publishing Company, 1911), 722.

47. *Biographical and Historical Memoirs of Eastern Arkansas* (Chicago: The Goodspeed Publishing Company, 1890), 608.

48. *Helena World* Souvenir Edition, 11 May 1904; *Arkansas Gazette*, 1 March 1908; *Arkansas Gazette*, 20 November 1919.

49. *Arkansas Gazette*, 31 August 1918.

50. Ibid., 20 November 1919.

51. Ibid.; see also 7 January 1922.

52. E. T. Brewster, *City of Little Rock Guide, 1890* (Little Rock: Guide Publishing Company, 1890), 74, 75 (hereafter cited as *Guide*).

53. *Biographical and Historical Memoirs of Central Arkansas* (Chicago: The Goodspeed Publishing Company, 1889), 305–06, 483 (hereafter cited as *Central Arkansas*).

54. Alvin Jacobson, interview with author, Little Rock, Ark., 26 March 1983; *Arkansas Gazette*, 7 March 1903, 2 October 1919.

55. Thomas, *Arkansas and Its People* 1: 60, 61.

56. *Arkansas Gazette*, 1 December 1906; Brown, *Romance*, 73.

57. One of the Siesel's daughters, Ruby, married Leo Pfeifer, and another daughter, Weetie, married Louis Pfeifer, Leo's cousin. Louis, son of Phil Pfeifer, later became owner of the M. J. Siesel Company. (Eugene M. Pfeifer Jr., interview with author, North Little Rock, Ark., 27 July 1982; *Arkansas Gazette*, 30 November 1933,.)

58. *Arkansas Gazette*, Special Edition, 18 April 1899.

59. Ibid., 30 January 1945.

60. Ibid., 19 March 1935, 3 February 1938.

61. *Arkansas Gazette*, 29 February 1908, 1 March 1936.

62. *Arkansas Democrat*, 31 August 1918; *Who's Who in Little Rock*, 90.

63. *Arkansas Gazette*, 8 October 1978; Jerry Russell and Bessie Butler Newsom

Allard, comps., *Arkansans of the Years*, vol. 6, *Who is Who in Arkansas*, vol. 2 (Little Rock: Allard House Publishers, 1968), 167.

64. Ferguson and Atkinson, *Historic Arkansas*, 258–60.

65. Maxwell Lyons II, interview with author, Little Rock, Ark., 14 December 1981.

66. Charles H. Elias, letter to author, 10 March 1992; *Arkansas Democrat*, 18 May 1958.

67. R. G. Dun & Co., "Arkansas" 6: 291, 359.

68. *Little Rock City Directory 1871* (Little Rock: Price & Barton, Printers, 1871), 82; *Arkansas Democrat*, 31 August 1918.

69. *Little Rock Board of Trade 22nd Annual Report, 1911*, 43–47; *Arkansas Gazette*, 30 September 1915.

70. R. G. Dun & Co., "Arkansas" 11: 223.

71. *Arkansas Gazette*, 20 June 1922, 20 July 1978; *Arkansas Democrat*, 17 May 1938.

72. *Arkansas Gazette*, 6 January 1911.

73. *Arkansas Gazette*, 17 January 1919.

74. *Little Rock Board of Trade 18th Annual Report, 1907*, 159, 160; *Arkansas Gazette*, 8 October 1914.

75. *Arkansas Democrat*, 16 January 1919.

76. *Arkansas Gazette*, 11 August 1939.

77. Ibid., 27 February 1979.

78. Ibid., 31 May 1903, 8 November 1917, 19 April 1936; Robert Heiman, interview with author, Blytheville, Ark., 25 November 1982.

79. *Arkansas Gazette*, 8 November 1917.

80. *Arkansas Democrat*, 14 April 1920.

81. Dallas T. Herndon, *Centennial History of Arkansas*, vol. 3 (Chicago–Little Rock: The S. J. Clarke Publishing Company, 1922), 279–80; *Arkansas Democrat*, 17 October 1936.

82. *Arkansas Gazette*, 15 September 1912.

83. R. G. Dun & Co., "Arkansas" 11: 188.

84. *Arkansas Gazette*, 4 July 1909, 15 September 1912. See also 12 September 1920; *Arkansas Democrat*, 20 December 1926, 22 December 1926.

85. *Arkansas Gazette*, 20 February 1956; Rosa (Pfeifer) Isacson, interview with author, Little Rock, Ark., 11 April 1983.

86. Dr. George F. Jackson, "Boys' Camp at Little Rock, Arkansas," *Kiwanis Monthly* (November 1931):1; *Arkansas Democrat*, 8 November 1931.

87. *Arkansas Gazette*, 25 October 1914, 16 July 1915; *Arkansas Democrat*, 21 September 1924.

88. See, for example, *Arkansas Gazette*, 12 July 1908; *Arkansas Democrat*, 26 August 1926.

89. *Arkansas Gazette*, 2 June 1960. The Donaghey Foundation was founded in 1929 by George W. Donaghey, who served as governor of Arkansas from 1909 to 1913, for the purpose of aiding higher education in Little Rock; Little Rock Junior College—subsequently known as the Little Rock University and UALR—has been the recipient.

90. Ibid., 17 August 1960.

91. Jill Feinstein, "Yesterday and Today, A History of Pfeifers' Department Store" (1954), Joseph Pfeifer, Family Histories File, AHC.

92. *Arkansas Gazette,* 16 December 1961; Isacson interview. Joseph Pfeifer's son, Albert, moved to New York in 1921.

93. *Arkansas Gazette,* 22 March 1931.

94. Jay Friedlander, "M. M. Cohn CEO: a Soft-spoken Man of Many Interests," *Arkansas Business* 2 (8 July–21 July 1985): 12. Unlike the other early Jewish settlers, who had immigrated from Central and Western Europe, Cohn came from Poland (he assumed the surname Cohn after coming to America; his name originally was Kaminsky). Cohn was quickly assimilated into the Reform German-Jewish community.

95. *Arkansas Gazette,* 18 April 1899.

96. Ibid., 11 September 1883.

97. *Arkansas Democrat,* 9 August 1911; *Arkansas Gazette,* 10 August 1911.

98. *Arkansas Gazette,* 4 September 1940; Raida (Cohn) Pfeifer Papers, Little Rock, Ark.

99. *Arkansas Gazette,* 14 July 1926.

100. Ibid., 4 September 1940. Samuel W. Reyburn, a native of the Magnet Cove area in Hot Spring County and a friend of the Cohn family, told of the high regard Kilbourne had for Cohn in a speech given at the formal opening of the new M. M. Cohn Company store in September 1940. Reyburn was then chairman of the board of the Associated Dry Goods Corporation. He had been a Little Rock banker who subsequently became president of Lord and Taylor of New York (see Samuel D. Dickinson, "John Rison Fordyce," *PCHR* 38 (1990): 45)

101. *Arkansas Gazette,* 14 July 1926; Miriam "Mimi" (Cohn) Phillips, interview with author, Little Rock, Ark., 9 December 1981.

102. Eli N. Evans, *The Provincials: A Personal History of Jews in the South* (New York: Atheneum, 1976), 70.

103. *Arkansas Gazette,* 31 March 1926, 19 November 1953.

104. Ferguson and Atkinson, *Historic Arkansas,* 74, 194.

105. *Central Arkansas,* 390–92.

106. Brewster, *Guide,* 44.

107. *Arkansas Democrat,* 13 January 1891.

108. Ibid., 31 August 1918.

109. *Arkansas Gazette,* 10 December 1911.

110. *Arkansas Democrat,* 31 August 1918.

111. Herndon, *Centennial History* 2: 23.

112. *Arkansas Democrat,* 9 January 1908.

113. *Arkansas Gazette,* 26 August 1913.

114. Ferguson and Atkinson, *Historic Arkansas,* 158, 203.

115. *Arkansas Gazette,* 8 September 1896, 9 September 1896, 7 April 1919; R. G. Dun & Co., "Arkansas" 11: 220; Ira E. Sanders and Elijah E. Palnick, comps. and eds., *One Hundred Years, Congregation B'nai Israel, 1866–1966* (Little Rock: n.p., 1966): 16.

116. Eugene M. Pfeifer Sr., "The Autobiography of Eugene M. Pfeifer," courtesy Mrs. E. G. Levy, Little Rock, Ark.; *Arkansas Gazette,* 27 July 1897.

117. Sarah C. Hudson, "Little Rock's Leadership: The First State Board of Health," *PCHR* 33 (1985): 26–39.

118. *Arkansas Gazette,* 1 March 1908.

119. Ibid., 6 June 1930.

120. *Arkansas Democrat,* magazine section, 1 April 1928.

121. *Arkansas Gazette,* 1 March 1908.

122. John Hugh Reynolds and David Y. Thomas, *History of the University of Arkansas* (Fayetteville: University of Arkansas, 1910), 379–80 (hereafter cited as *University of Arkansas*); *Arkansas Gazette,* 6 February 1901; Hempstead, *Historical Review of Arkansas* 2: 787.

123. *Arkansas Gazette,* 1 September 1871.

124. Reynolds and Thomas, *University of Arkansas,* 379, 380.

125. At his death, Morris Cohn was said to be the oldest member of the American Bar Association in Arkansas and one of the ten oldest in the nation (*Arkansas Gazette,* 4 April 1922).

126. *Book of Arkansas* (Little Rock: Arkansas Gazette, 1913), 16.

127. *Arkansas Gazette,* 4 April 1922.

128. Tribute by the Little Rock Bar Association to Morris Cohn, 24 June 1922, as published in the *Arkansas Gazette,* 25 June 1922.

129. *Arkansas Gazette,* 17 December 1881; *Arkansas Democrat,* 6 August 1880.

130. According to Daniels' grandson and namesake, Dan Daniels of Hot Springs, Daniels ran for mayor at the beginning of the Klan's heyday in Arkansas, and although the Klan endorsed his candidacy, he received backing from only two Little Rock Jews—businessman Harry B. Solmson Sr. and fledgling lawyer Henry Spitzberg. Daniels was so disappointed in the lack of support from the Jewish community of Little Rock that he moved to Shreveport, La., where he remained until his death in 1931. (Dan Daniels, interview with author, Hot Springs, Ark., 13 July 1982.) Evidently, the Jews of Little Rock were apprehensive that they might offend members of the dominant group (see Leonard Dinnerstein and Mary Dale Palsson, eds., *Jews in the South* [Baton Rouge: Louisiana State University Press, 1973], 20.)

131. *Arkansas Gazette,* 15 September 1885, 19 April 1914, 31 March 1918, 23 May 1921; *Arkansas Democrat,* 22 June 1907, 17 April 1914; *Little Rock Board of Trade 23rd Annual Report, 1912,* 72–73.

132. *Arkansas Gazette,* 25 January 1908. David Menkus, grandson of Jacob Menkus, interview with author, Little Rock, Ark., 22 April 1985.

133. John Hallum, *Pictorial History of Arkansas,* vol. 1 (Albany, N.Y.: Weed, Parsons & Company, 1887), 479; *Arkansas Gazette,* 20 October 1892; *Central Arkansas,* 456.

134. *Little Rock City Directories,* 1871–1910.

135. For insight into this seemingly incongruous situation, see Raymond Arsenault, "Charles Jacobson of Arkansas, a Jewish Politician in the Land of the Razorbacks," in Nathan M. Kaganoff and Melvin I. Urofsky, eds., *Turn to the South* (Charlottesville: University Press of Virginia, 1979), 55–75.

136. Hempstead, *Historical Review of Arkansas* 2: 702–04.

137. *Arkansas Gazette,* 15 July 1957.

138. Ibid., 21 January 1906.

139. Arkansas Secretary of State Records, Book 5, 141–43; E. F. Chesnutt, "Little Rock Gets Electric Lights," *AHQ* 42: 3 (1983): 238–53.

140. *Arkansas Gazette*, 11 April 1914, 9 July 1914.

141. Ibid., 13 December 1917.

142. Ibid., 7 July 1865, 27 October 1882; Ehrenberg interview.

143. *Arkansas Gazette*, 15 September 1885; R. G. Dun & Co., "Arkansas" 11: 236.

144. *Arkansas Gazette*, 30 November 1908, 24 June 1922, 7 December 1937, 4 January 1983.

145. Ibid., 10 November 1933.

146. *Arkansas Gazette*, 27 May 1920.

147. *Little Rock Board of Trade 14th Annual Report*, 1903, 114.

148. *Little Rock Board of Trade 23rd Annual Report*, 1912, 65.

149. *Little Rock Board of Trade 14th Annual Report*, 1903, 154, 155; *Little Rock Board of Trade 23rd Annual Report*, 1912, 77; *Arkansas Democrat*, 15 December 1916; *Arkansas Gazette*, 4 November 1918.

150. *Arkansas Gazette*, 2 May 1936.

151. Ibid., 1 February 1933; Claire (Samuel) Levy, interview with author, Little Rock, Ark., 9 February 1984.

152. Herndon, *Centennial History* 2: 23.

153. Thomas, *Arkansas and Its People* 4: 528–29; *Arkansas Democrat*, 3 April 1923.

154. Thomas, *Arkansas and Its People* 3: 272.

155. *Arkansas Gazette*, 10 June 1928.

156. *Arkansas Democrat*, 25 June 1964.

157. *Arkansas Gazette*, 13 February 1983.

158. Ibid., 21 September 1954.

159. Ibid., 29 December 1914.

160. Ibid., 11 August 1953.

161. *Central Arkansas*, 506–09; *Arkansas Gazette*, 1 March 1908.

162. *Little Rock Board of Trade 23rd Annual Report*, 1912, 151–52.

163. *Arkansas Gazette*, 6 August 1921, 25 September 1966; Frances T. Friedler, daughter of Sidney Thalheimer, interview with author, New Orleans, La., 17 November 1982.

164. *Arkansas Democrat*, 6 September 1889.

165. Ibid., 31 August 1918, 17 November 1940; *Arkansas Gazette*, 23 July 1915, 22 January 1920, 18 March 1940, 19 May 1951.

166. *Arkansas Democrat*, 29 August 1900; *Arkansas Gazette*, 3 November 1918.

167. *Arkansas Gazette*, 23 September 1925, 16 June 1932, 25 August 1965.

168. *Arkansas Gazette*, 18 August 1913.

169. *Pine Bluff Daily Graphic*, 23 August 1889.

170. *Arkansas Gazette*, 3 September 1882, 11 September 1883, 22 October 1885; *Arkansas Democrat*, 9 April 1884.

171. *Arkansas Gazette*, 19 February 1949.

172. *Arkansas Gazette*, 2 November 1895.

173. *Arkansas Democrat*, 17 September 1879; *Arkansas Gazette*, 1 February 1922.

174. *Arkansas Gazette*, 20 November 1919.

175. *Arkansas Democrat*, 8 December 1904; *Arkansas Gazette*, 9 August 1914.

176. *Arkansas Gazette*, 23 September 1914.

177. Ibid., 15 September 1885.

178. *Little Rock Board of Trade 14th Annual Report, 1903*, 68; *Arkansas Gazette*, 25 September 1986.

179. Joe and Carolyn (Summerfield) Tenenbaum, interview with author, Little Rock, Ark., 12 December 1981; *Arkansas Gazette*, 16 December 1938.

180. *Arkansas Gazette*, 1 February 1933, 12 December 1940.

181. Ibid., 19 September 1983.

182. Thomas, *Arkansas and Its People* 3: 205–06.

183. *Arkansas Democrat*, 4 April 1987.

184. "Block Family History," courtesy Glenn Block, Little Rock, Ark.; *Arkansas Gazette*, 17 July 1892.

185. *Arkansas Gazette*, 4 September 1940.

186. Ibid., 31 May 1908; 1 September 1915; *Little Rock Board of Trade 23rd Annual Report, 1912*, 94.

187. James Moses Jr., telephone interview with author, Little Rock, Ark., 15 November 1991.

188. *Little Rock Board of Trade 22nd Annual Report, 1911*, 43–47; *Arkansas Gazette*, 30 September 1915; Larry T. Menefee, "The Death of A Road Show Town: Little Rock, Arkansas, 1899–1921," dissertation presented to the Graduate School of Arts and Sciences, University of Denver, in partial fulfillment of the doctor of philosophy degree, March 1977.

189. *Arkansas Gazette*, 15 August 1922.

190. *Arkansas Democrat*, 31 August 1918; *Arkansas Gazette*, 12 January 1943.

191. *Arkansas Gazette*, 30 May 1924.

192. Chester C. Allard, comp., Bessie Butler Newsom Allard, ed., *Arkansans of the Years*, vol. 5, *Who is Who in Arkansas, vol. 1* (Little Rock: Allard House Publishers, 1959), 206.

193. *Arkansas Gazette*, 1 January 1971; Harry Gray, "'Bronco Billy' Anderson," *The California Parade* (Vallejo City Unified School District) (September 1975): 107–09 (Western Jewish History Center, Judah L. Magnes Memorial Museum, Berkeley, Calif.).

194. *Arkansas Gazette*, 16 June 1915, 2 May 1936, 31 March 1939. The team was known as the Little Rock Travelers after the turn of the century to 1915; it then joined the Southern League and was known as the Arkansas Travelers. Jim Bailey, *Arkansas Travelers: Seventy-nine Years of Baseball* (Little Rock: Arkansas Travelers Baseball Club, Inc., 1980), 3.

195. *Arkansas Gazette*, 4 November 1869.

196. Ibid., 24 March 1944; Brunette (Fox) Billstein, telephone interview with author, Toledo, Ohio, 8 February 1985.

197. *Arkansas Gazette*, 9 September 1951.

198. Herndon, *Centennial History* 3: 325.

199. C. Allard and B. Allard, *Who is Who in Arkansas* 1: 205; *Arkansas Gazette*, 28 September 1969. Rosenblum served as a captain in World War I, and he formed a close friendship with a fellow soldier, Harry S Truman, after whom he later named his only son.

200. *Arkansas Gazette*, 8 May 1953, 12 May 1986.

201. *Arkansas Democrat*, 20 December 1944; Herndon, *Centennial History* 2: 565–66.

202. *Arkansas Gazette*, 24 June 1916.

203. Ibid., 9 March 1931.

204. Hempstead, *Historical Review of Arkansas* 3: 1410–12.

205. *Arkansas Gazette*, 18 November 1917, 26 August 1946; Herndon, *Centennial History* 2: 844–45.

206. *Arkansas Democrat*, 25 November 1963; *Arkansas Gazette*, 25 November 1963; Mrs. Lawrence Berger, interview with author, North Little Rock, Ark., 1 May 1983.

207. E. Charles Eichenbaum, interview with author, Little Rock, Ark., 26 February 1985.

208. Ibid.; Don W. Pittman, "The Founding of Dyess Colony," *AHQ* 29: 4 (1970): 313–26.

209. Henry Sanders, "Henry Sanders Autobiography," courtesy Arthur Sanders, Little Rock, Ark.; *Arkansas Gazette*, 11 September 1909.

210. *Arkansas Democrat*, 31 March 1930.

211. *Arkansas Gazette*, 18 February 1935.

212. Ibid., 8 September 1927.

213. Arthur Sanders, interview with author, Little Rock, Ark., 10 March 1983; Janet (Sanders) Salston, letter to author, 3 December 1983; Jewish Welfare Agency Resolution, 13 August 1947, courtesy Arthur Sanders; *Arkansas Gazette*, 11 June 1947, 8 January 1974. For further data on Sanders' firm, see F. Hampton Roy, *Charles L. Thompson and Associates, Arkansas Architects, 1885–1938* (Little Rock: August House, 1982).

214. *Arkansas Gazette*, 28 November 1938, 11 June 1948. See also "House of Morris B. Sanders, New York," *The Architectural Forum* (March 1936); "Tailor-Made Furniture," *LIFE* 21 (23 September 1946): 128–33.

215. Thomas, *Arkansas and Its People* 4: 481; *Who's Who in Little Rock*, 126; *Arkansas Gazette*, 5 August 1961.

216. *Arkansas Gazette*, 3 May 1985.

217. Ibid.; Fay Williams, *Arkansans of the Years*, vol. 4 (Little Rock: C. C. Allard & Associates, Publishers, 1954), 27–34.

218. *Arkansas Gazette*, 14 June 1987; *Arkansas Democrat*, 14 June 1987.

219. Jonathan James Wolfe, "Background of German Immigration," part 1, *AHQ* 25: 2 (Summer 1966): 169; *Arkansas Gazette*, 1 March 1971.

220. *Arkansas Gazette*, 8 November 1870, 22 January 1875, 2 December 1892.

221. Eugenia (Stifft) Frank, "Our Family, Five Generations—Four Families, 1878–1963," Biographies File, Stifft Family Folder, AJA (hereafter cited as "Five Generations").

222. *Arkansas Gazette*, 10 August 1904.

223. Ibid., 28 August 1926, 5 February 1939; *Book of Arkansas*, 25.

224. *Little Rock Board of Trade 23rd Annual Report, 1912*, 153–54.

225. For an insight into Jewish family life in Little Rock around the turn of the century, see the biographical account by Frank, "Five Generations."

226. *Arkansas Gazette*, 16 April 1897, 16 September 1934; Samuel Lyons, interview with author, Little Rock, Ark., 14 December 1981.

227. Thomas, *Arkansas and Its People* 3: 248–49; Herndon, *Centennial History* 2, 889–91; *Arkansas Gazette*, 12 June 1932.

228. *Arkansas Gazette*, 24 July 1941.

229. *Arkansas Gazette*, 6 November 1870; Ferguson and Atkinson, *Historic Arkansas*, 97, 136.

230. *Arkansas Gazette*, 5 March 1967.

231. Ibid., 5 August 1909.

232. Ibid., 9 March 1937, 26 June 1939, 7 August 1938.

233. Ibid., 20 February 1909; Family descendants later changed the name to Shack (*Arkansas Gazette*, 1 July 1971).

234. *Little Rock City Directory 1871*, 63.

235. Ephraim and Sally Epstein were met with triple tragedies; all three of their sons committed suicide in their mid-twenties (*Arkansas Gazette*, 2 January 1914, 12 November 1914, 26 February 1921, 29 April 1935).

236. *Arkansas Gazette*, 28 June 1904.

237. Ibid., 13 May 1947, 22 May 1960.

238. Ibid., 8 May 1907.

239. *Arkansas Democrat*, 4 December 1913; *Arkansas Gazette*, 2 May 1911, 3 October 1955, 27 December 1958.

240. *Arkansas Gazette*, 11 January 1926.

241. *Arkansas Gazette*, 15 September 1909.

242. *Arkansas Democrat*, 25 March 1903, 22 December 1923, 9 August 1947, 18 January 1951, 6 July 1970.

243. Terence O'Dougherty and Frank M. Sarchet, comps., *Combined Directory of Little Rock, Hot Springs, Pine Bluff, Eureka Springs, and Fort Smith, 1881–2* (Little Rock: Union Printing & Publishing Co., 1881), 226–27.

244. *Arkansas Democrat*, 24 January 1891.

245. *Arkansas Gazette*, 19 November 1903, 4 March 1928, 5 March 1966.

246. Ibid., 17 August 1937.

247. F. Hampton Roy, Charles Witsell Jr., and Cheryl Griffith Nichols, *How We Lived* (Little Rock: August House, 1984), 151.

248. *Arkansas Democrat*, 31 March 1880.

249. In 1896 Sol Gans built a gray granite home in Richardsonian Romanesque style (named for architect Henry Richardson) at 1010 West Third Street; it was constructed of stone generally used for public or commercial buildings (see Roy, Witsell, and Nichols, *How We Lived*, 130). The house was included in the National Register of Historic Places and was restored in 1992 by Little Rock attorney Charles Hicks (*The Chronicle* [Little Rock] 19 [February–March 1992]: 9).

250. *Arkansas Gazette*, 12 July 1891, 31 May 1895; *Arkansas Democrat*, 29 August 1900; *Arkansas Gazette*, 3 November 1918.

251. *Arkansas Gazette*, 6 August 1907.

252. Ibid., 29 December 1899.

253. Ibid., 27 June 1888, 21 February 1909, 10 November 1945.

254. Ibid., 26 September 1889.

255. Ibid., 17 December 1943; Herndon, *Centennial History* 2: 1002.

256. *Arkansas Gazette*, 22 November 1957.

257. Ibid., 13 June 1955.

258. A return trip by Louis Bernays from St. Louis to Little Rock was touted in a local paper as one of the quickest trips ever made between the cities; it took thirty-six hours (*Arkansas Gazette*, 15 September 1871).

259. For example, see *Arkansas Gazette*, 28 September 1881.

260. Ralph F. Bernays, letter to author, 7 October 1986.

261. *Arkansas Gazette*, 3 September 1882; *Arkansas Democrat*, 16 July 1922.

262. *Arkansas Gazette*, 29 May 1921.

263. Quapaw Quarter Association Research in Little Rock City Directories, courtesy Nancy Lowe, researcher, 9 April 1982.

264. *Arkansas Gazette*, 9 August 1922.

265. Ibid., 5 July 1925.

266. Ibid., 6 April 1915.

267. Ibid., 24 September 1870.

268. Ibid., 15 September 1885.

269. Ibid., 22 January 1937.

270. Ibid., 6 November 1870.

271. Ibid., 7 December 1904, 8 December 1904, 23 January 1917.

272. Ibid., 14 October 1954.

273. Ibid., 9 August 1936, 5 April 1983.

274. Ibid., 3 October 1894.

275. Ibid., 4 October 1894.

276. Examples are *Abraham Friedheim v. Aaron Friedheim* (*Arkansas Gazette*, 29 November 1884); *Hirsch, Lowenstein & Levy v. Levinston-Friedheim Co.* (*Arkansas Gazette*, 31 January 1895); *Thalheimer v. Gans* (*Arkansas Gazette*, 21 May 1907).

277. *Arkansas Gazette*, 23 August 1884.

278. *Arkansas Democrat*, 5 April 1932; For a history of the Nathan Adler family, see Marie Adler Kessel, *A World of Differences* (Fayetteville: University of Arkansas Press, 1990).

279. *Arkansas Gazette*, 21 August 1951.

280. Ibid., 16 July 1950.

281. Ibid., 24 April 1941.

282. Ibid., 25 November 1977.

283. *Arkansas Democrat*, 1 November 1914.

284. *Arkansas Gazette*, 12 August 1940.

285. Ibid., 7 December 1930, 8 December 1930.

286. Ibid., 19 January 1929; Claire (Samuel) Levy, interview with author, Little Rock, Ark., 25 May 1991.

287. *Arkansas Democrat*, 24 February 1938; *Arkansas Gazette*, 25 February 1938.

288. *Arkansas Gazette*, 11 January 1962.

289. Billstein interview.

290. *Arkansas Gazette*, 16 April 1927.

291. *Arkansas Democrat*, 20 September 1928.

292. *Arkansas Gazette*, 24 August 1919.

293. Ibid., 24 June 1977.

294. *Arkansas Democrat*, 30 December 1958.

295. Ibid., 5 February 1980.

296. *Arkansas Gazette*, 25 August 1920.

297. Gladys (Ottenheimer) Hirsch, interview with author, Little Rock, Ark., 4 April 1983; *Arkansas Gazette,* 26 October 1983.

298. *Arkansas Gazette,* 23 March 1923.

299. Ibid., 17 May 1916.

300. Ibid., 13 May 1974.

301. Ibid., 11 October 1915, 12 October 1915.

302. Ibid., 6 January 1911.

303. Ibid., 24 June 1945.

304. Ibid., 14 July 1979.

305. Ibid., 18 April 1936.

306. Ibid., 22 April 1897, 18 April 1897, 20 November 1919.

307. *Arkansas Democrat,* 3 June 1939.

308. *Arkansas Gazette,* 13 January 1978.

309. Ibid., 20 February 1956.

310. Ibid., 23 March 1951.

311. Ibid., 4 March 1946.

312. Ibid., 18 September 1932.

313. Ibid., 17 January 1974.

314. Ibid., 19 March 1961.

315. *Arkansas Democrat,* 5 May 1982.

316. Betty (Eichenbaum) Wiener, letter to author, 26 February 1985; *Arkansas Gazette,* 24 March 1926.

317. *Arkansas Gazette,* 14 September 1959.

318. *Arkansas Gazette,* 11 September 1883, 28 August 1884, 11 September 1883; Annie (Narkinsky) Miller, interview with author, Little Rock, Ark., 21 July 1982.

319. Miller interview; *Arkansas Gazette,* 15 September 1885.

320. *Little Rock Board of Trade 23rd Annual Report, 1912,* 113–14; *Arkansas Gazette,* 29 January 1991.

321. *Arkansas Gazette,* 24 November 1926, 18 April 1931.

322. *Arkansas Democrat,* 13 May 1963; *Arkansas Gazette,* 5 June 1988.

323. *Arkansas Democrat,* 31 August 1918.

CHAPTER 8

German Migration in Eastern Arkansas

1. David Y. Thomas, ed., *Arkansas and Its People,* vol. 2 (New York: American Historical Society, Inc., 1930), 394, 455.

2. Marie (Adler) Kessel (Simon Adler's granddaughter), letter to author, 19 March 1983,.

3. Nancy Zilbergeld and Nancy Britton, "The Jewish Community in Batesville, Arkansas, 1853–1977," *The Independence County Chronicle* 21: 3 (April 1980): 9–11 (hereafter cited as "Batesville").

4. Ibid., 12–15, 26.

5. *Batesville Guard,* 29 December 1880; Zilbergeld and Britton, "Batesville," 19.

6. Zilbergeld and Britton, "Batesville," 9–10; *Batesville Guard,* 27 February 1880.

7. *Batesville Guard*, 14 October 1904; Zilbergeld and Britton, "Batesville," 24.

8. *Biographical and Historical Memoirs of Northeast Arkansas* (Chicago: The Goodspeed Publishing Company, 1889), 869, 870 (hereafter cited as *Northeast Arkansas*).

9. P. K. Holmes, letter to author, 30 July 1991; P. K. Holmes, "Jewish Merchants of Newport: Wolff-Goldman Mercantile Company, 1880–1927," *The Stream of History* 28: 4 (1991): 2–9.

10. *Arkansas Gazette*, 19 January 1909; Fay Hempstead, *Historical Review of Arkansas*, vol. 3 (Chicago: The Lewis Publishing Company, 1911), 1192–93; Norman J. "Tom" Wolff Jr., letter to author, 17 June 1991.

11. Mrs. William H. (Emma Wolff) Schield, letter to author, 19 April 1983.

12. Zerlena (Meyer) Salinger of Brinkley, interview with author, Little Rock, Ark., 15 April 1982.

13. *Northeast Arkansas*, 898–99; Julia (Shoffner) Phelps, interview with author, Little Rock, Ark., 2 November 1982 (The family did not know A. E. Shoffner was Jewish until a granddaughter, Julia S. Phelps, sought out the information.)

14. *Arkansas Gazette*, 6 April 1887; *Arkansas Democrat*, 22 March 1900.

15. *Northeast Arkansas*, 869, 870.

16. George Heinemann, interview with author, Jonesboro, Ark., 9 November 1982.

17. "Arkansas-Oklahoma Report" (January 1909) 135, 136, R. G. Dun & Co. Collection, Baker Library, Harvard University Graduate School of Business Administration (hereafter cited as R. G. Dun & Co., "Arkansas-Oklahoma").

18. Leonard Dinnerstein and Mary Dale Palsson, eds., *Jews in the South* (Baton Rouge: Louisiana State University Press, 1973), 163.

19. *Northeast Arkansas*, 801–02; *Arkansas Gazette*, 20 November 1919.

20. Ibid.; Carole A. Buffington, letter to author, 16 July 1985.

21. *Arkansas Gazette*, 20 November 1919, 17 March 1901.

22. *Jonesboro Enterprise*, vol. 8, Special Edition, April 1903; Thomas, *Arkansas and Its People* 2: 844.

23. *Jonesboro Enterprise*, vol. 8, Special Edition, April 1903.

24. *The Jewish Times*, 24 July 1936.

25. *Jonesboro Daily Tribune*, Special Edition, 26 October 1937.

26. W. J. Ivie, *A Message to the Homeseeker* (Jonesboro, Ark.: W. J. Ivie Publisher, 1941), 8, courtesy Emma Henry, Little Rock, Ark.

27. Heinemann interview.

28. *Jonesboro Enterprise*, vol. 8, Special Edition, April 1903.

29. Ibid.

30. *Jonesboro Daily Tribune*, Special Edition, 26 October 1937.

31. Dorothy Betty (Sales) Levy, interview with author, New Orleans, La., 17 November 1982.

32. Undesignated newspaper article, TIAJ; *Arkansas Gazette*, 10 April 1943; *Jonesboro Daily Tribune*, Special Edition, 26 October 1937.

33. Sadie Schoenfield, interview with author, Jonesboro, Ark., 9 November 1982.

34. *Jonesboro Enterprise*, vol. 8, Special Edition, April 1903.

35. Ibid.; Lee Hummelstein, interview with author, Jonesboro, Ark., 9 November 1982.

36. Hummelstein interview.

37. Pearl Hummelstein, interview with author, Jonesboro, Ark., 9 November 1982; Lee Hummelstein, interview with author, Jonesboro, Ark., 9 November 1982; (also quoted by Fern Allen and Roberta Elliott, "Jewish Presence in Rural South Dwindling But Steadfast," *Jewish Week* [13 February 1987]).

38. Mrs. Harry (Thelma Meyer) Scharff, letter to author, 3 October 1983.

39. *Jonesboro Enterprise*, vol. 8, Special Edition, April 1903.

40. C. W. Starnes, "Settlement of Northeastern Greene County," *Greene County Historical Quarterly* 6: 1 (1971): 9–29.

41. *Arkansas Democrat*, 14 March 1904, 14 December 1926; *Arkansas Gazette*, 20 April 1945.

42. *Northeast Arkansas*, 151; Dr. Tom Stern, interview with author, Memphis, Tenn., 4 December 1992.

43. *Arkansas Gazette*, 23 April 1939.

44. *Arkansas Democrat*, 14 March 1904; *Arkansas Gazette*, 12 December 1939, 27 January 1965.

45. Rosalind (Unterberger) Sarason, letter to author, 25 May 1982.

46. Pauline Crockett, interview with author, Rector, Ark., 11 November 1982.

47. Rosalind (Unterberger) Sarason, letter to author, 15 February 1982.

48. *Pocahontas Star Herald*, 10 September 1956; Edith Dodson (granddaughter of Isaac Hirst), interview with author, Pocahontas, Ark., 2 March 1985; Jean Traub (granddaughter of Jacob Hanauer), letter to author, 23 February 1983.

49. M. Drew Bowers, interview with author, Little Rock, Ark., 19 July 1986; *Pocahontas Star Herald*, 28 March 1923.

50. *Pocahontas Star Herald*, 23 September 1948, 2 May 1963; Bowers interview.

51. Dodson interview.

52. Charles E. Joseph, interview with author, Little Rock, Ark., 2 February 1992; Helen (Sternberg) Stern, telephone interview with author, Tucson, Ariz., 18 April 1992; *Arkansas Gazette*, 17 November 1916.

53. Joseph interview.

54. Mrs. Siegbert (Eva) Jiedel, interview with author, Blytheville, Ark., 25 June 1982.

55. Jo Ann (Rosenberg) Ashley, letter to author, 29 February 1992; Oscar Fendler, letter to author, 13 February 1992.

56. For a comprehensive study of the town of Wittsburg, see Richard L. Hartness Sr., *Wittsburg, Arkansas: Crowley's Ridge Steamboat Riverport, 1848–1890* (Little Rock: Rose Publishing Company, 1979).

57. *Biographical and Historical Memoirs of Eastern Arkansas* (Chicago: The Goodspeed Publishing Company, 1890), 337–39 (hereafter cited as *Eastern Arkansas*).

58. *Wynne Daily Star-Progress*, Cross County Bank 50th Anniversary Edition, 5 June 1941.

59. *Eastern Arkansas*, 340–41.

60. *Arkansas Gazette*, 27 January 1965.

61. Ben and Ruth Meyer, interview with author, Wynne, Ark., 23 June 1982.

62. Hartness, *Wittsburg*, 87.

63. *Eastern Arkansas*, 346, 347; *Wynne Daily Star-Progress*, 24 December 1937.

64. Leona Furst, interview with author, West Memphis, Ark., 28 June 1982.

65. Thomas, *Arkansas and Its People* 2: 778; U.S. Bureau of the Census, *Tenth Census of the United States, 1880* (Washington, D.C.: Government Printing Office, 1883).

66. Kirke Lewis family, letter to author, 17 August 1982.

67. *Forrest City Times*, Souvenir Supplement, 19 September 1905.

68. *Eastern Arkansas*, 604.

69. *Forrest City Times*, Souvenir Supplement, 19 September 1905.

70. *Forrest City Times*, 8 May 1914.

71. *Eastern Arkansas*, 555.

72. *Arkansas Gazette*, 23 August 1883; Mrs. Ted Callahan, "This Is Your Life, Harold Goldberg," courtesy Mrs. Ted Callahan.

73. *Arkansas Gazette*, 11 February 1914, 1 July 1931.

74. *Arkansas Gazette*, August 1883 (full citation unavailable); Arkansas Democrat, 8 November 1884; Ted. R. Worley, "Early History of Des Arc and It's People," *White River Journal* (March 1956 to March 1957):15–45, 74–76.

75. *Eastern Arkansas*, 699; *Arkansas Democrat*, 28 November 1884. According to some tenant farmers, the Gates brothers had buried gold on their farm during the Civil War, and years later the farmers tried to have some of Ferdinand Gates' sons attempt to locate it (Richard Gates, "Gates Family History," courtesy Louise [Gates] Dickerson, Hot Springs, Ark.)

76. *Eastern Arkansas*, 699; *Arkansas Democrat*, 28 November 1884; Gates, "Gates Family History." The Gates family left the DeValls Bluff store around 1911.

77. *Arkansas Gazette*, 19 June 1930. Jake Gates was a friend of U.S. Senator Joe T. Robinson (D-Ark.), and Robinson and his wife would stay in the Gates' home in Lonoke when campaigning in the area (Louise [Gates] Dickerson, letter to author, 27 January 1986, Hot Springs, Ark.).

78. *Arkansas Democrat*, 20 January 1917.

79. John L. Ferguson and J. H. Atkinson, *Historic Arkansas* (Little Rock: AHC, 1966), 265.

80. Gates, "Gates Family History"; Louise (Gates) Dickerson, letter to author, 21 December 1985; *Arkansas Gazette*, 5 May 1937.

81. E. T. Brewster, *City of Little Rock Guide, 1890* (Little Rock: Guide Publishing Company, 1890), 91.

82. Dan Daniels (grandson of pioneer Dan Daniels), interview with author, Hot Springs, Ark., 13 July 1982.

83. Madeleine W. Lowens (granddaughter of Gus Straus), letter to author, 3 September 1982.

84. *Arkansas Gazette*, 14 August 1938.

85. Ibid., 12 February 1905, 16 January 1938.

86. *Eastern Arkansas*, 699.

87. Dallas T. Herndon, *Centennial History of Arkansas,* vol. 2 (Chicago–Little Rock: The S. J. Clarke Publishing Company, 1922), 658.

88. Ibid.; *Arkansas Gazette*, 27 August 1932.

89. R. G. Dun & Co., "Arkansas-Oklahoma," 115. Another Jacob Frolich (1837–1890) migrated from Germany and settled in Eastern Arkansas in 1866. He established the *White County Record*, serving as editor, and became known

statewide. He served as secretary of state from 1878 to 1884. This Jacob Frolich listed himself as a Presbyterian, and he married Mollie G. Finley, an Episcopalian. It has not been determined to date if he had Jewish forebears (*Biographical and Historical Memoirs of Central Arkansas* [Chicago: The Goodspeed Publishing Company, 1889], 453 [hereafter cited as *Central Arkansas*]; *Arkansas Democrat*, 11 April 1884.)

90. Thomas, *Arkansas and Its People* 2: 660.

91. Herbert Frenkel, interview with author, Conway, Ark., 11 August 1982.

92. *Arkansas Democrat*, 2 February 1948; *Arkansas Gazette*, 14 December 1973.

93. Thomas, *Arkansas and Its People* 2: 730.

94. Doris (Goldstein Shaul) Schoenberger, interview with author, Marked Tree, Ark., 10 November 1982. Lee Shaul married Doris Goldstein, daughter of I. Goldstein of Paragould, in 1918.

95. Ibid.; R. G. Dun & Co., "Arkansas-Oklahoma," 122.

96. *Helena World*, Souvenir Edition, 11 May 1904.

97. R. G. Dun & Co., "Arkansas-Oklahoma," 122.

98. *Acts of the Eighth Session of the General Assembly of the Territory of Arkansas*, 8 November 1833, 74–79.

99. Ted R. Worley, "Helena on the Mississippi," *PCHQ* 5 (June 1967): 39.

100. Ferguson and Atkinson, *Historic Arkansas*, 102.

101. Ibid., 126; Thomas, *Arkansas and Its People* 2: 843.

102. Thomas, *Arkansas and Its People* 2: 843, 844; *Helena World*, Souvenir Edition, 11 May 1904.

103. *Eastern Arkansas*, 788; *Arkansas Gazette*, 15 May 1914. Aaron and Johanna Meyers had four children, and when Johanna died in 1877, Aaron married one of her sisters, Bianca, and had another child.

104. Dorothy James, "Court House of Phillips County," *PCHQ* 3 (June 1965): 1–3; *Helena Weekly World*, 18 November 1895; Undated Helena newspaper article (full citation unavailable), Solomon family papers, courtesy David Solomon Jr., Helena, Ark.

105. David Solomon Jr., interview with author, Helena, Ark., 1 July 1982.

106. Hempstead, *Historical Review of Arkansas* 2: 829–30; *Helena World*, 24 August 1927; Solomon family papers.

107. Joseph Solomon obituary (1927), Solomon family papers.

108. David Solomon Jr. interview; *Arkansas Gazette*, 3 February 1938.

109. *Helena World*, 27 April 1898.

110. David Solomon Jr. interview.

111. The Solomon brothers bought ten thousand acres of land from the Fathauer Lumber Company but had to let it go when the 1927 flood destroyed the crops. The land was purchased by (non-Jew) Jessie Peter, husband of Lily Peter; Lily Peter became known statewide as a benefactor of the arts in eastern Arkansas (David Solomon Jr. interview).

112. Ibid.

113. Joe S. Metz, letter to author, 12 March 1992.

114. *Helena World*, 1 December 1949; Pete Goldsmith's sister Rett married Lafe Solomon.

115. Louise Goldsmith, interview with author, Helena, Ark., 30 June 1982.

116. *Helena World,* 21 December 1948, 17 November 1963.

117. *Helena World,* Souvenir Edition, 11 May 1904,.

118. Lillian C. Feldman, "Dr. Montague Fink," *PCHQ* 8 (December 1969): 9; *Arkansas Democrat,* 2 March 1957; Solomon Feldman, interview with author, Helena, Ark.,30 June, 1982. Henry Fink also had three daughters, Mrs. Baruch (Rosa) Seelig, Mrs. Sam (Sallie) Levy, and Eva.

119. *The Arkansas Banker* 11 (1927): 22.

120. Hon. Gerald W. Heaney, "Jacob Trieber: Lawyer, Politician, Judge," *University of Arkansas at Little Rock Law Journal* 8 (1985–86): 439–55 (hereafter cited as "Trieber").

121. *United States v. Morris,* 125 F. 322 (E.D. Ark. 1903): 330–31.

122. Heaney, "Trieber," 442–49; *Hodges v. United States,* 203 U.S. 1 (1906), overruled; *Jones v. Alfred H. Mayer Co.,* 392 U.S. 409, 443 n. 78 (1968).

123. Heaney, "Trieber," 448, 449.

124. Ibid., 455–59.

125. Bowers interview. Data also collected from Judge Jacob Trieber Papers, courtesy J. Marshall Trieber (grandson of Judge Trieber), Fayetteville, N.C.

126. *Eastern Arkansas,* 768.

127. *Helena World,* 6 February 1939; Dr. Leslie Mundt (son of Seelig Mundt), interview with author, New Orleans, La., 5 November 1982.

128. *Helena World,* 6 February 1939.

129. "Arkansas, 1840s–1870s" 9: 257, 267, 338, R. G. Dun & Co. Collection, Baker Library, Harvard University Graduate School of Business Administration (hereaftercited as R. G. Dun & Co. "Arkansas").

130. Mundt interview.

131. *Helena World,* 24 January 1922.

132. *Eastern Arkansas,* 798; *Helena World,* 26 October 1927.

133. *Helena World,* 27 September 1928; Elaine Goldman, interview with author, New Orleans, La., 17 November 1982.

134. *Helena World,* Souvenir Edition, 11 May 1904.

135. Ibid.

136. *Helena World,* 17 October 1926, 9 July 1957.

137. Ibid., 5 January 1949.

138. Allen A. Warsen, "B'nai B'rith in Action," *Michigan Jewish History* 7 (July 1967): 26. The article incorrectly states that the tragedy occurred at Poplar Bluff, Ark.

139. *Helena Weekly World,* 24 July 1895.

140. Ibid., 26 February 1896.

141. *American Israelite,* 19 March 1880.

142. *Helena World,* 16 August 1945.

143. Gladys Halpern (daughter of D. A. Halpern), interview with author, Helena, Ark., 30 June 1982; *Helena World,* 2 November 1931.

144. *Helena World,* 20 November 1957.

145. "Street Directory of Helena, 1909," *PCHQ* 3 (December 1964): 17–20; "Helena Banks," *PCHQ* 5 (June 1967): 10; Dana White, "The Helena Grand Opera House," *PCHQ* 9 (June 1971): 13–20.

146. *Helena World*, 20 May 1934. Almost every obituary of Helena's Jewish population commended them as valuable citizens.

147. Alvin Solomon, interview with Dr. Berkley Kalin, Memphis State University Oral History Research Project, 18 June 1968, courtesy Alvin Solomon.

148. Ibid.; Alvin Solomon, interview with author, Helena, Ark., 1 July 1982. According to family members, the Moses Solomon and Sam Solomon families were not related.

149. Mundt interview.

150. *Helena Weekly World*, 7 August 1895, 17 July 1895, 24 July 1895.

151. Sarah Weiss (daughter of Henry Weiss, former employee of the Krow & Neumann firm, Marvell, Ark.), interview with author, Memphis, Tenn., 9 November 1985.

152. R. G. Dun & Co., "Arkansas" 9: 338; Thomas, *Arkansas and Its People* 2: 756.

153. *Helena World*, Souvenir Edition, 11 May 1904.

154. *Helena World*, 6 April 1951; Mrs. Max (Minnie Ruth Eisenkramer) Hirsch, telephone interview with author, Little Rock, Ark., 14 April 1983.

155. *Helena World*, 8 May 1974.

156. *Arkansas Gazette*, 20 November 1919.

157. *Eastern Arkansas*, 809.

158. *Arkansas Gazette*, 20 November 1919.

159. Thomas, *Arkansas and Its People* 2: 756.

160. Dr. Albert A. Horner, "One Boy's Helena in the Nineties," part 2, *PCHQ* 15 (March 1977): 9.

161. Fred Miller, interview with author, Helena, Ark., 30 June 1982.

162. Landon Neumann, telephone interview with author, Helena, Ark., 10 June 1983.

163. *Helena World*, Souvenir Edition, 11 May 1904, 26 August 1930, 27 August 1930, 11 May 1904.

164. Thomas, *Arkansas and Its People* 2: 745.

165. Data from Bank of Holly Grove calendar, August 1983, courtesy Bank of Holly Grove, Ark.

166. *Helena World*, 21 November 1940, 22 November 1940. See also Rue Abramson, sec. IV.

167. Thomas, *Arkansas and Its People* 2: 745, 746.

168. Margaret J. Lee, letter to author, 4 March 1987.

169. Mrs. Jacob (Mildred Bondi) Steinberg, letter to author, 20 November 1982.

170. *Arkansas Gazette*, 30 October 1898.

171. Leonard Kern Jr., telephone interview with author, Clarendon, Ark., 30 July 1991.

172. *Arkansas Democrat*, 24 February 1907; *Arkansas Gazette*, 8 July 1909; R. G. Dun & Co., "Arkansas-Oklahoma," 32.

173. *Arkansas Gazette*, 28 February 1963; data courtesy Norbert Zeno, letter to author, Little Rock, Ark., 20 May 1985.

174. Ross L. Silberstein, interview with author, Star City, Ark., 12 May 1982; Nettye Bush, interview with author, Star City, Ark., 12 May 1982.

175. *Biographical and Historical Memoirs of Southern Arkansas* (Chicago: The

Goodspeed Publishing Company, 1890), 955 (hereafter cited as *Southern Arkansas*); E. M. Dreidel, "Temple Meir Chayim: A Century-Old Need," *Programs of the Desha County Historical Society* (Spring 1978): 29–35.

176. William Downey, ed., "Hoover & Company," *Arkansas City Democrat* Historic Edition (ca. 1910).

177. Louis Reitzamper, "Early Ordinances Detail Arkansas City's History," *Desha County Historical Society* 7 (1981): 17–27; *Desha County News*, 6 June 1914.

178. Thomas, *Arkansas and Its People* 2: 697–99.

179. *Pine Bluff Commercial*, 7 September 1916.

180. Mrs. William (Joan) Hamburger, interview with author, Memphis, Tenn.,10 May 1983; *Arkansas Gazette*, 13 May 1984.

181. Elsie (Hamburger) Phillips, interview with author, Dumas, Ark., 7 May 1982.

182. *McGehee Times*, 4 September 1975; Rosa Belle Dreyfus, interview with author, McGehee, Ark., 9 May 1982; Lewis P. Dreyfus, interview with author, McGehee, Ark., 9 May 1982.

183. Elbert T. Cashion Sr., *A History of Eudora, Arkansas, Chicot County* (Lake Village, Ark.: James Printing Company, 1977), 25 (hereafter cited as *Eudora*).

184. Cashion, *Eudora*, 13.

185. Thomas, *Arkansas and Its People* 2: 675, 676.

186. Alvin Meyer Sr., interview with author, Readland, Ark., 10 May 1982; Carroll Meyer Sr., interview with author, Eudora, Ark., 11 May 1982.

187. Cashion, *Eudora*, 25; Adolph Meyer's brother Burdolph had a store at Sikeston, Mo., and his brothers Rudolph and Max had stores at Jonesboro, Ark.

188. Alvin Meyer Sr. interview.

189. Ibid. Alvin Meyer Sr. married Dorothy Morrice, a Catholic, and their three children were raised in the mother's faith.

190. Milton Sandstein, letter to author, 9 January 1986.

191. Cashion, *Eudora*, 10–31.

192. Lena Rexinger, interview with author, Russellville, Ark., 1 June 1983.

193. Thomas, *Arkansas and Its People* 2: 677.

194. *Arkansas Gazette*, 6 July 1941.

195. Mrs. Roy (Alberta Kimpel) Balantine Sr., interview with author, Memphis, Tenn., 10 May 1983.

196. Undesignated newspaper obituary of Dave Kimpel, 23 May 1929 (full citation unavailable); Bertha Kimpel Shafsky obituary, *Pine Bluff Commercial* (full citation unavailable).

197. Balantine interview.

198. For data on Ben Kimpel Sr., see this section, chap. 9, and on Ben Kimpel Jr., see sec. V, chap. 18.

199. *Pine Bluff Daily Graphic*, 26 January 1927, 23 October 1918; *Southern Arkansas*, 1052.

200. *Pine Bluff Daily Graphic*, 26 January 1927, 23 October 1918; *Southern Arkansas*, 1052. Gus W. Herrman, letters to author, 15 May 1984, 24 May 1984.

201. Thomas, *Arkansas and Its People* 2: 826.

202. *Pine Bluff Daily Graphic*, 8 July 1898.

203. Undesignated Pine Bluff newspaper, 1933 (full citation unavailable), Sam J. Altschul Papers, courtesy Sam J. Altschul, Pine Bluff, Ark.

204. *Pine Bluff Commercial*, 9 March 1923.

205. Adolph Altschul married Maggie Carson in 1880 (see Julius Lester, *Lovesong, Becoming a Jew* [New York: Henry Holt & Company, 1988], 11).

206. Altschul Papers.

207. *Pine Bluff Weekly Graphic*, 8 August 1896; *Pine Bluff Daily Graphic*, 12 December 1908.

208. Hempstead, *Historical Review of Arkansas* 2: 725–26; *Pine Bluff Daily Graphic*, 11 April 1914.

209. *Pine Bluff Daily Graphic*, 11 April 1914.

210. *Pine Bluff Commercial*, 25 April 1927; *Arkansas Gazette*, 12 April 1932.

211. *Arkansas Gazette*, 8 March 1936.

212. *Pine Bluff Press*, 9 November 1876.

213. *Pine Bluff Weekly Press*, 29 August 1872.

214. "Trailblazers of the Trans-Mississippi West," AJA 8: 2 (October 1956): 70–71. Adolphe Cremieux was a member of France's provisional government. He was founder and president of the Alliance Israelite Universelle, an organization that defended human rights of Jews worldwide (Solomon Grayzel, *A History of the Jews: From the Babylonian Exile to the Present* [New York: The New American Library, 1968], 507–08, 545–546, 573, 632).

215. Isaac Altschul, who had been quite successful, was financially ruined in the 1890s. *Pine Bluff Daily Graphic*, 8 June 1898.

216. Ibid., 8 April 1895. Sol Franklin was so revered by his friends that one of them, Mrs. Joseph Altheimer, penned a memorial to him (*Pine Bluff Weekly Commercial*, 14 April 1895):

"No royal blood was coursing through his veins,
Upon the battlefield no laurels did he win
His reputation, though, was spotless, without stains,
Beloved was he at large, by friends and kin.
A patriarch he reigned at Noble Lake,
For years and years he ruled his grand estate,
In vain he struggled, and his heart did break,
When it was torn from him by cruel fate.
'Sic transit gloria mundi' weep, oh weep!
Deserving is he of each falling tear,
Our noble Sol, if here he could not reap,
He'll find reward beyond the higher sphere."

217. *Pine Bluff Commercial*, 19 September 1946.

218. *Pine Bluff Daily Graphic*, 7 November 1919; *Arkansas Gazette*, 21 February 1937.

219. *Pine Bluff Press*, 9 September 1873.

220. James W. Leslie, *Pine Bluff and Jefferson County* (Norfolk, Va.: The Donning Company, 1981), 43.

221. *Pine Bluff Graphic*, 26 May 1893; *Pine Bluff Commercial*, 6 August 1885.

222. *Pine Bluff Press*, 27 July 1880.

223. *American Israelite*, 1 May 1876.

224. *Pine Bluff Graphic*, 26 May 1893.

225. *Pine Bluff Commercial*, 7 October 1926.

226. *Arkansas Democrat*, 16 June 1881; *Pine Bluff Graphic*, 12 April 1895.

227. *Pine Bluff Graphic*, 12 April 1895.

228. R. G. Dun & Co., "Arkansas" 3: 16; 7: 208, 243–16 [author's note: 243–16 is correct. The pages are numbered in an odd way].

229. *Pine Bluff Commercial*, 6 October 1915.

230. *Arkansas Democrat*, 2 April 1902; *Pine Bluff Weekly Commercial*, 5 April 1902; Bill Firestone, letter to author, 6 July 1991.

231. *Arkansas Gazette*, 21 April 1908; Herndon, *Centennial History* 3: 193; *Pine Bluff Daily Graphic*, 6 October 1915.

232. Herndon, *Centennial History* 2: 100–101; Russell Bearden, "Jefferson County's Worst Disaster: The Flood of 1927," *AHQ* 43:4 (1984): 333.

233. *Pine Bluff Daily Graphic*, 4 December 1917; *Central Arkansas*, 197–98.

234. Leslie, *Pine Bluff*, 49.

235. Ibid.; see also Leon and Evelyn Turitz, *Jews in Early Mississippi* (Jackson: University Press of Mississippi, 1983), 32.

236. Elizabeth Arnold Stone, *Uinta County: It's Place in History* (Laramie, Wyo.: Laramie Printing Company, 1924), 155–56; I. S. Bartlett, ed., *History of Wyoming*, vol. 2 (Chicago: The S. J. Clarke Publishing Company, 1918), 275.

237. *Pine Bluff Daily Graphic*, 9 March 1915.

238. Dolf Kastor, interview with author, Pine Bluff, Ark., 4 April 1985; see also *Arkansas Gazette*, 1 September 1985.

239. *Central Arkansas*, 150; *Pine Bluff Daily Graphic*, 19 February 1910.

240. *Pine Bluff Daily Graphic*, 9 April 1895, 29 November 1910; *Temple Anshe Emeth One Hundredth Anniversary, 1867–1967* (Pine Bluff, Ark.: n.p., 1967), 12, Anshe Emeth Archives, Pine Bluff, Ark.

241. R. G. Dun & Co., "Arkansas" 7: 180, 181.

242. *American Hebrew*, 11 April 1913.

243. Glenwood newspaper (full citation unavailable), 17 July 1914, Clipping 1.263, M/F File, AHC.

244. Ibid.

245. *Pine Bluff Commercial*, 10 March 1915; *Pine Bluff Daily Graphic*, 24 August 1902.

246. Herndon, *Centennial History* 2: 23–24.

247. *Pine Bluff Daily Graphic*, 4 October 1922, 30 April 1938; *Arkansas Gazette*, 25 September 1919.

248. *Pine Bluff Daily Graphic*, 30 April 1938, 29 April 1938.

249. R. G. Dun & Co., "Arkansas" 7: 199, 207, 234.

250. *Pine Bluff Daily Graphic*, 29 March 1889, 6 March 1900, 13 May 1892.

251. Altschul Papers.

252. R. G. Dun & Co., "Arkansas" 3: 264.

253. *Pine Bluff Commercial*, 28 March 1934.

254. R. G. Dun & Co., "Arkansas" 3: 290, 295; Herndon, *Centennial History* 2: 136.

255. *Pine Bluff Semi-Weekly Graphic*, Special Edition, August 1896; *Arkansas Gazette*, 1 March 1908.

256. *Pine Bluff Daily Graphic*, 25 September 1905.

257. R. G. Dun & Co., "Arkansas" 13: 114; 7: 201.

258. *Pine Bluff Press Eagle*, 29 August 1872. Isaac Wise Miller, a partner with the Rosenbergs, married a Chicago girl who could not adjust to small town life in Arkansas, and one by one the Miller family moved to Chicago (Harriett Miller, letter to author, 6 April 1985).

259. R. G. Dun & Co., "Arkansas" 7: 201, 230, 234–1, 234–q [author's note: 234–1 and 234–q are correct. The pages are numbered in an odd way].

260. Part of a letter written in 1877 by Sol Rosenberg of Pine Bluff and addressed to a future generation. The letter was found sealed in a bottle and placed in the foundation of a building being constructed that year by him and his partners, the Altheimer brothers, Joseph and Louis. The bottle was discovered in 1948 when the foundation for another building was being excavated. (Undesignated Pine Bluff newspaper article, 1948 [full citation unavailable], courtesy Mrs. Carl [Dorothy Jacobs] Frankel, granddaughter of Joseph Altheimer, Toronto, Canada.)

261. *Pine Bluff Daily Graphic*, 1 January 1892, 14 May 1920; *Pine Bluff Commercial*, 6 May 1936.

262. R. G. Dun & Co., "Arkansas" 7: 243d; *Pine Bluff Press Eagle*, 8 January 1883.

263. *Pine Bluff Commercial*, 12 April 1948.

264. *Central Arkansas*, 213; *Pine Bluff Daily Graphic*, 18 November 1892.

265. *Pine Bluff Commercial*, 9 November 1881.

266. *Pine Bluff Press*, 8 April 1875; Louis Bram, interview with author, Pine Bluff, Ark., 24 April 1982; *Pine Bluff Commercial*, 14 April 1887, 6 February 1932.

267. *Pine Bluff Commercial*, 19 December 1916.

268. *Pine Bluff Daily Graphic*, 10 March 1902.

269. *Pine Bluff Press*, 16 December 1875.

270. *Pine Bluff Commercial*, 9 September 1916.

271. *Pine Bluff Daily Graphic*, 27 July 1894.

272. Ibid., 15 September 1910.

273. Ibid., 30 March 1902.

274. *Pine Bluff Daily Graphic*, 22 March 1912.

275. R. G. Dun & Co., "Arkansas" 7: 241k–243k; *Pine Bluff Daily Graphic*, 10 December 1900, 11 April 1890.

276. *Pine Bluff Commercial*, 16 August 1916.

277. *Pine Bluff Daily Graphic*, 10 May 1922; *Pine Bluff Commercial*, 27 October 1958.

278. *Arkansas Gazette*, 4 October 1946; *Pine Bluff Daily Graphic*, 24 July 1909.

279. Herndon, *Centennial History* 2: 895; *Pine Bluff Daily Graphic*, 11 November 1923; *Pine Bluff Commercial*, 25 August 1950.

280. *Pine Bluff Commercial*, 21 July 1881.

281. Terence O'Dougherty and Frank M. Sarchet, comps., *Combined Directory of Little Rock, Hot Springs, Pine Bluff, Eureka Springs, and Fort Smith, 1881–2* (Little Rock: Union Printing & Publishing Co., 1881), 350–51.

282. Leslie, *Pine Bluff*, 70.

283. *Pine Bluff Daily Graphic*, 28 October 1892.

284. Ibid., 21 October 1901, 22 October 1901.

285. Harry B. Solmson Jr., interview with author, Memphis, Tenn., 9 May 1983; Undesignated newspaper article, 17 January 1938, Solmson family papers, courtesy Harry B. Solmson Jr., Memphis, Tenn.

286. Henry Marx, interview with author, Pine Bluff, Ark., 23 April 1982; Herndon, *Centennial History* 3: 748.

287. Bernard Levi, interview with author, Dermott, Ark., 10 May 1982.

288. *Pine Bluff Commercial*, 28 January 1932.

289. *Arkansas Gazette*, 8 November 1941.

290. *Pine Bluff Commercial*, 15 December 1945, 22 October 1973.

291. *Pine Bluff Commercial*, 18 March 1953; Louis Bram, telephone interview with author, 24 September 1982.

292. *Pine Bluff Daily Graphic*, 29 October 1901.

293. *Pine Bluff Commercial*, 24 October 1954.

294. Ibid., 24 February 1969; Herndon, *Centennial History* 2: 659.

295. *Arkansas Gazette*, 23 April 1956, 24 April 1960.

296. *Arkansas Gazette*, 21 February 1940, 18 March 1984.

297. The birth year of Louis Altheimer is given variously from 1847 to 1850.

298. Louis Altheimer, "Col. Louis Altheimer, Empire Builder," *Arkansas Gazette*, 20 November 1919.

299. Ibid.

300. *Arkansas Gazette*, 17 September 1916.

301. Altheimer, "Col. Louis Altheimer."

302. Weston Arthur Goodspeed, ed., *The Province and the States*, vol. 7 (Madison, Wis.: The Western Historical Association, 1904), 178–79.

303. *Who's Who in Little Rock, 1921* (Little Rock: Who's Who Publishers, 1921), 20.

304. *Arkansas Gazette*, 12 November 1937.

305. Alan J. Altheimer, letter to author, 14 November 1983.

306. Letter written by Louis Altheimer in 1877 to a future generation and placed in a sealed bottle (see note 260).

307. R. S. Barnett Jr. (a trustee of the Ben J. Altheimer Foundation), letter to author, 19 December 1984.

308. *Arkansas Gazette*, 30 May 1936.

309. E. W. Freeman (owner and publisher of the *Pine Bluff Commercial*), letter to Mrs. Matilda Altheimer, 6 May 1931, courtesy R. S. Barnett Jr., Altheimer, Ark.; "Dedication Program of the Altheimer Laboratory," Agricultural Experiment Station, UofA, 31 October 1980.

310. Data courtesy R. S. Barnett Jr., Altheimer, Ark., and John Stern, Chicago, Ill., trustees of the Ben J. Altheimer Foundation; *Arkansas Democrat*, 16 December 1986.

311. Thomas, *Arkansas and Its People* 2: 724.

312. Emanuel Cohn (son of Jacob Cohn), letter to author, Memphis, Tenn., 13 October 1983.

313. *A Collection of Memories in Bicentennial Salute to the People of Arkansas* (4-H Club Publication) (De Witt, Ark.: DeWitt Publishing Company, Inc., 1976), De Witt, Ark., Public Library.

314. *Stuttgart Daily Leader & Arkansawyer*, 25 March 1939.

315. *Pine Bluff Daily Graphic*, 7 May 1921, 21 September 1933.

316. R. C. Bryant, interview with author, Altheimer, Ark., 7 April 1984.

317. *Pine Bluff Daily Graphic*, 21 September 1933.

318. Ibid., 7 May 1921; Family member Lizzette Latz Waldstein (1820–1899) is buried in the family plot in Hot Springs.

319. Rabbi Samson A. Shain, "Arkansas Jewish Place Names," Hot Springs, Ark., Temple Beth Israel Scroll of Honor, Nearprint File, Arkansas, AJA; Arkansas maps, courtesy David Bizzell, North Little Rock, Ark.

320. Fred Miller, interview with author, Helena, Ark., 30 June 1982.

321. *Helena Weekly World*, 24 July 1895.

322. Emma Foster, telephone interview with author, Marvell, Ark., 27 August 1984.

323. L. R. Parmelee, "Helena and West Helena, A Civil Engineer Reminisces," *PCHQ* 1 (December 1962): 9; Helen Mosby, letter to author, 17 January 1984.

324. Mosby letter.

325. *Who's Who in American Jewry, 1928* (New York: The Jewish Biographical Bureau, Inc., 1928), 153, 154; *Pine Bluff Commercial*, 10 March 1939.

326. Data courtesy Mrs. Carl (Dorothy Jacobs) Frankel (granddaughter of Matilda Altheimer), Toronto, Canada; Graham Storey, *Reuters' Century* (New York: Crown Publishers, 1951), 3.

327. Thomas, *Arkansas and Its People* 2: 827.

328. *Pine Bluff Commercial*, 16 March 1935.

329. Undesignated Pine Bluff newspaper articles (full citation unavailable), courtesy Dorothy Frankel; Matilda Altheimer, *Pastime Poems* (Pine Bluff, Ark.: The Commercial Printing Company, [1932?]); *Pine Bluff Commercial*, 16 March 1935.

CHAPTER 9

German Migration in Western Arkansas

1. David Y. Thomas, ed., *Arkansas and Its People*, vol. 2 (New York: American Historical Society, Inc., 1930), 751; J. E. Gaughan, "Historic Camden," *AHQ* 20: 3 (1961): 247, 249.

2. Adolph Felsenthal, "Nearly Threescore and Ten," part 2, *Arkansas Gazette*, magazine section (1934) (full citation unavailable) Camden, Ark., Nearprint File, AJA.

3. *Arkansas Democrat*, 13 August 1903.

4. Donald V. Brady, "The Theatre in Early El Paso, 1881–1905," *Southwestern Studies* 4: 1 (1966): 3–39.

5. Felsenthal "Nearly Threescore," part 2; Sifford's Scrapbook, no. 3, Camden, Ark., Public Library.

6. Felsenthal, "Nearly Threescore."

7. David Felsenthal had six children by his first wife; when she died, he married her sister and had three more. (Data on Felsenthal family, courtesy Evelyn [Levy] Rosenbaum, letter to author, 15 January 1983, and Martha [Felsenthal] Hainsfurther, letter to author, 19 September 1985.)

8. *Arkansas Gazette*, magazine section, 18 July 1943.

9. Dallas T. Herndon, *Centennial History of Arkansas*, vol. 2 (Chicago–Little Rock: The S. J. Clarke Publishing Company, 1922), 984–85.

10. *Camden Beacon,* 6 October 1931.

11. *Arkansas Gazette,* 11 April 1942.

12. Editorials from Camden, Ark., El Dorado, Ark., and Hope, Ark., newspapers, April 1942 (full citation unavailable), courtesy Evelyn Rosenbaum, St. Louis, Mo.; *Arkansas Gazette,* 11 April 1942; *Arkansas Democrat,* 11 April 1942.

13. Felsenthal, "Nearly Threescore," part 2.

14. Ibid.; Harry B. Solmson Jr., interview with author, Memphis, Tenn., 9 May 1983.

15. Sifford's Scrapbook, no. 1, Camden, Ark., Public Library; Herndon, *Centennial History* 2: 494.

16. "Arkansas, 1840s–1870s" 13: 108, 170, R. G. Dun & Co. Collection, Baker Library, Harvard University Graduate School of Business Administration (hereafter cited as R. G. Dun & Co., "Arkansas").

17. Solmson interview.

18. *Camden News,* 4 September 1931, 4 January 1950.

19. *Camden News* editorial, 5 September 1931; Thomas, *Arkansas and Its People* 2: 751.

20. *Camden News,* 4 September 1931.

21. Camden Chamber of Commerce Letter of Commendation, 9 October 1931, courtesy Helen Berg, Camden, Ark.

22. Felsenthal, "Nearly Threescore," part 2.

23. *Arkansas Gazette,* 3 December 1884, 24 August 1899; *Biographical and Historical Memoirs of Southern Arkansas* (Chicago: The Goodspeed Publishing Company, 1890), 666; Camden Scrapbook, Book 1, Camden, Ark., Public Library.

24. Herndon, *Centennial History* 4, 1740.

25. *Arkansas Gazette,* 6 September 1903; Mose Stern obituary, Camden, Ark., newspaper (1925) (full citation unavailable), Solmson family papers, courtesy Harry B. Solmson Jr., Memphis, Tenn.

26. Undesignated newspaper articles (full citation unavailable), courtesy Leonard M. Stern Jr.; Leonard M. Stern Jr., interview with author, Little Rock, Ark., 14 March 1983; Herndon, *Centennial History* 4: 1740–41.

27. Felsenthal, "Nearly Threescore," part 2; Evelyn (Levy) Rosenbum, letter to author, 15 January 1983.

28. *Arkansas Gazette,* Special Edition, 18 April 1899; Felsenthal, "Nearly Threescore," part 1.

29. Felsenthal, "Nearly Threescore," part 1; *Arkansas Gazette,* 6 September 1903; Dorothy (Heller) Goldman, interview with author, New Orleans, La., 4 November 1982.

30. *Camden News,* 7 July 1943.

31. Helen Berg, interview with author, Camden, Ark., 29 October 1982.

32. Mayor J. T. "Pete" Young, interview with author, Felsenthal, Ark., 29 October 1982.

33. *Arkansas Democrat,* 12 April 1905; Young interview; *Arkansas Gazette,* 10 May 1991.

34. Thomas, *Arkansas and Its People* 2: 841.

35. John L. Ferguson and J. H. Atkinson, *Historic Arkansas* (Little Rock: AHC, 1966), 248; Thomas, *Arkansas and Its People* 2: 841.

36. Martha (Felsenthal) Hainsfurther, letter to author, 19 September 1985; Herndon, *Centennial History* 2: 747; El Dorado *Daily News*, 22 February 1939; *Camden News*, 22 February 1939.

37. Rose (Burd) Berk, interview with author, El Dorado, Ark., 29 October 1982.

38. *Arkansas Gazette*, 14 October 1944.

39. Ibid., 4 November 1944.

40. *R. L. Polk's El Dorado (Union County, Arkansas) City Directory* (Dallas: R. L. Polk & Company, Publisher, 1937).

41. Ferguson and Atkinson, *Historic Arkansas*, 248.

42. Thomas, *Arkansas and Its People* 2: 839.

43. Barbara Overton Chandler and J. Ed Howe, *History of Texarkana* (Shreveport, La.: J. Ed Howe Publisher, 1939), 236.

44. *Arkansas Democrat*, 19 September 1929.

45. Chandler and Howe, *Texarkana*, 336; Louis Josephs Folder, Autobiographies File, AJA.

46. Data to author courtesy Rabbi David Max Eichhorn, who assisted Judge Josephs in the case, Satellite Beach, Fla., 31 January 1983. The case is also found in Eichhorn's book, *Joys of Jewish Folklore: A Journey from New Amsterdam to Beverly Hills* (Middle Village, N.Y.: Jonathan David Pubs., Inc., 1981). See also, *Texarkana Gazette*, 13 February 1957.

47. R. G. Dun & Co., "Arkansas" 6: 249, 272.

48. Jo Ann (Rosenberg) Ashley, letter to author, 29 February 1992; *Arkansas Gazette*, 9 May 1911.

49. *Arkansas Gazette*, 26 March 1908.

50. For a history of Washington, Ark., see Francis Irby Gwaltney, "A Survey of Historic Washington, Arkansas," *AHQ* 17: 4 (1958): 337–96; Mary Medearis, *Washington, Arkansas: History on the Southwest Trail* (Hope, Ark: Etter Printing Company, 1976).

51. Gwaltney, "Washington, Arkansas," 338–95

52. *Washington Telegraph*, 18 November 1871.

53. Ibid., 20 December 1871.

54. See Fay Hempstead, *Historical Review of Arkansas*, vol. 1 (Chicago: The Lewis Publishing Company, 1911), 1597, 1598.

55. Dr. Joseph L. Rosenzweig, interview with author, Hot Springs, Ark., 6 April 1982; "Arkansas-Oklahoma Report" (January 1909): 7,8, R. G. Dun and Co. Collection, Baker Library, Harvard University Graduate School of Business Administration.

56. Felsenthal, "Nearly Threescore," part 2.

57. *Biographical and Historical Memoirs of Southeastern Arkansas* (Chicago: The Goodspeed Publishing Company, 1890), 260, 274; Lucille Westbrook, letter to author, 18 February 1982.

58. Thomas, *Arkansas and Its People* 2: 760.

59. Ernest Badt, letter to author, 2 September 1982.

60. For a short history of the park, see *Arkansas' Happy Hunting Grounds, Crater of Diamonds State Park* (Murfreesboro, Ark.: n.p., n.d.).

61. Thomas, *Arkansas and Its People* 2: 830–832.

62. *Arkansas Gazette*, 7 May 1910.

63. *Hot Springs Sentinel-Record*, 29 May 1939.

64. R. G. Dun & Co., "Arkansas" 6: 286, 293.

65. Ibid., 9: 155, 6: 187, 287; Inez E. Cline, "Four Score and Five," *The Record* (Hot Springs–Garland County Historical Society Journal) 7 (1979): 65–76a.

66. *Hot Springs Sentinel-Record*, 4 July 1936, 3 August 1941.

67. Ibid., 18 May 1959.

68. *Arkansas Gazette*, 23 October 1904.

69. *Hot Springs Sentinel-Record*, 29 May 1939.

70. Ibid., 11 April 1919.

71. Herndon, *Centennial History* 3: 1468; John L. Ferguson, *Arkansas Lives: The Opportunity Land Who's Who* (Hopkinsville, Ky.: Historical Record Association, 1965), 499.

72. Hempstead, *Historical Review of Arkansas* 2: 733.

73. Fannie (Benedikt) McLaughlin, interview with author, Hot Springs, Ark., 6 April 1982; Mrs. Alexander (Lore) Benedikt, interview with author, Hot Springs, Ark., 20 April 1982.

74. *Arkansas Democrat*, 10 September 1912; *Arkansas Gazette*, 19 August 1921.

75. Hubert Mendel, interview with author, Hot Springs, Ark., 5 April 1982.

76. Mrs. Joseph Rosenzweig, "House of Israel," *The Record* (1970 Yearbook of the Hot Springs–Garland County Historical Society) 11 (1970): 73–75.

77. *Arkansas Democrat*, 16 June 1900.

78. Lewis Goltz, interview with author, Hot Springs, Ark., 21 April 1982; *Hot Springs New Era*, 25 November 1937.

79. *Arkansas Gazette*, 6 December 1938.

80. Herndon, *Centennial History* 2: 699–700.

81. Mrs. Joseph Rosenzweig, "House of Israel," 65–74; Data to author courtesy Dr. Joseph L. Rosenzweig, Hot Springs, Ark.

82. Thomas, *Arkansas and Its People* 2: 714–15.

83. *Arkansas Gazette*, 4 January 1893.

84. *Arkansas Gazette*, 18 November 1926; *Malvern Daily Record*, 2 February 1976.

85. Fred H. Lang, "Two Decades of State Forestry in Arkansas," *AHQ* 24: 3 (1965): 211, 212. *Malvern Daily Record*, 3 July 1939.

86. Lang, "Two Decades," 211, 212. *Malvern Daily Record*, 3 July 1939. Strauss family members of Malvern have attempted to determine if Theodore Strauss was Jewish. If so, the family intermarried and embraced the Christian faith (Mrs. T. J. Strauss, letter to author, 18 January 1986).

87. Data courtesy Mary L. Cheatham, librarian, Arkansas Regional Library, Malvern, Ark., in letters to author, 27 November 1985, 30 December 1985.

88. Thomas, *Arkansas and Its People* 2: 816, 819, 821.

89. Terence O'Dougherty and Frank M. Sarchet, comps., *Combined Directory of Little Rock, Hot Springs, Pine Bluff, Eureka Springs, and Fort Smith, 1881–2* (Little Rock: Union Printing & Publishing Co., 1881), 393–420, 426–27.

90. Al Cohn, interview with author, Fort Smith, Ark., 26 April 1983.

91. Thomas, *Arkansas and Its People* 2: 819–20.

92. R. G. Dun & Co., "Arkansas" 7: 243h.

93. *Fort Smith Elevator*, 30 June 1899.

94. Leah (Cohn) Arndt, telephone interview with author, Oklahoma City, Okla., 27 April 1983.

95. See Charles Leroy Reed, "The Last Choctaw Chief," *Sturm's Oklahoma Magazine* 3 (1907): 13.

96. Arndt interview.

97. *Fort Smith Southwest American*, 3 February 1927; Benno S. Friedman, interview with author, Memphis, Tenn., 11 May 1983.

98. George Tilles, "A History of Fort Smith," courtesy Ella (Tilles) Falk, Fort Smith, Ark.

99. Jerome Ney, interview with author, Fort Smith, Ark., 19 August 1982; Friedman interview.

100. *Fort Smith Times-Record*, 21 March 1930.

101. Ibid.; Al Cohn interview.

102. Al Cohn interview.

103. Ibid.; *Fort Smith Times-Record*, 7 April 1940.

104. George H. Shirk, *Oklahoma Place Names* (Norman: University of Oklahoma Press, 1965), 225.

105. Herndon, *Centennial History* 2: 763–64; *Fort Smith Southwest American*, 25 February 1921.

106. Cyrus Adler, *I Have Considered the Days* (Philadelphia: Jewish Publication Society of America, 1945), 3–7.

107. Clifton E. Hull, *Shortline Railroads of Arkansas* (Norman: University of Oklahoma Press, 1969), 47–48.

108. William S. Speer and John Henry Brown, eds., *Encyclopedia of the New West* (Marshall, Tex.: The United States Biographical Publishing Company, 1881), 250–51; *Fort Smith Elevator*, 1 October 1886.

109. *Arkansas Gazette*, 8 December 1889.

110. *Fort Smith City Directory* (n.p., 1900), 62.

111. *Arkansas Gazette*, 29 January 1909.

112. *Fort Smith Southwest Times-Record*, 20 October 1929.

113. Frances Fuller Weinstock (granddaughter of Aaron Fuller), letter to author, 23 April 1983.

114. *Fort Smith Southwest Times-Record*, 20 October 1929.

115. Ney interview.

116. Jack Moseley, editor of the *Fort Smith Southwest Times*, interview with author, Fort Smith, Ark., 26 April 1982.

117. Jack Moseley, "Boston Store Closing Touches City," *The Journal* (Fort Smith Historical Society) 2 (September 1986): 32–34.

118. Herndon, *Centennial History* 2: 396; *Sebastian County News*, 14 February 1939.

119. *Fort Smith Times-Record*, 13 August 1953; Maxine (Langfelder) Chapman, interview with author, Fort Smith, Ark., 17 August 1982.

120. *Fort Smith Elevator*, 30 March 1906; Morton B. Marks Jr., letter to author, 10 June 1985.

121. *Fort Smith Southwest American*, 21 August 1916; *Fort Smith Times-Record*, 21 August 1916.

122. *Fort Smith Southwest American*, 30 March 1926, 5 January 1931.

123. In the 1970s the Tilles home was restored. Much to the consternation of

Tilles family members, it was designated the Roger-Tilles Home. The hyphenated name was selected on the assumption that Louis Tilles had not been the sole builder of the house. According to the Tilles family, it was built by Louis Tilles alone. (Ella [Tilles] Falk, interview with author, 17 August 1982.)

124. George and Ella Tilles had five children; when Ella died in 1899, George married Ella's younger sister, Lillian, and they had one child, a daughter, Ella. (Falk interview.)

125. Mary Stolberg, "Telephone Company in Fort Smith," *The Journal* (Fort Smith Historical Society) 1: 2 (1970): 50–54.

126. *Pine Bluff Daily Graphic*, 23 September 1902; *Fort Smith Southwest American*, 8 March 1910.

127. *Fort Smith Times-Record*, 27 November 1929.

128. Letter in possession of Ella (Tilles) Falk, Fort Smith, Ark.

129. *Physicians and Medicine, Crawford and Sebastian Counties, Arkansas, 1817–1976* (Fort Smith, Ark.: Sebastian County Medical Society, 1976), 335.

130. *Fort Smith Times-Record*, 27 November 1929.

131. Svend Peterson, "Arkansas State Tuberculosis Sanatorium: The Nation's Largest," *AHQ* 5: 4 (1946): 36.

132. *Fort Smith Southwest Times-Record*, 19 November 1972.

133. Falk interview. For years a statue of a World War I doughboy stood at the entrance to Tilles Park.

134. Herndon, *Centennial History* 2, 590–91.

135. Morton B. Marks Jr., interview with author, Fort Smith, Ark., 16 September 1982.

136. *Fort Smith Southwest American*, 31 July 1943.

137. *Fort Smith Times Record*, 12 May 1924, 5 April 1927.

138. *Fort Smith Weekly New Era*, 3 June 1874.

139. Data on Dr. Goldstein taken from *Fort Smith Southwest Times-Record*, 23 February 1969, 14 June 1980; Herndonn *Centennial History* 2: 145–46; *Physicians and Medicine*, 352–53; "Golden Deeds Award" (1954 speech given at Fort Smith Exchange Club, Fort Smith, Ark., in honor of Dr. Davis W. Goldstein), courtesy Mrs. Leona Goldstein.

140. *Fort Smith Southwest American*, 21 January 1927.

141. Bertha (Levinson Sternberg) Tilles, interview with author, Fort Smith, Ark., 26 April 1983; Irvin Sternberg, letter to author, 27 April 1992; Herndon, *Centennial History* 2: 507.

142. *Physicians and Medicine*, 170, 635; Herndon, *Centennial History* 2: 248.

143. Morton B. Marks Jr., letter to author, 28 February 1985.

144. *Fort Smith Times-Record*, 9 October 1918, 10 October 1918.

145. *Fort Smith City Directory, 1894–1895* (n.p.:Maloney Directory, n.d.).

146. Fort Smith *Southwest American*, 25 June 1919.

147. Ibid., 4 August 1910.

148. *Fort Smith Times-Record*, 12 June 1914.

149. *Fort Smith Elevator*, 16 February 1900.

150. *Fort Smith Southwest American*, 25 June 1958.

151. Ibid., 18 July 1949.

152. Mrs. Elizabeth S. Plaut, letter to author, 6 October 1985.

153. *Fort Smith Southwest American*, 17 April 1958.

154. Undesignated article (full citation unavailable), Goldman Hotel File, Special Collections, FSPL.

155. *Fort Smith Times-Record*, 14 November 1915.

156. *Fort Smith Southwest American*, 6 September 1910, 24 March 1924.

157. Harry L. Oppenheimer, letter to author, 18 April 1985.

158. Brunette (Fox) Billstein, letter to author, 5 March 1985.

159. U.S. Bureau of the Census, *Ninth Census of the United States. The Statistics of the Population of the United States*, vol. 1 (Washington, D.C.: Government Printing Office, 1872); Thomas, *Arkansas and Its People* 2: 785.

160. *History of Benton, Washington, Carroll, Madison, Crawford, Franklin, and Sebastian Counties, Arkansas* (Chicago: The Goodspeed Publishing Company, 1890), 455.

161. *Fayetteville Daily Democrat*, 23 February 1934; William S. Campbell, *100 Years of Fayetteville, 1828–1927* (Fayetteville, Ark.: Washington County Historical Society, 1977), 13, 36, 56; Baum Family, Fayetteville, Ark., Folder, Small Collections File, AJA.

162. *Fayetteville Daily Democrat*, 6 December 1922.

163. Gustine Weber (granddaughter of Moses Baum), letters to author, 15 March 1983, 1 May 1983.

164. Weber letter, 15 March 1983.

165. *Fayetteville Northwest Arkansas Times*, 14 June 1955, 15 May 1961.

166. Robert A. Leflar, interview with author, Fayetteville, Ark., 20 August 1982; Ferguson and Atkinson, *Historic Arkansas*, 331–34.

167. *Fayetteville Northwest Arkansas Times*, 18 September 1943; *Arkansas Gazette*, 19 September 1943, 8 May 1983. Julian Waterman married Evangeline Archer, a non–Jew.

168. Thomas, *Arkansas and Its People* 2: 772.

169. Izola (Rainbolt) McCoy, "Dampf Family History," Tahlequah, Okla.

170. *Marshall Mountain Wave*, 28 January 1898.

171. Ibid., 22 August 1914.

172. Ibid.; McCoy, "Dampf family history." Other Jews settled in some of the small Northwest Arkansas towns, and their history has yet to be written. The town of Bergman in Boone County, for example, was named for Edith Bergman, who may have been Jewish. Dr. Bergman, a female, donated the town site on condition it bear the name of her daughter, Edith. Dr. Bergman built the first hotel there in 1905, and Edith was the first postmaster. The town was first incorporated in 1904; it was reincorporated in 1968. Gladys Marler and Bonnie Mears, comps., *Bergman—Then and Now, 1904–1976* (Bergman, Ark: Bergman Homemakers Extension Club, 1976).

173. *Biographical and Historical Memoirs of Central Arkansas* (Chicago: The Goodspeed Publishing Company, 1889), 677, 678 (hereafter cited as *Central Arkansas*).

174. Dr. Gordon David Frank, telephone interview with author, Dallas, Tex., 11 July 1991; Ferguson, *Arkansas Lives*, 167.

175. Robert L. Gatewood, *Faulkner County, Arkansas, 1778–1964* (Conway, Ark.: n. p., 1964), 39.

176. *Conway Log Cabin Democrat*, 5 August 1952, 24 November 1978; Gladys (Frauenthal) Gates, interview with author, Little Rock, Ark., 6 January 1982; Ruth (Frauenthal) Krone (daughter of Max Frauenthal), interview with author, Little Rock, Ark., 6 January 1982. Two of Jacob Frauenthal's sons met tragic fates: Isaac was killed while serving with a posse attempting to catch thieves near Conway, Ark., and Maurice drowned when his foot became entangled in a stirrup after his horse stumbled in Cadron Creek (Gates interview).

177. Because of the outstanding success of the Frauenthal store of Conway, Ark., some criticism has developed (in hindsight) of its growth. Some have said lands were acquired at the expense of farmers who could no longer pay their bills. One writer, Robert K. Doolos, went so far as to say that Max Frauenthal could be classified with the robber barons that Hal Bridges describes as "avaricious rascals who habitually cheated and robbed investors and consumers . . ." Doolos notes, however, that the failure of so many farms between 1865 and 1900 was not caused by the merchants but rather was the result of "too many farmers and a surplus of farm commodities." The merchants were simply carrying on business as the times demanded. Doolos notes that it was fairly easy to begin a business in those early days, but it took farsightedness to be able to continue through depressed times. He also notes that Max Frauenthal was a significant part of entrepreneurial history in Arkansas, for he "geographically changed the commercial center of a town, thereby forever altering its history." (Robert K. Doolos, "Max Frauenthal: An Early Conway Entrepreneur," *Faulkner Facts & Fiddlings* 13 [1971]: 41, 42; Hal Bridges, "The Robber Baron Concept in American History," in Abraham Seldin Eisenstadt, ed., *American History: Recent Interpretations*, vol. 2 [New York: Thomas Y. Crowell Company, 1962], 58.)

178. Alex McPherson, *History of Faulkner County* (Conway, Ark.: Conway Times Plant, 1927), 58–59; *Conway Log Cabin Democrat*, 16 September 1944.

179. Edith White, "Early Conway," *Faulkner Facts & Fiddlings* 4 (December 1963): 15.

180. Eugene Nolte, "Jo Frauenthal, Opie Read, and the Spyglass: Some Unpublished Letters," *AHQ* 22: 2 (1963): 171–76.

181. *Arkansas Gazette*, 11 August 1947; Walter L. Brown, "Arkansas' Flag Is Fifty Years Old," *AHQ* 22: 1 (1966): 4. *Conway Log Cabin Democrat*, 11 August 1947.

182. Gates interview.

183. Krone interview; *Arkansas Democrat*, 9 March 1914; Hempstead, *Historical Review of Arkansas* 3: 1653–54; Louis Moore, "Notes on Frauenthal & Schwarz Store" (1977), Julian Frauenthal Papers, Little Rock, Ark.

184. Thomas, *Arkansas and Its People* 4: 646; Charles L. Ward, "Sugar Loaf Mountain, Once Scene of Red Man's Defeat, Now Popular Tourist Spot," undesignated newspaper article (full citation unavailable), Julian Frauenthal Papers, Little Rock, Ark. Max Frauenthal's picture was later removed from the courthouse rotunda, and his contributions to the area were mostly forgotten by later generations. (For an extensive history of Cleburne County, Ark., and Heber Springs, Ark., see Evalena Berry, *Time and the River* [Little Rock: Rose Publishing Company, 1982].)

185. Krone interview.

186. Gladys (Frauenthal) Gates, interview with author, Little Rock, Ark., 16 December 1981.

187. *Arkansas Gazette*, 5 December 1935; Hempstead, *Historical Review of Arkansas* 2: 653–54; Gatewood, *Faulkner County*, 104.

188. *Conway Log Cabin Democrat*, 8 February 1921; *Arkansas Gazette*, 20 April 1966.

189. *Central Arkansas*, 733–34.

190. *Arkansas Democrat*, magazine section, 23 November 1958.

191. White, "Early Conway," 16.

192. Thomas, *Arkansas and Its People* 4: 552.

193. *Arkansas Gazette*, 14 August 1938.

194. Doug Smith, "Oh, THAT Thyra," *Arkansas Gazette*, 22 December 1977.

195. *Arkansas Gazette*, 19 November 1933.

196. *Arkansas Gazette*, 22 August 1955, 19 November 1933.

197. Ella (Tilles) Falk, interview with author, 17 August 1982.

198. Maxine (Langfelder) Chapman, interview with author, Fort Smith, Ark., 17 August 1982.

199. Ferguson, *Arkansas Lives*, 167; *Arkansas Gazette*, 6 January 1942; Dr. Gordon David Frank, telephone interview with author, Dallas, Tex., 11 July 1991.

CHAPTER 10

East European Migration in Central Arkansas

1. Rabbi Louis Wolsey, letters to Industrial Removal Office, New York, N.Y., 6 September 1907, 30 September 1907, Industrial Removal Office (IRO) Papers, Arkansas, I–91, Box 29, AJHS; (see also sec. II).

2. Robert Itzkowitz, interview with author, North Little Rock, Ark., 4 April 1983.

3. According to relatives, Abe Back sold his store to M. M. Cohn and moved to New York; Pincus Back also had two other sons—Louis (1862–1950) and Morris (1870–1953). (Edward Back, interview with author, Little Rock, Ark., 4 August 1983.)

4. *Arkansas Gazette*, 3 March 1950.

5. Ibid.; *Arkansas Gazette*, 11 November 1911.

6. *Arkansas Gazette*, 7 October 1979; *Who's Who in Little Rock 1921* 1 (Little Rock: Who's Who Publishers, 1921), 17, 18; Mrs. Phil (Alice Lasker) Back, interview with author, Little Rock, Ark., 6 November 1981.

7. *Who's Who in Little Rock 1921* 1: 99; *Arkansas Gazette*, 24 December 1922, 11 February 1927.

8. Ben Kluglose, interview with author, Little Rock, Ark., 11 April 1983.

9. *Arkansas Gazette*, 8 January 1924.

10. Sam Storthz Jr., interview with author, Little Rock, Ark., 2 August 1982; *Arkansas Gazette*, 23 February 1932.

11. Sam Storthz Jr. interview; Fay Hempstead, *Historical Review of Arkansas*,

vol. 2 (Chicago: The Lewis Publishing Company, 1911), 861, 862; *Arkansas Gazette*, 3 May 1948.

12. Joe Storthz Jr., interview with author, Little Rock, Ark., 14 April 1983.

13. *Arkansas Gazette*, 17 January 1907.

14. Ibid.; *Arkansas Gazette*, 17 September 1911.

15. Joe Tenenbaum, interview with author, Little Rock, Ark., 12 December 1981; *Arkansas Gazette*, 7 February 1990; Pearl (Tenenbaum) Carvalho, telephone interview with author, Little Rock, Ark., 5 May 1983.

16. Adele Sanders, interview with author, Little Rock, Ark., 9 March 1983; *Arkansas Gazette*, 22 April 1946.

17. Gussie Alman, interview with author, Little Rock, Ark., 12 April 1982.

18. *Arkansas Gazette*, 19 December 1969.

19. Ibid., 7 September 1939.

20. Louis Barg, interview with author, Forrest City, Ark., 21 June 1982.

21. *Arkansas Gazette*, 1 March 1908.

22. Fannie (Bennett) Kaufman, interview with author, Little Rock, Ark., 6 April 1983.

23. Ruth (Goldman) Kretchmar, interview with author, Little Rock, Ark., 5 December 1982; Fay Williams, *Arkansans of the Years*, vol. 4 (Little Rock: C. C. Allard & Associates, Publishers, 1952–54), 113–22 (hereafter cited as *Arkansans*).

24. Robert Itzkowitz interview.

25. *Arkansas Gazette*, 12 December 1987, 17 April 1963.

26. Morris Lulky, interview with author, North Little Rock, Ark., 27 July 1982.

27. *Arkansas Gazette*, 17 January 1947.

28. Edith Breier, interview with author, Little Rock, Ark., 11 March 1983; *Arkansas Gazette*, 5 November 1978.

29. Mrs. Herbert (Gertrude) Latkin, interview with author, Little Rock, Ark., 16 April 1982; *Arkansas Gazette*, 16 February 1916, 18 February 1916; Annie (Narkinsky) Miller, interview with author, Little Rock, Ark., 21 July 1982.

30. *Arkansas Democrat*, 29 January 1951; *Arkansas Gazette*, 30 May 1963, 2 December 1963. Morris and Bessie Granoff also had three daughters.

31. Hattie Besser, interview with author, Little Rock, Ark., 14 April 1983.

32. Joe Bernhard, interview with author, Little Rock, Ark., 16 March 1983; Ben Kluglose, interview with author, Little Rock, Ark., 11 April 1983; *Arkansas Gazette*, 13 May 1933, 17 May 1933.

33. *Arkansas Gazette*, 12 March 1926, 24 December 1948.

34. Undesignated newspaper clippings (full citations unavailable), Charles Kluglose scrapbook, Little Rock, Ark.

35. Louis Barg, interview with author, Forrest City, Ark., 21 June 1982; Brigadier General A. W. Catlin, *With the Help of God and a Few Marines* (New York: Doubleday, 1919), 357.

36. *Arkansas Gazette*, 7 January 1942.

37. Ibid., 24 November 1910; Besser interview.

38. *Arkansas Democrat*, magazine section, 27 January 1952.

39. Arnold and Janet (Grundfest) Mayersohn, interview with author, Little Rock, Ark., 24 April 1985.

40. Such marriages were fairly rare at the time. Until after World War II, many German Jews and East European Jews did not mingle freely.

41. Edward Festinger, interview with author, Lake Village, Ark., 11 May 1982.

42. *Arkansas Gazette,* 3 March 1929, 24 January 1946.

43. Ibid., 13 December 1920, 11 March 1963.

44. Rosa Belle Dreyfus, interview with author, McGehee, Ark., 8 May 1982; *Arkansas Gazette,* 17 March 1911. Ellis Yout had a third son, Sam, who moved to New York, and J. Feinstein had a son, H. Julius, who settled at Monroe, La.

45. *Arkansas Gazette,* 7 November 1933, 10 November 1956; Sarah Korenblat, interview with author, Little Rock, Ark., 6 April 1983.

46. Z. Bensky, interview with author, Sarasota, Fla., 15 February 1984.

47. *Arkansas Gazette,* 3 August 1962, 28 April 1963.

48. Marion "Mooch" Safferstone, interview with author, Little Rock, Ark., 10 March 1983.

49. *Arkansas Democrat,* 31 December 1950; *Arkansas Gazette,* 19 June 1952, 8 December 1957, 1 January 1971.

50. *Arkansas Gazette,* 23 July 1963, 17 May 1966.

51. Ibid., 9 June 1952, 10 June 1952.

52. Ibid., 23 July 1885.

53. *Arkansas Democrat,* 25 June 1904.

54. Louis Rosen, interview with author, Little Rock, Ark., 18 February 1983.

55. *Arkansas Democrat,* 7 June 1920, 8 June 1920. Insurance was not automatically carried on policemen at the time.

56. *Arkansas Gazette,* 1 November 1913.

57. Ibid., 22 July 1932.

58. Ibid., 25 July 1937.

59. *Arkansas Democrat,* 2 July 1936. Lena Kassoff's daughter, Carrie, married Ben Besser.

60. *Arkansas Gazette,* 5 July 1897, 6 July 1897, 7 July 1897.

61. Ibid., 21 June 1972; Adele Sanders and Jennie (Sanders) Loket, interview with author, Little Rock, Ark., 9 March 1983.

62. *Arkansas Gazette,* 10 July 1966; *Arkansas Democrat,* 10 July 1966.

63. Ibid., 23 June 1916, 9 January 1964.

64. *Arkansas Democrat,* 24 July 1922; *Arkansas Gazette,* 10 May 1971.

65. *Arkansas Democrat,* 31 August 1918.

66. *Arkansas Gazette,* 22 February 1911, 4 January 1916.

67. Ibid., 1 March 1943; Henry Spitzberg, interview with author, Little Rock, Ark., 17 December 1981.

68. *Arkansas Gazette,* 8 May 1989. Sam and Jennie Spitzberg had two daughters, Ruth (Vogel) and Louise (Thalheimer) Rosenberg. The Forty and Eight was a fun-making body of the American Legion. It was formed after World War I and took its name from the standard French railroad (box) cars that held 40 men and 8 horses. It was devoted to good works, but it also brought humor to Legion meetings and parades. Col. John R. Elting, *A Dictionary of Soldier Talk* (New York: Charles Scribner's Sons, 1989), 115; Raymond Moley Jr., *The American Legion Story* (New York: Meredith Publishing Company 1966), 148.

69. Spitzberg interview.

70. *Arkansas Gazette*, 22 July 1980.

71. F. Williams, *Arkansans* 2: 338–47; *Arkansas Gazette*, 21 July 1957, 18 June 1958.

72. Leonard Scott, telephone interview with author, Little Rock, Ark., 10 July 1991.

73. *Arkansas Democrat*, 2 April 1924; *Arkansas Gazette*, 30 July 1953.

74. Latkin interview; *Arkansas Gazette*, 16 February 1916, 17 February 1916, 18 February 1916.

75. Latkin interview; *History of the Arkansas Press Association* (Little Rock: Parke-Harper Company, 1930), 78.

76. *Arkansas Gazette*, 6 June 1946; H. F. Barnes, ed., Lex B. Davis, comp., *Among Arkansas Leaders* (Little Rock: Lex B. Davis, 1934), 43; *Arkansas Gazette*, 29 September 1959.

77. *Arkansas Gazette*, 30 August 1982.

78. F. Williams, *Arkansans* 2: 358–67.

79. Belle Lipman, interview with author, Memphis, Tenn., 3 May 1982.

80. *Arkansas Gazette*, 8 October 1946.

81. *Arkansas Gazette*, 18 March 1965.

82. Erma (White) Gray (former Pulaski County public school teacher), interview with author, Little Rock, Ark., 3 May 1983.

83. Latkin interview; Mrs. Ora P. Nix, interview with author, Little Rock, Ark., 9 March 1982; Lena Latkin Memorial Library Association Dedication Program, 16 December 1934; *Arkansas Gazette*, 19 March 1933.

84. *Arkansas Democrat*, 5 May 1940; Latkin interview.

85. *Arkansas Gazette*, 31 July 1975; 22 September 1971.

86. Ibid., 4 June 1970.

87. Mary Herr Bernhard, unpublished autobiography, Joe Bernhard Papers, courtesy Joe Bernhard, Little Rock, Ark.; *Arkansas Gazette*, 19 June 1942.

88. Sherrie Fleischer Davidson and Doris Tenzel Fleischer, *Pauline Tenzel: The Life Story of a "Lady Doctor"* (New York: Impact Media Special Edition, Biblio Press, 1992); W. David Baird, *Medical Education in Arkansas, 1879–1978* (Memphis: Memphis State University Press, 1979).

89. Adele Sanders interview; *Arkansas Gazette*, 31 January 1989.

CHAPTER 11
East European Migration in Eastern Arkansas

1. Kenneth Libo and Irving Howe, *We Lived There Too* (New York: St. Martin's/Marek, 1984), 32.

2. "Arkansas-Oklahoma Report" (January 1909): 235, 136, R. G. Dun & Co. Collection, Baker Library, Harvard University Graduate School of Business Administration (hereafter cited as R. G. Dun & Co. "Arkansas-Oklahoma"; *Golden City Messenger*, November 1925, Jewish Children's Home Collection—180, Sec. 8, Special Collections, Tulane University Library.

3. Irving I. Edgar, "Some Early Jewish Physicians of Michigan: Dr. Simon Levin–Dr. Joseph Beisman," *Michigan Jewish History* 7 (July 1967): 8.

4. The Brownsteins had a brother, Sinai H. Brownstein, who married Hattie Grundfest of Cary, Miss. (Gus Brownstein, interview with author, Newport, Ark., 8 November 1982).

5. Susan (Levit) Plough, letter to author, 28 October 1991.

6. Paul Clayton, telephone interview with author, Tuckerman, Ark., 23 April 1992.

7. Mrs. Almus Matthews, letter to author, 10 November 1982; *Arkansas Democrat-Gazette*, 7 December 1991; *Newport Daily Independent*, 9 December 1991.

8. Sarah Steinberg and Ann Graber, interview with author, Corning, Ark., 11 November 1982.

9. Jerrold Graber, telephone interview with author, Memphis, Tenn., 29 July 1991.

10. *Jonesboro Enterprise*, Special Edition, April 1903.

11. Interviews by author with Isaac Goldstein's granddaughters: Marguerite (Arndt) Culver, interview with author, Jonesboro, Ark., 9 November 1982; Louise (Goldstein) Wolchansky, telephone interview with author, New Orleans, La., 17 November 1982.

12. Lena Mae (Wainman) Rubenstein, granddaughter of Nathan Blecker, interview with author, Memphis, Tenn., 11 May 1983.

13. George Heinemann, interview with author, Jonesboro, Ark., 9 November 1982; Guy "Cotton" Rubenstein, interview with author, Memphis, Tenn., 11 May 1983.

14. Bette (Grossman) Greenberg, letter to author, 11 November 1982; Sue (Berger Bressler) Dent, interview with author, Memphis, Tenn., 11 May 1983. Hyman Grossman moved to St. Louis, Mo.

15. Perry Cooperman and his son, Harold, interview with author, Steele, Mo., 26 June 1982; "This Is Your Life, Perry Cooperman" (testimonial to Perry Cooperman at Temple Israel, Blytheville, Ark., 1961), courtesy Harold Cooperman. Perry Cooperman also had furniture stores at Caruthersville, Mo., and Steele, Mo.

16. Oscar Fendler, letter to author, 20 July 1987.

17. Darlene (Feinberg) Goldberg, letter to author, 14 November 1991.

18. Luba (Tooter) Cohen, interview with author, Blytheville, Ark., 25 June 1982.

19. Hal Rand (born Harold Rosenthal), letter to author, 21 February 1983.

20. Hal Rand (born Harold Rosenthal), "Weinberg Family History," New York, N.Y., 28 July 1980, courtesy Carrol S. Meyer Jr., San Antonio, Tex.; Fendler letter.

21. Rand letter; Fendler letter.

22. Ramelle Applebaum, letter to author, 27 July 1987; *Arkansas Gazette*, 2 August 1938.

23. M. Gordon Tiger, letter to author, 9 February 1992.

24. William "Bill" and Pearl Borowsky, interviews with author, Manila, Ark., 24 June 1982, 27 June 1982; Jane (Borowsky) Ettingoff, interview with author, Memphis, Tenn., 11 May 1983.

25. Fendler letter; Bill and Pearl Borowsky interview.

26. Fendler letter.

27. Guy "Cotton" Rubenstein interview.

28. Ruth (Goldberg) Wigdor, granddaughter of I. Harwarg, letter to author, 15 March 1983.

29. See Ted R. Worley, "Early Days in Osceola," *AHQ* 24: 2 (1965): 119–26.

30. Wigdor letter (Tillie Harwarg died, and the three Harwarg children were sent to the Jewish orphan's home in Cleveland for several years).

31. Guy "Cotton" Rubenstein interview.

32. Lionel Silverfield, interview with author, Osceola, Ark., 26 June 1982.

33. Dr. Morris Nickol, interview with author, Osceola, Ark., 26 June 1982.

34. Melvin Lapides, interview with author, Osceola, Ark., 3 August 1991.

35. "Dedication Services of the New Temple Israel, Blytheville, Arkansas," 7 September 1947, TIAB; *Temple Israel Chronicle* (29 November 1936): 2, 3, courtesy Rabbi M. Lyons, St. Louis, Mo.; *Arkansas Gazette*, 31 May 1987.

36. Jeanette Evensky, interview with author, West Memphis, Ark., 29 June 1982; Plough letter.

37. Dorothy (Warshaw) Lowenstein, interview with author, Memphis, Tenn., 10 May 1983.

38. *Marked Tree Tribune*, 18 June 1967. When Jake Schoenberger's first wife, Emma Pohl, died, he married Doris (Goldstein) Shaul, widow of Lee Shaul of Marianna, Ark. (Doris [Goldstein Shaul] Schoenberger, interview with author, Marked Tree, Ark., 10 November 1982.)

39. Shirley B. Cohen, telephone interview with author, St. Louis, Mo., 23 January 1986.

40. Albert Bindursky, interview with author, Lepanto, Ark., 24 June 1982.

41. Eve B. Coleman, daughter of Herman Bindursky, letter to author, 22 January 1986.

42. *The McCrory Leader*, 24 December 1986.

43. I. N. Arnof, interview with author, McCrory, Ark., 10 November 1982; Ann (Arnof) Fishman, telephone interview with author, New Orleans, La., 19 November 1982; Ian Arnof, telephone interview with author, New Orleans, La., 19 November 1982.

44. Joe Wilenzick, interview with author, New Orleans, La., 20 November 1982; Undesignated newspaper clipping, 1 November 1921 (full citation unavailable), courtesy Joe Wilenzick.

45. David "Dave" Blumberg, interview with author, Richmond, Va., 5 November 1984.

46. *Wynne Star-Progress*, 10 August 1934; David Drexler, interview with author, Wynne, Ark., 23 June 1982.

47. Drexler interview; John L. Ferguson, *Arkansas Lives: the Opportunity Land Who's Who* (Hopkinsville, Ky.: Historical Record Association, 1965), 130, 131.

48. Isadore Steinberg and Morris Steinberg, interview with author, Wynne, Ark., 23 June 1982.

49. Libo and Howe, *We Lived*, 32.

50. David Reagler, interview with author, Wynne, Ark., 23 June 1982; Elouise (Reagler) Cohen, interview with author, Forrest City, Ark., 22 June 1982;

Mildred "Mickey" (Reagler) Rubens, interview with author, West Memphis, Ark., 28 June 1982; Miriam (Bornstein) Baer, interview with author, Memphis, Tenn., 13 May 1983.

51. David Drexler, letter to author, 12 August 1991.

52. Isadore Baer, son of Nathan Baer, interview with author, Memphis, Tenn., 12 May 1983.

53. Margaret Woolfork, letter to author, 8 July 1982; *American Israelite,* 15 January 1920.

54. Meyer Brick and his son Phillip, interview with author, Marion, Ark., 28 June 1982.

55. Jake Tupper and his first wife, Sarah, had four children; after she died, he married Fannie (Cohen Bursk), widow of Frank Bursk (and sister of Rebecca Snyder of Forrest City, Ark.); Fannie had three children by Frank Bursk (Sol and Lena [Tupper] Bursk, interview with author, Earle, Ark., 24 June 1982).

56. Stanley Lee and Irmazell (Harris) Lee, telephone interview with author, Memphis, Tenn., 12 May 1983; *Memphis Commercial Appeal,* 8 June 1954.

57. Mrs. George Stein and son George Raymond Stein, interview with author, Earle, Ark., 24 June 1982; *West Memphis Accelerator,* Souvenir Edition (undated article ca. 1930s, full citation unavailable), courtesy Mrs. George Stein.

58. *The Crawfordsville, Ark. Rotarian* (9 December 1952).

59. Dorothy (Warshaw) Lowenstein, interview with author, Memphis, Tenn., 10 May 1983.

60. L. H. Greene, interview with author, Crawfordsville, Ark., 13 May 1983.

61. Lowenstein interview.

62. Mike and Sadie Levitch, interview with author, West Memphis, Ark., 28 June 1982.

63. Jerrold Weisburd, telephone interview with author, West Memphis, Ark., 28 June 1982.

64. Ibid.; Levitch interview; Isadore Baer interview.

65. *Forrest City Times,* Souvenir Supplement, 19 September 1905.

66. *American Israelite,* 15 January 1920.

67. Jeanette (Warshavsky) Bernstein, "A Grateful Thread, A Family Journal," 4 January 1957, Arkansas, Jeannette Bernstein Folder, Box 1784, AJA.

68. Louis and Gertrude Barg, interview with author, West Memphis, Ark., 21 June 1982. Louis Barg was the son of Sam and Bella (Snyder) Barg; Bella was a sister of Esrael Snyder.

69. Harold Sharpe, interview with author, West Memphis, Ark., 22 June 1982.

70. William Cohn, interview with author, Forrest City, Ark., 22 June 1982.

71. Max and Elouise Cohen, interview with author, Forrest City, Ark., 22 June 1982.

72. Rose (Burd) Berk, interview with author, El Dorado, Ark., 29 October 1982.

73. *Crowley Ridge Chronicle,* 2 May 1940, Newspaper clipping 6.1072, M/F File, AHC.

74. Theodore Zuckerman, interview with author, Hughes, Ark., 29 May 1982; Mary Medearis, letter to author, 25 August 1984.

75. Robert Sakon, interview with author, Little Rock, Ark., 8 September 1986.

76. Robert Sakon, interview with author, England, Ark., 9 August 1984.

77. Ibid., Clara Burta, interview with author, Little Rock, Ark, 10 August 1982.

78. *Arkansas Gazette*, 25 May 1917, 30 July 1918, 19 January 1939.

79. *Pine Bluff Commercial*, 24 April 1935; Phyllis Scharff, telephone interview with author, Little Rock, Ark., 5 August 1991.

80. Gladys (Frauenthal) Gates, interview with author, Little Rock, Ark., 16 December 1981.

81. "Arkansas Postcard Past," *Arkansas Gazette*, 17 July 1986, 16 February 1987.

82. Reggie Goins, "Our Ancestors' Hand-Me-Downs," *Cat-Chat* (1980), Lee Academy, Marianna, Ark.; J. Edward Wise, son of Naomi (Lewis) Wise, letter to author, 4 October 1991.

83. Dr. Gary Strasberg, interview with author, Memphis, Tenn., 10 May 1983; Sylvia (Alperin) Greif, interview with author, Memphis, Tenn., 12 May 1983.

84. Edith (Davidson) Reiter, letter to author, 8 April 1985 (Edith Davidson married Murray Reiter of New York, and Dorothy married Dr. Benjamin Berger of Shaker Heights, Ohio); see also, Robert R. Logan, "Notes on the First Land Surveys in Arkansas," *AHQ* 19: 3 (1960): 260–70; *Arkansas Democrat*, 31 March 1959.

85. *Helena World*, 18 November 1940.

86. Solomon Feldman, interview with author, Helena, Ark., 30 June 1982.

87. Sam "Sonny" Ciener Jr., interview with author Helena, Ark., 30 June 1982; *Helena World*, 11 June 1962.

88. *Helena World*, 25 February 1974.

89. Elaine (Hyman) Handelman, interview with author, Helena, Ark., 30 June 1982.

90. *Helena World*, 11 February 1946.

91. Ibid., 19 April 1976.

92. Maurice Abowitz, interview with author, McGehee, Ark., 9 May 1982; Stephen Abowitz, interview with author, 10 May 1982; Shirley (Abowitz) Sherman, interview with author, Little Rock, Ark., 11 December 1981.

93. Mrs. R. Reitzhammer, interview with author, Arkansas City, Ark., 9 May 1982; Maurice Raphael, letter to author, 16 October 1989.

94. David Y. Thomas, ed., *Arkansas and Its People*, vol. 2 (New York: American Historical Society, Inc., 1930), 698.

95. Louise (Goldstein) Wolchansky, telephone interview with author, New Orleans, La., 17 November 1982; Helen (Wolchansky) Sabin and Roy Wolchansky, letters to author, 20 November 1982, 17 November 1983; *McGehee Times*, 25 November 1953.

96. Charles Fleisig's other daughter, Frances, moved out of state (Seymour and Edith Fleisig, interview with author, McGehee, Ark., 9 May 1982).

97. Jay and Faye (Marcus) Lewis, interview with author, Fayetteville, Ark., 29 April 1983.

98. Fay Hempstead, *Historical Review of Arkansas*, vol. 2 (Chicago: The Lewis Publishing Company, 1911), 1000.

99. Bertha Meyer married Reuben Kaplan and lived out of state (Jay and Faye [Marcus] Lewis interview).

100. Mannie Dreidel, interview with author, McGehee, Ark., 9 May 1982; Isadore Small, interview with author, Memphis, Tenn., 10 May 1983.

101. Mendel Pinkus, interview with author, Dermott, Ark., 10 May 1982.

102. Ibid.

103. Joe Dante, son of Eli Dante, telephone interview with author, Winnsboro, La., 12 April 1984.

104. Bernard and Louise Levi, interview with author, Dermott, Ark., 10 May 1982.

105. Pinkus interview. (Isadore Pinkus's daughter Fannie married Sol Meyer of McGehee, Ark., and his son Leon [1903–1960] married non-Jew Camille Shamoon of Lake Village, Ark.)

106. Ruth K. Abroms, interview with author, Miami, Fla., 23 May 1982; Barry and Marjorie Brunner, interview with author, Dermott, Ark., 10 May 1982.

107. *Arkansas Gazette,* 17 January 1947; R. G. Dun, "Arkansas-Oklahoma," 43, 44.

108. S. S. Forte, interview with author, Lake Village, Ark., 11 May 1982.

109. Sam Epstein Angel, interview with author, Lake Village, Ark., 11 May 1982; Mr. and Mrs. Ed Festinger and son Steve, interview with author, Lake Village, Ark., 11 May 1982. (Sam Epstein married Becke Ruth Eisenberg of Little Rock, Ark., and they had three daughters, Mrs. Harold [Helen] Kantor, Mrs. Ben [Sylvia] Angel, and Mrs. Ed [Melvyn] Festinger.)

110. Harry Hurt III, *Texas Rich* (New York,: W. W. Norton & Company, 1981), 49.

111. Dr. Joseph L. Rosenzweig, interview with author, Hot Springs, Ark., 6 April 1982.

112. Michael Rankin, former Lake Village, Ark., citizen, letter to author, 20 July 1985.

113. According to family members, Louis's brother, Mert Bloom of Tallulah, La., was suspicious over Louis's death and visited Lake Village, Ark., to investigate. Mert was attacked and left for dead. James Rankin, a family member at Lake Village, Ark., later found that Louis had been killed by a drunken Klan member, and it was the man's brother who had attacked Mert. The Klan had threatened to burn down Mert's store in Tallulah because he had rented another store to a Chinese family. Mert stood in front of the store with a shotgun, and the Klan left him alone after that (Michael Rankin, letters to author, 10 July 1981, 24 June 1985).

114. Ouida Cassali, Chicot County Deputy Sheriff, letter to author, 14 November 1985; Rankin letter, 20 July 1985.

115. Bess (Brockman) Weinberg, interview with author, Hot Springs, Ark., 19 April 1982.

116. See Elbert T. Cashion Sr., *A History of Eudora, Arkansas, Chicot County* (Lake Village, Ark.: James Printing Company, 1977).

117. Harold Hart, interview with author, Eudora, Ark., 10 May 1982.

118. Mrs. Bernard J. (Naomi Dante) Tanenbaum Sr., interview with author, Dumas, Ark., 12 May 1982; Bernard J. "Jerry" Tanenbaum Jr., interview with author, Dumas, Ark., 12 May 1982; *Arkansas Democrat,* magazine section, 28 November 1954.

119. Charles H. Dante, interview with author, Dumas, Ark., 7 May 1982; Judy (Dante) Grundfest, interview with author, Little Rock, Ark., 7 July 1982. Helen (Dante) Kahn moved out of state.

120. Bernard J. "Jerry" Tanenbaum Jr., interview with author, Dumas, Ark., 7 May 1982 (for more data on the Dante-Tanenbaum families, see sec. V).

121. Harry and Elsie Phillips, interview with author, Dumas, Ark., 7 May 1982.

122. Haskell and Elaine Wolff, interview with author, Dumas, Ark., 7 May 1982.

123. Louis Bram, interview with author, Pine Bluff, Ark., 24 April 1982.

124. Ibid.; Dr. Joseph L. Rosenzweig, interview with author, Hot Springs, Ark., 6 April 1982.

125. Bram interview; Adah B. Sonnenschein, interview with author, Pine Bluff, Ark., 22 April 1982; *Arkansas Democrat*, 14 December 1989.

126. The poignant story of the Soltz family was printed on the front page of the *St. Louis Post-Dispatch*, Sunday magazine, 29 October 1900.

127. Burton Schlosberg, interview with author, Pine Bluff, Ark., 23 April 1982.

128. *Pine Bluff Commercial*, 13 August 1917.

129. *Arkansas Gazette*, 25 April 1982.

130. *Pine Bluff Commercial*, 9 December 1943, 20 November 1958.

131. Maurice Cohen, interview with author, Pine Bluff, Ark., 23 April 1982.

132. Bram interview; *Pine Bluff Commercial*, 2 October 1973.

133. *Dumas Clarion*, 25 July 1979.

134. Charles Dante, Bernard J. "Jerry" Tanenbaum, and Mrs. Bernard J. (Naomi) Tanenbaum interviews; numerous newspaper clippings, Jerry Tanenbaum Papers.

135. See *Arkansas Democrat*, magazine section, 25 August 1957; *Lepanto News Record*, 1 April 1960; *Arkansas Gazette*, 26 May 1960; Coleman letter.

136. *Pine Bluff Daily Graphic*, 10 March 1940; *Pine Bluff Commercial*, 24 August 1966.

CHAPTER 12
East European Migration in Western Arkansas

1. Bessie (Phillips) Cooper, letter to author, 20 August 1987; *Camden News*, 5 November 1964.

2. Burton F. Zavelo, telephone interview with author, Little Rock, Ark., 25 July 1991.

3. Marjorie (Miller) Miron, letter to author, 19 November 1985.

4. *El Dorado News-Times*, 8 December 1980. Morris Lewis married Molly Solomon of Houston, Tex., and their daughter, Isabelle, moved to Nashville, Tenn. (Mrs. Morris Lewis, interview with author, El Dorado, Ark., 29 October 1982).

5. Jeannette (Warshavsky) Bernstein, "A Grateful Thread, A Family Journal," 4 January 1957, Arkansas, Jeannette Bernstein Folder, Box 1784, AJA.

6. *El Dorado News-Times*, 24 May 1976; Philip Pesses, interview with author, Magnolia, Ark., 30 August 1984.

7. Rose (Burd) Berk, telephone interview with author, El Dorado, Ark., 29 November 1982; *El Dorado News-Times*, 3 November 1969.

8. *El Dorado News-Times*, 27 August 1940.

9. *Arkansas Democrat-Gazette*, 30 November 1992.

10. "Arkansas, 1840s–1870s," 8: 8-a, 30, R. G. Dun & Co. Collection, Baker Library, Harvard University Graduate School of Business Administration; H. F. Barnes, ed., Lex B. Davis, comp., *Among Arkansas Leaders* (Lex B. Davis, 1934), 51.

11. *Arkansas Democrat*, 26 September 1940; Charlotte Finberg, letter to author, 6 August 1983.

12. Barbara Overton Chandler and J. Ed Howe, *History of Texarkana* (Shreveport, La.: J. Ed Howe Publisher, 1939), 360, 374. Another brother, Jacob Scherer, and a sister, Hannah, remained in Poland (*Texarkana Gazette*, 22 May 1938).

13. Max Wexler married Marguerite Goldstein in 1923, and they had two children, son Ralph, who became a Denver, Colo., physician, and daughter Marlene Lerner, who married a Denver physician (Max Wexler, interview with author, Texarkana, Ark., 28 October 1982).

14. Ibid.

15. Chandler and Howe, *Texarkana*, 309.

16. Ralph Brody, interview with author, Texarkana, Ark., 27 October 1982; Anne (Kusin) Gold, interview with author, Texarkana, Ark., 27 October 1982.

17. Wexler interview; Brody interview.

18. Billie Richmond, Foreman, Ark., librarian, letter to author, 26 September 1988.

19. *DeQueen Bee*, Pictorial Edition Supplement, 20 November 1903.

20. *Hot Springs Sentinel-Record*, 24 February 1935.

21. Robert Gartenberg, interview with author, Hot Springs, Ark., 20 April 1982.

22. Bess (Brockman) Weinberg, interview with author, Hot Springs, Ark., 18 April 1982.

23. *Who's Who in American Jewry, 1928* (New York: The Jewish Biographical Bureau, Inc., 1928), 501; Helen Wilma Moss, "A Link With Yesterday," 141, Arkansas File, Helen Wilma Moss Folder, AJA; *New York Times*, 1 April 1947.

24. *Hot Springs Sentinel-Record*, 28 December 1942; *Hot Springs New Era*, 12 October 1938.

25. *Hot Springs Sentinel-Record*, 27 May 1942, 8 December 1952.

26. A Wal-Mart store was later built on the dairy site (Elizabeth [King] Kallsnick, interview with author, Hot Springs, Ark., 21 April 1982).

27. Ibid.

28. *Hot Springs Sentinel-Record*, 28 February 1934.

29. Dallas T. Herndon, *Annals of Arkansas*, vol. 2 (Hopkinsville, Ky.: The Historical Record Association, 1947), 804–07. Ben King's grandfather, Leon Kingsburg, had served as a rabbi in Poland for sixty years. He emigrated to Mea Shearim, Palestine, at age 71 and continued his rabbinical duties until his death at age 102 (Kallsnick interview).

30. Kallsnick interview.

31. Maurice Cohen, interview with author, Pine Bluff, Ark., 22 April 1982; Max Cohen, interview with author, Forrest City, Ark., 22 June 1982.

32. *Hot Springs Sentinel-Record*, 11 July 1942.

33. Ibid., 8 January 1935, 10 July 1939.

34. Walter and Helen (Falk) Kleinman, telephone interview with author, Hot Springs, Ark., 12 September 1991; *Hot Springs Sentinel-Record*, 4 August 1941.

35. Lewis Goltz, interview with author, Hot Springs, Ark., 21 April 1982; Dr. Joseph L. Rosenzweig, interview with author, Hot Springs, Ark., 6 April 1982.

36. Bonnie L. Edens, "What Is Kosher?" *The Record* (Hot Springs–Garland County Historical Society Journal) 21 (1980): 88, 89.

37. Ibid., 89.

38. Frances Koppel, letter to author, 16 June 1982.

39. Troy A. Flake, son of former Coal Hill, Ark., miner, Alexander V. Flake, interview with author, Coal Hill, Ark., 16 April 1983.

40. *Fort Smith Southwest American*, 4 September 1944; *Bench and Bar of Arkansas, 1935* (n.p.: B. F. Pace Publishing Company, 1935), 111.

41. *Fort Smith Elevator*, 16 August 1901.

42. Muriel H. Wright, "Iser Nakdimen," *Chronicles of Oklahoma* 22: 3 (Autumn 1944): 366–69; *Fort Smith Tribune*, 23 April 1943.

43. Wright, "Iser Nakdimen," 369.

44. City National Bank (Fort Smith, Ark,) brochure (n.d.), 8.

45. Rae Stern, niece of Iser Nakdimen, interview with author, Oakland, Calif., 29 January 1986.

46. Herndon, *Annals of Arkansas* 4: 1704–07; *Fort Smith Tribune*, 23 April 1943.

47. According to a relative, when Hiram Nakdimen died, his son, Iser H. Nakdimen II, was quite small; Nakdimen's widow remarried and changed the son's name to Stephen and raised him as a Methodist (Joanne [Mendel] Pollock, granddaughter of I. H. Nakdimen, interview with author, Fort Smith, Ark., 18 August 1982).

48. *Fort Smith Southwest American*, 21 October 1955.

49. Yechiel Nakdimen, letter to author, 4 January 1986.

50. Eugene Feenberg, letter to Dr. E. C. Kemble, Harvard University, 4 April 1933, Eugene Feenberg Papers, courtesy Hilda Feenberg and Ben Feenberg; Ben Feenberg, letter to author, 24 May 1987.

51. Morton B. Marks Jr., interview with author, Fort Smith, Ark., 16 August 1982.

52. Simon Yaffe was married three times and had a number of children, several of whom remained in Fort Smith, Ark., and were associated with the Yaffe firm (Dorothy [Yaffe] Miller, interview with author, Fort Smith, Ark., 16 August 1983).

53. *Fort Smith Southwest American*, 13 June 1982.

54. Hugo Miller died in 1929 of an infected tooth; five days after his death, his wife, Pauline (Spiro) Miller, committed suicide. Their two young children were cared for by other family members (*Fort Smith Southwest American*, 15 June 1929, 20 June 1929; Ted and Dorothy Miller, interview with author, Fort Smith, Ark., 16 August 1983).

55. Miller interview.

56. Marks interview.

57. Ibid.

58. *Fort Smith Southwest Times Record*, 28 July 1968.

59. Marks interview.

60. Edith (Kasten) Rubin, letter to author, 7 January 1987.

61. Stephen Nosoff, "The Goal: From Russia to America," high school term paper (3 January 1973), courtesy Reba (Kasten) Nosoff, New York, N.Y.

62. Maurice Kasten, interview with author, Fort Smith, Ark., 18 August 1982.

63. Ibid.

64. *Fort Smith Times-Record,* 23 May 1922.

65. Verna Soifer, interview with author, Fort Smith, Ark., 28 April 1983.

66. Benno S. Friedman, son of Irving and Elizabeth Friedman, interview with author, Memphis, Tenn., 10 May 1983.

67. Rose Bogoslavsky, letter to author, 26 January 1986.

68. News Service press release, UofA, 11 November 1960; Dr. Joseph Rosenberg, UofA, letter to author, 23 August 1983; Dr. L. O. Warren, UofA Department of Entomology, letters to author, 26 November 1984, 4 April 1988; Dr. Barnett Sure File, Special Collections, UofA Library.

69. Mrs. Elizabeth Cane, interview with author, Siloam Springs, Ark., 30 April 1983.

70. David Y. Thomas, ed., *Arkansas and Its People,* vol. 2 (New York: American Historical Society, Inc., 1930), 674, 675.

71. Cora Pinkley-Call, *Pioneer Tales of Eureka Springs and Carroll County* (Eureka Springs, Ark.: n.p., 1930), 48.

72. Ibid.

73. Eureka Springs was one of only four cities in Arkansas to avail itself of Carnegie Library Grants. More than twenty-five hundred had been built nationwide by 1907, at which time the grant offer was closed (June Westphal and Catharine Osterhage, *A Fame Not Easily Forgotten* [Conway, Ark.: River Road Press, 1971], 155–58).

74. *Eureka Springs Fountain,* fragment, Misc. Eureka Springs newspapers, M/F File, AHC.

75. Pinkley-Call, *Pioneer Tales,* 76.

76. Michael Rankin, letter to author, 12 April 1983.

77. *Arkansas Democrat,* 29 February 1931.

78. J. Arthur "Art" Sarason, letter to author, 20 April 1982.

79. Meyer Prensky Anglicized his last name to Prentis. He became director of numerous subsidiary companies of the General Motors Corporation. One of the high points of his career was in negotiating a one-billion-dollar GM V-loan bank credit during World War II, which was the largest line for credit arranged for the war production program. He was an early supporter of brightly colored automobiles and drove an orange Cadillac in the early 1920s. His business, civic, and charitable activities were almost without number (*Who's Who in American Jewry, 1928* [New York: The Jewish Biographical Bureau, Inc., 1928], 546; *Detroit Free Press,* 15 July 1970.; Meyer Prentis, Personal Papers, Meyer Prentis File, Burton Historical Collection, Detroit, Mich., Public Library.)

80. Sarason letter.

81. Correspondence and data to author courtesy Sarason family members, 1982 through 1986.

82. Harry Sarason became a "born-again" Christian and wrote many poems about his Christian faith and love for God, which, he said, were "written by the Holy Spirit, not copyrightable by humans" (Harry Sarason, Austin, Tex., poems and data to author, 1982–85)

83. Nosoff, "The Goal"; Sarah Kasten and son Maurice Kasten, interview with

author, Fort Smith, Ark., 18 August 1982; Reba (Kasten) Nosoff, interview with author, Fort Smith, Ark., 15 August 1991

84. Rose (Sherman) Weinberger, interview with author, Fort Smith, Ark., 17 August 1982; *Fort Smith Southwest Times-Record*, 25 June 1978, 7 February 1982; *Arkansas Democrat*, 10 February 1986, 9 April 1986.

CHAPTER 13
The Arkansas "Kehillah," 1930s

1. One other state, North Carolina, established an association similar to the Arkansas Jewish Assembly. The North Carolina Association of Jewish Women was formed in January 1921 under the leadership of Mrs. Sol Weil of Goldsboro, N.C. Its original purpose was to draw together North Carolina's Jewish women from Judaism's various branches. The Association later included male membership, and its name was changed to reflect this. Its projects included a traveling library, a circuit rabbi, and the Blumenthal Jewish Home at Clemmons, N.C. The Association continued into the 1990s. Emma R. Edwards, "History of the North Carolina Association of Jewish Women," paper presented at the 1942 North Carolina Association of Jewish Women Conference; Hilda Wallerstein of Greensboro, N.C., interview with author, Savannah, Ga., 3 December 1983; Morris Speizman, letter to author, 18 November 1983.

2. Financial data from John L. Ferguson and J. H. Atkinson, *Historic Arkansas* (Little Rock: AHC, 1966), 294, 295.

3. Ibid., 299.

4. Rabbi A. B. Rhine, "The Why of the Arkansas Jewish Assembly," *Arkansas Assembly Bulletin* 11 (December 1941): 4.

5. Ibid.

6. Rabbi Ira E. Sanders, interview with author, Little Rock, Ark., 23 March 1983.

7. Arkansas Jewish Assembly Convention Minutes, 24 April 1932, unpublished papers, BIA (hereafter cited as Convention Minutes).

8. "Assembly Constitution," Convention Minutes, 23 April 1933.

9. Convention Minutes, 24 April 1932.

10. Convention Minutes, 23 April 1933.

11. William Rosenzweig, letter to Rabbi Teitelbaum, 8 August 1934; Convention Minutes, 24 April 1938.

12. Arkansas Jewish Assembly Board Minutes, 7 October 1934, unpublished papers, BIA (hereafter cited as Board Minutes).

13. *Arkansas Assembly Bulletin* 4 (September 1938): 1.

14. Rabbi Teitelbaum, letter to Cyrus Adler, 4 April 1934. (In 1950 Rabbi Martin M. Weitz of Hot Springs quoted an Assembly census as showing there were eight thousand Jews in Arkansas. This evidently was a misprint, for no Assembly records show more than three thousand, with an estimated one thousand not counted. Rabbi Weitz also said that the number of Arkansas Jews given in the *American Jewish Year Book* 1947–48 (Philadelphia: American Jewish com-

mittee, 1948), listed at 6,510, was "probably inaccurate" [Rabbi Martin M. Weitz, *Diamond Jubilee Bibilog . . . Temple Beth Israel, May, 1950* (Hot Springs, Ark.: n.p., 1950), 10].)

15. Sanders interview.

16. Contribution cards of Arkansas donors to the Jewish Children's Home, New Orleans, La., 1918–77, courtesy Mrs. Viola Weiss.

17. I. J. Friedman, "A Challenge to Arkansas Jewry," *Arkansas Assembly Bulletin* 4 (September 1938): 2.

18. John L. Ferguson and J. H. Atkinson, *Historic Arkansas* (Little Rock: AHC, 1966), 342–45.

19. Convention Minutes, 1932; I. J. Friedman, letter to Rabbi A. B. Rhine, 11 November 1932, BIA; Rabbi Teitelbaum, letter to Mrs. Jesse Heiman, 18 December 1934, BIA; Rabbi Teitelbaum, letter to Rabbi Rhine, 26 April 1938, BIA.

20. I. J. Friedman, letter to Rabbi Sanders, 15 March 1933, BIA.

21. Rabbi Carl Miller, letter to Rabbi Teitelbaum, 7 March 1935, BIA; Leo Rosten, *The Joys of Yiddish* (New York: Pocket Books, 1968), 14.

22. Mrs. Ora P. Nix, interview with author, Little Rock, Ark., 9 March 1982.

23. *Arkansas Gazette*, 23 April 1935.

24. Nix interview.

25. *Arkansas Gazette*, 25 June 1934.

26. Nix interview.

27. Mrs. Herbert (Gertrude) Latkin of Santa Barbara, Calif., interview with author, Little Rock, Ark., 16 April 1982.

28. Joe Tenenbaum, interview with author, Little Rock, Ark., 12 December 1981.

29. *Arkansas Democrat*, 4 November 1930; Sanders interview.

30. Eula Spivey, letter to Temple B'nai Israel's Men's Club, 13 April 1952, BIA.

31. Ira E. Sanders and Elijah E. Palnick, comps. and eds., *One Hundred Years, Congregation B'nai Israel 1866–1966* (Little Rock: n.p., 1966), 50.

32. Convention Minutes, 23 April 1933, BIA.

33. Convention Minutes, 24 April 1938, BIA.

34. Rabbi Teitelbaum, letter to Rabbi Joseph Shapiro, 14 March 1935, BIA.

35. Rabbi Shapiro, letter to Rabbi Teitelbaum, 19 March 1935, BIA.

36. Sanders interview.

37. Convention Minutes, 1932.

38. Bernard H. Barnett, letter to Rabbi Teitelbaum, 6 August 1934, BIA (Barnett was president of the Southern Jewish Youth Assembly at the time).

39. Sam Shuman, letter to Rabbi Teitelbaum, 12 October 1937; Board Minutes, 3 April 1938; Convention Minutes, 1938. (Little Rock's Congregation B'nai Israel had organized its own Junior Congregation in 1929 [Sanders and Palnick, *One Hundred Years*, 50].)

40. Rabbi Teitelbaum, letter to author, 17 May 1983.

41. *Arkansas Assembly Bulletin* 2 (January 1938).

42. Daisy Phillips, letter to Frances Grossel, Menorah Association of New York, 5 July 1928, Menorah Association of New York correspondence with Menorah Chapter, Fayetteville, Ark., MSS Col #2, 68/10, File 2767, University of Arkansas, 1928–1929, AJA.

43. Oscar Fendler, letter to Frances Grossel, Menorah Association of New York, 4 March 1929, Menorah Association of New York correspondence with Menorah Chapter, Fayetteville, Ark., MSS Col #268/10, File 2767, University of Arkansas, 1928–29, AJA.

44. Oscar Fendler to Frances Grossel, Menorah Association of New York, 20 May 1929, Menorah Association of New York correspondence with Menorah Chapter, Fayetteville, Ark., MSS Col #268/10, File 2767, University of Arkansas, 1928–29, AJA.

45. Rabbi Samuel Teitelbaum, "The Hillel Society of the University of Arkansas," *Arkansas News Bulletin* 2 (January 1938).

46. *Arkansas Assembly Bulletin* 2 (January 1938).

47. Ibid.

48. Handwritten speech delivered by unknown Hillel member, 1938, Assembly Papers, BIA.

49. Louis Cohen followed Rabbi Rhine as Assembly president. Other presidents during the 1930s were Mrs. Jesse Heiman, 1935; Dr. L. J. Kosminsky, 1936; H. B. Solmson Sr., 1937; Mrs. W. E. Marks, 1938; and I. J. Friedman, 1939.

50. Dallas T. Herndon, *Centennial History of Arkansas,* vol. 2 (Chicago–Little Rock: The S. J. Clarke Publishing Company, 1922), 396.

51. Ibid.; *Sebastian County News,* 14 February 1939.

52. Marie (Cohen) Storthz, interview with author, Little Rock, Ark., 10 August 1982.

53. Rabbi Teitelbaum, letter to Sam Levine, Pine Bluff attorney, 23 October 1934, BIA.

54. Harold Schwartz, letter to Rabbi Teitelbaum, 21 January 1935, BIA.

55. Rabbi David Max Eichhorn, letter to Rabbi Teitelbaum, 2 December 1936, BIA.

56. Rabbi Teitelbaum, letter to Abram Sachar, 5 October 1937, BIA.

57. Rabbi Teitelbaum, letter to I. Miller, president of B'nai B'rith Lodge, Blytheville, Ark., 2 November 1937, BIA.

58. Convention Minutes, 5 April 1937.

59. Samuel B. Schleifer, letter to Rabbi Teitelbaum, 26 October 1937, BIA.

60. Handwritten speech delivered by unknown Hillel member, 1938, Assembly Papers, BIA.

61. Board Minutes, 11 February 1934.

62. *Arkansas Assembly Bulletin* 4 (September 1938).

63. Rabbi Carl Miller, letter to Rabbi Teitelbaum, 28 March 1935; Board Minutes, Little Rock, 3 February 1935.

64. Convention Minutes, 25 April 1936; "Dedication Services of the New Temple Israel, Blytheville, Arkansas," 7 September 1947, TIAB.

65. Board Minutes, 22 November 1936.

66. Rabbi Morris Clark, *My Scrapbook* (self-published, ca. 1958), 69.

67. Board Minutes, 2 December 1936.

68. Convention Minutes, 4 April 1937.

69. *Camden News,* 4 January 1950.

70. Board Meeting, 3 October 1937.

71. Board Meeting, 2 April 1938.

72. Convention Minutes, 24 April 1938.

73. *Arkansas Gazette*, 30 October 1938.

74. *Camden News*, 4 January 1950.

75. Information from B'nai B'rith International Archives, Washington, D.C.

76. Convention Minutes, 15 April 1934.

77. Arkansas Jewish Assembly Report, 1 March 1937, BIA.

78. Board Minutes, 3 October 1937.

79. Rabbi Miller, letter to Rabbi Teitelbaum, 1 June 1934, BIA.

80. Oscar Leonard, letter to Rabbi Teitelbaum, 3 October 1934, BIA.

81. Board Minutes, 3 February 1935.

82. Rufus Learsi, *The Jews in America: A History* (New York: KTAV Publishing House, Inc., 1972), 212–13, 260–64, 316.

83. Board Minutes, 5 April 1935; Convention Minutes, 7 May 1935.

84. Rabbi Teitelbaum, letter to Stephen S. Wise, 16 April 1935, BIA.

85. Convention Minutes, 26 April 1936.

86. Rabbi Clark, letter to Rabbi Teitelbaum, 23 February 1938, BIA.

87. Board Minutes, 11 February 1934.

88. Rabbi Eichhorn, letter to Rabbi Teitelbaum, 3 November 1937, BIA.

89. Board Minutes, 13 November 1938.

90. *Arkansas Assembly Bulletin* 8 (November 1939).

91. Convention Minutes, 23 April 1933.

92. Convention Minutes, 15 April 1934.

93. Sanders interview.

94. Ibid.; *Arkansas Democrat*, 16 May 1974.

95. Rabbi Ira E. Sanders Papers, BIA.

96. Sanders interview.

97. Convention Minutes, 7 April 1935.

98. *Assembly Blah!* (6 April 1935), BIA.

99. Board Minutes, 9 June 1935.

100. Convention Minutes, 26 April 1936.

101. Rabbi David Max Eichhorn, leader of Texarkana's Mt. Sinai Congregation 1935–38, letter to author, 2 March 1983; *Texarkana Democrat*, 6 March 1937.

102. Eichhorn letter; *Texarkana Democrat*, 6 March 1937.

103. Paul D. Haynie, "Religion and Morals at the University of Arkansas in the 1920s," *AHQ* 45: 2 (1986): 164. Mannie Riesenberg, letter to Rabbi Teitelbaum, 8 November 1937, BIA.

104. Rabbi Teitelbaum, letter to Max Schwartz, 6 November 1937, BIA; Rabbi Teitelbaum, letter to Rabbi Miller, 15 November 1937, BIA.

105. Sidney Faden, Chancellor of Tau Kappa Chapter of Tau Epsilon Phi Fraternity, Fayetteville, Ark., letter to Rabbi Teitelbaum, 8 November 1937, BIA.

106. Rabbi Teitelbaum, letter to Sidney Faden and Mannie Riesenberg, Fayetteville, Ark., 22 November 1937, BIA.

107. *Arkansas Assembly Bulletin* 4 (September 1938).

108. Ibid.

109. Convention Minutes, 24 April 1938.

110. Ibid.

111. Ibid.

112. *Arkansas Assembly Bulletin* 4 (September 1938): 1.

113. Clark, *My Scrapbook,* 93.

114. Arthur D. Morse, *While Six Million Died: A Chronicle of American Apathy* (New York: Random House, Inc., 1968), 232.

115. Ibid., 230–50.

116. Sanders and Palnick, *One Hundred Years,* 54.

117. Ibid.

118. *Arkansas Gazette,* 30 October 1938.

119. Harry B. Solmson Jr., interview with author, Memphis, Tenn., 9 May 1983.

120. H. B. Solmson Sr., letter to Rabbi Teitelbaum, 22 November 1934; Board Minutes, 13 October 1935.

121. Undesignated newspaper article (full citation unavailable), 21 October 1933, Solmson family papers, courtesy Harry B. Solmson Jr., Memphis, Tenn.

122. Ibid.; Solmson interview.

123. Board Minutes, 13 November 1938.

124. *Arkansas Assembly Bulletin* 4 (September 1938).

CHAPTER 14

World War II—the Perspective Changes, 1940s

1. Arkansas Jewish Assembly Board Minutes, 7 December 1940, 3 April 1938, unpublished papers, BIA (hereafter cited as Board Minutes); Rabbi Teitelbaum, letter to Herbert Weil, 21 April 1938, BIA; *Arkansas Gazette,* 15 January 1940.

2. *Arkansas Assembly Bulletin* 10 (December 1940).

3. Isabel Lappin, "A Junior Writes," *Arkansas Assembly Bulletin* 8 (November 1939): 3.

4. *Arkansas Assembly Bulletin* 10 (December 1940).

5. Board Minutes, 7 December 1940.

6. *Arkansas Assembly Bulletin* 14 (November 1948).

7. *Arkansas Gazette,* 27 October 1982.

8. Arkansas Jewish Assembly Records, BIA; Mrs. Simon (Janice Abramson) Feldman and Ralph Abramson, interview with author, Holly Grove, Ark., 12 May 1984.

9. *Arkansas Gazette,* 10 August 1941.

10. Arkansas Jewish Assembly Convention Minutes, 7 December 1941, unpublished papers, BIA (hereafter cited as Convention Minutes).

11. Board Minutes, 17 December 1940.

12. Charles Dante Papers, courtesy Bernard J. "Jerry" Tanenbaum Jr., Dumas, Ark.

13. Harry Phillips, interview with author, Dumas, Ark., 7 May 1982.

14. Herbert Frenkel, interview with author, Conway, Ark., 11 August 1982.

15. Morton B. Marks Jr., interview with author, Fort Smith, Ark., 17 August 1982; *Arkansas Assembly Bulletin* 11 (December 1941).

16. *Arkansas Business* 3 (28 April–11 May 1986).

17. "State of Israel Bonds Tribute to Eric Nussbaum" (given at State of Israel Bonds Dinner, Synagogue Agudath Achim, Little Rock, Ark., 17 November 1991).

18. Louis Rhein, interview with author, Little Rock, Ark., 2 May 1984.

19. Mr. and Mrs. Joseph Spitzer, interview with author, Hot Springs, Ark., 21 April 1982; Mr. and Mrs. Abraham Jacubowicz, interview with author, Little Rock, Ark., 2 December 1985.

20. Rabbi Ira E. Sanders, interview with author, Little Rock, Ark., 25 March 1983.

21. Morton B. Marks Jr., interview with author, Fort Smith, Ark., 16 August 1982; Mrs. James Kempner (Assembly president in 1941), telephone interview with author, Little Rock, Ark., 17 May 1990; Dr. Maurice Friedman, interview with author, Little Rock, Ark., 1 March 1984; David Solomon, interview with author, Helena, Ark., 1 July 1982, Lewis Goltz, interview with author, Hot Springs, Ark., 21 April 1982; interviews with other former Assembly members.

22. *Arkansas Assembly Bulletin* 10 (December 1940).

23. Simon "Sammy" Feldman, letter to Lewis Goltz, 8 October 1942, BIA.

24. Louis Cohen, letter to Lewis Goltz, 22 October 22, BIA.

25. According to records of the Jewish War Veterans, U.S.A. National Memorial, Inc., Washington, D.C. (whose records of Jewish servicemen in World War II is incomplete); World War II data courtesy Jewish congregations of Arkansas.

26. Mrs. Herbert (Gertrude) Latkin of Santa Barbara, Calif., interview with author, Little Rock, Ark., 16 April 1982.

27. Sanders interview.

28. Latkin interview.

29. Ibid.; Harry Solmson Jr., letter to author, 13 October 1990.

30. *Arkansas Assembly Bulletin* (December 1940–December 1950).

31. For a history of Hadassah, the world's largest single Zionist organization, see Marlin Levin, *Balm in Gilead, The Story of Hadassah* (New York: Schocken Books, 1973).

32. Isadore Scrinopski, "Short History of the Scrinopski Family," courtesy Isadore Scrinopski; Sanders interview.

33. Hadassah Papers, Little Rock, Ark.

34. Eli N. Evans, *The Provincials: A Personal History of Jews in the South* (New York: Atheneum, 1976), 101.

35. Sanders interview.

36. When the Jewish Federation of Little Rock began holding an annual Holocaust memorial in the 1980s, Nathan Steppach was often called upon to read this letter as a reminder of the catastrophe from a firsthand witness.

37. Simon Feldman, letter to Max Wexler, 3 April 1946, BIA; Charles Dante, letter to Simon Feldman, 5 April 1946, BIA; Siegbert Jiedel, letter to Simon Feldman, 7 April 1946, BIA.

38. Edith R. Lerner, Directory Coordinator, Union of American Hebrew Congregations, letter to author, 31 January 1986.

39. Bill Borowsky, letter to Siegbert Jiedel, 8 September 1947, TIA.

40. "Dedication Services of the New Temple Israel, Blytheville, Arkansas," 7 September 1947, TIAB.

41. *Arkansas Assembly Bulletin* 16 (April 1950): 7.

42. E. M. Dreidel, "Temple Meir Chayim: A Century-Old Need," *Programs of the Desha County Historical Society* (Spring 1978): 29–35.

43. Marjorie M. Miron (daughter of J. B. Miller), letters to author, March and October, 1986; Joe and Janet Stuart, interview with author, El Dorado, Ark., 29 October 1982.

44. Convention Minutes, 27 October 1946.

45. Ibid.

46. Ibid.

47. Rufus Learsi, *The Jews in America: A History* (New York: KTAV Publishing House, Inc., 1972), 316.

48. Samuel Rothstein, chairman, Committee on Elections, American Jewish Conference, letter to Mrs. Simon Feldman, 24 October 1947, BIA; *Arkansas Assembly Bulletin* 13 (January 1948).

49. From an article that appeared in an Osceola, Ark., newspaper quoting the mayor of that city and reprinted in *Arkansas Assembly Bulletin* 14 (November 1948).

50. *Arkansas Assembly Bulletin* 16 (April 1950).

51. Ibid.

52. *Arkansas Assembly Bulletin* 14 (November 1948).

53. Ibid.

54. *Arkansas Assembly Bulletin* 9 (November 1939); *Arkansas Assembly Bulletin* 12 (October 1946).

55. Board Minutes, 23 January 1949.

56. *Arkansas Assembly Bulletin* 12 (October 1946): 5.

57. Rabbi H. Cerf Strauss, "A Warning Signal," *Arkansas Assembly Bulletin* 13 (January 1948): 3.

58. *Arkansas Assembly Bulletin* 13 (January 1948).

59. *Arkansas Assembly Bulletin* 17 (November–December 1950).

60. Ibid.

61. *Arkansas Assembly Bulletin* 16 (April 1950).

62. *Arkansas Assembly Bulletin* 17 (November–December 1950).

63. Ibid.

64. *Hot Springs Sentinel-Record*, 19 May 1951; Peggy Botnick, widow of Jack Botnick, telephone interview with author, Dallas, Tex., 8 April 1984.

65. *Arkansas Assembly Bulletin* 17 (November–December 1950).

66. Interviews or correspondence by author with Rabbis Sanders, Teitelbaum, Eichhorn, and Weitz, and laymen Dr. Maurice J. Friedman, Ralph Brody, Morton B. Marks Jr., Mrs. James Kempner, David Solomon Jr., Lewis Goltz, et al.

67. *Arkansas Assembly Bulletin* 17 (November–December 1950).

68.: Ibid., 2.

Section V Introduction

1. John L. Ferguson and J. H. Atkinson, *Historic Arkansas* (Little Rock: AHC, 1966), 303.

2. U.S. Bureau of the Census, *1980 Census of Agriculture*, vol. 1, no. 4, *Arkansas State and County Data* (Washington, D.C.: Government Printing Office, 1987), 15.

3. Ferguson and Atkinson, *Historic Arkansas*, 303.

4. Ibid., 304-06.

5. Ibid., 345.

6. *Road and Street Mileages* (Little Rock: Arkansas State Highway and Transportation Department Planning and Research Division, 1991).

7. Max I. Dimont, *The Jews in America* (New York: Simon & Schuster, 1978), 166.

8. When Edna Eilbott of Pine Bluff married non-Jew C. B. Blanks, a local paper noted that it was "no ordinary romance" since one party was a Jew and the other a Gentile, and when Clifton Dreyfus married non-Jew Edith Stewart, it was a "chief topic of conversation" at the time (*Pine Bluff Daily Graphic*, 18 October 1901, 20 October 1901, 3 December 1901; *Arkansas Democrat*, 3 December 1901).

CHAPTER 15
Congregational Histories

1. *Arkansas Gazette*, Sunday magazine, 8 May 1955.

2. "B'nai Israel's Quarter Century Celebration," 14 September1984, BIA.

3. Rabbi Ira E. Sanders, interview with author, Little Rock, Ark., 25 March 1983.

4. Irving J. Spitzberg Jr., *Racial Politics in Little Rock: 1954–1964* (New York: Garland Publishing Company, 1987), 151.

5. Rabbi Elijah E. Palnick, interview with author, Little Rock, 18 March 1982; Rabbi Elijah E. Palnick Papers, courtesy Rabbi Elijah E. Polnick.

6. Letters file, BIA.

7. Jana Jacobson, "A Look at the Temple's New Rabbi: Rabbi Eugene Levy," *ACTION* (Publication of the Jewish Federation of Little Rock, Ark.) 11 (Summer 1987): 1.

8. Rabbi Palnick interview.

9. Charles Elias, letter to author, 11 May 1992.

10. "Our Dreams Fulfilled" (Dedication Program of Agudath Achim, Little Rock, April–May 1976), 4. (When writing the name of God, the Orthodox traditionally omit the letter "o.")

11. Eric Nussbaum, letter to author, 11 May 1992.

12. *ACTION* (Publication of the Jewish Federation of Little Rock, Ark.) 14 (Spring 1990): 2.

13. Ibid., 12 (Winter 1988): 2.

14. The Hasidic movement began in Eastern Europe with Rabbi Israel Baal Shem Tov ("Master of the Divine Name") (1700–1760). Some of its features were inwardness, joyful awareness of God in nature, exultation, and the acceptance of menial tasks of life as divine challenges (Leo Trepp, *A History of the Jewish Experience* [New York: Behrman House, Inc., 1973], 247–59, 356–61; see also, Edward Hoffman, *Despite All Odds* [New York: Simon & Schuster, 1991]; Naftali Loewenthal, *Communicating the Infinite: The Emergence of the Chabad School* [Chicago: University of Chicago Press, 1990]).

15. James W. Leslie, "History of Congregation Anshe Emeth, 1867–1977," Anshe Emeth Archives, Pine Bluff, Ark.; Selma Golden, letter to author, 9 May 1992.

16. Golden letter; Selma Golden, telephone call to author.

17. Data on Helena's Beth El Congregation, courtesy David and Miriam Solomon, Helena, Ark.

18. Cited by Rufus Learsi, *The Jews in America: A History* (New York: KTAV Publishing House, Inc., 1972), 31.

19. *Camden News*, 29 December 1989.

20. Data on Beth Israel Congregation, El Dorado, Ark., courtesy Joe and Janet Stuart, El Dorado, Ark., and Mrs. Si (Marjorie Miller) Miron, Lake Jackson, Tex.

21. Mrs. Joseph Rosenzweig, "House of Israel," *The Record* (1970 Year Book of the Hot Springs–Garland County Historical Society) 11 (1970): 67, 68.

22. Dr. and Mrs. J. L. Rosenberg, letter to author, 28 September 1991.

23. Eugene "Gene" Kirsch, interview with author, Hot Springs, Ark., 5 April 1982.

24. For a history of Leo N. Levi Hospital, see Dale E. Wagoner, *Levi Arthritis Hospital: More Lasting Than Marble Or Stone* (Hot Springs, Ark.: Levi Hospital, 1984).

25. Minutes of Texarkana American Legion Posts 25–58, 16 November 1971, Texarkana—Mt. Sinai Folder, Congregation—Misc. File, AJA.

26. Barbara Glick, ed., *Centennial Journal of Mount Sinai Congregation, 1885–1985* (Texarkana, Ark.: n.p., 1985), 30.

27. Ibid., 23, 24.

28. Data on Texarkana's Mt. Sinai Congregation courtesy Ralph and Billie Brody, Texarkana, Ark.

29. All data on UHC of Fort Smith courtesy Morton B. Marks Jr., Fort Smith, Ark.

30. *Fort Smith Southwest American*, 30 April 1956.

31. Data on Temple Israel are taken from TIAJ.

32. The interviewee asked that her name be kept confidential.

33. Barbara Weinstock, letter to author, 7 October 1991.

34. "Memoriam to Dr. Alfred Vise," (Blytheville Air Force Base Program, 1957), TIAB.

35. "Silver Anniversary Program, Congregation Temple Israel, Blytheville, Arkansas, 1947–1972," TIAB.

36. Ibid.

37. Oscar Fendler, letter to author, 20 July 1987.

38. "Silver Anniversary Program, Temple Israel."

39. E. M. "Mannie" Dreidel, letter to author, 27 December 1985.

40. Data on McGehee's Meir Chayim Congregation courtesy Mrs. Elsie Phillips, Dumas, Ark.

41. Data on Temple Shalom and the Fayetteville Jewish community courtesy Dr. Wilma Sacks and Mrs. Jay (Faye) Lewis, Fayetteville, Ark., 28–30 April 1983.

42. *The Razorback Hillel Newsletter* 1 (Fall 1989).

43. *ACTION* (Publication of the Jewish Federation of Little Rock, Ark.) 14 (Spring 1990): 6.

CHAPTER 16
Central Arkansas

1. *Arkansas Gazette*, 23 May 1947.

2. *Arkansas Gazette*, 29 July 1960.

3. Arthur Phillips, interview with author, Little Rock, Ark., 9 December 1981.

4. *Arkansas Gazette*, 29 July 1960.

5. Copy of Rabbi Sanders speech to the state legislature, 18 February 1957, courtesy Rabbi Ira E. Sanders; Correspondence to Rabbi Sanders, 1957, Rabbi Ira E. Sanders Papers, BIA.

6. The four bills were: HB 322, which would create a state sovereignty commission with many duties " . . . necessary to protect the sovereignty of Arkansas and other states from encroachments by the Federal government"—this became Act 83 and was later repealed; HB 323, which "would make attendance noncompulsory in integrated schools"—this became Act 84 and was later superseded; HB 324, which "would require persons and organizations engaged in certain activities to register with the state and make regular reports of their income and expenses" (it would apply particularly to the National Association for the Advancement of Colored People)—this became Act 85 and was later repealed; and HB 325, which "would allow school boards to use school money to hire lawyers" for integration suits—this became Act 86 and remains as part of Arkansas law. (*Arkansas Gazette*, 18 February 1957, 19 February 1957, 27 February 1957; *Arkansas Code of 1987 Annotated*, Tables [Charlottesville, Va.: Michie Company, 1987], 260; *Arkansas Code of 1987 Annotated*, vol. 4, title 6 [Charlottesville, Va.: Michie Company, 1987], 271–86.)

7. *Arkansas Democrat*, 4 October 1957; *New York Times*, 4 October 1957.

8. *Arkansas Democrat*, 13 October 1957.

9. Rabbi Ira E. Sanders, interview with author, Little Rock, Ark., 25 March 1983.

10. Tony Freyer, *The Little Rock Crisis: A Constitutional Interpretation* (Westport, Conn.: Greenwood Press, 1984), 46.

11. Rabbi Ira E. Sanders, "The Journal of a Southern Rabbi," courtesy Rabbi Ira E. Sanders.

12. Irving J. Spitzberg Jr., *Racial Politics in Little Rock: 1954–1964* (New York: Garland Publishing Company, 1987), 21.

13. Irene Samuel, telephone interview with author, Little Rock, Ark., 11 October 1991.

14. Spitzberg, *Racial Politics in Little Rock*, 16–19, 111–12.

15. Elijah E. Palnick, "Southern Jewry and Civil Rights," *CCAR Journal* 13 (June 1965): 62.

16. Spitzberg, *Racial Politics in Little Rock*, 93.

17. Ibid., 93–94.

18. Samuel interview.

19. Patrick J. Owens, "The Gentleman Rebel," *ADL Bulletin* (September 1965): 7.

20. Ibid.

21. Samuel interview; Spitzberg, *Racial Politics in Little Rock*, 153–54.

22. *Arkansas Gazette*, 3 July 1983, 1 June 1986; *ACTION* (Publication of the Jewish Federation of Little Rock, Ark.) 10 (Winter 1986); Jane Mendel, telephone interview with author, Little Rock, Ark., 11 October 1991.

23. Shimon Weber, "How Has the School Conflict Affected the Jews in Little Rock?" *Jewish Daily Forward,* 19 October 1957.

24. Sam B. Strauss Sr., interview with author, Little Rock, Ark., 16 September 1983; Fay Williams, *Arkansans of the Years*, vol. 1 (Little Rock: C. C. Allard & Associates, Publishers, 1952–54), 374–79.

25. *Arkansas Gazette*, 25 November 1990.

26. *Arkansas Democrat*, 21 January 1964; *Arkansas Gazette*, 6 January 1977.

27. *Arkansas Gazette*, 10 April 1962, 9 September 1962.

28. Jay Friedlander, "M. M. Cohn CEO: a Soft-spoken Man of Many Interests," *Arkansas Business* 2 (8 July–21 July 1985): 12–14.

29. Ibid.

30. Arnold and Janet (Grundfest) Mayersohn, interview with author, Little Rock, Ark., 24 April 1985; John L. Ferguson, *Arkansas Lives: The Opportunity Land Who's Who* (Hopkinsville, Ky.: Historical Record Association, 1965), 202; Chester C. Allard, comp., Bessie Butler Newsom Allard, ed., *Arkansans of the Year*, vol. 5, *Who is Who in Arkansas*, vol. 1 (Little Rock: Allard House Publishers, 1959), 119, 120.

31. *Arkansas Democrat*, magazine section, 27 January 1952.

32. *Arkansas Gazette*, 22 February 1957.

33. *Arkansas Democrat*, "Profile," 16 February 1986.

34. *Arkansas Gazette*, 25 November 1984.

35. *Arkansas Gazette*, 26 April 1987; *Arkansas Democrat-Gazette*, 12 January 1992.

36. *Quapaw Quarter Chronicle* (Little Rock) 15 (October–November 1988): 1.

37. Eugene M. Pfeifer Jr., interview with author, North Little Rock, Ark., 27 July 1982.

38. *Arkansas Business* 7 (19 November 1990): 17; *Arkansas Democrat-Gazette,* 29 February 1992.

39. *Arkansas Gazette*, 3 August 1985.

40. *Arkansas Democrat*, 20 April 1986; *Arkansas Gazette*, 27 April 1986.

41. Charles Elias, letter to author, 6 February 1992; *Arkansas Democrat*, 18 May 1958.

42. Charles E. Joseph, interview with author, Little Rock, Ark., 21 February 1992.

43. David Goldberg, telephone interview with author, Little Rock, Ark., 28 September 1991; Dan Schwartz, telephone interview with author, Little Rock, Ark., 28 September 1991.

44. Louis Snyderman, interview with author, Little Rock, Ark., 13 March 1984.

45. F. Williams, *Arkansans* 3: 236–45; *Arkansas Gazette*, 22 October 1980.

46. Selwyn and Rose Loeb, telephone interview with author, Little Rock, Ark., 7 August 1991.

47. *Arkansas Gazette*, 20 October 1970; Dorothy Goldberg, interview with author, Little Rock, Ark., 29 July 1982.

48. Little Rock Police Department detective Gray LeMaster, interview with author, Little Rock, Ark., 13 April 1987.

49. *Arkansas Business* 8 (7 January 1991): 20.

50. George Brown of Little Rock, Ark., and Scott, Ark., interview with author, North Little Rock, Ark., 4 April 1983.

51. *Arkansas Democrat*, 18 July 1984.

52. Adele Sanders and Jennie (Sanders) Loket, interview with author, Little Rock, Ark., 9 March 1983; *Arkansas Gazette*, 21 June 1972.

53. *Arkansas Business* 3 (28 April–11 May 1986): 12–15; *Arkansas Business* 8 (4 March 1991): 22, 23.

54. Sam Storthz Jr., interview with author, Little Rock, Ark., 2 August 1982.

55. *Arkansas Gazette*, 7 December 1976; Partners in the AMR firm in 1991 were Moses, John Allison, Rick Reddin, and Jim Nosari (James "Jim" Moses Jr., telephone interview with author, Little Rock, Ark., 15 November 1991).

56. *Arkansas Gazette*, 26 March 1985.

57. Louis Rhein, interview with author, Little Rock, Ark., 2 May 1984. Liane "Lee" (Rhein) Humble, telephone interview with author, Little Rock, Ark., 25 May 1993; Liane "Lee" (Rhein) Humble, data to author 27 May 1993.

58. *Arkansas Gazette*, 8 October 1978.

59. *Arkansas Gazette*, 24 January 1984.

60. *Arkansas Gazette*, 14 June 1987.

61. Bob Wimberly, telephone interview with author, Little Rock, Ark., 18 September 1991.

62. Robert Brooks, who established the Brooks-Pollard company in 1915, was not related to Sidney M. Brooks, and there was no connection between the two companies (Wimberly interview).

63. *Arkansas Gazette*, 26 April 1987.

64. *Arkansas Democrat-Gazette*, "High Profile Section," 16 February 1992.

65. *Arkansas Gazette*, 8 April 1985.

66. *Arkansas Gazette*, 29 September 1959; H. F. Barnes, ed., Lex B. Davis, compl, *Among Arkansas Leaders* (Little Rock: Lex B. Davis, 1934), 43; Gus "Buddy" Shrader, telephone interview with author, Little Rock, Ark., 6 August 1991.

67. Ferguson, *Arkansas Lives*, 318; *Arkansas Gazette*, 17 September 1978, 17 August 1985; C. Allard, and B. Allard, *Who Is Who in Arkansas* 1: 160.

68. Ferguson, *Arkansas Lives*, 283; *Arkansas Gazette*, 7 August 1986; Jerry Russell and Bessie Butler Newsom Allard, comps., *Arkansans of the Years*, vol. 6, *Who is Who in Arkansas*, vol. 2 (Little Rock: Allard House Publishers, 1968), 146.

69. *Arkansas Gazette*, 8 May 1989.

70. Dr. Benjamin Saltzman, interview with author, Little Rock, Ark., 1 March 1984.

71. *Arkansas Gazette*, 19 September 1982.

72. Dr. Maurice J. Friedman, interview with author, Little Rock, Ark., 1 March 1984.

73. *Arkansas Democrat*, 14 August 1987.

74. *Arkansas Gazette*, 4 May 1974; "In Memoriam—A. Allen Weintraub," *Comment & Commentary*, St. Vincent's Infirmary, Little Rock, Ark.; publication) 1 (Spring 1974).

75. Ibid.

76. Lisa Fitzhugh, General Registry, CARTI, letter to author, 11 October 1991.

77. *Arkansas Gazette*, 29 September 1972.

78. Marion "Mooch" Safferstone, interview with author, Little Rock, Ark., 10 March 1983.

79. *Arkansas Democrat*, 2 September 1990.

80. Louis Rosen, interview with author, Little Rock, Ark., 18 February 1983.

81. *Arkansas Gazette*, 18 September 1969.

82. Noland Blass Jr., interview with author, Little Rock, Ark., 4 September 1985; *Arkansas Democrat-Gazette*, "High Profile Section," 17 November 1991.

83. Data from UAMS nomination of Betsy Blass for the USA Volunteer of the Year award, 1991, courtesy Noland Blass Jr.

84. *Arkansas Democrat*, "Profile Section," 25 October 1987.

85. *Arkansas Gazette*, 18 November 1984.

86. *Arkansas Gazette*, 23 October 1979.

87. Harry B. Solmson Jr., letter to author, 24 August 1984; *Arkansas Gazette*, 5 May 1985.

88. *Arkansas Democrat*, 8 August 1988.

89. *Arkansas Democrat*, 11 June 1990.

90. Mark Lipman, interview with author, Memphis, Tenn., 12 May 1983; Belle Lipman, interview with author, Memphis, Tenn., 12 May 1983; Ira A. Lipman, interview with author, Memphis, Tenn., 13 May 1983; Current data (1991)on Ira Lipman and Guardsmark, Inc., courtesy Ira A. Lipman, 16 September 1991; *Memphis Commercial Appeal*, 4 May 1982.

91. Mark Lipman, *Stealing* (New York: Harper's Magazine Press, 1973).

92. *U.S. News & World Report* 100 (26 May 1986): 36; *Arkansas Gazette*, 26 November 1989.

93. Sol Thalheimer Jr., interview with author, 14 March 1985.

94. *Arkansas Gazette*, 26 November 1989.

95. *Arkansas Democrat*, 31 March 1991.

CHAPTER 17
Eastern Arkansas

1. Marty Buchman, interview with author, Paragould, Ark., 11 November 1982.

2. Reba Stallcup, interview with author, Paragould, Ark., 11 November 1982.

3. Mrs. Jesse Banks, telephone interview with author, Jonesboro, Ark., 2 October 1991.

4. Sadie Schoenfield, interview with author, Jonesboro, Ark., 8 November 1982.

5. Mercantile Bank of Jonesboro brochure, TIAJ; *Arkansas Gazette*, 10 April 1943; *Jonesboro Daily Tribune*, Special Edition, 26 October 1937.

6. Hazel J. Deutsch, interview with author, Jonesboro, Ark., 10 November 1982.

7. Guy "Cotton" Rubenstein, interview with author, Memphis, Tenn., 11 May 1983.

8. Pearl Hummelstein, interview with author, Jonesboro, Ark., 9 November 1982; Lee Hummelstein, interview with author, Jonesboro, Ark., 9 November 1982; *Arkansas Gazette*, 25 August 1986.

9. Members of Jonesboro Industries, Inc., in 1945 included A. M. Herringer, Eric Rogers, Dr. P. W. Lutterloh, Dr. H. A. Stroud, Dr. H. H. McAdams, J. D. Weatherly, and Morris Schoenfield; Joe C. Young was the attorney representative (Gordon MacKenzie, comp., *Frolic Footwear History* [Frolic Footwear, Jonesboro, Ark.; publication, n.d.]; Lee Harlan, Frolic Footwear personnel director, telephone interview with author, Jonesboro, Ark., 3 October 1991.).

10. Ibid.; *Jonesboro Sun*, 17 December 1976.

11. MacKenzie, *Frolic Footwear History*.

12. Ibid.

13. Debbie (Blindman) Lazarov, telephone interview with author, Memphis, Tenn., 8 October 1991; Abe Blindman, telephone interview with author, Jonesboro, Ark., 11 October 1991.

14. Paul Clayton, telephone interview with author, Tuckerman, Ark., 23 April 1992.

15. Oscar Fendler, letter to author, 20 July 1987.

16. William "Bill" Borowsky, interview with author, Manila, Ark., 27 June 1982.

17. Fendler letter.

18. George and Norma Fisher, interview with author, Blytheville, Ark., 25 June 1982.

19. Robert and Hattie Heiman, interview with author, Blytheville, Ark., 25 June 1982.

20. *Arkansas Gazette*, 10 June 1963.

21. Fendler letter.

22. Ibid.

23. Lionel Silverfield, interview with author, Osceola, Ark., 26 June 1982.

24. *Arkansas Gazette*, 5 February 1983. A letter from the author to American Greetings in 1990 seeking to verify that Sapirstein had taken into consideration how Jews were treated in Arkansas before placing the plant in the state was answered by John A. Hernandis, corporate communications director. In his reply, he discounted the story. However, Richard "Dick" Prewitt, Osceola, Ark., mayor from 1971 to 1990, and Ben Butler, who had served as mayor for twenty-six years prior to Prewitt, verified that a deciding factor in Sapirstein's selection of Osceola as a site for his factory was how Jewish people were treated there (Dick Prewitt and Melvin Lapides, interview with author, Osceola, Ark., 3 August 1991).

25. *Arkansas Democrat*, 20 January 1990; Melvin Lapides, interview with author, Osceola, Ark., 3 August 1991.

26. Meyer Brick and his son Phillip, interview with author, Marion, Ark., 28 June 1982.

27. *Arkansas Democrat*, magazine section, 25 August 1957; *Lepanto News Record*, 1 April 1960.

28. *McCrory Leader*, 24 December 1986; I. N. Arnof's son, Ian, became president of one of the larger banks of New Orleans.

29. Max F. Baer, "New Man With an Old Mission," *The National Jewish Monthly* (November 1971): 18–22; David "Dave" Blumberg, interview with author, Richmond, Va., 5 November 1984.

30. David Drexler, interview with author, Wynne, Ark., 23 June 1982.

31. Ben and Ruth Meyer, interview with author, Wynne, Ark., 23 June 1982.

32. Raphael H. Andrews, interview with author, Wynne, Ark., 23 June 1982.

33. David Reagler, interview with author, Wynne, Ark., 23 June 1982.

34. Isadore and Morris Steinberg, interview with author, Wynne, Ark., 23 June 1982.

35. Bette Greene, *Summer of My German Soldier* (New York: Bantam Books, 1973).

36. Stanley and Irmazell (Harris) Lee, telephone interview with author, Memphis, Tenn., 12 May 1983; *Memphis Commercial Appeal*, 8 June 1954.

37. Sol and Lena (Tupper) Bursk, interview with author, Earle, Ark., 24 June 1982.

38. Mrs. George Stein and son George Raymond Stein, interview with author, Earle, Ark., 24 June 1982.

39. Isadore Baer, interview with author, Memphis, Tenn., 12 May 1983.

40. Ibid.

41. William Cohn, interview with author, Forrest City, Ark., 22 June 1982.

42. Harold Sharpe, interview with author, Forrest City, Ark., 22 June 1982.

43. Max and Elouise Cohen, interview with author, Forrest City, Ark., 24 June 1982.

44. Louis and Gertrude Barg, interview with author, Forrest City, Ark., 22 June 1982.

45. Zerlena (Meyer) Salinger, interview with author, Little Rock, Ark., 15 April 1982.

46. Dr. Hyman Harberg and daughter Dr. Evelyn Harberg, interview with author, Brinkley, Ark., 21 June 1982.

47. Mildred "Mickey" (Reagler) Rubens, interview with author, West Memphis, Ark., 28 June 1982.

48. Theodore Zuckerman, interview with author, Hughes, Ark., 29 June 1982.

49. See *Arkansas Gazette*, 19 June 1971, 27 July 1972, 1 August 1972, 7 August 1972.

50. J. Edward Wise (grandson of Morris Lewis), letter to author, 4 October 1991. Max O'Mell, who was Jewish, was said to have been helped by an Irish bartender in selecting an American name (Dorothy [O'Mell] Lewis, interview with author, Marianna, Ark., 1 July 1982).

51. David Solomon Jr., interview with author, Helena, Ark., 1 July 1982.

52. *Arkansas Gazette*, 13 October 1991.

53. *Twin City Tribune*, 23 June 1982.

54. Ibid.

55. L. R. Parmelee, "Helena and West Helena, A Civil Engineer Reminisces," *PCHQ* 1 (December 1962): 9; Helen Mosby, letter to author, 17 January 1984.

56. *Helena World*, 2 February 1982.

57. Walter Roberts, letter to the editor, *Arkansas Gazette*, 15 March 1985.

58. Edith (Davidson) Reiter, letter to author, 8 April 1985; Robert R. Logan, "Notes on the First Land Surveys in Arkansas," *AHQ* 19: 3 (1960): 260–70.

59. *Arkansas Gazette*, 6 September 1972, 7 September 1972.

60. Mrs. Max (Minnie Ruth Eisenkramer) Hirsch, telephone interview with author, Little Rock, Ark., 14 April 1983.

61. *Helena World*, 8 April 1951.

62. Hirsch interview.

63. Ralph Abramson, interview with author, Holly Grove, Ark., 12 August 1984; Janice (Abramson) Feldman, interview with author, Holly Grove, Ark., 12 August 1984.

64. Leonard Kern Jr., telephone interview with author, Clarendon, Ark., 30 July 1991.

65. *Arkansas Gazette,* 18 September 1969.

66. Sam Epstein Angel, interview with author, Lake Village, Ark., 11 May 1982.

67. Mr. and Mrs. Ed Festinger and son Steve, interview with author, Lake Village, Ark., 11 May 1982.

68. Mike Rankin, letter to author, 24 June 1985.

69. Carrol Meyer Jr., letters to author, 29 August 1982, 7 September 1982 (though Carroll Meyer Sr. spelled his name with two *l*s, he gave Carrol Meyer Jr. only one *l*). Charles L. Meyer, "Autobiography of Charles L. Meyer" (1982). Charles L. Meyer, letters to author, 14 December 1982, 18 February 1983, 9 February 1984, 16 February 1984, 15 August 1988, 18 August 1989, 25 August 1989, 7 December 1989.

70. *Arkansas Gazette,* 23 October 1984.

71. "Resolution" to Julian F. Haas, Arkansas Broadcasting Association, 19 April 1974, courtesy Mrs. Julian Haas Jr., Jackson, Tenn.

72. Bernard Levi, interview with author, Dermott, Ark., 10 May 1982.

73. Barry and Marjorie Brunner, interview with author, Dermott, Ark., 10 May 1982.

74. Isadore Small, interview with author, Memphis, Tenn., 12 May 1983.

75. Seymour and Edith Fleisig, interview with author, McGehee, Ark., 8 May 1982.

76. *Dumas Clarion,* 21 January 1970; Bernard J. "Jerry" and Pat Tanenbaum, interview with author, Dumas, Ark., 6 May 1982; Bernard J. "Jerry" Tanenbaum, interview with author, Dumas, Ark., 7 May 1982; Charlotte Schexnayder, telephone interview with author, Dumas, Ark., 7 May 1982.

77. Charles H. Dante, grandson of pioneer settler Charles Dante, interview with author, Dumas, Ark., 7 May 1982.

78. *Pine Bluff Commercial,* editorial, 7 January 1981; *Dumas Clarion,* 7 January 1981.

79. Bernard J. "Jerry" Tanenbaum, letter to author, 21 August 1991.

80. Haskell Wolff, interview with author, Dumas, Ark., 7 May 1982.

81. Harry and Elsie Phillips, interview with author, Dumas, Ark., 7 May 1982.

82. Victor Ray, former managing editor of the *Pine Bluff Commercial,* letter to author, 3 June 1983.

83. Patrick J. Owens, "The Gentleman Rebel," *ADL Bulletin* (September 1965): 7.

84. Julius Lester, *Lovesong, Becoming a Jew* (New York: Henry Holt & Company, 1988).

85. Jerome Glatstein, interview with author, Pine Bluff, Ark., 16 September 1986.

86. Mrs. Milford Sonnenschein, interview with author, Pine Bluff, Ark., 24 April 1982; Mrs. David (Kay Baim) Shapiro, telephone interview with author, Pine Bluff, Ark., 11 May 1992.

87. *Arkansas Gazette,* 25 April 1982.

88. Henry F. Marx, interview with author, Pine Bluff, Ark., 23 April 1982; *Arkansas Democrat,* 10 April 1987.

89. *The Arkansas Researcher,* 5 (February 1991): 1.

90. Charles E. Joseph, interview with author, Little Rock, Ark., 21 February 1992.

91. *Arkansas Gazette,* 2 May 1983.

92. *Arkansas Democrat,* 8 February 1990.

93. Donald R. Katz, "Good Times Coming In Arkansas," GEO (Gruner & Jahr, USA, Inc., Edition) 2 (June 1980): 35–56.

94. *Arkansas Gazette,* 28 April 1983.

95. *Arkansas Gazette,* 2 June 1988.

CHAPTER 18
Western Arkansas

1. *Camden News,* 11 November 1974.

2. *El Dorado News-Times,* 24 May 1976; Jules and Johanna Feinberg, interview with author, El Dorado, Ark., 29 October 1982.

3. Feinberg interview.

4. Ibid.; Joe and Janet Stuart, interview with author, El Dorado, Ark., 29 October 1982.

5. Fred Smith, retired administrator, Warner Brown Hospital, El Dorado, Ark., telephone interview with author, 3 October 1991.

6. Stuart interview.

7. J. T. "Pete" Young, Felsenthal, Ark., mayor, interview with author, Felsenthal, Ark., 29 October 1982; *Arkansas Democrat,* 27 May 1987. By 1988, however, continued work on the Ouachita River was considered as excessive by some (see *Arkansas Gazette,* 26 October 1988; *Arkansas Democrat-Gazette,* 1 November 1991).

8. Texarkana Jewry data courtesy Ralph and Billie Brody and from Barbara Glick, ed., *Centennial Journal of Mount Sinai Congregation, 1885–1985* (Texarkana, Ark.: n.p., 1985), 71–127

9. Ellen Kaufman, letter to author, 16 October 1991.

10. Billie Richmond, librarian, Foreman, Ark., Public Library, letter to author, 26 September 1988.

11. *Arkansas Democrat,* 12 September 1986.

12. Cathy Kunzinger Urwin, *Agenda for Reform: Winthrop Rockefeller as Governor of Arkansas, 1967–71* (Fayetteville: The University of Arkansas Press, 1991), 71, 107–08.

13. Jeanne Kahn, interview with author, Hot Springs, Ark., 20 April 1982.

14. Harold Gottlieb, interview with author, Hot Springs, Ark., 20 April 1982.

15. Victoria Leiber, interview with author, Hot Springs, Ark., 6 April 1982.

16. Dr. Joseph L. Rosenzweig, interview with author, Hot Springs, Ark., 6 April 1982.

17. *Arkansas Democrat,* 6 July 1986, 27 January 1988.

18. *Fort Smith Southwest Times-Record*, 4 December 1960; *The United Hebrew Temple Tablet* (October 1986): 2.

19. Leona Goldstein, interview with author, Fort Smith, Ark., 18 August 1982.

20. *Physicians and Medicine, Crawford and Sebastian Counties, Arkansas, 1817–1976* (Fort Smith, Ark.: Sebastian County Medical Society, 1976), 626–27.

21. Otto Henry Zinke, UofA professor of physics, letter to author, 1 September 1982. Zinke was a former student of Dr. Feenberg's.

22. Washington University *W.U. Record* (2 March 1975): 1; *St. Louis Post-Dispatch*, magazine section, 21 June 1987.

23. Data on Eugene Feenberg courtesy Ben Feenberg, Tamarac, Fla., and Mrs. Eugene (Hilda) Feenberg, La Jolla, Calif.

24. Legalities associated with the Cohn estate, such as back taxes, were later found, and it was uncertain how much of the estate would eventually be received by the Fort Smith library (*Arkansas Democrat*, 31 October 1990).

25. Benno S. Friedman, interview with author, Memphis, Tenn., 10 May 1983.

26. Jack Moseley, interview with author, Fort Smith, Ark., 29 April 1983.

27. *Fayetteville Northwest Arkansas Times*, 15 May 1961.

28. George S. Brewer, letter to the editor, *Arkansas Gazette*, 20 June 1986.

29. *Arkansas Gazette*, 21 April 1983; *Arkansas Democrat*, 30 April 1983; *Arkansas Democrat*, magazine section, 10 August 1986.

30. *Arkansas Democrat*, magazine section, 10 August 1986.

31. *Eureka and North Arkansas Journal*, 5 June 1986.

32. *Arkansas Democrat*, 18 January 1987.

33. *Arkansas Gazette*, 13 September 1935.

34. *Arkansas Interfaith Conference* (Summer 1991): 4. For more information on Gerald L. K. Smith's "sacred projects" at Eureka Springs and how he almost received a federal grant to build a road leading directly to his tourist projects, see "Gerald Smith's Road," in Arnold Forster and Benjamin R. Epstein, *The New Anti-Semitism* (New York: McGraw-Hill Book Company, 1974), 19–48.

35. *Arkansas Democrat*, 23 June 1991.

36. John L. Ferguson, *Arkansas Lives: The Opportunity Land Who's Who* (Hopkinsville, Ky: Historical Record Association, 1965), 167.

37. *Conway Log Cabin Democrat*, 5 August 1952.

38. Bill Heiligers, interview with author, Conway, Ark., 11 August 1982; *Arkansas Democrat*, 13 February 1987.

39. Frances Koppel, interview with author, Little Rock, Ark., 26 May 1982.

BIBLIOGRAPHY

Abbreviations used in Bibliography:

AHC Arkansas History Commission
AHQ *Arkansas Historical Quarterly*
AJA *American Jewish ARCHIVES* [Journal]
AJA American Jewish Archives, Cincinnati, Ohio
AJH *American Jewish History*
AJHQ *American Jewish Historical Quarterly*
AJHS American Jewish Historical Society, Waltham, Mass.
BIA Congregation B'nai Israel Archives, Little Rock. Ark.
CAL Central Arkansas Library, Little Rock, Ark.
FSPL Fort Smith, Ark., Public Library
PAJHS *Publications of American Jewish Historical Society* (predecessor of AJH)
PBPL Pine Bluff, Ark., Public Library
PCHQ *Phillips County Historical Quarterly*
PCHR *Pulaski County Historical Review*
PCPL Phillips County, Ark., Public Library
SARA Southwest Arkansas Regional Archives, Washington, Ark.
TIAB Temple Israel Archives, Blytheville, Ark.
TIAJ Temple Israel Archives, Jonesboro, Ark.
UofA University of Arkansas, Fayetteville
UALR University of Arkansas at Little Rock
UHCA United Hebrew Congregation Archives, Fort Smith, Ark.

Books

Acts of Arkansas, 1866–1877.
Acts of the Eighth Session of the General Assembly of the Territory of Arkansas, 8 November 1833.
Adler, Cyrus, ed. *The American Jewish Yearbook*, 1899–1900. Philadelphia: Jewish Publication Society of America, 1900.
———. *I Have Considered the Days*. Philadelphia: Jewish Publication Society of America, 1945.
Allard, Chester C., comp., Bessie Butler Newsom Allard, ed. *Arkansans of the*

Year, vol. 5, *Who is Who in Arkansas,* vol. 1 Little Rock: Allard House Publishers, 1959.

Altheimer, Matilda. *Pastime Poems.* Pine Bluff, Ark.: The Commercial Printing Company, [1932?].

Anstruther, Ian. *Dr. Livingstone, I Presume.* New York: E. P. Dutton & Company, 1957.

American Artists of Renown, 1981–1982. Gilmer, Tex.: Wilson, 1980.

American Jewish Year Book 1947–48. Philadelphia: American Jewish Committee, 1948.

Arkansas Code of 1987 Annotated. Tables. Charlottesville, Va.: Michie Company, 1987.

Arkansas Code of 1987 Annotated. Vol. 4, title 6. Charlottesville, Va.: Michie Company, 1987.

Arkansas' Happy Hunting Grounds, Crater of Diamonds State Park. Murfreesboro, Ark.: n.p., n.d.

Ashkenazi, Elliott. *The Business of Jews in Louisiana 1840–1875.* Tuscaloosa: University of Alabama Press, 1988.

Auerbach, Dr. B. D. *Berith Abraham.* Frankfurt, Germany: Berlag von Kauffmann, 1880.

Bailey, Jim. *Arkansas Travelers: Seventy-nine Years of Baseball.* Little Rock: Arkansas Travelers Baseball Club, Inc., 1980.

Baird, W. David. *Medical Education in Arkansas, 1879–1978.* Memphis: Memphis State University Press, 1979.

Barnes, H. F., ed., Lex B. Davis, comp. *Among Arkansas Leaders.* Little Rock: Lex B. Davis, 1934.

Bartlett, I. S., ed. *History of Wyoming.* Vol. 2. Chicago: The S. J. Clarke Publishing Company, 1918.

Bayme, Steven, and Gary Rubin, comps. *American Jewry and Judaism in the Twentieth Century.* New York: Hadassah, The Women's Zionist Organization of America, Inc., 1980.

Bell, James W. *The Little Rock Handbook.* Little Rock: James W. Bell, 1980.

Bench and Bar of Arkansas, 1935. N.p.: B. F. Pace Publishing Company, 1935.

Berman, Myron. *Richmond's Jewry, 1769–1976: Shabbat in Shockoe.* Charlottesville: University Press of Virginia, 1979.

Berry, Evalena. *Time and the River.* Little Rock: Rose Publishing Company, 1982.

Biographical Directory of the U.S. Congress, 1774–1989. Washington, D.C.: U.S. Government Printing Office, 1989.

Biographical and Historical Memoirs of Central Arkansas. Chicago: The Goodspeed Publishing Company, 1889.

Biographical and Historical Memoirs of Eastern Arkansas. Chicago: The Goodspeed Publishing Company, 1890.

Biographical and Historical Memoirs of Northeast Arkansas. Chicago: The Goodspeed Publishing Company, 1889.

Biographical and Historical Memoirs of Southern Arkansas. Chicago: The Goodspeed Publishing Company, 1890.

Biographical and Historical Memoirs of Western Arkansas. Chicago: The Goodspeed Publishing Company, 1889.

Books of Arkansas. Little Rock: *Arkansas Gazette*, 1913.

Brewster, E. T. *City of Little Rock Guide, 1890*. Little Rock: Guide Publishing Company, 1890.

Brown, Francis J., and Joseph S. Roucek. *One America: The History, Contributions, and Present Problems of Our Racial and National Minorities*. 3d ed. Englewood Cliffs, N.J.: Prentice-Hall, Inc., 1952.

Brown, Robert J. *Romance of the City of Roses*. Little Rock: n.p., n.d.

Campbell, William S. *100 Years of Fayetteville, 1828–1927*. Fayetteville, Ark.: Washington County Historical Society, 1977.

Cashion, Elbert T., Sr. *A History of Eudora, Arkansas, Chicot County*. Lake Village, Ark.: James Printing Company, 1977.

Catlin, Brigadier General A. W. *With the Help of God and a Few Marines*. New York: Doubleday, 1919.

Chandler, Barbara Overton, and J. Ed Howe. *History of Texarkana*. Shreveport, La.: J. Ed Howe Publisher, 1939.

Chowning, Robert W. *History of Cross County*. Wynne, Ark.: *Wynne Progress*, 1955.

Clark, Rabbi Morris. *My Scrapbook*. N. P., self-published, [1958?].

Cohen, George. *The Jews in the Making of America*. Boston: The Stratford Company, 1924.

Davidson, Gabriel. *Our Jewish Farmers and the Story of the Jewish Agricultural Society*. New York: L. B. Fischer, 1943.

Davidson, Sherrie Fleischer, and Doris Tenzel Fleischer. *Pauline Tenzel: The Life Story of a "Lady Doctor."* New York: Impact Media Special Edition, Biblio Press, 1992.

Davis-Dubois, Rachel, and Emma Schweppe. *The Jews in American Life*. New York: Thomas Nelson & Sons, 1935.

De Kruif, Paul. *Life Among the Doctors*. New York: Harcourt, Brace & Company, 1949.

deMan, George E. N., comp. and ed. *Helena: The Ridge, the River, the Romance*. Little Rock: Pioneer Press, 1978.

Dimont, Max I. *The Jews in America*. New York: Simon & Schuster, 1978.

Dinnerstein, Leonard. *The Leo Frank Case*. New York: Columbia University Press, 1968.

Dinnerstein, Leonard, and Mary Dale Palsson, eds. *Jews in the South*. Baton Rouge: Louisiana State University Press, 1973. Reprint, Athens: University of Georgia Press, 1987.

Dragonwagon, Crescent. *Message From the Avocadoes*. Little Rock: Parkhurst/Little Rock Publishers, 1982.

Eichhorn, Rabbi David Max. *Joys of Jewish Folklore: A Journey from New Amsterdam to Beverly Hills*. Middle Village, N.Y.: Jonathan David Pubs., Inc., 1981.

Eisenstadt, Abraham Seldin. *American History: Recent Interpretations*, Vol. 2. New York: Thomas Y. Crowell Company, 1962.

Elovitz, Mark. *A Century of Jewish Life in Dixie: The Birmingham Experience*. Tuscaloosa: University of Alabama Press, 1974.

Elting, Col. John R. *A Dictionary of Soldier Talk*. New York: Charles Scribner's Sons, 1989.

Evans, Eli N. *The Provincials: A Personal History of Jews in the South*. New York: Atheneum, 1976.

Ezekiel, Herbert T., and Gaston Lichtenstein. *The History of the Jews of Richmond, from 1769 to 1917*. Richmond, Va.: Herbert T. Ezekiel, 1917.

Feingold, Henry L., ed. *The Jewish People in America*, 5 vols. Baltimore: The Johns Hopkins University Press, 1992.

Feldman, Abraham J. *The American Jew: A Study of Backgrounds*. Rev. ed. New York: Bloch Publishing Company, 1959.

Ferguson, John L. *Arkansas Lives: The Opportunity Land Who's Who*. Hopkinsville, Ky.: Historical Record Association, 1965.

Ferguson, John L., and J. H. Atkinson. *Historic Arkansas*. Little Rock: AHC, 1966.

Foreman, Grant. *Indians and Pioneers*. Norman: University of Oklahoma Press, 1974.

Forster, Arnold, and Benjamin R. Epstein. *The New Anti-Semitism*. New York: McGraw-Hill Book Company, 1974.

Fort Smith City Directory. N.p., 1900.

Fort Smith City Directory, 1894–1895. N.p.: Maloney Directory, n.d.

Freyer, Tony. *The Little Rock Crisis: A Constitutional Interpretation*. Westport, Conn.: Greenwood Press, 1984.

Friedenwald, Herbert, ed. *The American Jewish Year Book, 1909–1910*. Philadelphia: The Jewish Publication Society of America, 1909.

Gatewood, Robert L. *Faulkner County, Arkansas, 1778–1964*. Conway, Ark.: n.p., 1964.

Gerstaecker, Frederick. *Wild Sports in the Far West*. Durham, N.C.: Duke University Press, 1968.

Glick, Barbara, ed. *Centennial Journal of Mount Sinai Congregation, 1885–1985*. Texarkana, Ark.: n.p., 1985.

Golden, Harry L. *Our Southern Landsmen*. New York: G. P. Putnam, 1974.

Goodspeed, Weston Arthur, ed. *The Province and the States*. Vol. 7. Madison, Wis.: The Western Historical Association, 1904.

Grayzel, Solomon. *A History of the Jews: From the Babylonian Exile to the Present*. New York: The New American Library, 1968.

Greene, Bette. *Get on Out of Here, Philip Hall*. New York: Dell Publishing Company, 1981.

———. *Morning Is a Long Time Coming*. New York: Pocket Books, 1978.

———. *Philip Hall Likes Me. I Reckon Maybe*. New York: Dial Press, 1974.

———. *Summer of My German Soldier*. New York: Bantam Books, 1973.

———. *Them That Glitter and Them That Don't*. New York: Alfred A. Knopf, 1983.

Grossman, Charles, comp. and ed. *Mount Sinai Jubilee*. Texarkana, Ark.: n.p., 1935.

Guide to Little Rock, 1890. N.p, n.d.

Hallum, John. *Pictorial History of Arkansas*. Vol. 1. Albany, N.Y.: Weed, Parsons & Company, 1887.

Harris, Leo A., Jr. *Merchant Princes: An Intimate History of Jewish Families Who Built Great Department Stores*. New York: Harper & Row, 1979.

Hartness, Richard L., Sr. *Wittsburg, Arkansas: Crowley's Ridge Steamboat Riverport, 1848–1890*. Little Rock: Rose Publishing Company, 1979.

Heller, James G. *Isaac M. Wise—His Life, Work and Thought*. New York: Union of American Hebrew Congregations, 1965.

Hempstead, Fay. *Historical Review of Arkansas*. 3 vols. Chicago: The Lewis Publishing Company, 1911.

———. *A Pictorial History of Arkansas*. New York: N. D. Thompson Publishing Company, 1890.

Herndon, Dallas T. *Centennial History of Arkansas*. 4 vols. Chicago–Little Rock: The S. J. Clarke Publishing Company, 1922.

———. *Annals of Arkansas*. 4 vols. Hopkinsville, Ky.: The Historical Record Association, 1947.

Hirshler, Eric E., ed. *Jews from Germany in the United States*. New York: Farrar, Straus & Cudahy, 1955.

History of Benton, Washington, Carroll, Madison, Crawford, Franklin, and Sebastian Counties, Arkansas. Chicago: The Goodspeed Publishing Company, 1890.

History of the Arkansas Press Association. Little Rock: Parke-Harper Company, 1930.

Hoffman, Edward. *Despite All Odds*. New York: Simon & Schuster, 1991.

Houston, Curtis A. *A History of the Bank of McCrory, 1903–1976*. McCrory, Ark.: n.p., 1976.

Hull, Clifton E. *Shortline Railroads of Arkansas*. Norman: University of Oklahoma Press, 1969.

Hurt, Harry III. *Texas Rich*. New York: W. W. Norton & Company, 1981.

Ivie, W. J. *A Message to the Homeseeker*. Jonesboro, Ark.: W. J. Ivie Publisher, 1941.

Janowsky, Oscar I., ed. *The American Jew: A Composite Portrait*. New York: Harper & Brothers, 1942.

Joseph, Samuel. *History of the Baron de Hirsch Fund: The Americanization of the Jewish Immigrant*. Philadelphia: Printed for Baron de Hirsch Fund by the Jewish Publication Society, 1935.

Kaganoff, Nathan M., and Melvin I. Urofsky, eds. *Turn to the South: Essays on Southern Jewry*. Charlottesville: University Press of Virginia, 1979.

Kaplan, Ben. *The Eternal Stranger: A Study of Jewish Life in the Small Community*. New York: Bookman Associates, 1957.

Karp, Abraham J. *Haven and Home: A History of the Jews in America*. New York: Schocken Books, 1985.

Katsh, Abraham I. *Hebraic Contributions to American Life*. New York: New York University Bookstore, 1941.

Kessel, Marie Adler. *A World of Differences*. Fayetteville: University of Arkansas Press, 1990.

Korn, Bertram Wallace. *American Jewry and the Civil War*. Philadelphia: The Jewish Publication Society of America, 1951.

———. *The Early Jews of New Orleans*. Waltham, Mass.: AJHS, 1969.

———. *Jews and Negro Slavery in the Old South*. Elkins Park, Pa.: Reform Congregation Keneseth Israel, 1961.

Landman, Isaac, ed. *The Universal Jewish Encyclopedia*. 10 vols. New York: Universal Jewish Encyclopedia Company, Inc., 1948.

Lavendar, Abraham D. *A Coat of Many Colors: Jewish Subcommunities in the United States*. Westport, Conn.: Greenwood Press, 1977.

Learsi, Rufus. *The Jews in America: A History*. New York: KTAV Publishing House, Inc., 1972.

Lerman, Antony, ed. *The Jewish Communities of the World: A Contemporary Guide*. New York: Facts On File, Inc., 1989.

Leslie, James W. *Pine Bluff and Jefferson County*. Norfolk, Va.: The Donning Company, 1981.

Lester, Julius. *Lovesong, Becoming a Jew*. New York: Henry Holt & Company, 1988.

Levin, Marlin. *Balm in Gilead, The Story of Hadassah*. New York: Schocken Books, 1973.

Levinger, Lee J. *A History of the Jews in the United States*. 4th ed. New York: Union of American Hebrew Congregations, 1954.

Libo, Kenneth, and Irving Howe. *We Lived There Too*. New York: St. Martin's/Marek, 1984.

Lipman, Ira. *How to Protect Yourself from Crime*. Chicago: Contemporary Books, 1989.

Lipman, Mark. *Stealing*. New York: Harper's Magazine Press, 1973.

Little Rock Board of Trade 12th Annual Report, 1900–1901.

Little Rock Board of Trade 14th Annual Report, 1903.

Little Rock Board of Trade 17th Annual Report, 1906.

Little Rock Board of Trade 18th Annual Report, 1907.

Little Rock Board of Trade 22nd Annual Report, 1911.

Little Rock Board of Trade 23rd Annual Report, 1912.

Little Rock City Directory 1871. Little Rock: Price & Barton, Printers, 1871.

Little Rock City Directories, 1872–1910.

Little Rock–Hot Springs Blue Book. Vol. 1. Little Rock–Chicago: The Blue Book Publishing Company, 1901.

Loewenthal, Naftali. *Communicating the Infinite: The Emergence of the Chabad School*. Chicago: University of Chicago Press, 1990.

McPherson, Alex. *History of Faulkner County*. Conway, Ark.: Conway Times Plant, 1927.

Marcus, Jacob Rader. *The American Jewish Woman, 1654–1980*. New York: KTAV Publishing House, Inc., 1981.

———. *Early American Jewry*. Vol. 2, *The Jews of Pennsylvania and the South, 1655–1790*. Philadelphia: The Jewish Publication Society of America, 1953.

———. *United States Jewry, 1776–1985*, 4 vols. Detroit: Wayne State University Press, 1991–92.

———, ed. *Memoirs of American Jews, 1775–1865*. 3 vols. Philadelphia: The Jewish Publication Society of America, 1955–56.

Marinbach, Bernard. *Galveston: The Ellis Island of the West*. Albany: State University of New York Press, 1983.

Marler, Gladys, and Bonnie Mears, comps. *Bergman—Then and Now, 1904–1976*. Bergman, Ark.: Bergman Homemakers Extension Club, 1976.

Masterson, James R. *Arkansas Folklore*. Little Rock: Rose Publishing Company, 1974.

May, Max B. *Isaac Mayer Wise*. New York: G. P. Putnam's Sons, 1946.

Medearis, Mary, ed. *Sam Williams: Printer's Devil*. Hope, Ark.: Etter Printing Company, 1976.

————. *Washington, Arkansas: History on the Southwest Trail*. Hope, Ark.: Etter Printing Company, 1976.

Moley, Raymond, Jr. *The American Legion Story*. New York: Meredith Publishing Company, 1966.

Morgan, James Logan. *Centennial History of Newport*. Newport, Ark.: Jackson County Historical Society, 1975.

Morse, Arthur D. *While Six Million Died: A Chronicle of American Apathy*. New York: Random House, Inc., 1968.

O'Dougherty, Terence, and Frank M. Sarchet, comps. *Combined Directory of Little Rock, Hot Springs, Pine Bluff, Eureka Springs, and Fort Smith, 1181–2*. Little Rock: Union Printing & Publishing Co., 1881.

Ornish, Natalie. *Pioneer Jewish Texans: Their Impact on Texas and American History for Four Hundred Years 1590–1990*. Dallas: Texas Heritage Press, 1989.

Physicians and Medicine, Crawford and Sebastian Counties, Arkansas, 1817–1976. Fort Smith, Ark.: Sebastian County Medical Society, 1976.

Pinkley-Call, Cora. *Pioneer Tales of Eureka Springs and Carroll County*. Eureka Springs, Ark.: n.p., 1930.

Postal, Bernard, and Lionel Koppman. *American Jewish Landmarks: A Travel Guide and History*. Vol. 2, *The South and Southwest*. New York: Fleet Press Corporation, 1979.

Proctor, Samuel, and Louis Schmier, eds. *Jews of the South, Essays from the Southern Jewish Historical Society*. Macon, Ga.: Mercer University Press, 1984.

R. L. Polk's El Dorado (Union County, Arkansas) City Directory. Dallas: R. L. Polk & Company, Publisher, 1937.

Reynolds, John Hugh, and David Y. Thomas. *History of the University of Arkansas*. Fayetteville: University of Arkansas, 1910.

Reznikoff, Charles, and Uriah Z. Engelman. *The Jews of Charleston, a History of an American Jewish Community*. Philadelphia: Jewish Publication Society of America, 1954.

Road and Street Mileages. Little Rock: Arkansas State Highway and Transportation Department Planning and Research Division, 1991.

Ross, Margaret. *Arkansas Gazette, The Early Years 1819–1866*. Little Rock: Gazette Foundation, 1969.

Rosten, Leo. *The Joys of Yiddish*. New York: Pocket Books, 1968.

Rothschild, Janice O. *As But a Day: The First Hundred Years 1867–1967*. Atlanta: The Hebrew Benevolent Congregation, 1967.

Roy, F. Hampton. *Charles L. Thompson and Associates, Arkansas Architects, 1885–1938*. Little Rock: August House, 1982.

Roy, F. Hampton, Charles Witsell Jr., and Cheryl Griffith Nichols. *How We Lived*. Little Rock: August House, 1984.

Rubin, Saul Jacob. *Third to None: The Saga of Savannah Jewry 1733–1983*. Savannah, Ga.: Rubin, 1983.

Russell, Jerry, and Bessie Butler Newsom Allard, comps. *Arkansans of the Years*. Vol. 6, *Who Is Who in Arkansas*. Vol. 2. Little Rock: Allard House Publishers, 1968.

Sacks, Dr. Jacob. *The Atom at Work*. New York: Ronald Press Company, 1952.

————. *Isotopic Tracers in Biochemistry and Physiology*. New York: McGraw-Hill, 1953.

Sanders, Ira E., and Elijah E. Palnick, comps. and eds. *One Hundred Years, Congregation B'nai Israel 1866–1966*. Little Rock: n.p., 1966.

Schachner, Nathan. *The Price of Liberty: A History of the American Jewish Committee*. New York: the American Jewish Committee, 1948.

Schmier, Louis, ed. *Reflections on Southern Jewry: The Letters of Charles Wessolowsky 1878–1879*. Albany, Ga.: Mercer University Press, 1982.

Sharfman, I. Harold. *Jews on the Frontier*. Chicago: Henry Regnery Company, 1977.

Shirk, George H. *Oklahoma Place Names*. Norman: University of Oklahoma Press, 1965.

Shpall, Leo. *The Jews of Louisiana*. New Orleans: n.p., 1936.

Silcox, Claris Edwin, and Galen M. Fisher. *Catholics, Jews, and Protestants: A Study of Relationships in the United States and Canada*. New York: Published for the Institute of Social and Religious Research by Harper & Brothers, 1934.

Simonhoff, Harry. *Jewish Participants in the Civil War*. New York: Arco Publishing Company, 1963.

Smith, Diann Sutherlin. *The Arkansas Handbook*. Little Rock: Emerald City Press, 1984.

Speer, William S., and John Henry Brown, eds. *The Encyclopedia of the New West*. Marshall, Tex.: The United States Biographical Publishing Company, 1881.

Spitzberg, Irving J., Jr. *Racial Politics in Little Rock: 1954–1964*. New York: Garland Publishing Company, 1987.

Stanley, Dorothy, ed. *The Autobiography of Sir Henry Morton Stanley*. Boston: Houghton Mifflin Company, 1909.

Staples, Thomas S. *Reconstruction in Arkansas, 1862–1874*. New York: Columbia University, 1923.

Stern, Malcolm H. *Americans of Jewish Descent: A Compendium of Genealogy*. Cincinnati: Hebrew Union College Press, 1960.

———. *First American Jewish Families: 600 Genealogies 1654–1977*. Cincinnati: AJA, 1978.

Stone, Elizabeth Arnold. *Uinta County: It's Place in History*. Laramie, Wyo.: Laramie Printing Company, 1924.

Storey, Graham. *Reuters' Century*. New York: Crown Publishers, 1951.

Temple Anshe Emeth One Hundredth Anniversary, 1867–1967. Pine Bluff, Ark.: n.p., 1967. Anshe Emeth Archives, Pine Bluff, Ark.

Thomas, David Y., ed. *Arkansas and Its People*. 4 vols. New York: American Historical Society, Inc., 1930.

Trepp, Leo. *A History of the Jewish Experience*. New York: Behrman House, Inc., 1973.

Turtiz, Leon and Evelyn. *Jews in Early Mississippi*. Jackson: University Press of Mississippi, 1983.

Urwin, Cathy Kunzinger. *Agenda for Reform: Winthrop Rockefeller as Governor of Arkansas, 1967–71*. Fayetteville: University of Arkansas Press, 1991.

U.S. Bureau of the Census. *1980 Census of Agriculture*. Vol. 1: no. 4, *Arkansas State and County Data*. Washington, D.C.: Government Printing Office, 1989.

———. *Compendium of the Ninth Census*. Washington, D.C.: Government Printing Office, 1872. Reprint, New York: Arno Press, 1976.

———. *Fourteenth Census of the United States, 1920.* Washington, D.C.: Government Printing Office, 1923.

———. *Ninth Census of the United States. The Statistics of the Population of the United States.* Vol. 1. Washington, D.C.: Government Printing Office, 1872.

———. *Tenth Census of the United States, 1880.* Washington, D.C.: Government Printing Office, 1883.

Wagoner, Dale E. *Levi Arthritis Hospital: More Lasting Than Marble or Stone.* Hot Springs, Ark.: Levi Hospital, 1984.

Weitz, Rabbi Martin M. *Diamond Jubilee Bibilog . . . Temple Beth Israel, May 1950.* Hot Springs, Ark.: n.p., 1950.

Westphal, June, and Catharine Osterhage. *A Fame Not Easily Forgotten.* Conway, Ark.: River Road Press, 1971.

Who's Who in American Jewry, 1928. New York: The Jewish Biographical Bureau, Inc., 1928.

Who's Who in Little Rock, 1921. Little Rock: Who's Who Publishers, 1921.

Who's Who in the South and Southwest, 1980–1981. Chicago: Marquis Who's Who, 1980.

Williams, Charlean Moss. *Washington Hempstead County Arkansas: The Old Town Speaks.* Houston: Anson Jones Press, 1951.

Williams, Fay. *Arkansans of the Years,* 4 vols. Little Rock: C. C. Allard & Associates, Publishers, 1952–54.

Winegarten, Ruthie and Cathy Schecter. *Deep in the Heart, the Lives and Legends of Texas Jews.* Austin: Eakin Press, 1990.

Winslow, Thyra Samter. *Blueberry Pie.* New York: Alfred A. Knopf, 1932.

———. *People Round the Corner.* New York: Alfred A. Knopf, 1927.

———. *Picture Frames.* New York: Alfred A. Knopf, 1923.

———. *Show Business.* New York: Alfred A. Knopf, 1926.

Wischnitzer, Mark. *Visas to Freedom: The History of HIAS.* Cleveland: The World Publishing Company, 1956.

Wolf, Simon. *The American Jew as Patriot, Soldier, and Citizen.* Philadelphia: The Levytype Company, 1895.

Periodicals, Manuscripts, Archival Materials, Brochures

ACTION (Publication of the Jewish Federation of Little Rock, Ark.) 10 (Winter 1986), 12 (Winter 1988), 14 (Spring 1990).

Agricultural History 24 (1950): 120–46

Allen, Fern, and Roberta Elliott. "Jewish Presence in Rural South Dwindling But Steadfast." *Jewish Week* (13 February 1987).

Altheimer, Louis. "Col. Louis Altheimer, Empire Builder." *Arkansas Gazette,* 20 November 1919.

Altschul, Sam J. Papers. Courtesy Sam J. Altschul, Pine Bluff, Ark.

"Annals of Arkansas 1866–1903." Gleaned from various sources, WPA Project 6715, AHC.

Anshe Emeth Archives, Pine Bluff, Ark.

"Arkansas, 1840s–1870s." R. G. Dun & Co. Collection, Baker Library, Harvard University Graduate School of Business Administration.

Arkansas Assembly Bulletin, nos. 1–4, 8–18.

The Arkansas Banker 11 (1927): 22.

Arkansas Business 3 (28 April–11 May, 1986): 12–15; 7 (19 November 1990): 17; 8 (7 January 1991): 20; 8 (4 March 1991): 22–23.

Arkansas Interfaith Conference (Summer 1991).

Arkansas Jewish Assembly Board Minutes, 1932–1950. Unpublished papers. BIA.

Arkansas Jewish Assembly Convention Minutes, 1932–1950. Unpublished papers. BIA.

Arkansas Jewish Assembly correspondence and reports. Unpublished papers. BIA.

Arkansas Jewish Assembly Records. BIA.

"Arkansas-Oklahoma Report" (January 1909). R. G. Dun & Co. Collection, Baker Library, Harvard University Graduate School of Business Administration.

The Arkansas Researcher 5 (February 1991): 1.

Arkansas Secretary of State Records, Book 5.

Arnold, W. H., Sr. "Historical Statement of Texarkana, Arkansas, to February 7, 1917." *AHQ* 5 (1946): 340–53.

Arsenault, Raymond. "Charles Jacobson of Arkansas, a Jewish Politician in the Land of the Razorbacks." In Nathan M. Kaganoff and Melvin I. Urofsky, eds. *Turn to the South*. Charlottesville: University Press of Virginia, 1979.

Assembly Blah! (6 April 1935). BIA.

"Assessments of All Members of the Congregation, September 1, 1989, to September 1, 1990." BIA.

Baer, Max F. "New Man With An Old Mission." *The National Jewish Monthly* (November 1971): 18–22.

Bank of Holly Grove calendar. Courtesy Bank of Holly Grove, Ark.

Baum Family, Fayetteville, Ark., Folder. Small Collections File. AJA.

Bearden, Russell. "Jefferson County's Worst Disaster: The Flood of 1927." *AHQ* 43 (1984): 324–38.

Bernhard, Joe. Papers. Courtesy Joe Bernhard, Little Rock, Ark.

Bernhard, Mary Herr. Unpublished autobiography. Joe Bernhard Papers. Courtesy Joe Bernhard, Little Rock, Ark.

Bernstein, Jeanette (Warshavsky). "A Grateful Thread, A Family Journal." 4 January 1957, Arkansas, Jeanette Bernstein Folder, Box 1784. AJA.

Berrol, Selma. "Germans Versus Russians: An Update." *AJH* 73 (1983): 142–56.

"Block Family History." Courtesy Glenn Block, Little Rock, Ark.

B'nai B'rith International Archives, Washington, D.C.

B'nai B'rith's Levi Arthritis Hospital, A Heritage of Caring. (Levi Hospital brochure, n.d.)

B'nai Israel Ladies Aid Society Folder, Temple B'nai Israel, Little Rock, Ark., Folder. AJA.

"B'nai Israel Minutes," 1873, 1880. BIA.

"B'nai Israel's Quarter Century Celebration." 14 September 1984. BIA.

Brady, Donald V. "The Theatre in Early El Paso, 1881–1905." *Southwestern Studies* 4: 1 (1966): 3–39.

Bridges, Hal. "The Robber Baron Concept in American History." In Abraham Seldin Eisenstadt, ed., *American History: Recent Interpretations* 2. New York: Thomas Y. Crowell Company, 1962.

Brister, Louis E. "The Image of Arkansas in the Early German Emigrant Guidebook: Notes on Immigration." *AHQ* 36: 3 (1977): 338–45.

Brockhoff, Dorothy. "Two-Day Symposium to Honor Retiring Physicist Eugene Feenberg." Washington University *W.U. Record* (20 March 1975): 2–3.

Brown, Walter L. "Arkansas' Flag Is Fifty Years Old." *AHQ* 22 (1966): 3–7.

Bukey, Evan Burr. "Frederick Gerstaecker and Arkansas." *AHQ* 31: 1 (1972): 4–14.

Callahan, Mrs. Ted. "This is Your Life, Harold Goldberg." Courtesy Mrs. Ted Callahan.

Camden Chamber of Commerce Letter of Commendation, 9 October 1931. Courtesy Helen Berg, Camden, Ark.

Carter, Pauline Booker. "Genealogical Memoranda of Abraham Block." Block File. SARA.

"Centennial Celebration of Congregation Beth El, Helena, Arkansas, 1867–1967." Churches Folder, PCPL.

Chambers' Historical Society 2 (1925). Abraham Block File. SARA.

Chesnutt, E. F. "Little Rock Gets Electric Lights." *AHQ* 42: 3 (1983): 238–53.

The Chronicle (Little Rock) 19 (February–March 1992): 9.

"The Churches of Helena." *Helena World*, 11 November 1923.

"Churches and Synagogues Historical Records Survey," Arkansas, Works Progress Administration (WPA), Box 434, Folders 1–2; Box 453, Folder 26. Special Collections, Mullins Library, UofA.

City National Bank (Fort Smith, Ark.) brochure. N.d.

Clark, Thomas D. "The Post–Civil War Economy in the South." *AJHQ* 55 (June 1966).

Cline, Inez E. "Four Score and Five." *The Record* (Hot Springs–Garland County Historical Society Journal) 7 (1979): 1–6a.

Cohen, Rev. Henry. "A Modern Maccabean." *PAJHS* 6 (1897): 31–37.

———. "Settlement of the Jews in Texas." *PAJHS* 2 (1894): 139–56.

A Collection of Memories in Bicentennial Salute to the People of Arkansas. (4-H Club Publication.) De Witt, Ark.: De Witt Publishing Company, Inc., 1976. De Witt, Ark., Public Library.

"Combined Directory of the Churches of Helena, Arkansas." 1 June 1926. Churches Folder, PCPL.

Contribution cards of Arkansas donors to the Jewish Children's Home, New Orleans, La., 1918–1977. Courtesy Mrs. Viola Weiss.

The (Crawfordsville) Rotarian (9 December 1952)

Dante, Charles. Papers. Courtesy Bernard J. "Jerry" Tanenbaum, Dumas, Ark.

"Dedication Program of the Altheimer Laboratory." Agricultural Experiment Station, UofA, 31 October 1980.

"Dedication Programme of Temple Israel of Jonesboro, Arkansas, Held Sunday, 2 January 1898." TIAJ.

"Dedication Services of the New Temple Israel, Blytheville, Arkansas." 7 September 1947, TIAB.

Dickinson, Samuel D. "John Rison Fordyce." *PCHR* 38 (1990): 42–50.

Dinnerstein, Leonard. "Leo M. Frank and the American Jewish Community." *AJA* 20 (November 1968): 107–26.

———. "A Neglected Aspect of Southern Jewish History." *AJHQ* 59 (September 1971): 52–68.

———. "Southern Jewry and the Desegregation Crisis, 1954–1970." *AJHQ* 62 (March 1973): 231–41.

Doolos, Robert K. "Max Frauenthal: An Early Conway Entrepreneur." *Faulkner Facts & Fiddlings* 13 (1971): 37–44.

Downey, William, ed., "Hoover & Company." *Arkansas City Democrat* Historic Edition, [1910?].

Dreidel, E. M. "Temple Meir Chayim: A Century-Old Need." *Programs of the Desha County Historical Society* (Spring 1978): 29–35.

Durning, Dan. "Attracting the German Immigrant." *PCHR* 28 (1980): 2–8.

Edens, Bonnie L. "What Is Kosher?" *The Record* (Hot Springs–Garland County Historical Society Journal) 21 (1980): 88–93.

Edgar, Irving I. "Some Early Jewish Physicians of Michigan: Dr. Simon Levin–Dr. Joseph Beisman." *Michigan Jewish History* 7 (July 1967): 2–12.

Edwards, Emma R. "History of the North Carolina Association of Jewish Women." Paper presented at the 1942 North Carolina Association of Jewish Women Conference.

Eichhorn, Rabbi David Max. "History of the Jews of Texarkana." In Charles Grossman, comp. and ed., *Mount Sinai Jubilee* (Texarkana, Ark.: n.p., 1935). Mt. Sinai Archives, Texarkana, Ark.

Feenberg, Eugene. Papers. Courtesy Hilda Feenberg and Ben Feenberg.

Feinstein, Jill. "Yesterday and Today, A History of Pfeifers' Department Store" (1954). Joseph Pfeifer, Family Histories File. AHC.

Feldman, Lillian C. "Dr. Montague Fink." *PCHQ* 8 (December 1969): 9–11.

Fels, Tony. "Religious Assimilation in a Fraternal Organization: Jews and Freemasonry in Gilded-Age San Francisco." *AJH* 74 (June 1985): 369–403.

Felsenthal, Adolph. "Nearly Threescore and Ten," Parts.1, 2. *Arkansas Gazette*, magazine section (1934) (full citation unavailable). Camden, Ark., Nearprint File. AJA.

Felsenthal, Adolph. "Threescore and Ten." Beth El Emeth, Camden, Ark., Folder. AJA.

"Fort Smith, Arkansas, B'nai B'rith 75th Anniversary, 1878–1953." 28 November 1953 brochure. UHCA.

Frank, Eugenia (Stifft). "Our Family, Five Generations—Four Families, 1878–1963." Biographies File, Stifft Family Folder. AJA.

Frauenthal, Julian. Papers. Little Rock, Ark.

Friedlander, Jay. "M. M. Cohn CEO: a Soft-spoken Man of Many Interests." *Arkansas Business* 2 (8 July–21 July 1985):12–14.

Friedman, I. J. "A Challenge to Arkansas Jewry." *Arkansas Assembly Bulletin* 4 (September 1938):2.

Gates, Richard. "Gates Family History." Courtesy Louise (Gates) Dickerson, Hot Springs, Ark.

Gaughan, J. E. "Historic Camden." *AHQ* 20 (1961): 245–55.

Goins, Reggie, "Our Ancestors' Hand-Me-Downs." *Cat-Chat* (1980). Lee Academy, Marianna, Ark.

Golden City Messenger. (1925–38.) Jewish Children's Home Collection—180, Sec. 8. Special Collections, Tulane University Library.

"Golden Deeds Award." 1954 speech given at Fort Smith Exchange Club, Fort Smith, Ark., in honor of Dr. Davis W. Goldstein. Courtesy Mrs. Leona Goldstein.

Golden, Harry. "Jew and Gentile in the New South." *Commentary* 20 (November 1955): 403–12.

Goldenstein, Rabbi Raphael, comp. and ed. "History and Activities of Congregation Anshe Emeth, 1867–1917." (1917). Anshe Emeth Archives, Pine Bluff, Ark.

Goldman Hotel File. Special Collections. FSPL.

Gray, Harry. "'Bronco Billy' Anderson." *The California Parade* (Vallejo City Unified School District) (September 1975): 107–09. Western Jewish History Center, Judah L. Magnes Memorial Museum, Berkeley, Calif.

Green, E. G. "A Brief History of West Helena." *PCHQ* 3 (June 1965): 20–22.

Griffin, M. L. "A Social History of Camden, Arkansas, 1824–1860." A paper submitted in partial fulfillment for the degree of master of arts in the School of Political Science and Philosophy of Columbia University. Camden, Ark., Public Library.

Gwaltney, Francis Irby. "A Survey of Historic Washington, Arkansas." *AHQ* 17: 4 (1958): 337–96.

Hadassah Papers. Little Rock, Ark.

Handwritten speech delivered by unknown Hillel member, 1938. Assembly Papers. BIA.

Hansbrough, Vivian. "The Crowleys of Crowley's Ridge." *AHQ* 13 (1954): 52–62.

Haynie, Paul D. "Religion and Morals at the University of Arkansas in the 1920s." *AHQ* 45: 2 (1986): 148–67.

Heaney, Hon. Gerald W. "Jacob Trieber: Lawyer, Politician, Judge." *University of Arkansas at Little Rock Law Journal* 8 (1985–86): 421–78.

"Helena Banks." *PCHQ* 5 (June 1967): 10.

Hempstead County Tax Record Book, 1826–32. SARA.

Herscher, Uri D., ed. "The East European Immigrant Jew in America (1881–1981)." *AJA* 33 (April 1981): 1–140.

"History of the Jews of Fort Smith." *Reform Advocate*, January 1914.

Hodges v. United States, 203 U.S. 1 (1906), overruled.

Holmes, P. K. "Jewish Merchants of Newport: Wolff-Goldman Mercantile Company, 1880–1927." *The Stream of History* 28: 4 (1991): 2–9.

Horner, Dr. Albert A. "One Boy's Helena in the Nineties." Parts 1, 2. *PCHQ* 15 (December 1976, March 1977):12–32, 1–22.

"House of Morris B. Sanders, New York." *The Architectural Forum* (March 1936).

Hudson, Sarah C. "Little Rock's Leadership: The First State Board of Health." *PCHR* 33 (1985): 26–39.

"In Memoriam—A. Allen Weintraub." *Comment & Commentary* (St. Vincent's Infirmary, Little Rock, Ark., publication) 1 (Spring 1974): 1–4.

Industrial Removal Office (IRO) Papers, Arkansas. I–91, Box 29. AJHS.

Isaacs Family Folder. Beth Ahabah Archives. Richmond, Va.

Jackson, Dr. George F. "Boys' Camp at Little Rock, Arkansas." *Kiwanis Monthly* (November 1931): 1.

Jacobson, Jana. "A Look at the Temple's New Rabbi: Rabbi Eugene Levy." *ACTION* (Publication of the Jewish Federation of Little Rock, Ark.) 11 (Summer 1987): 1–2.

James, Dorothy. "Court Houses of Phillips County." *PCHQ* 3 (June 1965): 1–3.

Jefferson County Land Records, Deed Book 44.

Jewish War Veterans, U.S.A. National Memorial, Inc. Washington, D.C.

Jewish Welfare Agency Resolution. 13 August 1947. Courtesy Arthur Sanders.

Jones v. Alfred H. Mayer Co., 392 U.S. 409, 443 n. 78 (1968).

Josephs, Louis. Folder. Autobiographies File. AJA.

Katz, Donald R. "Good Times Coming in Arkansas." *GEO* (Gruner & Jahr, USA, Inc., Edition) 2 (June 1980): 35–56.

Kluglose, Charles. Scrapbooks. Little Rock, Ark.

Kohut, George A. "Arkansas." *PAJHS* 6 (1897): 158

Korn, Bertram W. "Jews and Negro Slavery in the Old South, 1789–1864." *PAJHS* 50: 3 (March 1961): 151–201.

Lang, Fred H. "Two Decades of State Forestry in Arkansas." *AHQ* 24 (1965): 208–19.

Lappin, Isabel. "A Junior Writes." *Arkansas Assembly Bulletin* 8 (November 1939): 3.

Latz, Rabbi Charles, Folder. File 1628. AJA.

Lee, W. D. "A Historical Sketch of Center Point." *AHQ* 12 (1953): 262–72.

Lena Latkin Memorial Library Association Dedication Program. 16 December 1934.

Leslie, James W. "History of Congregation Anshe Emeth, 1867–1977." Anshe Emeth Archives, Pine Bluff, Ark.

Letters file. BIA.

Levitt, Sam. "A History of Temple Israel, Jonesboro, Arkansas." *The Craighead County Historical Quarterly* 3 (1965): 7–12.

Logan, Robert R. "Notes on the First Land Surveys in Arkansas." *AHQ* 19: 3 (1960): 260–70.

MacKenzie, Gordon, comp., *Frolic Footwear History*. (Frolic Footwear, Jonesboro, Ark., publication, n.d.)

McCartney, W. A., Sr. "The Story of Dr. Charles Goldberg, 1820–1890." AJA.

McCoy, Izola (Rainbolt). "Dampf Family History." Tahlequah, Okla.

Marriage Book of Hempstead County, A-245. SARA.

"Mary Lee Chapter #87 United Daughters of the Confederacy." Small Manuscript Collection, AHC.

"Memoriam to Dr. Alfred Vise." Blytheville Air Force Base Program, 1957. TIAB.

Menefee, Larry T. "The Death of A Road Show Town: Little Rock, Arkansas, 1899–1921." Dissertation presented to the Graduate School of Arts and Sciences, University of Denver, in partial fulfillment of the doctor of philosophy degree, March 1977.

Menorah Association of New York correspondence with Menorah Chapter, Fayetteville, Ark. MSS Col #2, 68/10, File 2767, University of Arkansas, 1928–1929, AJA.

Mercantile Bank of Jonesboro brochure. TIAJ.

Meyer, Charles L. "Autobiography of Charles L. Meyer" (1982).

Minutes of Texarkana American Legion Posts 25–58, 16 November 1971. Texarkana—Mt. Sinai Folder, Congregation—Misc. File. AJA.

Misc. Eureka Springs newspapers, M/F. AHC.

Montgomery, Donald Ray. "Simon T. Sanders: Public Servant." *AHQ* 39: 2 (1980): 159–68.

Moore, Louis. "Notes on Frauenthal & Schwarz Store." 1977. Julian Frauenthal papers. Little Rock, Ark.

Moseley, Jack. "Boston Store Closing Touches City." *The Journal* (Fort Smith Historical Society) 2 (September 1986): 32–34.

Moss, Helen Wilma. "A Link With Yesterday." Arkansas File, Helen Wilma Moss Folder. AJA.

Neiditch, Michael. "Watering the Desert: The Role of B'nai B'rith International in the Development of the Jewish Communities in the South, 1850–1880." Paper presented at the Southern Jewish Historical Society's Fifteenth Annual Conference, Jackson, Miss., 4 November 1990.

Nelson, Karen Y. "Another Life for the Remmel Building." *The Chronicle* (Little Rock) 19 (February–March 1992): 9.

Newberry, Farrar. "The Grand Old Roman." *AHQ* 18: 1 (1959): 26–43.

"Newspaper Report." *Allgemeine Zeitung des Judenthums* 47 (1883): 534–37.

News Service press release, U of A, Fayetteville. 11 November 1960.

Nolte, Eugene. "Jo Frauenthal, Opie Read, and the Spyglass: Some Unpublished Letters." *AHQ* 22: 2 (1963): 171–76.

Nosoff, Stephen, "The Goal: From Russia to America." High school term paper (3 January 1973). Courtesy Reba Kasten Nosoff, New York, N.Y.

Nuclear Physics A317: 1 (1979).

The Occident 15:2 (May 1857)

The Occident Advertiser (1859).

"Our Dreams Fulfilled" (Dedication Program of Congregation Agudath Achim, Little Rock, April–May 1976).

Owens, Patrick J., "The Gentleman Rebel." *ADL Bulletin* (September 1965): 6–7.

Palnick, Elijah E. "Southern Jewry and Civil Rights." *CCAR Journal* 13 (June 1965): 62.

Palnick, Rabbi Elijah E. Papers. Courtesy Rabbi Elijah E. Palnick.

Parmelee, L. R. "Helena and West Helena, A Civil Engineer Reminisces." *PCHQ* 1 (December 1962): 1–28.

Peterson, Svend. "Arkansas State Tuberculosis Sanatorium: The Nation's Largest." *AHQ* 5 (1946).

Pfeifer, Eugene M., Sr. "The Autobiography of Eugene M. Pfeifer." Courtesy Mrs. E. G. Levy, Little Rock.

Pfeifer, Raida (Cohn). Papers. Little Rock, Ark.

Pittman, Don W. "The Founding of Dyess Colony." *AHQ* 29: 4 (1970): 313–26.

Popkin, Juliet G. "Eugene Feenberg." Courtesy Hilda Feenberg, La Jolla, Calif.

Prentis, Meyer. Personal Papers, Meyer Prentis file. Burton Historical Collection. Detroit, Mich., Public Library.

"Proceedings of the 1902 and 1903 Conventions, District Grand Lodge No. 7," B'nai B'rith International Archives, Washington, D.C.

"Program of Dedication, 18 September 1892," UHCA.

Pulaski County Marriage Book B. AHC.

Quapaw Quarter Association Research in Little Rock City Directories. Courtesy Nancy Lowe, researcher. 9 April 1982.

Quapaw Quarter Chronicle (Little Rock) 15 (October–November 1988).

Rand, Hal "Weinberg Family History." New York, N.Y., 28 July 1980. Courtesy Carrol S. Meyer Jr., San Antonio, Tex.

"Razing of Synagogue Marks Passing of Landmark." Camden newspaper clipping, Sifford's Scrapbook no. 6, M/F File, AHC.

The Razorback Hillel Newsletter 1 (Fall 1989).

Record of Interments, Cemetery, Dispersed of Judah, Touro Synagogue File 224, vol. 2, Special Collections, Tulane University Library.

Reed, Charles Leroy. "The Last Choctaw Chief." *Sturm's Oklahoma Magazine* 3 (1907): 11–13.

Reform Judaism (September 1973).

Reitzammer, Louis. "Early Ordinances Detail Arkansas City's History." *Desha County Historical Society* 7(1981): 17–27.

"Resolution" to Julian F. Haas, Arkansas Broadcasting Association, 19 April 1974. Courtesy Mrs. Julian Haas Jr., Jackson, Tenn.

Rhine, Rabbi A. B. "The Why of the Arkansas Jewish Assembly," *Arkansas Assembly Bulletin* 11 (December 1941): 4.

Richards, Ira Don. "Little Rock on the Road to Reunion, 1865–1880." *AHQ* 25 (1966): 313.

Rosenzweig, Dr. Joseph. "The Story of Leo N. Levi Memorial Hospital." *Hospital Heartbeat* (Levi Hospital publication) (1951): 2–36. Hot Springs, Nearprint File, Misc. Collection. AJA.

Rosenzweig, Mrs. Joseph. "House of Israel." *The Record* (1970 Yearbook of the Hot Springs–Garland County Historical Society) 11 (1970): 65–76a.

The (Crawfordsvile, Ark.) Rotarian (9 December 1952).

Saloutos, Theodore. "The Agricultural Problem and Nineteenth Century Industrialism." In Abraham Seldin Eisenstadt, ed., *American History: Recent Interpretations* 2. New York: Thomas Y. Crowell Company, 1962.

Sanders, Henry. "Henry Sanders Autobiography." Courtesy Arthur Sanders, Little Rock, Ark.

Sanders, Rabbi Ira E. "The Journal of a Southern Rabbi." Courtesy Rabbi Ira E. Sanders.

Sanders, Rabbi Ira E. Papers. BIA.

Schoenberger, Rosa. "Dedication Programme of Temple Israel of Jonesboro, Ark., Held Sunday, January 2, 1898." TIAJ.

Schoenfield, Morris. "Talk by Morris Schoenfield on the Occasion of the 75th Anniversary Celebration of Temple Israel, Jonesboro, Arkansas," 14 December 1973, Jonesboro, Ark., Temple Israel Folder, Misc. File, AJA.

Schwartz, Dale. "Justice Delayed, Justice Denied: The Case of Leo Frank." Paper delivered at the Southern Jewish Historical Society Conference, Richmond, Va., 4 November 1984.

Scrinopski, Isador. "Short History of the Scrinopski Family." Little Rock, Ark., Hadassah Papers.

Sevier County Records, Sevier County, Ark.

Shain, Rabbi Samson A. "Arkansas Jewish Place Names." Hot Springs, Ark., Temple Beth Israel Scroll of Honor. Nearprint File, Arkansas, AJA.

———. "The Story of Arkansas Jewry, 1836–1953." Arkansas Folder, Histories File. AJA.

Shinkle, Florence. "Eugene Feenberg: Physics Was His Passion." *St. Louis Post-Dispatch,* magazine section, 21 June 1987.

"Short History of Second Baptist Church, Little Rock." Second Baptist Church Archives.

Shpall, Leo. "Jewish Agricultural Colonies in the United States." *Agricultural History* 24 (1950): 120–46.

Sifford's Scrapbooks, Nos. 1, 3, 4, 6. Camden, Ark., Public Library.

"Silver Anniversary Program, Congregation Temple Israel, Blytheville, Arkansas, 1947–1972." TIAB.

"Sixtieth Anniversary Services of Temple Israel, Jonesboro, Arkansas, 1898–1958." TIAJ.

"A Sketch of Congregation B'nai Israel," Board of Directors Meeting, 4 May 1880. Ladies Temple Aid Society Folder, Little Rock, Ark., Box X-38. AJA.

Smith, Doug. "Oh, THAT Thyra." *Arkansas Gazette,* 22 December 1977.

Solmson family papers. Courtesy Harry B. Solmson Jr., Memphis, Tenn.

Solomon, B. M. "Jewry in Helena Dates From 1867." *Arkansas Assembly Bulletin* 16 (April 1950): 7.

Solomon family papers. Courtesy David Solomon Jr., Helena, Ark.

Starnes, C. W. "Settlement of Northeastern Greene County." *Greene County Historical Quarterly* 6: 1 (1971): 4–29.

"State of Israel Bonds Tribute to Eric Nussbaum." Given at State of Israel Bonds Dinner, Synagogue Agudath Achim, Little Rock, Ark., 17 November 1991.

Stewart-Abernathy, Leslie, and Barbara Ruff. "A Good Man in Israel: Zooarcheology and Assimilation in Antebellum Washington, Arkansas." December 1985. Courtesy Leslie Stewart-Abernathy.

Stolberg, Mary. "Telephone Company in Fort Smith." *The Journal* (Fort Smith Historical Society) 1: 2 (1977): 50–54.

Stolz, Joseph. Collection. Nearprint File. AJA.

Strauss, Rabbi H. Cerf. "A Warning Signal." *Arkansas Assembly Bulletin* 13 (January 1948): 3.

"Street Directory of Helena, 1909." PCHQ 3 (December 1964): 17–20.

Sure, Dr. Barnett. File. Special Collections, UofA Library.

"Tailor-Made Furniture." *LIFE* 21 (23 September 1946): 128–33.

Teitelbaum, Rabbi Samuel. "The Hillel Society of the University of Arkansas." *Arkansas News Bulletin* 2 (January 1938): 1–4.

Temple Israel Chronicle (1936-1937). Courtesy Rabbi M. Lyons, St. Louis, Mo.

This Is B'nai B'rith. 1979 brochure. B'nai B'rith International Archives, Washington, D.C.

"This Is Your Life, Perry Cooperman." Testimonial to Perry Cooperman at Temple Israel, Blytheville, Ark., 1961. Courtesy Harold Cooperman.

Tilles, George. "A History of Fort Smith." Courtesy Ella (Tilles) Falk, Fort Smith, Ark.

"Trailblazers of the Trans-Mississippi West." *AJA* 8: 2 (October 1956): 59–130.

Trieber, Judge Jacob. Papers. Courtesy J. Marshall Treiber, Fayetteville, N.C.

"Twentieth Century Club Easter Edition." *Helena World,* 20 April 1930.

UHC Judaica Exhibit Paper (1982), UHCA.

United Hebrew Temple. (Printed history of the United Hebrew Congregation.) N.p., n.d. UHCA.

The United Hebrew Temple Tablet (October 1986).

United States v. Morris, 125 F. 322 (E.D. Ark. 1903).

U.S. News & World Report 100 (26 May 1986): 36.

Ward, Charles L. "Sugar Loaf Mountain, Once Scene of Red Man's Defeat, Now Popular Tourist Spot." Undesignated newspaper article (full citation unavailable). Julian Frauenthal papers. Little Rock, Ark.

Warranty Deed of the United Hebrew Congregation's Cemetery Association's Incorporation, 3 October 1887. UHCA.

Warsen, Allen A. "B'nai B'rith in Action." *Michigan Jewish History* 7 (July 1967): 23–28.

Washington University *W.U. Record* (2 March 1975).

Weber, Shimon. "How Has the School Conflict Affected the Jews in Little Rock?" *Jewish Daily Forward,* 19 October 1957.

Wheeler, Elizabeth L. "Isaac Fisher: The Frustrations of a Negro Educator at Branch Normal College, 1902–1911." *AHQ* 41: 1 (Spring 1982): 3–50.

White, Dana. "The Helena Grand Opera House." *PCHQ* 9 (June 1971): 13–20.

White, Edith. "Early Conway." *Faulkner Facts & Fiddlings* 4 (December 1963): 13–16.

Willner, Nancy E. "A Brief History of the Jewish Community in Charlottesville and Albemarle." *The Magazine of Albemarle County History* 40 (1982): 1–24.

Wilson, Mrs. W. E. "The Changing Face of Social Work." Paper given in 1951. Graduate School of Social Work File, UALR.

Wolfe, Jonathan James "Background of German Immigration." Parts 1, 2, 3. *AHQ* 25: 2, 3, 4 (Summer, Autumn, Winter 1966): 151–82, 248–78, 354–85.

———. "The Peopling of Pulaski County. Pulaski County Population Sources and Composition, 1850–1860." *PCHR* 21 (September 1973): 51–67.

Works Progress Administration (WPA) Churches and Synagogues Historical Records Survey, Arkansas, Boxes 434, 453. Special Collections, UofA Library.

Worley, Ted R. "Early Days in Osceola." *AHQ* 24: 2 (1965): 119–26.

———. "Early History of Des Arc and Its People." *White River Journal* (March 1956–March 1957): 1–80.

———. "Helena on the Mississippi." *PCHQ* 5 (June 1967): 30–44.

Wright, Muriel H. "Early Navigation and Commerce Along the Arkansas and Red Rivers in Oklahoma." *Chronicles of Oklahoma* 8 (March 1930): 65–88.

———. "Iser Nakdimen." *Chronicles of Oklahoma* 22: 3 (Autumn 1944): 367–69.

Zilbergeld, Nancy, and Nancy Britton. "The Jewish Community in Batesville, Arkansas, 1853–1977." *The Independence County Chronicle* 21: 3 (April 1980): 1–32.

Newspapers

American Hebrew
American Israelite
Arkansas City Democrat
Arkansas Democrat
Arkansas Democrat-Gazette
Arkansas Gazette
Batesville Guard
Camden Beacon
Camden News
Conway Log Cabin Democrat
Crowley Ridge Chronicle
DeQueen Bee
Desha County News
Detroit Free Press
Dumas Clarion
El Dorado Daily News
El Dorado News-Times
Eureka and North Arkansas Journal
Eureka Springs Fountain
Fayetteville Daily Democrat
Fayetteville Northwest Arkansas Times
Felsenthal Press
Forrest City Times
Fort Smith Elevator
Fort Smith News Record
Fort Smith Southwest American
Fort Smith Southwest Times
Fort Smith Southwest Times-Record
Fort Smith Times-Record
Fort Smith Tribune
Fort Smith Weekly New Era
Hebrew Standard
Helena Weekly World
Helena World
Hot Springs New Era
Hot Springs Sentinel-Record
Jewish Daily Forward
Jewish Review of Cleveland

Jewish Times
Jewish Week
Jonesboro Daily Tribune
Jonesboro Enterprise
Jonesboro Sun
Lepanto News Record
Malvern Daily Record
Marked Tree Tribune
Marshall Mountain Wave
McCrory Leader
McGehee Times
Memphis Commercial Appeal
Newport Daily Independent
New Orleans Daily Picayune
New Orleans Jewish Ledger
New York Times
Pine Bluff Commercial
Pine Bluff Daily Graphic
Pine Bluff Dispatch
Pine Bluff Graphic
Pine Bluff Herald
Pine Bluff Press
Pine Bluff Press Eagle
Pine Bluff Semi-Weekly Graphic
Pine Bluff Weekly Graphic
Pine Bluff Weekly Press
Pine Bluff Weekly Commercial
Pocahontas Star Herald
Reform Advocate
Sebastian County News
St. Louis Post-Dispatch
Stuttgart Daily Leader & Arkansawyer
Texarkana Democrat
Texarkana Gazette
Twin City Tribune
Washington Telegraph
West Memphis Accelerator
Wynne Daily Star-Progress
Wynne Star-Progress

Aschaffenberg, 27, 56, 178
  D., 42
  David, 58, 183
  Leopold, 183
Ashkenasim, xx
Ashley
  Jo Ann (Rosenberg), 158
  William E., 468 (n.13)
Assyrians, xix
Astrachan
  Rabbi George, 369
  Rabbi Jeffrey, 369
Ati' Day Yisroel Nursery School (Little Rock),
  357–58
Atkins, Gov. Homer M., 221
Atlas, Rabbi Seymour, 355
Atlas Finance Company, 113
Auerbach
  A. K., 42, 58, 139
  H. R., 39
  Dr. J. J., 129
  Murray A., 63
Austin, Stephen, 6

Babylonians, xix, xx
Bach, M., 152
Bacharach
  Edgar, 169
  Sigmund, 150
Back
  Abraham, 230
  Alice (Lasker), 376
  Edward, 388
  Joseph D., 230
  Louis, 519 (n.3)
  Morris, 519 (n.3)
  Phillip G., 230–31, 354, 355, 376–77, 388,
    396–97
  Pincus, 230
  William, 81, 230
  William and Sophia (Goldstein), 230
Back Family, 137
Backel
  Sam, 240
  Sayde (Simon), 240
Badinelli, J. E., 159
Badt
  Arnold, 204
  Ernest J., 204
  Jesse, 204
  Mendel, 204
  Sam, 204
  Sybil (Lyons), 204
Badt Family, 134
Baer
  Abe, 84, 284
  Bernhard, 31, 45–46, 73, 211–12, 219

C., 184
Miss Carrie, 85
F., 31
Ferdinand, 187, 188
Freda (Adler), 212
H., 211
Herman, 73
Herman [of Turrell], 264, 425
Isadore, 425
Jacob, 216
Jake, 425
Julius, 212
L., 31
Lewis, 31
Mary, 212
Max, 263
Morris, 263
Nathan, 263–64
Robert, 425
Ronald, 425
Ruth (Levitch), 263
S., 73
Samuel, 211
Sigmund, 212
Baer stores, 431
Baer Family, 207
Bailey, Gov. Carl, 145, 221, 231
Baim
  Aaron, 282, 438–39
  Adah, 282
  Bennie, 282, 438–39
  Charles, 282, 438–39
  Eugene, 282, 438–39
  Kenneth, 359, 438–39
  Leo, 282, 438–39
  Mrs. Leo, 333, 335
  Milton, 317–18
  Samuel, 84
  Samuel, 438–39
  Samuel Baer, 282
  Sarah (Fink), 282
Baker, 27
  C., 38
Balfour Hotel (Hot Springs), 294
Balkin, Susie, 357
Ball
  Albert, 168
  Stella, 273
Bamberger
  Jake, 189–90
  Simon, 189–90
Banking in Arkansas
  Jewish involvement in, 116–17, 150, 151,
    154, 156, 159, 160, 163, 165, 166, 167,
    169, 172, 175, 176, 177, 178, 181, 184,
    196–98, 205, 208, 211, 224, 253, 254, 256,
    296

Jake, 154
Joe M., 75
Joseph, 114
Lawrence J., 130, 208
Louie, 255
Marcus, 75, 153
Marcus and Henrietta (Less), 114
Morris, Jr., 153–54
Morris, Sr., 75
S. Lewis, 246
Sarah (Grossman), 255
Berger Family, 111, 125
Bergman, Edith, 517 (n.172)
Berk
  B. H., 90
  Ben, 200, 289
  Benjamin, 444
  Isadore, 200, 444
  Isadore, 269, 289
  Joe, 289
  Rose (Burd), 200, 289
Berkowitz, Jessie, 255
Berland, I., 363
Berlinger, Bero, 71
Berman
  P., 73
  Pincus, 218
Bernath
  Henry, 185
  Joseph, 185
  Moses, 185
Bernays
  Louis C., 138
  Phillip H., 138
Bernhard
  Ely, 248
  Evelyn, 237, 399
  Joseph, 237, 248, 399
  Mary (Herr), 248
  Melanie, 357, 399
  Sam, 81, 236, 248, 399
  Susie, 399
Bernhard Family, 240
Bernstein
  H., 83, 152
  L., 172
  Martin, 288
  Mrs. Martin (Jeannette Warshavsky), 288
Bershoff, Maurice, 452–53
Bertig
  A. D., 155–56
  Saul, 155–56
Besser
  Ben, 236, 237
  Isadore, 236, 387
  Joseph, 236
  Leopold, 81, 235–36, 237

Lippman, 81, 235–36, 237, 387
Maurice, 355
Morris, 242
Rose (Ruff), 236
Besser Family, 240, 387
Beth El Emeth (Camden). *See* Congregations
Beth Israel (House of Israel). *See* Congregations
Beth Jacob Synagogue (Hot Springs). *See* Congregations
Billstein
  Alfred, 143
  Brunette (Fox), 143
Billstein Family, 219
Bilsky
  Charles, 270
  Fretha, 270
  Hannah, 270
  Isaac, 270
  Jeanette (Adler), 270
  Dr. Lester J., 409
  Maurice, 270
  Max, 270
  Solomon, 270
  William, 84, 270
Bindursky
  A. B., 260, 423
  Mrs. A. B. (Addie Kaplan), 273, 423
  Albert, 260, 423
  Esther, 260, 285–86, 423
  Eve, 260
  Herman, 260
  Meyer, 260, 285
  Milton Bernard, 260
  Minnie (Iskiwitch), 260, 285
Binstock, Rabbi Louis, 75
Biondo, Dr. Raymond V., 358, 402
Bishin Family, 271
Bishkin
  Gloria (Kusin), 446
  Leo, 364, 446
  Mrs. Leo, 364
Biskin, Mrs. William C., 272
Biton, Dr. Victor, 400–401
Black, James, 6
Black and White Food Stores, 135
Blacker, A., 172
Blackman Family, 303
Bland, W. H., 162
Blank
  David, 17
  Moses, 17
Blanks, C. B., 539 (n.8)
Blass
  Alvin, 113
  Betsy, 410
  Company. *See* Gus Blass Company

Ralph, 261–62
Rose (Davis), 261
Blumenfield, Dr. Samuel, 341
Blumensteil
    Alice (Kempner), 205
    Sam, 205
    Simon, 205
Blumenthal, Max, 150
Bluthenthal
    Adele, 334
    Adolph, 58, 178, 187
    David, 38, 181–82
    David M., 38, 43, 181–82
    David M. and Sophie (Simons), 182
    David S., 181–82, 381
    Harold E., 182
    Henry and Marmel ("Amalie" Rothschild), 38, 181
    Mrs. Herbert, 57
    Josephine, 55, 182
    May, 55
    Mrs. Sam, 56
    Samuel, 43, 181
Bluthenthal Family, 178
Bluthenthal Hotel, 38, 181
Blytheville Chamber of Commerce, 256
B'nai B'rith in Arkansas
    Blytheville, 86–87, 337
    Camden, 53–54
    El Dorado, 90
    Forrest City, 89
    Fort Smith, 53–54, 74
    Helena, 53–54
    Hot Springs, 53–54, 68–69
    Jonesboro, 81, 366
    Little Rock, 54, 139, 358
    McGehee, 83, 369
    Pine Bluff, 53–54
    Texarkana, 364–65
    Wynne, 89
B'nai B'rith (IOBB), 70, 424, 426
B'nai B'rith Home for the Aged (Memphis), 316, 356–57
B'nai Israel Congregation, Little Rock. See Congregations
Board of Trade Restaurant and Saloon, 125
Bogen, Rabbi Joseph, 72
Bogoslavsky
    Abe, 301
    Gerald, 301, 366
    Dr. Lance, 405
    Leonard, 301
    Rose (Gampol), 301
Boies, W. D., 183
Bondi
    August, 44
    Edward, 172, 431

Ike, 172, 431
Isadore, 172
Sam, 172
Sol, 172
Boone
    Daniel, 4
    Thomas L., 474 (n.43)
Boone Family, 138
Borden's Dairy, 126
Borg, Alexander, 65
Born, Joe, 318
Bornstein
    Cecile (Goldman), 263
    Herman, 88, 262–63
Borowsky
    Benjamin, 419
    Boris, 257
    Colman, 419
    Fruma, 419
    Leona, 257
    Leslie, 419
    Max, 257, 337, 419–20
    Pearl, 257, 420
    William, 87, 257, 336, 337, 368, 419–20
Boston Store, 212, 452
Botnick, Jack, 335, 341–42
Bott
    Augusta, 25
    George, 25
    Henrietta, 120
    Isaac, 24, 25, 37, 120, 125, 133
    J., 58
    Leo P., 25, 133
    Leo P., Jr., 133
Bott Family, 118
Bowie, Jim, 6
Bowman, Mrs. Mattie, 68
Bracha, Dr. H. Stefan, 402
Bragg, Dr. Junius N., 43
Bram
    Barnett, 84, 281
    David, 58, 359
    Harris, 84, 281
    Louis, 84
Branch Normal College (University of Arkansas at Pine Bluff), 56
Brandeis Family, 240
Brav, Rabbi Louis, 57
Braverman, Rabbi J. D., 75
Brazil, Pernambuco (Recife), xx
Breckenridge, Congressman Clifton, 100, 183
Breier
    Bertha, 82, 234–35
    Edith, 235
    Matthews, 235
    Nancy, 235
    Samuel, 81, 234–35

B'nai Israel, 84
Temple Israel, 57
Texarkana, Mt. Sinai, 71–72, 89–90, 363–65
Wynne, Ahavath Achim, 88–89
Conservative Judaism, xxii, 80, 483–84 (n.16)
Conway, Joel, 6
Conway Chamber of Commerce, 223
Conway Cotton Oil Company, 105
Cook
Mrs. Meyer (Ella Solomon), 165
Nathan, 186
Cook Family, 186
Cooke, E. V., 390
Coolidge, Pres. Calvin, 146, 292
Cooper
Isabel, 356
Morris, 276
Cooper Clinic, 216, 217, 453–54
Cooper Family, 125
Cooperman
Mary (Friedman), 255
Perry, 255
Cornblatt, Dave, 279
Cotton farming and handling in Arkansas
Jewish involvement in, 16, 23, 26, 38, 45,
105, 108–110, 152, 156, 157, 158, 159,
160, 163, 164–65, 166, 171, 174, 175, 177,
179, 182, 183, 188, 202, 219, 226, 255,
256, 259, 273, 274, 278
Couch, Harvey C., 197, 224
Coulter
C. E., 259
Mrs. C. E., 86
Council of Jewish Women (Little Rock), 142,
145
Covenant, The Sword and the Arm of the
Lord (CSA), 459–60
Cravens, Congressman Ben, 295–96
Cremieux, Adolphe, 179, 507 (n.214)
Crockett, Davy, 6
Cross, Edward, 6
Cross County Bank, 159
Crowley, Benjamin, 29–30
Culture and entertainment in Arkansas
Jewish involvement in, 127–28, 150, 167,
168, 169, 182, 192, 223, 288, 382, 456
Cunniff, Dr. Chris, 403
Currick, Rabbi Max C., 74
Curtis, Gen. Samuel R., 41
Czarnikow
Edward, 12, 14–15, 73, 210
Louis, 15
Rose (Happek), 210

Dachau (concentration camp), 336, 397
Dally, Harry P., 217
Dalton Gang, 204

Daltroff
Rosa (Ackerman), 159
Shields, 47, 159
Willie (Malone), 159
Dampf
Max, 46, 221–22
Samuel and Matilda (Apple), 221
Sarah C. (Hollis), 221
Daniel
David, 475 (n.74)
Dennis, 294
Janet, 294
Daniels, Dan, 65, 119–20, 162, 493 (n.130)
Daniels and Straus, 162
Dante
Camille, 435–36
Charles, 58, 270, 279–80, 284, 331, 333,
337, 359, 369, 435–36, 437
Mrs. Charles (Antionette Stiel), 232,
284–85
Charles and Toney, 239
Charles H., 280, 435–37
Charles [son of Charles H.], 435–36
Eli, 82, 270, 274, 276
Gladys (Wilenzick), 261
Helen, 280, 285
Mrs. Jack (Rose Mae Herrman), 280,
437
Jack Stiel, 280, 285, 435–36, 437
Jacob, 241–42
Jo Ann (Meyers), 435–36
Joe, 261
Joseph, 241–42
Julianne "Judy," 383
Naomi, 280, 285
Sarah, 270
Toni, 435–36
Danziger, Abe, 359
Darch
Louis, 294–95
Sol, 294–95
Darrow, Clarence, 315
David Family, 247
Davidson
Abe J., 272, 430–31
Bell (Simon), 267
Buddy, 431
Carrie, 142
Dorothy, 272
Edith, 272
Ely, 272
Fannie (Bernstein), 272
Isaac, 271–72
Dr. J. S., 272
Joe, 431
M., 267
Samuel J., 271–72

Goldman Hotel, 126, 218, 454–55
Goldsmith
    Abe, 165, 429
    Adolph, 202, 203
    George, 429
    Helena (Rosenberg), 202
    L., 73
    L. E., 137, 183, 188
    Louise (Hurst), 429
    Milton W., 165
    S., 171
    Selig, 164–65
Goldstein
    Bernard, 266
    Dr. Davis Woolf, 216, 298–99, 453
    Doris, 155
    Edgar L., 216
    Ethel (Finkel), 254
    Florence (Pahotski), 298
    Florette, 216
    Harry, 254
    I., 75
    Ike, 90
    Isaac, 254
    Jaime, 254
    Joseph, 277, 369
    Leona (Heilbron), 453
    Marx, 216
    Rosa (Woolf), 216
    Dr. Samuel, 355, 401–2
    Velma (Lazarus), 254
Goldweber
    Aaron, 283, 359
    Sam, 58
Goltz
    Bernice (Lockwood), 450
    Lewis, 362, 450
Goodkin
    Joseph, 289, 444
    Sam, 366
Goodman
    Adolph, 161
    Arnold, 354
    H., 71
    Herman, 475 (n.74)
    Mike and Sara, 289
    Mr., 69
    Rose, 289
    Saul, 233
Goodman Family, 207, 236
Gordon Family, 236
Gore, Al, 463
Gottfried, D., 155
Gottlieb
    Harold, 450
    Henry, 363
    Max, 187

Graber
    Abraham, 253–54
    Dave, 254
    Gordon and Fannie (Froma Solomon), 253
    Joe, 254
    Louis, 253–54
    Max, 253–54
    Meyer, 253–54
    Sam, 253–54
Graber Family, 416
Gradus, M., 359
Grand-Leader firm, The, 212
Grand Opera House Saloon, 125
Granoff
    Bessie, 235
    Edward M., 235
    Max, 235
    Morris, 235, 388
Grant, Pres. Ulysses S., 43, 52, 104
Grauman
    Dave, 166
    Edward, 165–66, 429
    Harry, 165–66, 171
Grauman Cotton Company, 165–66
Graves, Guy, 285
Gray, Dr. E. M., 404
Grayboys, Rabbi Angela, 362
Great Depression, 68, 104, 130–31, 140–41,
    154, 157, 182–83, 219, 234, 238, 239, 257,
    271, 275, 287, 310, 313, 314, 315, 320,
    328, 453
Green
    Gertrude, 247–48
    Marcus and Minnie (Back), 230, 247
    Milton, 385
    Morris, 81
    Teanie, 247–48
Greenbaum
    Abe, 395
    Abram and Nellie, 407
    David, 355, 407
Greenberg
    H., 82, 277
    I., 85, 294
    Irving, 71, 362
    Paul, 359, 440, 464
Greenblatt, Rabbi Meyer, 55
Greene, Bette (Evensky), 425
Greenfield, 88
Greenwald, Joseph, 291
Gregson, Dr., 318
Grey, Rabbi Ernest, 338, 339
Griffenhagen, Dr. Henry, 401
Grober, Victor, 276
Groner, Rabbi Irwin, 355
Gross
    Bernard "Billy," 69, 71, 205–6

Isaacson
Henrietta (Spiro), 211
I., 73
Isaac, 211
J., 73
Isaacson Family, 296
Isken
Max, 363
Islam, xx
Israel
Northern Kingdom, xix
Southern Kingdom, xix
State of, 342
Itzkowitz
Joseph, 230, 234
Judy, 389
Leon, 234
Marvin, 389
Max, 81, 230, 234
Max, 234, 389
Robert, 234, 355, 389
Rose (Zarik), 234
Ruth (Schweig), 389
Itzkowitz Family, 240
Izenberg, James, 318–19

Jabotinsky, Vladimir, 256, 420
Jack, Rabbi Emanuel J., 63
Jackson, Pres. Andrew, 6, 14–15
Jacobi
Albert Cohen, 14
Henry, 12, 13–14
Hirsch, 14
Mrs. Hirsch (Amalia Kahn), 147
Jacobie, Jacob, 30
Jacobs
David, 218
Henrietta (Altheimer), 194
I. B., 194
Jeremiah, 9
Joseph, 9
Julius, 73, 367
Marguerite, 76
Michael, 83, 150, 415
Rabbi Peiser, 66
Rose, 415
Jacobson
Adolph, 110
Charles, 62, 63, 110, 120–21
Jacob, 110, 120
Dr. William, 409
Jacobson Family, 107, 139, 180
Jacubowicz, Mr. and Mrs. Abraham, 333
Jaffe
E. M., 336
I., 75
James, Jesse, 204

Jasin, Rabbi Joseph, 56, 63
Jastrawer, A., 160
Jefferson, Thomas, 4
Jennings, Orville, 38
Jensen, Hans D., 455
Jett
Benjamin P., 37–38, 40
Emma, 40–41
Hester (Block), 37–38, 40
Jewish Children's Home of New Orleans, 120, 241, 312, 316
Jewish Federation of Little Rock, 343, 356–57, 408
Jewish Theological Seminary of America, 26
Jewish War Veterans of the United States, 537 (n.25)
Arkansas Post No. 436, 348
Jiedel
Eva, 169
Jacob, 169, 255
Raphael, 169
Richard, 158, 169, 255, 320, 336, 368
Siegbert, 87, 158, 169, 255, 320, 335, 336, 368
Joe's Hobby Shop, 237
Joel
Joseph, 218–19
M., 73, 218–19
Moses, 211
Mrs. S., 74
Simon, 73, 218–19
Joffe, E. M., 259
Johl, Sol H., 126
Johl Family, 122
Johnson
J. S., 321
John M., 153–54
Nunnally, 226
Joint Distribution Committee, 323, 328
Joliet, Louis, xv
Jones
Daniel W., 6
G. W., 200
Heber, 224
James K., 6
John T., 224
Virgil, 318
Jonesboro Hide and Fur Company, 154
Josaphat
Emma, 193
Israel Beer, 193
Sigmund and Fredricka (Meyer), 193
Joseph
Charles E., 158, 386–87
E., 186
N., 82
Olga (Sternberg), 158

Sam, 158, 255, 386–87, 440
Mrs. Sam, 86
Setta (Goldman), 156
Simeon, 24, 26
Simon, 58, 158
Simon L., 156
Simon S., 440
Joseph Pfeifer Kiwanis Camp, 114, 380
Josephs, Judge Louis, 201–2, 311, 440
Judah, Dr. Leopold N., 401

Kaelter, Rabbi Walter, 338, 339, 361
Kahn
    Abe, 85, 175–76
    Adolph, 140, 141
    Adrianne, 439
    Dr. Alfred, Jr., 397, 402
    Alfred, Sr., 105, 391, 397, 402
    Andrew, 283, 439
    Bess, 439
    Rabbi Emanuel, 74
    Herman, 63, 65, 104–5, 117, 119, 126, 394
    Mrs. Herman, 145
    Herman and Jean, 449
    Herman and Marion "Mamie," 105
    Hugo, 238
    Lehman, 298–99
    Louis, 168
    Louis and Nellie (Grauman), 168
    Lucian, 298–99
    Marion (Cohn), 104
    Mosler, 168
    Mr., 45
    Redith (White), 402
    Roger, 449
    Rosalind (Buchman), 449
    Sidney L., Sr., 65, 105, 117, 397
    Stanley, 439
Kahn Family, 119
Kaiser, Charles W., 136
Kalderon, Dr. Albert E., 400
Kalischer, S., 475 (n.74)
Kalisha, S., 31
Kallsnick
    Aaron, 293
    Aaron and Ethyl, 85
    Abe, 293
    Dave, 293
    Elizabeth (King), 293
    Ethyl, 293
    Joseph, 293
    Maurice, 293
    Sam, 293
    Sarah, 293
Kaltenborn, H. V., 316
Kantor
    Harold, 432

Mrs. Helen (Epstein), 432
Kaplan
    Freda, 273
    Miriam, 273
    Philip E., 353, 355, 407, 463
    Regina, 70, 363, 450
    Ruthe, 407
    Samuel, 272–73
    Rabbi Solomon, 359, 365
Kaplan Family, 427
Karatofsky, J., 69, 85, 294
Kass, Warner, 363
Kasselberg, Adolph, 139
Kassoff
    Lena, 241
    Leon, 245
Kassoff Family, 236
Kasten
    Abe, 299
    Anne, 299
    Isadore, 299
    Louis, 299, 305, 451–52
    Louis and Sarah, 87
    Mary, 299
    Maurice, 299
    Pinia, 299
    Reba, 299
    Sarah (Churgin), 299, 304–5, 451–52
    Sussman (Zussman), 299
Kastor
    Dolph, 182–83, 438
    Florence (Meyer), 182
    Isador, 182
    Leo, 181
Kastor Family, 219
Katrovitz, Morris and Goldie (Unger), 241
Katz
    Arthur, 207
    Charles, 367
    Donald R., 440
    Leon, 172
Katzenberg
    Jennie (Mandlebaum), 125
    Louis, 125
Katzenberger, Mrs. William, 146
Katzenellenbogen, Rabbi Samuel, 81–82
Katzenstein
    Aaron, 137
    M., 117
    Moses, 137
    Mr., 163
    Samuel, 187
Katzenstein Family, 118
Katzer
    Ben, 454
    Rose S., 297
    Sander, 297, 454

Maurice, 239, 398
Perla "Pauline," 248–49
Robert, 398
Scott, 398
Kornfeld
Rabbi Joseph, 55, 181–82
Josephine (Bluthenthal), 181–82
Kory
Dr. Roscoe C., 129
Mrs. Roscoe C. (Rose Bernwald), 146,
335
Kosberg
Mary, 401
Dr. Oscar, 401
Kosminsky
Joseph, 289
Dr. Leonce J., 289–90, 325, 534 (n.49)
Marks, 71–72
Nettie (Friede), 289–90
Kossover
A. D., 81
Aaron, 236
Jake, 237
Melvyn, 340, 342
Kossover Family, 240, 247
Kosten
Joe, 81
Joseph, 236
Kraft, 39
Krain, Dr. Mark, 409
Kramer
Adaline (Reichardt), 118
Carl, 289
Frederick, 25, 117–18, 119–20
Rose (Goodman), 289
William S., 245, 397–98
Kramer School, 118
Krane, Harold, 362
Kretchmar
Lee, 233, 395
Ruth (Goldman), 395
Kristallnacht, 327–28, 338
Krock, Dr. Fred, 298
Krokow, Abe, 85, 294
Kroll Family, 245, 270
Kronberg Family, 112
Krone
Lucian, 224
Ruth (Frauenthal), 224
Krone Family, 158, 219
Kroner, Abraham J., 246
Krouse, Leo, 72, 291
Krow
Bertha, 192
Ira, 171, 192, 431
Josephine, 192
Rose (Ricka Seelig), 192

Sallie, 192
Simon, 171, 192
Krumpner, 84
Joe K., 186
Ku Klux Klan (KKK), 100, 155, 165, 167, 196,
198, 204, 209, 243, 256, 258, 270, 276,
279, 459–60, 493 (n.130), 527 (n.113)
Kuhn, Sigismund, 475 (n.74)
Kuperman, Dr. Irving, 355, 403
Kupperman, Harry, 71, 362
Kurtz, Hyman, 259
Kusin
Anne (Brody), 290–91, 446
David, 290–91, 446
Gloria, 290
Melvin, 290, 364, 446
Sherman, 290, 364, 446
Kuttner
Edward, 127–28
Joseph, 127
Othelia, 127
Kuttner's Orchestra, 128

La Salle, xvi
Ladies Aid Societies. See Temple Sisterhoods
Lafferty
Monsignor Claiborne, 448, 474 (n.43)
Mabel (Morgan), 474 (n.43)
Rose, 474 (n.43)
Thomas, 474 (n.43)
Lamar, Julian, 227
Landau, Rabbi Moses M., 364
Landsberg
L., 58
Solomon, 120, 139
Lane
Elsie (Scher), 240
Louis, 240
Laney, Gov. Ben, 305
Langfelder
L. L. and Blanche Wilheminia
(Heymann), 213, 217
Ludwig L., 73, 213
Maxine, 213
Lanoue, Ron, 357
Lansky, Louis, 255
Lapides
Louis, 259, 422
Melvin, 259, 422
Lappin
Bernard, 298
Isabel, 298, 332
Israel, 298
Joseph, 298
Rea (Levy), 298
Larkin, Sam and Jean, 437
Laser, Dave, 70–71